Medical Emergencies in Dentistry

An Abridged Edition of
Emergencies in Dental Practice, *THIRD EDITION*

FRANK M. McCARTHY, B.S., M.S., M.D., D.D.S., Sc.D., F.A.C.D., F.I.C.D., F.A.D.S.A.

Professor and Chairman, Section of Anesthesia and Medicine
University of Southern California School of Dentistry;
Director, Dental Anesthesia Service,
Los Angeles County-University of Southern California Medical Center

1982

W. B. SAUNDERS COMPANY

Philadelphia   London   Toronto   Mexico City   Rio de Janeiro   Sydney   Tokyo

W. B. Saunders Company: West Washington Square
Philadelphia, PA 19105

1 St. Anne's Road
Eastbourne, East Sussex BN 21 3UN, England

1 Goldthorne Avenue
Toronto, Ontario M8Z 5T9, Canada

Apartado 26370 — Cedro 512
Mexico 4, D.F. Mexico

Rua Coronel Cabrita, 8
Sao Cristovao Caixa Postal 21176
Rio de Janeiro, Brazil

9 Waltham Street
Artarmon, N.S.W. 2064, Australia

Ichibancho, Central Bldg., 22-1 Ichibancho
Chiyoda-ku, Tokyo 102, Japan

Library of Congress Cataloging in Publication Data

Main entry under title:

Medical emergencies in dentistry.

1. Medical emergencies.   2. Dental emergencies.
I. McCarthy, Frank M.   II. Emergencies in dental
practice. [DNLM: 1. Dentistry.   2. Emergencies.
WU 100 E53]

| RC86.7.M43 1982 | 616'.025'0246176 | 81–48094 |
| ISBN 0–7216–5879–2 | | AACR2 |

Medical Emergencies in Dentistry   ISBN   0–7216–5879–2

Last digit is the print number: 9   8   7   6   5   4   3   2   1

To Judy

CONTRIBUTORS

W. HOWARD DAVIS, D.D.S., F.A.C.D. Clinical Professor, University of Southern California School of Dentistry; Associate Professor, Loma Linda University School of Dentistry; Consultant, Long Beach Veterans Administration Hospital, Long Beach Naval Hospital; Staff, Downey Community Hospital, Long Beach Memorial Hospital, St. Mary's Hospital, Long Beach, California.

Emergency Drugs and Allergy.

JOHN HAGEN, D.D.S., M.S., F.A.C.D., F.A.D.S.A. Late Clinical Associate Professor, Section of Anesthesia and Medicine, University of Southern California School of Dentistry; Senior Attending Staff, Los Angeles County/University of Southern California Medical Center, Los Angeles.

Basic Life Support and Parenteral Drug Administration (with Stanley F. Malamed).

CEDRIC L. HAYDEN, D.M.D. Formerly Head, Department of Anesthesia, Port of Spain Community Hospital, Port of Spain, Trinidad, West Indies; Presently in private practice of dentistry and anesthesia for dentistry.

Monitoring (with Thomas F. Mulkey).

JESS HAYDEN, JR., D.M.D. Ph.D. Clinical Professor, Department of Surgical Dentistry, University of Colorado Medical Center, Denver; Consultant in Pedodontics, Denver General Hospital, Denver, Colorado.

Complications from Local Analgesia (with Niels Bjorn Jorgensen).

NIELS BJORN JORGENSEN, D.D.S., F.A.C.S., M.R.S.H. Late Emeritus Professor of Oral Surgery, Anesthesia Division, Loma Linda University School of Dentistry.

Complications from Local Analgesia (with Jess Hayden, Jr.).

LEO KORCHIN, B.S., D.D.S., M.S., F.A.C.D. Professor of Oral Surgery and Assistant Dean, University of Puerto Rico School of Dentistry; Attending Oral Surgeon, University Hospital, San Juan, Puerto Rico.

Establishing an Emergency Airway.

JOHN J. LYTLE, M.D., D.D.S., F.A.C.D. Clinical Professor and Chairman, Section of Oral and Maxillofacial Surgery, University of Southern California School of Dentistry; Chief of Oral and Maxillofacial Surgery, Department of Dentistry, Los Angeles County/University of Southern California Medical Center, Los Angeles; Chief of Staff, Memorial Hospital of Glendale, Glendale, California.

Cardiovascular and Other Medical Emergencies.

STANLEY F. MALAMED, D.D.S. Assistant Professor, Section of Anesthesia and Medicine, University of Southern California School of Dentistry, Los Angeles, California.

Basic Life Support and Parenteral Drug Administration (with John Hagen).

FRANK M. McCARTHY, B.S., M.S., M.D., D.D.S., Sc.D., F.A.C.D., F.I.C.D., F.A.D.S.A. Professor and Chairman, Department of Surgical Sciences and Anesthesia and Medicine Section, Assistant Dean for Hospital Affairs, University of Southern California School of Dentistry; Director, Dental Anesthesia Service, Los Angeles County/University of Southern California Medical Center; Guest Lecturer, Loma Linda University School of Dentistry; Consultant, Orthopaedic Hospital of Los Angeles.

Sudden Death. Physical Evaluation and Treatment Modification.

JOHN B. McVEIGH, D.D.S., M.S., F.I.C.D. Coordinator, Oral Surgery Residency Training, Alameda County Hospital, Oakland; Chief, Department of Dentistry, Providence Hospital, Oakland; Associate Staff, Children's Hospital, Merritt Hospital, and Perralta Hospital, Oakland, California.

General Anesthetic Emergencies and Complications.

THOMAS F. MULKEY, D.D.S. Clinical Professor, University of Southern California School of Dentistry; Senior Attending Staff, Los Angeles County/University of Southern California Medical Center; Chief, Dental Service, Orthopaedic Hospital of Los Angeles; Attending Staff, Daniel Freeman Memorial Hospital, Inglewood, California.

Monitoring (with Cedric L. Hayden).

THOMAS W. QUINN, D.M.D. Clinical Professor of Oral and Maxillofacial Surgery, Tufts University·School of Dental Medicine, Boston; Director, Department of Dentistry, Chief of Oral Surgery, Carney Hospital, Boston; Chief of Oral Surgery, Quincy City Hospital, Quincy, Massachusetts.

Cardiopulmonary Arrest.

LAWRENCE W. RICHARDSON, D.D.S., M.D. Board of Governors, School of Medicine, Stanford University; Lecturer equivalent to Associate Professor, School of Dentistry, School of Medicine, University of California at Los Angeles; Clinical Assistant Professor, University of Southern California School of Dentistry; Assistant Visiting Attending, University of California at Los Angeles Hospital; Senior Attending Dentist, Los Angeles County/University of Southern California Medical Center, St. John's Hospital, Santa Monica, California.

Physical Diagnosis.

GERALD A. SHEPPARD, B.A., L.L.B. Clinical Assistant Professor, University of Southern California School of Dentistry; Guest Lecturer, University of California at Los Angeles School of Dentistry and Loma Linda University School of Dentistry; Member Los Angeles County Bar Association, State Bar of California, and American Bar Association; Practitioner before the Bar of the United States Supreme Court.

Legal Aspects of Emergencies.

ROBERT BRUCE STEINER, D.M.D., B.S., F.A.C.D., F.I.C.D. Clinical Professor, University of Southern California School of Dentistry; Senior Attending Staff, Los Angeles County/University of Southern California Medical Center; Chief of Dental Section, Children's Hospital of Los Angeles; Staff, Hollywood Presbyterian Medical Center, St. Joseph's Hospital, Sunset Boulevard Hospital, Hollywood Community Hospital, Hollywood, California.

Drugs: Use and Abuse.

PREFACE

This abridged version of the third edition of *Emergencies in Dental Practice* responds to numerous requests from students, educators, general practitioners, specialists, hygienists, and dental assistants for a softcover edition limited to medical emergencies.

Parts I and II of *Emergencies in Dental Practice*, prevention and treatment of serious medical emergencies, are reproduced without change, except for the deletion of five chapters on sedation. Part III, prevention and treatment of surgical and operative emergencies, is deleted completely, as is Part IV, complementary topics, with the exception of legal aspects of emergencies. Medicolegal defense measures are an integral part of both prevention and postincident action and are thus included without change.

The reader will find definitive coverage of every conceivable serious medical emergency, with the emphasis on prevention. Brevity, clarity, and relevance were the watchwords in choosing topics and preparing the chapters. Both simple and complex emergencies are reviewed thoroughly, without verbosity.

Prevention of emergencies is based first upon recognition of the medically compromised patient. Emergencies rarely occur if there is proper physical evaluation and subsequent indicated modification of treatment. This book is not an exhaustive catalog of signs, symptoms, and treatment that rarely can be remembered during the exigencies of the moment. Instead, it gives sensible, practical attention to the treatment of emergencies. It does not demand performance approaching the level of the emergency room physician from dental health practitioners, most of whom have had very limited practical experience both in treating medical emergencies and in utilizing the intravenous route. It would be absurd to recommend an enormous number of emergency drugs, some requiring administration by the intravenous route, when an emergency may demand no more than a basic understanding of the disease process and immediate application of basic life support measures. In many cases, few if any drugs are desirable before the speedy transfer of the patient to medical or paramedical personnel. It is the author's firm belief that lack of understanding of the basic disease process and of preventive measures, plus compulsive and possibly unwise use of drugs during an emergency, leads to dangerous confusion and complication after the event. For those practitioners who are frequently exposed to potential life-threatening emergencies and are experienced in using the intravenous route, detailed material is included for study.

It is suggested that the reader first become familiar with the chapters on sudden death, physical evaluation and treatment modification, and legal aspects. He or she should then proceed to basic life support and parenteral drug administration, cardiopulmonary arrest, emergency drugs and allergy, cardiovascular and other medical emergencies, and complications from local analgesia. The chapters on monitoring and drugs outline essential background information, while the chapter on physical diagnosis serves as a bridge between physical evaluation and comprehensive physical diagnosis as practiced in medicine. The chapters on the emergency airway and general anesthetic complications are designed for those practitioners who treat patients when intravenous sedation or general anesthesia is utilized in the office or hospital.

FRANK M. MCCARTHY

CONTENTS

Part 1

PREVENTION OF SERIOUS MEDICAL EMERGENCIES

SUDDEN DEATH

FRANK M. McCARTHY

INTRODUCTION

The ultimate catastrophe in the dental office, death of a patient, requires an in-depth understanding of sudden death.

Until advances were made in external cardiopulmonary resuscitation (ECPR) during the 1960's, sudden and unexpected death remained virtually a statistical observation, not a treatable problem, with the rare exception of open-chest cardiac resuscitation performed during anesthesia and surgery. The nonsurgical mode of ECPR allows the reversal of many deaths which formerly were felt to be final, unexplained, and untreatable.

DEFINITION OF SUDDEN DEATH

There are about two million nonaccidental deaths per year in the United States.[1] Approximately one million of these are relatively sudden (cardiovascular and cerebrovascular diseases). Very nearly 20 per cent of all nonaccidental deaths, or 400,000, are sudden *and* unexpected. The mean age of the victims is 45 years.

Sudden, unexpected death occurs from nonaccidental causes in persons who previously appeared to be in good health and who had no history of disease. By various temporal definitions, sudden death occurs from up to one hour to 24 hours after collapse of the individual. Timing from collapse to death is rather academic since most sudden deaths are *instantaneous*.[2] Cardiovascular disease is the major cause, and almost all sudden deaths occur outside of the hospital.

Persons dying *instantaneously* of coronary artery disease differ to a considerable degree from persons dying *suddenly* of coronary artery disease.[3] They rarely exhibit acute symptoms or signs before death, more than one half die during physical stress, death results from a primary arrhythmia (ventricular fibrillation), and their hearts rarely show an acute lesion (myocardial infarction). A disconcerting number of sudden deaths cannot reasonably be accounted for at necropsy (postmortem examination).

CAUSES OF SUDDEN DEATH

The more common causes of sudden, unexpected death are coronary artery disease, cerebrovascular accidents, myocardiopathies, and cardiac conduction defects. These disorders may or may not have an increased familial incidence.

Doyle's review of the causes of sudden, nontraumatic death is outlined in Table 1–1.[2] Two additional causes of sudden death have recently been suggested. One involves the sudden formation of platelet aggregates in small pulmonary arteries and arterioles, with extreme respiratory distress and death in one to 30 minutes.[4] The other involves a progressive atrioventricular conduction defect in three generations of a large family.[5] Clinical findings included a slow heart rate and episodes of syncope. Progression to complete heart block was usually slow, but occasionally a fulminant course led to sudden death within two to three years. None of these deaths was unexpected.

MECHANISMS OF SUDDEN DEATH

The mechanism of sudden death is usually derangement of heart rhythm. In the hospital cardiac care unit (CCU), sudden death is most fre-

TABLE 1–1 CAUSES OF SUDDEN, NONTRAUMATIC DEATH

CARDIAC	Cor pulmonale
Coronary artery disease	acute
Morgagni-Adams-Stokes syndrome	chronic
Aortic stenosis	Status asthmaticus
Floppy mitral valve syndrome	
Primary myocardial disease	EXTRACARDIAC
Acute myocarditis	Dissecting aneurysm of aorta
Acute pericardial tamponade	Exsanguinating hemorrhage
Coronary embolism	Intracranial hemorrhage
Prolonged Q-T interval syndrome	
Congenital heart disease	MISCELLANEOUS
	Sudden infant death syndrome
PULMONARY	Pokurri disease; Bangungut
Asphyxia ("cafe coronary")	Unexplained

quently the result of ventricular fibrillation. If treatment is immediately instituted, the patient usually survives.

Unconsciousness occurs in healthy young experimental human subjects in an average of 6.8 seconds after occlusion of the cerebral circulation. Syncope is the presenting manifestation of sudden death and *implies circulatory arrest.*[2]

Seventy-five per cent of deaths from acute myocardial infarction (MI) take place during the *first hour.* Hospitalization must be expedited, as must admission to the CCU. One third of all patients with MI are detained in the emergency area for more than three hours until a diagnosis is securely established, thus resulting in a significant number of deaths from preventable cardiac arrest. A normal electrocardiogram (ECG) is perfectly compatible with the presence of an MI that may be fatal within minutes.

HEREDITARY FACTORS

Ten instances have been reported of the occurrence in three generations of sudden, unexpected death associated with stress and attributable to minor anatomical defects of the cardiac conduction system that could predispose to fatal arrhythmias. Pathological examinations were normal except for semiserial conduction studies by the Lev–Shanklin–Laite technique, a method that should be utilized in similar instances of unexplained death in persons with hearts that are grossly normal at necropsy. This type of death is probably far more common than can be proved on the basis of present evidence.

An uncommon type of QT prolongation (see electrocardiographic background in Chapter 4, Monitoring) is heritable and occurs most often in children with congenital deafness or with normal hearing. It is associated with syncopal episodes and sudden death. Asymmetrical sympathetic neural stimulation of the ventricular myocardium may lead to gross changes in the T wave and a prolonged QT interval. Prolongation of the QT interval represents delayed ventricular repolarization and an increase in the susceptibility to ventricular dysrhythmia. In the presence of a prolonged QT interval, premature ventricular contractions (PVCs) may lead to ventricular fibrillation.

If the medical history of a child with or without congenital deafness reveals *frequent syncope,* an ECG to investigate possible QT prolongation would be indicated.

Survival to adulthood by children with heritable QT prolongation indicates the termination of the conduction defect without further risk of sudden death.

With the exceptions of congenital heart disease and heritable conduction defects already covered, heredity has little influence on the development of common varieties of heart disease that can result in sudden, unexpected death. In disorders such as arterial hypertension and rheumatic fever, several genes may influence the disease, but environmental factors are far more important.

ENVIRONMENTAL FACTORS

Respiratory infections kill thousands of people of all ages who have chronic illness, especially old people and those with heart disease. Death rates vastly increase during the winter and in association with cold waves.

The same mortality increase in patients with chronic illness is seen during the summer for almost the entire United States.[6] Deaths from cardiac disease literally soar during hot and humid weather.

When the environmental temperature is at a comfortable level, heat loss at the skin surface occurs primarily by convection and radiation, with some by conduction. If the thermal gradient between the body and the environment becomes too little, or is actually reversed so that the temperature of the environment exceeds that of the body, then heat loss by usual means becomes inadequate or even ceases, and body heat must be lost by evaporation of sweat from the skin surface. If evaporative heat loss is impaired because of humidity, body temperature will rise. For heat loss to occur by evaporation, saturation of the surrounding atmosphere with water (relative humidity) must be less than 100 per cent.

Cardiac output in patients with heart disease is fixed at relatively low maximal levels. Cardiac output at total rest averages 3 to 4.5 liters per minute. In a hot and humid environment with thermal regulatory demands requiring a cardiac output of 20 to 30 liters per minute for any sustained period of time, the diseased heart will fail.

Patients with heart disease must be instructed to avoid hot and humid environments. For some patients with severe heart disease, air-conditioning is essential during dental treatment.

EMOTIONAL FACTORS

Regulatory inhibition of cardiac rate is enhanced by purposeful action and is diminished in situations that appear to be overwhelming and without hope, such as severe dejection or sudden fear. The loss of inhibition provides the death mechanism. Being frightened to death is literally possible.

In a study of 530 out of 817 episodes of acute myocardial infarction, it was possible to determine that 104 (20 per cent) occurred during sleep. Ten patients known to have nocturnal attacks of angina pectoris were monitored during sleep for 12 full nights, 39 episodes of angina pectoris with significant ECG changes being recorded. The dreams involved strenuous exertion, fear, anger, or frustration.

A medicolegal application of the stress response was demonstrated by a $500,000 professional negligence verdict in the hospital general anesthesia death of a 13-year-old male who, it was claimed, was in a state of panic preoperatively and was therefore not a fit candidate for anesthesia or surgery.

The role of emotional stress associated with anesthesia and dentoalveolar surgery has been recognized as a cause of death by leading dental authorities in the United Kingdom.[7, 8] Emotional as well as physical stress is capable of precipitating complications in individuals with heart disease.[9]

It is my opinion that emotional stress is responsible for more deaths related to dental therapy than any other single factor.

AGE AND DEATH

Age at each end of the spectrum strongly influences the incidence of sudden death.

Sudden, unexpected infant deaths occur at a markedly high rate in the 10-day to 16-week age group, leveling off at six months of age.

Sudden, unexpected death rates increase proportionally with age until the middle years, when the rate increases in direct relationship to the diseases of aging. In an analysis of 328 fatally injured drivers, there was no significant correlation between accident responsibility and disease, but the proportion of drivers 60 years of age or older was five times as high among those killed as among those who survived multi-vehicle crashes. The aged had a markedly increased incidence of death from complications of existing disease, such as coronary atherosclerotic heart disease.

Age alone has a marked influence on hospital fatalities. Patients less than 60 years of age average 12 per cent fatalities, and older patients show a steadily increasing fatality percentage up to 50 per cent in the oldest age group. Patients hospitalized in facilities with CCUs have *slightly lower* fatality rates than other patients. Monday admissions substantially exceed fatalities on other days of the week.[10]

INDIVIDUALS AT RISK

The identification of the individual at greatest risk of sudden death merely represents the delineation of his or her coronary risk profile; for example, male sex, relative youth, arterial hypertension, overweight, glucose intolerance, hypercholesterolemia, indolence, and heavy smoking.[2] I hasten to add that hypercholesterolemia may be removed from the preceding profile. Clinicians remain unconvinced that the low fat, low cholesterol, polyunsaturated diets promoted since 1950 have any effect on coronary heart disease. No diet therapy has been shown effective for the prevention or treatment of coronary heart disease, and there is no safe and efficacious drug known for the management of hypercholesterolemia.[11] Low fat diets at least have not been harmful to those following the latest trend, though dogs subsisting on table scraps in such families have commonly developed mange (fat deprivation).

Evidence suggests that fit and active people are spared the complications of coronary artery atherosclerosis. Studies of the Masai indicate that exercise makes even atherosclerotic vessels enlarge so that the capacity of coronary vessels increases despite an increase of atherosclerosis.[11]

If the electrocardiographic pattern of left ventricular hypertrophy (LVH) is added to the usual coronary risk profile, the risk of sudden death increases as much as sixteen-fold between individuals at opposite ends of the risk factor scale.[12]

There are few characteristics associated specifically with a likelihood of sudden death. PVCs are common in the general population, increase in frequency with age, and have little significance in healthy individuals. However, PVCs are universally observed during myocardial infarction and are often a precursor to ventricular fibrillation, and are therefore of prognostic significance in individuals *with* heart disease.[2]

The possibility of impending sudden death should be considered with the appearance of inappropriate bradycardia (heart rate less than 60 beats per minute) or significant PVCs during dental treatment. Sudden death rates among persons over age 30 with PVCs is six times that of persons over age 30 without PVCs.

REVERSAL OF DEATH

Successful reversal of sudden death in the dental office demands immediate and effective treatment before transportation to the hospital. Approximately 70 per cent of patients dying from coronary atherosclerotic heart disease (CAHD) never reach the hospital. Death is frequently instantaneous. About 60 per cent of all sudden deaths occur in patients with CAHD.

According to Jude and Nagel,[13] sudden total circulatory collapse in the operating room can be expected to have a 60 to 75 per cent survival via ECPR; in the cardiac catheterization laboratory, success is 95 to 100 per cent; in the CCU, sudden arrhythmic death can be reversed in 50 to 60 per cent of cases; in the general hospital setting, 8 to 15 per cent are successfully resuscitated.

No reliable statistics are available for successful reversal of the out-of-hospital death (OHD), although fragmentary evidence is disappointing. In a study on delay in the prehospital phase, delay due to inappropriate patient behavior was the most important component. However, 60 to 75 per cent of OHDs occur so rapidly that their prevention by reduction of prehospital delay seems impossible.[14] In another mortality study the median patient delay, from onset of symptoms until hospital arrival, was 5.6 hours.[15] Public education and a vast increase of mobile and other ancillary medical facilities will be necessary in order to significantly further reduce OHDs.

It is interesting to note that the age-adjusted death rate from coronary artery disease declined between 1963 and 1968, while at the same time an epidemic of coronary artery disease has been claimed, based only upon crude death rates. This discrepancy is due to a shift in the age composition of the population. The increase in crude death rates will continue so long as gains in life expectancy result in a bigger population in the older ages, even though there may be a decrease in mortality for every individual age group.[16] There is an approximate five-year time lag in the publication of U.S. government age-adjusted mortality rates.

CARDIAC CARE UNIT

The cardiac care unit (CCU), sometimes known by the more general term intensive care unit (ICU), proliferated vastly in the 1970s. Originally established as a special area where MI patients could be provided with continuous ECG monitoring and specially trained nurses, the typical CCU now requires the use of complex diagnostic, physiologic, and therapeutic procedures. Burch feels that MIs can be treated very well with simple bedside procedures and therapy. He quotes a 12.3 per cent mortality rate among 253 unselected MI patients treated only by ECG monitoring and close observation in the CCU compared to mortality rates of 13 to 21 per cent in other U.S. institutions. Burch objects to invasive monitoring techniques; for example, the placement of catheters to record central venous pressure, systemic venous pressure, capillary wedge pressure, and pulmonary or systemic arterial pressure. He feels that the catheters are not only hazardous but are uncomfortable and frightening to many patients, and that they interfere with rest.[17] Since stress increases the number of PVCs in the infarcted heart,[18] it is probable that CCUs will revert to less involved monitoring for an increasing number of patients. Further, the cost-effectiveness of invasive monitoring is being questioned.

Some hospitals are introducing intermediate cardiac care unit (ICCUs), to which patients at less risk are transferred very early from the CCU and monitored in less intensive, less heavily staffed areas, rather than being transferred to general medical wards where nursing coverage may be sparse and monitoring nonexistent. The subacute areas of these ICCUs utilize radiotelemetry to allow early ambulation.

OTHER MORTALITY RATES

We have examined sudden death mortality rates in and out of the hospital. For a more comprehensive understanding of death, we will review myocardial infarction related to general anesthesia, general anesthesia mortality in the hospital, and general anesthesia mortality in the dental office.

GENERAL ANESTHESIA AND MIs

Patients who have had an MI are at high risk of reinfarction under general anesthesia, 6.6 per cent experiencing another MI during the first postoperative week. There is no relationship between incidence of reinfarction and type or duration of anesthesia, although operations on the thorax and upper abdomen are followed by three times as many reinfarctions as operations at other sites.[19]

Patients who are operated on within three months of infarction have a 37 per cent reinfarction rate. This rate decreases to 16 per cent in patients at three to six months after infarction, and remains at 4 to 5 per cent over six months. Over 50 per cent die as a result of reinfarction.[19]

GENERAL ANESTHESIA MORTALITY

Approximately 15 million general anesthetics are administered yearly in hospitals in the United States. Forty per cent of the anesthetics are ad-

TABLE 1-2 GENERAL ANESTHESIA MORTALITY

Dental offices, U.S.	−1:400,000
Dental offices, South. Calif.	−1:400,000
Dental offices, U.K.	−1:300,000
Large teaching hospitals, U.S.	−1:1500
Suburban hospitals, U.S.	−1:9000
T & A, hospitals, U.S.	−1:40,000

ministered by trained anesthesiologists (MD), 40 per cent by certified registered nurse anesthetists (CRNA), and 20 per cent by other personnel.[20] Approximately five million general anesthetics are administered yearly in dental offices in the United States. Seventy per cent of the anesthetics are administered by trained dental practitioners, 4 per cent by anesthesiologists, 10 per cent by CRNAs, and 16 per cent by other personnel.[21]

Table 1–2 demonstrates the general anesthesia mortality experience in dental offices in the United States[21], Southern California[22], and the United Kingdom.[23] Comparison is made with general anesthesia mortality in large teaching centers[24] and suburban hospitals[25] in the United States. The tonsillectomy and adenoidectomy (T & A) mortality rate of 1:40,000 is quoted, as it is the most favorable report I have discovered in the literature, although the national T & A general anesthesia mortality rate is 1:20,000.[21] The Southern California survey reported a 100 per cent response.

It would appear that general anesthesia in the dental office is at least 10 to 20 times safer than general anesthesia in the hospital. It is improper, however, to make comparisons without stressing the great differences between hospital general anesthesia and dental office general anesthesia. General anesthesia in the dental office is purely elective and is available only to favorable risk patients; duration of anesthesia is comparatively short; the treatment can be terminated instantly in an emergency; operative delays are uncommon; and the anesthetic depth is ultralight, rarely approaching surgical depth with depression or obtundation of protective reflexes.

Mortality greatly increases if the preoperative physical status of the patient is unfavorable, and it increases again for emergencies as compared to elective procedures.[26] In a computerized analysis of postanesthetic deaths, the prime determinants of mortality were considered to be the physical status of the patient and the judgment and skill of the physician.[27] In this same study, which reported an overall general anesthesia mortality of 1.82 per cent, mortality of Class I and Class II physical status patients (favorable risk) was 1.70 per cent, and this despite the fact that 30 per cent of the Class I and Class II patients were emergencies.

DENTAL OFFICE MORTALITY

There are no totally reliable national or regional records of patient deaths in dental and medical offices, and there does not seem to be much chance of accurate surveys being made, except under unusual control circumstances.[22]

Coroner records are unreliable, as the deceased may be certified in the medical office or hospital emergency room and thus not become a coroner's case. National and regional surveys are questionable, as doctors are reluctant to divulge information, and reporting is usually incomplete. Liability insurance records are both privileged and subject to distortions.

In my opinion, based purely upon informed speculation, the average dental doctor will experience one or two patient deaths during his or her practice lifetime, occurring either in the office or within a 24-hour post-treatment period, and there will be an additional known four or five patient deaths occurring within one week of treatment. These deaths are probably unrelated to therapy and occur at random, although treatment stresses may represent contributing factors.

In closing this section on mortality associated with dental therapy, allow me to quote Mark Twain: *There are lies, damned lies, and statistics.* The reader must make the judgment.

SUDDEN DEATH AND TRENDS IN DENTISTRY

A review of current trends in dental care related to mortality or serious morbidity in the office will be limited to medicolegal pressures. In California there is an average of one wrongful death medical lawsuit per month with judgment of one million dollars or more. Wrongful death dental lawsuits in California have reached a top of $300,000 as of this writing and are certain to go higher. Risk-free therapy is impossible, yet the public has been educated by the news media to expect a perfect result as a norm. The reader is referred to Chapter 13 for a comprehensive review of the disturbing legal aspects of the situation.

As patient mortality closely related to dental treatment reaches the point of ultimate catastrophe, we note increases in the following areas: publicity, malpractice charges, malpractice awards, and criminal negligence charges (negligent homicide). These pressures are influencing the dental doctor, consciously or unconsciously, to avoid treatment which might be a basis for a malpractice claim.

In the arena of medical emergencies and possible morbidity or mortality involving the risk patient, local analgesic agents without vasoconstrictors are being arbitrarily chosen, although depth of analgesia may suffer and the risk of toxic overdose is increased; high risk patients are being hospitalized for dental care under general anesthesia, thus subjecting them to enormous risk, while the same procedure could be performed far more safely in the dental office with local analgesia and perhaps sedation for anxiety control; sedation via the inhalation and intravenous routes is being used less commonly for the risk patient in order to avoid possible claims, whereas the risk patient vastly benefits from sedation. Lastly, an increasing number of dental practitioners are flatly refusing to treat the risk patient. All of these alterations in treatment standards work to the distinct detriment of the medically compromised patient.

WHEN YOUR OFFICE PATIENT DIES

When your patient dies in the office, it is a shattering experience not only to the deceased's relatives but also to you and to your office staff. It can be damaging to your professional reputation, it can result in a wrongful death malpractice suit, and it can result in a charge of criminal negligence. Conviction of criminal negligence usually absolves your professional liability insurance carrier of any financial obligation resulting from subsequent malpractice action.[28]

Humane and practical considerations are five in number:[29]

1. Preplan your resuscitative procedures with your office staff. Practice simulated emergencies. If your procedures are not preplanned and rehearsed, you will perhaps treat a life-threatening emergency in a less than adequate manner. Keep your resuscitative kit updated and handy for instant use. If your patient does not survive, despite your prompt and definitive treatment, you will be able to demonstrate that you did everything that could reasonably be expected of you.

2. Take extreme care when informing the next-of-kin of a death. Tell the relative in the privacy of your office that the patient collapsed, that everything possible was done, but to no avail. It is virtually impossible to extend too much grief and sympathy *without admitting liability*. Avoid any statement about the cause of death until you have had time to review and complete your records. Just say *sudden collapse*.

3. Have the patients in your reception room excused, with only *serious emergency* as explanation.

4. Compile a complete record — the patient's appearance, the probable cause of death, and the resuscitative efforts. It is mandatory in most states to report such a death to the coroner's office. Also, certain liability insurance carriers require that they be notified immediately of any event that could result in a claim. Sudden death in the office is a leading cause of large judgments.

5. Guard your reputation. You will have to fend off pointed questions by the deceased's relatives and friends. Silence on your part will intrigue the relatives and fortify suspicions about your possible responsibility. Repeat your shock and grief, offer sincerest sympathy, but simply say that the deceased suddenly collapsed.

Always accompany the patient to the hospital. If you are refused transportation in the emergency vehicle, proceed in another vehicle. Do not remain in the office under any circumstances.

Proper resuscitative efforts, even though ultimately unsuccessful, will usually result in transportation to the hospital while living. Do not discontinue ECPR in the office. It is also possible that the death may be certified by the emergency room physician, thus obviating the need for a coroner's report.

Preparation before the fact is the key in order to weather such a catastrophe in a proper, humane, and practical manner.

PREVENTION OF DEATH

In the general community, success in reducing the incidence of sudden death rests mainly with the individual seeking early medical assistance, with discouraging results to date. For example, despite the biennial physical examinations in the Framingham study, 50 per cent of all subjects who died suddenly had no prior clinical diagnosis of heart disease.[30] The authors concluded that the only road to a substantial reduction of coronary heart disease mortality is prevention of coronary heart disease.

All is not gloom, however. Coronary care ambulances have shown great promise. In one study, highly motivated ambulance personnel were trained so that they achieved a high degree of accuracy in ECG interpretation, and by persistent vigorous ECPR combined with defibrillation were able to salvage seven out of 14 patients, all of whom were subsequently discharged from the hospital.[31]

In the dental community, a high degree of success in the prevention of sudden death during dental treatment can be achieved. Three areas of primary importance include proper physical evaluation before therapy, adequate pain/anxiety control, and knowledgeable treatment of medical emergencies by a team composed of the doctor and assistants.

COMMENT

The incidence of sudden, unexpected death is so high that a significant number of such deaths can and do occur coincidentally in the dental office or soon after treatment. Furthermore, since most primary causes of sudden, unexpected death can be influenced by physical or emotional stress, it is probable that such deaths in the dental office could be secondarily related to treatment stress. This is strong justification for adequate pain/anxiety control for dental patients who are in apparent good heatlh, and is obvious justification for an in-depth grasp of the prevention, recognition, and treatment of life-threatening emergencies.

REFERENCES

1. Vital Statistics Report — Annual Summary for the United States, 1970. Rockville, Maryland, U.S. Public Health Service, 1970, p. 3.
2. Doyle, J. T.: Mechanisms and prevention of sudden death. Mod. Conc. Cardiov. Dis., 45:111–116, 1976.
3. Friedman, M., et al.: Instantaneous and sudden deaths. J.A.M.A., 225:1319–1328, 1973.
4. Editorial: Sudden death — a new syndrome. J.A.M.A., 230:1018, 1974.
5. Lynch, H. T., et al.: Hereditary progressive atrioventricular conduction defect — a new syndrome. J.A.M.A., 225:1465–1470, 1973.
6. Burch, G. E., and Giles, T. D.: The burden of a hot and humid environment on the heart. Mod. Conc. Cardiov. Dis., 39:115–120, 1970.
7. Goldman, V., Los Angeles Times, July 24, 1970.
8. Drummond-Jackson, S. L.: A tragic story. Newsletter SAAD, 2:195, 1974.
9. Hockwald, R. S.: Can emotional stress cause atherosclerosis? J.A.M.A., 218:1308, 1971.
10. Peterson, D. R., et al.: Ischemic heart disease prognosis, a community wide assessment (1966–1969). J.A.M.A., 219:1423–1427, 1972.
11. Mann, G. V.: Diet–heart: end of an era. New Engl. J. Med., 297:644–650, 1977.
12. Kannel, W. B., et al.: Precursors of sudden coronary death. Circulation, 51:606–613, 1975.
13. Jude, J. R., and Nagel, E. L.: Cardiopulmonary resuscitation 1970. Mod. Conc. Cardiov. Dis., 39:133–139, 1970.
14. Gillum, R. F., et al.: Delay in the prehospital phase of acute myocardial infarction. Arch. Intern. Med., 136:649–654, 1976.
15. Feinleib, M., and Davidson, M. J.: Coronary heart disease mortality. J.A.M.A., 222:1129–1134, 1972.
16. Walker, W. J.: Coronary mortality: what is going on. J.A.M.A., 227:1045–1046, 1974.

17. Burch, G. E.: A reappraisal of coronary care units. Resident & Staff Physician, 5:51–54, 1977.

18. Lown, B., and Verrier, R. L.: Neural activity and ventricular fibrillation, New Engl. J. Med., 294:1165–1170, 1976.

19. Tarhan, S., et al.: Myocardial infarction after general anesthesia. J.A.M.A., 220:1451–1454, 1972.

20. Jenkins, M. T.: Anesthesiology. J.A.M.A., 211:282–285, 1970.

21. Driscoll, E. J.: ASOS anesthesia morbidity and mortality survey. J. Oral Surg., 32:733–738, 1974.

22. Lytle, J. J.: Anesthesia morbidity and mortality survey of the Southern California Society of Oral Surgeons. J. Oral Surg., 32:739–744, 1974.

23. Tomlin, P. J.: Death in outpatient dental anesthetic practice. Anaesthesia, 29:551, 1974.

24. Beecher, H. K., and Todd, D. P.: A Study of Deaths Associated with Anesthesia and Surgery. Springfield, Charles C Thomas, 1954, p. 43.

25. Mannix, A. J.: Medicolegal implications of operating room deaths. New York J. Med., 60:683, 1960.

26. Vacanti, C., et al.: A statistical analysis of the relationship of physical status to postoperative mortality in 68,388 cases. Anesth. Analg., 49:564–566, 1970.

27. Marx, G. T., et al.: Computer analysis of postanesthetic deaths. Anesthesiology, 39:54–58, 1973.

28. McCarthy, F. M.: When your office patient dies. In Archer, W. H.: Oral and Maxillofacial Surgery. Philadelphia, W. B. Saunders Co., 1975, pp. 1544–1545.

29. Aarons, E. F.: What if a patient dies in your office. Med. Econ., 195: (Jan. 19), 1970.

30. Gordon, T., and Kannel, W. B.: Premature mortality from coronary heart disease — the Framingham study. J.A.M.A., 215:1617–1625, 1971.

31. Rose, L. B., and Press, E.: Cardiac defibrillation by ambulance attendants. J.A.M.A., 219:63–68, 1972.

PHYSICAL EVALUATION AND TREATMENT MODIFICATION

FRANK M. McCARTHY

PHYSICAL EXAMINATION

PHYSICAL EVALUATION

DEFINITION

Physical evaluation in dentistry consists of the establishment of a basic medical risk factor, without necessarily reaching a definitive diagnosis, prior to dental therapy.[1]

The art and science of physical evaluation utilizes a medical history, which is usually completed by the patient, and applicable physical examination, sometimes assisted by function tests and laboratory tests. On the other hand, physical diagnosis in medicine establishes a medical diagnosis in response to a complaint and usually leads to therapy; the medical history is usually conducted verbally by the health practitioner; and a more complete physical examination may be performed. Physical evaluation and physical diagnosis are markedly similar, differing only in the degree of application of methods for general diagnosis, since medical risk factor orientation alone is the goal of the former.

There follows an outline of the various parts of physical evaluation compared to physical diagnosis:

Physical Evaluation	*Physical Diagnosis*
1. Medical history	1. Medical history
2. Physical examination	2. Physical examination
3. Function tests	3. Function tests
4. X-rays and lab tests	4. X-rays and lab tests
5. Establish physical status	5. Establish diagnosis
6. Modifications to therapy	6. Treat illness
7. Mitigate fears and anxieties	7. Mitigate fears and anxieties

INTRODUCTION

Routine physical evaluation of the patient prior to dental treatment has become a standard of care in the United States during the past 20 years. This has come about because of the increased morbidity and mortality risks with longer dental treatments, the adoption of sophisticated sedation techniques, the increasing numbers of geriatric dental patients, the introduction of external cardiopulmonary resuscitation, and the normal elevation of standards for the public good. Proper evaluation is a legal obligation as well as a moral responsibility. No longer is the casual question, "Are you in good health?" considered to be an adequate pretreatment evaluation in dentistry.

Knowledge by the dental practitioner of an effective evaluation technique is desirable because death, serious illness, and minor physical reactions may be directly related to dental treatment. Such complications are preventable in large part by proper pretreatment evaluation.

In addition, patients consult the dental practitioner five times more frequently than the physician. This represents a marvelous opportunity for valuable health screening and is a highly significant health service. As one example, early detection of arterial hypertension usually allows effective treatment, while late detection after serious damage to target organs (heart, kidneys, brain), may represent a virtually hopeless treatment situation.

A review of 4785 consecutive medical histories at the Temple University dental clinic revealed that only 877 patients of that group had consulted a physician within the past year, 25 per cent had a chronic illness, 10.8 per cent had more than one medical problem, and 18.5 per cent were taking routine medications.[2]

GOAL OF PHYSICAL EVALUATION

The doctor's goal in evaluation is simply to determine the physical and emotional ability of a particular patient to tolerate a specific dental procedure in comfort and relative safety. The goal is not to diagnose or treat the medical problem, although accurate diagnoses will be achieved by the use of a proper evaluation technique and by experience. We wish to produce an evaluation factor by which it is determined whether we may proceed with dental treatment in relative safety or that medical consultation is indicated before treatment.

FUNCTION OF PHYSICIAN

The function of the physician is to reach a diagnosis and treat the medical problem. When any doubt exists regarding the medical status of a dental patient, the physician should be consulted. The physician is a vital member of the health team, and will be more than willing to discuss dental treatment plans as they relate to the specific medical problems of the patient. The dental practitioner has a responsibility to the patient to consult the physician when indicated and to be guided but not directed by the advice. The final responsibility to the dental patient cannot be equally shared by the physician except under unusual circumstances. The practitioner should receive the physician's advice with an open mind, and should discuss the treatment plan and anticipated problems. Most misunderstandings occur as a result of lack of communication.

In most cases, consultation with the physician will result in little alteration of the treatment plan. In some cases it may be markedly altered, and in the rare instance it may be necessary to delay treatment or postpone it indefinitely. It makes little sense to rehabilitate dentally a patient with terminal cancer, nor does it make better sense to subject a high-risk cardiac patient to prolonged, stress-producing restorative dentistry. The dental doctor must be prepared to justify anything except emergency dental treatment for the high-risk patient.

EVALUATION TECHNIQUE

The evaluation technique described here is designed to be used by all practitioners, regardless of past training or experience. The general practitioner may utilize the health questionnaire only. As experience is gained, and particularly if he or she supplements knowledge by continuing education, the doctor will progress further into full evaluation of the patient. Depending on background and interest in the subject, the general practitioner may readily develop the ability to make a detailed and highly accurate judgment of the patient's physical status. I urge the doctor to reach a tentative conclusion and treatment plan following a *full* history and physical examination *before* calling the physician in consultation, rather than calling the physician at the first mention of a potential health problem. This will give the practitioner experience in evaluation and will prepare him or her to discuss the problem with knowledge and insight.

The medical history that follows can be used by all dental practitioners, regardless of type of practice. The oral surgeon is obligated to make a detailed analysis, particularly when general anesthesia is to be used; yet the general practitioner should not feel that he or she is excused from the obligation of evaluation. The risk of local analgesia or any dental treatment in a particular case may be very high; mortality reports in the general dental office support this recommendation.

MEDICAL HISTORY QUESTIONNAIRE

Synonyms or euphemisms for the medical history in dentistry have included the following terms: health questionnaire, health history, health review, and health analysis. Since the dental practitioner obtains a comprehensive though relatively brief medical history, and since it is commonly more comprehensive than the history obtained in the average medical practice, it is refreshing to observe the present trend to use of the proper term, medical history.

Every dental patient should be required to complete a medical history questionnaire. For a basic, risk-factor evaluation by the experienced practitioner, I suggest the short-form medical history taken from the 1977-78 edition of *Accepted Dental Therapeutics* (Fig. 2–1).[3] It has been kept as brief and as simple as possible in order to facilitate patient accuracy and understanding. Four of the questions apply only to the patient who is to receive general anesthesia or sedation.

HEALTH QUESTIONNAIRE

Date _____

Name _____ Address _____
  Last   First   Middle   Number & Street

City _____ State _____ Zip Code _____ Home & Business Phone _____
Age _____ Sex _____ Height _____ Weight _____ Occupation _____

Married _____ Spouse _____ Single _____

Closest Relative _____ Phone _____

If you are completing this form for another person, what is your relationship to that person?

_____

PLEASE ANSWER EACH QUESTION   CIRCLE

1. Have you been a patient in a hospital during the past 2 years?   Yes No
2. Have you been under the care of a physician during the past 2 years?   Yes No
3. Have you taken any kind of medicine or drugs during the past year?   Yes No
4. Are you allergic to penicillin or any drugs or medicine?   Yes No
5. Have you ever had any excessive bleeding requiring special treatment?   Yes No
6. Circle any of the following which you have had:

    heart trouble   jaundice   arthritis
    congenital heart lesions   asthma   stroke
    heart murmur   cough   epilepsy
    high blood pressure   diabetes   psychiatric treatment
    anemia   tuberculosis   sinus trouble
    rheumatic fever   hepatitis

7. (Women) Are you pregnant now?   Yes No
8. Have you had any other serious illnesses?   Yes No

   TO BE ANSWERED ONLY BY PATIENTS RECEIVING SEDATION OR GENERAL ANESTHESIA.

9. Have you had anything to eat or drink within the last 4 hours?   Yes No
10. Are you wearing removable dental applicances?   Yes No
11. Are you wearing contact lenses?   Yes No
12. Who is to drive you home today?

   a. Name _____

Reviewed by _____ Signature _____

P1-HQ1

Figure 2–1. Short-form medical history, taken from the 1977-78 edition of *Accepted Dental Therapeutics*.

HEALTH QUESTIONNAIRE

Date _____

Name _____ Address _____
     Last   First   Middle   Number & Street

City _____ State _____ Zip Code _____ Home & Business Phone _____

Date of Birth _____ Sex _____ Height _____ Weight _____ Occupation _____

Married _____ Spouse _____ Single _____

Closest Relative _____ Phone _____

If you are completing this form for another person, what is your relationship to that person?

_____

In the following questions, circle yes or no, whichever applies. Your answers are for our records only and will be considered confidential.

1. Has there been any change in your general health within the past year .... YES   NO

2. My last physical examination was on_____

3. Are you now under the care of a physician.. YES   NO
   a. If so, what is the condition being treated _____

4. The name and address of my physician is _____
   _____
   _____

5. Have you had any serious illness or operation .... YES   NO
   a. If so, what was the illness or operation_____

6. Have you been hospitalized or had a serious illness within the past five (5) years .... YES   NO
   a. If so, what was the problem _____

7. Do you have or have you had any of the following diseases or problems.
   a. Rheumatic fever or rheumatic heart disease... YES   NO
   b. Congenital heart lesions... YES   NO
   c. Cardiovascular disease (heart trouble, heart attack, coronary insufficiency, coronary occlusion,
      high blood pressure, arteriosclerosis, stroke)... YES   NO
      1) Do you have pain in chest upon exertion .... YES   NO
      2) Are you ever short of breath after mild exercise... YES   NO
      3) Do your ankles swell... YES   NO
      4) Do you get short of breath when you lie down, or do you require extra pillows when you sleep... YES   NO
   d. Allergy... YES   NO
   e. Sinus trouble... YES   NO
   f. Asthma or hay fever... YES   NO
   g. Hives or a skin rash .... YES   NO
   h. Fainting spells or seizures... YES   NO
   i. Diabetes.. YES   NO
      1) Do you have to urinate (pass water) more than six times a day .... YES   NO
      2) Are you thirsty much of the time .... YES   NO
      3) Does your mouth frequently become dry .... YES   NO
   j. Hepatitis, jaundice or liver disease .... YES   NO
   k. Arthritis... YES   NO
   l. Inflammatory rheumatism (painful swollen joints)... YES   NO
   m. Stomach ulcers .... YES   NO
   n. Kidney trouble... YES   NO
   o. Tuberculosis .... YES   NO
   p. Do you have a persistent cough or cough up blood... YES   NO
   q. Low blood pressure... YES   NO
   r. Venereal disease .... YES   NO
   s. Other _____

(over)

Figure 2–2. Long-form medical history, taken from the 1977-78 edition of *Accepted Dental Therapeutics.*

8. Have you had abnormal bleeding associated with previous extractions, surgery, or trauma . . . . YES NO
   a. Do you bruise easily . . . . YES NO
   b. Have you ever required a blood transfusion . . . . YES NO
      If so, explain the circumstances _____

9. Do you have any blood disorder such as anemia . . . . YES NO
10. Have you had surgery or x-ray treatment for a tumor, growth, or other condition of your mouth or lips . . YES NO
11. Are you taking any drug or medicine . . . . YES NO
    If so, what _____
12. Are you taking any of the following:
    a. Antibiotics or sulfa drugs . . . . YES NO
    b. Anticoagulants (blood thinners) . . . . YES NO
    c. Medicine for high blood pressure . . . . YES NO
    d. Cortisone (steroids) . . . . YES NO
    e. Tranquilizers . . . . YES NO
    f. Antihistamines . . . . YES NO
    g. Aspirin . . . . YES NO
    h. Insulin, tolbutamide (Orinase) or similar drug . . . . YES NO
    i. Digitalis or drugs for heart trouble . . . . YES NO
    j. Nitroglycerin . . . . YES NO
    k. Other _____
13. Are you allergic or have you reacted adversely to:
    a. Local anesthetics . . . . YES NO
    b. Penicillin or other antibiotics . . . . YES NO
    c. Sulfa drugs . . . . YES NO
    d. Barbiturates, sedatives, or sleeping pills . . . . YES NO
    e. Aspirin . . . . YES NO
    f. Iodine . . . . YES NO
    g. Codeine or other narcotics . . . . YES NO
    h. Other _____
14. Have you had any serious trouble associated with any previous dental treatment . . . . YES NO
    If so, explain _____

15. Do you have any disease, condition, or problem not listed above that you think I should know about . . . YES NO
    If so, explain _____

16. Are you employed in any situation which exposes you regularly to x-rays or other ionizing radiation . . . YES NO
17. Are you wearing contact lenses . . . . YES NO

WOMEN

18. Are you pregnant . . . . YES NO
19. Do you have any problems associated with your menstrual period . . . . YES NO

Remarks:

_____
SIGNATURE OF PATIENT

_____
SIGNATURE OF DENTIST

P1-HQ

Figure 2-2. Continued.

The recommended short-form medical history (now slightly modified) was created in 1956 by the six oral surgeons who originally made up the Dental Anesthesia Service, Los Angeles County/University of Southern California Medical Center, and is routinely used in their offices. The dependability of the form is attested to by their having administered a total of over 720,000 office general anesthetics through 1978 with but one contributing general anesthetic mortality (subarachnoid hemorrhage in a patient with polycythemia vera).

The long-form medical history in *Accepted Dental Therapeutics* (Fig. 2–2) is adequate for physical evaluation. It also serves as a reliable teaching aid and as an excellent departure point for physical diagnosis.[4]

A guide to a complete dialogue medical history may be seen in the chapter on *physical diagnosis*. This is a suggested form for physical diagnosis, and will not be considered further in this chapter.

OTHER QUESTIONNAIRES

Other medical history questionnaires are equally applicable. I feel, however, that a questionnaire designed primarily to produce a basic evaluation and risk factor can be entirely *too* detailed, resulting in annoyance to the patient, inattention, and inaccuracies. Some questionnaires are unnecessarily long and confusing to the patient. Although medicolegal considerations tempt the practitioner to utilize a voluminous health questionnaire, in my opinion the accuracy of a brief and simple questionnaire is in the best interests of the patient. I do not think that a highly detailed questionnaire is indicated for most purposes in other than a teaching environment, and I therefore recommend a short-form questionnaire to the experienced practitioner, to be followed by a dialogue history as indicated.

A programmed medical history was introduced in medicine in 1966,[40] followed by a programmed physical examination in 1971.[41] Such complexity is not required for our purposes.

RELIABILITY OF QUESTIONNAIRE

Well controlled surveys have shown that a self-administered medical history is reliable and readily accepted by patients. Although questionnaires are superior to the conventional dialogue history in terms of providing a recorded data base, they have not been shown to be superior with respect to initial diagnostic and therapeutic decisions. It is my feeling that the method of history-taking described in this chapter, a self-administered questionnaire followed by a dialogue history conducted by the practitioner, is the most accurate, least time consuming, and least annoying to the patient of any method to date.

Some practitioners prefer to personally make the queries directly from the questionnaire (or have the assistant do so), feeling that accuracy is enhanced. While this claim is unproven at the moment, the routine is to be recommended if time allows, as it notably improves rapport early in the treatment relationship, and gives the doctor or assistant the opportunity to explain any question that is confusing or appears to be irrelevant.

The relatively unstructured verbal inquiry has been demonstrated to be deficient compared to a structured patient-completed questionnaire.[39]

CHECKING THE QUESTIONNAIRE

It is the policy of the LAC/USC Dental Anesthesia Service to have the new patient complete the medical history questionnaire and other standard records in the reception room, after which the dental assistant reviews the questionnaire with the patient to make certain that it is complete. The patient and assistant sign the dated form, and the practitioner then has proof that the history was taken and is accurate. We do not feel that it is necessary for the doctor or assistant to personally ask the history questions, although this may be done if desired.

TIME LAPSE IN TREATMENT

When the doctor meets the patient in consultation, the medical history is reviewed and evaluation proceeds as indicated. When the patient returns to the office after a period of time, it is my custom to have the assistant ask the patient if he or she has had any health problems or is taking any medication not previously discussed. Such changes are noted on the record and initialed by the assistant. A new questionnaire is not necessary.

DIALOGUE HISTORY

The detailed, follow-up, or dialogue history is verbally conducted by the doctor after reviewing the questionnaire. This includes further specific evaluation of positive information obtained via the preliminary patient-completed form. If the medical history discloses areas for further investigation, and the doctor is unable or unwilling to proceed further, he or she should consult the patient's physician at this time. I do not believe, however, in slavish, automatic medical consultations for potentially serious diseases such as arterial hypertension and coronary heart disease when the doctor is competent through training and experience to make a proper judgment and conduct therapy in an approved manner.

To assist in continuing with a dialogue history, certain broad categories of disease will be reviewed, and questions will be suggested for their evaluation in dentistry. Only the most common relevant diseases will be covered. I have also granted myself a certain license for the purpose of describing the medical background of each disease entity. First we will review the medical consultation and an evaluation system, then proceed to systems review.

MEDICAL CONSULTATION

When indicated by physical evaluation (either abnormal history or physical findings), the dental doctor is responsible for initiating a medical consultation. Slavish, automatic consultation without good cause is *not* called for. Your responsibilities are as follows:

1. Receive the physician's advice with an open mind.
2. Be *prepared* to discuss your treatment plan and anticipated problems.
3. Do not call until after performing a *complete* physical evaluation.
4. You are solely responsible for your treatment plan and treatment risks. Responsibility can rarely be shared with the physician. If you knowingly follow incorrect advice, you are liable. The physician advises but does not direct. It is your responsibility to follow a proper standard of care.

Friction between dental doctor and medical doctor during consultation is not common, but a review of the usual causes is in order, with advice on comportment:

1. Fatigue or bad manners by either party.
2. Lack of communication skills by either party.
3. Inadequate preparation by the dental practitioner.
4. Don't argue — educate. If education of a physician is not possible, remain courteous. An argument solves nothing and is not in the best interests of the patient. Exceptionally improper behavior on the part of the physician which *materially interferes* with proper patient care may be reported to the Grievance Committee of the local medical society, if the physician is a member, or to the State Board of Medical Examiners. This action would very rarely be indicated. Be forgiving—we all have bad days.
5. Accept the physician's advice in good grace, then treat in the patient's best interests.

USC PHYSICAL EVALUATION SYSTEM

INTRODUCTION

The author conceived the University of Southern California School of Dentistry Physical Evaluation System to assist in categorizing dental patients from the standpoint of risk-factor orientation.* The system was introduced as a limited pilot program in 1975, and was adopted school-wide in 1977. Certain sections of narrative are taken from the school manual, and I have further modified the system to make it easily adaptable to the needs of private practice.

The purpose of this system is to quickly and easily place each patient in an appropriate medical-risk category and to thereby provide dental therapy in comfort and relative safety. During the original physical evaluation the patient is placed in one of four physical status classes devised by the

*Grateful acknowledgement is made to Dr. Stanley Malamed for his support in expanding methodology, and to the Physical Evaluation Task Force for its invaluable critique of the first draft in 1975. The task force was composed of Drs. Albert Abrams, Arlos Aduddel, Marianne Alessio, Donald Cooksey, Randy Gates, Barbara Mills, Kit Neacy, Thomas Pallasch, and Robert Ziehm.

American Society of Anesthesiologists. The physical status classification then serves as a helpful guide to the level of dental therapy, suggested management, and treatment modification for the medically compromised patient.

ASA Physical Status Classification System

In 1940 the American Society of Anesthesiologists (ASA) conceived this system to classify the physical status of a patient about to undergo general anesthesia and surgery. The system has proved to be so valuable that it is used to classify all patients prior to surgery, manipulation (casting), or diagnostic studies of any kind utilizing any type or combination of anesthesia/sedation modalities.

Table 2–1 shows the ASA system on the left; on the right are general considerations for dental therapy modification. The system is very valuable in determining relative risk prior to dental treatment and the possible need for treatment modification.

Stress Reduction

In Table 2–1 and in the systems review section to follow, stress reduction merely refers to consideration of a psychosedation modality to relieve anxiety, possibly prescribing medication for sleep the night before treatment, limiting treatment to morning hours when functional reserve is at its highest, limiting the duration of treatment, avoiding elective treatment during unusually hot and humid weather, and giving special attention to post-treatment pain/anxiety control. Stress and sudden death walk hand in hand. While stress reduction for the ASA Class I patient is surely in order if indi-

TABLE 2–1

ASA Physical Status Classification	Therapy Modification
I. A normal healthy patient	None (stress reduction as indicated).
II. A patient with mild to moderate systemic disease	Possible stress reduction and other modification as indicated
III. A patient with *severe systemic disease* that *limits activity* but is not incapacitating	Possible strict modifications; stress reduction and medical consultation prioritized
IV. A patient with *severe systemic disease* that *limits activity* and is a *constant threat to life*	Minimal emergency care in office; hospitalize for complicated treatment; medical consultation urged
V. A moribund patient not expected to survive 24 hours with or without operation.	Treatment in the hospital is limited to life support only, e.g., airway and hemorrhage management

(An emergency operation is preceded by an E – e.g., E I, E IV, etc. – which is an admission that we do not have the necessary facts to make an accurate estimate of the patient's physical status).

cated, it is of paramount importance for the ASA Class II to IV patients if there is the slightest indication.

CLASSIFICATION GUIDELINES

Guidelines for ASA classification will be given for relevant diseases under systems review. Brief examples, any *one* of which calls for ASA Class II placement, are as follows: present history of allergic rhinitis (hay fever), history of any drug allergy or hypersensitivity, history of hepatitis B that is currently antigen-positive, history of arrested pulmonary tuberculosis without disability, history of rheumatic fever with heart murmur and no disability, history of heavy smoking with chronic bronchitis, chronic pulmonary emphysema without significant disability, history of corrected congenital heart disease without disability, history of chronic glomerulonephritis or pylonephritis without disability, history of controlled arterial hypertension without disability, history of controlled diabetes mellitus without disability, history of controlled chronic glaucoma, history of possible attitudinal problems with health care (as negative experiences with prior practitioners), and history of behavioral problems with health care (as moderate to extreme anxiety). Many of the preceding diseases or conditions could become Class III or IV, depending upon the history and physical examination. Some doctors drop the patient one class if there are two or more diseases, none of which is disabling; for example, a patient with allergic rhinitis, penicillin allergy, and chronic glomerulonephritis could be placed in ASA Class III rather than Class II. This is a judgment decision and is based upon your perception of physical status related to treatment stresses.

A Class II designation noted on your patient's record is a red flag indicating that special care may be in order. It alerts the doctor and staff to the possible necessity of anxiety control, avoidance of possibly lethal drugs, possible antibiotic prophylaxis to guard against bacterial endocarditis, and so forth. The importance of a Class III or IV designation goes without saying.

It is suggested that the Table 2–2 chart be added as a permanent part of your patient records, and that the appropriate designation be circled during the original physical evaluation. This can be changed up or down as circumstances dictate. For example, a post-MI patient would be considered Class IV at three months, yet probably revert to Class III or even Class II at six months if the disease were no longer considered to be a constant threat to life, or if significant disability did not exist.

TABLE 2–2

ASA Physical Status	*Reason(s) For Status Selection*
Class— I	(Write in)
Class— II	
Class—III	
Class— IV	
(Circle appropriate class)	

In closing this section on the USC Physical Evaluation System, may I emphasize that ASA numbers cannot substitute for knowledge and good judgment. Recommended physical status categories and treatment modifications should not be considered as absolutes but merely as guides. While the guidelines may appear to be inflexible, they should not be considered so. Deviation from the recommendations is often justified and is expected.

SYSTEMS REVIEW

INTRODUCTION

Also known as system review, review of systems, inventory of systems, and systemic review, the traditional method of understanding disease is to study the diseases involving the various body systems; that is, blood, eye, heart, and other systems. By understanding disease, we are able to prevent most emergencies, and, when necessary, treat the rare life-threatening emergency that is unavoidable.

Dentistry is the most disciplined of all the health sciences. We are trained to be utter perfectionists* — witness the horror evoked by an imperfect margin or a retained root tip. Since the treatment of emergencies is admittedly peripheral to dental care (and something we could all do without), we naturally tend to search for a highly disciplined, treat-by-the-numbers approach; for example, if the patient is short of breath, administer oxygen and call the paramedics. Under such circumstances, the patient with hyperventilation syndrome may eventually desist, owing to boredom, fatigue, or muscle cramps, but the patient with advanced pulmonary emphysema may die. We treat chronic pulpitis by understanding the disease and therefore the treatment options; we do not treat symptoms *per se*. In this chapter we shall, therefore, approach prevention and recognition of emergencies by understanding the disease process. Unfortunately, there is no simple by-the-numbers or by-the-symptoms method.

My choice of systems and diseases is of necessity pragmatic. It is limited to those diseases that, in my view, are particularly relevant to oral health care and potential medical emergencies. For serious students of physical evaluation, a textbook of medicine, such as Beeson-McDermott, is recommended. It makes fascinating reading in small doses, is ideal for the insomniac and hypochondriac, and will vastly increase your skills and pleasures in the health sciences.

VIRAL DISEASES

Of general interest to the practitioner is the third most common disease known to man, the common cold (acute coryza). It is caused by at least 88 different viruses and some nonviral agents; immunity to a specific virus exists for one to two years; one is contagious for one to two days before

---

*A perfectionist is one who takes great pains in executing a task, and who produces great pain in all those involved with the task.

symptoms develop and throughout the symptom phase (nasal discharge and sneezing); repeated infections can produce chronic bronchitis and pulmonary emphysema; and the chance of contagion is 10 per cent with close contact.

Of equal general interest under viral diseases is the dental doctor who predicts measles (rubeola) in a young patient by observing Koplik's spots one to four days before the skin rash, and who will thus become known in the neighborhood as a diagnostician akin to Sir William Osler.

Other viral diseases require little comment other than the proper evaluation of residual disability, if any, following poliomyelitis or viral encephalitis. Minor motor disability would indicate ASA Class II designation, as would the patient who is hepatitis B antigen-positive (the doctor and staff requiring masking and double-gloving, and special attention being paid to sterilization).

BACTERIAL DISEASES

Again little comment is called for with this group. The doctor will not be treating patients with active bronchopneumonia, meningitis, or rheumatic fever, and he or she will be evaluating the degree of disability, if any, resulting from these diverse bacterial diseases, placing the patient in ASA Class I to IV as indicated.

One type of bacteria that merits mention is the beta-hemolytic group A streptococcus that causes up to 3 per cent rheumatic fever and 20 per cent glomerulonephritis in infected patients (throat or skin), resulting in dental management concerns. To assist in ASA placement some examples are given:

ASA Class I — history of rheumatic fever, negative for rheumatic heart disease.

ASA Class II — rheumatic heart disease, no disability.

ASA Class III — rheumatic heart disease, congestive heart failure, mild to moderate disability.

ASA Class IV — rheumatic heart disease, severe congestive heart failure, barely ambulatory.

Modification to therapy would include antibiotic prophylaxis with a history of rheumatic heart disease. ASA Class II and III would require any or all stress reduction factors mentioned under *stress reduction* during review of the USC Physical Evaluation System. An ASA Class IV patient is offered emergency office treatment only.

EYE, EAR, NOSE AND THROAT DISEASES

A past history of acute glaucoma (narrow-angle) calls for the avoidance of drugs in dental treatment that can cause dilatation of the pupil, such as atropine, scopolamine, or diazepam (Valium), and thus cause an acute attack. Untreated acute glaucoma results in permanent blindness in two to five days. Chronic glaucoma (open-angle) under medical treatment requires no special therapy modification, though the doctor should be aware that emotional stress may accentuate the disease process, and thus sedation could be considered (Valium is acceptable).

Meniere's disease is caused by dilatation of the cochlear duct at about age 40 to 60, and is marked by recurrent severe vertigo and possibly nausea and vomiting. Utilization of sedation during active episodes of the disease could further handicap the patient.

Acute maxillary sinusitis may result from acute dental infection, and sometimes is misdiagnosed as acute dental pain. Chronic maxillary sinusitis is often of dental origin, estimated at up to 70 per cent of all cases.

Acute pericoronitis associated with a partially erupted mandibular third molar is sometimes misdiagnosed by the medical doctor as acute pharyngitis, acute tonsillitis, or acute peritonsillar abscess.

Foreign Bodies — Laryngeal, Bronchial, and Esophageal

Dental instruments, devices, and materials may act as foreign bodies, and the outcome can be lethal. The use of a rubber dam may avoid most episodes, but some are totally unavoidable.

Foreign bodies in the larynx and bronchi produce initial coughing and respiratory distress, and possibly complete obstruction of the airway with asphyxia. With a bronchial foreign body, the initial coughing is followed by a "silent" period of hours, months, or years, then obstruction or inflammation occurs, with cough, atelectasis (lung collapse), wheezing, and bronchopneumonia. See Chapter 12 for treatment of laryngeal and bronchial foreign bodies by the *Heimlich maneuver* and for treatment of laryngeal foreign bodies by *cricothyrotomy* should the Heimlich maneuver fail. Direct laryngoscopy in the hospital could be necessary for either of these types of foreign bodies.

Esophageal foreign bodies cause initial coughing, gagging, and pain, with subsidence of symptoms if the foreign body reaches the stomach. Perforation of the esophagus during passage or by retention of the foreign body in the esophagus may lead to mediastinal infection, which has a 50 per cent mortality rate.

If there is the slightest question of a foreign body, immediate x-rays should be taken to determine location, after which competent medical advice should be followed.

Depending upon circumstances, any one of these three foreign bodies could place the patient temporarily (or permanently) in ASA Class II to V.

Bronchopulmonary Diseases
Terms

A review of common terms is in order prior to a review of this section.

Dyspnea — shortness of breath, difficult or labored breathing; further subdivided into exertional dyspnea and rest dyspnea; rest dyspnea is characteristic of congestive heart failure, while exertional dyspnea is characteristic of either pulmonary emphysema or congestive heart failure.

Orthopnea — difficulty in breathing except in the upright position (sitting or standing); characteristic of congestive heart failure.

Cough — the most common symptom of respiratory disease, representing inflammation of one or more areas from the oropharynx to the terminal bronchioles; may be dry or productive; a paroxysmal cough suggests bronchial obstruction, such as productive bronchitis, emphysema, tumor, bronchopneumonia, bronchiectasis, lung abscess, or foreign body.

Expectoration — mucoid (white) sputum, tracheobronchitis and bronchial asthma; purulent sputum (yellow or green), bacterial infection; foul-smelling sputum, anaerobic infection, lung abscess; pink, frothy sputum, acute pulmonary edema, characteristic of advanced congestive heart failure.

Wheezing — occurs during *expiration* only, characteristic of bronchial narrowing; forced expiration or expiration after exercise may produce wheezing that is normally absent; the wheezing of bronchial asthma is paroxysmal; localized wheezing indicates local bronchial obstruction.

Chest Pain — the lung and visceral pleura (pleura covering lung surface) are insensitive to pain; the pain of lung disease is due to involvement of parietal pleura (pleura covering chest wall) or the chest wall itself; cardiac pain is usually substernal (precordial), and may radiate.

Hemoptysis — coughing of blood may occur with bronchitis, tuberculosis, tumor, and bronchiectasis; fatal hemorrhage is rare.

Cyanosis — blue skin color due to reduced hemoglobin in blood over 5 gm per 100 ml; normal adult hemoglobin is 12 to 18 gm per 100 ml; in the patient who is severely anemic, cyanosis may not occur even as a terminal sign.

Bronchiectasis

Bronchiectasis is much less common due to the early treatment of pneumonia, pertussis, and tuberculosis. It is caused by chronic dilatation of smaller bronchi and terminal bronchioles, with dependent pooling of pus. There is a very productive, purulent cough; rales and rhonchi are heard over the lung bases on auscultation; diagnosis is by bronchogram, which demonstrates bronchial dilatations.

A rale is a sound produced by air moving through liquid in the bronchus or lung. A rhonchus is a coarse, very loud rale heard over a partially obstructed bronchus.

ASA classification of bronchiectasis will be discussed under functional reserve classification of congestive heart failure. If the disease is particularly active and the body temperature is 101°F or higher, drop to the next lower ASA class (see temperature discussion under Vital Signs). Follow therapy modifications in Table 2–1; for the ASA Class II or III bronchiectatic patient, oxygen therapy during dental treatment is beneficial (such as 3 L/min via nasal cannula).

Pulmonary Emphysema

Heredity and smoking are major causative factors in pulmonary emphysema. There may be a hereditary defect in pulmonary elastic tissue, or the disease may be secondary to chronic bronchial obstruction (acute or chronic bronchitis, bronchial asthma, silicosis).

The pathologic physiology is twofold. First, the lung is made up of millions of tiny air sacs (pulmonary alveoli) where gas exchange occurs — oxygen in, carbon dioxide out. If these pulmonary alveoli were laid flat, they would cover the surface of a tennis court. The healthy individual therefore has the square footage of a tennis court for essential gas exchange. In emphysema the walls (septa) between alveoli break down; hundreds and even thousands of pulmonary alveoli form larger chambers, and the square footage for gas exchange markedly decreases. The individual with moderate emphysema may have the alveolar membrane square footage of one fourth of a tennis court; the person with advanced emphysema has far less. Shortness of breath results. Secondly, the elasticity of the smaller bronchi and terminal bronchioles is impaired. On expiration, the bronchi and bronchioles collapse, and the air in the larger air sacs cannot be expelled. We therefore have a patient with greatly reduced lung tissue for gas exchange, plus trapping of oxygen-deficient waste gases in the lungs.

The characteristics of pulmonary emphysema are:

1. Diffuse distention and over-aeration of alveoli.
2. Loss of intra-alveolar septa.
3. Loss of pulmonary elasticity.
4. Partial obstruction of smaller bronchi.
5. Impaired pulmonary function.

Exertional dyspnea and chronic productive cough are the primary symptoms and signs of emphysema. Their onset is insidious and is usually not noticed until the disease is moderately advanced. There are frequent intercurrent respiratory infections (bronchitis, bronchopneumonia), which may prove to be fatal. A barrel chest develops late in the disease; the chest becomes fixed in the inspiratory position. Prolonged, wheezing expirations are noted. Late in the disease, accessory muscles of respiration (shoulders, neck) are used. At this time a chest x-ray will demonstrate overaerated lung fields and a flattened diaphragm from lung expansion in the inspiratory position.

Emphysema can be differentiated from congestive heart failure and bronchial asthma by history and examination.

Function tests such as timed forced expiratory volume, match test, and breath-holding test are discussed under Physical Examination in this chapter. They will allow you to make an accurate estimate of the physical status of your emphysema patient. ASA classification will be reviewed under *functional reserve classification* of congestive heart failure.

Follow therapy modifications in Table 2–1, and stress reduction as indicated. Oxygen therapy is beneficial during dental treatment for the ASA Class II and III emphysema patient (3 L/min via nasal cannula). Respiratory cripples are ASA Class IV (rest dyspnea), and only minimal emergency care should be provided in the office. *Oxygen therapy is not indicated,* unless you are trained in advanced life support and are able to supply 30 per cent oxygen in the inspired air. Patients with advanced emphysema tolerate a very high arterial carbon dioxide tension. When the administration of 100 per cent oxygen lowers the carbon dioxide tension, breathing may cease, and artificial ventilation may be required.

Bronchial Asthma

This is marked by *paroxysmal* attacks of expiratory wheezing, dyspnea, cough, and production of mucoid sputum, and is caused by reversible bronchial constriction (constriction with emphysema is *not* reversible); rales and expiratory wheezing are heard on auscultation. The extrinsic type is responsible for 50 per cent of the cases (allergy; antigen-antibody response), and 50 per cent are intrinsic (response to infection, exercise, irritating inhalants, emotional stress).

Stress during dental treatment is also a factor in the extrinsic type, and many asthmatic episodes in the dental operatory, whether extrinsic or intrinsic in origin, can be rapidly controlled by moving the patient from the operatory, or can be prevented by adequate sedation.

ASA Class II is proper for most asthmatics. Stress reduction is in order. An asthmatic will temporarily become an ASA Class III during an attack. Progression to ASA Class IV is rare (status asthmaticus), but sudden death is remotely possible under these circumstances.

CARDIOVASCULAR DISEASES

Terms

Atrium — one of a pair of smaller cavities of the heart, from which blood passes to the ventricles. The right atrium receives systemic venous blood; the left atrium receives pulmonary venous blood.

Ventricle — one of a pair of larger cavities of the heart, with thick muscular walls. The right ventricle propels blood through the lungs; the left ventricle propels blood through the systemic arterial system.

Paroxysmal nocturnal dyspnea — sudden, severe nocturnal dyspnea occurring in the supine position, characteristic of acute congestive heart failure.

Palpitation — patient awareness of a rapid or irregular heart beat. The term is not plural, though lay people usually make it so (palpitations).

Edema — accumulation of *intercellular* fluid.

Heart Failure: Pathologic Physiology

The heart is a complex pump that can suffer from disease for years before failing in its function of delivering an adequate supply of blood to body tissues.

The heart fails in three common ways:

1. A portion of heart muscle supplied by a diseased coronary artery may become ischemic (not necrotic) and temporarily lose its contractile ability while the heart still delivers an adequate supply of blood to other body tissues. This is the clinical syndrome of angina pectoris and does not represent systemic failure.

2. With cardiac standstill or ventricular fibrillation (both called cardiac ar-

rest), there is immediate syncope and the patient dies. See Chapter 9, on *cardiopulmonary arrest.*

3. More commonly, the diseased heart loses it ability to effectively pump blood to peripheral tissues, resulting in the slow development of the clinical picture called congestive heart failure.

Failure of circulation occurs when the heart is unable to pump sufficient blood for body needs. The heart may be unable to pump out blood returned to it by the great veins (heart failure), or venous return may be inadequate (peripheral circulatory failure; see Shock in Chapter 11, on *general anesthetic emergencies*).

The clinical picture of heart failure is produced by:

1. Inadequate blood supply to peripheral tissues (forward heart failure).
2. Inadequate venous drainage of peripheral tissues, with accumulation of excess blood in tissues and organs (backward heart failure).

Forward and backward heart failure must occur together, but the signs and symptoms of congestion (backward heart failure) are clinically more evident.

The amounts of blood pumped from the left and right heart are normally identical. When left ventricular output is decreased by disease, right ventricular output overloads the pulmonary vascular bed and the lungs become congested and edematous. This is called left heart failure. When right ventricular output is decreased, the left ventricular output overloads the peripheral vascular bed and there are signs of systemic congestion and edema. This is called right heart failure. Clinically, right and left heart failure usually occur together, but the signs and symptoms of either pulmonary venous congestion (left heart failure) or systemic venous congestion (right heart failure) may predominate. The clinical syndrome of congestive heart failure includes both right and left heart failure.

In patients with *predominant left heart failure*, congestion is mainly in the lungs whereas in patients with *predominant right heart failure*, congestion occurs in the abdominal viscera and lower extremities, observed as peripheral venous distention (jugular vein distention), hepatomegaly (enlarged liver), ascites (fluid in peritoneal cavity, with abdominal distention), and peripheral edema (pitting edema of ankles).[5]

Compensatory mechanisms in heart disease include concentric hypertrophy of the heart (larger contractile cells) and dilatation of the heart (increased fiber length). Both of these mechanisms increase the force of contraction.

The treatment of congestive heart failure includes rest (decreases heart load), diet (bland, low caloric, salt restricted), digitalis, and diuresis (eliminate excess fluids).

Congestive Heart Failure

This is known also as heart failure or cardiac decompensation. The patient with a failing heart represents one of the commonest risks treated in the dental office.

The main symptoms and signs of congestive heart failure (CHF) are dyspnea (shortness of breath) and undue fatigue. For our purposes, evaluation by degree of dyspnea and fatigue is exceptionally accurate.

Other causes of exertional dyspnea include advanced age, debility, poor physical conditioning (indolence), obesity, chronic pulmonary disease, ascites from any cause, advanced pregnancy, and bronchial asthma.

The term *undue fatigue* may appear rather general for specific evaluation application, but it must be remembered that the usual case of chronic congestive heart failure has been developing for months or years before obvious symptoms and signs appear. For months or years the nutritional requirements of the patient's vital organs and skeletal muscles have not been completely satisfied. For months or years the intercostal muscles have labored to move wet, congested lungs. Although this patient may not present with the classic complaints of exertional dyspnea, paroxysmal nocturnal dyspnea, and orthopnea, he or she will tire easily with little exertion, thus making undue fatigue a most important clinical sign in evaluation.

The *clinical picture* of congestive heart failure results from diverse varieties of heart *disease*, such as congenital, rheumatic, and coronary heart disease (ischemic heart disease), arterial hypertension, certain cardiac arrhythmias, pericarditis, myocarditis, endocarditis, and aortic aneurysm. Most of these specific diseases do not require individual discussion with respect to either physical evaluation or emergency treatment. Some will be covered where applicable in Chapter 3, Physical Diagnosis, and the reader may consult a textbook of medicine for detailed background.

EVALUATION OF CHF

Here are some recommended questions in the evaluation of congestive heart failure:

1. Can you carry on your usual normal activities without shortness of breath or undue fatigue?
Comment: Represents a good risk if other points are negative. No point in evaluation is more important than the fact that the functional capacity of the patient allows him or her to carry on normal activities.

There is a marked mortality increase from congestive heart failure and myocardial infarction associated with recent significant life changes, such as recent serious illness, loss of a job, health or marital concerns, and death or divorce of a spouse.[6] Such a history would merit temporarily dropping the patient one ASA physical status classification, as from ASA Class II to III or ASA Class III to IV.

During your queries about dyspnea, specifically inquire into possible dyspnea occurring after *climbing one flight of stairs*. This gives more valuable information than a general inquiry about exertional dyspnea.[7] See also the following functional reserve classification in this section.

2. Can you climb a flight of stairs without resting?
Comment: Good risk if other points are negative. In past years in dentistry this question was virtually the only evaluation by the practitioner prior to inhalation anesthesia. The mortality record was excellent.

3. Do your ankles swell as the day progresses?
Comment: Compensatory mechanism in chronic right heart failure (systemic venous congestion).

4. Have you ever awakened at night short of breath?
Comment: Known as paroxysmal nocturnal dyspnea, a serious symptom; the result of acute left heart failure with pulmonary edema. Consultation with physician advised.

5. Must you remain in a sitting position in order to breathe comfortably?
Comment: Known as orthopnea (the inability to breathe in comparative comfort except in the upright position); a serious symptom; compensatory mechanism to confine

pulmonary edema to the lung bases and to keep ventilatory capacity at a maximum. Consultation recommended.

6. How many pillows do you use for breathing comfort while sleeping?

Comment: Two or three pillows indicate orthopnea.

7. Have you had a recent large weight gain?

Comment: May indicate rapid fluid accumulation and onset of acute failure. This patient will present with swollen ankles and legs and possibly with a distended abdomen. Consultation recommended.

8. Are you taking medication?

Comment: If taking a diuretic, suspect chronic heart failure. If taking digitalis or a digitalis glycoside (Digoxin, Digitoxin, Lanoxin, etc.), you may assume an episode of failure past or present. Digitalis increases the contractile force of the heart whether it is in frank failure or not. See the chapter on *drugs*. If the patient has resumed normal activities since digitalization, and other points are negative, the failure is compensated and the patient is a good risk.

The following functional reserve classification is an aid in determining the current cardiovascular status in cardiac failure cases and is of assistance in dental treatment planning. This classification is also helpful when there is a history of pulmonary disease, such as lung abscess, tuberculosis, emphysema, bronchial asthma, and bronchiectasis.

This classification system has been in use by the Dental Anesthesia Service at LAC/USC Medical Center since 1956. It correlates exactly with the ASA physical status classification system; that is, FR Class 2 becomes ASA Class II, FR Class 3 becomes ASA Class III, and FR Class 4 becomes ASA Class IV for the purpose of categorizing congestive heart failure. The same correlation is correct with respect to dyspnea and undue fatigue for the purpose of ASA classification of the bronchiectatic or emphysematous patient.

Follow Table 2–1 for therapy modification of congestive heart failure; further recommendations follow.

FUNCTIONAL RESERVE CLASSIFICATION (MCCARTHY)

Class 1. No dyspnea or undue fatigue with normal exertion.

Class 2. Mild dyspnea or fatigue with exertion; may rest at the top of a flight of stairs.

Comment: Assuming that other points are negative, both Classes 1 and 2 represent good risks for all dental treatment. If the Class 2 patient is quite apprehensive, consider sedation to reduce emotional and physical stress. See the chapters on *psychosedation*.

Class 3. Dyspnea or undue fatigue with normal activities; comfortable at rest in any position; may have a tendency toward orthopnea, and may have a history of paroxysmal nocturnal dyspnea; rests before reaching the top of a flight of stairs.

Comment: This patient represents a definite risk; consultation is recommended. Sedation during dental treatment is strongly recommended. Keep appointments short; do not carry treatment to the limit of tolerance. Avoid elective treatment during hot and humid weather unless your office is air-conditioned. Cardiac output of 20 to 30 liters per minute (normal resting output varies from 3 to 4.5 liters per minute) may be required by thermal regulatory demands.

Class 4. Dyspnea, orthopnea, and undue fatigue at all times. The patient will rest on numerous occasions when climbing a flight of stairs, if he or she is able to negotiate them at all.

Comment: A serious risk; only emergency dental treatment should be considered. The patient's physician should be in attendance if possible, or at least within call. Oxygen therapy throughout treatment should be considered.

Coronary Heart Disease

Coronary heart disease (CHD) is a clinical entity presenting as either angina pectoris or acute myocardial infarction. It is related entirely to marked narrowing (at least one third of normal) or complete occlusion of a coronary artery lumen. With the rare exception of syphilitic aortitis, the pathologic entity of coronary heart disease or ischemic heart disease is coronary atherosclerosis, thus accounting for the common clinical term of coronary atherosclerotic heart disease (CAHD).

ANGINA PECTORIS

Angina pectoris is also known as paroxysmal cardiac pain and as anginal syndrome. This patient represents a considerably greater risk than the average case of heart failure. There is at least a 30 per cent higher mortality rate than the average. You must remember that the attack can become irreversible, proceeding to acute myocardial infarction and possibly death.

The cause of angina pectoris is temporary lack of oxygen (ischemia) in the heart muscle, related to narrowing of the coronary arteries, increased cardiac output (exertion, excitement, meals), and increased work load (as with rheumatic/valvular heart disease and arterial hypertension).

The patient will have a history of recurrent attacks of precordial (substernal) pain, varying from mild to severe. There is often radiation of pain to the left shoulder or arm; infrequently to the right shoulder and back. The pain often is precipitated by exertion, anger, emotional stress, anxiety, or meals, and usually is relieved by rest in less than 15 minutes. It usually is not the intense, crushing pain of acute myocardial infarction. The patient usually has taken nitroglycerin for relief of pain. Consultation with the patient's physician regarding the planned dental treatment may be desirable.

The history may indicate a recent significant life change (see comment under congestive heart failure), in which event the risk is increased.[6] Certain factors in your dialogue history of angina pectoris are of great discriminatory value: the risk is increased if anginal pain is incompletely relieved by nitroglycerin, if there is a frequent relationship of anginal pain to exertion, and if there is radiation of pain to the left arm.[8] There is real diagnostic value in inquiring into possible precordial pain related to *climbing a flight of stairs,* rather than a general question about chest pain.[7]

ASA Classification of Angina Pectoris

The following classification is recommended. It is modified by the author from the New York Heart Association Classification of Angina Pectoris.

ASA Class II: *Ordinary physical activity does not cause angina.* Angina may occur with *strenuous* or *prolonged* exertion or with sexual relations. Angina may occur with rapid walking, walking uphill, or climbing stairs rapidly, or by walking more than two blocks on the level or climbing more than one flight of stairs at a normal pace.

ASA Class III: *Marked limitation of ordinary physical activity.* Angina may occur by walking one or two blocks on the level or climbing one flight of stairs at a normal pace. Comfortable at rest.

ASA Class IV: *Inability to carry on any physical activity without discomfort.* Angina may be present at rest.

Therapy modification should follow Table 2–1 and *stress reduction* recommendations previously covered, as well as the following protocol.

Recommended Management of the Angina Patient

1. Routine sedation is strongly advised. These patients do not tolerate emotional stress well.
2. Make every effort to achieve effective local analgesia; use the proper injection technique as outlined in the chapter on *complications from local analgesia.*
3. Premedicate with nitroglycerin sublingually about five minutes before starting local analgesia. Use the patient's supply of nitroglycerin if possible. A significant number of angina patients (estimated at up to 10 per cent) will exhibit a paradoxical reaction to nitroglycerin when taken in a dosage higher than they normally find effective, and an anginal attack will ensue. If the patient is not carrying his or her usual supply, use nitroglycerin in the dosage of .30 mg (1/200 gr). I do not recommend that the higher dosage forms of nitroglycerin, .45 mg (1/150 gr) and .60 mg (1/100 gr), be stocked. The smallest dose of .15 mg (1/400 gr) is rarely utilized. Nitroglycerin should be replaced six months after the bottle is opened, as it deteriorates.
4. Keep the procedure as short as possible, and make every effort to avoid reaching the limit of tolerance.
5. Remember that the average angina patient's risk level is about the same as that of the cardiac patient in Class 3 functional reserve (ASA Class III).
6. If the patient has daily episodes of chest pain, especially associated with meals, exertion, or emotional stress, consider him or her to be a serious risk. Emergency dental treatment only is recommended (ASA Class IV).

Nitroglycerin: Action, Prophylaxis, and Potency

Only one mechanism for increasing oxygen supply to the heart muscle on demand is of significance, and that is augmentation of blood flow in the coronary arteries. The capacity of the normal coronary circulation to *dilate* and maintain flow is so great that even with prolonged hypotension, infarction is rare.[9]

Nitroglycerin (TNG) dramatically improves the regional perfusion of an ischemic portion of heart muscle while not affecting total coronary flow.[10] It also produces general venous dilatation, which results in a decreased cardiac work load. TNG significantly increases exercise tolerance when taken prophylactically.[11] Long-acting nitrites have not proven more effective than TNG, and there is some doubt that they are equally effective.[9] TNG improves the exercise performance of patients with coronary heart disease, markedly decreasing the frequency of arrhythmias.[12]

TNG is unstable when stored or dispensed improperly.[13, 14, 15] In a study by Edelman,[15] loss of potency at 201 days was less than 5 per cent when tablets were stored in amber or clear glass vials; over the same time period up to 30 per cent loss of potency occurred with polystyrene vials, and 72 per cent loss with polystyrene pillboxes; there was up to 90 per cent loss with individual strip packaging (often used in hospital clinics). Nitroglycerin should be stored, dispensed, and maintained in tightly sealed glass vials, and should never be transferred to pillboxes.[16]

Fresh nitroglycerin produces immediate sublingual burning and a greater systemic effect, while aged TNG produces absent or decreased burning and decreased systemic effect. The burning sensation is a practical index of potency.[17]

ACUTE MYOCARDIAL INFARCTION

Acute myocardial infarction is also known as coronary occlusion and coronary thrombosis or as a "coronary." This patient, as with the anginal case, represents at least a 30 per cent greater mortality risk than the average. About 75 per cent of myocardial infarctions are caused by coronary thrombosis. Infarction may develop in the absence of fresh coronary occlusion, and coronary artery thrombosis can occur without necessarily causing infarction. In the first instance, coronary circulation may be so deficient that coagulation necrosis (infarction) occurs without complete occlusion of the coronary artery; in the latter instance, even in the presence of complete coronary artery occlusion, acquired collateral circulation may be sufficient to prevent infarction.

Recently it has been suggested that coronary thrombosis is the result rather than the cause of infarction. However, substantial evidence supports the classical concept of the primary causal role of coronary thrombosis in the pathogenesis of myocardial infarction.[18]

Long-term survival of the post-MI patient is related to the presence of other chronic diseases and to the presence or absence of angina related to exertion, congestive heart failure, and left ventricular hypertrophy (ECG interpretation). Complete clinical and ECG recovery is compatible with survival for 10 to 15 years. Patients with residual CHF following MI usually die within one to five years.

At onset, symptoms of acute myocardial infarction are similar to those of angina pectoris, but the precordial (substernal) pain is not relieved by nitrites or rest, and dyspnea and weakness are common. Most post-infarction patients will be able to supply you with the proper diagnosis during your dialogue history. If they are not aware of a diagnosis, it is easily established by reviewing the history of the heart problem. In addition to the foregoing, there usually will be a history of hospitalization followed by some weeks or months of inactivity at home. Consultation with the physician is desirable prior to treatment planning.

While it is generally accepted that coronary atherosclerotic heart disease is the primary cause of myocardial infarction, a recent explanation for the Prinzmetal type of variant angina pectoris emphasizes the risk factor of emotional stress.[19, 20] Variant angina occurs at rest and without severe fixed coronary stenosis. It is due to coronary arterial spasm,[20] and is relieved by nitroglycerin. Sir William Osler predicted the cause of this variant type in 1910. Paul Dudley White emphasized the basic risk factor related to stress in the highly nervous sensitive individual, and he predicted that this type of coronary artery disease, as opposed to atherosclerosis, may become more common in these stressful days.[19] The proof of coronary arterial spasm related to stress demonstrates the value of sedation for the anginal or post-MI patient.

ASA Classification for Post-Myocardial Infarction Patient. Any documented MI of less than six months duration is automatically ASA Class IV. A post-MI patient beyond six months who has no current history of angina and whose history and physical is otherwise negative is ASA Class II. Utilize the previously recommended ASA classification of angina pectoris for your further classification of the post-MI patient, related to angina and degree of exertion.

It is emphasized that post-MI patients often develop congestive heart failure (CHF). In fact, CHF is one of the common complications of MI during the acute phase, along with shock and cardiac arrest. If your post-MI patient appears to be ASA Class II, yet the CHF functional reserve classification also places him or her in ASA Class II, then drop to ASA Class III.

Therapy modification follows Table 2–1, with emphasis upon stress reduction and the following protocol. No patient is a more likely candidate for sudden death in the dental office than the post-MI patient under stressful treatment.

Epinephrine. The use of epinephrine in dental local analgesic solutions continues to cause confusion despite the fact that clear guidelines from the New York Heart Association and latterly the American Heart Association (AHA) have existed for almost 30 years. While the subject will be examined in several other areas of this book, let me say now that the AHA states that there is no hazard for a cardiac patient if not more than .04 mg of epinephrine is utilized at a single dental appointment. You may use two 2.0 ml cartridges at a concentration of epinephrine 1:100,000, and four cartridges at 1:200,000. This guideline assumes proper instrumentation and technique, and it applies both to the post-MI and anginal patient. Please see review in Chapter 10, Complications from Local Analgesia, for detailed information.

Recommended Management of the Post-Myocardial Infarction Patient. Routine management of the post-infarction patient exactly duplicates management of the anginal patient, with three exceptions:

1. Routine premedication with nitroglycerin is open to debate, and therefore is not recommended. However, it is definitely recommended if the patient has current episodes of angina pectoris. Dosage forms are the same as in angina.
Recent reports have suggested that TNG might reduce the degree of ischemic injury in some patients during the acute phase of MI.[21] It has not been proven, however, and since TNG can produce severe hypotension (quickly reversed with leg elevation), particularly in patients not in left ventricular failure, it is not recommended as prophylaxis in the post-MI patient at this time.
2. Do not perform any elective dental treatment for the post-infarction patient for at least six months after the attack. It takes that long for these patients to heal and stabilize. The ban on elective dental care includes dental prophylaxis and minor restorative procedures, even though conducted in a hospital dental department and with the attending physician's approval. The post-infarction patient is extremely intolerant of stress early in the recovery period, and the hospital environment does not provide an umbrella of safety to prevent a recurrent infarction or possibly a fatal dysrhythmia.
3. If the patient is taking an anticoagulant (heparin, dicumarol, Coumadin, Hedulin, etc.), and many post-infarction patients do so for a time after the attack, dental treatment during which even mild bleeding may occur should be avoided until his or her status has been discussed with the physician.

Anticoagulant Therapy Post-MI. At present, exodontia is frequently performed at a prothrombin level of 20 to 30 per cent, so that the anticoagulant will not have to be withdrawn and thus subject the patient to possible recurrent coronary thrombosis. The surgical routine includes the following, as indicated: hemostatic socket dressing, multiple sutures, intraoral pressure dressings, ice packs, avoidance of mouth rinses and drinking straws, and a soft diet for 48 hours. Hospitalization is not necessary in the usual case. Menadione (vitamin K) under the direction of the physician may be necessary if these measures are not effective in controlling bleeding. There is no clinically demonstrable risk of rebound thromboembolism from use of vitamin K.

Anticoagulant therapy may reduce the death rate during the first three years after infarction. Survival rates of anticoagulant treated and untreated post-infarction patients converge after the third year, and by the fifth year there is no difference in survival of treated and untreated groups.

Recent studies show that anticoagulants are effective in lowering morbidity in the first weeks after MI, particularly the incidence of thromboembolic complications in patients at high risk, as those with CHF, marked obesity, and severe varicosities.[22] When close follow-up of the patient cannot be maintained, the risk of hemorrhage may outweigh the possible benefit. Another study has shown no reinfarction risk when anticoagulant therapy is discontinued.[23]

CORONARY ARTERY SURGERY AND THE BYPASS PATIENT

Coronary artery bypass surgery has become increasingly popular, 50,000 operations having been performed in 1974 alone. While both enthusiastic and pessimistic positions are taken, there is no doubt that the procedure improves the quality of life by relieving symptoms.[24] It remains to be firmly established whether coronary bypass operations improve long-term survival.[25]

Several of Corday's conclusions on the status of bypass surgery will be repeated in part for your general information:[24]

1. Coronary bypass surgery relieves angina.
2. Life expectancy appears increased in the subgroups of *impending infarction* and *high-risk lesions* (italics mine).
3. Because the life expectancy of patients with stable angina pectoris is relatively good, coronary bypass should be reserved for those patients with *uncontrollable angina* (italics mine).
4. Because the long-term fate of the saphenous vein or the intrinsic coronary arteries following the bypass is not yet known, the operation *cannot be considered a prophylactic procedure* (italics mine).

ASA physical status classification of the patient who has had coronary bypass surgery would depend upon the history and probable medical consultation. ASA Class II designation would be uncommon but possible, ASA Class III probable, and ASA Class IV possible.

Management of the bypass patient would follow Table 2–1 and the anginal and post-MI recommendations, as indicated. There is no special protocol. If antibiotic prophylaxis is advised by the physician, no harm should be done; such a routine is not a standard of care at this time. There need be no time delay for elective dental care following bypass surgery, subject to the physician's advice.

CARDIAC PACEMAKERS

There are two types of cardiac pacemakers: the fixed-rate type (asynchronous), which stimulates the heart continuously at a predetermined rate, and the demand type (synchronous), which stimulates the heart only when the rate varies from a predetermined norm. Most pacemakers are of the demand type. The fixed-rate pacemaker is less sensitive to disturbance.[26] Electromagnetic radiation can inhibit the normal function of demand-type pacemakers. Simon states that fixed-rate pacemakers are influenced only by very intense electromagnetic fields, and that no precautions are necessary in the dental office other than the avoidance of electrosurgery, or, when necessary, using it for short bursts (one second or less) spaced 10 or more seconds apart.[27] When the demand pacemaker is inhibited by external electromagnetic energy, the unit reverts to a fixed-rate mode; normal operations resume when the patient moves from the electromagnetic field. Improvements in pacemaker circuitry and design have lessened the risk.

No firm guidelines exist at this time for the conduct of dental therapy in the patient with a demand-type pacemaker. Simon's recommendations will be reviewed in part for your information:[27]

1. The type of pacemaker should be recorded in your medical history.
2. The patient's physician should be contacted for guidance.
3. Follow previously reviewed precautions for electrosurgery.
4. If doubt exists, conversion of the demand pacemaker to a fixed-rate mode may be indicated. This is done by placing a strong magnet over the pulse generator.
5. Persons who wear a pacemaker and work near induction casting equipment should be evaluated on an individual basis.
6. Caution should be exercised with pulp testers and ultrasonic cleaners, although they demonstrated no interference in Simon's limited observations.
7. Tensing of the pectoralis major may inhibit pacemakers. The patient should be cautioned to avoid muscle tension of the upper extremities. Convert to fixed-rate mode if necessary.

While no fixed guidelines exist, one fact is beyond question — over one million patients in the United States wear cardiac pacemakers. The dental practitioner should consult the physician and proceed with caution.

Arterial Hypotension

Hypotension, or *low* blood pressure, does not exist in the healthy conscious patient. Life insurance statistics demonstrate that life expecatancy increases as blood pressure decreases. The *ideal* blood pressure is the lowest pressure a person can tolerate without going into shock.

Arterial Hypertension

Arterial hypertension is defined as a measurement that is consistently higher than 140/90 mm Hg. Pressure elevations 30 per cent above normal are not uncommon in the dental office. A borderline measurement should be rechecked several times before the physician is called in consultation.

When the patient has a history of hypertension, you should first investigate the possible existence of heart failure or angina pectoris. It is natural to think of stroke first when confronted with a hypertensive history, but the fact is that 65 per cent of hypertensives die of heart disease, whereas only 20 per cent demonstrate predominantly cerebral symptoms. This is not true of black people, however. They develop hypertension earlier in life, it is frequently more severe, and it results in a higher mortality at a younger age, more commonly from stroke than from coronary heart disease.[28]

The complications of hypertension include the following: congestive heart failure, angina pectoris, myocardial infarction, cerebral hemorrhage, cerebral thrombosis, and kidney failure.

ASA physical status classification is made according to the clinical syndrome resulting from hypertension, and it will be discussed further in the section on blood pressure under *vital signs*. The same is true of treatment modification. Follow Table 2–1.

Other Heart Diseases

Congenital heart disease represents 2 per cent of all adult heart disease. Congenital lesions consist of narrowing of vessels or valves, septal defects between atria or ventricles, and others.

Rheumatic heart disease results from a single or repeated attacks of rheumatic fever which produce deformity of valve cusps and fusion of valve commissures. Deformity or fusion produces valve stenosis or insufficiency or both; the mitral valve is involved in 50 to 60 per cent of cases, the mitral and aortic in 20 per cent, and the aortic alone in 10 per cent. There is a history of rheumatic fever in only 60 per cent of the cases of rheumatic heart disease, so 40 per cent of the cases must develop from subclinical or unrecognized rheumatic fever.

Antibiotic prophylaxis aside (bacterial endocarditis prevention), the common denominator of congenital heart disease and rheumatic heart disease is a pump that will fail from intolerably increased work loads. The patient will most likely develop congestive heart failure, although both angina pectoris and myocardial infarction are possible.

Aortic aneurysm is a localized dilatation of the ascending aorta as the result of syphilitic cardiovascular disease. Complications include aortic valve insufficiency (development of congestive heart failure), occlusion of the coronary artery ostia (development of angina pectoris or myocardial infarction), rupture of the aorta (sudden death), and dissecting aneurysm with rupture.

ASA classification of these three diverse types of heart disease depends upon the clinical picture, and the same is the case for treatment modification. Follow Table 2–1.

CEREBROVASCULAR DISEASES

Terms

Thrombus — an aggregation of blood factors (platelets, fibrin, and cells) causing vascular obstruction at the point of origin.
Embolus — a clot or other plug brought by the blood from another vessel and forced into a smaller one, causing obstruction.

Hemiplegia — paralysis of one side of body.

Quadriplegia — paralysis of all four limbs.

Infarct — an area of coagulation necrosis (cell death) in a tissue due to local ischemia from circulatory obstruction. The *process* of forming an infarct is called infarction.

Hypesthesia — decreased skin sensitivity.

Occlusive Cerebrovascular Disease – General

Degenerative arterial diseases are primarily caused by arteriosclerosis, most marked after age 40, and with strong predisposition related to diabetes mellitus and arterial hypertension. Raised arterial pressure produces accelerated atherosclerosis of major arteries. *Sustained* hypertension causes the normally reversible arteriolar narrowing to become *permanent* as the result of intimal thickening and muscle hypertrophy. The clinical picture of degenerative arterial diseases, whether cardiovascular or cerebrovascular, is that of a weakening of the arterial wall and a gradual narrowing and ultimate occlusion of the artery.

Occlusive cerebrovascular disease is characterized by three distinct clinical stages:

1. Gradual mental deterioration.
2. Dizzy spells, visual defects, transient weakness of face, arm, or leg.
3. Sudden complete hemiplegia (stroke).

Extracranial arteries are commonly involved in occlusive cerebrovascular disease, such as the common carotid bifurcation (origin of internal and external carotids), the vertebral artery, and intrathoracic segments of aortic branches.

Transient Cerebral Ischemia (TCI)

TCI represents a transient, reversible episode of cerebral ischemia (temporary cerebral artery insufficiency) lasting for 10 seconds to one hour, marked by headache, drowsiness, syncope, mental confusion, speech defect, muscle weakness, and focal hypesthesia. These temporary episodes do not constitute a true cerebrovascular accident (CVA) or stroke, but are prodromal only.

When taking the dialogue history of the patient who has already indicated a past history of CVA on the questionnaire, or the older patient with hypertension, inquire of the patient if there have been symptoms and signs that would indicate TCI. Such information is rarely volunteered. The TCI patient is managed in the dental office as if he or she has had an actual stroke, with the exception of treatment timing (see next section).

Cerebrovascular Accident

A stroke is also called cerebrovascular accident, CVA, and cerebral apoplexy. CVA is caused by cerebral hemorrhage, thrombosis, or embolism, and is marked by the sudden onset of neurologic complaints: focal motor (extremity or face weakness), focal hypesthesia (skin numbness), speech defects, vomiting, convulsions, headaches, and nuchal rigidity (neck), with or without recovery.

Early clinical findings may be sudden and devastating, the patient falling to the ground unconscious with hemiplegia, and there are lesser grades of CVA ranging from slight derangement of speech to muscle weakness and memory loss. Loss of consciousness is not necessary.

Occasionally your CVA or TCI patient will be taking an anticoagulant, and this must be considered in your dental treatment planning (see discussion under *myocardial infarction*). While the evidence does not warrant anticoagulation for patients with a completed stroke, it is of value as prophylaxis in recurrent emboli to the brain (as in rheumatic valvular disease), and it may assist the patient with TCI or progressive stroke.[29]

ASA Classification

The ASA classification for a patient with a history of CVA or TCI and otherwise negative history and physical findings would be Class II; a history of TCI as well as CVA would drop the patient to Class III. Modification of dental therapy follows Table 2–1 and the following recommendations.

Recommended Management of the Post-CVA and TCI Patient

1. A medical consultation is desirable if the patient's physical status is doubtful.
2. No elective dental treatment for at least six months after the episode (CVA only).
3. Keep appointments short.
4. Sedation is highly desirable, but should be used with great care and should not be carried to the point of extreme drowsiness or depression. Deep sedation depresses cerebral circulation and can initiate cerebral thrombosis.

KIDNEY DISEASES

Glomerulonephritis and Pyelonephritis

Most cases of glomerulonephritis are the result of immunologic reactions (immune complex disease), with antigen or antibody excess directly damaging the kidney. The disease is usually poststreptococcal (beta-hemolytic group A). Complications of the acute phase include CHF (salt and water retention), CHF with hypertension, hypertensive brain damage (convulsions), and kidney failure.

Pyelonephritis is an acute or chronic bacterial urinary tract infection producing nephrosclerosis (kidney scarring) in the final stages that is indistinguishable from late glomerulonephritis. Both diseases may terminate in kidney failure.

Chronic Renal Insufficiency

Chronic kidney failure is treated by diet and fluids (protein limitation), electrolyte replacement, transfusions, extracorporeal dialysis (kidney machine), and kidney transplant.

With dialysis, there is an 87 per cent one-year survival rate, 73 per cent two-year survival, and 60 per cent six-year survival. With kidney transplant, the kidney of a parent or sibling remains functional for one year in 74 per cent of the cases, and for three years in 70 per cent. A cadaver transplant remains functional for one year in 50 per cent of the cases, and for three years in 42 per cent.

Hemodialysis and Kidney Transplant

ASA classification of the patient in chronic kidney failure depends upon the degree of associated complications such as hypertension, anemia, and congestive heart failure. Renal impairment alone would place the patient in ASA Class II, while the addition of CHF would drop the patient to ASA Class III. Follow the recommendations in Table 2–1, with special attention to stress reduction.

Consultation with the physician is advisable, particularly in regard to drugs you may prescribe.[30] Care should be used with aspirin and acetaminophen; phenacetin and the tetracyclines should be strictly avoided; erythromycin, local analgesics, oxacillin, codeine, barbiturates, and benzodiazepines (Valium) are safe.[31] The physician may wish to advise a prophylactic antibiotic before dental therapy for the patient receiving dialysis or the recipient of a kidney transplant.

DIGESTIVE SYSTEM DISEASES

Peptic Ulcer

Peptic ulcer is a benign ulcer occurring in a portion of the digestive tract which is accessible to gastric acid secretions (stomach or duodenum). A duodenal ulcer is five times more common than gastric ulcer, occurs in 10 per cent of all people at some time, and tends to recur; 10 per cent require surgery. A gastric ulcer has the same prognosis.

The history of an active peptic ulcer would place the patient in ASA Class II. Follow Table 2–1 recommendations, with special attention to stress reduction.

Regional Enteritis and Ulcerative Colitis

Regional enteritis (regional ileitis) is a chronic inflammatory disease of the small intestine. It afflicts the young adult as a rule, and is marked by an insidious onset, intermittent diarrhea, and low fever. It may be low grade or fulminating.

Nonspecific ulcerative colitis is a chronic inflammatory disease of the colon afflicting young adults most commonly. It is characterized by bloody diarrhea, cramps, weight loss, and fever. It is usually low grade, but may be fulminating.

ASA designation would be Class II for either disease unless it were in a fulminant stage, in which case Class III or IV would be possible. Follow Table 2–1 modifications, with special attention to stress reduction.

Corticosteroids are often used in treating either disease, and your history should be concerned with dosage and duration. See adrenocortical insufficiency, discussed under *endocrine diseases*.

LIVER DISEASES

Acute Hepatitis

The dental doctor would normally not treat the patient with acute hepatitis A (infectious hepatitis) or acute hepatitis B (serum hepatitis). In the event of emergency care, special attention should be paid to self and staff protection (masking and double-gloving), sterilization to prevent cross-contamination, and post-exposure prophylaxis for self and staff (immune serum globulin for type A and special immune serum globulin for type B).

Chronic Hepatitis

Chronic hepatitis consists of a chronic inflammatory reaction of the liver demonstrated by abnormal liver function tests and illness beyond six months. It may be the result (sequela) of hepatitis A, hepatitis B (the patient remaining antigen-positive), or may be due to drugs.

Alcoholic hepatitis is the most common type, with parenchymal necrosis from alcohol abuse. Heavy drinking is essential; drunkenness is not. The disease may be reversible, depending upon liver function. If prothrombin time is unduly prolonged, the mortality rate is 40 per cent.

The patient may present for dental care with nothing but a positive history, or there may be anorexia (loss of appetite), nausea, hepatomegaly (enlarged liver), jaundice, ascites, debility, and peripheral edema. Liver failure proceeds to coma and death.

Depending upon signs and symptoms and medical consultation, if indicated, ASA classification may range from II to IV. Follow Table 2–1. Special attention should be paid to stress reduction and to possible bleeding tendencies.

ENDOCRINE DISEASES

Diabetes Mellitus

Diabetes mellitus is a clinical syndrome of disordered metabolism and *hyperglycemia* (abnormally high blood sugar) due to insulin deficiency *or* reduction of insulin effectiveness. Being familiar with the basic three types of diabetes is of assistance in physical evaluation and treatment modification.

Types of Diabetes

1. Insulinopenic Type I — insulin is reduced or absent.
   a. Insulinopenic Type IA (severe) — juveniles and nonobese adults; insulin production is absent; diet and insulin required in treatment. This type is often "brittle" and difficult to control; can be high risk.
   b. Insulinopenic Type IB (mild to moderate severity) — nonobese adults; insulin production is reduced; treatment by diet and perhaps oral hypoglycemic agent.
2. Insulinoplethoric Type II (mild severity) — obese adults; insulin is normal; treatment by diet. Due to chronic overeating, there is ineffective insulin action, with overdistention of storage depots and reduced ability to clear nutrients; there is sustained beta cell (pancreas) stimulation and *hyperinsulinism*, which induces receptor insensitivity.

The common clinical features of Type I diabetes are:

1. Polydipsia (increased thirst and water intake)
2. Polyuria (increased urine output)
3. Polyphagia (ravenous appetite, with weight loss)

The common clinical features of Type II diabetes are:

1. Peripheral neuropathy (as numbness of soles of feet)
2. Often no symptoms
   Diseases commonly associated with diabetes are cataracts, retinopathy, retinal hemorrhage and detachment, lower extremity occlusive vascular disease, renal hypertension, coronary atherosclerosis, cerebral atherosclerosis, and neuropathies. There are two types of diabetic coma: hypoglycemic coma (insulin shock) and hyperglycemic coma (diabetic acidosis).

MANAGEMENT OF DIABETIC

Do not treat the uncontrolled diabetic. The health picture makes the patient a poor candidate for withstanding dental stress, and it has been shown that emotional stress increases glycemia and the tendency to diabetic acidosis and coma.

Most diabetics can give an accurate estimate of their current status, since they commonly test their urine for sugar. If the urine test is negative, shows a trace, or is 1+ for sugar, little problem with dental treatment would be expected. If the patient is doubtful regarding control, question regarding abnormal thirst, abnormal urine output, and weight loss. These are all signs of uncontrolled diabetes. If doubt still exists, a medical consultation is in order. It should be noted that the brittle diabetic cannot readily be controlled by such insulin substitutes as oral Diabinese, Orinase, Dymelor, and DBI. If the patient is taking one of these substitutes, or is controlled by diet alone, you may assume that the disease is not severe.

Since oral hypoglycemic agents have been associated with an increased risk of cardiovascular mortality in maturity-onset diabetics, physicians are relying more on diet in treating such patients.[32] All diabetics must be careful of their diets, some to avoid the need for insulin and others, who require insulin, to avoid hypoglycemia.

There is a marked tendency toward early development of arteriosclerosis in the diabetic, whether controlled or not. In evaluating the diabetic it is well to inquire into possible symptoms of heart failure and angina pectoris. A comprehensive 10-year study of 370 diabetics and 370 matched controls showed the death rate of diabetics to be 2.5 times that of the controls. The excess mortality was accounted for primarily by a higher prevalence of cardiovascular and renal disease, and, secondarily, by the severity of the diabetes as indicated by high insulin dosage (40 units or more daily), onset of the disease before age 45, and recurrent glycosuria, a definition of the "brittle" diabetic.

Frequently the meal before a dental appointment is inadequate or is missed entirely due to apprehension, and in these days of quadrant dentistry it is common to miss another meal or even two after the appointment. If the contemplated dental procedure may result in several meals being missed, I direct the patient to decrease insulin by half on the day of treatment in order to diminish the possibility of insulin shock. An elevated blood sugar for a short period is harmless. Anesthesiologists normally follow this same routine, either reducing insulin dosage at the time of surgery or withholding insulin entirely until the postoperative period.[22]

The brittle diabetic should pay special attention to urine sugar and acetone postoperatively. After considerable stress-producing treatment in such a patient, I recommend that he or she test the urine for sugar and acetone four times a day for four days and report any unusual deviations to the dental doctor and the medical doctor so that remedial action can be taken after consultation.

ASA CLASSIFICATION

The well controlled diabetic without associated additional disease is ASA Class II, the brittle diabetic with severe control problems is Class III; associated diseases such as CHF, MI, etc., may drop the diabetic to Class III or even IV. Follow Table 2–1, with special attention to stress reduction and the recommendations in the preceding paragraphs.

Hypothyroidism

Thyroid hormone affects all cellular metabolism. Hypothyroidism since infancy (cretinism) causes irreversible metabolic and growth changes. Hypothyroid adults under treatment rarely are a management concern in dentistry, even to the extreme of myxedema with slow pulse, brittle hair, dull facies, nonpitting edema of the face, and lethargic behavior. An enlarged tongue could be a technical problem, but these advanced cases are rarely encountered any more. The myxedematous patient may display signs and symptoms of CHF, and is very sensitive to sedatives.

ASA Class II would be correct for most hypothyroids, unless severe disease exists.

Hyperthyroidism

For our purposes, a history of hyperthyroidism should suggest the possibility of heart failure and angina pectoris. In addition, the moderately severe hyperthyroid suffers from tachycardia, sweating, headache, and nervous manifestations which make him or her a poor candidate for usual dental care.

The treated hyperthyroid would be placed in ASA Class II or lower if other significant disease exists. The untreated, severe hyperthyroid should be considered as Class IV temporarily. Follow Table 2–1.

Adrenocortical Insufficiency

The classic example of chronic adrenocortical insufficiency is Addison's disease, a deficiency of hormones concerned with glyconeogenesis (formation of carbohydrates from amino acids and fatty acids) and with mineral metabolism.

Tuberculosis is the cause of Addison's disease in 50 per cent of the cases, and 50 per cent result from idiopathic (cause unknown) atrophy of the adrenal glands. The patient suffers from weakness, anorexia, skin pigmentation, hypotension, and small heart. Treatment is by steroid replacement therapy (cortisone acetate).

Acute adrenocortical insufficiency is an emergency caused by an insufficient supply of adrenocortical hormones. Adrenal crisis may occur following treatment stress or following withdrawal of the hormone, with chronic insufficiency or with normal adrenals that are temporarily insufficient because of suppression due to recent use of a steroid for other purposes.

MANAGEMENT

There has been reported a near fatal adrenal crisis in an adrenalectomized patient for whom dental extractions were performed.[33] The patient had been prepared with 100 mg cortisone the night before surgery and a like dosage immediately before surgery. Profound shock occurred 90 minutes after surgery. You must assume the possibility of adrenal insufficiency if the patient has taken an adrenocortical hormone (cortisone, hydrocortisone, etc.) within the preceding two years. Irreversible shock may occur with such minor stress as a local analgesic injection or a simple dental extraction. You may consult the patient's physician, and he or she may reinstitute the steroid prior to dental treatment or make other arrangements to supplement. In assessing whether or not a steroid is required, I follow the Rule of Twos (McCarthy): if a patient has taken 20 mg of cortisone or equivalent for at least two weeks during the past two years, I assume the possibility of adrenal suppression. Admittedly the Rule of Twos is very conservative and restrictive, but it is safe.

Adrenocorticals are commonly utilized for the following: chronic collagen disorders (rheumatoid arthritis, lupus erythematosus), dermatologic diseases, rheumatic disorders, allergic states, ophthalmic diseases, respiratory diseases, hematologic disorders, neoplastic disorders, pemphigus, and postoperative inflammations.

The patient may be taking an adrenocortical hormone for chronic collagen disorder, such as rheumatoid arthritis, lupus erythematosus (L.E. disease), or other autoimmune diseases. The physician may wish to increase the dosage of the steroid temporarily if extensive dental therapy is planned and where an increased "stress reaction" would possibly be expected.

ASA CLASSIFICATION

ASA placement for the Addison's disease patient would depend upon signs and symptoms, replacement therapy success, and other diseases. It could range from Class II-IV, with possible strict modification of dental therapy in addition to steroid supplementation. ASA status for the uncomplicated patient to which the Rule of Twos applies would be Class II.

DISEASES OF THE BLOOD

Anemia

Anemia is characterized by one of the following:

1. Reduction below normal in the number of erythrocytes (red cells) — megaloblastic, pernicious, folic acid deficiency, aplastic.
2. Reduction in quantity of hemoglobin — iron deficiency, sickle cell.
3. Reduction in volume of packed red cells — bleeding or destruction (hemolytic).

The signs and symptoms of anemia include easy fatigability, dyspnea, pallor, palpitation, angina pectoris, tachycardia, brittle hair, and brittle nails. Normal adult hemoglobin is 12 to 18 gm per 100 ml; anemia is assumed to be significant at a hemoglobin of 9 grams or less. While a patient in renal failure will often tolerate a 5 gram hemoglobin remarkably well, you will elicit a history of exertional dyspnea, easy fatigability, etc.

ASA designation depends upon the type of anemia and signs and symptoms, relying upon the functional reserve classification primarily. With a 9 gram hemoglobin, ASA Class II would be appropriate, while below 9 grams Class III would be considered. Follow Table 2–1 for therapy modification. Stress reduction is in order, and oxygen supplementation during dental treatment can be helpful (as 3 L/min via nasal cannula). As with all anemias, bleeding tendencies during dental treatment must be considered.

Sickle Cell Anemia

This disease is covered separately because a crisis can occur during dental treatment. Nine per cent of U.S. blacks and 45 per cent of central African blacks display the sickling phenomenon, a marked insolubility of *reduced* HbS (hemoglobin S). The reduced HbS crystallizes from solution within the red cells into a sickle-shaped crystal. Infarction of the liver, kidney, brain, or long bones may occur with *extremely low oxygen tension* (flying, inhalation sedation, general anesthesia).

It is emphasized that there is a vast difference between sickle cell anemia, where the hemoglobin is all of the sickle type (SS), and the sickling phenomenon or sickle cell trait, where the S hemoglobin is linked with normal hemoglobin (AS).[34] Only one in 600 U.S. blacks has sickle cell anemia, characterized by HbSS, and this patient is our only concern. The sickle cell trait, characterized by HbAS, is a benign condition.[35] Mass screenings for the sickle cell trait have magnified the problem out of proportion since the sickling phenomenon is definitely a nondisease.

The patient with sickle cell anemia will give a history of fever, and pain in the arms, legs, or abdomen since early childhood. Anemia is severe. Scleral icterus (jaundiced white of eye) is common. The disease is disabling due to recurrent crises, with infarction of bones, joints, and organs. Complications include leg ulcers, hematuria (blood in urine), and heart enlargement. Many victims die in childhood from cerebral hemorrhage; some live beyond age 50; progressive renal damage is common (kidney failure).

ASA placement depends upon signs and symptoms, with the bulk of the patients being Class III. Follow Table 2–1 modifications, with special attention to stress reduction. Adequate oxygen delivery to the patient is essential to inhalation sedation, never falling below 30 per cent. Outpatient general anesthesia would represent a formidable endeavor.

Polycythemia Vera

This is caused by an overproduction of red cells, white cells, and platelets, with symptoms resulting from increased blood viscosity, characterized by malaise, fatigue, weakness, florid face, dusky red mucosa, and headache. Complications include GI hemorrhage, cerebral thrombosis, and pulmonary thrombosis. Excessive bleeding during dental treatment is common. Average survival is 13 years.

Most of these patients would be ASA Class III, depending upon history and signs and symptoms. Follow Table 2–1, with possible oxygen during treatment.

Leukemia

Properly falling under diseases of the white blood cells and reticuloendothelial system, leukemia will be considered here for convenience.

There is a proliferation of abnormal white cells in both acute and chronic leukemia, and most signs and symptoms are due to anemia: weakness, malaise, anorexia, pallor, fever, lymph node enlargement, and splenomegaly (enlarged spleen). Remission of up to one to three years is possible in 50 per cent of acute cases, and there is a life expectancy of three to four years in chronic cases with remissions.

Patients would be placed in ASA Class II to IV, as your judgment dictates. The advice under *anemia* applies, with special concern regarding bleeding.

Hodgkin's Disease

Here we see a proliferation of white cells in one or more lymph nodes, spreading to contiguous lymphatic structures. Lymph nodes are enlarged and nontender; there is fever and fatigue, and the disease is marked by exacerbations and remissions. Early treatment of the disease includes chemotherapy and possibly splenectomy. Late treatment is limited to irradiation. Up to 25 per cent of early cases are cured; overall five-year survival is 30 per cent.

ASA classification and treatment modification follow the anemias.

CONVULSIVE DISORDERS

This discussion is modified from the USC Physical Evaluation Manual. Convulsive disorders are characterized by abrupt transient symptoms of a motor, sensory, psychic, or autonomic nature, frequently associated with changes in consciousness. Epilepsy may be of an idiopathic nature (cause unknown) or be symptomatic of pathological states (brain tumor). The onset of idiopathic epilepsy is usually before age 30; onset thereafter usually suggests organic disease. In patients with classic epilepsy, anxiety and fear play a trigger role.

Convulsive disorders are classified as follows:

1. Grand mal epilepsy (major epilepsy) — 50 per cent of epileptics; loss of consciousness occurs and the patient undergoes generalized skeletal muscle contractions for several minutes, regaining consciousness with a headache and weakness. The seizure is usually preceded by a premonitory sign called an "aura," such as a bright light.
2. Petit mal epilepsy (minor epilepsy) — 10 per cent of epileptics; characterized by brief blank periods without falling or convulsions; most common in children. Neither the patient nor observers may be aware of the episode, which may appear as a brief lapse of attention.
3. Other types of epilepsy include Jacksonian (focal convulsions, consciousness retained), psychomotor disturbances (odd focal seizures, possible amnesia), status epilepticus (constant severe seizures that may be fatal), and febrile convulsions (associated with fever, especially in children).

ASA classification ranges from II to IV, depending upon the history of seizure frequency and severity. Grand mal well managed by medication would be Class II; poorly managed by medication — Class III; frequent seizures associated with dental therapy could merit Class IV and possible hospitalization.

Modification of treatment would include strict adherence to stress reduction, and doctor and staff should be prepared to manage a seizure (see Chapter 8, Cardiovascular and Other Medical Emergencies).

PHYSICAL EXAMINATION

INTRODUCTION

The medical history questionnaire, plus the indicated dialogue history, will provide you in most cases with an adequate pretreatment physical evaluation in dentistry. However, no physical evaluation is complete without a physical examination. Measurement and recording of vital signs is the first part of a physical examination, but will be considered after inspection.

INSPECTION

Inspection of the patient represents the most important part of every physical examination. You have been doing this, perhaps without realizing it, since you became a dental health professional.

Train yourself to actually *see* the patient when checking the medical history questionnaire or taking the dialogue history. Several points to observe are:

1. The color of the skin:
   Cyanosis — heart disease, polycythemia.
   Pallor — anemia, fear, tendency toward syncope.
   Flushing — fever, atropine overdosage, apprehension, hyperthyroidism.
   Jaundice — liver disease.
2. The eyes:
   Exophthalmos — hyperthyroidism.
3. The conjunctiva:
   Pallor — anemia.
   Jaundice — liver disease.
4. The hands:
   Tremor — hyperthyroidism, apprehension, hysteria, paralysis agitans, epilepsy, multiple sclerosis, senility.
5. The fingers:
   Clubbing — cardiopulmonary disease.
   Cyanosis of nail beds – cardiopulmonary disease.
6. The neck:
   Jugular vein distention — right heart failure.
7. The ankles:
   Swelling — varicose veins, right heart failure, kidney disease.
8. The respiratory rate, particularly with heart failure:
   Normal adult — 16 to 18 per minute.
   Normal child — 24 to 28 per minute.
9. The abdomen:
   Ascites — hepatic cirrhosis, right heart failure.
10. Appearance, demeanor, attitude, behavior:
    Is the patient in acute distress (pain or dyspnea); acutely anxious, fearful, antagonistic, belligerent; does the patient appear to be reliable and well informed. Any observed deviation from the norm should be recorded.

VITAL SIGNS

While no clear standard of care exists at the present time regarding what vital signs, if any, should be determined prior to dental therapy, it would appear that determination of blood pressure in adults at the initial physical evaluation is approaching a mandatory status. From the standpoint of comprehensive health care, it is urged that the following three vital signs be measured at the original physical evaluation of all patients:

1. Blood pressure
2. Pulse rate and rhythm

3.   Body temperature

It is further urged that the remaining three commonly measured vital signs also be recorded at the initial examination: height, weight, and respiratory rate.

It is also urged that the dental doctor dedicated to comprehensive health care measure and record at least the blood pressure, and preferably pulse rate and body temperature as well, prior to subsequent dental treatment during which medication of any kind is to be administered (includes local analgesia) or during which significant emotional or physical stress may be encountered by the patient.

Blood pressure measurement before inhalation sedation is highly desirable, and it is mandatory before intravenous sedation. See elsewhere in this book for the technical aspects of *vital sign determination*.

Blood pressure should be redetermined after a lapse of six months or longer, and both blood pressure and pulse rate are highly desirable in cases of suspected cardiovascular or cerebrovascular disease.

Blood Pressure

You may easily train your assistant to do this as a matter of routine, although you may wish to check personally if the reading is abnormal.

You will be gratified by the number of undiagnosed and often asymptomatic cases of hypertension which this routine will disclose. Your patients will be most appreciative of this health service, but more importantly your alertness can result in the early and effective medical treatment of hypertension, and your own treatment plan may well be altered by the discovery.

The blood pressure varies up to 140/90 mm in the normal adult. Since it may vary as much as 20 to 30 mm over a short period due to exertion or excitement, take several readings when in doubt, and assume that the lowest is normal for that patient.

There is no simple way of estimating by blood pressure measurement alone whether the patient's hypertension is mild or severe. Such an evaluation must depend on the blood pressure and, more important, on the overall evaluation of the patient. A patient who is taking an antihypertensive drug, and who has a history of a stroke and a blood pressure of 160/100, may be a far greater risk under treatment than a patient with untreated essential hypertension, a reading of 190/120, and a total lack of symptoms referable to hypertension. If any doubt exists regarding the propriety of treatment, consult the physician.

ASA Class II is merited for a pressure consistently in the area of 140 to 160/90 to 95, Class III for 160 to 200/95 to 115, and Class IV over 200/115. A systolic pressure consistently over 200 may be considered a medical emergency. Rechecking by the physician away from the dental environment may demonstrate consistently lower pressures, in which event you should adjust the ASA classification and treatment modification. Three or more consecutive recordings above 140/90 justifies a medical consultation. Follow Table 2–1 therapy modifications, with special attention to stress reduction. Patients taking antihypertensive drugs should be protected against abrupt postural changes, as sitting up or standing. Alter the operating chair position slowly so that the cardiovascular system adapts and postural hypotension with syncope does not occur.

Pulse Rate and Rhythm

Bradycardia — heart rate slower than 60 beats per minute.
Tachycardia — heart rate faster than 100 beats per minute.

Pulse considerations are as follows:

1. Pulse rate varies from 60 to 90 per minute in the normal adult, and 80 to 120 per minute in the normal child. In the endurance athlete, the pulse rate may be as low as 50 to 60 per minute. Loss of consciousness usually occurs below a rate of 40 per minute.
   Comment: A rate of less than 60 or more than 110 in the adult should be viewed with suspicion, and usually is sufficient evidence to justify a medical consultation.
2. The pulse rate should be within normal limits and should be both strong and regular.
3. Any irregularity of the pulse, other than a very occasional premature ventricular contraction (extrasystole, dropped beat), is an indication for medical consultation.
   Examples:
   a. Complete irregularity of the pulse (complete arrhythmia, pulsus irregularis perpetuus) usually indicates atrial fibrillation; may or may not be serious in respect to dental treatment.
   b. Pulsus alternans, which is regular alternation in the size or strength of the pulsations, indicates severe myocardial damage.

As was stated in the chapter on *sudden death*, premature ventricular contractions (PVCs, skipped beats) are common in the healthy adult and are of no significance. When noted in the patient with cardiovascular disease (CHF, CAHD, hypertension), PVCs can be significant. Notation of five PVCs or more per minute in a post-MI patient would be grounds for ASA Class IV designation until a medical consultation dictated a lesser designation. This same is true of a pulse rate in the adult consistently over 110 or less than 60 until explained satisfactorily by medical consultation or by circumstances (athlete). Pulsus alternans is an automatic Class IV. Atrial fibrillation could range from Class II to IV, depending upon the cause and signs and symptoms.

Pulse rate or rhythm alone is not a terribly reliable method for ASA classification, the final designation relying on the disease or condition responsible for the abnormal finding. Follow Table 2–1 for appropriate modification.

Temperature

Body temperature ranges from 96.8 to 99.4° F in the healthy individual, with a "normal" of 98.6° F. Actual body temperatures rise above individual setpoints in warm environments or during work and fall below setpoints in cold environments.[36] The variation range is probably wider, pending investigation of larger groups.

Normal rectal or vaginal temperature is 1° F higher than the oral temperature, and the normal axillary temperature is 1° F lower. Oral, nasal, and axillary temperatures are subject to errors by evaporative cooling, and the rectal site is encumbered by thermally inert masses and is influenced by microbial heat production. In fever there is an upward shift of the individual setpoint by depressing action of the pyrogen, for example, bacterial end products.[36] An individual with a low setpoint could have a 2° fever and still demonstrate a 98.8° F measurement, well within the range of "normal," while an individual with a high setpoint could demonstrate an oral temperature of 101.4° F with the same 2° fever.

As can be seen, body temperature is unreliable as to specific numbers, but an elevated temperature speaks volumes in determining the physical status of a patient. Routine measurement of body temperature by the dental practitioner is called for if comprehensive health care is the goal. It is certainly indicated for an obviously ill patient suffering from oral or nonoral systemic infection.

ASA classification based upon body temperature alone is of necessity empiric and is more wisely based upon the specific disease process. The following guidelines are suggested:

ASA Class II — 99.5 to 101°F — cause of elevated temperature should be sought; no elective therapy if signs of respiratory infection; elective treatment otherwise OK, depending upon evaluation of individual patient; use of psychosedation or general anesthesia is a judgment decision; stress reduction and treatment duration limitation indicated.

ASA Class III — 101 to 104°F — medical consultation; emergency dental treatment only.

ASA Class IV — over 104°F — medical emergency.

Height/Weight

Normal weight may vary 10 to 15 per cent above or below standard weight tables. *Any* recent weight gain or loss may be significant in evaluating the physical status prior to dental therapy. Recording height and weight can be very valuable, especially since loose clothing can mask a considerable overweight problem.

Weight gain may be produced by:

1. Overeating
2. Endocrine dysfunction (hypothyroidism)
3. Edema associated with:
    a. congestive heart failure
    b. hepatic (liver) failure
    c. renal (kidney) insufficiency

Weight loss may be produced by:

1. Dieting
2. GI dysfunction (peptic ulcer, gall bladder disease, etc.)
3. Endocrine dysfunction (hyperthyroidism)
4. Malignancy
5. Neurosis

Consideration should be given to dropping one ASA classification for either gross overweight or gross underweight (wasting). Gross overweight is especially important in classifying the patient with cardiovascular diseases; an angina pectoris patient in ASA Class II would surely be dropped to Class III in this situation. Follow Table 2–1 modifications and stress reduction.

Respiratory Rate

Observe the type, rate, and depth of breathing at rest. Normal for the reasonably apprehensive adult in the dental environment is 16 to 18 per minute; for the child 24 to 28 per minute. Respiratory depth and rhythm are regular. Rate increases 4 per minute for each 1°F temperature elevation.

Respiration in males is primarily diaphragmatic (abdominal); pronounced use of the chest muscles could indicate air hunger. The reverse is true of females, whose breathing is primarily costal (chest); pronounced use of the diaphragm (abdomen) could indicate dyspnea. Use of the accessory muscles of respiration (neck, shoulders) could indicate dyspnea.

Breath odors can be of value. A fetid (foul, putrefactive) breath may be noted with lung abscess or bronchiectasis. An acetone odor (sweet, fruity) could indicate diabetic acidosis and perhaps threatened hyperglycemic coma. The odor of ammonia may indicate uremia (kidney failure). In liver failure the breath may have a musty odor (fetor hepaticus; methyl mercaptan). The odor of alcohol may indicate self-medication on a sedative or compulsive basis, and is good reason for a thorough evaluation of possible anxiety or a drinking problem.

The respiratory rate does not lend itself to ASA physical status classification. A demonstrated hyperventilation syndrome would be designated as ASA Class II, while the Kussmaul breathing of diabetic acidosis (rate — 30 to 40/min) would classify as ASA Class IV and would be considered a medical emergency.

AUSCULTATION OF HEART AND LUNGS

Although it is not mandatory that the dental doctor be experienced in auscultation of the heart and lungs, this examination is well within the standard of practice in dentistry. Many states have dental practice acts which specifically mention physical evaluation as being within dental standards of practice, while in other states its legality may be taken for granted, as the technique can be a necessary adjunct to the safe practice of dentistry.

Stethoscopic examination of the heart and lungs as an aid in physical evaluation may be made with perfect propriety by the dental practitioner who is competent through training and experience. I consider the following guidelines to be essential to this examination:

1. Regardless of the sex or age of the patient, a dental assistant should be present with the patient and doctor throughout the examination. The claim of sexual impropriety by the unbalanced adult or fantasizing child or teenager, even though unsubstantiated, can be extremely damaging to the

doctor's reputation. I am aware of criminal charges being filed in such instances. This same advice is sound when the axilla is examined, as such has been interpreted as a sexual caress.

2. Reasonable justification is essential to the examination; that is, there must be reasonable concern regarding the possibility of cardiovascular or bronchopulmonary disease. Exceptions to this advice include the teaching environment, the patient being examined prior to general anesthesia or admission to the hospital, and the patient for which complete physical evaluation is being performed by the practitioner.

An impression of chronic congestive heart failure gained by the dialogue history may be supported by rales heard over the lung bases on auscultation. A history of possible valvular heart disease may be supported upon auscultation of the heart. It is probable that in the future heart sounds will be analyzed by an office telephone connection with a computer. In a study of 3797 children, no known cases of heart disease were missed by the computer, the false-positive ratio was 5.6 per cent, and the computer picked up eight previously unknown cases of heart disease out of a grand total of 16 for the group.

Auscultation of the heart and lungs has been taught in all advanced oral surgery training programs in the United States for many years. At the University of Southern California a continuing education course in advanced physical diagnosis has been presented to general dental practitioners since 1961. Auscultation has been taught to the predoctoral student and the dental hygiene student at USC since 1976, and the examination has been adopted as a routine for selected patients in the dental clinic since 1978, all predoctoral students participating on a required basis.

Inasmuch as complete physical diagnosis is the next step for meaningful progress in physical evaluation in dentistry, and since such advancement is in the public interest, the following chapter is devoted exclusively to that subject so that the advanced student of physical evaluation will have dental-oriented material available. It is suggested that the reader at least review the material on the significance of heart sounds and breath sounds.

FUNCTION TESTS

Introduction

At the completion of the medical history and applicable physical examination, you may have serious reservations about the functional reserve of a patient with cardiovascular or bronchopulmonary disease. Should the patient be placed in ASA Class II, III, or IV, and what therapy modifications are therefore in order. The Anderson Breath-Holding Test is very valuable in this instance. It serves as a test flight of stairs in the dental office.

The suspicion of bronchopulmonary disease may be very strong, but you need function tests to reinforce your impression of lower airway obstruction (pulmonary emphysema). The Match Test and Timed Forced Expiratory Volume are of great assistance. They may allow an unnecessary medical consultation to be avoided, or may give you valuable information with which to initiate a medical consultation.

Anderson Breath-Holding Test

Technique:

1. The patient takes a deep breath.
2. The patient pinches the nostrils together in order to prevent exhalation; also some patients may inadvertently breathe through the nose.
3. The breath is held as long as is reasonably comfortable, and you time the interval. It is my practice to stop the test at 20 seconds.

Interpretation:

1. The upper limits vary greatly and may be beyond 35 to 45 seconds.
2. 20 seconds or more—excellent

   15 seconds or less — caution

   10 seconds or less — great caution

A test result of 15 seconds or less should be viewed with suspicion, especially if there is evidence of cardiovascular or bronchopulmonary disease. Repeat the test at least once if the result is questionable. An observation of 10 seconds or less would militate against elective therapy and indicate a medical consultation, as an ASA Class IV designation is in order, at least temporarily. Patients with congestive heart failure or emphysema in Class III will usually achieve a test result of 15 seconds.

Match Test

The Match Test is of great value in respiratory system evaluation. The patient attempts to blow out a half-burned match held at 6 inches from the mouth with lips parted wide, not pursed. Failure to pass this test indicates FEV per second (see next test for explanation) in the area of 1 liter (L), or a peak flow rate of under 100 liters per minute,[37] a serious situation. Further evaluation by pulmonary function tests would be in order.

Timed Forced Expiratory Volume

Vital capacity (VC) is the maximum expelled volume of air after a maximum inspiration. Forced vital capacity (FVC) is normally expelled in 3 seconds or less with effort; if the timed expulsion is 5 seconds or more, bronchial obstruction exists (emphysema, asthma, other). You may time the forced expiration in the office. While the use of a spirometer would improve accuracy, it is not necessary to support your impression.

Forced expiratory volume (FEV) is the maximum expelled volume in a timed interval, as 1, 2, 3, 4, or 5 seconds. The expelled volume may be expressed as a percentage of FVC or in liters (L). The following are percentage values for the normal healthy patient:

$$FEV \text{ 1 sec, or } FEV_1 = 83\% \text{ of actual VC}$$
$$FEV \text{ 2 sec, or } FEV_2 = 97\% \text{ of actual VC}$$
$$FEV \text{ 3 sec, or } FEV_3 = 99\% \text{ of actual VC}$$

Here are examples of expelled volume (requiring a spirometer) for the normal healthy patient. In this patient the total lung capacity (TLC) is 5.08 L, the residual volume (RV) is 1.54 L, and the FVC is 3.33 L:

$$FEV_1 = 2.23 \text{ L}$$
$$FEV_2 = 2.84 \text{ L}$$
$$FEV_3 = 3.21 \text{ L}$$

Reduction to 60 to 75 per cent of estimated normal is indicative of obstructive lung disease (emphysema); reduction to 40 to 60 per cent of normal represents a very serious functional loss. The most useful test is FEV_1. Failure to expel 60 per cent of the 3 second FEV in the first second indicates trouble.[37] Examples of risk patients are: high risk — FEV_1 = 1.64 L; very high risk — FEV_1 = 1.20 L.

Estimate the FEV in your office over a timed interval of 5 seconds. The maximum volume should be expelled in 1 to 2 seconds. If the patient is still expelling significant volume at 5 seconds, and if the medical history is suspicious, a consultation and possible pulmonary function tests would be in order.

Further, if the patient's maximal chest expansion is over one inch, it is unlikely that restrictive disease of the thoracic cage exists.[37]

Double Two-Step Exercise Test

While this test will be performed in the medical office, it is extremely valuable in the diagnosis and prognosis of coronary artery disease. Robb concludes that a nonischemic ECG response to exercise practically excludes coronary disease of a type that will cause premature death, and the exercise test is more reliable than the medical history in the diagnosis of silent coronary disease.[42]

LABORATORY TESTS

For years hospitalized patients have had prior to general anesthesia a minimum laboratory examination consisting of a routine urinalysis and a complete blood count. In dental offices such examinations have never become routine, although a small minority of offices perform a hemoglobin or hematocrit determination and check the urine for sugar. It is doubtful if such routine examinations add significantly to the usual basic evaluation outlined here, although they are a significant public service as a health screen.

Routine health screening is assisted by a microhematocrit (packed cell volume), hemoglobin, and basic urinalysis (sugar and protein), all of which are simple to perform at small cost in the dental office. Urinalysis is cost-effective as a health screen, while the other tests are not considered so by public health authorities for general screening in public clinics. This reasoning does not apply to the dental office.

Regarding urinalysis, a positive result for protein (albumin) would not contraindicate usual dental treatment or even outpatient general anesthesia but would suggest a medical consultation to investigate possible kidney disease. A positive sugar in the patient with diabetes indicates possible control problems, while possible diabetes should be investigated in the event of a negative history.

It is suggested that a hematocrit below 30 per cent or hemoglobin below 10 grams is a contraindication to outpatient general anesthesia.[38] Normal adult hemoglobin is 12 to 18 gm per 100 ml. I consider a hemoglobin of 9 grams or less to be significant and worthy of investigation. A hemoglobin as low as 5 grams will usually be accompanied by exertional dyspnea, tachycardia, palpitation, and undue fatigue.

If you are not performing screening tests in the office, and if you have doubts regarding possible kidney disease, anemia, bleeding tendencies, diabetes, etc., it would be wise to refer the patient to a clinical laboratory, depending upon your background and experience in interpreting such tests, or refer to a physician for appropriate examination, tests, and opinion.

COMMENT

Adequate physical evaluation is the most important method by which the dental practitioner is able to prevent life-threatening emergencies during therapy, and is followed closely in importance by proper stress reduction and other indicated modifications to therapy. You must first be dedicated to prevention, and, understanding the hows and whys of prevention, you will then understand the treatment of extant emergencies, treating appropriately by knowledge of disease, rather than blindly utilizing by-the-numbers, by-the-symptoms cookbook therapy.

REFERENCES

1. McCarthy, F. M.: Physical evaluation. Dent. Clin. North Amer., 17:191–209, 1973.
2. Halpern, I. L.: Patient's medical status — a factor in dental treatment. Oral Surg., 39:216–226, 1975.
3. Accepted Dental Therapeutics. Chicago, American Dental Association, 1977–78, p. 9.
4. Ibid, pp. 7–8.
5. Yu, P. N.: Lung water in congestive heart failure. Mod. Conc. Cardiov. Dis., 40:27–32, 1971.
6. Rahe, R. H., et al.: Recent life changes, myocardial infarction, and abrupt coronary death. Arch. Intern. Med., 133:221–228, 1974.
7. Hershberg, P. I., et al.: The medical history question as a health screening test. Arch. Intern. Med., 127:266–272, 1971.
8. Horwitz, L. D.: The diagnostic significance of anginal symptoms. J.A.M.A., 299:1196–1199, 1974.
9. Lesch, M., and Gorlin, R.: Pharmacological therapy of angina pectoris. Mod. Conc. Cardiov. Dis., 42:5–10, 1973.
10. Becker, L. C., et al.: Effect of ischemia and antianginal drugs on the distribution of radioactive microspheres in the canine left ventricle. Circ. Res., 28:263–269, 1971.
11. Medical Letter on Drugs and Therapeutics: Drugs for prophylaxis of angina pectoris, 17:57–58, 1975.
12. Gey, G. E., et al.: Exertional arrhythmia and nitroglycerin. J.A.M.A., 226:287–290, 1973.
13. Medical Letter on Drugs and Therapeutics: Disintegration and storage of nitroglycerin tablets, 13:13–14, 1971.
14. Editorial: Nitroglycerin tablets: loss of potency, J.A.M.A., 216:878, 1971.
15. Edelman, B. A., et al.: The stability of hypodermic tablets of nitroglycerin packaged in dispensing containers. J. Amer. Pharmaceut. Assoc., NS11:30–33, 1971.
16. FDA Drug Bulletin: Nitroglycerin packaging affects potency. February, 1972.
17. Copelan, H. W.: Burning sensation and potency of nitroglycerin sublingually. J.A.M.A., 219:176–179, 1972.
18. Chandler, A. B.: Relationship of coronary thrombosis to myocardial infarction. Mod. Conc. Cardiov. Dis., 44:1–5, 1975.
19. White, P. D.: The historical background of angina pectoris. Mod. Conc. Cardiov. Dis., 43:109–112, 1974.

20. Carleton, R. A., and Johnson, A. D.: Coronary artery spasm. Mod. Conc. Cardiov. Dis., *43*:87–91, 1974.
21. Medical Letter on Drugs and Therapeutics: Nitroglycerin in acute myocardial infarction. *18*:37–38, 1976.
22. Medical Letter on Drugs and Therapeutics: Anticoagulants in myocardial infarction. *16*:17–19, 1974.
23. Michaels, L.: Incidence of thromboembolism after stopping anticoagulant therapy. J.A.M.A., *215*:595–599, 1971.
24. Corday, E.: Status of coronary bypass surgery. J.A.M.A., *231*:1245–1247, 1975.
25. Medical Letter on Drugs and Therapeutics: Coronary arteriography and coronary artery surgery. *18*:57–59, 1976.
26. Rezal, F. R.: Dental treatment of patient with a cardiac pacemaker. Oral Surg., *44*:662–665, 1977.
27. Simon, A. B., et al.: The individual with a pacemaker in the dental environment. J.A.D.A., *91*:1224–1229, 1975.
28. Finnerty, F. A.: Hypertension is different in blacks. J.A.M.A., *216*:1634–1635, 1971.
29. Medical Letter on Drugs and Therapeutics: Anticoagulants in the prevention of strokes caused by occlusive vascular disease. *13*:27–28, 1971.
30. Westbrook, S. D.: Dental management of patients receiving hemodialysis and kidney transplants. J.A.D.A., *96*:464–468, 1978.
31. Heard, E., et al.: The dental patient with renal disease: precautions and guidelines. J.A.D.A., *96*:792–796, 1978.
32. Medical Letter on Drugs and Therapeutics: Some notes on diet in the management of diabetics. *13*:58–59, 1971.
33. Brontsas, M. G., and Seldin, R.: Adrenal crisis after tooth extractions in an adrenalectomized patient: Report of case. J. Oral Surg., *30*:301–302, 1972.
34. Hussey, H. H.: Sicklemia. J.A.M.A., *229*:192, 1974.
35. Bristow, L. R.: The myth of sickle cell trait. Western J. Med., *121*:77–82, 1974.
36. Benzinger, T. H.: What is normal body temperature. J.A.M.A., *218*:603, 1971.
37. Chase, H. F.: To operate or not to operate — what is the risk. Resident & Staff Physician, 65–77, May 1978.
38. Allen, G. D.: Dental Anesthesia and Analgesia. Baltimore, Williams & Wilkins Co., 1972, p. 22.
39. Rothwell, P. S., and Wragg, K. A.: Assessment of the medical status of patients in general dental practice — a comparative survey of a questionnaire and verbal injury. Brit. Dent. J., *133*:252–255, 1972.
40. Slack, W., et al.: A computer-based medical history system, New Engl. J. Med., *274*:194–198, 1966.
41. Kanner, I. F.: The programmed physical examination with or without a computer, J.A.M.A., *215*:1281–1291, 1971.
42. Robb, G. P., and Seltzer, F.: Appraisal of the double two-step exercise test. J.A.M.A., *234*:722–727, 1975.

SUPPLEMENTAL READING

Bates, B.: A Guide to Physical Examination. 1st ed., Philadelphia, J. B. Lippincott Co., 1974.
Beeson, P. B., and McDermott, W.: The Textbook of Medicine. 14th ed., Philadelphia, W. B. Saunders Co., 1975.
Cain, H. D.: Flint's Emergency Treatment and Management. 6th ed., Philadelphia, W. B. Saunders Co., 1980.
Davis, K.: Training Manual for Oral and Maxillofacial Surgery Assistants. 1st ed., Chapel Hill, N.C., Training Manual Publishing Co., 1979.
DeGowin, E. L., and DeGowin, R. L.: Bedside Diagnostic Examination. 3rd ed., New York, Macmillan Publishing Co., Inc., 1976.
Delp, M. H., and Manning, R. T.: Major's Physical Diagnosis. 9th ed., Philadelphia, W. B. Saunders Co., 1980.
Dunn, M. J., and Booth, D. F.: Internal Medicine/Systemic Emergencies – Module 4, Dental Auxiliary Practice. 1st ed., Baltimore, The Williams & Wilkins Co., 1975.
Irby, W. B., and Baldwin, K. H.: Emergencies and Urgent Complications in Dentistry. 1st ed., St. Louis, C. V. Mosby Co., 1965.
Krupp, M. A., and Chatton, M. J.: Current Medical Diagnosis and Treatment. 18th ed., Los Altos, Cal., Lange Medical Publications, 1979.
Krupp, M. A., et al.: Physician's Handbook. 19th ed., Los Altos, Cal., Lange Medical Publications, 1979.
Malamed, S. F.: Handbook of Medical Emergencies in the Dental Office. 1st ed., St. Louis, C. V. Mosby Co., 1978.
Schijatschky, M. M.: Life-Threatening Emergencies in the Dental Practice. 1st ed., Chicago, Buch- und Zeitschriften-Verlag "Die Quintessenz," 1975.

PHYSICAL DIAGNOSIS

LAWRENCE W. RICHARDSON

INTRODUCTION

The chapter on *physical evaluation* dealt primarily with the establishment of a basic medical evaluation in which the risk factor only was determined prior to dental therapy. This chapter will present material covering the subject of physical diagnosis that has general application to dentistry. Some overlap with other chapters must be accepted for clarity.

The serious student will also find that this fundamental, dental oriented approach makes for a simple transition from physical evaluation to a textbook on comprehensive physical diagnosis.

Either the short-form or the long-form medical history illustrated in Chapter 2 can serve as a departure point for physical diagnosis. The dialogue medical history that will be presented here is not a patient-completed questionnaire, but is a suggested outline from which the practitioner can choose pertinent material for investigation.

This chapter encompasses a brief discussion of physical diagnosis with specific reference to signs, symptoms, and pathogenesis of some of the more common or interesting diseases the practitioner may encounter. Emphasis has been placed on changes in organ function.

The patient comes to the health practitioner because he wants a checkup, knows he is ill, or has a variety of fears and is worried. The practitioner's responsibility is threefold: (1) to establish a diagnosis, (2) to treat the illness, and (3) to mitigate the patient's fears and anxieties.

SYMPTOMS AND SIGNS

Disease manifests itself by abnormal sensations and events known as symptoms, and by changes in structure or function known as signs. Symptoms, being subjective, must be described by the patient and obtained in his history. Signs are objective, and are discovered by the examiner by means of physical examination, laboratory tests, and x-ray. The information obtained from the history and physical examination is of value only when one is able to select and correlate the pertinent facts and recognize the clinical picture that they indicate. Abnormal symptoms and signs should be completely investigated. Mistakes are just as often caused by lack of thoroughness as by lack of knowledge. The history of a patient is absolutely essential in making a diagnosis. In some diseases a physical examination is of great importance whereas a laboratory examination is of little value; in other diseases the reverse is true; but in all diseases the history is of great importance. In some diseases the diagnosis is made entirely from the history. In pulmonary tuberculosis, the history of loss of weight and night sweats and afternoon fever may be of greater value than any physical findings. In angina pectoris the diagnosis is often entirely made from the history of pain under the sternum, which radiates to the left arm and is accompanied by a sensation of impending death.

HISTORY TAKING

Taking of a history includes not only taking the patient's medical history but also his or her personal and social history. During the time utilized in obtaining a history, one also strives to develop a good rapport with the patient, and has the opportunity to make a psychological evaluation and to determine the patient's mental status.

First are recorded name, residence, age, sex, race, marital state, nationality, and occupation. Next is obtained the *chief complaint,* which asks for the nature and duration of the symptoms that brought the patient to the practitioner. *Present illness* (analysis of chief complaint) will include detailed information concerning the current symptoms. This should be a logically developed story, accurately describing the time and mode of onset, duration, severity, location, progress, character, and relation to physiologic function. *Past history* should include diseases of childhood, serious illnesses, injuries, previous surgery and hospitalizations, previous radiation therapy, allergies, blood transfusions, familial diseases, medications now being taken, and habits regarding alcohol and tobacco. Following this is the systems review, which is a methodical questioning about each system of the body with specific questions to remind the patient of symptoms. The systems review is shown in Table 3–1.

PHYSICAL EXAMINATION

The five basic procedures used in conducting a general physical examination are indicated below. These are supplemented by special methods for testing neurologic function.

Inspection — looking at the body.

Palpation — feeling the various parts.

Percussion — listening to the sounds produced and noting the degree of resistance encountered when a region is tapped.

TABLE 3-1 SYSTEMS REVIEW

Head: headache, vertigo, lightheadedness, fainting
Eyes: glasses, vision, pain
Ears: hearing, tinnitus, pain, discharge
Nose: head colds, epistaxis, smell
Mouth: salivation, lesions, pain, sense of taste, swallowing, hoarseness, tonsillitis
Neck: stiffness, venous distention, pulsations, swellings
Respiratory: cough, hemoptysis, sputum, night sweats
Cardiac: pain in chest, palpitation, dyspnea, orthopnea, ankle edema
Gastrointestinal: appetite, nausea, vomiting, diarrhea, hematemesis, jaundice, color of stools, abdominal pain
Genitourinary: pain on urination, hematuria, frequency, purulent urine, incontinence, penile discharge
Menses: age at onset, frequency, regularity, duration, pain, amount, date of last period
Neuromuscular: convulsions, paresthesia, weakness, paralysis, incoordination of movements
Weight: amount and any recent change

Auscultation—listening to the sounds produced within the body.

Smell — odors of a disease may be characteristic.

Examination by these methods is performed after the history has been taken. Those parts of the body to which the history has directed suspicion require detailed investigation; however, it is the responsibility of the practioner to give a thorough physical examination. Pathology frequently exists without producing subjective manifestations and is often found incidentally on examination. The form presented in Table 3–2 is recommended as a guide for general physical examination.

SKIN

Inspection of the skin and mucous membranes is the simplest of all procedures. Only with diseases of the skin can one have such a complete view.

Many skin conditions are associated with general systemic disease, whereas others are skin diseases *per se* and belong entirely within the domain of dermatology.

Color. The color of the skin is one of the first characteristics that should be studied. The conjunctiva and sclera of the eye are excellent sites to observe change in color. Extreme pallor of the skin and mucous membranes may be indications of anemia. Abnormal redness can be a sign of polycythemia vera, which is an overproduction of red blood cells. Jaundice, or yellow discoloration, usually indicates infectious hepatitis or obstructive disease of the bile ducts, such as with neoplasms and gallstones. Cyanosis, a bluish color of the skin, is associated with diminished oxygen-carrying capacity of the blood. It may be present with cardiac or pulmonary disease. With Addison's disease (adrenocortical insufficency) there is a bronze-like discoloration of the skin.

Hemorrhage. Subcutaneous bleeding, occurring spontaneously or after minor trauma, is often an indication of a systemic disease. Lesions less than 2 mm. in diameter are referred to as petechiae, from 2 to 5 mm. as

TABLE 3-2 OUTLINE OF PHYSICAL EXAMINATION

1. Vital signs: pulse, blood pressure, respirations, temperature, weight
2. General appearance: stature, posture, nutritional state
3. Skin: color, texture, moisture, turgor, pigmentation, lesions
4. Head: shape, size, distribution of hair
5. Eyes: conjunctivae and sclera; size and shape of pupils; reaction of pupils to light and accommodation; funduscopic examination of retina for hemorrhage, exudate, vessels, and optic disks; vision
6. Ears: external examination for tophi; tympanic membrane examined for inflammation, exudate; auditory acuity
7. Nose: septum, turbinates, polyps
8. Mouth and throat: teeth, tongue, tonsils, lesions, lips
9. Neck: lymph nodes, thyroid, engorgement of veins, abnormal pulsations, masses, midline trachea
10. Chest: contour, symmetry, equal expansion, axillary lymph nodes
11. Lungs: breath sounds, respiratory rate, fremitus, rales, wheezes, friction rub
12. Breasts: size, masses, secretion, pigmentation, tenderness
13. Heart: point of maximal impulse, thrills, pulse rate, heart sounds, murmurs, rhythm
14. Abdomen: contour, scars, dilated veins, rigidity, tenderness, liver, spleen, kidneys, bladder, masses, fluid, inguinal lymph nodes
15. Male genitalia: discharge, lesions, testicular masses, inguinal hernia
16. Female genitalia: inspection of perineum, cervix, bimanual examination of uterus and adnexa, Pap smear.
17. Rectum: hemorrhoids, masses, prostate
18. Extremities: color of palms, clubbing of fingers, cyanosis, joint swelling or deformity, pulses
19. Back: curvature, mobility
20. Nervous system: deep tendon reflexes, pathologic reflexes, cranial nerves, sensory examination

purpuric spots, and larger ones as ecchymosis. If there is enough bleeding to cause a palpable mass, the lesion is a hematoma. Hemorrhage may occur spontaneously with thrombocytopenic purpura, a disease in which the blood platelets are prematurely destroyed in the spleen; leukemias and lymphomas in which there is a deficiency in platelet formation; aplastic anemia; infections with streptococcus or meningococcus; severe liver disease with a decreased production of prothrombin; and in patients who are taking anticoagulant medications such as Coumadin or dicumarol. When subacute bacterial endocarditis is suspected, the conjunctivae should be frequently inspected for the appearance of petechial hemorrhages.

Edema. Edema is a collection of fluid in the subcutaneous tissue. The skin is tense and shiny, and pits on pressure. An impression made on the skin by pressure with the fingers does not immediately disappear after the fingers are removed. Edema may be due to congestive heart failure; liver failure in which there is too little production of blood proteins such as albumin; renal insufficiency, in which blood proteins are lost in the urine; and starvation. A localized area of edema may be due to trauma, infection, or interference with venous blood or lymph flow.

Subcutaneous Emphysema. The presence of air or gas in the subcutaneous tissue gives an edematous appearance. On palpation there is a crackling sensation (crepitation) under the skin. Air blown into the root canal of a tooth, or around the crevicular margins of a tooth preparation; puncture wounds of the trachea or lungs; the rupture of emphysematous blebs of the lungs; or infection of a wound by a gas-producing organism can cause subcutaneous emphysema.

Primary Lesions of the Skin

MACULES. These are flat, circumscribed changes in skin color, such as with freckles, petechiae, and flat moles.

PAPULES. These are circumscribed elevations not over a centimeter in size.

NODULES. These are circumscribed solid lesions in the subcutaneous tissue which may be inflammatory or neoplastic.

WHEALS (HIVES). These are morphologically papules, sharply circumscribed, and produced by acute edema.

VESICLES. These are sharply circumscribed, small elevations, containing clear fluid.

BULLAE. These are large vesicles, greater than 0.5 cm.

PUSTULES. These are circumscribed lesions containing free pus.

SCALES. These are loose fragments of an incompletely shed, dead, keratinized layer of skin.

ULCER. This is a destruction of the skin extending beneath the epidermis. When an ulcer heals, it always leaves a scar.

SCAR (CICATRIX). This is a permanent skin change formed of fibrous tissue, replacing the normal tissue lost, following damage. A fresh scar may be temporarily accentuated, but with passage of time scars contract and become less evident. When there is progressive hypertrophy, instead of contraction, a keloid forms.

KELOID. This is a fibrous tissue tumor, arising in predisposed persons, following a break in the skin. Keloids are seen predominantly in Negroes. Surgical incisions in predisposed patients will heal with keloid formation.

Skin eruptions are present with many systemic diseases. Scarlet fever resulting from a hemolytic streptococcal infection presents with fever, sore throat, and a small fine, vividly red macular rash that disappears on pressure. Measles appear as a red macular rash that coalesces to give a blotchy appearance.

Seborrheic Dermatitis (Dandruff). This is a chronic scaling eruption, usually in hairy areas that are rich in sebaceous glands. Exacerbations may be related to anxiety, whereas hot and humid weather may cause improvement.

Warts (Verrucae). These are papular lesions that are caused by a viral infection. They are contagious, and when present on a man's face may be readily spread by shaving nicks.

Drug Eruptions. Drug eruptions may present themselves as almost any cutaneous lesion. They are usually widespread in distribution, because they result from a circulating agent; are rapid in onset; may occur as edema in the form of vesicles, bullae, and hives; and commonly appear as an inflammatory response with itching. The history is very important in making a diagnosis.

Actinic (Senile) Keratosis. These begin as brownish macules that become papular and keratotic in areas that are chronically exposed to sunlight. Bald-headed men are particularly prone to this lesion. Although these keratoses are related to aging, they are precipitated by sunlight, and so deserve the term actinic.

Squamous Cell Carcinoma. Squamous cell carcinoma of the skin can usually be prevented because it arises from actinic keratoses. They are firm and show little anaplasia; metastases occur late, in contrast to squamous cell carcinoma of the mucous membrane which metastasizes early.

Basal Cell Carcinoma. This tumor develops most frequently on the exposed surfaces of the skin, the face and scalp. There is practically no tendency to metastasis, but the tumor may kill by direct invasion. It begins as a slightly elevated papule that ulcerates, heals over, and then breaks down again. The crusting ulcer develops a smooth, rolled border that represents the tumor cells spreading laterally beneath the skin.

Spider Angioma. This is a central red papule from which superficial fine blood vessels radiate (legs). The lesions are arterial and a pulsation may be felt in the center. The legs will blanch when the center is pressed. They are related to increased estrogen levels and may be present in pregnant women. They are, however, most characteristic for chronic liver disease when there has been parenchymal destruction such as with cirrhosis.

Syphilis. Syphilis is a chronic, systemic infection transmitted by direct and intimate contact with moist infectious lesions of the skin and mucous membranes. Sexual contact is the most common means of infection, but it can be spread through skin abrasions.

A primary lesion, the chancre, develops at the site of inoculation. The chancre is an ulceration of the skin or mucous membrane that heals spontaneously.

Secondary syphilis, occurring about six weeks after the primary lesion, presents as an erythematous macular or papular rash. Superficial painless erosions on the oral mucosa which may be covered with a grayish exudate are mucous patches.

Latent syphilis is that stage of the disease in which there are no clinical signs or symptoms of the infection. Diagnosis is dependent upon serologic testing.

Signs and symptoms of late destructive syphilis occur up to five to 20 years later. Late syphilis of the skin may appear as either small nodules or ulcerating gummas. The gumma begins as a subcutaneous tumor that softens and ruptures, exuding a gummy material. A gumma may produce a painful destructive lesion of the palate and nasal septum. Cardiovascular syphilis is an aortitis, causing either dilatation of the aorta with aortic insufficiency or a saccular aneurysm. Neurosyphilis causes destruction of the posterior roots of the spinal nerves with resulting ataxia, and a psychosis with dementia, hallucinations, memory loss, poor judgment, and gradual change in personality.

Congenital syphilis results from the passage of the spirochete through the placenta from mother to fetus.

WEIGHT

Charts indicating the normal weight for persons of a given height, age, sex and race are useful as guides. Normal weight may vary from 10 to 15 per cent above or below the given standard. Deviation from the average in a normal individual depends upon food intake, energy output, heredity, size of bony framework, temperament, and differences in endocrine gland activity.

Any recent weight gain or loss may be significant. Weight gain, when not caused by overeating, may be due to an endocrine disturbance such as myxedema (hypothyroidism) or edema as in cases of cardiac, hepatic or renal insufficiency.

Weight loss may be an indication of disturbances of digestion, endocrine disorders such as hyperthyroidism, or malignant disease.

TEMPERATURE

The temperature may be normal, subnormal or increased. Body temperature varies to a degree in different persons and from time to time in the same person. Oral temperature above 96.8°F by mouth and below 99.4°F is regarded as normal.

Fever is present if the temperature is over 99.4°F by mouth. It may be caused by infection, inflammation, malignant tumors, disturbance of the heat-regulating mechanism in the basal ganglia as in cerebral hemorrhage, trauma, or hemorrhage.

A chill manifests by a sensation of coldness and shivering, followed by an abrupt rise in temperature. Chills commonly mark the onset of certain infectious diseases, such as pneumonia.

When sweating occurs with a fever there is an abrupt fall in temperature. Chills and sweating are a means for the body to change temperature.

HEAD AND NECK

The size and shape of the head should be noted. In hydrocephalus the large head with the bulging forehead is very striking. In Paget's disease (osteitis deformans) bone changes cause the head to be disproportionately enlarged in relation to the face. The head and face are both enlarged in acromegaly.

In children with hypertrophied adenoid tissue there may be a history of mouth-breathing, frequent colds, and ear infections.

With myxedema the face is swollen, but in contrast to true edema it does not pit on pressure. The skin is coarse and dry, and the hair is dry and scanty.

With hyperthyroidism, exophthalmus (prominence and bulging of the eyes), warm, moist skin, loss of weight, and goiter (enlargement of the thyroid gland) may be present.

Palpation of the neck for enlarged lymph nodes should be carefully performed. Nodes to be examined are the preauricular, mastoid, suboccipital, submandibular areas, anterior and posterior triangles, supra- and infraclavicular fossae, and axillary. Inflammation of the mouth, particularly a mandibular third molar pericoronitis, or tonsillitis may produce swelling and tenderness of the submandibular nodes. Metastatic tumor from cancer of the mouth, tongue, nasopharynx, oral pharynx, hypopharynx, or thyroid gland may first be diagnosed from a biopsy of a discrete hard node. Lymphoma may first present as a nontender, firm, discrete, multiple lymph node enlargement. Other causes are infectious mononucleosis, leukemia, syphilis, and tuberculous lesions.

Rigidity of the neck (nuchal rigidity) is seen in meningitis. There is a boardlike rigidity of the neck, and the body can be raised from a reclining position by lifting the head.

EYES

The eyes give significant information about a patient and provide clues to the diagnosis of systemic disease. Ptosis (drooping) of the upper lids can result from paralysis of the oculomotor nerve. There is marked feebleness of the upper eyelid in myasthenia gravis. In Bell's palsy with facial paralysis of the orbicularis oculi, the individual is unable to close the eye on the affected side. The eyelids are markedly swollen and the eyes nearly closed in angioedema or edema of nephritis, thyrotoxicosis, myxedema, diabetes, anemia, and acute sinusitis. There is usually protrusion of the eyeballs (exophthalmos) in hyperthyroidism.

Glaucoma is an increase in intraocular pressure causing the eyeball to feel hard. Symptoms include pain, often severe and extending over the head, clouding of the cornea, dilatation of the pupil, and reduction of vision.

Cataract is an opacity of the lens usually coming on in later life causing a decrease and blurring of vision.

The conjunctiva is stained yellow in jaundice. Petechiae commonly appear in the conjunctiva with bacterial endocarditis, leukemia, and aplastic anemia.

Examination of the retina with an ophthalmoscope can disclose (1) papilledema or choked disc, a sign of increased intracranial pressure; (2) arteriosclerosis, readily recognized by narrowing of arterioles at certain points; (3) hypertension demonstrated by a nicking of the retinal veins where they are crossed by arterioles, a condition in which the vein appears to taper down or stop abruptly on either side of the arteriole; (4) diabetic retinopathy associated with arteriosclerosis; and (5) optic atrophy.

CHEST

For convenience in describing the surface anatomy of the chest, imaginary lines are drawn. The midclavicular line is drawn through the middle of the clavicle. On the sides of the chest the anterior axillary line is drawn downward from the origin of the anterior axillary fold.

Inspection and palpation of the chest often reveals much information, such as the barrel-shaped chest often seen with emphysema, enlargement of the axillary lymph nodes as seen with carcinoma of the breast, Hodgkin's disease or other lymphomas, leukemia, and infections of the hand or arm. Carcinoma of the breast is a stony hard mass with distortion of the breast and retraction of the nipple.

Kyphosis is an abnormal curvature of the spine with a dorsal prominence; scoliosis is a lateral curvature of the spine.

Auscultation of the lungs and radiographic examination are the most important methods of detecting pulmonary disease. Auscultation, or listening to the lungs with a stethoscope, can tell much about pathology only after one is completely familiar with the normal sounds. Rales are pathologic sounds produced during inspiration or expiration by the passage of air through any liquids present in the bronchi or lungs. Rhonchi are coarse rales caused by partial obstruction of large bronchi. These rales are usually heard in inflammation of the mucous membranes of the bronchi, and are due to the tenacious mucus that partially occludes the bronchus. Moist rales are not continuous but are short, crackling sounds. Fremitus is a palpatory examination of the lungs produced by placing the hands symmetrically upon the chest and asking the patient to speak. The spoken voice sets up a resonance in the lungs and chest wall which can be felt by the hands. The vocal fremitus is produced by vibrations produced in the larynx passing down the bronchi so that the lungs and chest wall vibrate. Abnormally increased fremitus is produced with a solid lung, as with consolidation, pneumonia, atelectasis, and when there is solid lung tissue between the bronchus and chest wall. Decreased fremitus is produced when there is an abnormal medium between the hand and bronchus such as with pleural thickening, pleural effusion, and bronchial obstruction.

A pleural friction rub is a rasping, harsh, rough sound heard during both inspiration and expiration, usually fairly localized, produced by friction of the movements of roughened visceral pleura over parietal pleura. The pleural friction rub is present with acute fibrinous pleurisy.

Kussmaul breathing is a tachypnea (increase in respiratory rate to as high as 30 to 40 per minute) which may be present with uncontrolled diabetes mellitus caused by acidosis and build-up of CO_2. The respirations are also increased in depth.

The hyperventilation syndrome is rapid breathing caused by an altered emotional state. The hyperventilation causes a lowering of the blood CO_2 with a resulting respiratory alkalosis, which may lead to paresthesia around the mouth and fingers and tetany. Cramps in the arms and legs are present.

Bronchiectasis. A dilatation of the small bronchi with sacculation results in pooling of secretions and chronic inflammation. The patient gives a history of coughing up large amounts of sputum in the morning owing to the overnight collecting of the exudate. Diminished breath and voice sounds are present with moist rales. Clubbing of the fingers is usually pronounced.

Pleural Effusion. Pleural effusion is the accumulation of an exudate in the pleural cavity between the visceral and parietal pleura. There are decreased fremitus and breath sounds, the area is dull to percussion, and there are probably no rales. The exudate is usually due to neoplasm or infection.

Atelectasis. All or part of a lung is deflated owing to impaired inflow from an airway obstruction such as tumor, foreign body, or exudate. Because there is no air in the lungs, there are diminished fremitus, absence of breath sounds, no rales, and dullness on percussion.

Pneumothorax. Air enters the pleural cavity, causing all or part of the lung to collapse. The lung is compressed by air in the pleural space. Adhesions of the lung to the thoracic wall prevent complete collapse. There are no breath sounds or rales, fremitus is diminished, and hyperresonance (tympany) occurs on percussion. Pneumothorax is usually caused by rupture of an emphysematous bleb or by trauma.

Pneumonia. Pneumonia is an acute infectious disease of the lungs. The patient has cough, fever, malaise, rust-colored sputum coughed up from the lungs, and chest pain caused by pleuritis. Breathing will be difficult not only because of the pain but because of the decreased vital capacity of the diseased parenchyma. Fremitus will be increased owing to consolidation of lung tissue. Rales will be heard, and there may be a pleural friction rub. Bronchopneumonia is inflammation of the terminal bronchioles distributed throughout the lungs, whereas lobar pneumonia is an infection involving all of one or more lobes of the lungs.

Bronchial Asthma. Bronchial asthma is an allergic disease characterized by expiratory dyspnea and expiratory wheezing. There is a contraction of the smooth muscle around the medium-sized bronchi, causing increased resistance to the flow of air. There are also edema and swelling of the mucous lining and production of mucus. The airways are smaller during expiration than inspiration owing to the difference in intrathoracic pressure; consequently the patient has more difficulty during expiration. With decreased oxygenation of the blood, the patient may become cyanotic; with decreased elimination of CO_2, somnolence and narcosis may develop.

Emphysema. Emphysema is a degenerative disease that usually occurs after the age of 50. The alveolar septa break down, resulting in formation of sacs. The supporting elastic fibers do not support small airways, so the airways will collapse on expiration to give complete obstruction. Progressive dyspnea is the predominant symptom; secondary infections are inevitable. Cyanosis results with clubbing of fingers. With obstruction to air passage on expiration and trapping of air in the lungs, the chest form becomes larger and larger. These patients develop a barrel chest with a large increase in anteroposterior diameter. On expiration, a little positive pressure on the airway will tend to prevent collapsing of the small airways. This positive pressure gives a pursed-lip expiration. On auscultation, breath sounds will be faint owing to decreased exchange of gas, and rales are usually present.

Tumor of the Lung. The majority of primary tumors of the lung arise from the epithelial lining of the bronchus. These bronchogenic carcinomas are usually of the squamous cell type. Metastatic tumors may be from the breast, stomach, pancreas, thyroid, kidney, prostate, uterus, or sarcoma, especially of bone. These tumors may occur as a single circumscribed mass or in an infiltrative form. Lymphomas may appear in multiple nodular or infiltrative form. Symptoms include a cough, which may be productive of blood-tinged sputum, hemoptysis (bleeding from the lungs); dyspnea when a large bronchus is obstructed; secondary infection; pleural effusion from extension of the tumor into the pleura; bronchial obstruction, causing atelectasis of the lung; and mediastinal obstruction with compression of the superior vena cava, resulting in decreased venous return from the face, neck and arms with edema. Generalized malaise, weight loss, and pain are also present.

Pulmonary Edema. Pulmonary edema, sometimes referred to as cardiac asthma, is acute congestion of the pulmonary vascular bed because of left-sided heart failure and decreased ability of the heart to pump blood. This usually occurs in patients with left ventricular failure caused by hypertension, lesions of the aortic valve, or myocardial disease such as myocardial infarction. The patient may have extreme dyspnea and a feeling of suffocation; if this occurs at night, the term paroxysmal noctural dyspnea is applied. Large quantities of pinkish, frothy sputum are coughed up. Rales may be so prominent as to obscure breath and heart sounds.

Pulmonary Embolism and Infarction. Pulmonary embolism is the lodging of any foreign material in a branch of a pulmonary artery, impairing blood flow. Embolism by clot is a complication in patients recovering from surgical operations; fat emboli occur as a result of injury to bones; a thrombus in the right atrium in long-standing heart disease, or valvular vegetation in a right heart chamber in acute or subacute bacterial endocarditis, may form emboli. Pain is a result of regional pleuritis, and the patient complains of a feeling of suffocation and tightness across the chest. Dyspnea is extreme. Blood pressure drops suddenly. Collapse and death may result.

Pleural Friction Rub. A pleural friction rub is a rasping, harsh, rough sound heard during both inspiration and expiration, usually fairly well localized, produced by friction of the movement of roughened visceral pleura over parietal pleura. Pleural friction rub is pathognomonic of acute fibrinous pleurisy.

HEART

Diseases of the heart, like diseases of other organs and tissues, can be categorized by the pathology present:

1. Inflammatory — endocarditis, myocarditis, pericarditis.
2. Neoplastic — tumors.
3. Degenerative — atherosclerotic, congestive heart failure, defect in the conduction system, hypertensive heart disease.
4. Congenital.
5. Hereditary.
6. Abnormal immune response — Rheumatic heart disease.
7. Trauma.
8. Metabolic.
9. Toxic.

In beginning the examination of the heart, the gross anatomy of the normal heart and the manner in which it is projected against the chest wall should be kept in mind.

On inspection and palpation of the heart we look first for the point of maximal impulse (PMI). This impulse that we see and feel on the normal chest wall is the impulse, not of the apex, but of the left ventricle proximal to the apex. The movements of the heart during systole push the heart against the chest wall.

Systole is the contraction of the heart that forces the blood from the ventricles into the systemic and pulmonary circulations, whereas diastole is the period in which the cardiac muscle is relaxing, allowing for filling of the ventricles. The PMI is normally located at the fifth intercostal space at the left midclavicular line. In valvular disease, and in congestive heart failure when there has been marked enlargement of the ventricles, the PMI will be displaced to the left and downward, indicating left ventricular hypertrophy (LVH).

Heart sounds is the term applied to the sounds caused by movements of the heart valves. The first sound is due to the sudden closing of the mitral and tricuspid valves, the valves between the ventricles and atria, when the heart contracts during systole. As the ventricles contract, the pressure within them moves the blood to close these valves and open the aortic and pulmonic valves. The second sound follows the first by a short pause, and is caused by the sudden closing of the aortic and pulmonic valves at the end of systole. This is the beginning of diastole when the ventricles are relaxed and the increased blood pressure in the systemic and pulmonary arteries close the valves.

Murmurs are extra sounds heard over the heart. Many murmurs indicate valvular or other defects within the heart, whereas some systolic murmurs are unimportant and do not imply the presence of a heart lesion. Murmurs are due to eddies formed in the bloodstream owing to a disturbance of the normal streamlined blood flow. Murmurs are either systolic or diastolic in time, occurring with either systole or diastole. They are also designated according to the valve area where they are best heard. A pathologic process may deform the leaflets so that complete closure does not take place, resulting in insufficiency or regurgitation of blood through the valve, in turn resulting in a murmur. Depending on the valve involved, the blood during systole flows backward from a contracting ventricle to a relaxing atrium (mitral or tricuspid insufficiency) or, during diastole, from the aorta or pulmonary artery into a relaxing ventricle (aortic or pulmonic insufficiency). Scarring of the valve leaflets prevents them from opening properly and causes the orifice to be narrowed. Scarring of the leaflets of the mitral valve prevents the normal flow of blood during diastole from the left atrium to the left ventricle — mitral stenosis. A diastolic murmur is heard. Narrowing (stenosis) of the aortic or pulmonic orifice, diminishing blood flow during systole from the ventricles into the aortic or pulmonic arteries, is aortic or pulmonic stenosis, causing a systolic murmur. If a chamber of the heart becomes dilated, the leaflets of one of its valves may fail to close completely, causing a relative insufficiency. The murmur produced by each valvular lesion is usually heard loudest over the valve area and has its own area of distribution. The mitral valve area is located in the fifth left intercostal space, the pulmonary valve area in the second left intercostal space, the aortic valve area at the right second rib and in the right second intercostal space, and the tricuspid area over the sternum at the junction of the corpus sterni with the xiphoid process (See Fig. 3–1). A systolic murmur is produced when a greater than usual amount of blood passes through an orifice, such as in anemia, hyperthyroidism, and after extreme exercise. Murmurs are also heard from abnormal communication between heart chambers or vessels, such as with a patent ductus arteriosus.

As blood passes through constrictions, the vibrations produced are not only heard as murmurs but may be felt as thrills. In aortic stenosis, a systolic thrill may be felt over the precordium with its maximum intensity at the aortic area.

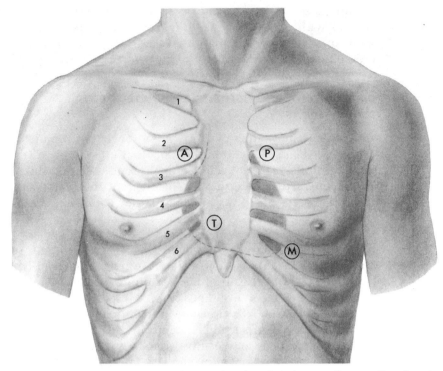

Figure 3–1.   Areas where the heart valves are best heard. A, Aortic valve area; P, pulmonic valve area; T, tricuspid valve area; M, mitral valve area.

Pulse

The average pulse rate in normal adults in the dental environment is 60 to 90 heart beats per minute. The pulse represents ventricular systole with the ejection of blood from the ventricles into the systemic and pulmonary circulations. The electrical impulse that starts the normal heart beat begins at the sino-atrial (S–A) node and spreads through the atrial musculature, causing it to contract. From the atria it extends to the atrioventricular (A–V) node, then along the bundle of His and its branches to the Purkinje fibers, through which it is distributed to the ventricular musculature. This conduction of the impulse can be measured on the ECG; in other words, the ECG represents the electrical activity of the heart. Normally the pulse rate is decreased during sleep and increased during excitement and exercise.

Cardiac Dysrhythmias or Arrhythmias

Dysrhythmias or arrhythmias can occur in the absence of detectable structural disease of the heart. Dysrhythmias can be irregularities of the heartbeat, disturbances of rate, or disturbances of conduction. Dysrhythmias frequently are caused by (1) a pathologic process in the myocardium, such as myocardial infarction, ischemia, rheumatic heart disease, or myocarditis; (2) a sudden drop in blood volume due to hemorrhage; (3) endocrine disturbances, such as thyrotoxicosis or pheochromocytoma; (4) drug toxicity, such as with digitalis; (5) fever and infections; (6) tumor; (7) rapid development of severe hypoxemia (decreased oxygen content) or hypercapnia (increased carbon dioxide); and (8) electrolyte disturbance.

CIRCULATORY DERANGEMENTS ASSOCIATED WITH DYSRHYTHMIAS

With a tachycardia of 160 or more beats per minute or a bradycardia of 40 or less beats per minute, cardiac output can be severely decreased, as stroke volume can not adequately compensate for this alteration in rate. With tachycardia there may be insufficient time for diastolic filling, resulting in too little blood in the ventricle for expulsion during ventricular contraction.

The atria should be considered booster pumps which augment ventricular filling. In many dysrhythmias the normal temporal sequence between atrial and ventricular systole is lost, and effective atrial contraction does not occur. The loss of the atrial booster pump can result in a lowering of cardiac output by as much as 40 per cent.

Coronary blood flow occurs predominantly during diastole, and since the total number of seconds of diastole per minute is reduced with tachycardia, a rapid heart rate can precipitate myocardial ischemia.

In ventricular fibrillation the myocardium contracts in such an irregular and chaotic manner that there is no coordinated contraction with sufficient pressure to propel blood forward.

SPECIFIC DISORDERS OF RATE AND RHYTHM

Paroxymal tachycardia may be auricular, A–V nodal, or ventricular in origin.

Sinus Tachycardia. Sinus tachycardia is an abnormally rapid heart rate, over 100 beats per minute, arising at the normal S–A pacemaker. Causes of sinus tachycardia include stimulation during light anesthesia, hypoxia, hypertension, exercise, anxiety, fever, anemia and thyrotoxicosis.

Atrial Tachycardia. Atrial tachycardia is a common cardiac arrhythmia with a rate of 150 to 300 per minute, arising from an ectopic focus in the atrium.

Atrial Fibrillation. During atrial fibrillation the atria does not contract as a whole. There are many small areas of muscle tissue stimulated at various times. The effect is to obliterate any effective contraction of the atria and to bombard the A–V node and ventricles with a very rapid and irregular series of impulses. The ventricles contract rapidly and with gross irregularity. With the absence of atrial contractions mural thrombi (clots) form in the atria. This patient then becomes subject to the hazard of embolism. Atrial fibrillation is present in a high percentage of patients with rheumatic or coronary heart disease.

Ventricular Tachycardia. Ventricular tachycardia is described as repeated ventricular premature beats occurring at a rapid rate. This premature discharge of impulses originates in the ventricular musculature. The ventricular musculature becomes hyperirritable and gives off an impulse which passes over the ventricle by abnormal pathways. It frequently occurs within a few days following the occurrence of a myocardial infarction.

Ventricular Fibrillation. Ventricular fibrillation is a result of a completely haphazard spread of impulses over the conduction network of the ventricle, causing a disorganized and inefficient contraction of the ventricular musculature with resulting circulatory failure.

Bradycardia. Bradycardia is a slowing of the heart rate and is caused by (1) increased vagal tone, as in sinus bradycardia, or (2) a block in the conduction system. With a block in the conduction system, sudden cessation of circulation often causes syncopal attacks (Stokes–Adams attacks). An A–V block can be caused by a myocardial infarction. With a block in the conduction system, the atria maintain their normal rhythm whereas the ventricles contract much slower. Treatment is by implantation of a pacemaker.

CONGESTIVE HEART FAILURE

The failure of adequate circulation, or cardiac decompensation, is a condition in which the cardiac output is too low for the metabolic needs of the body and too low in relation to the venous return. The heart loses its ability to effectively pump blood to peripheral tissues, resulting in the slow development of the clinical picture called congestive heart failure.

Two theories have evolved: forward failure and backward failure. The former holds that because of myocardial weakness cardiac output becomes incapable of meeting the metabolic demands of the body. Blood flow through the kidneys is reduced, resulting in retention of electrolytes and water in the body. The backward failure theory contends incomplete emptying of the heart due to myocardial weakness results in dilatation of the chambers and increase in intracardiac pressure. With increased intracardiac pressure there is decreased filling of the heart, with increased venous pressure and venous stasis. The venous stasis causes impaired renal function with retention of electrolytes and water; and increased pressure in the capillaries causes loss of fluid into the tissue. The retention of electrolytes and fluid is the most important factor in congestive heart failure.

The symptoms and signs of congestive heart failure are based on the accumulation of fluid. Dyspnea, or shortness of breath, is due to fluid within the lungs preventing adequate ventilation. Ankle edema and enlargement of the liver are present. The neck veins (jugular) are distended and prominent. Ascites is the accumulation of fluid within the abdomen.

Treatment is to reduce the excess fluids by the use of diuretics, and to strengthen the cardiac muscle.

CORONARY HEART DISEASE

Heart disease resulting from coronary atherosclerosis is frequent in many patients beyond middle life. Localized narrowing of the coronary blood vessels reduces the blood flow causing an imbalance between the oxygen requirements of the myocardium and the oxygen supply.

Angina pectoris is a syndrome of paroxysmal cardiac pain, substernal in nature. This pain may radiate to the left shoulder and arm, and infrequently to the right shoulder, back, neck, and jaw. Angina pectoris is caused by a temporary lack of oxygen in the myocardium to meet the present needs; consequently the pain is often precipitated by exercise and emotional stress. Relief is obtained by reducing or stopping activity and by the use of coronary vasodilators.

Myocardial infarction is necrosis (death) of the myocardium caused by coronary artery occlusion, embolism in a coronary vessel, or prolonged myocardial ischemia where there is continued diminished blood flow. The necrotic myocardium can no longer contract. Death may result from diminished cardiac output (shock), massive congestive heart failure with pulmonary edema, destruction of the impulse conduction in the myocardium resulting in ventricular fibrillation, or rupture of the necrotic myocardium. The usual symptoms are agonizing crushing substernal pain, dyspnea, and peripheral circulatory failure with fall of blood pressure. The patient's skin becomes cold, clammy, grayish, and cyanotic with perspiration. With lack of blood to the brain the patient becomes confused and unresponsive. Renal shutdown occurs with prolonged shock. Treatment is directed toward relief of pain, reduction of pulmonary edema, relief of shock, oxygenation of the cardiac muscle, and rest.

HYPERTENSIVE HEART DISEASE

Blood pressure is dependent upon the following factors: (1) the cardiac output from the left ventricle into the systemic circulation, (2) elastic recoil of the aorta and large arteries, which propels the blood down the arterial tree during diastole, (3) the peripheral resistance of the arterioles, (4) the volume and viscosity of the blood.

During ventricular contraction (the period of maximum ejection) blood enters the circulation more rapidly than it escapes from the arterioles. As a consequence, the volume of blood in the reservoir increases; potential energy is stored in walls of the vessels, and the blood pressure rises to a maximum — the systolic pressure. During the phase of cardiac relaxation, the rate of arterial drainage exceeds the blood that enters and the pressure falls to a minimum — the diastolic pressure. The normal systolic pressure ranges up to 140; the normal diastolic pressure ranges up to 90.

Hypertensive heart disease is applied to cases that show ventricular hypertrophy caused by increased peripheral hypertension. Peripheral resistance of the blood vessels is increased by decreased elasticity of the vessels, degenerative changes in the intima of the vessels, and deposition of atherosclerotic plaques and calcium. The left ventricle must hypertrophy in order to exert enough force to eject sufficient blood for the body demands against this increased resistance. As a result there may be cardiac failure caused by an insufficient coronary blood supply to meet the demand of the hypertrophied myocardium; cerebral hemorrhage, because the cerebral arterioles cannot tolerate the increased pressure; or renal disease.

ARTERIOSCLEROSIS

Arteriosclerosis is a degenerative condition in which the walls of the arteries become thickened, narrowing the lumen and decreasing the amount of blood flow through the vessel. This increase in peripheral resistance and decreased blood flow leads to coronary insufficiency, hypertension, and secondary hypertensive heart disease.

RHEUMATIC HEART DISEASE

Rheumatic fever is an inflammatory complication that may follow group A beta-hemolyic streptococcal infection. The basic lesion is degeneration of fibrinoid, which is a substance resembling fibrin. These areas of fibrinoid degeneration when surrounded by inflammatory cells are referred to as Aschoff nodules. Aschoff nodules are found in the heart and joints. This entire disease process may be attributed to a breakdown in the immune mechanism and represent a disease of hypersensitivity. Rheumatic fever is a leading cause of chronic illness, invalidism, and death in children; the morbidity is very high due to the residual effects on the heart. The major clinical manifestations are pathognomonic: migratory polyarthritis, chorea, carditis, subcutaneous nodules, erythematous nonpruritic skin rash.

The larger joints (ankles, knees, hips, wrists, elbows, and shoulders) are involved, often in succession. The joint becomes swollen, hot, red, and tender to touch. Active and passive motion is painful.

Specific cardiac lesions are:

1. Acute pericarditis with a serofibrinous exudate between the epicardium and pericardium. This infiltrate contains leukocytes.
2. Myocarditis consists of Aschoff nodules and fibrinoid necrosis in the connective tissue between the muscle fibers. The action of the muscle fibers is severely limited, and cardiac failure can result.
3. Endocarditis is the result of lesions of verrucae composed of fibrin and blood cells along the borders of the valves and chordae. As these lesions heal they may resolve completely or the lesion may undergo organization and scarring, causing valve leaflets to fuse together to narrow an orifice (stenosis). The valve most often affected is the mitral valve. With mitral stenosis, a diastolic murmur is heard during diastole as blood is passing through the stenosed mitral valve from the left atrium to the left ventricle. Lesions on the chordae may cause shortening of the chordae, preventing a valve from closing completely; may cause a dilatation of the valve ring; and may cause destruction of valve substance, all resulting in an insufficiency of the valve. With mitral insufficiency, a systolic murmer will be heard when blood passes in a reverse manner from the contracting left ventricle into the relaxed atria during systole.

Chorea is a disorder of the central nervous system characterized by purposeless movements and muscular weakness. The attacks are recurrent and often prolonged but eventually recovery is complete.

In the skin rheumatic nodules occur near large joints. They are freely movable firm masses, and are large areas of fibrinoid necrosis with inflammatory infiltrate.

SUBACUTE BACTERIAL ENDOCARDITIS

This is a prolonged, febrile, often fatal disease resulting from streptococcal or other infection of a heart valve or a prosthetic valve. Bacterial infection is established on a valve which has been previously damaged by rheumatic fever or congenital heart disease. Roughening of the endocardial surface predisposes to implanation of the bacteria, which are carried to the heart in the blood stream.

Symptoms include fever, chills, sweating, weakness, malaise, heart failure, and paralysis.

Petechial hemorrhages may be visible on the mucosal surfaces, especially the conjunctiva of the lower eyelid or, less frequently, on the skin covering any part of the body.

The bacterial vegetations on the heart valves are friable, and fragments are broken off by the current of blood passing over them. The usual cause of death is embolism of a bacterial vegetation to the brain, heart, or other organ or progressive, intractable cardiac decompensation (failure).

SHOCK

Circulatory failure, or shock, can be either central, when the heart fails to pump a sufficient amount of blood, or peripheral (hypovolemic shock), when there is an acute reduction in the circulating volume. Hypovolemic shock can be due to blood loss caused by a laceration, bleeding ulcer, crushing injury, ruptured spleen, or ectopic pregnancy; it can result from plasma loss, as with a burn or peritonitis, or a water loss, such as from vomiting and diarrhea.

The classic diagnostic signs of shock are a drop in blood pressure, rapid heart rate, pulse feeble and brief in duration, sweating in the axilla, upper lip, forehead, and palmar region, skin coldness, skin color changes, and coma or vagueness of response in the patient.

SYNCOPE

Syncope is caused by a decrease in the vascular motor tone. The circulatory failure is brief and does not become irreversible, and the individual will recover by being left alone in a horizontal position. The blood vessels have become relaxed, the total blood volume remains the same but is distributed over a greater vascular capacity. The individual becomes light-headed and faints because the cerebral circulation has not been adequate. The most effective therapy is not with the head between the knees but rather the Trendelenburg position, with the individual prone or supine and the legs raised.

ABDOMEN

Abdominal examination is best performed with the patient lying on his back on a table or firm bed. For the purpose of describing and localizing lesions in various parts of the abdomen it is usually divided into nine regions. Two vertical lines on each side extend upward from a point midway between the anterosuperior spine of the ilium and midline; and two horizontal lines, one crossing the abdomen at the lower level of the tenth costal cartilages and the lower horizontal line at the level of the anterosuperior iliac spines. The upper third is divided into epigastrium and right and left hypochondria; the middle third, into umbilical region and right and left lumbar regions; and the lower third into hypogastrium and right and left iliac regions (See Fig. 3–2).

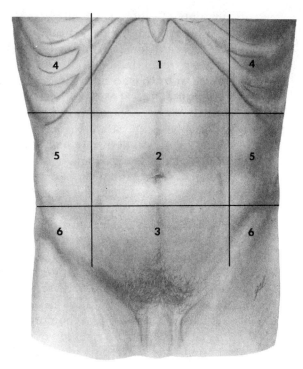

Figure 3–2. Regions of the abdomen. (1) Epigastric; (2) umbilical; (3) pubic; (4) right and left hypochondriac; (5) right and left lumbar; (6) right and left iliac.

Inspection and palpation are the two primary methods of physical examination of the abdomen.

One looks for abnormal general contour, pulsations, local prominence, cutaneous lesions, dilated veins, and abnormalities of the umbilicus.

Two of the most common causes of generalized abdominal enlargements are ascites and ovarian cyst. Ascites is the accumulation of fluid within the abdomen and may be due to cardiac failure, cirrhosis of the liver, nephrosis, and tumors of abominal organs.

A pulsation of the epigastrium is seen in aneurysm of the abdominal aorta.

Palpation of the abdomen in the normal individual yields nothing tangible.

Acute Peritonitis. Acute peritonitis is a suppurative process caused by spread of infection to the peritoneum from a diseased intra-abdominal organ. The most common causes are acute appendicitis, acute cholecystitis, salpingitis, perforation of peptic ulcer, perforation of the intestinal wall such as from diverticulitis, ulcerative colitis, cancer, or necrosis of bowel wall from impairment of its circualtion as with mesenteric thrombosis or volvulus. Pain is usually present at the site of the underlying lesion. Involuntary rigidity of the abdominal wall is present in the region of the lesion. When especially severe it may cause the patient to lie with knees drawn up, to relieve tension on the irritated muscles. Fever, rapid pulse, increased respiration, nausea, and vomiting may also be present. Rebound tenderness, which is pain experienced momentarily when pressure is released after withdrawing the palpating hand, is often present.

Gastritis. Gastritis is the most common of all gastrointestinal diseases and is commonly due to an overindulgence in food or alcohol, excessive amounts of aspirin, or food poisoning. The usual symptoms are of epigastric discomfort and tenderness, nausea, vomiting, and diarrhea.

Peptic Ulcer.   Peptic ulcer occurs in the tissues of the stomach and the first section of the duodenum (beginning of the small intestine), the tissues of which are exposed to the hydrochloric acid present in the gastric juice. The depth of the ulcer varies from a shallow erosion confined to the mucosa to a full thickness destruction of the wall with perforation into the peritoneal cavity. Symptoms are heartburn, belching, intolerance to certain foods, vague diffuse abdominal discomfort, and periodic relief of discomfort by the ingestion of alkalis and bland foods. The complications of peptic disease are hemorrhage, perforation with secondary peritonitis from food and gastric secretions emptying into the peritoneum, and obstruction.

Appendicitis.   Appendicitis is an inflammation of the vermiform appendix. It can be caused by various infectious processes or by obstruction. When the appendix becomes obstructed, for example, by a fecalith, pressure within the lumen of the appendix causes inflammation and edema, obstruction of venous return, and impairment of arterial flow, which leads to gangrene, necrosis, and perforation. Abscess or peritonitis can occur. The first symptom in an otherwise well individual is abdominal pain; this is followed by anorexia, nausea, or vomiting. When inflammation occurs in the adjacent peritoneum the pain shifts to the right lower quadrant of the abdomen causing tenderness, spasm of the muscles, and rebound tenderness.

LIVER

If the lower border of the liver extends below its normal level, it can be located by palpation. Hepatic enlargement is present if the lower border is felt below the costal margin in the right hypochondrium. Hepatic enlargement can be caused by fatty infiltration, congestive heart failure when there is impairment of return blood flow (right heart failure), hepatitis, cirrhosis, neoplasm, biliary tract obstruction, and parasitic infestation.

Jaundice.   Jaundice, the term applied to the yellow pigmentation of the tissues of the skin and mucous membranes, is associated with an increase in the bilirubin content of the plasma. Jaundice results from one of three general situations: (1) when bilirubin is presented to a normal liver at a rate which exceeds the ability of the liver to conjugate and excrete the pigment into the biliary system (prehepatic jaundice), (2) when the liver cells are functionally impaired and cannot conjugate and excrete a normal amount of bilirubin presented to them (hepatic jaundice), and (3) when the free flow of conjugated bilirubin through the biliary system is impaired (posthepatic jaundice).

In prehepatic jaundice resulting from a hemolytic disease, the fundamental abnormalitiy is an increased rate of destruction of red cells, an overproduction of bilirubin. The plasma bilirubin is mainly of the indirect type (unconjugated). Since the bilirubin present in the plasma is in the insoluble form as free bilirubin, it is not filtered by the kidneys.

In hepatocellular disease both unconjugated and conjugated bilirubins are increased in the plasma.

In posthepatic jaundice the fundamental defect is in the passage of conjugated bilirubin through the biliary system. In hepatocellular disease and with obstruction of the bile passage, conjugated bilirubin will be regurgitated into the plasma and excreted in the urine, resulting in dark urine. Since there are decreased or no bilirubin by-products in the gastrointestinal tract, the stools will be clay colored.

Hepatitis B. Hepatitis B is an acute systemic viral infection that affects the liver. There are degeneration and necrosis of the liver parenchymal cells with proliferation and swelling of the reticuloendothelium. The symptoms are fever, headache, anorexia, weakness, nausea, vomiting, indigestion, and abdominal pain. Jaundice appears and is accompanied by bilirubin in the urine (dark urine) and clay-colored stools. The more severe cases can lead to liver failure with development of central nervous system changes, somnolence, disorientation, delirium, convulsions, and coma. The liver can no longer metabolize alcohol and any intake may cause further destruction of the parenchymal cells and relapse.

Transmission of the virus is via the fecal-oral route, the parenteral route resulting from transfusions, or the use of nonsterile instruments, and there is some evidence that suggests transmission can occur through saliva.

The hepatitis carrier becomes the greatest obstacle to the control of the disease. It is generally assumed that those who retain the hepatitis antigen in their blood are potentially infective, although this risk is extremely slight. The antigen appears during the incubation period of the disease and is most often cleared from the blood by three months after recovery; however, some patients may remain antigen-positive for years. The identification of non-A and non-B hepatitis viruses has introduced even greater doubt regarding the hepatitis B "carrier" state.

Cirrhosis. Cirrhosis is a diffuse fibrosis that destroys the normal lobular architecture of the liver and causes degeneration and necrosis of the parenchymal cells. As the cirrhotic process advances, signs of liver failure and portal hypertension appear. Blood can no longer pass through the liver to the vena cava; consequently, alternate venous return develops in the form of esophageal and abdominal varices. As liver cells fail to function, serum albumin, prothrombin, and fibrinogen levels fall, detoxification decreases, bilirubin builds up and is not conjugated, glycogen storage decreases, and there is a breakdown in protein, carbohydrate, and lipid metabolism. Blood coagulation will be decreased owing to a deficiency of prothrombin and other clotting factors. Patients may have massive bleeding from esophageal varices. The clinical signs of cirrhosis include jaundice, edema, pleural effusion and ascites due to low levels of plasma proteins and increased venous pressure, spider nevi, palmar erythema, gynecomastia, low grade fever, nausea, vomiting, diarrhea, and abdominal pain. The liver becomes enlarged, the skin has a grayish hue, and there is a sickeningly sweet odor to the breath. The patient has a wasted appearance, and develops a flapping tremor and other neurologic changes.

The common types of cirrhosis are:

1. Laennecs's cirrhosis, caused by malnutrition or chronic alcoholism, or both.
2. Postnecrotic cirrhosis, usually a sequela to hepatic necrosis following hepatitis.
3. Biliary cirrhosis, which develops as a result of prolonged obstruction of the extrahepatic bile ducts, and usually has a relatively benign course for a

number of years, during which there are few clinical or laboratory signs of hepatocellular failure.

4. Cardiac cirrhosis, which results from passive congestion of the liver with blood secondary to heart failure. Engorgement of the sinusoids with blood results in atrophy and degeneration of the parenchymal cells.

Carcinoma.   Primary carcinoma of the liver may arise from either the parenchymal cells or the intrahepatic bile duct epithelium. Cirrhosis appears to be an important predisposing factor.

Metastatic neoplasms occur at least 20 times as frequently as primary carcinoma; hepatic metastases are found in approximately one third of all malignancies. Metastasizing cells gain easy access to the liver because of its double circulation — hepatic arterial and portal venous. Gastrointestinal, pancreatic, breast, uterine, ovarian and renal carcinomas often metastasize to the liver first. Clinical signs include cachexia, abdominal pain, jaundice, and ascites as well as enlarged liver.

KIDNEYS

In diseases of the kidneys the most significant findings are often those discovered in examination of blood and urine.

Nephrotic Syndrome (Nephrosis).   This is a degenerative, noninflammatory lesion confined to the tubules; it may occur with a number of pathologic lesions. Clinically the patient has severe proteinuria (loss of albumin in the urine), low serum protein, secondary edema with pleural effusion, and probably no elevation of blood pressure. This may occur with the nephrotic stage of glomerulonephritis, renal vein thrombosis, diabetic glomerulonephrosclerosis, lupus erythematosus, and multiple myeloma.

Pyelonephritis.   Pyelonephritis, either acute or chronic, is an infectious process of the kidneys. It is more common in females, and the usual infecting agent is the colon bacillus. The clinical signs and symptoms are fever, chills, lumbar pain, pain on urination with increased frequency, and moderate to extreme tenderness in the costovertebral angle. Long-standing disease causes damage to the parenchyma and impaired kidney function. Uremia, serious hypertension, and renal failure may result. Hypertension caused by impaired function is due to renal vascular damage. The urine is loaded with white blood cells and bacteria.

Kidney Stones.   Renal stones may exist for years without causing symptoms, but, when they descend to the ureter, extreme pain (renal colic) will be felt in the lower quadrant of the abdomen and flank. Gross hematuria (blood in the urine) and urgency caused by reflex bladder irritation are present. Calcium stones occur with hyperparathyroidism, prolonged immobilization, high milk intake, and idiopathic hypercalcinuria. Uric acid stones may be present with gout.

Renal Failure.   Renal failure is the impaired ability of the kidneys to clear the blood of metabolites. Urea, creatine, and other nonprotein nitrogens build up in the blood, leading to uremia. The signs and symptoms of uremia are a yellowish-brown discoloration of the skin, pallor resulting from anemia, pruritis, purpura secondary to increased capillary permeability, urea frost on the skin, depression of erythropoiesis, hypertension with secondary heart failure, Kussmaul breathing (deep respirations with slight tachypnea) secondary to a metabolic acidosis, anorexia, nausea, and eventual onset of coma.

Renal failure can occur whenever the kidneys are damaged, such as with malignant hypertension, fulminating pyelonephritis, shock associated with circulatory failure, the degenerative stage of the nephrotic syndrome, or a toxic insult.

Diabetes Mellitus. Diabetes mellitus is a disorder of carbohydrate metabolism caused by an absolute or relative insulin deficiency. Insulin deficiency leads to inability of the body to transfer glucose into the cells, with resultant hyperglycemia (excessive glucose in the blood) and glycosuria (glucose in the urine). Owing to lack of utilization of glucose, fatty acids and proteins are metabolized to ketone bodies to supply the energy needs of the body. As ketone bodies are acids, metabolic acidosis results. The glycosuria causes diuresis and resultant dehydration. Diabetic coma is due to the effects of acidosis, ketosis, and dehydration on the central nervous system.

Vascular lesions are present; atherosclerosis, arteriosclerosis, calcification of the vessels, and decrease in capillary lumen size occur. These lesions cause the individual to have an increased incidence of coronary artery insufficiency, cerebrovascular accidents, impaired renal function, and gangrene of the toes and feet.

Considering diabetes as an imbalance between ingested carbohydrates and available body insulin, therapy is directed toward dietary restriction and augmentation of insulin effects. Insulin administration does check the hyperglycemia and ketosis but has no influence on the progress of the degenerative disease of the blood vessels.

The more uncontrolled the disease, the more susceptible the individual is to infection. Infections also have a disastrous effect on diabetes, readily changing a controlled state to an uncontrolled state.

Symptoms of the disease are polyuria, polydipsia, polyphagia, dry hot skin, and an emaciated appearance.

THYROID

The function of the thyroid gland is to produce a hormone which is capable of stimulating the rate of metabolism of the tissues, according to the needs of the body.

Hypothyroidism. Hypothyroidism may be either primary, owing to thyroid gland failure, or secondary, owing to lack of thyroid stimulating hormone from the pituitary gland. Primary hypothyroidism dating from birth is known as cretinism and is a result of genetic defects or a deficiency of iodine. The clinical picture is that of a dwarfed, stocky, somewhat overweight, mentally retarded child, with eyes set apart owing to failure of naso-orbital development, coarse features, thick lips, and protruding tongue. Myxedema characterizes hypothyroidism in the adult. The clinical picture shows a typical facies with a dull uninterested expression and puggy eyelids; alopecia of the outer third of the eyebrows is characteristic, as are dry and rough skin, coarse, brittle, and dry hair, hoarse speech, slowing of mental and physical activity, and poor muscle tone. The relaxation time of the deep tendon reflexes is prolonged.

Hyperthyroidism. Also known as Graves' disease, this condition results from diffuse hyperplasia of the thyroid gland. Enlargement of the gland is called goiter. There is a peculiar involvement of bulbar tissue which begins with edema of the loose connective tissue, followed by a proliferative fibrosis. This edema and fibrosis lead to displacement of the eye bulb forward, known as exophthalmos. The patient also suffers from the following: fine tremor of the extended fingers and tongue; increased nervousness, irritability, and emotional instability; sweating; hyperkinesis; loss of weight and strength without loss of appetite; intolerance to heat; warm, moist skin; increased metabolic rate; and cardiac findings which include a wide pulse pressure between the systolic and diastolic pressures, tachycardia or atrial fibrillation, frequent systolic murmur, and heart failure. These individuals have soft, silky hair.

ADRENAL CORTEX

The adrenal cortex produces three types of hormones, all steroids. The glucocorticoids promote gluconeogenesis, which brings about the destruction of protein and its conversion to carbohydrate. The amino acids are diverted toward carbohydrate metabolism at the expense of protein synthesis. The mineralocorticoids cause urinary retention of sodium and water and increased urinary output of potassium and phosphorus The sex hormones, estrogen, progesterone and androgens, contribute to the development of secondary sex characteristics, play some part in skeletal maturation, and promote protein synthesis.

Hypofunction may exist as a primary problem of the cortex known as Addison's disease or secondary to hypopituitarism and lack of cortical stimulating hormones of the pituitary gland. The most common cause of primary progressive adrenal cortical destruction is adrenal tuberculosis. Clinical signs and symptoms are a bronze darkening of the skin due to deposition of melanin, weakness, hypotension, weight loss, anorexia, and hypoglycemia due to lack of glucocorticoids.

Hyperfunction due to bilateral adrenal cortical hyperplasia or adrenal tumor is known as Cushing's syndrome. Clinical signs and symptoms are weight gain, hirsutism, amenorrhea, redistribution of fat producing the characteristic "moon" facies, supraclavicular fat pads, obesity of the trunk and thin extremities, hypertension, muscular weakness due to breakdown of proteins, some evidence of masculinization in females. There is generalized osteoporosis due to increased gluconeogenesis with a breakdown of proteins to carbohydrates. Fractures are seen, with greatest frequency in the vertebra, and the lamina dura around the teeth is often missing. Diabetes may occur. There is a generalized atherosclerosis, well advanced in relation to age.

PARATHYROIDS

Hyperparathyroidism. This is a disease in which excessive parathormone is produced, causing symptoms of the skeletal, muscular, gastrointestinal and renal systems. Excessive parathormone is produced by an adenoma, carcinoma, or hyperplasia of the parathyroid glands. This hormone stimulates osteoclastic activity, causing osteoporosis. Spontaneous fracture may occur. As a result of mobilization of the calcium and phosphates from bone, renal stones will form; the calcium passing into the gastrointestinal tract causes nausea, vomiting, anorexia, and gastric and duodenal ulcers. Muscle weakness and decreased muscle tone result from the increased circulating calcium.

HEMATOLOGY

ANEMIA

Anemia is a condition caused by an insufficient amount of erythrocytes with a resulting decrease in the total oxygen carrying capacity. Anemia can be a result of a loss of blood inside or outside the body, a failure to manufacture erythrocytes, or a shortened red cell life span, the disease known as hemolytic anemia.

Sickle Cell Anemia. Sickle cell anemia, a hemolytic anemia hereditary in nature, is found only in blacks and is a result of the manufacture of abnormal hemoglobin. The anomaly is inherited as a mendelian dominant characteristic in which each parent having the "trait" transfers the abnormal gene to his or her offspring. The erythrocytes instead of being concentric assume the shape of a half-moon (sickle) when the hemoglobin is in the reduced state. Thus, if a person with the disease is temporarily deficient in oxygen, such as during a plane trip or under general anesthesia, many cells will assume the crescentic form. In the homozygous state the erythrocytes contain sufficient abnormal hemoglobin to bring about sickling within the physiologic range of oxygen tensions. Because of this shape the viscosity of the blood and the mechanical fragility of the erythrocytes are significantly increased, and hemolysis results. Also the sickleshaped cells become enmeshed, forming a mass and causing thrombotic episodes. Because there are many erythrocytes in the sinusoids of the spleen, a splenic thrombotic episode will be very painful, suggesting an abdominal emergency. These individuals have chronic hemolytic anemia, develop thrombosis, infarction, and necrosis in the lungs, spleen, and nervous system, are jaundiced and weak, and often have episodes of aching pain in the joints; x-ray examination of the skull shows a "hair-on-end" appearance of the marrow due to the demand for erythrocyte production.

Iron Deficiency Anemia. Lack of iron can be a result of insufficient iron in the diet or impaired absorption but is usually caused by a chronic loss of blood. Excessive menstruation and occult bleeding from the gastrointestinal tract are common causes. The symptoms are those common to all chronic anemias and may include a variety of vague gastrointestinal complaints such as anorexia, sore tongue, dysphagia, and neuralgic pains.

Pernicious Anemia. Pernicious anemia is a disorder brought about by the body's failure to manufacture erythrocytes. It is a familial disease, occurring usually in middle life. A lack of gastric acid in the stomach prevents absorption of Vitamin B_{12} and folic acid. These vitamins act as coenzymes at different stages in the synthesis of nucleoproteins within the hemoglobin. Neurological abnormalities are also present, since these vitamins are also necessary for the synthesis of proteins within the central nervous system. Individuals with this disease may experience tingling and numbness.

Leukemia.   Leukemia is a progressive, malignant disorder characterized by abnormal proliferation of white blood cells and their precursors. This is in contrast to the benign, controlled proliferation that occurs after hemorrhage and during infection. The circulating cells are immature and have deranged serum proteins, thus greatly diminishing their antibody-making capability. Control of infection is a continuous problem in leukemia victims. Because of the massive amounts of tumor cells within the bone marrow, there is a decrease in thrombocytes, causing these individuals to be subjected to abnormal bleeding. The signs and symptoms include great fatigue, weakness, fever, bone pain, purpura, nose bleeds, severe anemia, and chronic periodontitis. Death usually results from an uncontrolled infection or from bleeding within the brain.

LYMPH NODES

The functions of the lymph nodes are to afford mechanical filtration for the lymph stream, removing cellular debris, foreign particles, and bacteria, and to serve as the site of formation of lymphocytes and antibodies.

Enlargement of nodes can be due to the following disorders: suppurative infections such as streptococcus or staphylococcus; antigenic challenge in serum sickness or systemic lupus erythematosus; granuloma formation in such diseases as tuberculosis, syphilis, histoplasmosis, and sarcoid; metastases of malignant disease such as carcinoma; congenital abnormalities as with a lymphangioma; or primary tumors, including Hodgkins disease, lymphosarcoma, and chronic lymphocytic leukemia. Nodes to be examined for enlargement are the cervical, post-auricular, supraclavicular, axillary, ulnar, and inguinal.

COMA

Coma is a prolonged state of unconsciousness in which there is no response to outside stimuli — the patient cannot be roused. When a comatose patient is first seen, certain therapeutic measures take precedence over diagnostic procedures. The comatose patient must have a clear airway; bleeding must be stopped if trauma has occurred, and adequate circulation must be ensured. Coma may occur with any lesion that damages the central reticular formation.

A few of the common causes of coma follow.

Cerebrovascular Accident (Stroke).   Cerebral hemorrhage is bleeding directly into the brain; the most common cause is hypertension associated with degenerative changes in the vessel walls. Hypertensive cerebral hemorrhage usually occurs in late middle life, whereas hemorrhage occurring during the first half of adult life is likely to be from a congenital vascular abnormality such as an aneurysm or angioma. The site of hemorrhage is occupied by a red clot, and the surrounding tissues are compressed and may be edematous. Later, if the victim survives, the clot is absorbed and is replaced by a neuroglial scar. A neurological deficit results depending upon the area of the brain where the neural tissue has been destroyed and replaced with scar tissue. The onset is always sudden. Usually the patient complains of a sudden severe headache, may vomit, becomes dazed, and loses consciousness.

Drug Poisoining.   In coma caused by drug poisoning the respirations are slow, and circulatory failure may develop, with a fall in blood pressure. The history is very significant. Narcotic and barbiturate drugs in excessive amounts cause coma.

Head Injury.   Concussion causes temporary unconsciousness lasting a few minutes after trauma. Coma that lasts longer than a few hours is usually a sign of contusion of the brain with cerebral edema or intracranial bleeding. Besides loss of consciousness, other signs of epidural or subdural hematoma are nausea, projectile vomiting, rise in blood pressure, slowing of the pulse, paralysis, fixed, dilated pupils, and slow, irregular breathing. In skull fracture the nose and ears are examined for blood or cerebrospinal fluid loss.

EPILEPSY

Epileptic convulsions result from a paroxysmal discharge of abnormal electrical impulses in some part of the brain. These discharges are likely to be repetitive. The first motor manifestation of the convulsion is a phase of tonic (sustained) spasm of the muscles which is usually symmetrical on both sides of the body. Owing to spasm of the respiratory muscles, breathing ceases during the tonic phase, which usually lasts less than half a minute. Progressive cyanosis occurs during the arrest of respiration but passes off when respirations are re-established. Repeated episodes of cyanosis will result in gradual deterioration of brain function and mentality.

In the second, or clonic, phase, the sustained contraction of the muscles give way to sharp, short, interrupted jerking movements. During the clonic phase the tongue may be bitten, foaming at the mouth may occur, and the individual is incontinent. Toward the end of the clonic phase the intervals between the muscular contractions become longer and the jerking motions finally cease. The individual remains in coma for a variable time, and on recovering consciousness sleeps for several hours.

The convulsion often begins with an aura, or warning of the attack. This is a symptom produced at the beginning of the epileptic discharge and perceived by the individual before consciousness is lost. Since the focus of origin of the attack may be situated in a variety of localities within the brain there is a corresponding variety of auras, which can take the form of a complex mental state, an emotion such as fear, or a hallucination in the sphere of one of the senses such as smell, taste, vision or hearing, or an abnormal feeling referred to some part of the body.

Consciousness is usually lost immediately after the aura.

HEADACHE

The principal pain-sensitive structures within the skull are the large blood vessels, and there is abundant evidence that many headaches are initiated by the effect of pressure or traction on these intracranial vessels. The most common causes are space-occupying lesions, such as a tumor or hematoma, meningeal irritation, such as with an inflammatory exudate, and hypertension. Pain in the head can also be referred from the eye, nasal sinuses, temporomandibular joint, thoracic or abdominal viscera or can be psychogenic.

CEREBRAL ISCHEMIA

There is a group of disorders in which the symptoms are due to insufficiency of the blood supply to the brain. The commonest of these is atheroma of the arteries supplying the brain. Infarction of the brain may occur as a result of the narrowing of an artery by atheroma without its complete occlusion or as the result of its occlusion by thrombosis or embolism.

Since the cerebral circulation depends directly upon the adequacy of the blood pressure, a fall in pressure from any cause, such as myocardial infarction, paroxysmal arrhythmia, or peripheral circulatory failure may render temporarily inadequate the circulation through a narrowed atheromatous vessel.

Mental symptoms are common and include reduction in intellectual capacity, impairment of memory especially for recent events, emotional instability, and attacks of confusion.

Cerebral embolism is a variety of ischemic cerebral disease in which the ischemia develops acutely as the result of some substance being carried in the circulation to lodge in one or more of the cerebral vessels. Embolism can be due to atheroma from an extracranial vessel, a blood clot from a paralyzed left atrium as a result of atrial fibrillation or mitral stenosis, or an infected vegetation breaking off from the aortic or mitral valve in subacute bacterial endocarditis.

HYDROCEPHALUS

Hydrocephalus is enlargement of the head occurring before birth or in early infancy and caused by an excess of cerebrospinal fluid under increased pressure. It is due to an obstruction to the circulation of the cerebrospinal fluid which prevents proper absorption of the fluid into the blood. These children are mentally defective, owing to compression and atrophy of the brain.

MULTIPLE SCLEROSIS

Multiple sclerosis is characterized by widespread occurrence of patches of demyelination of the nerve tracts within the central nervous system. The demyelination is followed by gliosis (scarring). There is a tendency for remissions and relapses, so that the course of the disease may be prolonged for years. Symptoms include blurred vision, double vision, numbness of some part of the body, weakness of a limb, and euphoria with a characteristic sense of mental and physical well being.

MENINGITIS

Acute meningitis is an infection of the pia mater and arachnoid which inevitably involves the subarachnoid space and the cerebrospinal fluid. It may be due to a fracture of the skull, extension to the meninges of a pyogenic infection from one of the nasal sinuses, the middle ear, or mastoid, or spread of infection through the blood stream which may be secondary to a focal infection such as with pneumonia, osteomyelitis, enteric infection or a bacteremia, as with meningococcal meningitis.

The subarachnoid space of the brain and spinal cord becomes filled with a greenish-yellow pus and the cerebrospinal fluid is under increased pressure and loaded with white cells. Cervical rigidity due to spasm of the extensor muscles of the neck is always present; delirium is common in the early stages. The patient also has headache, fever, increased pulse rate, drowsiness, and stupor. Convulsions are common in children. Coma occurs in later stages.

RHEUMATOID ARTHRITIS

Rheumatoid arthritis is a chronic systemic disease in which there are inflammatory changes in the joints causing characteristic deformities. There is chronic inflammation, edema, proliferation of capillaries, and infiltration of inflammatory cells which may progress to the formation of granulation tissue and fibrosis. The layers of granulation tissue covering each surface of the joint interdigitate with their opposing layers to form fibrous adhesions and ankylosis. The clinical manifestations of joint inflammation are pain, swelling, redness, heat, and deformity. Subcutaneous nodules are frequently found near tendon sheaths, and an arteritis may be found in the synovial membrane, muscles, heart, and other organs.

DEGENERATIVE JOINT DISEASE

Degenerative joint disease, also known as osteoarthritis, is a disease related to the physiologic process of aging in which there is degeneration of the articular cartilage and hypertrophy of adjacent bone. There are no systemic manifestations. Pain is present when the joints are used and subsides with rest. Stiffness results from prolonged rest in a fixed position and disappears after resuming activity. The enlarged joints, when present, feel hard and knobby, unlike the soft, fluctuant swelling in rheumatoid arthritis.

CONCLUSION

It is not the intent of this abbreviated discussion of disease processes and significant symptoms and signs to prepare the reader to be an astute diagnostician but merely to familiarize him or her with the method of approach to disease.

Sir William Osler stated: "To study the phenomena of disease without books is to sail an uncharted sea, while to study books without patients is not to go to sea at all. . ."

The dental health professional interested in furthering his or her knowledge of physical evalution/physical diagnosis and dental treatment modification is invited to become thoroughly familiar with chapters 1 to 3. If more detailed information is desired, proceed to textbooks of medicine, physical diagnosis, and physicial examination, and participate in advanced physical diagnosis continuing education courses.

If you feel that dental patients are not sufficiently medically compromised to provide experience for you, per the Osler quotation, it is suggested that you look again. There is a wealth of relevant clinical material in the dental office for the diligent observer. Once you learn to recognize and evaluate disease, you will be staggered by the large percentage of ASA physical status Class II and III patients who merit proper evaluation and modification to dental therapy, yet whom you otherwise have classified as healthy, normal patients prior to your development of expertise in physical evaluation/physical diagnosis (see chapter on *physical evaluation* regarding ASA classification). Interest, dedication, the powers of observation, and experience are the keys to further development.

REFERENCES

1. Bates, B.: A Guide to Physical Examination. 1st ed., Philadelphia, J. B. Lippincott Co., 1974.
2. Beeson, P. B., and McDermott, W.: Textbook of Medicine. 14th ed., Philadelphia, W. B. Saunders Co., 1975.
3. DeGowin, E. L., and DeGowin, R. L.: Bedside Diagnostic Examination. 3rd ed., New York, Macmillan Publishing Co., Inc., 1976.
4. Delp, M. H., and Manning, R. T.: Major's Physical Diagnosis. 8th ed., Philadelphia, W. B. Saunders Co., 1975.
5. Dineen, J. J.: What constitutes appropriate training in physical diagnosis and medicine for oral surgeons. J. Oral Surg., 33:740–742, 1975.
6. Laskin, D. L., and Lemke, G. W.: Teaching of physical diagnosis to dental students and oral surgery residents. J. Oral Surg., 33:736–739, 1975.
7. Trieger, N., and Goldblatt, L.: The art of history taking, J. Oral Surg., 36:118–124, 1978.

MONITORING

THOMAS F. MULKEY
and CEDRIC L. HAYDEN

INTRODUCTION

Consciously or unconsciously, every practitioner evaluates the patient before, during, and after each operation and procedure. As Adriani informs us, "The term monitoring refers to the overall surveillance of the patient by methods employing the senses of touch, sight, hearing or smell or by means of devices which operate chemically, physically or electronically to measure the adequacy of the various physiological functions."[1]

This chapter will first review all direct observation monitoring that applies to conscious-patient sedation or ultralight general anesthesia in the office. The same monitoring background is also vital with respect to the conduct of a high-risk case or in the treatment of an emergency. The general practitioner is invited to carefully review this chapter.

Later we will cover biomedical and mechanical monitoring, some of which is impractical at this time for office use. Yet, some applications can be made at present in the occasional case, and, as enormous strides are being made in instrument design, we feel that the information should be made available. In this section the general dental practitioner will find the following of greatest interest and most possible application: the "fail-safe" style of gas pressure monitor for the anesthesia or sedation machine, the electronic pulse monitor, and the monaural stethoscope for breath sounds, heart sounds, and blood pressure. The cardioscope is also of interest, as is the general discussion of the more common cardiac arrhythmias.

Monitoring of vital signs is a necessary function during all dental therapy, regardless of the anesthesia utilized. *The degree of surveillance is in direct relation to the degree of pain/anxiety control,* and therefore it varies from the totally unmedicated patient through local analgesia alone, the conscious-patient sedation techniques, ultralight outpatient general anesthesia, and hospital-type, surgical depth general anesthesia in which an endotracheal tube can be tolerated for restorative dentistry or the peritoneum can be incised. *The degree of surveillance also increases with an emergency or with serious disease.*

If we analyze the definition of conscious-patient sedation, we observe:

Conscious — awake to one's own existence, sensations; cognition, having the mental faculties awake.
Sedation — that which causes one to be sedate.
Sedate — calm, quiet or composed, sober, undisturbed by passion or emotion.

To transpose these definitions to a patient about to receive treatment, we have a patient who has received a chemical substance by the oral, inhalation, or intravenous route which has rendered him calm, composed, and undisturbed by his emotions, yet able to respond knowledgeably to question or command, and without depression of protective reflexes.

Analyzing the term ultralight general anesthesia we observe:

Ultra — beyond the ordinary
Light — of small amount, force or intensity.
General anesthesia — general insensibility to pain, with loss of consciousness.

To transpose, we have a patient who is generally insensitive to pain, but of exceedingly small intensity; a patient who is unconscious with no significant muscle relaxation and whose protective reflexes, such as lash, lid, gag, laryngeal, and cough, are depressed either not at all or only momentarily.

Monitoring is in a state of change in dentistry, and few standards can be recognized at the present time. In an attempt to clarify the situation, Table 4–1 shows our estimate of present minimal application of various monitoring techniques. It is assumed that the patient is in excellent health, that there are no emergency problems, and that a routine physical evaluation with blood pressure, pulse, and temperature has been performed. Additional monitoring modalities would be applied as indicated in an emergency or for the high-risk patient.

Direct observational techniques for monitoring the patient are inspec-

TABLE 4-1

	Preop Temp. & Resp.	Preop B.P. & Pulse	Periodic B.P. & Pulse	Continuous B.S. & H.S.	Continuous B.P. & Pulse	Card.
Unmedicated	No–D	No–D	No	No	No	No
Local analgesia only	No–D	No–D	No	No	No	No
Conscious-patient oral sedation	No–D	No–D	No	No	No	No
Conscious-patient inhalation sedation	No–D	No–D	No	No	No	No
Conscious-patient intravenous sedation	No–D	Yes	No–D	No	No	No
Ultralight general anesthesia	Yes	Yes	D	D	Opt.	Opt.
Surgical depth general anesthesia	Yes	Yes	Yes	Yes	Yes	Opt.

B.P. = blood pressure.   D = desirable.
B.S. = breath sounds   Opt. = optional.
H.S. = heart sounds.   Card. = cardioscope.

tion, palpation, auscultation, and percussion. The physiological functions that lend themselves to monitoring and are significant in determining the well being of the patient at any time during anesthesia include those of three organ systems: the central nervous system, the respiratory system, and the cardiovascular system.

The early Egyptian physicians were familiar with the concept of inspection. And one Victorian physician-turned-author, Sir Arthur Conan Doyle, created an unsurpassed detective with tremendous powers of inspection and analysis, Sherlock Holmes. The literary character is said to be based upon an actual physician whose uncanny powers of observation had greatly impressed the young physician Doyle. Although the ancients, including Hippocrates, had some conception of auscultation, this method of diagnosis did not become important until the discovery of the stethoscope by Laennec in the early nineteenth century. Today's anesthetist will sometimes percuss the abdomen to see if the anesthetic gas or air has been forced into the stomach, thereby distending it, or he will use palpation when feeling the pulse.

From the beginning, however, inspection was one of the most important methods used for the assessment of patient health, and it remains so today. It is easily the most significant patient evaluation technique used by health practitioners. By using the main methods of physical diagnosis, the surgeon/anesthetist and the general dental practitioner may monitor patients with great safety.

A brief anatomical description of the three main organ systems mentioned above might be appropriate at this time. The central nervous system pertains to the brain, spinal cord, and the many afferent and efferent nerve fibers that carry the impulses from the sensory surfaces to the reflex centers and back, thus giving us the reflex actions which we monitor. The respiratory system, as referred to in this chapter, includes the nose, pharynx, trachea, lungs, thorax, and respiratory muscles, including the diaphragm and intercostals. These components interact to move the oxygen into the system and waste carbon dioxide out of the body. The cardiovascular system includes the heart, the various categories of vessels, and the blood, functioning together as a transport system for oxygen and carbon dioxide within the body.

At this time we wish to consider the various signs to be assessed by the doctor and his team of trained auxiliary personnel. By using the information received from monitoring the three systems by direct observation, he can give the patient safe, comfortable dental care. In succeeding pages we will introduce the electronic and mechanical devices that have been developed and that are capable of second-to-second monitoring of many vital functions simultaneously.

DIRECT OBSERVATION MONITORING

Central Nervous System

The reflex actions of the central nervous system indicate the degree to which a particular physiological function has been affected during an emergency, conscious-patient sedation, or general anesthesia.

Reflex actions of the eye, including those of the lash, lid, and pupil, are examples of reflex activity that can be evaluated continuously by the team during a procedure in order to determine the physiological status of the patient.

Starting with the structures that are anatomically most superficial, we encounter the lash reflex. This is the blinking of the eye that occurs whenever the upper or lower eyelash is stroked gently with the finger. This stroking is a very weak stimulus, and for this reason the reflex is lost early in the induction phase of anesthesia. Many dentistry procedures that are not particularly painful may be performed when this reflex is still present. For example, suturing of a mucosal incision at the end of a surgical procedure may be completed while this reflex is present. However, elevating a mucoperiosteal flap might not be possible when this reflex is active. The lid reflex is the next we encounter, and this occurs when the eyelid loses its ability to close voluntarily after it has been opened. This reflex is usually seen with the patient in a surgical plane of anesthesia when one is using an intravenous barbiturate. Coordinated movement of the eyeballs when the lids are lifted together is usually seen during the lighter stages of dental anesthesia. It will disappear as the anesthesia deepens.

The pupil of the eye also offers many varied signs to determine the depth of anesthesia. The reaction of the pupil to light in the unpremedicated patient is a sign that may be interpreted very accurately. If the patient has lost the pupillary reaction to light, then he is in a *deeper plane of anesthesia than is usually needed for dental procedures*. The pupil size is another indication of depth of anesthesia. It becomes smaller with increasing depth and is usually constricted in the late surgical plane of anesthesia. Painful stimulation during light anesthesia will cause a dilatation of the pupil. Dilated pupils may indicate either light anesthesia or very deep anesthesia and anoxia. As an indication of adequacy of cerebral oxygenation, *pupillary constriction and dilatation is one of the more reliable signs that we have.*

Muscle activity and response to stimulation is another means of determining the status of the central nervous system during anesthesia. Muscle control diminishes as the anesthesia deepens and relaxation increases. Muscle activity is a result of muscle tone and will, of course, vary with the age, physical status, and muscular development of the patient. Usually the unpremedicated patient will respond to a painful stimulation in a light plane of general anesthesia by movement away from the point of stimulation, or by movement of an extremity. These responses, which may not interfere with a relatively short procedure, are frequently seen in dental ambulatory anesthesia. Such movements would not be acceptable in an abdominal procedure, but they would not present a problem in the short dental procedure. Another reflex muscular activity used in determining the depth of anesthesia is that of swallowing. In barbiturate anesthesia we see depression of the swallowing reflex following the induction phase and continuing throughout most of the surgical plane of anesthesia, with a return as the anesthesia lightens.

In summary, observation of the reflex activity reveals the degree of depression or stimulation and provides essential information in a simple and expeditious manner when properly interpreted and correlated with other data.

Respiratory System

Oxygen is the most important single factor in life. An adult body reserves only about 1 liter of oxygen, which is used up at the rate of 200 to 300 cc. per minute under resting circumstances and at a much faster rate during muscular activity. The elimination of the waste product, carbon dioxide (CO_2), is also of great importance. The respiratory system provides the first step in ensuring that adequate oxygen is available for the needs of the body and the means for the final elimination of the carbon dioxide.

In monitoring the respiratory system we are constantly aware of the movement of the chest and abdomen. We are able to observe, and if necessary feel, if they are moving in a rhythmical manner. We can check the amplitude of each inspiration and expiration. We are also able to observe the movement of the reservoir bag on the anesthesia or sedation machine as another means of evaluating the respiration rate, rhythm, and amplitude (Fig. 4-1). We are able to evaluate the events that occur, such as the deep sigh and transient apnea frequently seen on induction of general anesthesia with an intravenous barbiturate. The increase in the rate of respiration becomes very apparent as the anesthetic plane lightens and the patient reacts to a painful stimulus. Conversely, as the anesthetic plane deepens and the respiratory rate decreases, we are able to detect these signs and withhold the anesthetic agent and assist respiration if necessary until the return of the rhythmical breathing seen in the surgical plane of barbiturate anesthesia.

Observation of the thoracic and abdominal movements during anesthesia quickly reveals any abnormal pattern, such as jerking of the diaphragm and heaving of the chest, during partial or complete obstruction, allowing this pattern to be corrected.

We are able to hear the movement of air in the nose and mouth as it

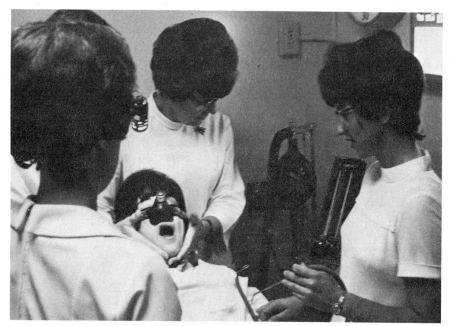

Figure 4-1   The anesthesia assistant can monitor the rate and amplitude of each inspiration and expiration by observing the reservoir bag on the anesthesia machine.

passes to and from the lungs (Fig. 4-2). Other sounds, also detectable during the anesthesia, make us aware of the minute-to-minute function of the respiratory system. These may include the gurgling sound from the passage of air over mucus or blood that has seeped past the pharyngeal partition, or the snoring as the tongue falls back in the oral pharynx and partially occludes the airway. The wheezing associated with bronchial constriction or the high-pitched crowing that may indicate partial laryngeal obstruction can easily be heard and quickly corrected.

Cardiovascular System

The second step in ensuring that the body has sufficient oxygen is having an adequate means of delivering oxygen to the cells. This is the major function of the cardiovascular system. Means available to monitor the cardiovascular system clinically include observation of the pulse rate, blood pressure, color of the skin, mucous membrane, and blood in the surgical field.

Monitoring the pulse is easily accomplished by palpating the radial, carotid, facial, or superficial temporal arteries. These are all within easy reach of the doctor or some member of the team. The strength and character of the pulse can be determined as well as the rate and rhythm. We will see an increase in the normal adult pulse rate during the induction stage, but the rate will usually return to near normal during the maintenance of ultralight anesthesia. The pulse rate will increase in response to painful stimuli, a carbon dioxide excess, and oxygen lack.

Palpation of the pulse may also reveal some of the more common arrhythmias encountered, such as premature beat and sinus arrhythmia, secondary to the patient's respiratory pattern; there are other arrhythmias which may only be detected through the use of the electrocardiograph, and these will be discussed later in the chapter.

The blood pressure must be taken prior to the intravenous administration of any medication for conscious-patient sedation or general anesthesia. Blood pressure is a function of heart action and vascular resistance. Any direct or indirect physiological, psychological or pharmacological action may have an effect on the blood pressure. The initial measurement will serve as a screening device for hypertension, as a preoperative evaluation, and as a baseline which we can compare with readings taken intraoperatively, at the completion of the procedure, or in the event of an emergency. The blood pressure will follow the pulse during the induction stages of anesthesia. It will rise with stimulation and return to the preanesthetic level during the maintenance of ultralight levels of anesthesia. Deeper planes of anesthesia will cause a lowering of the blood pressure and light planes an increase. It will also increase during episodes of hypoxia and carbon dioxide accumulation. There is little chance of misinterpreting the cause of a rise in blood pressure; movement of the extremities will often be seen during light anesthesia, and the blood pressure will be elevated. When hypoxia or carbon dioxide retention is the factor causing an increased blood pressure, there will be no movement of the extemities.

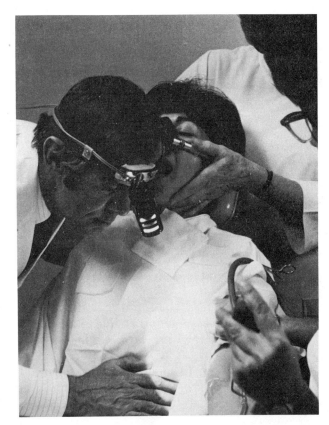

Figure 4–2 The doctor can hear the movement of air in the nose and mouth as it passes to and from the lungs. He is also able to feel the movement of the abdomen and chest in evaluating the respiratory system.

From the color of the skin, mucous membrane, or the blood in the surgical field, we can gain much valuable information. Well-oxygenated blood will appear bright red in the wound, and as the oxygen content diminishes the blood will become a darker red. The color of the mucous membrane can give us an indication of the degree of oxygenation of the blood. The well-oxygenated mucosa will have a healthy pink color. Mucosa with decreased arterial oxygen values appears bluish or dusky. Normal blood contains about 12 to 18 gm. of hemoglobin per 100 ml. Lunsgaard found that the capillary blood must contain approximately 5 gm. of reduced hemoglobin per 100 ml. before cyanosis will appear.[2] Because of this finding, a patient with a low hemoglobin value will not appear dusky or cyanotic in the early stages of hypoxia.

THE SURGEON/ANESTHETIST AND THE ANESTHESIA TEAM CONCEPT

Throughout the section on direct observation monitoring of the patient during general anesthesia, reference was made to the surgeon/anesthetist and the anesthesia team. This concept has been endorsed by the Council on Dental Therapeutics of the American Dental Association, as evidenced by the following statement from the 37th edition of Accepted Dental Therapeutics:

> General anesthetics for the ambulatory dental patient can be effectively administered by a qualified team, which may be supervised by the surgeon providing he is thoroughly trained in general anesthesia. Utilization of a separate trained anesthetist is also encouraged. The safety of the patient is paramount and, regardless of the method used, the physical status of the patient must be continuously monitored to assure this safety.[3]

Utilizing this technique, which has been mentioned by Hubbell and Krogh,[4] and described by Hagen and McCarthy,[5] one can observe carefully and constantly the physical status of the patient. Each member of the team has a specific function with regards to monitoring during the anesthetic as well as during an emergency, as described by Hagen and McCarthy.[6] The anesthesia assistant has the primary function of maintaining a patent airway and monitoring the rate, character, and amplitude of the respirations. This is accomplished by maintaining the mandible in a proper position and observing the movement of the patient's chest, abdomen, and the reservoir bag attached to the anesthesia machine. This assistant is also able to monitor the pulse and report any irregularities to the surgeon.

The surgical assistant has the primary function of keeping the field free of blood and mucus which would tend to interfere with the normal respiratory pattern. From her position, she is able to aid in the monitoring of respiration, color, pulse, and blood pressure (Fig. 4–3).

The surgeon has the ultimate responsibility for the patient undergoing any surgical procedure, whether in an office or hospital environment. Because of his background the surgeon/anesthetist is well qualified to train his team in monitoring techniques. Use of a highly qualified team under the supervision of the surgeon will enhance patient safety during the anesthetic. Patient safety, as stated by the Council on Dental Therapeutics,[7]

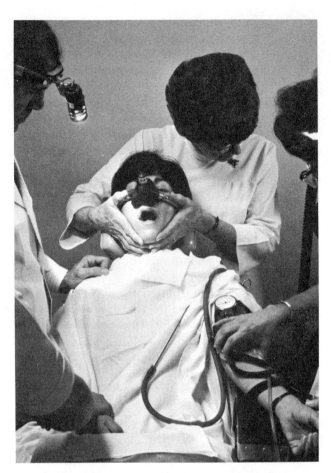

Figure 4–3 The surgical assistant has the primary function of keeping the field free from blood and mucus, and from her position she is able to monitor respiration, color, pulse rate, and blood pressure.

must be the paramount issue. In like manner, it is the responsibility of the general practitioner to train his or her assistants in observation monitoring so that they may act as a smoothly functioning team both in routine treatment and in the treatment of emergencies.

BIOMEDICAL ELECTRONIC AND MECHANICAL MONITORING

In most instances, the individual to be evaluated is immediately adjacent to the evaluator. However, we are now at a point when it is possible to place men in space, in the caverns of the earth, or in the depths of the sea. For various reasons, it has been necessary to measure the physiological functions of these explorers. One spelunker spent six months alone underground in a cave to ascertain the effect of such isolation on the human body. He was monitored by hardwire connections to the surface. The astronauts provide another example of long-distance monitoring; they, of course, are monitored by telemetry. Through the use of these advanced electronic and mechanical monitors it is possible not only to monitor individuals who are very distant from the evaluator but also to follow equally well the vital signs of a patient a few steps away in the recovery room, or immediately at hand in the dental operatory. As the science of physiological monitoring advances, the practitioner should find himself using more and more of these aids to supplement the information supplied him by direct observation of the patient. Legal considerations may make it prudent to use the instruments the industry makes available to us. A recent large judgment against an anesthesiologist who failed to monitor the patient's pulse, with untoward consequences, is a case in point.

Hospital dental patients treated under general anesthesia (and likewise some restorative office cases) may often require a treatment duration of four to six hours, or more. Keeping patients anesthetized for such an amount of time creates physiological and biochemical problems not ordinarily seen in shorter anesthetic procedures. An increased level of patient monitoring, including lab tests, may be indicated in some of these cases. Also, use of supplemental aids for monitoring the anesthetized patient assumes increasing importance with the advent of four-, six-, and eight-handed dentistry, in which time and motion efficiency experts have urged the practitioner to train his eyes on the operative area, often to the relative exclusion of the "whole" patient. Although constant visual observation of the patient's general physiological state can be partially delegated to other members of the team, use of supplemental monitoring aids will be important, particularly when the doctor is training a new team or orienting a new team member. Many dental offices will in the course of one day administer general anesthestics to more patients than the local community hospital, and each individual treated must be evaluated in some manner preoperatively, as well as during the procedure and throughout the postoperative period. To a large degree, biomedical electronic monitoring can supplement the technique of direct observation, though not replace it. As stated by the ADA Council of Therapeutics, "the safety of the patient is paramount and, regardless of the method used, the physical status of the patient must be continuously monitored to assure this safety."[8]

Our attention will now turn to various types of monitors commercially available to the practitioner.

A number of these products are listed at the end of this chapter for ease in contacting representative manufacturers. Most types of products are manufactured by several competitive companies, and the prospective purchaser may be wise to contact several suppliers prior to purchase, rather than limiting himself to the manufacturers mentioned in this chapter. It should be noted that the instruments mentioned in these pages may not always be identical to the ones illustrated but will be generally similar to them in nature. Some monitors mentioned are used with anesthetic techniques not commonly used by the general practitioner. Other monitors are of equal value to the general practitioner and the surgeon. Understandably, this presentation includes only a very few of the many monitoring devices available. For more information, the reader is referred to the current literature or to trade journals dealing with biomedical electronic monitors.[9]

TEMPERATURE MONITORING

Temperature monitoring and evaluation are important to any patient receiving an intravenous anesthetic. Temperature variations from "normal" can be a result of many different factors; for example, dehydration, infection, exercise, diet, and so forth. The basal metabolic rate is increased 7 per cent for each 1° F increase in the body temperature. This becomes significant when a patient, with a temperature of 103° F, receives an ultralight general anesthesia for the removal of an infected tooth. There has been an increase of 30 per cent in the basal metabolic rate, necessitating a demand for 30 per cent more oxygen. Temperature monitoring is also important in order to ascertain large fluctuations in body temperature. It is unlikely that extreme temperature variations will occur during the shorter dental procedures, such as those performed in oral surgery offices. However, with the increased use of general anesthetics in restorative dentistry, procedures taking several hours or more are not uncommon, and the possibility of significant temperature variations should be considered. Should any change occur, it would usually be a decrease in body temperature (hypothermia), which can be easily controlled by warming the room and covering the patient with blankets. Although significant cooling must occur in the adult before any marked decrease in respiration will occur, such decrease has been noted during prolonged anesthesia. In rare instances, the temperature may increase under general anesthesia (malignant hyperthermia), a condition which seems to be related more to the type of anesthetic given than to the length of procedure or any other consideration known to us. Significantly for dental anesthetics, this condition is not noted with nitrous oxide–oxygen anesthesia, although it has been seen with Fluothane and other anesthetics often used in dental surgery.[10] Malignant hyperthermia is a life-threatening situation of which every anesthesia team member should be aware.

Oral Thermometer

The most generally used method to monitor oral temperature is the glass-mercury thermometer, which is placed sublingually for three to five minutes and read from the scale. An improvement in this technique has been made by the availability of sterile disposable plastic sheaths (TEMP-AWAY),[9A]* which come individually packaged. (Fig. 4–4).

A second and more recent improvement in taking oral temperatures is the use of a system of chemical mixtures* (TEMPRA-DOT),[9B] which melt and recrystallize at a very specific temperature (Fig. 4–5). As the mixture recrystallizes it changes color. The temperature is read on a scale to the last recrystalized dot. The system is disposable and comes sterile and ready for use. The temperature may be read after the system has been in the sublingual area only 30 seconds.

Electronic Thermometer

The third method is by electronic thermometers,[9C] which are used for the continuous monitoring of patients under anesthesia as well as in the

---

*Superscript letters refer to the Manufacturers' List found at the end of this chapter.

TEMP-AWAY Thermometer Sheaths. A single patient thermometer system.

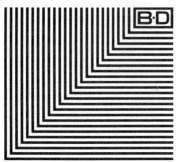

Note: Rectal TEMP-AWAY Sheaths are pre-lubricated.

1 Shake down a Security Bulb Thermometer in the usual way. The B-D thermometer has a tab top. You can shake more vigorously.

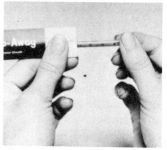

2 Insert the thermometer tip into the the preformed opening. You'll find this opening on the end where the written instructions are printed. Push the thermometer in until you feel a "spongy" resistant feeling.

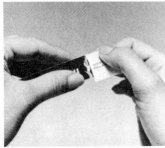

3 Grasp package as shown. Then with thumb and forefinger of each hand, twist package with each hand twisting in the opposite direction. The package will tear at the dotted line.

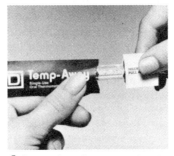

4 As you twist, pull paper away from the tab top of the thermometer. The paper will slide off, leaving the TEMP-AWAY Sheath covering the thermometer shaft.

5 The remaining paper on the plastic sheath is your handle to place the thermometer in the patient's mouth in the usual way.

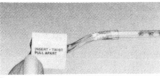

6 After temperature is taken, remove sheath by pulling the paper handle toward the thermometer tip while twisting slightly. The sheath will reverse, turning itself inside-out and encapsulating most contamination.

7 Dispose of the sheath in your usual way. Reversed, the TEMP-AWAY Sheath also helps protect housekeeping personnel from cross-contamination.

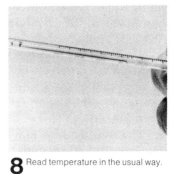

8 Read temperature in the usual way.

Note: When thermometers are used to take temperatures from patient to patient (not being a single-patient thermometer system) the thermometer must be disinfected prior to each patient use.

B·D BECTON-DICKINSON
Rutherford, New Jersey 07070
Division of Becton, Dickinson and Company
In Canada: Becton, Dickinson and Co. Canada Ltd. Mississauga, Ontario

B-D and TEMP-AWAY are trademarks of Becton, Dickinson and Company
Printed in U.S.A.   TWC/76-2001-2

Figure 4–4

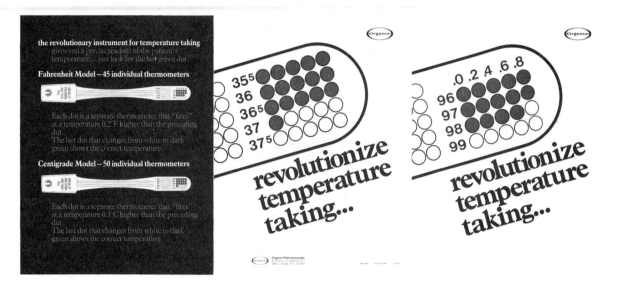

New **Tempa-DOT**
single use oral thermometer

☐ fast

☐ accurate

☐ easy to read

☐ unbreakable

☐ free from cross-infection risks

☐ no shaking down

☐ no after-use washing

☐ no sterilizing

☐ completely disposable

**Revolutionize
temperature taking
...just 3 simple steps**

ready... aim... fire...

Simply break handle seal at the score mark by bending it up and down. Pull thermometer straight out toward you without twisting or side-to-side motion.

Insert sensor end of the Tempa-DOT Thermometer under either side of tongue, well back alongside the frenum. Have patient hold the stem with teeth, press tongue down on it, and keep mouth closed for a minimum of 30 seconds.

Remove from mouth and read temperature — the last dot that "fires" to dark green. Discard the Tempa-DOT Thermometer. (This example shows a temperature of 98.6° F.)

Faster, easier, safer, accurate, and economical... with no risk of cross-infection or reinfection because the Tempa-DOT Thermometer is a single-use instrument.

Figure 4–5

**Here's the Tempa-DOT
Single Use Oral Thermometer
that can revolutionize temperature
taking in your hospital**

Organon provides an extended in-service program with members of the nursing staff to assure complete understanding of the Tempa-DOT Thermometer and the technique of using it.

Your Organon Hospital Specialist will be glad to demonstrate the Tempa-DOT Thermometer and arrange for its evaluation in accordance with whatever evaluation procedures are used in your hospital.

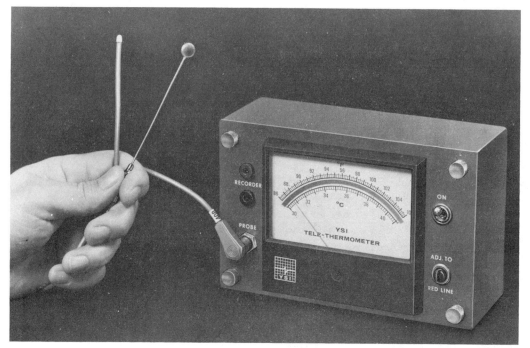

Figure 4–6

recovery room (Fig 4–6). Any change of more than one half to one degree above the initial stabilized temperature should be observed carefully and cooling procedures instituted if the patient becomes hyperpyrexic. A newer technique for taking temperature that may be of interest in dental anesthesia records the temperature of the ear canal. This location has the advantage of being removed from the oral cavity, but without the difficulties of placing a temperature probe esophageally or rectally.

RESPIRATORY SYSTEM MONITORING

One of the more common anesthetic emergencies is that of hypoxia. It is insidious in that it may be difficult to recognize in the earliest stages. Monitoring of the gas exchange can provide significant information about the pulmonary status. When using an anesthesia or sedation machine to deliver medical gases one may obtain efficient guarding of the oxygen supply by installing an oxygen pressure monitor on the oxygen delivery line or anesthesia machine. When the oxygen pressure drops to dangerous levels, the battery-powered monitor will sound an alarm and flash a red light. This battery-powered device operates independently of the gas pressures and will give an alarm signal when oxygen pressures drop. Unfortunately, when the batteries deteriorate the device will become inoperative. It should be checked each morning to ensure that the audible and visual alarms are functional. It is advisable to check tank pressures of oxygen and nitrous oxide at the same time to ensure a safe supply for the day. A second type of gas pressure monitor is a whistle alarm,[9D] an accessory installed in the an-

Figure 4-7

esthesia machine. If the oxygen supply pressure falls to a predetermined level, a whistle will sound. The device is self-checking, in that any time the oxygen pressure rises from near zero to its normal value, a brief "peep" attests that the alarm is functioning. A small reservoir stores enough oxygen to blow the whistle for at least five seconds. No other source of power is required. An anesthesia machine is often equipped with a device that will cut off the flow of all other gases and vapors when the oxygen supply pressure drops below a predetermined level. This minimizes the chance of delivering a hypoxic mixture to the breathing circuit. The reduced flow of fresh gas may also alert the doctor to the depletion of the oxygen supply, but the alarms described above are probably more reliable. One unwise monitoring practice that is to be avoided is "sniffing" gas flows to determine that the proper anesthetic mixtures are being delivered. This can lead to dependence upon inhalation anesthetics.

Carbon Dioxide Analyzer

An extremely useful monitoring tool is the carbon dioxide analyzer, or capnograph[9E] (Fig. 4-7). Expiratory carbon dioxide is measured by this instrument. The adapter lead is easily inserted into the airway tubing at some readily accessible point close to the patient's airway. It may be used in conjunction with an endotracheal tube, a nasopharyngeal tube, or a nasal or full-face mask. An increase in the amount of expired carbon dioxide may indicate hypoventilation and relative hypoxia. Hyperventilation will cause a decrease in the amount of CO_2 recorded. In the event of cardiac arrest, perfusion of blood to the lungs will cease, thus stopping the excretion of carbon dioxide from the lungs, and the CO_2 analyzer will indicate zero per cent carbon dioxide. A zero per cent indication might also be seen in the event of an airway obstruction; if this occurs, immediate action is indicated. Medical Gas analyzers $9E_2$ (Fig. 4-8) are available that not only will monitor CO_2 but, by using interchangeable pickup heads, will measure nitrous oxide or halothane also.

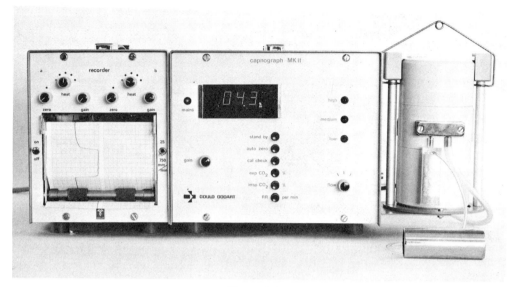

Figure 4-8

Oxygen Alarm Monitor

It is technically quite easy to continuously monitor the percentage of oxygen in the gases being delivered to the anesthetized patient. An oxygen alarm[9F] monitor may be placed in line between the anesthesia machine and the patient (Fig. 4-9). The monitor will sense any amount of oxygen from 0 to 100 per cent and an audio-visual alarm system is activated when the partial pressure of oxygen falls below a preset limit. The alarm is battery operated, less than six inches long, and weighs less than three pounds. It can be calibrated on room air or 100 per cent oxygen and is extremely accurate.

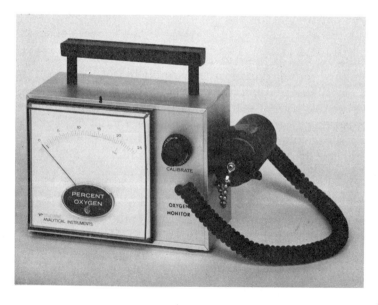

Figure 4-9

Spirometer

Various instruments are available to monitor respiratory rate, tidal volume (amount of air passing in or out of the lungs during each breath), and minute volume (amount of air passing in or out of the lungs in one minute). Tidal and minute volume values are probably of greater importance to the doctor than is respiratory rate. A person breathing at a "normal" respiratory rate is not necessarily inspiring the amount of oxygen necessary to prevent hypoxia. A person with normal tidal and minute volumes is likely to have adequate gas exchange.

Oximeter

Although gas percentages are easily ascertained in the respiratory gas flow, modern technology is providing simple and inexpensive methods of measuring arterial blood gas saturations. This more direct but noninvasive method of measuring the physiological status of patients deserves at least academic attention. An oximeter[9G] measures the arterial oxygen saturation by colorimetric changes in the arterial circulation of the pinna of the ear (Fig. 4–10). This spectrophotometric instrument is about 16 inches in its greatest dimension and weighs about 37 pounds. Operating independently of skin color and unaffected by motion, it continuously measures arterial oxygen saturation without the necessity of calibration or mathematical manipulation of the readout. Oxygenated hemoglobin absorbs one light spectrum and reduced hemoglobin another. When the loosely fitting earpiece is attached (without skin penetration) a light beam is transmitted through the ear and picked up on the other side by the sensor. Alteration in light intensities at eight different wave lengths is instantly interpreted by the instrument as per

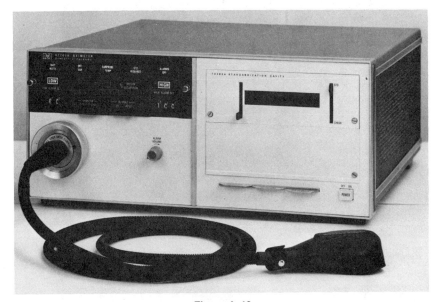

Figure 4–10

cent oxygen saturation. A patient with a satisfactory arterial oxygen saturation is unlikely to suffer the ill effects of hypoxia.

When facilities permit, as on a Hospital Dental Service, micro-blood samples may be taken and quickly processed in a nearby clinical laboratory to determine blood tensions of oxygen and carbon dioxide, the pH, the concentration of electrolytes, and other serum chemistries that can give important information on the status of the patient.

TRACE GASES

Though not of importance to the health of the patient, one should be aware that health personnel who are exposed to trace concentrations of anesthestic gases over long periods of time during multiple exposure might be at some physical risk. The technology is available to measure and monitor anesthetic trace gases in the dental operatory utilizing gas chromatography and infrared spectrometry; scavenging systems can be installed to eliminate the possible problem.

CARDIOVASCULAR SYSTEM MONITORING

The status of the cardiovascular system is of enormous importance during general anesthesia and, fortunately, is easily monitored at a number of anatomical points with many different types of monitors. A few of these methods will be presented now.

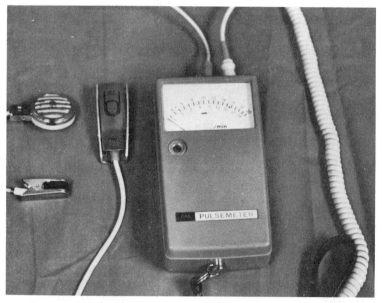

Figure 4–11 Pulse monitor. Showing finger tip pickup and earlobe/nostril pickup (lower left). Acoustic signal is heard from speaker (upper left). Pulse rate per minute is read on the dial, as a light beneath the dial flashes with each pulse beat.

The pulse is probably the easiest physiological sign to monitor in the dental outpatient. Hands and fingers are completely exposed for the application of the pulse monitor. Few if any patients find terror in the application and use of a pulse monitoring device, particularly if its action and function are briefly described as similar to the photoelectric cells often found on elevator doors which respond to interruption of a light beam. In the case of the pulse monitor[9H], the photoelectric beam is interrupted by the blood flow through the finger following each heartbeat, creating a visual and/or audible signal (Fig. 4–11). Available models include a lightweight portable monitor powered by a rechargeable battery. Optional pickups will clip onto a toe, nostril, or earlobe, in addition to the fingertip. Advanced models will portray a visible waveform on the oscilloscopic screen, count the pulse automatically, and emit an audible signal with each heartbeat.

Monaural Stethoscope and Cardiac Audio Monitor

The heart may be monitored effectively by a stethoscope placed just below the trachea in the suprasternal or pretracheal position. In this position, the stethoscope will transmit both cardiac and breath sounds. These are of great interest, and the intensity, rate, rhythmicity and quality provide much information. It is quite convenient to monitor the heart sounds with the use of a custom-fitted ear mold[9I] connected to the chest piece by 5 or 6 feet of lightweight plastic tubing (Figs. 4–12 and 4–13). Should one find the tubing restrictive to motion, the stethoscope may be connected to a microphone pick-up and amplifier and broadcast into the room. This has the advantage of allowing every member of the team to be conscious of the patient's cardiac tones; the doctor is free to move unencumbered by any connection to the patient.

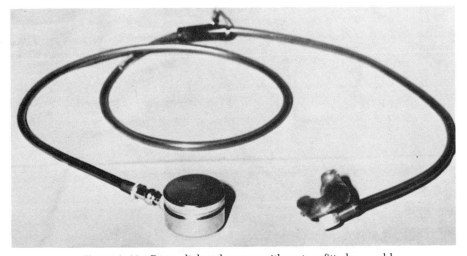

Figure 4–12 Precordial stethoscope with custom-fitted ear mold.

Figure 4–13   Cardiac audio monitor. Microphone (lower left) amplifies heart sounds picked up by stethoscope (lower right). Stethoscope is inexpensively made from heavy pipe fitting. Weight keeps stethoscope in position on the chest.

Esophageal Stethoscope

In some cases it may be difficult to hear satisfactory heart sounds with the precordial or suprasternal stethoscope. An alternative would be the esophageal stethoscope, particularly with the patient who has been intubated (Fig. 4–14). The esophageal stethoscope may be quickly placed by the oral or nasal route. This provides optimum cardiac and pulmonic tones. When a nasal route

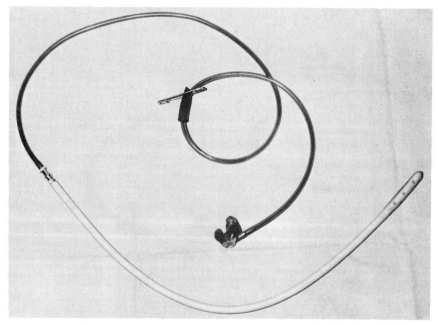

Figure 4–14   Esophageal stethoscope with custom earpiece.

of insertion is chosen, the main precaution to be observed is the prevention of bleeding. A well-lubricated esophageal stethoscope will usually cause no problem if inserted gently. However, children in their teens and younger may have hypertrophic adenoid tissue which can be easily traumatized. Some adults may have friable blood vessels in the anterior portion of the nostril, but adenoid tissue is greatly diminished after adolescence and unlikely to be a problem. Should one nostril seem occluded, perhaps from a deviated septum, the esophageal stethoscope can often be inserted easily in the other nostril.

Oscilloscopes

The oscilloscope is widely and commonly used to give a visual representation of various parameters, including but not limited to the electrocardiograph (ECG), pulse rate, respiratory rate, blood pressure, and electroencephalograph (EEG). All these wave forms may be presented simultaneously on some models, or individually at the discretion of the operator in others. It is probably unwise to use the ECG mode as the sole measure of cardiac activity, as it provides no direct information on the vital characteristics of cardiac output. If the patient is healthy, and has no history of cardiac disease, one might find that monitoring the pulse and blood pressure would do more to avoid unexpected and untoward complications. The ECG will, of course, provide early detection of arrhythmias, and the alert clinician will remember that PVCs are a possible precursor to ventricular fibrillation. The oscilloscope is connected to the patient by painless, easily attached adhesive electrodes.

ECG displays are available in several types. The conventional "bouncing ball" is familiar to most. In this instance, the bright spot moves across the screen from left to right, vanishing at the right only to reappear again at the left. A second type of display is the "moving window" wherein a pattern of steady brightness fills the entire width of the screen, and moves from right to left. Current information enters the screen on the right edge. This is a "non-fade" display, as is the "erase bar" depiction. The "erase bar" also has full screen width and steady brightness but the pattern does not move as a whole. Instead, a narrow gap in the ECG moves across the screen from left to right. Fresh data are found at the left of the gap, and information is erased at the right edge of the gap. Various optional features are available with non-fade displays, such as the "freeze" or "hold" feature. With this tool, one may hold the display on the screen for an indefinite period of time in order to study the ECG. Trend-plotting is available on some models, where the sweep speed is very slow, and a number of cardiac contractions will be represented on the screen at one time. A "cascade" non-fade display allows a number of sweeps of the oscilloscope to be preserved on the screen for a period of time. The sweeps are depicted one above another, on different channels, providing a "cascade."

Monitors are also available which will store physiological information in a solid state memory and give an "instant replay" when desired; in other models a tracing can be "frozen" on the screen, moved to a different channel, and compared with the new tracings flowing across the oscilloscope screen on the original channel. The conventional bouncing ball display will probably meet the needs of most practitioners treating dental patients on an outpatient basis.

Recorders: Telephone ECG Systems

In many instances, for diagnostic or legal purposes, it will be desirable to make hard-copy or permanent records of physiological signs. In these cases it is easy to connect the monitors to recorders and inscribe tracings on paper. This tracing might be filed with the patient's chart for future reference, or shown to a consultant for diagnosis. If one wishes to record an entire lengthy procedure, it might be advisable to use a trend recorder, which is a paper recorder used at very slow speed; a two-hour procedure would be recorded on perhaps two inches of paper.

ECG signals can be transmitted across the phone lines from the patient to the appropriate receiver. Many individuals wearing pacemakers are monitored at regular intervals in this manner to ascertain that the pacemaker is functioning properly. This tool could be available to the dental office; it would be useful for requesting immediate interpretation of questionable tracings during an anesthetic. Preanesthetic and postanesthetic tracings might be transmitted for evaluation by a consultant.

Automatic Blood Pressure Monitor

Blood pressure is most commonly measured by means of a blood pressure cuff applied to the upper arm, though the upper thigh can be used with good results if the situation requires it. During a procedure blood pressures are often taken on a regular time schedule of every five minutes by trained ancillary personnel. Although this is a quick and efficient method, increased reliability can be obtained by use of an automatic indirect blood pressure monitor. This machine, which uses a conventionally applied cuff about the arm, will display at any desired time interval from one to 15 minutes the usual indirect blood pressure measurement, both systolic and diastolic. After the cuff has been placed on the patient's arm and the time interval has been selected, blood pressures will be automatically taken and displayed in lighted numerals depicting millimeters of mercury. The lighted numerals can be easily read by all team members and will be held on the display board for reference until the next automatic reading. The machine does not forget to take the readings in moments of stress. The information has high credibility, as it is taken in a uniform, objective "machine" manner.

The maxillofacial surgeon or other individual concerned with team treatment of patients with traumatic injuries will probably be exposed to invasive techniques of blood pressure monitoring. One fairly common technique involves the cannulation of the radial artery with a percutaneous indwelling 20 gauge Teflon catheter. This can be connected to a transducer to allow beat by beat oscilloscopic display of the pulse contour for determining blood pressure and heart rate. Determination of stroke volume can be made; arterial blood samples can be obtained for blood gas analysis. Alternatively, the same catheter could be connected to a pressure infusor and simple aneroid manometer to provide a cheap, simple, and reliable measure of the blood pressure. Samples could also be drawn. The major disadvantage is that no hard copy record would be available.

Perometer

Measurement of fluid and blood volume is an important consideration when monitoring the cardiovascular system. It is possible for blood loss from some dental procedures, notably oral surgery and periodontal surgery, to exceed one or more units of blood (a unit of blood is equivalent to 500 ml).[11] Though this is not necessarily a significant loss for the healthy adult patient, some patients cannot afford such blood loss, and occasionally a postoperative transfusion is indicated. Methods of evaluating the amount of blood loss include measuring the blood in suction bottles and estimating the blood contained in wet and dry sponges and drapes, gowns, and gloves. Sponges of a known weight, containing only blood and no saline or irrigating solution, may be weighed to determine the amount of blood contained in them. A more satisfactory method for determining blood loss involves use of a "perometer."[9J] This is essentially a washing machine, complete with a spin dryer, and containing a colorimetric device for the measurement of hemoglobin. The hemoglobinometer is set to the known presurgical hemoglobin values of the patient, as determined by the routine preoperative hemoglobin laboratory test. As the operation progresses, all fluid and blood-stained articles are placed in the machine. The blood-laden water from the washing machine is constantly circulated through the hemoglobinometer, and the amount of blood loss in liters or fractions of a liter is read out on a dial. By this technique the doctor may be apprised of the amount of blood loss on a frequent basis, and the blood lost may be replaced precisely by transfusion if indicated.

Doppler

An extremely sensitive and accurate method for indirect, noninvasive blood pressure monitoring is provided by the ultrasonic Doppler flow detector.[9K] This instrument is used for making difficult systolic pressure measurements, and can detect systolic pressures as low as 10 millimeters of mercury. The Doppler probe consists of two crystals, one of which sends a beam of ultrasound energy into the skin, while the other receives the reflected waves. These reflected waves come from underlying tissue and from the moving red cells. Since the underlying tissue is stationary, the frequency of waves reflected from it is exactly the same as the frequency of the transmitted waves. However, the reflected waves from anything in motion (blood) are of a different frequency owing to the Doppler effect. What one hears from the speaker is the frequency difference between the transmitted and received waves. Because of the random velocity of the blood cells, the sound is not a pure tone, but a hissing noise. The pitch of this noise is proportional to the velocity of the moving blood.

To use the Doppler in instances when an ordinary stethoscope will not function, one simply applies an ordinary blood pressure cuff above the elbow. The flat Doppler probe is placed over the radial artery before the cuff is inflated. The cuff is inflated above the systolic pressure and then deflated. A pulsing flow sound is heard during that portion of the cardiac cycle that represents systole. Diastolic pressures are not easily measured with this device.

CENTRAL STATION MONITORING

The greatest utilization of biomedical electronic and mechanical monitoring is found in the intensive care and cardiac care units. Here patients with cardiac disease not only are under the constant observation of trained ancillary personnel but are also connected to electronic and mechanical instruments which determine their physiologic state from minute to minute. This monitoring is made easier by use of a console that will receive information from the various individual instruments. The information is registered on the display area of the console for easy viewing. Parameters such as pulse rate, ECG, blood pressure, temperature, and respiration can be followed. Many of the instruments are of modular design to permit rapid replacement of a defective instrument. Closed circuit television is also being used to monitor the patient visually and to assist in prevention of problems which can only be detected by direct observation.

Computers are being used by many hospitals to monitor patients in intensive care and cardiac care units, as well as in the operating rooms. The computer is programmed to scan the sensors on a group of subjects in sequence. If abnormal data are received from one patient, a signal will immediately alert hospital personnel, start emergency equipment, or provide other programmed services. The computer is also being used as a diagnostic and treatment aid. The day is rapidly approaching when simple automatic corrective procedures will be instituted when the physiological event exceeds preset limits; for example, a computer may be programmed to give blood when the arterial pressure is low. Computers are also good for automatic measurement acquisition, display, storage, retrieval, and charting of information for medical records.

ELECTROCARDIOGRAPHY

As was mentioned earlier in the text, the electrocardioscope may be used as an aid in monitoring the cardiovascular system during ultralight general anesthesia. In utilizing the electrocardioscope and electrocardiogram to monitor the conduction system of the heart, we are most interested in recognition of the normal and abnormal rate and rhythm patterns. We are also interested in what clinical significance these patterns will have and how they affect the administration of a safe anesthetic to our patients. It is not our desire or our need to go into the subtleties of electrocardiologic diagnosis or treatment of these abnormalities. Our purpose for inclusion of this material is to make the members of the team aware of another aid that may be of assistance in monitoring selected patients during general anesthesia.

As interpretation of the information provided by the ECG is less obvious than that provided by other monitoring devices discussed in this chapter, additional explanatory material will be presented.

The electrocardioscope is differentiated from the electrocardiogram in that the latter provides a permanent electrocardiographic record on paper, whereas the former presents to the observer only a transient tracing on the oscilloscope screen. As continual monitoring of the patient by the electrocardiogram would be impractical, the electrocardioscope is commonly used for routine continuous monitoring, and a permanent record is made of only the more important tracings noted.

Electrophysiology

Whenever muscle activity occurs, electrical activity must also occur, and this is what is recorded by the ECG. The inside of any muscle cell carries a negative charge and the outside of the cell a positive one. The resting polarized cell has no potential difference between any two points of the cell. At a point of stimulation the cell potential drops to zero because the cell membrane becomes electrically permeable and the charges on the two sides neutralize each other. A wave of excitation is then created, which spreads over the muscle cell, producing a potential difference between any two points on the cell until the entire surface of the muscle has lost its positive charge and is depolarized.

Since the heart is a pump made up of muscle cells, when one point is stimulated the wave of propagation spreads until the entire surface loses its positive charge and becomes depolarized. The normal pathway for this wave of propagation is formation of the impulses in the sinoatrial (S-A) node, lying in the wall of the right atrium near the mouth of the superior vena cava. It spreads over the wall of the atrium to the atrioventricular (A-V) node near the coronary sinus. From here it spreads toward the ventricle through the A-V bundle of His to the left and right conduction bundles passing down the septum. The wave reaches the Purkinje fibers under the endocardium and spreads outward through the myocardium to the epicardium, reaching the apex first, then the lateral wall of the right and left ventricles and base of the heart, where it terminates.

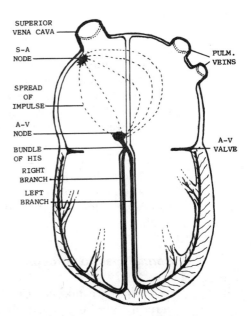

Figure 4–15 Electrical excitation of heart. Normal pathway of impulses from S-A node to myocardium. (Hopkins, H. U.: Leopold's Principles and Methods of Physical Diagnosis. 3rd ed. Philadelphia, W. B. Saunders Co., 1965.)

From early fetal life until death this electrical stimulation and subsequent beating of the heart continues automatically and rhythmically. Interruptions of this usual rhythm are referred to as dysrhythmias or arrhythmias. They are important clinically because they can produce important clinical symptoms, disability, and death. The clinical significance of some rhythm disturbances has been misappraised and has led to needless disability.

As was mentioned earlier in the chapter, the ECG is the means by which many of the arrhythmias can be recognized. In order to recognize the abnormal, we must first be able to recognize the normal. Certain standards have been developed and accepted in the use of the ECG. These standards include the placement of electrodes and the paper which receives the tracing of the cardiac activity.

Leads

Because the total potential developed in the heart at any one time can be expressed as a vector, the form of any ECG tracing obtained will depend to a great extent on the placement of the electrodes. The voltage recorded is the difference between the voltage at these two points. Using the principles of the equilateral triangle as suggested by Einthoven, the three standard limb leads evolved. The difference in potential between the right and left arms is called lead I, that between the right arm and left leg lead II, and that between the left arm and left leg lead III. These are called bipolar leads because they record the difference between the two potentials.

There are also unipolar leads which record the actual potential and not the difference between the two potentials. Greater sensitivity is obtainable with the unipolar leads, and for that reason they are used more for diagnostic purposes than in surgery, where drapes and activity about the patient make these leads difficult to use.

Paper

ECG paper is standardized, and when a direct record is made the various intervals and amplitudes can be easily measured by inspection or with calipers for evaluation of the tracing and diagnosis of the patient's cardiac condition. The standard machine moves the paper at a rate of 25 mm per second. Each small box enclosed by faint vertical lines on the paper represents 0.04 second. Each large box of five small horizontal boxes represents 0.2 second and is enclosed by the heavy vertical lines. Each vertical large box is 5 mm tall (Fig. 4–16). One millivolt equals 10 mm or two large vertical boxes. When using the electrocardioscope as a monitoring device, one finds that these measurements are not as readily apparent as tracings on paper. If precise values are desired, the cardioscope is connected to a direct writer and a tracing is made on ECG paper.

Normal Electrocardiogram

When we take an ECG on an individual with a normal, healthy heart, certain definite deflections occur in the tracing. Each of these deflections

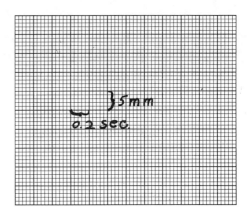

Figure 4–16 Electrocardiogram paper.

indicates certain actions of the heart. Because the cause of the deflections was unknown originally, the developer of the device, Einthoven, ascribed to them the letters P,Q,R,S, and T. The first wave of the complex, the P wave, is caused by the depolarization of the atria when the stimulus starting in the S-A node passes over them. The atria actually contract right after the beginning of the P wave. Then there is an interval of little or no deflection. This is followed by another group of deflections called the QRS complex. This group of deflections is caused by the depolarization which occurs as the impulse from the AV node passes over the ventricular musculature. Following the QRS group, there is another period of little or no potential which is called the S-T interval. This is followed by the T wave, which is caused by the repolarization of the

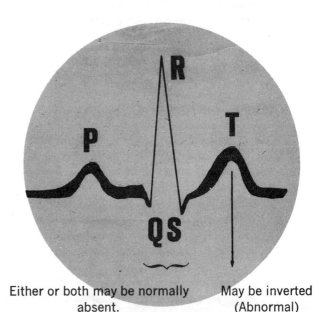

Figure 4–17 Normal ECG complex. (Figures 4–17 through 4–27 are taken from the arrhythmia chart prepared in cooperation with Walter S. Graf, M.D., and The Daniel Freeman Hospital, Inglewood, California, by Dallon Instruments, a Division of International Rectifier Corp., El Segundo, California.)

Either or both may be normally absent.

May be inverted (Abnormal)

ONE HEART BEAT

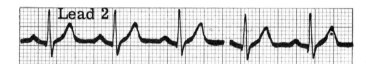

Figure 4–18   Normal ECG tracing — lead II.

ventricles. As has been previously discussed, it is possible to take tracings from a number of different leads (12 or more) by placing the electrodes at various points on the body. For monitoring purposes one lead is selected to monitor throughout the entire case. The best lead for monitoring during anesthesia, according to Wylie,[12] is lead II (Fig. 4–18).

PHYSIOLOGICAL SINUS RHYTHM AND ARRHYTHMIAS

The usual discharge of impulses from the S-A node is between 60 and 100 times a minute. Below 60 times a minute is termed bradycardia and above 100 times a minute is termed tachycardia.

Sinus Arrhythmia (Fig. 4–19)

Sinus arrhythmia is the name given to the minor benign changes associated with respiration. The heart rate increases during the early part of the inspiration and slows during expiration. It is attributed to varying degrees of vagal stimulation and disappears when the breath is held or under general anesthesia. It is not a disease process and seldom causes any untoward clinical symptoms

Sinus Tachycardia (Fig. 4–20)

Sinus tachycardia is an abnormally rapid heart rate, over 100 beats per minute, arising at the normal S-A pacemaker. Causes of sinus tachycardia include stimulation during very light anesthesia, hypoxia, hypotension, exercise, anxiety, fever, and anemia. Sinus tachycardia may or may not be of clinical significance and is not, in itself, indicative of cardiac disease. If severe or prolonged, the tachycardia may lead to cardiac failure.

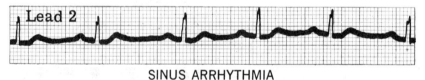

SINUS ARRHYTHMIA
Figure 4–19   Sinus arrhythmia tracing.

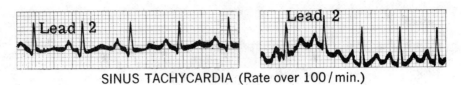

SINUS TACHYCARDIA (Rate over 100/min.)

Figure 4–20   Sinus tachycardia tracing.

Sinus Bradycardia (Fig. 4–21)

Sinus bradycardia is a slow sinus rhythm of less than 60 beats per minute. It is frequently seen in highly trained athletes, probably owing to an increase in vagal tone. Other causes of increased vagal tone include hypotension secondary to hemorrhage and pressure on the eyeballs or carotid sinus. Cyclopropane and halothane anesthesia can also induce sinus bradycardia.

PATHOLOGICAL ARRHYTHMIAS

Premature Contractions

Any region of the heart can prematurely discharge the impulse for contraction with the resultant atrial, nodal, or ventricular premature beat. The exact origin of the premature beat is discernible only after viewing the ECG. Atrial and nodal premature beats are often seen during anesthesia and surgery. The QRS is normal and the prematurities apparently have no special significance. Premature ventricular contractions will be discussed later.

Paroxysmal Tachycardia

Paroxysmal tachycardia is a term applied to attacks of rapid heart action in which ventricular contraction responds to regular impulses arising in a focus removed from the S-A node. The ectopic focus may be in the atria, the A-V node, or the ventricles. The heart rate is 100 beats per minute or more. The paroxysm begins suddenly, may last for minutes or days, and ends abruptly. The beats are absolutely regular. Vagal stimulation may change the rate or stop the paroxysm completely.

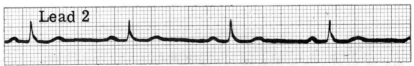

SINUS BRADYCARDIA (Rate less than 60/min.)

Figure 4–21   Sinus bradycardia tracing.

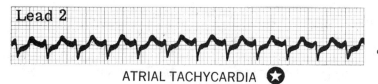

ATRIAL TACHYCARDIA ⭐

Figure 4-22 Atrial tachy-cardia tracing.

Atrial Tachycardia (Fig. 4-22)

Atrial tachycardia is a common cardiac arrhythmia. The rate is 150 to 300 beats per minute with the ventricles responding to each atrial beat. The rapid heart rate tends to make the patient dyspneic and weak owing to decreased arterial blood pressure. The ECG shows a rapid succession of abnormal P waves that are deformed because of the fact that the contraction commences in a focus removed from the S-A node. The QRS complexes are equally rapid but regular and normal in form. The paroxysm may stop abruptly, either spontaneously or with vagal stimulation. There is no temporary slowing with this arrhythmia, in contrast to sinus tachycardia. Atrial tachycardia either will resume slow normal contractions with treatment or it will be unaltered. Syncope is not uncommon during an attack. Clinically, most patients have no organic heart disease and the arrhythmia is purely functional.

Atrial Flutter (Fig. 4-23)

In atrial flutter the atria are contracting at a rate of 230 to 360 times a minute and therefore 230 to 360 P waves are observed on the ECG tracing. The ventricles cannot respond to every impulse, so that there is usually either a 2:1, 3:1, or 4:1 block between the atria and the ventricles, resulting in a ventricular rate of one half, one third, or one fourth the atrial rate. The ECG shows characteristic sawtooth arrangements of the P waves. The P-R interval is absent and the ventricular rate may be regular or irregular.

Atrial Fibrillation (Fig. 4-24)

During atrial fibrillation the atria do not contract as a whole. Small areas of the muscle tissue are stimulated at various times so that there are no true P waves. However, there is usually sufficient potential developed so that we see small "f" (or fibrillary) waves appearing in the tracing. As the impulses reach the A-V node, it is stimulated. It sends its impulse to the bundle of His; if the bundle of His is not in a refractory period, the impulse is transmitted to the

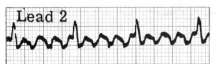

ATRIAL FLUTTER with ⭐
4:1 block

Figure 4-23 Atrial flutter with 4:1 block tracing.

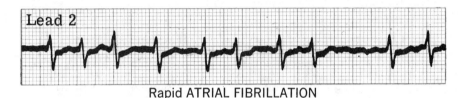

Rapid ATRIAL FIBRILLATION

Figure 4–24   Atrial fibrillation tracing.

ventricles, and this gives a normal QRS and T complex. The QRS and T complexes are unevenly spaced owing to irregularity of the ventricular rate. Usually only one of every four impulses excites the ventricles, so the ventricular rate is one fourth that of the atria. Atrial fibrillation is seen in coronary atherosclerotic heart disease and many other heart diseases and also may be observed in a clinically normal heart.

Premature Ventricular Contractions (PVCs)

As was mentioned earlier, because of the possibility of premature discharge of the impulse, contractions can originate in the ventricular musculature. These contractions may occur in normal healthy persons during excitement, breath-holding, anxiety, fatigue, and smoking, as well as during anesthesia with hypoxia and elevated CO_2 content in the bloodstream.

In PVCs some point in the ventricle becomes hyperirritable and gives off an impulse which passes over the ventricle by an abnormal pathway. When this occurs we ‚see an *abnormal QRS complex*. It is wide, slurred, and notched. The T wave is in the opposite direction from the QRS. There is no P wave preceding a PVC. When impulses from ventricular foci occur regularly with every second beat, the arrhythmia is known as bigeminy; with every third beat, trigeminy. There is also a compensatory pause which assists in the recognition of the PVC. The explanation of the compensatory pause is as follows:

In the beat preceding the PVC, the impulse begins in the S-A node, giving rise to the P wave. This impulse then strikes the A-V node and gives rise to QRS and T complexes. Then, before the atrium can stimulate the ventricle again, the ventricular premature contraction occurs with its abnormal QRS and T complex. When the S-A node now gives off its next impulse, a P wave results. Although the A-V node is stimulated and gives off an impulse, the ventricle is in a refractory period and cannot respond to this stimulus. Therefore, there is a pause until the next impulse leaves the S-A node and reaches the ventricle which reacts and gives the normal QRS and T complex.

A common cause of PVCs is the excessive use of the drug digitalis. The patient may notice a "thumping in the chest" or a "flip-flop heart." An occasional PVC may be innocuous. However, they must be looked upon as *potential precursors of impending ventricular tachycardia and ventricular fibrillation*. Premature ventricular contractions are considered dangerous when they occur in runs of two or more, fall on the T wave, *occur more fre-*

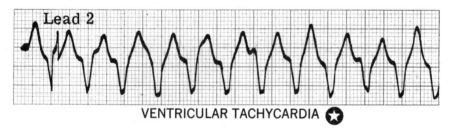

VENTRICULAR TACHYCARDIA ⭐

Figure 4–25 Ventricular tachycardia tracing.

quently than five per minute, or are multifocal as indicated by different shapes to the abnormal QRS complexes.

Experience has shown that placing the patient on 100 per cent oxygen and temporarily terminating the procedure will eliminate the PVCs which are occasionally seen during surgical stimulation in light planes of anesthesia or in episodes of hypoxia. If the abnormal QRS complexes persist, 50 mg of lidocaine is administered intravenously over a one-minute period. Lidocaine should not be used when there is a history of pre-existing complete heart block, since it may cause ventricular arrest.

Ventricular Tachycardia (Fig. 4–25)

Ventricular tachycardia may be described as repeated ventricular premature beats characterized by the aforementioned changes in the QRS and T complex. The rate will usually be from 180 to 250 per minute with a rapid onset. This condition is strongly suggestive of cardiac disease in patients in whom it has not been precipitated by the use of digitalis or other drugs. It sometimes precedes ventricular fibrillation.

Ventricular Fibrillation (Fig. 4–26)

Ventricular fibrillation, the result of a completely haphazard spread of the impulse over the conduction network, causes disorganized and inefficient contraction of the ventricular musculature with resulting circulatory failure. If not corrected immediately, fibrillation will result in death. It may be the terminal event in coronary artery disease or in other forms of heart failure. It will, however, occasionally occur in a healthy patient following minor myocardial infarction, after electric shock, or during general anesthesia in which cyclopropane or halothane has been used, particularly when they have been used with epinephrine.

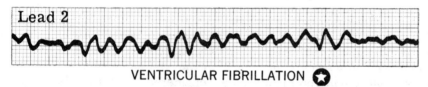

VENTRICULAR FIBRILLATION ⭐

Figure 4–26 Ventricular fibrillation tracing (terminal).

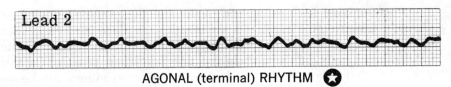

AGONAL (terminal) RHYTHM ⭐

Figure 4–27 Agonal (terminal) rhythm.

Cardiac Standstill

This may be primary or follow ventricular fibrillation. The impulses are no longer functional, and we obtain the agonal rhythm on the cardioscope or ECG tracing (Fig. 4–27). Death is immediate.

Improvements in instrumentation have transformed the electrocardio-scope from a bulky, somewhat awkward device into a compact, portable instrument, which is suitable for use in the dental office. There are certain problems encountered when using the instrument on the patient undergoing ultralight general anesthesia.

The major problem associated with its use on patients receiving ultralight general anesthesia is the distortion of the tracing that is caused by the movement of the patient or slight shifting of the electrodes. The lightly anesthetized patient may respond to a stimulus by extremity movement, and this will cause considerable distortion of the tracing as it moves across the screen. However, with training and experience, team members will quickly be able to differentiate these distortions from arrhythmias which may occur during treatment. Other distortions occasionally seen in dental offices are those caused by the use of x-ray equipment in the area and by a drop in the line voltage common to large medical-dental buildings. These problems have been partially corrected by the use of electronic filters, but as reported by Arbeit et al.[13], these filters may further distort the tracing, and any abnormality detected on the scope must be checked by the ECG tracing taken directly from the patient and not through the filtered cardioscope.

DISCUSSION OF COMBINED MONITORING SYSTEMS

An individual may choose one or several biomedical monitors to supplement the essential direct observation of the patient by himself and other members of the team.* After visual inspection of the patient, a precordial or suprasternal stethoscope is placed. The sounds are transmitted to the ear of the anesthetist via five or six feet of plastic tubing. The anesthetist wears a custom-molded earpiece for sustained comfort. A blood pressure cuff is placed on the patient's arm, and the finger monitor is taped to a finger of the same arm. When used, the electrocardiograph leads of an oscilloscope are connected to the patient, using adhesive electrodes. The carbon dioxide

---

*A hypothetical monitoring system with multiple tools is presented here to demonstrate coordination of many monitoring devices.

analyzer lead is inserted in the anesthesia tubing system near the patient's airway. An electric temperature lead is placed at a convenient point, such as the ear canal. The audio signal of the finger pulse monitor is tuned to a convenient level and the oscilloscope situated so that the visual wave can be easily seen. The number of pulse beats per minute can be seen and heard on the monitor. The oximeter is placed on the ear to monitor arterial blood oxygen. When the blood pressure is to be checked, the cuff is inflated, either manually or with a semiautomatic valve that needs only the touch of a finger or foot to inflate the cuff. As the cuff is inflated above the systolic blood pressure, the audiovisual pulse signals cease owing to the lack of circulation in the lower arm and finger. When the cuff pressure is deflated to the systolic pressure and circulation again reaches the finger pulse monitor, the audio signal is heard, and the pulse wave forms are seen. At this moment the doctor may glance at the conspicuously mounted blood pressure dial to check the systolic pressure. Should it prove difficult to obtain, the Doppler could be used to double-check the systolic pressure. The heart and breath sounds are monitored constantly via the stethoscope and monaural earpiece. If it is desirable to broadcast these sounds to the dental operatory at large, the plastic tubing from the chest piece is connected to a cardiac audio-monitor, which will amplify the heart sounds and enable the entire team to be conscious of the respiratory and cardiac status of the patient. If tidal volume needs to be known, a respirometer can be attached to the expiratory breathing tube. When desired, the oscilloscope is switched from the finger pulse lead to the ECG lead and the electrocardioscopic tracing is seen on the screen, together with an audible "beep" at each heartbeat. The oscilloscope may be connected to a paper writer recorder if a permanent tracing is desired. The CO_2 analyzer indicates the carbon dioxide output of each breath; this, too, is often traced on paper by a recorder — usually a trend recorder operating at a very slow paper speed to conserve paper. The electric thermometer constantly displays the body temperature. A "fail-safe" warning system guards the medical gas supply pressure, and the oxygen alarm monitor follows the percentage of oxygen being delivered.

Desirable variations in this procedure might include the use of an automatic indirect blood pressure monitor to record systolic and diastolic pressure in an automatically activated visual display. A small computer could be used to coordinate all this physiological information by monitoring, alarming, displaying, and printing anesthesia records.

Ploss System

While the doctor is using his sense of sight primarily in the operative field, his auditory sense is available for acoustical monitoring. An interesting and economical system has been developed by Ploss,[14] which allows continuous acoustic monitoring of the patient (Fig. 4–28). A lightweight rubber stethoscope pickup is placed over the brachial artery under the blood pressure cuff. The precordial or pretracheal stethoscope is placed on the chest, and the two stethoscopes are connected to the Ploss Automatic Switch Valve[L]. This valve is activated by cuff inflation pressures to exclude heart and lung sounds while the blood pressure is being determined by auscultation. Imme-

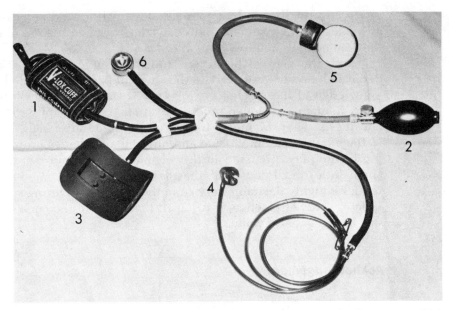

Figure 4–28 Ploss automatic switch valve (center). As the blood pressure cuff (1) is inflated by the squeeze bulb (2), Korotkoff sounds are heard through the rubber acoustic pickup (3) which would be positioned over the brachial artery. These sounds are transmitted to the earpiece (4) and the blood pressure is read on the aneroid manometer (5). As the blood pressure cuff is deflated, the heart sounds are heard from the precordial stethoscope (6).

diately upon cuff deflation, the valve automatically switches back to the heart and lung sounds. The valve can be used with conventional sphygmomanometer squeeze bulbs or operated by the Side-Kick[D] semi-automatic blood pressure cuff inflator. With this system, heart, breath, and pulse sounds may be evaluated acoustically and with a minimum of detraction from the operative procedure. Use of the automatic switch valve described above frees the operator's hand for other duties. If this extreme efficiency is not necessary, a simple plastic or metal three-way valve may be used to channel the sounds manually with equally good acoustic results.

As most vital signs are taken relative to time, it is helpful to have a large electric clock with a sweep second hand prominently located for timing the various measurements.

An anesthesia record detailing the treatment rendered and the vital signs during the procedure is of importance in recapitulating cases at any later date.

SUMMARY AND CONCLUSIONS

Consideration has been given to various methods of evaluating the patient under general anesthesia. These include the fundamental principles of patient observation as well as monitoring by biomedical electronic and mechanical methods. Every doctor is, by virtue of training and experience, almost instinctively aware of the significance of many physiological signs observed visually and by auscultation, palpation, and percussion. Increased awareness of the patient's status can come through the use of one or more of the commercial monitors available.

Both the general practitioner and the surgeon in practice today have dedicated a number of years to the study of basic and applied science. Their knowledge of these sciences, together with the manual dexterity innate in every dental practitioner, predisposes to make them apt students of the art of anesthesia. They are highly trained and skilled individuals. Those interested in the administration of office and hospital anesthetics utilizing the monitoring techniques discussed in this chapter should find that a period of time spent in a formal course of anesthesia training will rapidly equip them to render a highly desirable service to their patients. During such training, and in later years of practice, it is hoped that some of the concepts presented in this text may be of value.

Acknowledgement

Electrocardiogram tracings used in this chapter are published with the permission of Dallon Instruments of El Segundo, California.

REFERENCES

1. Adriani, J.: Techniques and Procedures of Anesthesia. Springfield, Ill., Charles C Thomas, 1964, p. 60.
2. Best, C. H., and Taylor, N. B.: The Physiological Basis of Medical Practice. 4th ed., Baltimore, Williams & Wilkins Company, 1945, p. 373.
3. General anesthesia. In Accepted Dental Therapeutics, 37th ed. Chicago, American Dental Association, 1977, p. 118.
4. Hubbell, A. O., and Krogh, H. W.: Management of intravenous anesthesia to control recovery time. J. Oral Surg. Oral Med. Oral Pathol., 9:403, 1956.
5. Hagen, J. O., and McCarthy, F. M.: General anesthesia for the ambulatory patient: The anesthetic team. J. South. California Dent. Assoc., 37:244, 1969.
6. Ibid.
7. Op. cit., General anesthesia.
8. Ibid.
9. See the manufacturers' list of instruments at the end of this chapter.
10. Quinn, J. R., Spatz, S., Shensa, D. R., and Esway, J. K.: Malignant hyperthermia during an oral surgical procedure; report of a case. J. Oral Surg., 27:266, 1969.
11. Gores, R. J., Royer, R. Q., and Mann, F. D.: Blood loss during operation for multiple extractions with alveoplasty and oral surgical procedures. J. Oral Surg., 13:299, 1955.
12. Wylie, W. D., and Churchill-Davidson, H. C.: A Practice of Anesthesia. 2nd ed., Chicago, Year Book, 1966, pp. 465–483.
13. Arbeit, S. R., Rubin, I. L., and Gross, H.: Dangers in interpreting the electrocardiogram from the oscilloscope monitor. J.A.M.A., 211:253, 1970.
14. Ploss, R. E.: Simple constant monitoring system. Anesthesiology, 16:466, 1955.

MANUFACTURERS' LIST

A. Temp-Away: Becton-Dickinson
                                     Division of Becton, Dickinson and
                                     Company
                                     Rutherford, New Jersey 07070

B. Tempra-Dot: Organon Pharmaceuticals
                                     A Division of Organon Inc.
                                     West Orange, New Jersey, 07052

C. Electronic Thermometer: Yellow Springs Instrument Co., Inc.
                                     Box 279
                                     Yellow Springs, Ohio 45387

D. Fail-Safe: Ohio Medical Products
   Ohio Side Kick: P. O. Box 7550
                                     Madison, Wisconsin 53707

E_1 Capnograph: Beckman Instrument Co.
                                     2500 Harbor Blvd.
                                     Fullerton, California 92634

E_2 Capnograph: Corpul Metrix Inc.
                                     6415 S. W. Canyon Court Suite 50
                                     Portland, Oregon 97221

F. Oxygen Alarm Monitor: Teledyne Analytical Instruments
                                     333 West Mission Drive
                                     San Gabriel, California 91776

G. Blood Gas Oximeter: Hewlett-Packard
                                     175 Wyman Street
                                     Waltham, Mass. 02173

H. Pulse Monitor: San-Ei Instrument Co., Ltd.
                                     1-89, Kashiwagi, Shinjuku
                                     Tokyo, Japan

I. Custom Monaural Ear-Mold: Royale Laboratories
                                     1238 E. Broadway
                                     Glendale, California 91205

J. Perometer: Particle Data Incorporated
                                     P. O. Box 265
                                     Elmhurst, Illinois 60126

K. Doppler: Parks Electronic Laboratory
                                     P. O. Box B.B.
                                     Beavertown, Oregon 97005

L. Ploss System: 3M Company, Medical Products Division
                                     3M Center
                                     St. Paul, Minnesota 55101

5

DRUGS: USE AND ABUSE

ROBERT BRUCE STEINER

INTRODUCTION

For those who have been exposed to the first and second editions, this introduction is repetitive, but it is also, I'm sorry to say, apropos! Things change and yet somehow remain basically the same. Greed and profound lack of respect and concern for fellow man is still the vanguard, creed, or philosophy (you choose) of a small group of manufacturers and retailers who, like the poor, it appears will always be with us.

The Food and Drug Administration (FDA), until lately a flickering candle of light on the horizon, has grown into a powerful beam searching into some of the darker recesses of the pharmaceutical industry. Unfortunately, it appears that its zeal and exuberance are overflowing (as is the case with most government entities) in certain questionable areas (as, for example, in the prohibitions on saccharin) but, nonetheless, some control is badly needed.

"For many years a vast system of medical empiricism, sustained by popular credulity and the sanction of government, has prevailed in this country to the serious detriment of the public health and morals.

"The increase of empiricism and of patent medicines within [this century] is an evil over which the friends of science and humanity can never cease to mourn."

A new and timely warning concerning our contemporary "medical specialists" on television? Hardly; this excerpt is taken from House Report No. 52, 30th Congress (2nd Session), 1849.

"Americans are now paying the greatest price they have ever paid for worthless nostrums, ineffectual and potentially dangerous devices, treatments given by unqualified practitioners, food fads, and un-needed diet supplements and other alluring products or services that make misleading promises of cure or end to pain.

"It is incredible that a wealthy nation, priding itself on enlightenment and its thirst for progress should pay such a heavy penalty for ignorance or lack of adequate enforcement."

More verbose and of a larger scope, but the basic theme and tenets are exactly the same. Is this another editorial from the nineteenth century? No, it is an excerpt from the report of the Williams Subcommittee, U.S. Senate, 89th Congress (1st Session), 1965.[61] It specifies, exemplifies, illuminates, and enumerates the odds we face and the progress we've made.

When you finish perusing this chapter you will probably be aware that it is basically negative in tone and content. Before becoming critical of this approach and comfortably certain of your ability to resist the medical hucksters, consider what they are offering: promises of a life free from worries, pain, insomnia, tension, constipation, tired blood, wrinkles, halitosis, weak teeth, body odor, and pimples. Goebbels' theory of conversion of the masses to a preplanned line of thought by continual, monotonous repetition of the big lie mesmerized not only the ignorant and uninformed but also the educated, many with IQ's near and in the genius category.

Dental practitioners are not immune. Because ours is a healing art, we have been trained and suffused with the desire to cure disease and/or alleviate suffering, and we may be more prone to succumb to these blandishments than are our lay brothers. It should not be our role to preach or foster distrust or disillusionment in our patients, but to leaven the euphoria with common sense and to substitute hard facts for wishful thoughts.

There is a moral, ethical, and legal responsibility we must accept with our diplomas — that of analyzing, dissecting, and then accepting or discarding the claims that come not only from Madison Avenue but also from our well-intentioned, but not always well-informed, detail persons. By virtue of didactic education and clinical practice, we know that quackery still flourishes, but that fluoridation is an explosive issue; that *some* drugs are really miraculous, but that *all* are protoplasmic poisons. But do our patients know this?

Do they know that of the approximately 400 new drug products which appear on counter shelves every year, roughly 20 are new compounds whereas the others represent new salts of the same drug, minor changes in structure (such as the exchange of one halogen [Cl] for another [Br]), and mixtures of old brand names? I doubt it!

It is still the popular lay concept that drugs will cure or alleviate almost any misery with great speed and complete safety, and many of us are guilty of subscribing to and encouraging this attitude. Aspirin and its prototypes relieve headache and hangover, antibiotics easily destroy bacteria, and tranquilizers reduce nervous tension. But this supposedly simple and safe alkali-neutralizes-acid kind of drug action is so rare as to be almost nonexistent. Aspirin can cause rash, asthma, and fatal allergic reactions in some persons. Antibiotics produce a swarm of serious disorders. And tranquilizers often give rise to a series of unwanted effects which range from muscular dysfunction to liver malfunctions.

It is an old medical axiom that the use of any drug is a carefully calculated risk. The lack of understanding by the general public that drug action is not simple, that totally unforeseen results can occur with the administration of any medicine, and that newly discovered drugs may have hidden and exotic toxicities which are not revealed until they are widely used, recently led our nation to the brink of what one writer has termed "drug hysteria." We emerged from this state of near-panic with some more federal laws, several scores of lawsuits, and a new anxiety named "drug safety."

Since 1938 no new medicinal agent has been marketed unless the Food and Drug Administration was satisfied that the compound was relatively safe when used according to directions. "Relatively safe" drugs appear to be the best that we can ever hope for. The Surgeon General of the United States has used the phrases "relatively quite safe," and "relatively completely safe." These terms reflect his considered opinion and post a warning that there is a calculated risk involved in the use of any drug or chemical compound.[8]

There is a general tendency to underestimate the toxicity of drugs. Diverse reasons are advanced to explain this phenomenon: overwhelming advertising, in which the patient invariably experiences a pleasing result from taking "medicine"; aesthetic design of both pill and package; natural optimism of the average human; difficulty in recognizing certain types of toxicity because of obscure symptoms; and reluctance of drug manufacturers to list apparent or potential toxic effects of a product.

Broad statistics on episodes of serious toxicity or deaths from drug reactions are either not available or nonexistent. This fact in no way leavens the magnitude of the problem. A significant clue is the sheer abundance of articles relating to toxicity in the medical and allied literature. If this seems undismaying, a survey made in one of our largest teaching medical centers revealed *that toxic reaction to drugs constituted the greatest single cause of hospitalization in the medical service of that institution.*

The avalanches of new products and concomitant advertising, plus the pressures from patients and salesmen alike, pose a problem of primary concern in the study of pharmacology and chemotherapy. The multiplicity of "Siamese" compounds that emerge in the wake of a new and unique drug, especially one which opens fresh vistas or approaches to the control of disease, is certainly an understandable, if not always meritorious, aspect of the free enterprise system, in which failure to compete may mean failure to exist.

Each pharmaceutical company feels that in order to remain competitive in a highly competitive field, it must produce a related or similar product. The end result of this is a spray of congeners which many times yield confusion and frustration to even the most perceptive of our colleagues in the dental, medical, and pharmaceutical professions.

One of the paradoxes of modern chemotherapy is that in our preoccupation with the formulation or discovery of new drugs we seem to forget that their safe and effective use rests ultimately on the practitioners' understanding of current pharmacologic concepts.

Drug intoxication as a topic or an entity must necessarily deal not only with the chemical or agent and its inherent properties but also with the existing state of health of the patient for whom it is prescribed. If a drug is to be used intelligently and safely for the prevention, treatment, or diagnosis of disease, it is imperative that the clinician have information or experience regarding its physiologic effects on both the healthy and the diseased organism.

One basic consideration or rule of thumb which may pre-empt all others is that the existing degree of irritability of the patient's central nervous system determines the amount or dosage of the drug prescribed for that patient. Conditions which *increase* irritability are fear, pain, fever, thyrotoxicosis, alcoholism, excessive musculature, and toxic phenomena → high BMR or higher doses. Conditions which *decrease* irritability are shock, hypothyroidism (myxedema), Addison's disease, senility, and asthenic or wasting diseases → low BMR or lower doses.

Other predominant factors in the choice and dosage of a drug if it is to be safely employed for therapy are race, sex, weight, temperament, environment, route and time of administration, heredity, allergy, and, of course, age.

Race

Orientals are ordinarily more sensitive to depressant drugs, and deeply pigmented races are much less sensitive than others to the mydriatic action of locally applied sympathomimetic amines. In the same vein, it would be futile to accept these or similar observations as more than a guide in attempting to adjust dosage or evaluate inherent sensitivity or toxicity because of, or on account of, specific racial background.

Sex

There are some indications that the sexes respond differently in quantitative terms to drugs, but according to most clinicians if these differences really exist they are slight and in the main relatively unimportant. Nevertheless, it is inadvisable to give the same dosage to a diminutive female as you would to a husky male, other things being equal. It is just the "other things" — temperament, environment, etc. — that matter, however. Of course, in the pregnant female, one has to consider the potential harmfulness of some drugs to the fetus when given in full dosage to the mother, or the toxic effect on the nursing infant through drugs excreted in the milk.

Weight

Empirical clinical practice proceeds on the assumption that it is only common sense to give smaller doses of potent drugs to emaciated, lethargic, or underdeveloped patients than to our corpulent citizens. Drugs are habitually researched and tested on the basis of dosage per kilogram of body weight, and we have been cozened into believing that this is the proper "scientific" approach. However, there is little real justification for the rigid acceptance of such a practice. The imponderables of the relationship of weight to blood volume, individual metabolism, and the inequalities in fat content in individuals of the same weight make a good case for a flexible approach in interpreting a patient's needs when weight is the only factor in determining drug dosage and toxicity.

Temperament

The firmly based clinical impression that individuals respond differently to drugs according to "temperamental makeup" is a dogma embraced by a large majority of practitioners and prescribers of medicines. Easily excited, unstable, neurotic people appear prone to react excessively, although sometimes their state of hyperexcitement and apprehension necessitates the use, in them, of stronger than normal premedication and therapeutic dosage of an appropriate agent.

Environment

Socioeconomic stress and strain are environmental factors that presumably may affect responses to certain types of drugs. Worry, undernourishment, and low resistance are indigenous to low income groups; therefore patients in this category may exhibit other than normal responses to the usual quantitative dosage prescribed.

Climate, humidity, and altitude may affect drug selection and application in many respects, some of which are not yet documented. But it is fairly well accepted that relative oxygen deprivation, from whatever cause, increases sensitivity to a great variety and number of agents.

Route of Administration

The way in which a drug is administered may have a profound influence on the effects achieved. Many agents are not reliable or efficacious when taken orally. Conversely, other agents cannot or should not be injected parenterally. Others must be inhaled to be useful. The astute therapist should have a thorough knowledge of a drug's assimilation before maximum benefit and avoidance of toxicity can be obtained from its use.

Time of Administration

The response expected from a drug after administration is modified favorably or unfavorably by the *time* of administration. Body physiology changes with time and activity, a consideration which determines the most propitious moment for the ingestion or application of the agent selected to impart the desired alteration or alleviation of a pathologic entity.

Heredity

Heredity can make the same drug a boon to one patient and a poison to another. Although knowledge of genetic factors is still rather primitive, the potential reactor can often be identified, too. Wide variations in the rate and pattern of drug metabolism are often accounted for by genetically determined enzyme systems. Half of the population are either fast or slow metabolizers of isoniazid, a drug widely used in the treatment of tuberculosis. This difference has definitely been proved to be inheritable, according to Dr. Bert LaDu of the New York University School of Medicine. Dicumarol is another drug in which dosage varies considerably because of other genetic factors. One 73-year-old man had to take 20 times the "normal" dose before the drug was effective.[29]

Allergy

Allergy has been defined as immunity gone wrong. Immunity relates to those processes in which the introduction of a foreign substance into the organism causes no clinically evident reaction.

For over 50 years histamine has been implicated in anaphylaxis. Recently other substances (SRS, kinins, and serotonin) have been indicated to help share the blame. One reason for enlarging the list of culprits is that antihistamine drugs are completely ineffective in some cases of allergy or altered acquired immunologic response.

Because of the rampant confusion and the differences in approach and treatment, the practical importance of distinguishing toxicity from true allergy is undebatable in these days of greatly expanded drug therapy. In dealing with a toxic or side effect, a simple reduction of the dose may relieve or eradicate untoward symptoms or problems and allow the important or desired therapeutic effect of the drug to be retained. In dealing with an allergy, dose size is almost totally unrelated to the magnitude of the effect, and the drug must be immediately and completely withdrawn and not repeated. The differential diagnosis of allergy from toxicity and idiosyncrasy in obscure cases depends on these factors when a drug is suspect:

1. If reducing the dose reduces or eliminates the symptoms, it is toxicity.
2. If the phenomena in question arise with the initial dose, it is probably idiosyncrasy.
3. If ensuing normal doses produce redness, rash, or hives on the skin, rather sudden edema of the limbs, face or trachea, asthma, or gastrointestinal cramps, it is allergy.

CBC studies are helpful to confirm a suspected allergy in that they usually show less than 30 round cells and an increase in eosinophils.

A better understanding of allergic phenomena and new techniques and drugs to interdict or negate the detrimental effects are in trial at this writing. (See Chapter 7 for a complete coverage of this entity.)

Age

Although drug dosage in infants and children is usually determined by Young's modulus or a similar body weight-age formula, dosage in the elderly is modified as a precautionary measure because the absorptive, distributive, metabolic, and excretionary functions of geriatric patients are often altered appreciably and can be widely divergent from the norm.

Pediatrics.   Children are not miniature adults! Their reactions to and tolerance of drugs are often uniquely pediatric. It is poor practice to halve the adult dose because the intended recipient is half the adult size!

Children, especially infants, have underdeveloped livers and enzyme systems—the principal areas for drug detoxification. An immature physiology cannot cope with some agents except in minimal amounts. Evidence suggests permanent damage to growth or maturation of specific organs and systems.

Modell has repeatedly warned that the younger the child, the more striking the problem. Fortunately the dental clinician seldom deals with infants, happily avoiding most of these problems. However, antibiotics, sedatives, and analgesics, three entities common in pedodontic practice, are categories in which child response may differ grossly from adult response.

Intensive or pervasive evaluation and identification of abnormalities, congenital or acquired, and prior and/or current pathosis will dictate the degree of need and influence the dose. The most accurate method of determining normal dosage which is basic for successful therapy is based on the exterior epithelial area of the child's body—ordinarily difficult to measure. A safe and rapid method, using weight and surface area data, is this formula: $0.7 \times$ weight $+ 10 = \%$ of adult dosage.

Lastly, in situations in which exactness is mandatory, the agent must be injected even though psychically traumatic and distasteful for all. Refusal to swallow, spitting, and vomiting make the oral route precarious and the ingested quantity unknown. Rectal suppositories or liquids are also unpleasant and unreliable, frequently precipitating instant bowel movements or uneven and faulty absorption.

Geriatrics.   Geriatrics is a fairly new term with many connotations, depending on one's viewpoint. The very word is paramount to some, and anathema to others. Suffice it to say here that it is accepted to mean those citizens (more than 10 per cent of our population) who are past the age of 65. Elderly people often present real problems for business and industry, their families, and their doctors. This appears to be a cruel and tragic simplification of a complex situation, but the premise is true, the people are here, and they must be dealt with. The rather archaic attitudes of industry regarding the usefulness of those over 65 are hopefully about to change. If one considers that the very nature of our efforts in all the healing arts is guaranteed to perpetuate the geriatric scene, it may generate more incentive to cope with the special problems indigenous to it. The usual geriatric patient has a major flaw—it may be physiologic, psychologic, or economic. Regardless of the source, it will affect his attitude toward you and the proposed therapy. Since drugs occupy or encompass a part of virtually all treatment plans and a patient's attitude may have a profound influence on his reactions to these drugs, we have returned full circle to our topic.

Besides his questionable response to the routine dental medicines, synergism, interaction, incompatibility, and additive and cumulative effects are always major considerations in the treatment program of a geriatric patient. It is rare to encounter an aged individual without a systemic malfunction requiring not just one but a planned regimen of drugs to regulate or maintain near-normal or adequate body physiology. Arthritis, hypertension, arteriosclerosis, angina, edema, emphysema, glaucoma, cataracts, menopause, prostatitis — some of these are part and parcel of the everyday existence of most senior citizens.

Steroids, salicylates, thiazides, digitalis, hypotensives, anticoagulants, tranquilizers, insulin, antibiotics, ointments — the roster is endless! The aged learn to live with discomfort, pain, and pills.

A dialogue history with special emphasis on prescription drugs is mandatory before therapy of any kind is attempted. Consultation with the patient's physician may be desirable.

The chart on drug interactions at the end of this chapter precludes a repetitive listing at this point.

Before leaving this topic, two important points are pertinent:

1. It is not unusual for an elderly person to have an ambiguous reaction to drugs (i.e., excitement from barbiturates or scopolamine). If anticipated, surprise will not be an unsettling or damaging factor, and restorative, supportive, or resuscitative therapy will be instituted without doubt or delay.

2. The elderly are perfect "pigeons" for over-the-counter panaceas, and this is not difficult to understand. Disillusioned and/or disappointed with a lack of efficacy or speed in the standard prescription remedies, they turn, often in desperation, to patent potions for relief. Most of these miracle compounds are ordinary, many are frauds, and some are dangerous.

A list of nonprescription remedies, their chemical formulae, and their frequency of use are a very important part of a geriatric patient's history. "To be forewarned is to be forearmed" is not a foolish cliché!

Pregnancy

Unnecessary or excessive medication of the pregnant patient should be stringently avoided. It is known that the fetus is incapable of metabolizing or detoxifying certain drugs that are nevertheless safe and effective in the mother. This is primarily due to immature liver and enzyme function. Most drugs will pass the placental barrier, especially the lipid soluble drugs (includes most anesthetics), and many of their effects are not yet fully known. (Only those drugs over 1000 molecular weight are immune.)

The agent ingested by the mother may directly affect the fetus (or its metabolites may be toxic) according to its distribution to or affinity for fetal tissue, or it may exert an indirect effect by interfering with metabolic processes in the mother. This results in the transmission of potentially toxic metabolites from mother to fetus or embryo. Organogenesis is a factor during the first trimester only.

Congenital malformations occur most readily during the stages of early cellular differentiation (10 to 15 days after conception). Phocomelia (thalidomide), narcotic addiction (heroin), and tooth discoloration (tetracyclines) are but three common and dramatic malformations among many that are known or thought to occur. Teratogenetics, the science of drug-induced birth defects, must be ever in mind when planning treatment for the pregnant patient. Only those agents known to be safe are considered, and all medications should be kept to that minimum required for effective therapy. Seventy-five per cent of all spontaneous abortions occur before the sixteenth week; the second trimester is the safest time for anesthetics and surgery.

But therapeutic nihilism arising from fear of jeopardizing the intrauterine patient by maternal medication is unjustified. In fact, there are times during pregnancy when the withholding of a drug would cause a much more serious consequence than the possible adverse effects to either the mother or child. It is an intolerable judgment if fear of adverse effects to the offspring deprives the mother of drugs that could be essential to her well-being and even to the successful outcome of the pregnancy itself.

Analgesics. Narcotic and non-narcotic analgesics all cross the placenta. The narcotics (especially morphine and heroin) may cause addiction in utero, and severe respiratory depression, miosis, and withdrawal symptoms at birth. Codeine is safe.

Hypnotics. Barbiturates yield a level in the fetus of up to 70 per cent of maternal level, but unless the mother suffers derangement of physiology during a general anesthetic or overdose of oral medication, there is no evidence of induced abortion or congenital malformations with this class of drugs.

Antibiotics. The penicillin family is safe in every area unless severe allergy rears its ugly head. Erythromycin is blameless too, but all other commonly used antimicrobials are either irrevocably harmful or restricted to certain periods during the pregnancy. Included are sulphonamides, the tetracycline family, streptomycin, lincomycin, Clindamycin, and Novobiocin. Consultation with the obstetrician is mandatory if severe or unyielding dental infection exists.

Antihistamines. Diphenhydramine and chlorpheniramine are known to be inert in the fetus and may be prescribed with safety. Diphenhydramine may also be useful as an antinauseant and mild soporific, two areas in pregnancy that frequently need alteration and medication.

Antacids. All aluminum salts containing antacids (Amphojel, Phosphaljel, Maalox) cannot cross the placenta; therefore, they are not a toxic factor. Kaopectate falls in the same category.

Tranquilizers. Many of this class are known to be dangerous, and others are highly suspect. Chlordiazepoxide (diazepam is thought to be similar in action) passes the barrier 100 per cent, and, although teratogenicity has not been proved, these drugs should be used with caution during the first trimester.

Chloral hydrate and the barbiturates ought to be given first consideration when sedation of the pregnant patient is desirable or mandatory.

Local Analgesics. Local analgesics, especially the aniline series, are not restricted when proper techniques (aspiration, etc.) are employed.

As an addendum to this general classification, I believe a listing of specific drugs that the dentist may use, or at least be interested in, is essential for the complete protection of our unborn children. The medication or agent is listed along with its adverse effects in Table 5-1, taken from Martin's Hazards of Medication, a textbook of infinite worth.

DRUGS IN LACTATING MOTHERS

Drugs administered during lactation follow a similar pattern of action and distribution as in pregnancy, with some startling exceptions. Morphine and codeine do not occur in milk at all, while other narcotics appear in sufficient strength to sedate the nursing infant.

ASA appears in moderate amounts. To negate any possible interactions, the mother should take the tablet just prior to nursing.

Barbital is completely absent, but NaP shows intraces (mgm), and phenobarbital may be present in high enough concentration to cause enzyme induction in the infant's immature liver.

Oxacillin is the only common antibiotic that does not appear in the milk, while penicillin in even trace amounts could precipitate sensitivity reactions in later life. Erythromycin is relatively innocuous, and it is often the drug of choice in most dental infections.

Diazepam may cause a noticeable sedative effect on the child, which could impair feeding.

Local anesthetics are generally innocuous.

As a general rule, all drugs that cause central nervous system depression are suspect until proved innocent, except ethanol, whose ingestion, unless gross, is not contraindicated. Analgesics, hypnotics, and tranquilizers, along with general anesthetics, fall in this class. *The dose is directly related to the effect.* Minimal effective amount for the shortest possible time is the paramount rule.

Teratogenicity is and should be a frightening word! The general welfare of the embryo, fetus, and neonate (along with the mother) must be the prime concern of every prescriber of medicine or chemotherapy. Since this topic is substantial enough for a tome of its own, only those drugs of a dangerous nature and those that can be prescribed and used with safety are mentioned. Many of the newer compounds are missing because insufficient data are available. Others are missing because they have no real place in the dental armamentarium.

When in doubt – don't!

Chronic Illness

All the previous factors are important and unavoidably pertinent in the treatment or therapy plans for our patients, but none more so than in the state of chronic illness. Here is probably the classic challenge to our therapeutic acumen. How best to approach the debilitated patient, whose well-being depends on a balanced regimen of drugs to maintain an acceptable plateau of health and well-being? The ever-burgeoning hordes of people whose function and comfort depend on delicately balanced programs of chemotherapy have every right to expect that their precarious existence will not be jeopardized by careless or ignorant administration of agents which disturb this balance or are incompatible with those drugs already in use.

DRUG DEFINITIONS

The following definitions may help dispel some of the foggy notions concerning all drugs.

TABLE 5-1 LIST OF MEDICATIONS AND ADVERSE EFFECTS
(FROM MARTIN, HAZARDS OF MEDICATION)

Drugs	Adverse Effects
Acetophenetidin	Methemoglobinemia
Alphaprodine (Nisentil)	Fetal respiratory depression
Anesthetics (Volatile)	Depressed fetal respiration
Androgens	Advanced bone age; clitoral enlargement; labial fusion; masculinization
Barbiturates	Depressed respiration
Bromides	Neonatal skin eruptions (bromoderma)
Chloral hydrate (large doses)	Fetal death
Chloramphenicol (Chloromycetin)	Fetal death; gray syndrome
Chlorpromazine	Neonatal jaundice; mortality; prolonged extra-pyramidal signs
Cortisone	Cleft palate
Ether	Neonatal apnea
Ganglionic blocking agents	Neonatal ileus
Iodides	Goiter
Lysergic acid diethylamide (LSD)	Chromosomal damage; stunted offspring
Mepivacaine (Carbocaine)	Fetal bradycardia; neonatal depression
Methadone	Fetal respiratory depression
Morphine	Initial neonatal addiction; respiratory depression; neonatal death
Nicotine (smoking)	Small neonates
Nitrofurantoin (Furadantin)	Fetal hemolysis
Nitrous oxide (anesthetic)	Inhibits fetal respiratory movement
Novobiocin (Albamycin)	Hyperbilirubinemia
Oral progestogens (Norlutin, Lutocylol, Pranone, Progestoral)	Clitoral enlargement; labial fusion; masculinization
Phenobarbital (in excess)	Neonatal hemorrhage and death
Phenylbutazone (Butazolidin)	Neonatal goiter
Potassium iodide	Cyanosis; goiter; mental retardation; respiratory distress
Reserpine	Nasal block; respiratory obstruction
Salicylates (aspirin)	Neonatal bleeding; severe hypoglycemia
Streptomycin	Hearing loss; micromelia; multiple skeletal anomalies; 8th nerve damage
Sulfonamides (long-acting)	Kernicterus; hyperbilirubinemia; acute liver atrophy; anemia
Tetracyclines	Discolored teeth, inhibited bone growth, micromelia; syndactyly
Thalidomide	Hearing defects; phocomelia; death
Thiazides (Chlorothiazide, Methychlothiazide, etc.)	Neonatal death; thrombocytopenia
Vitamin A (large doses)	Cleft palate; congenital anomalies; eye damage; syndactyly
Vitamin D (large doses)	Hypercalcemia; mental retardation
Vitamin K Analogues (large doses)	Hyperbilirubinemia; kernicterus

Psychological dependence (habituation) is an altered psychic or mental state in which a drug and its effects on the conditions associated with its use assume undue importance (almost necessity) for the maintenance of an optimal state of comfort and well-being (tobacco, coffee, sweets, etc.).

Physical dependence (biological craving) is an altered physiological state created by repeated use which necessitates the continued administration to prevent a stereo-typed syndrome (withdrawal) which results in objective illness (days to weeks) (narcotics, phenothiazines, tricyclics, amphetamines, and alcohol).

Addiction is a behavioral pattern of compulsive drug use characterized by both *physical* and *psychological* dependence so strong that the addict's whole existence revolves around the procurement and ingestion of the drug, and all of life's normal pursuits are excluded or relegated to an inferior level.

Tolerance (tachyphylaxis) is a reduced physiologic response to a given dose of the agent in question, necessitating larger doses, sometimes to the toxic level, to obtain the effects observed with the original or average dose.

Rebound phenomenon is an exaggerated, negative, or unwanted effect due to increasing tolerance from larger and repetitive doses, resulting not only in ineffectiveness but also in an aberrant increase in the symptoms or complaint, for the reversal of which the original therapy was designed or prescribed.

SELECTION OF DRUGS FOR DISCUSSION

It will soon be apparent to those who read on that many basic drugs and proprietary compounds are not mentioned in the following pages. There has been no conscious intent to exclude or to malign some products or to promote or subsidize others, except in cases where a preponderant number of those colleagues or texts consulted dictated such tactics or opinions. Nor has there been a conscious attempt to impress the reader with a presumptuous knowledge of the intricacies of molecular chemistry and body physiology, which admittedly are not within the author's purview.

With these limitations always in mind, and ever aware of the infinite scope of the subject, the reader should evaluate this chapter as nothing more than a list of commonly prescribed drugs, some of the conditions or situations which modify their actions, and the toxic manifestations which arise or may be encountered when they are used separately or together in the treatment of our patients.

CARDIOVASCULAR DRUGS

The increase in life expectancy of the average patient, while eminently desirable and the certain goal of the healing arts, creates a host of problems which demand perceptiveness and alertness on the part of the practitioner. Nowhere are these problems more pertinent than in the therapy for cardiovascular diseases. There are drugs which stimulate the myocardium; there are others which depress the myocardium. Hypertension is controlled by agents which decrease the blood pressure; hypotension is treated with agents which elevate the blood pressure. Other compounds or chemicals are administered to influence the cardiovascular system by indirect or remote actions; for example, the diuretics, nitrites, and atropine. The clinician is embroiled in these problems because many drugs employed in everyday dental office practice are incompatible, interfere with, or increase the toxicity of the agents used by the physician to control cardiovascular disease.

The *digitalis glycosides* are universally administered to patients to combat myocardial insufficiency or congestive heart failure. Digitalis, digitoxin, digoxin, ouabain, and cedilanid are the generic names for this group of drugs, all of which are naturally occurring and not yet synthesized. The details and ramifications of their actions are hardly within the scope of this chapter, but the necessity of a cautious approach in the application of the drugs required for ordinary dental treatment on the digitalized patient is worthy of comment and consideration.

Digitalis is itself a highly toxic drug which requires intensive care and regulation in determining the proper dosage. The therapeutic dose and the toxic dose are, in many cases, very close. Potassium ion depletion is common in digitalized patients, and gives rise to paroxysmal atrial tachycardia and heart block. Diabetics receiving insulin plus glucose are often low in K ion and therefore hard to control or stabilize. Thyroidectomized persons using thyroxin for maintenance therapy must be alert to possible toxic complications.

Some drugs used frequently in dental treatment which can increase the toxicity of digitalis are atropine, steroids, and the adrenergic agents. Atropine can be dangerous through excessive vagal depression yielding undesirable bouts of tachycardia. Steroids often exert untoward influences which, although vague and difficult to discern, are distressing and sometimes dangerous to digitalis users. The adrenergic drugs, especially epinephrine and ephedrine, sensitize the myocardium, and in combination with digitalis, which has already increased cardiac muscle tone in its host, may precipitate arrhythmias or a fatal ventricular fibrillation. Endogenous epinephrine, released into the cardiovascular system as a direct result of stimuli from painful or psychically traumatic dental procedures, can and does elicit the same toxic phenomena.

Occasionally it becomes mandatory to depress the cardiac muscle tone in certain abnormal states such as arrhythmias and chronic tachycardias. Quinidine, procainamide, and potassium chloride are the agents of choice for this purpose. These drugs exhibit many toxic manifestations of their own which are primarily the concern of the physician, but preparations or dental procedures which are depressant or hypotensive in nature should be approached with caution or avoided. Also, many arrhythmias are worsened by anxiety, which, if severe enough, may negate the therapeutic effect of these agents.

Hypertensive patients are controlled or treated with the rauwolfia alkaloids (reserpine and deserpidine), barbiturates, ganglionic-blocking compounds, and, occasionally, tranquilizers. The barbiturates and tranquilizers are mentioned elsewhere, as are the rauwolfias. The ganglionic-blocking drugs are a potent group employed only in severe hypertensives and used cautiously in deference to their often extreme potency and toxicity. Ansolysen, Veriloid, Apresoline, and Ecolid are the proprietary or familiar names of the more popular of these agents.

Usurping the ganglionic blockers when possible, because of lower toxicity, fewer side effects, and less labile doses, guanethidine (Ismelin) and methyldopa (Aldomet) are more desirable antihypertensives. With a mode of action resembling rauwolfia (because they interfere with the natural catecholamines) but differing in approach (storage and displacement), they are still prone to produce postural hypotension and interactions with other depressors to the extent that a cauldron of trouble awaits the unwary.

Clonidine HCl (Catapres), a fairly new anti-hypertensive, acts differently from any existing drug in this category because it acts centrally on the brain to reduce or suppress sympathetic output. In other respects it is similar to methyldopa (interactions, etc.).

Propranolol (Inderal) is a beta adrenergic receptor blocking agent and as such is enjoying increasing usage in various cardiopathies. After initial employment for prophylaxis of paroxysmal atrial tachycardia and other arrhythmias, some patients suffering from hypertrophic aortic stenosis, angina pectoris, and hypertension are being treated with this potent agent. Regardless of the questionable nature of this form of therapy it behooves all clinicians to be aware of the dangers involved when treating anyone who is currently taking this drug.

Inderal's action prevents the heart from responding to sympathetic stimulation and circulating catecholamines and could precipitate asthmatic attacks in susceptible individuals. All this is germane to the stress inherent or generated in the performance of our profession (daily tasks). Inderal's appearance on a history form should indicate to the doctor that he or she is dealing with a risk patient, thereby provoking a conservative or cautious appraisal of the treatment plan. Isoproterenol is the drug of choice in overcoming beta adrenergic blockade.

Consultation with the physician may be advisable when patients on any "blood pressure medicine" report for dental treatment.

Chronic hypotension is seldom a serious situation except when associated with a definite pathologic state, such as myxedema or Addison's disease. Sudden acute hypotension, of course, is dangerous. It usually results from a toxic response to a drug or a traumatic experience (shock) and must be treated with a vasopressor or similar analeptic. Adrenalin, Phenylephrine, Ephedrine, Vasoxyl, Aramine, Wyamine, and Levophed are the trade names of commonly used vasopressors.

The knowledgeable therapist employs sympathomimetic amines only when it is certain that hypotension is due largely to vasomotor paralysis and not oligemia. Otherwise, serious toxic effects such as acute tubular necrosis (ATN) of the kidneys may result. Also he differentiates between the two distinct vascular actions and the cardiac action, and whether direct rather than indirect agents are appropriate.

Selection of the best one for a particular circulatory problem is easily done in the textbooks, but clinically it is a guessing game. Circulatory measurements and the comprehensive physiologic and pharmacologic data necessary for exactness are seldom available at the instant of decision.

All the currently used adrenergics share five actions but differ quantitatively to a great degree in their amplification: vascular excitatory for alpha receptors which cause constriction; vascular inhibitory for beta receptors which cause dilatation; cardiac excitatory; metabolic excitatory; and CNS excitatory. The variance in strength or propensity for each or all of these five actions should govern the selection of the pressor agent. Some agents act indirectly by releasing vessel and end plate stores of norepinephrine; others act directly on the receptors; and still others have both indirect and direct actions or manifestations.

Indirect alpha — Tyramine, Amphetamine, nasal decongestants (Naphazoline, Oxymetazoline, Phenylpropanolamine)
Direct alpha — Phenylephrine, Methoxamine

Direct beta — Isoproterenol
Indirect and direct alpha — Ephedrine, Metaraminol, Mephentermine
Direct alpha and beta — epinephrine and norepinephrine

Since cocaine prevents release of norepinephrine from vessel sites and effector organs whereas reserpine acts by depleting them, an indirectly acting agent would be useless in restoring vascular tonus or integrity.

In the whole sphere of pharmacotherapeutics, no area of greater controversy exists than that covered by the vasopressors. Each clinician or author invariably adopts a favorite drug, confers on it powers that others fail to perceive, and defends his pet vigorously, often demeaning others in the process.

These sympathomimetic agents are all very potent and can produce serious toxicities of their own, such as acute anxiety, pulmonary edema, and cardiac arrhythmias, including fibrillation. The hazard of these aforementioned toxic responses is grossly magnified for those patients who need emergency vasopressor therapy and are already afflicted with hyperthyroidism, arteriosclerosis, or one of the cardiopathies.

Diuretics

Diuretics are the most prominent indirect agents in the treatment of myocardial insufficiencies. These drugs increase urine flow and promote excretion of Na ions in the kidneys, thereby relieving the edema which is pathognomonic of congestive heart failure. The early diuretics displayed varied and numerous toxic effects, but only the thiazides will be considered here, because chlorothiazide (Diuril) and its congeners are first choice for the majority of patients, while furosemide and ethracrynic acid are more specific and limited in use. These drugs are potent, yet low in direct toxicity. *However, they exert a hypotensive effect which can be markedly enhanced if combined with other such agents.* This factor is of particular interest when IV barbiturates, synergistic with chlorothiazide, are considered for sedation or anesthesia in the dental treatment of such a patient.

Nitrites and Nitrates

These drugs could be considered to have both a direct and indirect effect on the myocardium. Nitroglycerin, amyl nitrite, and Peritrate are most commonly prescribed. Isordil is a long acting form. Their primary use is in the relief of pain in patients suffering from angina pectoris. Nitrites accomplish this feat by relaxing the smooth or involuntary muscle in the walls of certain hollow structures, especially the coronary arteries and veins, thereby increasing the blood flow to the hypoxic myocardium. (Controversy exists over the exact mechanism or mode of action.) This sudden rush of blood perfuses the oxygen-starved cardiac tissues and relieves the pain. Since the appearance of these drugs is not uncommon in the dental office, the symptoms of nitrite intoxication should be listed. Usually precipitated only after large or overdoses, they are throbbing headache, flushing of the face, palpitation, and fainting.

Heparin and the Coumarins

As the number of patients with cardiac and vascular disorders increases, anticoagulants assume a larger role in the scheme of things. This group of drugs is important to the clinician in that they are a factor in the total therapy picture. Allergic responses to heparin, Coumadin, and Dicumarol are extremely rare, and toxicity occurs only with overdose. Compatibility with dental drugs is not a problem, but vitamin K and its analogs will negate the therapeutic effect of the coumarins. Conversely, K can control the toxic effects if or when overdosage creates a problem.

ANALGESIC DRUGS

Relief of pain is one of the great objectives in the healing arts. Drugs whose predominant action is pain relief are termed analgesics, and are loosely divided into three categories: addictive, nonaddictive, and speculatory.* The addictive analgesics are narcotics, whether natural or synthetic, and their use is regulated by the Harrison Act.

ADDICTIVE

Pharmacologic studies have proved that a basic similarity exists among all the narcotic drugs, and because of its great potency, morphine is still used as a standard of comparison for this group.

Morphine

The chief alkaloid of opium, this analgesic has many and various uses in control of pain, reduction of metabolic rate, abolishment of fear and anxiety, relieving pulmonary edema, and eradication of the cough reflex. Despite its many virtues, morphine is a dangerous and extremely toxic drug, and it behooves the practitioner to be thoroughly familiar with its pharmacology. The chief effects are exerted on the central nervous system, the respiratory system, and the gastrointestinal tract.

CNS.   Morphine produces profound analgesia and, in large doses, sleep. In addition there are euphoria, emotional placidity, and easing or lessening of muscular tremors. These desirable characteristics are chiefly responsible for addiction, which leads progressively to toxic overdose and dangerous alteration of body physiology.

Respiration.   Morphine exerts a powerful depressing effect on the respiratory center in the brain (medulla), causing a diminution of both respiratory rate and volume. This depression can occur even in very small doses, and could be significant in patients with respiratory ailments such as emphysema, bronchiectasis, and the pneumoconioses. Bronchial constriction may occur in asthmatics, sometimes to a lethal degree.

---

*Author's relative designation.

Gastrointestinal Tract.   Morphine constricts the sphincters of the gastro-intestinal tract, increases muscle tone in the bowel (spasm), causing constipation, and irritates the chemoreceptor trigger zone in the medulla, which results in nausea and vomiting.

Delay in gastric emptying due to spasm of the pyloric sphincter is a dangerous factor when administration of general anesthetics is contemplated.

Morphine increases intracranial pressure and is contraindicated in patients with head injuries. Hyperglycemia often follows morphine injection and could be toxic to advanced diabetics.

Since this drug is detoxicated in the liver, patients with cirrhosis may experience a prolonged effect. It should be used with caution during pregnancy because morphine readily passes the placental barrier and may have a profound effect on fetal respiration. Hypothyroidism, Addison's disease, anemia, and severe debilitation are other disease states in which narcotics can exert a deleterious or toxic effect in normal dosages.

Acute morphine toxicity presents the following picture and, with few exceptions, exhibits the general diagnostic signs common to all forms of CNS poisoning from natural or synthetic narcotic drugs: irregular mixed stimulation and depression of the central nervous system with selective depression of the respiratory center; slow, shallow or sighing respiration, with unconsciousness, cyanosis, and pupilloconstriction (Argyll Robertson pupil). As depression deepens, and respirations slow and become less adequate, there is a gradual onset of prostration with loss of reflexes and muscular relaxation. The skin becomes pale, cold, and moist, and the pupils dilate; the heartbeat may be slow at first, but later it becomes irregular, rapid, and weak, and the blood pressure drops. There may be convulsions just before paralysis and death.

An interesting study in 1977 has shown that combining dextroamphetamines with morphine sulfate increases potency and euphoria and decreases toxicity.

Dilaudid

An oxidation product of morphine, hydromorphone, exhibits all the properties, bad and good, of the parent drug, except that it may be used in much smaller doses (2 to 4 mg) to gain analgesia, and has considerably less effect on the gastrointestinal tract.

Codeine

This alkaloid of opium is widely prescribed by clinicians, and as such is an important pain remedy. It depresses respiration less than morphine, but has a better antitussive effect, causes less constipation but more nausea, and elicts little, if any, spasm of the gastrointestinal tract.

The analgesic effect of codeine is roughly one-sixth that of morphine, and it fails to produce progressive sedation with increasing doses. This factor, together with a lack of euphoria (except in Percodan), lessens the chances of addiction to codeine. Its greatly reduced toxicity when compared with morphine makes it a much safer drug for nursing or pregnant patients, diabetics, and patients with chronic respiratory ailments, head injuries, and cirrhosis. However, cerebral and cord hyperirritability are more pronounced with codeine, so that before coma supervenes, there may be delirium, and after coma, convulsions. Empirin Compound, Phenaphen, Fiorinal, etc., all depend on codeine for their practical analgesic effect.

Percodan

Percodan is a favorite analgesic of many clinicians, but they should be aware that it contains APC and oxycodone in the HCl and terepthalate salts and is not yet cleared for use in pregnant patients. Oxycodone is derived from thebain, one of the original opium alkaloids, and chemically is considered to be stronger and longer acting than plain codeine, which it closely resembles. Dosage varies, with 1 tablet (containing approximately 5 mg of oxycodone, ASA 224 mg, phenacetin 160 mg and caffeine 32 mg) prescribed q 4 to 6 h and doubled if necessary.

Synalgos DC

This is another analgesic compound which is avidly promoted as superior to codeine sulfate in relief of pain. Synalgos DC is formulated with drocode (dihydrocodeine ¼ gr [16 mg]), promethazine 6.25 mg and APC — it has yet to be cleared for teratogeneity, which negates its value in pregnancy.

It appears to be more potent than plain codeine or its compounds and, as such, probably deserves a trial for a spot in your armamentarium against pain. Dosage is one capsule q 4 h and doubled if necessary in resistant pain syndrome.

Meperidine (Demerol)

A synthetic narcotic which is most popular, this analgesic is not as toxic as morphine, nor is it nearly as potent, ranging from one tenth to one eighth as effective in comparative doses.

Despite conflicting reports, most clinicians consider it equal to morphine as a depressant of respiration, but, since it is a bronchodilator (considered controversial — it would be more correct to say it is not a constrictor as in MS), it should be safer for use on asthmatic patients. Its gastrointestinal activity is similar to morphine but exerted to a lesser degree. It has little effect on the motility of the bowel; therefore, constipation is not a problem.

Demerol appears to be more closely related to atropine than to morphine, because in addition to its analgesic effect it has parasympatholytic actions such as dryness of the mouth, flushing of the face and cervical areas, and bronchodilatation. The pupil of the eye is not affected by Demerol.

This drug is rapidly and almost completely destroyed by the liver; therefore, its use in patients with hepatic disease demands caution and close observation.

Anileridine (Leritine)

This synthetic drug is related to meperidine but is reported to be more potent. It has similar toxic effects, so when administered, the same rules of caution observed with meperidine should prevail.

Phenazocine (Prinadol)

A synthetic analog which earlier showed great promise by being four times as active as morphine, has, in later trials, failed to offer any significant advantages because its addictive and toxic effects are very similar to morphine. However, there is less nausea, and this factor may be an important consideration in certain patients.

Alphaprodine (Nisentil)

This wholly synthetic analgesic compound appears to be more potent than Demerol with less respiratory depression and more rapid onset, usually within five minutes. Its action is of short duration — one to two hours — and this is a paramount consideration in the ambulatory dental patient. It produces negligible euphoria and little sedation, so the average patient remains alert and aware of his surroundings. Nisentil causes fewer side effects and is generally *less toxic* than Demerol.

Fentanyl (Sublimaze)

Fentanyl (Sublimaze) is another synthetic (piperidine) analgesic of great potency, rapid onset (three to eight minutes), and short duration (one-half to one hour, depending on the route of administration). It very much resembles Nisentil in its basic nature and actions, and as such offers a choice.

It is being touted for a secondary effect which is also important — the relief of postanesthetic emergence delirium. If true, this may supersede its primary function. There is a surplus of good narcotic analgesics. There is a dearth of good agents to combat delirium without undue depression.

Methadone (Dolophine)

This synthetic analgesic most closely resembles morphine in potency for pain relief, but has less emetic and constipating actions. Sedation and euphoria are slight, thus limiting its use in preanesthetic medication. Respiratory depression is comparable with morphine, but methadone is less addictive and less toxic. Considering the above factors, methadone is ordinarily confined to use as an analgesic for treatment of severe or traumatic pain.

Methadone is addictive — a narcotic in the true sense as we know it. But it replaces the craving for heroin and morphine and allows the user to work and function normally. In addition, it is inexpensive, requires but one dose per day to alleviate an addict's suffering, and causes much less derangement of normal physiology. Although controversial at this time, methadone, as a controlled substitute for more dangerous drugs, is gaining momentum as the newest weapon in the programs for rehabilitation of addicts.

Hycodan, Numorphan, Metopon, and Pantopon are all morphine congeners with similar uses and toxicity, but without significant advantages and differences which would recommend their general substitution for morphine except in selected cases.

Nalorphine (Nalline); Levallorphan (Lorfan); Naloxone (Narcan); Naltrexone

Although derivatives of certain opiate drugs, Nalline and Lorfan antagonize practically all of the effects of morphine and the other narcotic compounds. Similar in every way, they may be used interchangeably. There are no known differences or specific advantages of one as compared with the other, and employment of either is a matter of personal choice.

The antidotal effects of these agents is thought to be due to competitive inhibition with replacement of potent drugs by a weak compound having higher affinity for the receptor. Nonetheless, they are effective and predictable, and have a wide range of use in negating the action of *all the narcotic drugs*.

However, the appearance of naloxone (Narcan) several years ago has rendered all this information academic. Its superiority is unquestioned for two reasons: it is basically nontoxic and it has no narcotic properties; therefore, if a patient's depression is misdiagnosed (i.e., hypnotic rather than narcotic in origin), Narcan, unlike Lorfan and Nalline, will not act as a narcotic and increase the depression to a lethal degree.

Naloxone (Narcan) dosage is 0.4 mg repeated every two or three minutes. If three doses fail to initiate improvement, the depression is other than narcotic.

It is only effective for two hours and an overdosage of some narcotics may persist for six or more hours, so the patient must not be permitted to leave the office until tests (Gestalt and others) assure CNS depression is eradicated.

Naltrexone, just released, appears to be even better in that it is more potent and much longer lasting (up to 48 hours). It is also non-agonistic except for slight pupillary dysfunction.[58]

NONADDICTIVE

This classification or group encompasses the drugs most frequently used by both professional and lay people. Consumption of salicylates and their congeners is so vast that the quantity must be calculated in tons (6500 tons of aspirin per year alone) rather than grains or grams. This phenomenon is credible and easily explained for the following reasons — effectiveness, wide range of use or application, availability, general low cost, and low toxicity.

In addition to their analgesic properties, many drugs in this group are also antipyretic, anti-inflammatory, antirheumatic, and uricosuric in action.

Salicylates

These analgesic compounds are those preparations related to salicylic acid, and include acetylsalicylic acid, sodium salicylate, and salicylamide.

The mechanism for the therapeutic actions of the salicylates is not well understood and less well explained, except for the uricosuric effect. This particular action increases the excretion of uric acid by inhibition of its resorption by the tubules of the kidneys.

Although the salicylates are considered remarkably safe drugs, they can produce severe adverse effects and even death. They are especially toxic to children, being the chief cause of poisoning in youngsters under three and etiologic in 16 per cent of the cases through 15 years of age. All coal tar analgesics are toxic to the CNS, and in continuous large dosages produce "salicylism," a condition characterized by tinnitus, vertigo, severe headache, and mental confusion. Salicylism, undiagnosed or untreated, progresses to a serious salicylate intoxication, recognized by the symptoms of hyperpnea, gastrointestinal irritation and bleeding, disturbances in the acid-base balance, and petechial hemorrhage. It is thought that the hemorrhagic tendency may result from interference with the formation of prothrombin and also from interference with release of ADP, which provides the "glue" in the clumping of platelets in rouleaux formation. ASA has recently been indicted as a causative factor in permanent alteration of albumin's molecular structure, and in vitro acetylation of gamma globulin, some hormones, and DNA. If widespread, these effects could be disastrous to the body's elemental functions.

Finally, some individuals exhibit true allergies to the salicylates and show anaphylactic reactions, usually of the urticarial or asthmatic type, following even the smallest doses of these drugs. A recent unexpected and startling report revealed that nearly 20 per cent of severely ill asthmatic patients in a famed respiratory disease hospital had aspirin intolerance.[29] Patients' claims to aspirin allergy are not to be ignored or denigrated. Fatalities, although rare, have been reported.

Aniline Derivatives

Acetophenetidin (phenacetin) is more widely used and less toxic than acetanilid, but has been replaced in popularity by N-acetyl-p-aminophenol (acetaminophen), which promises certain advantages over both of these drugs, especially in pediatric use. More and more pharmaceutical houses are dropping phenacetin from their formulation and most pharmacists consider this a wise decision. There is a paucity of studies or literature in support of either additive or potentiating effect of APC compounds over pure ASA (acetylsalicylic acid, aspirin).

Although serious toxic reactions rarely occur, acetanilid and acetophenetidin have a proclivity or potential for producing hemolytic anemia, acidosis, and methemoglobinemia following prolonged usage. At present, acetaminophen (Percogesic, Tylenol) appears to be innocent of these toxic effects, and is enjoying increased employment as an analgesic in adult and pediatric therapy. As another plus, it does not irritate gastric mucosa.

The aniline derivatives are effective analgesics and antipyretics, but lack uricosuric and antirheumatic actions, and have yet to demonstrate any superiority to the generally less toxic salicylates.

Excedrin

This is a lavishly promoted "extra strength" compound about which at present there is a dearth of available reliable evidence regarding potency or toxicity. The formula is interesting: 190 mg of ASA, 130 mg of salicylamide, 90 mg of acetaminophen, and 60 mg of caffeine. "Assuming that one equates acetaminophen as being roughly as potent as aspirin, two tablets of Excedrin would contain the equivalent of 560 mg of aspirin (less than the amount in two USP tablets)." Presumably then, the "extra strength" is accounted for by the 260 mg of salicylamide. This premise is questionable, however, because salicylamide, in such a subtherapeutic dose, probably has little, if any, therapeutic value! The "extra strength pain reliever" appears to be possibly as effective as but certainly not more effective than two USP aspirin tablets.[27] Available reports (admittedly scattered and inconclusive) give us little reason to believe that Excedrin produces increased analgesic effect without a corresponding increase in toxicity. Multiple-ingredient medicines should be suspect until proved innocent, because if these products cause toxic or allergic problems, who can name the culprit?

Lately there is an increasing tendency to question the necessity or desirability of adding anilines to salicylates to form analgesic compounds. Recent studies lend support of those clinicians who claim that aspirin alone is as efficacious as and less toxic than any non-narcotic compound of which it forms a part.

Many knowledgeable investigators insist that 10 grains of aspirin at one time is sufficient to gain the maximum analgesic effect obtainable with non-narcotic drugs, and that higher doses or additive compounds are relatively useless for most patients.

The presence of caffeine in most of the proprietary mixtures mentioned above is "justified" on the basis that the cerebral effects of caffeine may relieve the tensions which contribute to certain kinds of headaches. It also may elevate the mood in some individuals.

Indomethacin (Indocin)

Promoted primarily for the treatment of gouty arthritis, Indocin has anti-inflammatory, antipyretic, and analgesic properties. Prescribed also for patients with rheumatoid arthritis, osteoarthritis, and spondylitis, it has enjoyed moderate success.

Although Indocin has been advocated by some for temporomandibular joint problems, its toxic effects — severe headache, peptic ulcer, and hematologic disorders — should suggest that its advocates look for safer medication.

Pyrazolone Compounds

This group includes aminopyrine and phenylbutazone, which exhibit analgesic, antipyretic and antiarthralgic properties but possess no significant advantage over other less toxic analgesic drugs.

Aminopyrine (Pyramidon) has little value in the dental armamentarium, and its use has led to the development of agranulocytosis in a significant number of patients.

Phenylbutazone (Butazolidin) is a newer pyrazolone derivative which is extensively used in the treatment of arthritis and other joint diseases. Although effective, it is much too toxic for general therapy and should be confined to special cases which do not respond to other medication. Its toxic manifestations include skin rashes, gastrointestinal irritation and ulceration, generalized hypersensitivity, bone marrow depression, hemorrhagic tendency, and jaundice.

Butazolidin has uncommon application in dentistry, but the practitioner should be aware of its nature when prescribing for patients who are taking this drug.

Ibuprofen

Ibuprofen (Motrin) is a new non-steroidal *anti-inflammatory agent.* It is derived from phenylalkanoic acid, which so far has produced a family of drugs which, although not yet released (except for Ibuprofen), are considered to be a possibly important breakthrough in the therapy for collagen diseases.

It should be employed only in the treatment of rheumatoid and osteoarthritis victims who do not respond to ASA mainly because its analgesic and antipyretic properties are considered weak.

Fortunately, serious untoward effects so far are rare and although mainly confined to the GI tract, there is less GI bleeding than with ASA. Despite a difference in chemical formulae, there is a similar antigenic determinant; therefore it is not safe to prescribe it for those patients allergic to ASA (dosage 400 mg TID).

A comparative study at Georgetown University (Cooper, Needle and Kruger, J. Oral Surg. 35, Nov. 1977) presented the rather surprising conclusion that Ibuprofen not only is more potent than ASA but has greater efficacy without any notable increase in adverse effects. They suggest additional clinical studies to confirm these results.

Propoxyphene (Darvon)

This synthetic drug, a derivative of methadone, has enjoyed exceptional growth in popularity since introduction, but its potency as an analgesic is conjectural and has been warmly debated by members of the health professions. Ideally it is supposed to approximate codeine in analgesic effect without the depression and respiratory and gastrointestinal side effects.

Although its allergenic potential is low (occasional skin rash), the manufacturer lists these adverse effects: dizziness, headache, sedation, somnolence, paradoxical excitement and insomnia and gastrointestinal disturbance (nausea, vomiting, abdominal pain, and constipation). The clinical picture of overdose parallels that of the true narcotics, plus the added distress of convulsions. Propoxyphene can be abused. Cases of tolerance and addiction are increasingly reported. Addicts discovered that the Darvon part of the compound capsule was in the form of a small pure pill: by splitting several capsules, enough pure Darvon was available for a "high" by intravenous injection. Recent revision by the manufacturer distributes the propoxyphene evenly through the powder, thereby negating this problem. Narcan is indicated and effective in cases of overdose or poisoning.

Propoxyphene is evidently synergized by APC, which is an integral part of Darvon Compound 65. It is also marketed with aspirin and called Darvon ASA.

Because of the instability factor with the hydrochloride salt when formulated as a powder, Lilly has discovered the napsylate salt (propoxyphene napsylate), which is more stable. However, because it lacks the molecular weight, a 100 mg dose of the napsylate salt is required to supply the amount of propoxyphene equivalent (in activity or potency) to that present in 65 mg of the hydrochloride salt. Darvon N is the designation of the new formula with 50 mg of propoxyphene napsylate, while Darvon N ASA has 325 mg of aspirin added. Darvocet–N and Darvocet–N 100 are the same new form with acetaminophen (325 mg and 650 mg respectively) replacing the ASA or APC in the compound.

In March, 1977, propoxyphene was placed in Schedule IV of the Controlled Substances Act. Drugs in this schedule are defined as those that "may lead to limited physical or psychological dependence."

Since it is structurally related or an analog of methadone and has been abused with resultant psychic and physical dependence (low grade) and tolerance, the F.D.A. has changed its classification. This is no way demeans the drug. Most agents which affect the CNS in any way may fall into this category.

Ethoheptazine (Zactane; Zactirin)

Another synthetic related to meperidine, Zactirin occupies the same spectrum as Darvon in the analgesic group of drugs. It is also relatively free from gastrointestinal side effects and respiratory depression, but Zactirin's potency is yet to be satisfactorily determined and must be evaluated by the clinician. Toxicity is minimal, and significant allergenic tendencies have not been reported.

The standard preparation includes APC or ASA in its formula, a factor that should be considered when prescribing this agent. Zactirin is combined with meprobamate to form a compound labeled Equagesic, which has properties and actions common to both drugs. It should have some value in dental office practice.

Measurin, Contac, et al.

Increasing emphasis, desirability, and somewhat garish publicity have pushed time acting or sustained release drug forms to the forefront, especially in the analgesic and cold tablet class. This type of packaging usually encompasses a towering quantity of a drug to be released in measured doses at measured intervals. This controlled action is predetermined by fractioning into sized particles and/or enteric coatings.

Knowing the vagaries of the gastrointestinal tract and the quality control of some manufacturers, prudence should dictate the policy in every instance.

SPECULATORY

The richest plum in the drug orchard, sought by all and as yet unplucked, is a potent analgesic which lacks habituating and addicting powers and does not depress respiration or other vital CNS functions.

There are four recent arrivals on the scene and several more hovering in the wings, all of which showed promise in this direction but are now considered controversial. Because they are new, and also because two of them hint of great merit, they will be discussed in detail. These drugs are labeled speculatory because, although three qualify as potent analgesics without addiction dangers, each has peculiarities which limit usage to specific situations and not general therapy for the average patient.

Methotrimeprazine (Levoprome)

A phenothiazine compound, Levoprome is also a potent non-narcotic analgesic. About half as strong as morphine on a milligram basis, it appears to cause less respiratory depression and finds its greatest use in relieving pain in acute and chronic conditions for those patients confined to bed, in traction, or recovering from major surgery.

Precautions. Like other new drugs, it must be considered to have teratogenetic potential until proved otherwise and thus should be restricted in pregnant patients. Since it has strong sedative effects, operation of autos or complicated machinery following its use is forbidden.

Adverse Reactions. These are numerous and often serious: disorientation, blurred vision, nasal congestion, dry mouth, difficult micturition, and intense pain at the site of injection, plus the usual extrapyramidal syndromes associated with phenothiazines.

Contraindications. Severe orthostatic hypotension which may last for 12 to 16 hours after the initial dose, along with the necessity for deep and painful IM injection (there is no oral form, and subcutaneous instillation causes irritation), practically cancels its value in dentistry.

Levoprome's only feasible use might be for postoperative pain in a major oral surgical case in which the patient is confined to bed and/or allergic to other strong analgesics.

Dosage. The usual dose is 20 mg IM, repeated every four to six hours.

Carbamazepine (Tegretol)

Another phenothiazine type with potent and specific action on pain, Tegretol is an extremely dangerous drug that must not be prescribed as a routine analgesic. Thorough familiarization with the adverse effects and precautionary measures is vital and may be obtained from the Physicians' Drug Reference or current texts on pharmacology.

Although Tegretol has been used in Europe since approximately 1962, its first appearance in American pharmacies occurred in 1968.

A tricyclic compound originally ticketed as an anticonvulsant (as Ponstel was classed as an anti-inflammatory), Tegretol soon exhibited its ability to eradicate the crushing pain of tic douloureux. Since no drug had ever been able to approach, much less achieve, this goal and still enable the patient to ambulate and retain his senses, this compound was hailed far and wide as the "answer." Then came the deluge of reports on side effects and the sobering second thoughts which invariably follow in the wake of a new "miracle" drug.

A CBC and platelet estimate should precede initial therapy and be repeated once a week for the first month, every two weeks for the second and third months, and at monthly intervals as long as the drug is employed. Variants from the norm at any time dictate immediate discontinuance.

Tegretol is remarkably effective, and initial relief is evident in 24 to 48 hours. In approximately 68 per cent of patients with severe symptoms, pain is virtually abolished, although this may take 10 to 14 days. Therapy has been extended for more than two years in some victims before remission is obtained. However, attempts to reduce dosage to the necessary minimum should be a continuing goal, no matter how long therapy is planned or needed. It can be used in conjunction with Dilantin in severe cases.

Evidence suggests that its mode of action is the inhibition of synaptic transmission with the spinal trigeminal nucleus. It is very useful in controlling psychomotor epilepsy — grand mal also responds.

Precautions. The benefit-risk ratio should be an ever-present guide or criterion in evaluation of the patient's welfare, especially in those with cardiac disease, hepatic pathosis or dysfunction, and borderline psychosis. Appropriate liver function tests are essential in long-term therapy.

Adverse Reactions. The minor side effects are nausea, dizziness, and drowsiness, which are transient and readily disappear when therapy is suspended. But patients should be made aware of the early signs of hematologic toxicity, such as fever, sore throat, mouth ulcers, and petechial or purpuric hemorrhage in the mucosa or skin. These symptoms precede or warn of the onset of agranulocytosis, thrombocytopenia, and leukopenia. Continued aggravation of the bone marrow could precipitate aplastic anemia with fatal results. Tegretol must never be used concurrently with MAO inhibitors because it is chemically related to Tofranil (a tricyclic) and interacts in the same severe way.

The multiplicity of the side effects and their extensive ramifications require constant vigilance and perception on the part of the prescriber and awareness and discipline on the part of the user.

Dosage. One hundred milligrams twice a day initially, increasing to 400 to 800 mg. in divided doses every 24 hours if necessary. As stated above, the dosage should be minimized or discontinued at the earliest feasible time, and close control is mandatory (visual and laboratory examinations) for the patient's welfare.

Mefenamic Acid (Ponstel)

I am not convinced that Ponstel belongs in this list, but because of its nature, a thorough airing is desirable. It is a fairly simple compound, but is unique in that it differs from all other agents used in the management of pain. According to the manufacturer, clinical trials have demonstrated that Ponstel is effective in relieving pain from bursitis, backache, sprains, toothache and dental surgery.

Ponstel was originally introduced as an anti-inflammatory agent. Now it is promoted as an analgesic. Distribution of this drug in the United Kingdom has provided most of the experience and data available. An estimated 25 million capsules have been prescribed there.

Precautions.   Ponstel should be administered with caution to patients with abnormal renal function or inflammatory disease of the gastrointestinal tract. If rash occurs, the drug should be promptly withdrawn. Acute exacerbations have been reported in asthmatics following administration of Ponstel. Caution and prudence are mandatory.

Adverse Reactions.   In controlled clinical studies of Ponstel at analgesic doses of up to 150 mg per day, associated side effects were relatively mild and infrequent. Complaints are dose related, being more frequent with higher doses.

In 3205 observations on 1985 subjects over periods of from one to 238 days, the most frequently reported side reactions were (in descending order) drowsiness, nausea, dizziness, nervousness, headache, and gastrointestinal tract discomfort. Upper gastrointestinal tract side effects can be appreciably reduced by taking medication during meals.[43]

As with the administration of any new drug, it is recommended that hematopoietic, renal, and hepatic function studies be done when extended usage is anticipated.

Contraindications.   Like other anti-inflammatory agents, Ponstel is not indicated for use in patients with intestinal ulcerations. However, in double-blind comparison with aspirin, Ponstel appears to be less liable to cause gastrointestinal bleeding. The prescribing of Ponstel to pregnant women and those of child-bearing potential is at present contraindicated. This drug should not be given to children under 14 years of age, because the pediatric dose is yet to be established.

Warning.   If diarrhea occurs, Ponstel should be *promptly* discontinued. The patient so affected is usually unable to tolerate the drug thereafter.

Dosage.   The recommended oral regimen for adults is 500 mg as an initial dose, followed by 250 mg every six hours as needed. Ponstel is indicated for short-term administration *not exceeding one week of therapy.* The margin of safety plummets with higher doses and longer administration.

At this writing Ponstel is still therapeutically controversial. Such an opinion should not be misconstrued as denigrating to this compound. It is certainly premature to make judgments before more data are available.

The original clinical studies of its efficacy were watered down by later FDA trials. These double-blind studies place the drug in the same spectrum as ASA or slightly better.

Consultation with colleagues and pharmacists has revealed a divergence of attitudes but no passionate commitments for either the positive or the negative position in evaluating Ponstel.

Those who report success (and some are enthusiastic) tend to initiate therapy immediately and prescribe the recommended dosage regularly at six-hour intervals through the time period when pain is normally expected. Others have not obtained the results so glowingly reported in the introductory pamphlet.

Pentazocine (Talwin)

Listed in the second edition as a speculatory drug, Talwin has certainly earned its place in the arena of pain control.

Medical people are, for the most part, grudging in their acceptance of a new drug, especially one that has been long sought or desperately needed.

This reluctance is partly engendered by past disappointment with similar panaceas and partly by the awareness of the responsibility shouldered by every doctor who treats patients with new, little-known, and potent medicines. This seemingly stodgy attitude usually works for the patient's benefit in the long run.

Despite the doubts of some and the reluctance of others, Talwin emerges as a highly impressive drug. It is the first really potent non-narcotic, non-phenothiazine analgesic that is relatively safe for ambulatory patients (does not produce severe postural hypotension) and for long-term therapy (drug tolerance does not develop). It has been used in some patients continuously for more than 300 days and discontinued abruptly without withdrawal or untoward symptoms of any kind.

Other advantages of Talwin may be listed as follows: (1) It has a wide range of use in mild, moderate, or severe pain from almost any source. (2) It is not tachyphylactic. (3) It is well tolerated systemically and locally. (4) It is rapid acting and long lasting in effect. (5) It has good shelf life and is free of narcotic controls.

Talwin's only unique and serious disadvantage stems from its secondary role as a weak narcotic antagonist. Because of this, Nalline and Lorfan are useless in combating overdosages and respiratory depression. If the latter occurs, it was treated with oxygen and Ritalin (methylphenidate), a central nervous system stimulant which is not nearly as effective as an antagonist. Narcan is effective and is the drug of choice.

Precautions. Although teratogenetic or embryotoxic effects have not been seen in extensive animal tests or reported in humans, Talwin, like all new drugs, should be given with caution to pregnant women until more data are available.

Since dizziness, sedation, and euphoria are not uncommon, regardless of dosage, ambulatory patients should be warned not to operate machinery, drive automobiles or unnecessarily expose themselves to hazards. This precaution is especially applicable to the unaccompanied dental patient who has probably driven himself to the dental office and intends to return to work after his appointment.

Conditions which result in reduced respiratory capacity from any cause will ordinarily preclude or minimize the use of Talwin. Asthma, pneumoconiosis, lung infections, obstructions, regular therapy with other depressant drugs, and cardiac disease are all capable of interfering with normal or adequate gaseous exchange in the lungs.

Because most drugs are detoxified and eliminated by the liver and kidneys in that order, Talwin should be used with care in patients who suffer from impaired hepatic or renal function.

Narcotic addicts or patients who are "on" morphine at the time should not be given Talwin by the clinician; otherwise withdrawal symptoms may result with their concomitant hazards.

There are a few other precautions which lie mainly in the province of the physician and need not be mentioned here.

Adverse Effects.   Nausea is the most frequent adverse effect and respiratory depression the most serious, although apnea is not a problem even with large doses.

According to The Medical Letter, "when given in equianalgesic doses, pentazocine produces as much sedation, grogginess, dizziness, nausea, vomiting, sweating and other minor subjective complaints as do morphine and other narcotics."

Contraindications.   Like other potent analgesics, Talwin should not be used on patients with head injuries, increased intracranial pressure, or brain pathology until a clearance has been given by the neurosurgeon. It can cloud the central nervous system symptoms and make diagnosis difficult or misleading.

Dosage.   The average parenteral dose is 30 mg, either IV or IM or subcutaneously, and may be repeated every three to four hours. Some patients require up to 60 mg (single dose) for relief, but in this range psychotomimetic reactions are possible and have occurred. The usual oral dose is 50 mg. Talwin is not recommended for children under 12 years of age because of insufficient data on this group.

HYPNOTIC DRUGS

Hypnotics encompass a large field of different drugs which can produce a state of depression of the CNS resembling natural sleep. In smaller divided doses, these same drugs, for the most part, induce a state of drowsiness, and in this capacity they are classified as sedatives. The practical difference between a hypnotic drug and an anesthetic drug is in degree of CNS depression, i.e., dosage. A therapeutic dose of a hypnotic produces sleep from which the patient can be roused, whereas an increased dose of the same agent results in an anesthetic state from which the patient cannot be roused until the drug has been metabolized. The anesthetic dose, with the possible exception of the ultra-short barbiturates, is dangerously close to the toxic and/or lethal dose. Some hypnotics are also listed as tranquilizers more out of deference to common acceptance than accuracy.

Over the past decade the concepts of the use of hypnotics and sedative tranquilizers have changed greatly owing to the intense interest in this field which has generated much useful information.

The indications, selection, and alternative regimens and contraindications are manifest, and primary nervous disorders and sleep disorders such as sleep apnea, nocturnal myoclonus, and circadian rhythm changes call for specific, not empiric, management.

The etiology needs to be determined (for example, depression, anxiety, alcoholism, tension tolerance) and a clear-cut diagnosis or plan developed before any patient is introduced to these drugs, *most* of which create dependency, interact with other drugs, are potent and expensive, and have numerous, often toxic, side effects.

Dr. Robert DuPont, director of N.I.D.A., conservatively estimates that sleeping pills are responsible for at least 5000 deaths and more than 25,000 trips to hospital emergency rooms each year.

The barbiturates, along with Doriden, Noludar, Placidyl, and Quaalude, are the chief offenders and should not be prescribed for the average dental patient. It is much wiser to prescribe one of the benzodiazepines, which are more effective, safer, and ordinarily do not cause the "hangover" feeling common with the other drugs.

Barbiturates

Eminently the most popular and, according to most investigators, the safest hypnotics are the barbiturates, a series of closely related compounds formed by combining urea and malonic acid. This happy marriage yields barbituric acid, which is modified by appropriate substitutions in position 5 of the molecule to produce the familiar drugs of this large group.

The barbiturates differ mainly in varying duration of action or rate of metabolism, thereby establishing their classification as ultra-short, short, intermediate, and long acting (Table 5–2).

Although toxic addiction (from large and protracted dosage) does occur, urticaria or allergic responses and neurologic changes are rare in normal therapy.

Acute toxicity from overdose of barbiturates is manifested primarily as depression of respiration to decreasing levels until cessation ensues. In some agitated, feverish, or elderly patients, barbiturates can evoke an ambiguous or contrary response and stimulate or excite these individuals to a state of delirium (hyperexcitability).

Probably the greatest hazard in the general use of barbiturates is their propensity for synergism with a multitude of other common drugs. Alcohol, reserpine, and antihistamines all intensify the action of barbiturates. When ingested together, sudden, unexpected, and severe depression may result.

Porphyria, a rare disorder involving excessive respiratory pigment, hematoporphyria, must always be considered in any discussion of toxicity. Ingestion of any barbiturate by a patient afflicted with this disorder will ordinarily yield drastic and/or fatal results.

Antidotal measures in the treatment of barbiturate poisoning no longer include convulsant drugs. Mild stimulants, good oxygenation, and maintenance of fluid and electrolyte balance are the accepted remedies for barbiturate intoxication. Analeptic drugs may only intensify the toxic effect or exchange one set of symptoms for another equally dangerous syndrome.

Physostigmine is usually effective and is the drug of choice for barbiturate antagonism.

Chloral Hydrate

Chloral hydrate is a desirable hypnotic, especially for elderly patients, and children, because it gives quick, relatively short sedation without the sequelae that often follow barbiturate ingestion. It is a central depressant, inducing calm, then sleep, without marked respiratory and cardiovascular depression.

Although a gastric irritant forbidden for use in patients with peptic and duodenal ulcers, its toxicity is relatively low in all other respects.

Chloral hydrate, its reputation somewhat tarnished (or enhanced, as the case may be) owing to its storied use by bartenders as a "Mickey Finn," is

TABLE 5–2 CLASSIFICATION, STRUCTURE, AND DOSAGE OF
COMMONLY USED BARBITURATES

Duration of Action	Names	Substituents in Position 5	Hypnotic Dose
Ultra-short (IV Anesthetics)	Thiopental° (Pentothal)	Ethyl 1-Methylbutyl	
	Thiamylal° (Surital)	Allyl 1-Methylbutyl	
	Methohexital† (Brevital)		
	Hexobarbital‡ (Evipal)	Methyl, Cyclohexenyl	
Short	Secobarbital (Seconal)	Allyl 1-Methylbutyl	
Intermediate	Pentobarbital (Nembutal)	Ethyl 1-Methylbutyl	0.1–0.2 gm
	Butabarbital (Butisol)	Ethyl Sec-butyl	0.1 gm
	Amobarbital (Amytal)	Ethyl Iscamyl	0.1–0.2 gm 0.05–0.2 gm
Long	Phenobarbital (Luminal)	Ethyl, Phenyl	0.1–0.2 gm
	Barbital (Veronal)	Ethyl, Ethyl	0.3–0.5 gm

°Thiobarbiturate.
†Oxybarbiturate.
‡A CH_3 group attached to the nitrogen.

nevertheless a valuable adjunct in the premedication of those persons who are overly sensitive or allergic to the barbiturates. Dosage is 75 mg per kg on a curve to a maximum of 1500 mg at 50 kg.

Paraldehyde

An excellent sedative, paraldehyde produces moderately prolonged sleep (eight to 12 hours) with little or no medullary or motor depression. It is a powerful CNS depressant, resembling alcohol in effect; but, despite this potency, it has a wide margin of safety when properly prescribed. This attribute (low toxicity) in combination with paraldehyde's powerful effect would enhance its value tremendously except for one thing — a strong, offensive odor which is disagreeable to the vast majority of patients.

Bromides

These compounds (NaBr and KBr), while formerly popular as sedatives and hypnotics, are now rarely prescribed by professionals. However, bromides deserve mention and consideration because they frequently appear as the principal ingredients in proprietary, over-the-counter, nonprescription sleeping pills. Cumulative in the body, these drugs are often highly toxic, causing a condition known as "bromism." This syndrome is characterized by signs of chronic motor and sensory depression and mental aberrations. Dermatitis is another common toxic symptom.

It is difficult to defend the use of such potentially dangerous drugs when superior agents are readily available.

Ethanol

Appropriately or not, many texts list this drug as a hypnotic. Each researcher should be exhorted to experiment with ethanol in the potion which suits him best and then form his own conclusions. Its toxic manifestations should be common knowledge and need no explanation. Intravenous ethanol can and has been used as a supplemental anesthetic for alcoholic patients. Despite its soothing powers on many citizens, alcohol can be a nightmare for others.

It is a sedative and a hypnotic, and in high doses (P.O. or I.V.) it can be an anesthetic.

Ethanol has additive effects on all CNS depressants and potentiates (more than doubles the action of) the barbiturates (especially Nembutal, Seconal, Butisol, Doriden, and Quaalude!) These are known to be deadly when taken with alcohol—there may be others, not yet defined, with similar action.

In addition, it induces the sulfonylureas (Diabinese, Orinase, Tolbutamide) by speeding up their metabolism approximately 50 per cent; increases the absorption of diazepam; and should not be used in conjunction with the phenothiazines, which inhibit alcohol dehydrogenase (the enzyme responsible for the reduction of C_2H_5OH into acetaldehyde and other metabolites), thereby prolonging and intensifying its negative or depressant action. Alcohol is a direct myocardial toxin, and cardiomyopathy is a clinical entity which affects approximately 1 per cent of the adult population in the U.S.A.

Higher Alcohols

This group is represented by three widely publicized, but otherwise undistinguished, drugs: methylparafynol (Dormison), ethylchlorvynol (Placidyl), and phenaglycodol (Ultran).

Generally speaking, they are weakly sedative in action, producing drowsiness in therapeutic doses.

Toxicity is negligible, but some cases of hepatic damage from Dormison have been reported.

Piperidinediones

This group of supposedly mild hypnotics is similar in effect to the short-acting barbiturates, but the mechanism of their action is less well understood and the toxic potential may in some cases be extreme.

Glutethimide (Doriden) frequently causes skin rash and fever, and psychosis and addiction have been reported after prolonged use. It is one of the most lethal drugs in the formulary because abusers do not respond to any known antagonistic, analeptic, or antidotal measures (physostigmine et al.)

Methyprylon (Nodular) may precipitate headache, nausea, and vertigo. Addiction is possible after long-term therapy.

Thalidomide (Kevadon), although never marketed in the United States, deserves mention if for no other reason than its reputation. Most of the professional and lay population are familiar with its toxic manifestations. Phocomelia and other bizarre birth defects are dreadful proof of the dangerous potential of this drug.

TRANQUILIZERS

Tranquilizing drugs are assuming ever greater importance in the practice of the healing arts. These agents can suppress anxiety and modify disturbed behavior in doses which are not profoundly hypnotic. Such characteristics would seem to be eminently desirable in the armamentarium of an office practice. But the sprawling range of potency, multiple actions, overlapping vague responses, plural potentiation, exotic and often severe ancillary effects, and the complex pharmacologic interrelationships among this class of drugs demand a prudent and restrictive approach to dental or medical use. This group may be said to have conceived and nourished that new and blooming specialty iatrogenics.

Tranquilizers act with multiple sites in the CNS, producing sedation, antipruritic activity, antiemetic activity, antihistamine activity, antiserotonin activity, alpha-adrenergic activity, adrenergic potentiation, and analgesia. They can control spasms and convulsions. There are almost 200 drugs which claim to qualify, and the combinations are myriad and bewildering.

It is assumed that any classification will be controversial and even provocative to some, but should be conciliatory, flexible, not too specific, and biphasic for all.

The two phases consist of an arbitrary major-moderate-minor division to denote strength and potency: a chemical or pharmacal grouping to enumerate related drugs whose actions are basically similar. This method is more resilient than perfect, but it offers a catalog as a guide from which drugs for specific needs may be selected. The rauwolfa alkaloids, butyrophenones, and phenothiazines as a class, regardless of individual differences, are proclaimed major tranquilizers. The benzodiazepines fall essentially into the moderate slot with the diphenylmethanes. The large, varied minor group encompasses carbamides, ureides, and higher alcohols.

MAJOR TRANQUILIZERS

Rauwolfias

The Rauwolfia alkaloids are reserpine (Serpasil), deserpidine (Harmonyl), rescinnamine (Moderil), syrosingopine (Singoserp), serpentina (Raudixin), and alseroxylon (Rauwiloid). Although relatively low in direct toxicity, they must be considered major tranquilizers, not only because of potency but also because of their indirect, delayed and long-lasting mode of action. Their pharmacology is complex and needs to be elucidated. They act as antihypertensives indirectly by depleting norepinephrine, epinephrine, and dopamine in vascular storage sites and as tranquilizers by releasing various amines from the brain and some peripheral tissues to depress the CNS. The threat of synergism is always present when hypnotics and other depressants are prescribed for patients "on" the rauwolfias. There are also numerous annoying autonomic side effects: miosis, bradycardia, and increased gastrointestinal activity (which creates an incompatibility with ulcer victims). Nasal stuffiness from mucosal edema rates high on the nuisance list and promotes overuse of decongestant sprays. The most pertinent hazard is the occasional development of severe, sometimes unyielding hypotension during a general anesthetic or IV sedation period.

Butyrophenones

The butyrophenones, relatively new but surging in popularity under the pseudonym "neuroleptic," are clamoring for attention and getting it. What initially seemed a breakthrough is, after close inspection, hardly more than a widening of the present horizon.

Haloperidol (Haldol) and droperidol (Inapsine), although matching the potency and increasing the versatility of the other major tranquilizers, also share their drawbacks.

Toxicity is relatively equal or synonymous with the phenothiazines in scope and intensity, differing only in frequency. Extrapyramidal syndromes are most common, with hematopoietic and cardiovascular problems next in order.

Allergic skin reactions, photosensitivity, and jaundice are minor and seldom reported. These agents, in conjunction with a potent analgesic, form the basis of the neuroleptanalgesia technique discussed further along in this chapter.

Phenothiazines

Although phenothiazine derivatives exhibit antihistaminic, antipruritic, and analgesic properties, their value in dental practice is primarily as tranquilizing agents and secondarily as antiemetics.

The tranquilizing action of the majority of the phenothiazines is similar, varying somewhat in depth and length of action. Chlorpromazine enjoys the widest latitude of use and is fairly representative of the remainder of the group.

Any classification of phenothiazines must, by the nature and complexity of the groups, be weak and arbitrary, blurred and imprecise.

There are roughly 30 separate derivatives of phenothiazine available — their only real differences being structural and quantitative, not qualitative. No more than five pheno-compounds are needed to completely cover the pharmacologic spectrum of this series.

The other derivatives, each with its share of confirmed disciples, present slight deviations in structure and action but some important differences in clinical application. But because of the escalating number of these derivatives and the extensive claims made for each, Table 5–3, attempting to differentiate and classify similar drugs in this category, is presented.

Originally conceived by Dr. Martin Gold in 1966, this table has been modified with additions and deletions by the author to fit current concepts.[24]

TABLE 5-3 PHENOTHIAZINE TRANQUILIZERS

I. PIPERAZINES

Prochlorperazine (Compazine)	Fluphenazine (Permitil, Prolixin)
Thiethylperazine (Torecan)	Acetophenazine (Tindal)
Trifluoperazine (Stelazine)	Carphenazine (Proketazine)
Thiopropazate (Dartal)	Butaperazine (Repoise)
Perphenazine (Trilafon)	Thioperazine (Vontil)

TOXICITIES:
Frequent: Parkinson's syndrome; akathisia; dystonic reactions; anticholinergic effects
Occasional: photosensitivity reaction; inhibition of ejaculation
Rare: cholestatic jaundice; blood dyscrasia; lenticular pigmentation; postural hypotensi
allergic skin reactions; ECG abnormalities (usually without cardiac injury)

II. PROMAZINES

Promazine (Sparine)
Chlorpromazine (Thorazine)
Triflupromazine (Vesprin)
Methoxypromazine (Tentone)

TOXICITIES:
Frequent: oversedation; anticholinergic effects; postural hypotension
Occasional: pigmentary retinopathy; Parkinson's syndrome; akathisia; dystonic reactions;
hibition of ejaculation; photosensitivity reaction
Rare: cholestatic jaundice; blood dyscrasia

III. PIPERIDINES (ALIPHATIC)

Pipamazine (Mornidine)	Piperacetazine (Quide)
Propiomazine (Largon)	Thioridazine (Mellaril)
Mepazine (Palatal)	

TOXICITIES:
Frequent: oversedation; postural hypotension; anticholinergic effects
Occasional: cholestatic jaundice; Parkinson's syndrome; akathisia; dystonic reactions; inhibit
of ejaculation; blood dyscrasia; photosensitivity reaction; allergic skin reactions
rare: lenticular pigmentation; ECG abnormalities (usually without cardiac injury)

IV. PHENOTHIAZINE (ANTIHISTAMINE)

Phenothiazine	Promethazine (Phenergan)
Diethazine (Diparcol)	Trimeprazine (Temaril)
Profenamine (Parsidol)	Methdilazine (Tecaryl)
Pyrathiazine (Pyrrolazote)	

It shows that potency (with toxicity usually paralleling) is determined by the type of side-chain addition. These additives categorize the analogs in synonymous groups and provide a method of relating and predicting their deviation from the parent drug, chlorpromazine.

These analogs are grouped and presented in Table 5-3 in a descending order of strength and effectiveness as tranquilizers, other actions being relative. Prominent specific toxicities as reported by The Medical Letter will be listed with each group. Unusual properties of individual members will be cited in succeeding paragraphs.

Although completely capable of tranquilizing, antiemetic and other actions, the fourth group in the table projects stronger antihistamine and antipruritic powers than most members of the family. Other things being relative or equal, such attributes should be known and should influence one's selection of a drug for a specific condition or illness.

Probably the least dangerous, but certainly the most dramatic, of all side effects of toxicities of the major tranquilizers (rauwolfias excepted) are the extrapyramidal syndromes—akathisia and dystonia. Bizarre is the only word to describe them.

Akathisia, characterized by inability to keep still, an irresistible urge to be in motion, and fright, is a prominent extrapyramidal tract symptom which appears frequently. The dystonic syndrome, involving tics, hypertonicity, or spasm of the muscles of the face, tongue, and neck with correspondingly bizarre facial expressions, and oculogyric syndrome (a contraction of the superior rectus muscles of the eye temporarily blinding the patient—only the white portion is visible to the observer) can and does occur in up to 10 per cent of patients on extended phenothiazine therapy. These rhythmical, intermittent muscle twitchings may be accompanied by anxiety and sweating. These toxic states — akathesia and dystonia — although not overly dangerous and ordinarily well controlled by anti-parkinsonian drugs, are disagreeable and very often frightening to the patient and his relatives and friends. However, tardive dyskinesia, which features vermiculation of the tongue muscles along with other symptoms heretofore described, is a lingering syndrome which some clinicians have declared a permanent disability.

MODERATE TRANQUILIZERS

Many categorizations are assailable — this one is no exception. Imitating the colors in a Madras print, the tranquilizers overlay and intermingle their intensities and toxicities to the extent that any designation is arbitrary and malleable. Mostly for the sake of clarity and comparison are the diazepines labeled moderate in action.

Since the publication of the second edition, the benzodiazepines have proliferated in numbers and swamped the sedative, anxiolytic, or neuroleptic muscle relaxant class in quantity by a vast margin. Diazepam (Valium) is the number one prescription item in our nation at this writing, and justly so when employed judiciously!

Chlordiazepoxide (Librium) exhibits both sedative and hypnotic effects on the CNS and has a selective action on the thalamus and hypothalamus which is thought to be the mechanism explaining its ability to suppress our anxious and aggressive tendencies. Librium in addition reduces cholinergic and adrenergic activity in the peripheral nervous system, thereby tending to lower blood pressure and tension. Diazepam (Valium) differs in that it has less effect on the CNS; nor is it a peripheral suppressor. Valium's primary targets seem to be the thalamus and hypothalamus, which should enhance its anti-anxiety effect while diminishing comcomitant CNS depression. Oxazepam (Serax) simulates diazepam in all its attributes, but seemingly has less anticonvulsant power.

Librium and Valium have demonstrated excellent anticonvulsant properties. In tests each exhibited strength enough to block strychnine-induced convulsions in animals, a feat not duplicated by chlorpromazine or reserpine, both reputed to be heavyweights in this field. Diazepines are premier agents for mild or moderate anxiety states, either parenterally or by mouth. They are occasionally used to reduce blood pressure in mild hypertension and show promise as a part of the multi-pronged efforts in rehabilitation of alcholics and addicts.

Flurazepam (Dalmane) is mainly proposed or prescribed for its hypnotic effects and is increasingly replacing other hypnotics because the results are as good with apparently less hazard of severe toxic effects. Although dependency and habituation are feasible (more psychological than physiological), considering the range and potency of the diazepines, their toxicity level is comfortably low.

The rapidity of onset and duration of action in this class of drugs is, of course, determined by metabolic degradation and the potency of the metabolites produced therein.

Rapid onset in approximate scale or order:
Diazepam (Valium) 2.5 — 10 mg T.I.D.
Oxazepam (Serax) 10 to 30 mg T.I.D.
Chlorazepate (Tranzene) 7.5 to 15 mg T.I.D.
Clonazepam (Clonopin) 0.5 to 6 mg T.I.D.
Chlordiazepoxide (Librium) 5 to 25 mg T.I.D.
Triazolam (Halcion); not used in U.S.

Slower onset:
Flurazepam (Dalmane) 15 to 30 mg H.S.
Prazepam (Vestran)

These are known to be slower in onset of clinical effects and therefore usually longer acting. These data should be considered arbitrary and based on rather sketchy observations, but this assumption has virtually confined their employment as hypnotics only. Newer analogs—medrazepam (Nobrium), nitrazepam (Mogadon) and fluctrazepam—either are in the testing stage or are unavailable in the U.S. at this writing.

Lorazepam (Ativan) is very similar to oxazepam, but its narrow dosage range, 3 to 4 mg (5 mg or more incites a high incidence of side effects), has so far limited its use to premedication for general or neuroleptic anesthesia. In this area it produces significant antegrade amnesia (lack of recall) and a higher degree of somnolence than Valium, Serax, or Librium. This would seem to nullify its value in outpatient therapy.

Review of the literatures continues to confirm safety of Valium et al. One attempted suicide recovered completely after a 1500 mg oral dose.[54]

Even though a cardiac or cardiorespiratory arrest was attributed to diazepam in a recent Journal of Orthopedic Surgery article (Aug. 1977), subsequent investigation and interpretation of the event has cast doubt on its authenticity; four other drugs were involved, which is certainly a mitigating factor in the case described.

In several studies Valium was found to produce significant amnesia only with dosage of 10 mg or more while sedation and anxiety relief were present at as little as 2.5 mg dosage.

Morphine, Demerol, and other drugs that are known to delay gastric emptying, and atropine (with its anticholinergic effect on gastric motility), decrease uptake of oral diazepam and becloud its efficacy.

Although the manufacturer advises against water, normal saline, or 5 per cent dextrose as diluents, this advice is based on the remote possibility of a thrombus formation from a precipitate formed with these mixtures. This precipitate is fine enough to pass through ordinary filter paper, and it requires a severe stretch of the imagination to believe that this precipitate poses a danger to the patient. The author has personal knowledge of routine injection into a port of a high flow IV infusion with normal saline and 5 per cent D/W without complications of any kind! However, to be medicolegally secure, it is wiser to use a 5 to 10 cc syringe and aspirate blood as a dilutent for the 1,2, or 3 cc (5 mg per cc) dosage range you may select.

The pH of Valium (6.8) and the propyleneglycol vehicle will occasionally cause burning pain and subsequent, usually transitory, thickening at or proximal to the injection site (especially true in small veins), undesirable side effects of IV administration even when mixed with blood. While not morbid, this factor may elicit patient complaints postoperatively.

Libman and others have stated that Valium combined with local anesthesia is the safest and most effective neuroleptic for outpatient dental practice.[32]

In conclusion, most Medical Letter consultants believe that Librium, now available in the generic (chlordiazepoxide) form, may compare in efficacy with any other of the listed benzodiazepines. This is an important factor to a cost-conscious public when savings of 50 per cent or more are involved without sacrificing therapeutic value.

The contraindications for benzodiazepine therapy are:
Known allergies
Pregnancy
Acute narrow angle glaucoma
Untreated wide angle glaucoma
Certain depressed or suicidal syndromes or psychotic psychoses
Infants
Shock
Cautionary indications include:
Kidney disease
Acute or severe cardiovascular disease and severe respiratory disease
Gross obesity (improves appetite)
C.N.S. depressants and stimulants, including alcohol

Diphenylmethanes (Tranquilizers)

Lauded by many, dismissed as relatively weak and ineffective by others, the diphenylmethane derivatives are placed in the moderate category more for their breadth of action and potential than for their exhibited strength.

These drugs are structurally similar, but frequently pharmacologically different. They are related to various anticholinergics, antihistamines, antiemetics, narcotics, and even muscle relaxants, which have the diphenylmethane structure. Most are somewhat weak CNS depressants with multiple side effects more similar in nature to the major than to the minor tranquilizers.

Because of its immense popularity with dental and medical doctors, hydroxyzine (Atarax, Vistaril) will be exemplified as representative of its group.

Rapid-acting and mild, hydroxyzine exhibits sedative and tranquilizing powers along with antihistaminic properties. It has been suggested that hydroxyzine may arrest ventricular arrhythmias. One of its more popular applications in dentistry was in the field of psychosedation. Alone or in polypharmacal combinations (Demerol, scopolamine, etc.) for IV injection, it was the leading agent until 1970, when reports of vascular irritation and pathosis led to recommendation for discontinuing IV usages. Nevertheless, this is a veteran drug of proved usefulness and remarkably low direct toxicity with a possible exception in pregnancy, in which it has been shown that hydroxyzine has definite teratogenetic effects on some animal fetuses. Enough data to establish safety for human use are not yet available.

Because the differences among the diphenylmethane tranquilizers are insignificant, the others are listed below, without comment.
Benactyzine (Suavitil)
Pipethanate (Sycotrol)
Captodiamine (Suvren)
Pipradrol (Meratran)
Azacyclonol (Frenquel)
Buclizine (Softran)

Minor Tranquilizers

Carbamides, Ureides, and Higher Alcohols

Although the major tranquilizers affect not only behavior but also the autonomic nervous system, the minor agents, carbamides, ureides, and higher alcohols, are sedative in nature, anticonvulsant, and reduce skeletal muscle tone without significant autonomic effects.

Within this subgroup these agents differ from the phenothiazines, the diphenylmethanes, and rauwolfia in significant ways: (1) there are a variety of chemical structures involved; (2) they are not ganglionic blocking, adrenolytic, antihistaminic, antiserotonin, or antiemetic and they do not exhibit analgesia; (3) they are relatively nontoxic and resemble their close relations, the barbiturates; and (4) generally, they are not considered antihypertensive in clinical dosage.

These drugs exhibit three fundamental pharmacologic properties: (1) CNS depression, (2) muscle relaxation, and (3) anticonvulsant action.

The muscle relaxant group resembles the tranquilizers in most respects and exhibits the same basic pharmacologic properties, with heavy emphasis on muscle relaxant activity. Many of the muscle relaxants have been withdrawn from the market because of toxicity.

Meprobamate exhibits all the main characteristics of its group with approximately equal force and will serve as the prototype.

Miltown and Equanil are interneuronal blockers: central muscle relaxants with attendant sedative, tranquilizing (taming effect), and anticonvulsant properites. These eminently desirable requisites, combined with low toxicity and lack of depression, have made meprobamate an extremely popular and useful product.

Despite the glowing reputation and apparent safety, habituation and addiction (invariably involving patients taking massive doses over an extended period) are not unknown among the members of this supposedly minor, rather innocuous chemical group. However, neither affliction is particularly difficult to break, and withdrawal symptoms are mild and without sequelae when the patient is gradually weaned from the drug. Nonetheless, sudden withdrawal after addiction may result in toxic symptoms of a severe nature — tics, convulsions, and other irritative exacerbations of the CNS.

The Mephenesin and Substituted Propanediol Derivatives

I. *Tranquilizers (primarily):*

Meprobamate (Miltown, Equanil)
Mebutamate (Capla)
Emylcamate (Striatran)
Hydroxyphenamate (Listica)
Promoxolane (Dimethylane)

Oxanamide (Quiactin)
Phenaglycodol (Ultran)
Mephenoxalone (Trepidone)
Amphenidone (Dornwal)

II. *Muscle relaxants (primarily):*

Mephenesin
Meprobamate (Miltown, Equanil)
Carisoprodol (Soma, Rela)
Chlorzoxazone (Paraflex)
Methocarbamol (Robaxin)

Styramate (Sinaxar)
Phenyramidol (Analexin)
Chlormezanone (Trancopal)
Metaxalone (Skelaxin)
Zoxazolamine (Flexin) (discontinued)

III. *Nonbarbiturate CNS depressants (sedatives):*

Methaqualone (Quaalude)
Ethinamate (Valmid)
Ethchlorvynol (Placidyl)
Methylparafynol (Dormison)
Methyprylon (Nodular)

Glutethimide (Doriden)
Carbromal (Adalin)
Ectylurea (Nostyn)
Thalidomide (Kevadon) (discontinued)

Methaqualone has become a leading drug in the abuse category.

Tranquilizers Which Are Stimulants

Since most of us are members of the anxiety cult with its overt fears, we tend to forget the depressed citizens with their covert fears. A tranquil state can be approached from opposite directions — a depressor, to calm an agitated patient, or a stimulant, to elevate the mood of a morose one.

The MAOI's are prime examples — stimulants of the CNS to resolve psychotic depressant states. Reams of papers and articles have established both the need for and the efficacy of the MAOI's.

The amine oxidase inhibitors:

Phenelzine (Nardil)
Isocarboxazid (Marplan)
Pargyline (Eutonyl)
Etryptamine (Monase)

Nialamide (Niamid)
Tranylcypromine (Parnate) (discontinued)
Ipronizaine (Marsilid) (discontinued)
Pheniprazine (Catron) (discontinued)

Introduced innocuously as antidepressants, the MAO inhibitors have surfaced as controversial. A rather heterogenous group of drugs, they share one common trait: the ability to block oxidative deamination of naturally occurring amines. MAO's have prolonged and cumulative effects — two to three weeks after discontinuance.

Now the caution light is blinking and in two cases the red light is on. The width and intensity of toxic manifestations and potentiation associated with coemployment of the inhibitors with other common drugs (and foods) are stunning. Aged cheese, beer, wine, and certain heavy breads which harbor excessive amounts of tyramine are forbidden. Severe hypertension, convulsions, narcosis, and death are all lurking just around the corner for the unwary therapist or the unwarned patient.

Because of the increased activity and exploration of depression states, and the pressing need for less dangerous control agents, the dibenzazepines soon surfaced and became a factor.

Dibenzazepine derivatives (tricyclic).

Imipramine (Tofranil)   Trimipramine (Surmontil)
Amitryptyline (Elavil)   Protriptyline (Vivactil)
Desipramine (Pertofrane)   Doxepin (Sinequan)
Nortriptyline (Aventyl)

Effective, somewhat milder, easier to control, and lacking the extreme potentiating power of oxidase inhibitors, these agents resemble the phenothinazines in depth and range of toxicity. Anticholinergic effects and hypotension (antagonizes guanethidine) are frequent; parkinsonian activity with extrapyramidal features, mild seizures, cholestatic jaundice, and agranulocytopenia have been seen, along with drowsiness and allergic rash. Other negative aspects include a long latent period (often two to four weeks) and necessity for close, even daily, observation of the patient.

Before leaving the hypno-tranquilizers, several other agents with CNS and peripheral depressant and stimulatory action deserve mention:

CNS Depressants

Trimethobenzamide (Tigan) is widely known for its antiemetic properties. It has a unique chemical structure, is not a true phenothiazine, and should not be substituted in place of one. Most agents to control nausea are ineffective or at least controversial. Tigan seems to be as good as the best and less toxic than most.

Phencyclidine (Sernylan), like ketamine, is a dissociative anesthetic type drug producing a pseudocataleptic state with high analgesia and as such is employed in veterinary medicine. Although analogs may prove useful in the future, P.C.P., at present, is too toxic for human use. However, as one would expect, the cultists discovered it had hallucinogenic powers and now it is a leading drug of abuse, known in street parlance as "Angel Dust," "crystals," etc. The terrifying aspect is that it is simple and inexpensive to manufacture, thereby extremely difficult to control and it may be ingested, snorted, smoked, or injected with results of equal intensity. Symptoms are blank stare, bizarre behavior, confusion, ataxia, stupor or even combative, spasmodic episodes and unusual physical strength.

It is always dangerous to the physiology and often lethal in larger doses.[20]

Thioxanthenes

Chlorprothixene (Taractan) and thiothixene (Navane) are thioxanthenes whose conglomerate properties are so similar to the phenothiazines that it would seem needless to use them as substitutes until more knowledge is available.

CNS Stimulants

Data regarding bemegride, ethamivan, doxapram, and methylphenidate appear under the section on stimulants.

HISTAMINES AND ANTIHISTAMINES

A pyramiding group of drugs which block the effects of histamine at various receptor sites are referred to as antihistamines. They are useful not only in allergic diseases, but also for prophylaxis in motion sickness and as light sedatives, tranquilizers, and antiemetics. Their wide range of action and low toxicity have catapulted these agents into a prominent place in the dental armamentarium.

Antihistamines prevent or minimize the physiological effects of histamine. Theoretically there are three ways in which a drug might do this. First, by physiological antagonism of histamine (Adrenalin is an example of a drug many of whose actions are directly the opposite of those of histamine). Second, the drug might destroy histamine. Substances which do this are formaldehyde, nitrates, and an enzyme, diamine oxidase, known as histaminase. With the exception of histaminase, none of these other substances has therapeutic value as an antihistamine. Third, drugs may compete with histamine at its sites of action in the body, a phenomenon known as "competitive antagonism." The latter is the way all the currently prescribed antihistamines are believed to act. It is thought that these drugs, because their chemical structure resembles that of histamine, are accepted by the histamine receptors in the effector cells, thereby blocking out histamine. The evidence that histamine is implicated in the pathogenesis of many of the allergic diseases is inferred rather than proved, and it is therefore not altogether surprising that therapy with antihistamine drugs is not uniformly successful. The best results are obtained in acute urticaria and seasonal hay fever. In both these conditions the great majority of sufferers obtain a high degree of relief from the proper use of antihistamine drugs. In perennial vasomotor rhinitis, chronic urticaria, angioneurotic edema, and allergic skin reactions due to various allergens, including drugs, the results of treatment with antihistamines are of symptomatic value only; they do not shorten the course of the disease. In acute anaphylactic type reactions the drug of choice is Adrenalin. Antihistamines are of secondary value. In the field of allergic diseases the most disappointing result has been the failure of antihistamine drugs to benefit the vast majority of patients with bronchial asthma. The allergic basis of asthmatic attacks is undoubted; antihistamines are, however, seldom of value for either the prevention or the treatment of the acute asthmatic attack.

Often the choice of an antihistamine drug involves the consideration of the multitude of other effects it may have upon the patient besides that effect which is desired. Clearly it is undesirable to use an antihistamine which causes sleepiness for the treatment of hay fever in those citizens who must drive or perform precision tasks while taking the drug. On the other hand, sedation is a valuable attribute in a drug for the treatment of an acute urticarial reaction in a patient who is confined to bed.

Diphenhydramine (Benadryl) and tripelennamine (Pyribenzamine) have definite blocking and anesthetic effects on peripheral nerves and may be substituted for procaine, lidocaine, etc., in patients who are allergic or hypersensitive to these drugs. They are employed in the same relative dosage, i.e., 2 to 3 cc USP.

The antihistamines can be placed arbitrarily into six groups. This classification is based mainly on their relationship to the aminoethyl side chain of histamine and has value in that it provides a method of cataloguing agents which differ just enough to offer a selection to meet individual patient variations and to focus on specific needs.

1. *Ethylurediamine series.* This large group of general purpose antihistamines contains some very familiar proprietary names, including Neoantergen, Pyribenzamine, Histadyl, Anahist, and Antistine.

2. *Aminoalkylether series.* This group is strongly sedative almost to the hypnotic stage, and many have been used in nonprescription sleeping potions. Benadryl and Decapryn are the well-known members.

3. *Alkylamine series.* This group contains some of the newer and more potent antihistaminics which as a rule have a wider range of action and produce less drowsiness and sedation than the others. Chlor-Trimeton, Dimetane, Pyronil, and Forhistal are prominent names in this series.

4. *Individual or other series.* This group, represented primarily by Thephorin and Periactin, shows no clear relationship to the aminoethyl side chain, but its members are effective antihistamines, especially against serotonins. Many pharmacologists believe a fifth, or phenothiazine, classification is necessary in the grouping of histamine H receptor antagonists. Many of the phenothiazines act as antihistamines, the foremost example of which is promethazine (Phenergan). Others are trimeprazine (Temaril) and profenamine (Parsidol).

A new and exciting class of antihistamine drugs, the histamine H_2 receptor antagonists, are looming as important and effective in various areas of therapy. They inhibit gastric acid secretions stimulated by histamine released in the allergic phenomena.

Cimetidine (Tagamet) is the first to be released. Surprisingly, it also blocks secretion normally induced by insulin, foods, or vagal reflex; therefore it not only is classed with the antihistamines but also is a gastrointestinal drug for therapy in all duodenal and peptic ulcers and other conditions associated with gastric acid. It appears, *from the limited data available* at this writing, to be very effective and low in toxicity.

Another group of antihistamines, used primarily as anti-motion sickness agents, is listed separately. The vestibular apparatus is the site of motion sickness, and depression of this area by these agents relieves the symptoms of vertigo and nausea and also controls Meniere's syndrome. This depressant action is not solely antihistaminic, because many good antihistamines are ineffective; nor is it purely antiemetic, because chlorpromazine, a good anti-emetic, is not a good anti-motion sickness agent. Dramamine, Marezine, and Bonine are able representatives in this class.

Side effects, although usually minor, may be unexpected and aggravating. Inability to concentrate, dizziness, and disturbances of coordination are fairly common. Dryness of the mouth, pharynx, and bronchial mucosa with an irritating dry cough may occur. Often unwanted gastrointestinal effects occur, surprisingly in view of the antiemetic effect of many antihistamines. Occasionally a vasovagal effect with syncopal attacks may occur, and rarely other bizarre reactions such as delirium, narcolepsy, fever, and dermatitis have been noted. Topical application is of questionable value, and may cause hypersensitivity.

It is wise to remember that antihistamines are more potent in preventing the actions of histamine than in reversing these actions once they develop. Antihistamines are synergistic with depressant drugs and as a rule cause drowsiness.

In comparison with other effective drugs, the toxic features of most antihistamines are remarkably benign. However, recent animal studies have revealed drug-induced fetal abnormalities following high dosages of hydroxyzine, meclizine, and buclizine. Clinical data in human beings are inadequate to establish safety in gestation, except for chlorphenaramine and diphenhydramine.

GENERAL ANESTHETIC AGENTS

General anesthesia is seldom used in the average dental office, but sedation, produced by the inhalation of anesthetic gases through special apparatus, is common enough to deserve mention. Nitrous oxide and occasionally trichlorethylene are the agents of choice. Greater than average care and skill are demanded of individuals contemplating or employing such a procedure. No other area of dental practice is fraught with more hazards. Recording the number of presedation precautions or steps necessary for safe administration of these agents and the side effects or number of toxic manifestations which may be encountered subsequent to their use is beyond the scope of this chapter. However, the basic properties of these drugs should be noted.

Nitrous oxide is inexorably linked with early dentistry, and still retains a lofty place in our favor. "Analgesia machines" invariably employ nitrous oxide as the chief agent. This gas, in combination with 30 per cent or more of oxygen, will produce good-to-excellent sedation with little if any direct toxic effects. But the hallucinations and struggling which can occur with improper administration may produce excitement and exertion which could be harmful to patients in a precarious state of health, or which could result in physical injury.

Recent reports have revealed an intensification of the hallucinatory effect when nitrous oxide sedation is employed on marijuana users. Although some are more placid, the usual response is heightened euphoria and exaggerated physical movements during administration, and prolonged after-effects. Consistent marijuana smokers require an increased percentage of nitrous oxide in the sedative mixture, leading to increased CNS initiation and increased difficulty of management, resulting in a generally ineffective and disruptive session in which little may be accomplished.

Trilene is one of the most potent analgesics in use today. It can be one of the most dangerous. Cardiac arrhythmias regularly appear, even with small concentrations, and cases of cardiac arrest have been reported during the analgesic state. Arrest can occur following sudden increase in concentration, even in the conscious patient. It is deceptively easy to administer and pleasant, and can be used alone or in conjunction with nitrous oxide and oxygen. Tachypnea is also an undesirable effect. A rebreather cannister containing either Ca or $MgOH_2$ must not be used anywhere in the anesthesia circuit. Phosgene, a lethal gas (used in WWI), is formed by mixing trichlorethylene and soda lime ($CaOH_2$). Trilene is not recommended.

The foregoing information may all be historical in nature, because at this writing, the FDA has proposed a ban on all uses of trichlorethylene because tests (1977) at the National Cancer Institute revealed liver cancer in mice after exposure to it.

FDA Proposes Ban on Trichlorethylene (Official Government Release)

The Food and Drug Administration has proposed a ban on the chemical trichlorethylene (TCE), in foods, drugs, and cosmetics. The substance has been shown to cause liver cancer in mice, according to tests performed by the National Cancer Institute. Trichlorethylene was once widely used to remove caffeine from coffee.

Trichlorethylene, under the name of Trilene, in the past was used quite commonly as a general anesthetic for dental surgery. In recent years its popularity has decreased owing to the use of newer, less-toxic agents.

Fluroxene (Fluoromar) should be listed because it enjoyed a flair of popularity, which then quietly expired. It resembles ethyl ether, but is less flammable, not as potent, and more toxic.

In fact, *Fluothane, Penthrane* and *Ethrane* are the only acceptable potent, nonexplosive, inhalation agents which are relatively safe for general anesthesia. *Ethyl ether* and *cyclopropane* are not only potent but highly flammable, and should be administered only by experienced personnel using proper equipment in a grounded room. *Chloroform* and *ethyl chloride*, while nonflammable, are cardiotoxic agents with a narrow margin of safety even in the best of circumstances. Their general use has been sharply curtailed.

Halothane (Fluothane) has replaced most of the other inhalation anesthetics because of its potency, nonexplosive nature, and lack of toxicity, even though some cases of hepatic damage have been reported.

Methoxyflurane (Penthrane) has been promoted largely for its analgesic properties. Disposable inhalers controlled by the patient are available to secure a high plane of analgesia for minimal procedures. Induction is slower; otherwise it approximates halothane in most respects.

Abbott Laboratories issued a warning about Penthrane late in 1970, concerning the increased incidence of renal tubular dysfunction, sometimes with a fatal termination. Long, deep anesthetics on obese or aged patients are mostly implicated, but of particular interest to clinicians is that *concurrent use of methoxyflurane on a patient who is taking tetracyclines may result in death from kidney failure.*

Enflurane (Ethrane) is another fluorinated hydrocarbon which is enjoying increasing use. It is very similar to halothane and methoxyflurane. Induction is fairly rapid and not unpleasant! Enflurane causes little nausea and vomiting, is chemically stable, and has minimal after effects. Like halothane it enhances the effect of non-depolarizing muscle relaxants.

Propanidid (Epontol) is an IV agent resembling ultra-short-acting barbiturates in induction and maintenance techniques. Its significant difference is a temporary stimulatory rather than depressive effect on respiration and blood pressure. Although widely used in Europe and Canada, it is little known in the U.S. Epontol may be substituted for barbiturates in patients with porphyria. It has been combined with methohexital, but the therapeutic value of the resultant mixture is highly questionable.

The ultra-short IV barbiturates (Pentothal and Brevital) are similar to the other barbiturates in action and toxicity except for their incredible speed in producing a state of unconsciousness and almost as rapid detoxification under normal physiologic conditions.

Neuroleptanalgesia Anesthesia

Neuroleptanalgesia is an anesthetic technique using a neuroleptic (major tranquilizer) and a narcotic analgesic in conjunction with inhalation anesthesia for induction and maintenance.

Innovar combines a potent major tranquilizer (droperidol) with a potent narcotic analgesic (fentanyl) to achieve the anesthetic state with or without premedication. Used by some anesthetists at 1 cc per 20 lbs and others at 1 cc per 50 lbs of body weight, Innovar provides the induction and basic control with nitrous oxide–oxygen as the supplemental agent. The technique is to give two-thirds of the total measured dose in one bolus, a muscle relaxant, intubation, then maintenance with 2:1 N_2O–O_2 and small increments of the remaining drug.

Toxic effects are the usual ones expected with CNS depression, plus a unique one: thoracic rigidity. Compliance of the lungs is reduced, and ventilation becomes a problem. This rigidity usually occurs with large doses and is susceptible to muscle relaxants; nevertheless, it is an annoying complication.

The main advantage is *professed* to be increased safety for poor risk patients in that profound analgesia and sedation are obtained without serious impairment of vital centers or function. However, Innovar has been condemned by Medical Letter as an unacceptable drug, not only because of its side effects but also because it is a potent compound with a fixed dose ratio which in this enlightened era of pharmacodynamics is not only frowned upon but subject to critical scrutiny from all angles.

It is possible to obtain a neuroleptic state without rigidity by judicious combinations of droperidol and fentanyl and other potent tranquilizers and analgesics. However, this is a jungle for the initiate or novice. Serious hypotension and respiratory depression along with other CNS problems often must be dealt with in this area of practice. The dental practitioner should be familiar with antagonists and analeptics, such as naloxone and physostigmine, and doxapram, and the selective employment of the proper vasopressors and/or analeptics in patients under MAO and trycyclic therapy, the restrictions involved with use of alpha (phenotolamine [Regitine]) and beta (propranalol [Inderal]) blockers, and other facts such as *possible epinephrine reversal with phenothiazines and occasionally with butyrophenones*. This information should be as familiar to you as is the use of O_2. Lack of knowledge concerning the alleviation and control of CNS vagaries with the proper agents and techniques should preclude ventures into this hazardous area of dental practice.

Disassociative Anesthesia

Disassociative anesthesia is another new technique defined as disassociation with profound analgesia in the presence of superficial sleep.

Ketamine HCl is the forerunner of what hopefully will be a new and exciting category of anesthetic agents. By definition it is not a true anesthetic. Its action is characterized by a peculiar state of unconsciousness in which sensory input is not blocked at the spinal or brain stem levels but afferent impulses received are interrupted in the association area of the cortex.

Outwardly the patient appears to be in a trance and unaware of painful stimuli; his eyes remain open, but he is oblivious to his surroundings.

The dosage is calculated by body weight and is injected *slowly* IV as a bolus, 1 mg per lb. Subsequent increments are at reduced strength (0.5 mg per lb). When excessive movements of the head or extremities occur (usually after 10 minutes) the injection of 0.5 mg per pound is repeated at these intervals until the surgery is completed.

The IM dose, which is especially useful for "hard-to-manage" children, is given in one quick "pop," 5 mg per lb. If additional anesthetic is needed, the strength is reduced to 2.5 mg per lb and repeated in 20 to 30 minutes.

Arbitrary limits for the number of repeated doses may be set at 15 for IV and five for IM.

There are several striking advantages evident in a ketamine anesthetic. The airway is not a major problem, because muscle tone and pharyngeal and laryngeal reflexes are largely unaffected. Cardiovascular and respiratory function are seldom impaired, and the CNS is not depressed significantly.

There is also a reverse and darker side of the coin. Sudden and drastic rise in blood pressure has been a factor often enough to curtail ketamine's use in hypertensive or arteriosclerotic patients. Mental complications are emerging in approximately 15 per cent of adult patients and are also prevalent in children. Delirium nightmares, hallucinations, and even schizoid reactions are seen during the recovery period. Although many are the result of improper handling, early aural, visual, or tactile stimulation must be avoided or kept minimal; the reactions are so strong and in some cases so persistent (for months) that ketamine's use should be restricted to specific cases until these psychic alterations can be eliminated or controlled. Valium has been used (with questionable success) by many investigators as a premedicant designed to reduce and/or negate these shattering psychic phenomena. At this time its value as a control remains controversial. Physostigmine will control most toxic phenomena.

The foregoing general anesthetic agents are included with brief comments only to maintain continuity and not with the intention of suggesting their use in any practice. Some — ether and cyclopropane — are too hazardous for office use; others — chloroform and ethyl chloride — are too hazardous for any use except in dire emergencies when other agents are unavailable. Fluothane and the IV barbiturates are potent drugs safe only in the hands of dentists properly trained in intratracheal anesthetic and resuscitative techniques.

LOCAL ANALGESIC AGENTS

The majority of local analgesics are esters of aromatic acids which usually contain an amino group and aliphatic amino alcohols. Ortho-amino, para-amino, meta-aminobenzoic acid, and benzoic acid esters are the predominant compounds. These ester types are primarily hydrolyzed in the plasma or in the liver by esterases. The aniline compounds, lidocaine (Xylocaine), propiticaine (Citanest) and mepivacaine (Carbocaine) compose the only other major local analgesic formulas suitable for injection. These drugs are not hydrolyzed in the plasma or liver, but depend on urinary excretion and redistribution into nonsensitive tissues for their detoxification.

The general aim in the synthesis of new anesthetic compounds is to produce more potent drugs with decreased systemic and local toxicity. In most cases, toxicity tends to rise as potency increases. If, however, the structural change responsible for the increased potency also increases the hydrolysis rate, then the toxicity of the new compound may be decreased. A good example of such a compound is 2-chloroprocaine (Nesacaine), which although twice as potent as procaine, is, because of its five times more rapid hydrolysis rate, less toxic. Since the temporary inhibition of conduction is the purpose of a local analgesic, diffusibility or the penetration of nerve sheaths in sufficient concentrations is a foremost consideration in determining its effectiveness.

Toxicity is a relative value. One local analgesic may initiate more frequent, even more severe episodes than another, but still not be as dangerous or lethal; for example, lidocaine is supposedly twice as toxic as procaine, but is not etiologic in nearly as many fatal or anaphylactic seizures.

Toxicity from overdose, yielding a blood level of the drug high enough to affect the vital centers, is caused either by intravascular injection, too large a volume, too concentrated a solution (percentage), or injecting rapidly into vascular areas.

A sparsely known fact of inestimable importance is that topical anesthetics are more rapidly absorbed from mucous membranes than from any other tissues. Blood level curves are similar to those following IV injection and grossly higher than subcutaneous or intramuscular infiltration. Vasopressors will not prevent or even retard absorption of the topical anesthetic, whether applied by swab or spray or gargle. Contrary to expectations, vasopressors offer no protection against sudden high levels.

The first symptoms of toxicity of the ester types are those of cerebral cortical stimulation characterized by talkativeness, restlessness, apprehension, excitement, and possibly convulsions. However, lidocaine and mepivacaine are different, causing cortical depression, lethargy, drowsiness, and sleep. If the toxic response is moderate to severe, medullary stimulation follows the cerebral cortical phase. Then, increased blood pressure, pulse rate, and respirations are evident. Nausea and vomiting also may occur. The final phase is medullary depression whose severity is directly proportional to the amount or degree of the previous stimulation. Blood pressure drops, pulse may become slow and thready, and respiration weakens or ceases. In almost all cases, death following a toxic overdose of a local analgesic drug is the result of respiratory depression or apnea.

While a great deal has been written concerning allergic reactions to local analgesic drugs, *true allergy is uncommon*. It has been extimated that only about 1 per cent of all reactions occurring during local analgesia are allergic in origin. However, when anaphylaxis strikes, manifested by sudden violent loss of vasomotor tonus (i.e., blood pressure and pulse), it is the most terrifying and hazardous reaction possible. Despite prompt and accurate treatment, even heroic measures, a fatal termination may be unavoidable.

Since it is a fact that some patients are allergic to local analgesics and that these allergies can be dangerous, it is also a fact that a patient who is allergic to any one drug usually will be allergic to every other drug of closely related chemical structure. Therefore, the local analgesics grouped according to their chemical structures are listed for edification and guidance in substituting one agent for another when allergy is suspected or confirmed.

    I.   Benzoic acid esters
          Piperocaine (Metycaine)
          Meprylcaine (Orocaine)
          Kincaine (Kincaine)
    II. Para-aminobenzoic acid esters
          Procaine (Novocaine)
          Tetracaine (Pontocaine)
          Butethamine (Monocaine)
          Propoxycaine (Ravocaine)
          2-Chloroprocaine (Nesacaine)
          Procaine and Butethamine (Duocaine)
   III. Meta-aminobenzoic acid esters
          Metabutethamine (Unacaine)
          Primacaine (Primacaine)
   IV. Para-ethroxybenzoic acid esters
          Diethoxin (Intracaine)
    V. Cyclohexylamino-2 propylbenzoate
          Hexylcaine (Cyclaine)
   VI. Anilide or Amide
          Bupivacaine (Marcaine)
          Etidocaine (Duranest)
          Lidocaine (Xylocaine)
          Mepivacaine (Carbocaine)
          Propiticaine (Citanest)
          Quanticaine (Tarracine)

A new anilide derivative, bupivacaine (Marcaine) is a potent and long-acting local analgesic with good tissue penetrating properties and low incidence of side effects. Surprisingly, when compared with lidocaine, bupivacaine is superior in all areas: lower toxicity in equipotent doses, greater potency, quicker onset, longer duration (2 to 4 times), latent pain-free period after return to normal sensation in many patients, *and no requirement of a vasoconstrictor for consistent profoundness.*

It is contraindicated in children and retarded patients because of the possibility of lip chewing or self-mutilation.

Etidocaine (Duranest) is another amide or anilide derivative which is so similar in every respect to bupivacaine that a repetitive dissertation on its properties is not needed. A preference between the two brands may be determined after a lengthier trial but at this time none can be found in the literature.[18, 28, 41]

Until now, tetracaine held the longevity record, but duration is not a prime factor in most dental procedures, whereas toxicity is! Since tetracaine is also the most lethal of local analgesics, it has not been a favorite for office-type practice despite its proved worth.

As a general rule, the potency of a local analgesic depends solely on its chemical structure, while the duration, although markedly influenced by the molecular configuration, can also be altered by the addition of a vasoconstrictor drug. This additive has an important and sometimes vitally necessary function when one remembers that all the local analgesic agents in use in dentistry today, with the possible exception of Xylocaine, Carbocaine, and Monocaine, are vasodilators and, as such, are rapidly absorbed into the systemic circulation, thereby increasing the possibility of toxic overdose and decreasing local potency and duration.

The addition of beta-receptor blocking agents such as propranolol HCl to local anesthetic agents, in order to minimize or counteract undesirable cardiovascular and CNS symptoms, has been tested without significantly favorable results.

VASOPRESSORS OR VASOCONSTRICTORS

Despite the controversies that continue to swirl around the use, non-use, and abuse of the vasoconstrictor drugs, they are an integral part of most of the local analgesic solutions used in dentistry. Of the five sympathomimetic drugs commonly present as vasoconstrictors in dental analgesic solutions, all provide satisfactory results, with epinephrine being the most efficient, followed in order by Levophed, Cobefrin, Neo-Cobefrin, and Neo-Synephrine.

The importance of the sympathomimetic agents cannot be overstressed, particularly when it is considered that, because of their vasodilatory effect which increases with an increase in strength, very few if any of the local analgesics would produce satisfactory anesthesia for dental procedures without the addition of a vasopressor drug. Yet it is unlikely that there exists a dental practitioner in this country who has not received a note from the physician of a patient with cardiovascular disease, admonishing against the use of an anesthetic containing an adrenergic agent. Again, who will deny that the anxiety and stress created by painful dental treatment may provoke an ungovernable and unmeasurable release of endogenous epinephrine into this same patient's vascular system? It is the considered and published opinion of most cardiologists and internists that vasopressors should be used with local analgesics in treating patients with cardiovascular disease. Rather than increasing the hazard, it enhances the safety and comfort of dental procedures for these simple and sufficient reasons: (1) an increase in depth with the attendant psychic and physiologic benefits; (2) prevention of too rapid or too quantitative absorption of a potentially toxic and/or lethal drug (local analgesic) into the circulation; (3) reduction of bacteremia by decreasing circulation in the area of septic surgery; (4) reduction of hemorrhage in hypertensive patients; and (5) reduction of local tissue damage inherent with repeated injections and large quantities of irritating solutions. Provided proper precautions are observed (instrumentation and technique), the use of epinephrine within prescribed limits is considered safe for most cardiac patients. Knowledge of the anatomy, selection of the proper site before injection, good technique, and aspiration ordinarily will create a satisfactory plane of anesthesia even with minimal amounts of weaker analgesic solutions. Since the goal of chemotherapy is to achieve optimum therapeutic results with minimum alterations of normal physiology, one can hardly quibble when a majority of internists and anesthesiologists agree that 1 per cent solutions containing 1:200,000 parts epinephrine will provide a sufficient degree of anesthesia for most dental operations when properly employed. The reader is referred to Chapters 2 and 10 for further discussions of epinephrine.

Another cogent factor, often blithely ignored or disregarded, is that compounds containing racemic epinephrine, used in packing gingival areas to facilitate impression-taking of teeth prepared for restorative dentistry, can be extremely dangerous. The rapid absorption of large quantities of epinephrine through the abraded tissues of the gingiva and adjacent capillary plexuses may precipitate a profound cardiovascular reaction or crisis. One need only remember the swift and potent response to nitroglycerin when placed on the normal mucosa of the sublingual area to appreciate the amplified effect possible when other strong drugs are applied to lacerated and bleeding tissues in the same area.

Undoubtedly many untoward systemic reactions are attributed to the local analgesic drugs when the constrictors are the real offenders. The symptoms arising from toxic overdose of a vasopressor are mainly palpitation, tachycardia, hypertension, and headache, which differ from the signs of CNS stimulation and/or depression synonymous with local analgesic toxicity.

True allergic manifestations from vasoconstrictor drugs are extremely rare or do not exist. Many authorities state that any direct reactions attributable to the vasopressor drugs are due to overdose or idiosyncrasy and may be limited to those four mentioned above. All other complications which may ensue, other than occasional tissue slough from ischemia at the site of injection, should be blamed on other sources or agents.

ANTIBIOTICS

Most discussions on antibiotics and their usage end in impasse: there are few phases of medicine which provoke more passionate commitments and denouncements — more heat and less light.

Many enthusiastic practitioners will defend overusage on the grounds of beneficial secondary effects, such as lowered incidence of rheumatic fever because of prophylactic penicillin in pediatric nasopharyngeal infections.

Others will condemn this practice on the basis of a growing resistance of bacteria engendered by promiscuous application of these drugs, and the pyramiding number of allergic and toxic reactions appearing in the literature. This chapter is of course concerned with the latter.

There are several types of antibiotic toxicity: anaphylaxis — shock or acute cardiovascular collapse; simple allergy — edema, hives, rashes, etc.; auditory — damage to eighth cranial nerve and cochlea; hematopoietic — marrow damage and aplastic anemia; renal and hepatic — tubular (kidney) damage and necrosis of the liver; superinfection — disruption of normal bacterial flora, degenerative intestinal mucosa changes, fungus overgrowth, or chronic or persistent diarrhea.

The condemnation of piggy-back antibiotic combinations, alluded to in the first edition because of their questionable value and inherent dangers, has intensified to the point that their manufacture and distribution have ceased (with a few exceptions) and the shotgun concept has been virtually discarded. Antibiotics should be used as a rifle rather than a scattergun because they have an amazing degree of specificity. Accurate evaluation is virtually impossible with such conglomerate packaging.

The use of antibiotics in dental practice is not and should not be confined only to infections in and about the oral cavity. It is difficult for most of us to envision the potential danger and the very real chance of tragic consequences from relatively simple dental procedures performed on a patient with a history of cardiac damage. In individuals with rheumatic or congenital heart disease, bacteria present in the blood may lodge on damaged heart valves or other parts of the endocardium because of the roughened cauliflower-like surface of the scar tissue there. Concentration of bacteria or bacteremia, even though transitory, constitutes a measurable threat of bacterial endocarditis — a potential crippling or even fatal infection which often does not respond to massive doses of antibiotics.

It is well established that transitory bacteremia does result from tooth extraction, oral surgical procedures, manipulation of periodontal tissues, and removal of tonsils and adenoids.

In patients with cardiopathies it is recommended that antibiotics be used routinely in conjunction with the aforementioned procedures to decrease the likelihood that bacterial endocarditis will occur.

The purpose of antibiotic therapy is, of course, a prophylactic weapon to prevent bacteremia or reduce the magnitude or duration should it occur and to eradicate bacteria that may implant on heart valves before a vegetation is formed. Penicillin is the drug of choice. Although broad-spectrum antibiotics may decrease bacteremia, they cannot be relied upon to eradicate initial bacterial implants and for this reason they are not recommended. Erythromycin is always the second choice if an allergy to penicillin exists. Sulfonamides are completely unsatisfactory.

ROUTE OF ADMINISTRATION

The oral route of administration for dental infections involving the mucous membranes, skin, other soft tissues, and the sinuses is usually sufficient. Serious bone infections require parenteral IM injections for high effectiveness, while gross phlegmons (cellulitis, Ludwig's, etc.), which interfere with respiration or a patent airway, septicemia, and endocarditis are always treated with maximum IV doses.

The last infections mentioned are naturally of high morbidity, and the IV therapy is usually a combination of a penicillin and an aminoglycoside (i.e., carbenicillin and tobramycin, which together are potent in action and broad in spectrum), unless, of course, the patient is allergic or sensitive to one class or the other.

Regardless, potentially lethal infections of the oral maxillofacial complex require a consultation with an internist trained or specializing in antimicrobial therapy.

Classification according to molecular mechanism of action has an important part in the better understanding of the goals in antibiotic therapy.

I. Agents that alter structure and function of the cell wall (protein synthesis):
    The penicillins
    Cephalothin and analogues
    Bacitracin
    Vancomycin
    Ristocetin
    Cycloserine
II. Agents that restrict function of the cell membrane (penetrate cell wall and cytoplasm):
    Nystatin
    Amphotericin B
    Polymyxin B
    Tyrocidin
    Gramicidin
    Colistin
III. Agents that impair translation of genetic information (ribosome code, RNA, etc.) into protein synthesis:
    The tetracyclines
    Erythromycin, Oleandomycin, and TAO
    Lincomycin and Clindamycin
    Chloramphenicol
    Neomycin
    Streptomycin
    Kanamycin
    Gentamicin
    Tobramycin
IV. Agents that impede replication of genetic information:
    Nalidixic acid
    Griseofulvin

Following is the list of the major and minor antibiotics in use at this time and the toxic effects which they may produce.

Penicillins

In many ways this drug is the most remarkable and effective weapon of modern medicine. Even with the extensive publicity given the newer "wonder drugs," penicillin remains the premier antibiotic. Were it not for its allergic potential, penicillin would be the safest and most useful agent of all. More research in the area of synthetic congeners may eliminate this danger.

Regardless of personal preference or safety reservations, penicillin is the standard by which most others are judged. Despite the knowledgeable air some therapists assume when the acquired resistance of bacteria to penicillin is discussed, there are, in fact, few significant data to support or structure this indictment. It still slaughters most streptococci and other gram-positive organisms with relative ease and impunity. However, penicillin-resistant staphylococci are a case apart.

Because of protein binding, acid sensitivity, and penicillinase problems, new analogs of penicillin have been evolved to solve or minimize the factors which render them weak or useless.

More data are certainly in order concerning the basic nature of antimicrobial agents, even though the majority of clinicians practicing today have been brought up in the antibiotic era. The penicillins act basically by interference with the biosynthesis of bacterial cell walls. Penicillin G, or benzylpenicillin, is the standard and exists in four therapeutic forms, aqueous, procaine, benzathine, and Oralpen. The *aqueous* form is given IV in million-plus unit doses and is effective for four to six hours, then must be repeated. Procaine is injected IM and lasts up to 24 hours. The procaine factor acts as an analgesic as well as a depot storage vehicle, therein slowing release of the penicillin. The usual dosage to maintain blood level is 600,000 to 1,000,000 units B.I.D. *Benzathine* is the long lasting (30 days) form permitting low dose (extended or continuous) for patients with rheumatic hearts and others who must have an effective blood level at all times in order to survive. The usual dose is 1.2 million units every 30 days. *Oralpen* is the ordinary Na or K form of penicillin G. These tablets must be used in high dosage forms, 1.5 million units or 1.5 to 2 gm, in order to provide adequate blood levels because exposure to gastric secretions destroys more than 50 per cent of the active drug.

Penicillin V, or phenoxymethyl penicillin, is the other form of the basic agent. Its primary virtue is the ability to resist degradation or destruction by gastric action to the point where 80 to 90 per cent of the oral dose remains effective.

Why, then, should penicillin V not be the drug of choice by the oral route? Scientifically it is, but economically it is not! Penicillin G is far less expensive than penicillin V, so even when two or three times as much is needed, it is still less costly. Physiologically, the amount makes little difference because penicillin is relatively nontoxic.

Methicillin is employed against penicillinase-producing staphylococcus. It is usually restricted to hospital use and must be given IV or IM. (Dosage 6–12 Grn/D IV.)

Carbenicillin (Carboxybenzylpenicillin) acts against the normal spectrum + penicillinase + gram negative bacilli (pseudomonas, proteus, and enterobacteria). It is frequently used in combination with gentamicin and tobramycin in potentially lethal infections. A great drawback in its employment is that bacteria develop resistance in a short time.

Cloxacillin and *dicloxacillin* are oral forms of synthetic or semisynthetic penicillins formulated to combat penicillinase-producing staphylococcus dosage: 250-500 mg Q.I.D.).

Oxacillin (Tegopen) and *Nafcillin* (Unipen), also in this group, are available in IM and IV formulation — 500 mg Q.I.D. Nafcillin (Unipen) yields better tissue levels in comparison. It is also mixed with aminoglycosides in therapy for highly morbid infections.

A good rule of thumb in suspected gram positive or staphylococcus infections is to start the patient on any one of these four agents before precise bacteriology is known, especially if the infection is a fulminating type!

Ampicillin (α-amino benzyl penicillin) and *amoxicillin* (same formula + H), which yield higher blood levels, are semisynthetic broad-spectrum penicillins which cover the penicillin G range plus many gram negative bacilli. However, they are ineffective against penicillinase-producing staphylococcus. The range includes *Escherichia coli, Proteus mirabilis, Salmonella, Shigella, Neisseria meningitides* and *Haemophilus influenzae*. Ampicillin is the drug of choice for influenza bacteria.

The ampicillins must be ingested at least 30 minutes before eating in order to prevent a decline or diminution of their effectiveness.

A majority of those colleagues who are really aware of all the vagaries and implications of penicillin therapy agree that the least expensive form of penicillin G if used in *large enough doses* will do the job as well as the more exotic and expensive relatives in its family. Penicillin should never be used topically, because ingestion through the skin, especially mucous membranes, greatly enhances the sensitivity effect. Toxic manifestation may be severe enough to be fatal (anaphylactoid shock and glottic edema) or mild enough merely to produce pruritus, rash, and hives. Toxic states with the severity of their symptoms somewhere between these extremes commonly occur. The signs may be immediate or may appear after a prolonged time, and their magnitude is variable and unpredictable.

Before we continue with other listings, a short dissertation on microbes will refresh your memory and aid substantially to your knowledgeable use of antibiotic compounds.

The five most common microorganisms found in odontogenic infections are, in order of frequency: *Streptococcus viridans, Neisseria catarrhalis, Staphylococcus albus* (DNase negative), *Staphylococcus aureus* (DNase positive), and anaerobic streptococci. These are all aerobic save the last and all are gram positive and therefore usually susceptible to the penicillins, the cephalosporins, erythromycin, and clindamycin.

Other common offenders are diphtheroids *Klebsiella, Hemophilus influenzae,* and occasionally *Proteus mirabilis,* H enterococci, *N. pharyngis,* and pneumococci. It would seem logical that most oral bacteria would be aerobic, but not so—over three fourths of mouth organisms extant are anaerobic. Since most cultures taken are only for aerobic tests, one can't help wonder if we are really aware of the true etiology in many head and neck infections. If moderate to *serious disease exists, it is wise to ask for and take anaerobic cultures with the special equipment needed.*

The most common anaerobics associated with oral and respiratory infections are *Bacteroides melaninogenicus,* fusobacteria (fusiform bacilli), and peptostreptococci. This group, along with others found in oral infection—*B. oralis, Clostridium* spp., and *Veillonella* spp.—are usually highly susceptible to penicillin G.

Cephalosporins

GROUP I

Cephalothin (Keflin), cephapirin (Cefadyl), and cephacetrile (Celospor) are all parenteral forms and are rapidly detoxified by the liver and excreted within 4 hours. This group is safe in most penicillin allergy cases. The IM dose is 500 mg every 8 hours, and the IV dose is 25 mg per kg every 3 to 6 hours. Higher or more frequent doses are mandatory in serious infections.

GROUP II

Cephaloridine (Loridine) and cefazolin (Kefzol, Ancef) are also parenteral forms but are long acting because of slow excretion and protein binding. They are considered best in meningitis, but are limited to a maximum dose of 4 gm per day because of their propensity for nephrotoxicity. Azotemia can be checked for with a Coombs' test.

GROUP III

Cephalexin (Keflex), cephaloglycin (Kafocin), and Cephadrine (Velosef, Anspor) are all oral forms with low protein binding and a high activity blood level. Kidney problems are minimal with unimpaired excretion.

As a group they are effective against penicillinase-producing staphylococci and are lower in allergic response.

In all serious infections where allergenicity is unknown and effectiveness against cell walls of gram positive or negative bacteria is needed, a cephalosporin is the drug of choice. They also will control *Staphylococcus epidermidis*, which is an increasingly morbid factor because it seems to have a predilection for metal. Heart valves, hip and other bone implants, and embedded mesh and wires are in jeopardy from this new manifestation in a formerly rather innocuous microbe.

All in all, the *broader spectrum* of the cephalosporins makes them more likely to *alter the normal microbial ecology of the host* and render him more susceptible to superinfections with resistant *Pseudomonas, E. coli,* and enterobacteria.

The Macrolides: Erythromycin (Ilosone, Erythrocin, E-mycin); Oleandomycin; TAO

Erythromycin operates best in the same bacterial spectrum (gram-positive) as penicillin and as such is used as a penicillin substitute. Although not as effective, it is much safer. Hypersensitivity reactions and bacterial resistance are rarely encountered. Toxicity to erythromycin is almost negligible except for mild gastrointestinal irritation and diarrhea. Reports of allergy are scattered and inconclusive. The estolate salt has been linked with cholestatic jaundice. However, because of erythromycin's proven safety it is often prescribed as a placebo to the detriment of the efficacious ratio and its future value.

Erythromycin is bacteriostatic in normal doses but frequently moves into the bactericidal range when employed in large increments. The dosage is 1–2 gm or more per day.

A big drawback is its incompatibility with almost all IV medications, including catecholamines, vitamins, barbiturates, phenothiazines, phenytoin (Dilantin), lactobinate salts, succinate salts, and other antibiotics. It also influences many lab tests to give false readings (especially liver profile tests); this may be an important factor in total patient therapy.

Oleandomycin and Triacetyloleandomycin (TAO) fall in the same spectrum and category as erythromycin but are being phased out because they are less active and more toxic. They are limited to 10-day usage, with hepatic and GI problems (nausea, vomiting, and colitis) a not infrequent deleterious effect. Anaphylaxis has been reported which, along with the above, certainly removes oleandomycin and TAO from consideration in dental therapeutics.

Lincomycin (Lincocin); Clindamycin (Cleocin)

Isolated from the fungus *Streptomyces lincolnensis*, these antibiotics are usually bactericidal against gram-positive pathogens and effective to some degree against the remainder of the organisms in this class. No serious hypersensitivity reactions (angioneurotic edema, anaphylaxis, etc.) have been reported at this date, but gastrointestinal irritation (nausea, diarrhea, and cramps), colitis, and superinfection appear to be the major toxic manifestations. Lincomycin (parenteral), Lincocin, and clindamycin (oral) (Cleocin) inhibit protein synthesis (ribosomes and polypeptides). Because of their affinity or predilection for bone infections* and undoubted effectiveness against staphylococci, these drugs were accepted as heaven sent by most clinicians who daily deal with bacterial osteitis and occasional osteomyelitis. They are effective but not as potent as first hoped. Still, if you respect the limitations, they are second (at least on a par with erythromycin) to penicillin and the cephalosporins in pharyngitis, otitis media, dental infections (bone and soft tissue), septicemia, cellulitis, osteomyelitis[34a] and some thoracic infections. *They are not affected by probenecid but are antagonized by erythromycin, and the two should never be used together.* Protein binding is low, therefore they present a fairly high level of activity early. It is the preferred drug in anaerobic penicillin resistant (or allergy) infections,* especially *B. fragilis.* As mentioned, allergy is not a big factor and toxicity is mainly confined to the bowel but it must be stressed that its manifestations can be extremely serious (bleeding, ulceration, and slough). More than 300 cases of clindamycin-induced colitis, including 20 deaths, have been reported.[42] The dosage is 150 to 300 mg four times per day.

Tetracycline (Achromycin, Tetracyn, etc.), Chlortetracycline (Aureomycin), Oxytetracycline (Terramycin), Demethylchlortetracycline (Declomycin), Methacycline (Rondomycin), Doxycycline (Vibramycin), Rolitetracycline (Syntetrin, Velacycline), Minocycline (Minocin)

These are the major members of a large group of closely related antibiotics known for their broad spectrum of activity. Although this wide range is certainly a desirable factor, tetracyclines, unlike penicillin, which is bacteriolytic, are bacteriostatic and consequently are ordinarily neither as rapid nor as effective in overcoming severe infections. They are not first choice for any dental or pharyngeal infection, with the possible exception of *parotitis*

---

*Conjectured, but accepted by most.

(salivary adenitis). Minocin has a predilection for salivary glands (unfortunately it also has a high ratio of allergenicity), and *osteoradionecrosis* where Vibramycin has been effective. A recent study found tetracycline to be useless in the treatment of most periodontal diseases. Toxic effects are usually manifested by gastrointestinal symptoms of nausea, vomiting, and diarrhea, which can preclude the more serious alimentary mucous membrane degenerative changes resulting from superinfection. This change in resident bacterial flora offers the chance for monilial growth and persistent diarrhea. A relatively new and, from the dental standpoint, serious finding is that ingestion of tetracyclines by pregnant women may result in a faulty development and yellow discoloration of the dentition of the fetus in utero and in early childhood which persists throughout life. The platitude, shared by many in the past, that tetracyclines were rather innocuous and could be prescribed with alacrity as a placebo with an "I must do something positive for the patient; it can't hurt, and may help" attitude has been shattered. Fatal anaphylaxis is not an unknown entity.

Aminoglycosides

The aminoglycosides encompass a large group of antibiotics including old standbys and some of the newest "wonder" drugs.

Streptomycin, neomycin, kanamycin, gentamicin, tobramycin, paramycin and *amikacin* are now used in therapy, while sisomycin and lividomycin are expected to be released within a year's time.

Administration covers all routes, with kanamycin, paramycin, and neomycin available PO, and the others parenterally. Neomycin, of course, is effective topically. Amikacin is new and is the drug of choice to combat gram-negative bacteria which appear to resist the aminoglycosides.

Antibiotics of this class are synergistic and compatible with the penicillins, and exhibit bacteriostatic action in low doses and lytic action in high doses, especially against gram-negative bacilli. However, because of their extreme side effects, dental use should be limited (except for topical neomycin) to life threatening maxillofacial infections. Permanent damage to the auditory nerve, cochlear and vestibular labyrinthitis, and lethal nephrotoxicity are common with unrestricted or careless use of aminoglycosides.

Pre-therapeutic renal function tests are mandatory when extended usage is planned. Dosage is 3 mg per kg per day for 24 hours in lethal infections and 2 mg per kg per day thereafter. Aminoglycosides are more active in an alkaline atmosphere (8–$60\times$) and less in high osmolality. Calcium ions (milk, etc.) may negate their action.

Spectinomycin (Trobicin)

This is very similar in all respects to the aminoglycosides, and, in addition, it builds up quick resistance. Its only use is for stubborn cases of gonorrhea where its effectiveness is determined by a definite and lethal affinity for the gonococci.

Chloramphenicol (Chloromycetin)

This drug exhibits a wide range of activity: gram-positive and gram-negative bacteria, rickettsias, typhoid, and some large viruses are susceptible to its action. It has a predilection for cerebrospinal fluid, and this and its broad spectrum make it valuable in bacterial meningitis. But the general usefulness of this potent agent is limited (except as a life-saving measure) because chloramphenicol has been found to produce blood dyscrasias and other gross degenerative changes. Although justification for the employment of Chloromycetin in any dental disease seems inconceivable, it should have a proper listing. Toxic effects are mainly concerned with marrow damage and resultant agranulocytosis or aplastic anemia, but newborn infants may be fatally poisoned by their failure to carry out the glucuronide conjugation necessary for metabolizing this agent. Temporary erythroid hypoplasia and gastrointestinal symptoms are other unwelcome side effects.

Carbomycin

Employed in the same situations and very similar to oleandomycin in action, this antibiotic precipitates minor gastrointestinal disorders, but dangerous toxicity has yet to be reported.

Novobiocin

Skin eruptions, jaundice-like discoloration of epithelium, possible liver damage, and blood dyscrasias are among the detrimental effects attributed to this antibiotic. These plus a narrow range of activity curtail its value.

Polymyxins

Reports of renal damage should provoke a hesitant attitude toward the general use of polymyxin B. It also causes postinjection pain.

The polymyxins A B C D E are all forms of this active group of antibiotics but only poly B and colistin (E) are in therapeutic use and then only topically, where they are bactericidal. Care is necessary because the toxic manifestations (nephrosis, peripheral neuropathy, and respiratory arrest) are severe.

Vancomycin

This is a dangerous nephrotoxic and ototoxic drug (resembling the aminoglycosides). Its use is restricted to treatment of coccal endocarditis and other morbid gram-positive coccal infections when the patient is allergic to all other appropriate antibiotics. Intermittent IV only with 1 gm every 12 hours.

Rifampin

Rifampin is an oral drug with great potential and low toxicity. It is effective against most gram-positive and gram-negative bacteria, some viruses, and *Mycobacterium tuberculosis*. Most experts in antimicrobial therapy feel its use should be limited to tuberculosis treatment, but it is effective in a broad spectrum, if needed.

Several of these listed antibiotics have little and often highly questionable application in dental infections, but are mentioned because of their popularity. Other new products, such as cycloserine, ristocetin, Coly-Mycin, nalidixic acid, fucidic acid, and viomycin, should also fall in this restricted category.

There are two other antibiotics whose primary value lies in topical application. They frequently appear in the form of lozenges, sprays, and creams in combination with many other agents. Despite their largely empirical employment, they do have therapeutic value. Bacitracin is effective on surface tissues against most of the gram-positive and some of the gram-negative cocci. It is not locally toxic or irritating.

Tyrothricin has a limited field of usefulness because its action is inhibited by the presence of gram-negative organisms, but it is bactericidal for streptococci and staphylococci in open wounds. This drug is remarkably low in sensitizing capacity to all tissues except the meninges. It is highly toxic when it is introduced accidentally or otherwise into the subarachnoid space. If such a possibility exists, the use of tyrothricin should be avoided.

Sulfonamides

Other agents used to control infections in the body are not true antibiotics, which by definition must be produced by living things, but synthetic compounds from the chemical laboratory. This chemotherapeutic group includes the sulfonamides, the antifungal drugs, the antiprotozoan drugs and the vermifuges. Only the first two classes are germane to dentistry and will be discussed.

Sulfadiazine is by consensus the most effective and least toxic of the sulfas, but sulfisoxazole (Gantrisin) and the triple sulfas are also widely and effectively employed, especially in urinary infections. Sulfas are highly bound in blood protein.

Sulfadimethoxine (Madribon) is another popular and potent product which has been accused of precipitating Stevens-Johnson syndrome (severe erythema multiforme with bulla formation) in a limited number of patients. Although rare, it is unfortunately a highly morbid disease.

In general, sulfonamides should be used guardedly and only after critical appraisal in patients with liver or renal damage, urinary obstructions, and blood dyscrasias. Skin rashes and angioneurotic edema do occur, but the major toxicity ordinarily encountered with the sulfas is crystalluria, which produces irritation of the kidneys and urinary tract and tubular obstruction. Adjuvant therapy with sodium bicarbonate will result in an alkaline urine, thus preventing crystal formation.

Fungicides and Fungistats

Three of the newer antifungal agents are widely, but not necessarily wisely, used in combination with the tetracyclines. Their effectiveness in short-term therapy is debatable.

Antifungal agents usually have a detergent-like effect on the fungal cell wall. In past years, a tetracycline-nystatin combination (Mysteclin F) was the antibiotic most commonly prescribed by the dental profession. No comment on the wisdom of this choice is necessary.

Amphotericin B is the best of the group for serious mycotic infection and is employed as an IV drip (50 mg every 6 hours). It is occasionally toxic to the kidneys and GI system, and can cause CNS depression with headache, fever, and chills.

Flucytosine is the safest of these agents and is the preferred choice for most mild to moderate cases. The dose is 500 mg four times a day by mouth.

Nystatin may be given orally or topically and is effective against *Candida* and *Monilia,* which is part of the normal flora. It is occasionally inactivated by gastric juice.

Griseofulvin is used primarily for dermatophytes (tinea) rather than systemic mycoses. It is taken orally for long periods, three to four weeks for skin infections and six to 12 months for nail infections. It acts by being deposited in the growing integument (keratin).

Nitrofurazone (Furacin)

A nitrofuran derivative, this agent is very effective against many organisms, both gram-negative and gram-positive, which are resistant to regular antibiotics and is bactericidal in a broad spectrum. It is applied topically in solution or ointment-like form. Continuous use for ten or more days often results in local tissue irritation and occasionally in generalized allergic skin reaction. In short term use, it is nontoxic, effective in blood or pus, and promotes healing. Furacin gauze is a favorite for packing infected antrums or covering wounds.

Other nitrofurans are nalidixic acid and methenamine.

Antiviral Agents

Like the Holy Grail, antiviral agents have been pursued assiduously but with little success, until recently, because viruses are intracellular and therefore difficult to eradicate without killing the cell itself. At present, there are 10 compounds under investigation.

The most recent and by far the most successful agent, *adenine arabinoside,* has quickened the pulse of the medical community. It has been employed successfully in 90 per cent of a group of patients with herpes encephalitis, which normally kills 70 per cent of its victims and leaves most survivors with serious neurological damage. At present, intensive studies are in progress to expand its horizons along with promising analogues of this "potential" miracle drug. Cytosine arabinoside appears effective in herpes genitalis. More data are needed and forthcoming.

Interferon is a long known antiviral factor produced by the tissue lymphocytes of the reticuloendothelial (immunological) system, but has a species specificity.

Rifampin, mentioned before, is primarily an antibacterial but has had some success against herpes and pox viruses.

Amantadine has been used with mixed (actually little) success against viral influenza.

Pyrimidine shows some activity in negating Herpes, while *Isatin* is, at present, investigational.

Anti-Protozoan Agents

Chloroquine, one of the few medications bound intracellularly rather than to blood protein, is active against malaria, amebiasis, trypanosomiasis, leishmaniasis, giardiasis, and toxoplasmosis. Fortunately the dental profession is not involved with these maladies and they are mentioned for clarification and academic interest only.

There are few areas of dental treatment in which more acumen is desirable and less is displayed than in the application of antibiotics.

Improper choice, employment of multiple or shotgun combinations, overuse of antifungal agents, reliance on highly toxic or potentially toxic agents when safer ones will suffice, inadequate and/or prolonged period of usage, and failure to secure identification and sensitivity tests from cultures are all errors of judgment common to most practices.

Thoughtful reflection on all the ramifications of antibiotic therapy and the setting of specific goals with specific weapons should replace the helter-skelter approach which presently relies on overblown claims and inadequate or inaccurate information as a substitute for cerebration.

Reproduced without change is a chart from *The Medical Letter,* listing toxicities (and their frequencies) of most of the major and minor antibiotics, fungicides, and fungistats.[56]

PRINCIPAL ADVERSE EFFECTS OF ANTIMICROBIAL DRUGS

Adverse effects of antimicrobial drugs can vary with dosage, duration of administration, concomitant therapy, age of the patient, and the state of the patient's renal and hepatic function. The principal adverse effects of antimicrobial agents are listed in the table on page 31 [of *Medical Letter*]. It is difficult to estimate the incidence of adverse effects from published reports alone; the frequencies indicated in the table are based on the experience of Medical Letter consultants as well. Major interactions of the drugs are also listed in the table.

ALLERGIC REACTIONS — Severe allergic reactions to antimicrobial agents are most likely to occur after parenteral administration. Penicillins frequently cause delayed allergic reactions such as drug fever, skin eruptions, and serum sickness; anaphylactic reactions are rare, especially with oral administration, and particularly in children. A person allergic to one penicillin should be considered allergic to all others. Ampicillin causes maculopapular rashes more frequently than other penicillins. Although the cephalosporins are often used in patients allergic to the penicillins, such patients may have allergic reactions to cephalosporins. Other antimicrobial drugs that are likely to cause allergic reactions are demeclocycline, flucytosine, nalidixic acid, novobiocin, the sulfonamides, and trimethoprim-sulfamethoxazole.

ADVERSE EFFECTS OF ORAL ADMINISTRATION — Oral antimicrobial drugs often cause gastrointestinal disturbances such as nausea, vomiting, and diarrhea. These effects are usually dose-related and may result from irritation, superinfection, or changes in flora; they can occur with parenteral as well as oral administration. Diarrhea is especially common with tetracyclines, ampicillin, lincomycin, clindamycin, or the cephalosporins. Clindamycin and lincomycin can cause severe diarrhea and pseudomembranous colitis; other antibiotics can also occasionally cause colitis. Serious systemic adverse effects sometimes result from the absorption of "nonabsorbable" antibiotics such as neomycin; the risk of such effects is greater in infants and in patients with renal failure, though they may occur in any patient with prolonged oral administration.

SUPERINFECTIONS — Antimicrobial agents administered by any route can predispose to superinfection in the gastrointestinal tract and other organs. Superinfection is most likely when large doses are taken repeatedly or when combinations of drugs are used; it is relatively frequent with the tetracyclines and other broad-spectrum drugs. Enterocolitis caused by Staphylococcus aureus and pneumonia and sepsis caused by staphylococci, gram-negative bacilli, or Candida are among the most serious superinfections. Stomatitis, glossitis, anal itching, and vulvovaginitis associated with oral administration of antimicrobials are often caused by fungi, particularly Candida species, though fungal cultures in patients with these symptoms may be negative.

RENAL DAMAGE AND RENAL INSUFFICIENCY — Many antimicrobial agents are excreted unchanged, mainly in the urine. Others are metabolized, and the metabolites, along with some unchanged drug, are excreted in the urine or through the biliary tract. Some antimicrobials excreted mainly by the kidneys can cause renal damage, leading to accumulation of the drug in the blood and further injury to the kidneys; these include bacitracin, neomycin, vancomycin, cephaloridine, trimethoprim-sulfamethoxazole, and the sulfonamides. Most patients with impaired renal function can tolerate the usual first dose of a drug excreted mainly by the kidneys; thereafter, to minimize the risk of toxicity, total daily dosage may be reduced by increasing the interval between doses or reducing the individual dose or both (F O'Grady, Br Med Bull, 27:142, 1971; WM Bennett et al, JAMA 230:1544, 1974). For specific dosage recommendations in renal insufficiency, see page 26 [of *Medical Letter*].

PREGNANCY — Although there is no firm evidence that any antimicrobial agent is teratogenic in humans, these drugs, like drugs generally, should be prescribed for pregnant women with special caution. Griseofulvin is embryotoxic and teratogenic in rats, and is contraindicated during pregnancy. Tetracyclines administered after the fourth month can produce staining and hypoplasia of the teeth in the newborn child. Parenterally administered tetracycline has caused severe liver damage in pregnant women. Sulfonamides given near term may contribute to the development of kernicterus in the newborn.

ADVERSE EFFECTS OF ANTIMICROBIAL DRUGS

°Relatively new drug; the possibility that other adverse effects will appear is greater than with older drugs.

AMANTADINE (Symmetrel)
  Frequent: livedo reticularis and ankle edema; insomnia; dizziness; lethargy
  Occasional: depression; psychosis; confusion; congestive heart failure; orthostatic hypotension; urinary retention; GI disturbance; rash; visual disturbance; increased seizures in epilepsy
  Rare: convulsions; leukopenia; neutropenia; eczematoid dermatitis; oculogyric episodes
  (INTERACTION: Hallucinations, confusion, nightmares with anticholinergics)

AMINOSALICYLIC ACID (PAS)
  Frequent: GI disturbance
  Occasional: allergic reactions; liver damage; renal irritation; blood dyscrasias; thyroid enlargement; malabsorption syndrome
  Rare: acidosis; hypokalemia; encephalopathy; vasculitis
  (INTERACTION: Increased toxicity with probenecid)

°*AMOXICILLIN*—see Penicillins

AMPHOTERICIN B (Fungizone)
  Frequent: renal damage; hypokalemia; fever; thrombophlebitis at site of injection
  Occasional: hypomagnesemia; normocytic, normochromic anemia
  Rare: hemorrhagic gastroenteritis; blood dyscrasias; rash; blurred vision; peripheral neuropathy; convulsions; anaphylaxis; arrhythmias; acute liver failure
  (INTERACTIONS: Concurrent use may increase toxicity of other nephrotoxic agents, curariform drugs, and digitalis glycosides)

AMPICILLIN — see Penicillins

AMPICILLIN-PROBENECID
  (Polycillin-PRB; Probampacin; Trojacillin-Plus) (Probably same as for ampicillin, except that either component can cause rashes, which therefore are likely to be more frequent)

BACITRACIN
  Frequent: renal damage; local pain with IM use; GI disturbance
  Occasional: blood dyscrasias; rash
  (INTERACTION: Concurrent use may increase toxicity of other nephrotoxic agents)

CAPREOMYCIN (Capastat)
  Occasional: renal damage; eighth-nerve damage; hypokalemia
  Rare: allergic reactions; neuromuscular blockade and apnea with large IV doses, reversed by neostigmine or calcium gluconate
  (INTERACTIONS: Increased toxicity with other ototoxic or nephrotoxic agents)

CARBENICILLIN — see Penicillins

CEPHALOSPORINS (cefazolin [Ancef; Kefzol]; cephalexin [Keflex]; cephaloglycin [Kafocin]; cephaloridine [Loridine]; cephalothin [Keflin]; *cephapirin [Cefadyl]; *cephradine [Anspor; Velosef])
  Frequent: thrombophlebitis with IV use; serum sickness-like reaction with prolonged parenteral administration
  Occasional: allergic reactions, rarely anaphylactic; GI disturbance
  Rare: hemolytic anemia; hepatic dysfunction; blood dyscrasias; renal damage (especially with cephaloridine)
  (INTERACTIONS: Toxic renal damage may be potentiated by concurrent use of aminoglycosides, probenecid, or rapid-acting diuretics such as furosemide or ethacrynic acid)

CHLORAMPHENICOL (Chloromycetin; and others)
  Occasional: blood dyscrasias, rarely aplastic anemia, possibly leukemia; gray syndrome in infants; GI disturbance
  Rare: allergic and febrile reactions; peripheral neuropathy; optic neuritis and other CNS injury.
  (INTERACTIONS: Antabuse-like symptoms with alcohol; increased anticoagulant effect with dicumarol; increased hypoglycemia with sulfonylureas; increased phenytoin toxicity)

CLINDAMYCIN (Cleocin)
  Frequent: diarrhea; allergic reactions
  Occasional: pseudomembranous colitis, sometimes fatal
  Rare: blood dyscrasias
  (INTERACTION: Neuromuscular blockade with curariform drugs)

CLOFAZIMINE (Lamprene)
  Frequent: red or red-purple skin pigmentation, gray-blue pigmentation of lesions, and urine discoloration with prolonged high dosage
  Occasional: epigastric distress; diarrhea; headache

COLISTIMETHATE — see Polymyxins

CYCLOSERINE (Seromycin)
  Frequent: confusion; coma
  Occasional: peripheral neuropathy; liver damage; malabsorption syndrome; folate deficiency
  Rare: seizures; psychosis
  (INTERACTION: Increased convulsions with chronic alcohol abuse)

DAPSONE (Avlosulfon)
  Frequent: rash
  Occasional: blood dyscrasias including hemolytic anemia; nephrotic syndrome; liver damage

DOXYCYCLINE — see Tetracyclines

ERYTHROMYCINS (Erythrocin; and others)
  Occasional: stomatitis; GI disturbance; cholestatic hepatitis with erythromycin estolate in adults
  Rare: allergic reactions; transient deafness

ETHAMBUTOL (Myambutol)
  Occasional: optic neuritis; allergic reactions; GI disturbance; mental confusion; precipitation of acute gout
  Rare: peripheral neuritis

ETHIONAMIDE (Trecator)
  Frequent: GI disturbance
  Occasional: liver damage; CNS disturbance including peripheral neuropathy; allergic reactions; gynecomastia
  Rare: hypothyroidism; optic neuritis
  (INTERACTION: May increase hypoglycemia with sulfonylureas)
FLUCYTOSINE (Ancobon)
  Frequent: GI disturbance; rash; hepatic dysfunction; blood dyscrasias, including pancytopenia
  Occasional: confusion; hallucinations
FURAZOLIDONE (Furoxone)
  Frequent: nausea; vomiting
  Occasional: allergic reactions, including pulmonary infiltration; headache; orthostatic hypotension; hypoglycemia; polyneuritis
  Rare: hemolytic anemia in G–6PD deficiency and infants less than one month
  (INTERACTIONS: Antabuse-like reaction with alcohol; possible hypertensive crises with other monoamine oxidase inhibitors, tyramine-containing foods or beverages, sympathomimetic amines such as phenylephrine, ephedrine, and amphetamines, and with levodopa; hyperpyrexia and convulsions with tricyclic antidepressants; hyperprexia, hypertension, or hypotension and coma with meperidine)
GENTAMICIN (Garamycin)
  Occasional: vestibular damage; renal damage; rash
  Rare: auditory damage; neuromuscular blockade and apnea, reversible with calcium or neostigmine
  (INTERACTIONS: Increased nephrotoxicity with cephalosporins, polymyxins; ototoxicity with ethacrynic acid; neuromuscular blockade with curariform drugs)
GRISEOFULVIN (Fulvicin-U/F; and others)
  Occasional: GI disturbance; allergic and photosensitivity reactions
  Rare: proteinuria; blood dyscrasias; mental confusion; paresthesias
  (INTERACTION: Decreased anticoagulant effect with warfarin)
*HYDROXYSTILBAMIDINE (Hydroxystilbamidine isethionate)
  Frequent: hypotension; vomiting; renal damage
  Occasional: liver damage; neuropathies

ISONIAZID
  Occasional: peripheral neuropathy; glossitis and GI disturbance; liver damage, particularly in patients more than 35 years old; allergic reactions; fever
  Rare: blood dyscrasias; psychosis; optic neuritis; hyperglycemia; folate and B_6 deficiency; pellagra-like rash; keratitis; lupus erythematosus-like syndrome
  (INTERACTIONS: Psychotic episodes, ataxia with disulfiram (Antabuse); enhances toxicity of phenytoin; increased incidence of hepatitis with alcohol; diminished isoniazid effect in some patients with chronic alcohol abuse)
KANAMYCIN (Kantrex)
  Occasional: eighth-nerve damage affecting mainly hearing that may be irreversible and may not be detected until after therapy has been stopped (most likely with renal impairment); renal damage
  Rare: rash; fever; peripheral neuritis; parenteral or intraperitoneal administration may produce neuromuscular blockade and apnea, not reversed by neostigmine
  (INTERACTIONS: Increased nephrotoxicity with cephalosporins, polymyxins; ototoxicity with other ototoxic drugs, ethacrynic acid, furosemide, or other rapid-acting diuretics; neuromuscular blockade with curariform drugs)
LINCOMYCIN (Lincocin)
  Frequent: diarrhea, sometimes progressing to severe pseudomembranous colitis
  Occasional: allergic reactions, rarely anaphylactic
  Rare: blood dyscrasias; hypotension with rapid IV injection
  (INTERACTION: Neuromuscular blockade with curariform drugs)
METHENAMINE MANDELATE (Mandelamine; and others) and METHENAMINE
HIPPURATE (Hiprex; Urex)
  Occasional: GI disturbance; dysuria; allergic reactions
*METHISAZONE (Marboran)
  Frequent: severe vomiting; nausea; anorexia
  Occasional: diarrhea; transient fluid retention; allergic reactions
  Rare: hyperbilirubinemia
  (INTERACTION: Increased adverse effects with alcohol)

MINOCYCLINE — see Tetracyclines
NALIDIXIC ACID (NegGram)
Frequent: GI disturbance; rash; visual disturbance
Occasional: CNS disturbance; acute intracranial hypertension in young children; photosensitivity reactions, sometimes persistent; convulsions
Rare: cholestatic jaundice; blood dyscrasias; arthralgia or arthritis
(INTERACTION: Increased effect of oral anticoagulants)
NEOMYCIN
Occasional: eighth-nerve and renal damage, same as with kanamycin but hearing loss may be more frequent and severe and may occur with oral, intraarticular, or topical use; GI disturbance; malabsorption with oral use; contact dermatitis with topical use
Rare: neuromuscular blockade and apnea that may be reversed by intravenous neostigmine or calcium gluconate
(INTERACTIONS: Increased nephrotoxicity with other nephrotoxic drugs; increased ototoxicity with ethacrynic acid and other ototoxic drugs; neuromuscular blockage with curariform drugs)
NITROFURANTOIN (Furadantin; and others)
Frequent: GI disturbance
Occasional: allergic reactions, including pulmonary infiltration and a lupus-erythematosus syndrome; blood dyscrasias; hemolytic anemia; peripheral neuropathy, sometimes severe
Rare: cholestatic jaundice
NOVOBIOCIN (Albamycin)
Frequent: cholestatic jaundice; allergic reactions; GI disturbance; neonatal hyperbilirubinemia
Occasional: severe blood dyscrasias
NYSTATIN (Mycostatin; Nilstat)
Occasional: allergic reactions; GI disturbance
OXOLINIC ACID (Utibid)
Frequent: CNS disturbance; nausea
Occasional: GI disturbance; anorexia; pruritus
Rare: allergic reactions; blood dyscrasias; photophobia
(INTERACTION: May increase effect of oral anticoagulants)

PENICILLINS (amoxicillin [Amoxil, Larotid, Polymox]; ampicillin [Polycillin; and others]; carbenicillin [Geocillin, Geopen, Pyopen]; cloxacillin [Tegopen]; dicloxacillin [Dynapen, Pathocil, Veracillin]; hetacillin [Versapen]; methicillin [Celbenin, Staphcillin]; nafcillin [Unipen]; oxacillin [Bactocill, Prostaphlin]; penicillin G, penicillin V, phenethicillin [Maxipen, Syncillin])
Frequent: allergic reactions, rarely anaphylactic; rash (more common with ampicillin than with other penicillins); diarrhea (most common with ampicillin)
Occasional: hemolytic anemia
Rare: muscle irritability and seizures, usually after high doses in patients with impaired renal function; renal damage; hyperkalemia and arrhythmias with IV potassium penicillin G given rapidly; bleeding diathesis; granulocytopenia or agranulocytosis with semisynthetic penicillins; pseudomembranous colitis with ampicillin; hepatic damage with semi-synthetic penicillins; abnormal behavior and neurological reactions with high doses of procaine penicillin G; hypokalemic alkalosis and/or sodium overload with high doses of carbenicillin; platelet dysfunction with carbenicillin
POLYMYXINS (colistimethate [Coly-Mycin]; polymyxin B [Aerosporin, Polymyxin B])
Occasional: renal damage; peripheral neuropathy; thrombophlebitis at IV injection site with polymyxin B
Rare: allergic reactions; neuromuscular blockade and apnea with parenteral administration, not reversed by neostigmine but may be by IV calcium chloride
(INTERACTIONS: Increased nephrotoxicity with aminoglycosides; neuromuscular blockade with curariform drugs)
PYRAZINAMIDE (Pyrazinamide)
Occasional: liver damage; hyperuricemia; GI disturbance
Rare: photosensitivity reactions
RIFAMPIN (Rifadin; Rimactane)
Occasional: liver damage; GI disturbance; allergic reactions
Rare: flu-like syndrome, sometimes

with thrombocytopenia, hemolytic anemia, and renal failure, particularly with intermittent therapy
(INTERACTIONS: Decreased effect of oral anticoagulants; decreased effect of oral contraceptives; toxicity enhanced by probenecid)

*RIFAMPIN-ISONIAZID (Rifamate; Rimactazid) — see individual drugs
(Although both drugs are hepatotoxic, it appears that hepatotoxicity is no greater than with isoniazid alone)

SPECTINOMYCIN (Trobicin)
Occasional: urticaria; dizziness; nausea; chills and fever; insomnia

STREPTOMYCIN
Frequent: eighth-nerve damage (mainly vestibular), sometimes permanent; paresthesias; rash; fever
Occasional: pruritus; anaphylaxis; renal damage
Rare: blood dyscrasias; neuromuscular blockade and apnea with parenteral administration, usually reversed by neostigmine; optic neuritis; hepatic necrosis; myocarditis
(INTERACTIONS: Increased nephrotoxicity with cephaloridine, cephalothin, polymyxins; ototoxicity with ethacrynic acid; neuromuscular blockade with curariform drugs)

SULFONAMIDES
Frequent: allergic reactions (rash, photosensitivity and drug fever)
Occasional: kernicterus in newborn; renal damage; liver damage; Stevens-Johnson syndrome (particularly with long-acting sulfonamides); hemolytic anemia; other blood dyscrasias; vasculitis
(INTERACTIONS [long/acting]: Increased effect of oral anticoagulants; increased hypoglycemia with sulfonylureas)

TETRACYCLINES (chlortetracycline [Aureomycin]; demeclocycline [Declomycin]; doxycycline [Vibramycin; and others]; methacycline [Rondomycin]; minocycline [Minocin; Vectrin]; oxytetracycline [Terramycin; and others]; tetracycline hydrochloride [Achromycin; and others])
Frequent: GI disturbance; bone lesions and staining and deformity of teeth in children up to 12 years old, and in the newborn when given to pregnant women after the fourth month of pregnancy

Occasional: malabsorption; enterocolitis; photosensitivity reactions (most frequent with demeclocycline); vestibular reactions with minocycline; increased azotemia with renal insufficiency (except doxycycline); parenteral doses may cause serious liver damage, especially in pregnant women and patients with renal disease receiving 1 gram or more daily
Rare: allergic reactions; blood dyscrasias; increased intracranial pressure in infants; fixed-drug eruptions; diabetes insipidus with demeclocycline
(INTERACTIONS: Nephrotoxicity with methoxyflurane; decreased tetracycline effects with oral antacids, iron; decreased doxycycline effects with barbiturates, carbamazepine)

*TOBRAMYCIN (Nebcin)
(Probably same as with gentamicin)

TRIMETHOPRIMSULFAMETHOX-AZOLE (Bactrim; Septra) (Same as sulfonamides, but possibly higher incidence of hematologic reactions and renal damage)

TROLEANDOMYCIN (Cyclamycin; TAO)
Occasional: stomatitis; GI disturbance; cholestatic jaundice
Rare: allergic reactions

VANCOMYCIN (Vancocin)
Frequent: thrombophlebitis; chills, fever
Occasional: renal damage; eighth-nerve damage (mainly hearing) especially with large or continued doses (more than 10 days), in presence of renal damage, and in the elderly
Rare: peripheral neuropathy; urticaria
(INTERACTION: Increased toxicity with other ototoxic or nephrotoxic agents)

VIOMYCIN (Viocin; Viomycin)
Frequent: eighth-nerve damage (vestibular and hearing) with large or continued doses (more than 10 days) or in presence of renal damage
Occasional: rash; renal damage; electrolyte disturbances
(INTERACTIONS: Increased toxicity with other ototoxic and nephrotoxic agents; neuromuscular blockade with curariform drugs)

ANTICHOLINERGIC DRUGS (BELLADONNA ALKALOIDS, ETC.)

Atropine and scopolamine are the most important of the parasympatholytic group, which includes hyoscyamine and the synthetics Tral, Banthine, and Pro-Banthine. They enjoy wide use in medicine for treating a varied and long list of maladies, including cardiopathies, parkinsonism, gastric dysfunction, intestinal spasm, and mydriasis. They are antidotal in combating excessive actions of some other drugs, including the respiratory depression of morphine and the barbiturates.

In dental practice, atropine, a CNS excitant, is employed as an anti-sialagogue in conjunction with local analgesics and to diminish secretions in the nasopharynx and the bronchial tree, which reduces the hazard of aspiration in the unconscious anesthetized patient. Scopolamine, a CNS depressant, has stronger antisecretory properties and in addition produces drowsiness, euphoria, and amnesia. Comparison would seem to place scopolamine above atropine in desirable qualities, and this would be true if it were not for the paradoxical effects — excitement, hallucinations, and delirium — often seen after scopolamine administration.

Serious toxicity to either drug is seldom experienced, even though the symptoms of poisoning with agents of this group are very violent. Dysphagia, great thirst, visual disturbance, flushing of face, neck, and chest, rise in temperature, tachycardia, and delirious excitement followed by giddiness and stupor are recorded. Despite this formidable array of toxic effects, most victims recover without sequelae. Atropine and scopolamine usually are contraindicated for use in patients with glaucoma because of their mydriatic and cycloplegic actions. Increase in the intraocular pressure may lead to rupture or damage of the eyeball. Atropine causes tachycardia by blocking vagal inhibitory action on the heart, and this is undesirable in some cardiac conditions. These drugs are always prescribed with caution to geriatric patients, for in their age bracket appear most of the ailments which restrict the use of the belladonna alkaloids.

Cholinergic Drugs (Pilocarpine, etc.)

The parasympathomimetic or cholinergic agents, methacholine, carbachol, and bethanechol, are potent drugs whose medical uses are restricted to conditions which demand rather drastic treatment, such as postoperative urinary retention, ileus, and delayed gastric emptying after vagotomy.

Pilocarpine, probably the weakest member of this group, is sometimes used in dentistry as a sialagogue. It very effectively combats the dry mouth experienced by many patients who are taking ganglionic blocking agents (veriloid, apresoline) for the treatment of hypertension. Besides xerostomia, which often prohibits denture wearing and drastically interferes with mastication and deglutition, other distressing complaints are constipation, dryness of the eyes, and difficulty in micturition. Pilocarpine overcomes all these symptoms and may be given orally. Its toxic manifestations are essentially the opposite of the ganglionic blockers, and include sweating, lacrimation, salivation, urinary urgency, and incipient pulmonary edema. Consultation with the patient's physician is desirable when the dental doctor considers this treatment for any "dry-mouth" patient.

STIMULANTS AND ANALEPTICS

Amphetamine (Benzedrine)

This drug and its family, including dextroamphetamine (Dexedrine) and methamphetamine (Desoxyn and Methedrine [speed]), probably are the most improperly used products in the entire formulary. To improve the mood or relieve the outward manifestations of depression in mildly disturbed patients is their primary mission. Occasionally they are indicated to temporarily curb the appetite (anorexia) in some obese patients or to induce wakefulness in others. They also have some value as a respiratory stimulant in barbiturate poisoning. But gross misuse and the toxic ramifications thereof have caused the beneficial effects of the amphetamines to be accepted with diminishing fervor when their potential for harm is considered.

Toxicity to large or continued dosages is rapid and severe. Symptoms include insomnia, hallucinations, mania, hyperpyrexia, and convulsions, which if persistent and unrelieved may lead to death. Subtle or less dramatic toxic manifestations are the loss of sound judgment (which in auto and truck drivers has precipitated many fatal accidents) and interference with reasoning ability and intelligence. This interference can delude a person on "pep-pills" ("uppers") into believing that all is well in life when in reality it is not. The possible tragic consequences of such an attitude can well be imagined. The last but not least danger is that amphetamines are habituating, and the number of addicts is large, growing, and widespread throughout the country.

Diphenylmethanes

These cerebral or psychic stimulants, although related to amphetamine, are much milder in function with greatly reduced toxicity. Meratran and Ritalin are known in dental practice and may be employed with less hazard than most other stimulants. Hyperexcitability, some irritability, and insomnia are the undesirable but not usually dangerous toxic effects which may appear in some patients.

Often mentioned or suggested as an antidote for barbiturate or other drug depression states, Ritalin is slow and so mild as to be relatively tepid for real analeptic action. However, it is also mild in toxicity rating and may be expedient as a mood elevator.

Diphenylhydantoin (Dilantin Sodium)

This agent is the best of a large group of anticonvulsants prescribed to control epilepsy and other similar disorders. It may also be used occasionally in cardiac patients to control arrhythmias. Since this convulsive dysfunction is fairly common, a dental article should find a niche, however small, for information concerning Dilantin and similar drugs used in grand mal patients. Surprisingly, these anticonvulsant agents do not ordinarily becloud the mind or depress cortical activity, but all exhibit some toxic reactions in the CNS at normal dose levels, and excessive doses yield incapacitation with frightening symptoms. Ataxia, blurred vision, nystagmus, hyperreflexia, lethargy, and coma, along with mental aberrations, degenerative epithelial changes, visceral dysfunction, and blood dyscrasias, are the general toxic manifestations which may arise subject to excessive or prolonged ingestion of Dilantin. There are fortunately no apparent incompatibilities with other agents which could precipitate an acute crisis in a dental office, although an increase in CNS excitation originating from apprehension to the forthcoming procedure could trigger a seizure. Another toxic factor important from the dental standpoint is the frequent, often gross and obstructive hyperplasia of the alveolar gingival tissues found in patients on long-term Dilantin therapy.

Caffeine

Belonging to the xanthine group, caffeine is certainly the world's premier stimulant, and the safest, too! Appearing naturally in coffee, tea, and cocoa, it is also available in tablet and injectable form with sodium benzoate. Regardless of the method of assimilation, it stimulates all parts of the CNS to produce alertness, wakefulness, and talkativeness. Other effects, which may or may not be desirable, depending on the patient, are increase in respiration and diuresis. Toxicity is seldom a problem, but restlessness, irritability, and insomnia can be dangerous in some patients.

Hydrazines

The hydrazines or monoamine oxidase inhibitors often are listed with the stimulants but have wide ranging effects in other areas. Isocarboxazid (Marplan) is the only popular, relatively nontoxic drug in this group at this time. It has little, if any, use in dentistry. (See Tranquilizer section.)

Bemegride (Megimide)

Bemegride was introduced as an antagonist of the barbiturates, via competitive inhibition, but this virtue has yet to be proved. Present evidence indicates that it stimulates respiration and other neural functions by mechanisms similar to older analeptics, but is milder and less toxic. As with most CNS stimulants, overdose yields convulsions.

Ethamivan (Emivan)

Touted mainly as a stimulant useful in hypoventilatory states associated with chronic pulmonary disease, Emivan may be employed for general respiratory stimulation when such an agent is called for. Although this drug has a good margin of safety, it is a convulsant in large doses.

Doxapram (Dopram)

This agent is a promising respiratory stimulant of low toxicity. It is unique in that the dose required for respiratory stimulation is below that necessary to evoke excessive cerebral cortical activity.

PSYCHOTOMIMETICS

Damned by the majority on definition alone — psychoto (deep, far-reaching, prolonged mental disorders), mimetic (to mimic or simulate) — these black sheep in the drug family are unfortunately popular enough to demand attention. They require space in this text on the strength of the unpredictable nature of the interactions possible when patients experimenting with these potent agents are given common dental prescriptions. To avoid unpleasant, frightening, or possibly violent incidents, it is wise to postpone treatment of any kind for those who are known or suspected "users" of (1) lysergic acid diethylamide, (2) cannabis, (3) mescaline, or (4) psilocybin.

Lysergic Acid Diethylamide

LSD is a synthetic and the most potent hallucinogen. Its only legitimate use has been in experimental psychiatry. It is thought to obtain its profound effects from an antagonistic action on serotonin and the direct effect of an unusual amine.

Toxicities are broad and not well established, but persistent psychoses and chromosomal damage are evident in chronic users.

Cannabis

Marijuana has become a household word. The mountains of publicity it has garlanded have not been adverse enough to suit this author. The bevy of entertainers and some highly placed members of the academic world who dismiss its harmfulness, condone it, or jest about its illegal use have brought a modicum of respectability to this prostitute of the drug family.

Its alleged psychological benefits must be weighed against its acknowledged destruction or disruption of the will to excel or even to compete in our society, and against mounting evidence of insidious pathosis.

In the frantic search by its advocates for virtues to legitimize its use, only one positive aspect has presented. Tetrahydrocannabinol, the active chemical ingredient, has, in some cases, successfully counteracted the nausea caused by antimetabolites and other chemotherapeutic agents used in therapy for malignant tumors.

Mescaline (Peyote)

Mescaline is obtained from the mescal cactus. The dried buttons when ingested produce a stuporous state accompanied by brilliant visual hallucinations.

Toxicity is thought to be low, but little is known at this time owing to lack of data.

Psilocybin (Mexican Mushrooms)

Psilocybin resembles LSD, but seems much milder in all respects.

HORMONES (NATURAL)

Hormones are substances secreted by the ductless glands which regulate most body processes. The natural hormones have a multitude of effects, many of which at this time are not well understood.

Hypothyroidism (myxedema), hypoinsulinism (diabetes), and hypopituitarism (dwarfism) are examples of diseases which result from inadequate production of hormones by the thyroid, pancreas and pituitary glands. In other conditions, the endocrine glands, although normal, do not secrete enough hormone to meet the extra demands the body makes in its efforts to overcome severe stresses. An example is the use of norepinephrine and epinephrine in the alleviation or reversal of shock.

One may well question the necessity or desirability of including these exotic drugs in a dental treatise. It should be unnecessary to remind the reader that an inordinate number of patients who present for dental treatment may be on thyroxin for weight loss, estrogens for menopausal disorders, progesterones for menstrual and associated disorders, and oxytocin (posterior pituitary extract) in pregnancy complications.

Patients with Addison's disease may need supplemental vasopressor therapy. Asthmatics may require control with these same agents. Such patients must be carefully evaluated before stressful dental procedures are attempted; otherwise, toxic conditions may be precipitated which are exceedingly difficult to control or reverse. These include gastrointestinal distress and cramps, uterine bleeding, tachycardia, retention of electrolytes and water, and skin disturbances.

HORMONES (SYNTHETIC)

The cortisone derivatives are used extensively in many therapeutic situations. At present they are for the most part synthetic in origin, diverse, often obscure in action, transitory rather than curative in nature, and *potent*! These agents are capable of producing dramatic temporary improvement, but rarely permanent relief, from many afflictions.

One fundamental action of cortisone is its ability to suppress the inflammatory and immunologic responses of the body. This requisite is the basis of most of the clinical applications of cortisone and related drugs. Its use in therapy for various dermatoses, arthritis and allied collagen diseases, and allergic manifestations is particularly widespread. Anti-inflammatory and antiallergic actions of corticosteroids include reduction of the exudation of leukocytes and plasma constituents, maintenance of cell membrane integrity, inhibition of lysozyme release from granulocytes, other modes of phagocytosis inhibition, and stabilization of intracellular lysosomal membranes. Glucocorticoids inhibit amino-acid transport into muscle and reduce new protein synthesis. Cortisol, the natural hormone secreted by the adrenal cortex, is required for liver gluconeogenesis utilizing amino acids. All the corticosteroids tend to cause hypokalemia by increasing urinary losses of potassium. Effects of glucocorticoids on the central nervous system and on blood cells are notable and sometimes deleterious.

On the question or category of allergy, now is the proper time to place the corticosteroids in correct perspective for the step-by-step treatment of an-

ORAL GLUCOCORTICOIDS

Drug	Anti-inflam-matory Potency	Mineralocorti-coid Potency	Equivalent Doses
Cortisone	0.8	0.8	25 mg
Cortone (Merck)			
Cortisone Acetate (Upjohn)			
Hydrocortisone	1.0	1.0	20 mg
Cortef (Upjohn)			
Hydrocortone (Merck)			
Prednisolone	4.0	0.8	5 mg
Delta-Cortef (Upjohn)			
Fernisolone (Ferndale)			
Prednicen (Central)			
Prednis (USV)			
Sterane (Pfizer)			
Prednisone	4.0	0.8	5 mg
Delta-Dome (Dome)			
Deltasone (Upjohn)			
Fernisone (Ferndale)			
Keysone (Hyrex-Key)			
Lisacort (Fellows-Testagar)			
Meticorten (Schering)			
Orasone (Rowell)			
Paracort (Parke, Davis)			
Pred-5 (Saron)			
Servisone (Lederle)			
Sterapred (Mayrand)			
Meprednisone	4.0	0	4 mg
Betapar (Parke, Davis)			
Methylprednisolone	5.0	0	4 mg
Medrol (Upjohn)			
Triamcinolone	5.0	0	4 mg
Aristocort (Lederle)			
Kenacort (Squibb)			
Paramethasone	10.0	0	2 mg
Haldrone (Lilly)			
Stemex (Syntex)			
Fluprednisolone	15.0	0	1.5 mg
Alphadrol (Upjohn)			
Dexamethasone	25.0	0	0.75 mg
Decadron (Merck)			
Deronil (Schering)			
Dexameth (USV)			
Dexone (Rowell)			
Gammacorten (Ciba)			
Hexadrol (Organon)			
Betamethasone	25.0	0	0.6 mg
Celestone (Schering)			

aphylaxis and other emergency situations. Contrary to many articles and popular opinion, steroids are too slow-acting to be life-saving in acute episodes, and are the last drugs administered in emergency procedures. Although essential in combating immunologic reactions and regaining homeostasis, they are virtually ineffective in those first precious moments of crisis. Deviation from this concept could cost a life.

Even discounting the multitude of patients ingesting steroid preparations as a regimen for the control of inflammatory symptoms, the escalating number of dental nostrums featuring hormones is sufficient reason for the clinician to be acutely aware of the potency of these agents.

The list of natural and synthetic steroids is vast, but the actions and the toxicity of virtually all closely approximate those of cortisone.

Mineralocorticoids

Used in adrenocortical insufficiency states (Addison's disease, etc.) and salt losing adrenogenital syndrome, deoxycorticosterone acetate (DOCA) is the only pure mineralocorticoid, with fluorocortisone (Florinef) not far behind.

They are employed in close conjunction with glucocorticoids, glucose, fluid and electrolyte control, and antibiotics (in case of infection) in order to retain hormonal and physiologic balance in the patient. The general principles of corticosteroid therapy are as follows:

1. Use only for an established diagnosis and when less harmful therapies have failed.
2. Use the smallest therapeutically effective dose.
3. Use alternate-day therapy whenever possible.
4. Teach patients about the need for higher steroid doses during stress. Procedures for cessation of therapy are recommended.

TOXICITY

Cortisone and other steroids can and do mask the objective and subjective symptoms of serious infections until they become unmanageable — conceivably to the point of extremis. Because of toxic influence on the CNS, steroids may initiate psychotic behavior in patients with a basic predisposition in this direction. Cortisone-induced disturbances in metabolism and electrolyte balance may produce osteoporosis in bone and lead to pathologic fractures.

In the presence of diseases in which body defenses are essential, such as tuberculosis and peptic ulcer, cortisone and other steroids are contraindicated. Simulated Cushing's syndrome (recognized by the following symptoms: moon face, acne, facial hirsutism, edema, weakness, and depression) often appears in patients during a course of hormone therapy. Fortunately, this syndrome is reversible and the signs disappear when treatment is discontinued.

Prolonged cortisone ingestion usually results in adrenal atrophy which may persist for six months *or longer* after the drug is discontinued. This factor is of prime importance when general anesthetics are indicated for dental treatment. A crisis during the anesthetic period may precipitate a state of acute adrenocorticotropic insufficiency with a fatal termination.

VITAMINS

Seemingly innocuous and out of place in a chapter on toxicity, this group of drugs may qualify as the most used, most abused, and least understood of

all the common therapeutic agents. Although relatively simple organic compounds which are essential nutrients required for normal metabolism, some
vitamins are highly toxic in large and extended doses. This attribute is especially true of A and D and to some extent the other fat-soluble vitamins
because they can be stored in the body. In contrast, the water-soluble vitamins, B complex and C, are rapidly excreted and exhibit minimal, if any,
harmful effects.

Vitamin A

The fat-soluble lipochromes, alpha, beta, and gamma carotene and cryp-
toxanthin, occur naturally in plants and animal tissues and are converted into
vitamin A in the intestinal mucosa and liver.

Vitamin A has a marked antikeratinizing effect on epithelial tissue and
has been suggested for use in oral troches to treat leukoplakia. The therapy
period is long, two to six months, but results appear to be promising, and no
toxicity has been reported. However, the small number of patients involved in
this particular research project precludes acceptance of the value of vitamin A
for this specific application until more data are available.

Dosage above the normal may be required in steatorrhea, hepatic disease,
or intestinal inflammation, but overdosage in the healthy patient produces
hypervitaminosis, which is characterized by anorexia, irritability, pruritus,
alopecia, cracked lips, hepatomegaly, and periosteal thickening.

Vitamin D

This fat-soluble vitamin occurs naturally in plant and animal tissues,
usually in the form of a precursor, ergosterol or 7-dehydrocholesterol. These
precursors are converted to the active form by ultraviolet light.

Large doses often yield severe toxic disturbances by increasing the renal
excretion of phosphorus and the intestinal absorption of calcium, thereby
upsetting the normal Ca-P balance in the body. This results in the mobilization of calcium from osseous structures, causing rarefaction and soft spots in
the bone and calcification in the muscles and kidneys. This metastatic calcification in vital organs is a dangerous and sometimes irreversible condition.

Vitamin E

Another fat-soluble vitamin occurring naturally as alpha-tocopherol in
plant and animal tissues, vitamin E has been linked to the fertility factor in
animals. Despite the fact that lack of E results in germinal atrophy and
defective development in some animals, its performance in humans is indefinite and equivocal.

There is no available evidence that overdosage can or does produce toxic
effects.

Vitamin K

This liquid-soluble vitamin occurs naturally as naphthoquinines in plant and animal tissues, and is synthesized as menadione and phytonadione salts, which are water soluble. These analogs are known commercially as Hykinone, Synkayvite, and Mephyton. Since vitamin K promotes the formation of prothrombin in the liver, its use is mainly in blood coagulant therapy when hypoprothrombinemia is a factor and in negating or controlling coumarin effects in patients with vascular disease.

It is directly toxic to premature infants, producing jaundice and fatal kernicterus in large doses, and indirectly toxic when it interferes with controlled anticoagulant therapy in adult patients.

B Complex Vitamins

This group of water-soluble vitamins includes thiamine, niacrin, riboflavin, pyridoxine, pantothenic acid, and biotin. Except for pantothenic acid and biotin, these are important agents in the maintenance of oral health. Further description is superfluous here, other than the citing of harmful effects.

The toxicity of the B vitamins is nil, even in extreme overdoses, but thiamine occasionally elicits an allergic response of low magnitude, and in large doses a ganglionic-blocking action with resultant hypotension is possible. Niacin may produce a transient vasodilatation causing flushed or hyperemic areas on the skin.

Vitamin C

This water-soluble vitamin (ascorbic acid) occurs naturally in plant and animal tissues and has been synthesized since 1932. Probably the single most important vitamin in the maintenance of oral soft tissue health, vitamin C cannot be stored by the body and should be ingested daily.

Serious toxic reactions have never been reported from ascorbic acid, regardless of the state of the patient's health or the size of the dose. Dr. Pauling's well publicized theories on the role of Vitamin C in the prevention of common colds are at this date still in doubt. An intensive and extensive study by a team from the University of Pittsburgh (1976–77) has negated most of Pauling's theory. Another problem, reported in J.A.M.A. 237 (8):768, 1977, concerns the increase in urinary oxalate which can and does lead to the formation of uroliths (urinary tract stones). The possibility of oxalate stones is always a consideration in users of excessive amounts (approximately 1 gm or more daily) of Vitamin C.

Fluorine-Vitamin Compounds

These compounds are becoming extremely popular as a safe, simple method for ingestion of fluorides in areas where natural water content of fluorine is nonexistent or insufficient to help control dental caries. At this printing, toxic effects, local or systemic, have not emerged or been reported.

ENZYMES

Enzymes are relatively new but assiduously promoted by many manufacturers, and as a result are increasingly employed in the practice of dentistry.

Hyaluronidase, streptokinase-streptodornase, papase, trypsin and chymotrypsin are the important enzymes and enjoy the widest use. Although they may seem quite innocuous by nature and physiologic in action, it should be remembered that because some are derived in most part from animal tissue and bacteria, they are capable of producing foreign-protein anaphylaxis. They also may be instrumental in the spread of infection by breaking down natural body defenses. Persistent, unexplained hyperpyrexia is a new phenomenon associated with long-term enzyme therapy. Leukocytosis is assumed to be an etiologic factor in this temporary and reversible condition. One must struggle to make a good case for their use in dental practice.

ANTACIDS

This classification of drugs should be mentioned because of the gross quantities consumed by the general public to allay ulcer pain and to relieve functional indigestion. These drugs fall into two main groups: the inorganic alkaline salts and the insoluble buffered salts.

The inorganic alkaline salts are represented by $NaHCO_3$, $CaCO_3$, and MgO, only one of which is toxic enough to cause concern. Sodium bicarbonate, while effective and rapid in action, produces rebound acidity and, with overuse, alkalosis.

The insoluble buffered salts are commonly called gels: aluminum hydroxide (Amphogel), aluminum phosphate (Phosphaljel), and mixtures of magnesium hydroxide (Maalox) are the well known products in this category. Their toxic potential is very low, thereby casting them in the favored role for long-term antacid therapy.

VACCINES

The use of vaccines, while in the embryonic stage, is becoming a useful modality in dental medicine.

Herpes simplex virus causes some of the most aggravating and painful lesions known to man. Autogenous vaccines and vaccinia (smallpox) vaccine are often employed in the treatment of herpetic infections, and the results have been encouraging. Tetanus antitoxin and/or toxoid should be a part of the rationale of therapy for puncture wounds of the face and oral cavity or when severe trauma causes gross contamination of this area by dirt and debris. But, as is the case with all foreign protein substances, injection may elicit a toxic response.

All the signs and symptoms of severe histamine poisonings, cutaneous flushing, dizziness, nausea, fainting, tachycardia, vascular hypotension, and asthma, may occur from the injection of these sera or vaccines. In addition, urticaria is a frequent complaint. The delayed reaction, five to seven days later, features joint and muscle pain.

GERMICIDES, DISINFECTANTS, AND ANTISEPTICS

Germicides which kill bacteria, disinfectants which either kill or render organisms inert, and antiseptics which prevent further growth are all employed, sometimes ignorantly, in dental offices to reduce the pathogen population on equipment, instruments, and living tissues. The very nature and purpose of this group of drugs ensures their toxicity, in varying degrees, to all viable cells. Many of these agents — phenol, mercurials, boric acid, and iodine — are highly poisonous and cause severe local or general symptoms when applied to the skin or when they are ingested by other routes, whereas Zephiran, pHisoHex and peroxide usually are quite benign in normal situations.

Phenol

Phenol or carbolic acid and related phenolic compounds should merit consideration in any discussion of drug toxicity. Creosote, eugenol, guaiacol, thymol, resorcinol, "Campho-Phenique," and other mixtures of phenolic compounds are often subjected to vigorous and indiscriminate use in dentistry with apparently little thought being given to the possible consequences of such use. Usually, phenol et al. have a self-limiting penetration when applied topically, but deep placement in the bone or soft tissues (e.g., root canal therapy, drains, and bone packing for deep seated infections) may result in serious toxicity. An early symptom of mild systemic poisoning is dark-colored urine. Moderate poisoning may produce delirium, then convulsions, collapse, and unconsciousness. With severe systemic toxicity, there is cerebral edema, cardiac dilatation, degeneration of the kidneys, and necrosis of the liver. Ordinarily, fatal or severe poisoning results only from oral ingestion of fairly large amounts, and local application produces little more than surface tissue necrosis. However, there are cases on record where the application of small amounts to the epithelium have resulted in some or all of the gross toxic manifestations listed above.

Organic Mercurial Compounds

Three of the oldest and best known antiseptics are in this class — Metaphen, Merthiolate, and Mercurochrome. Despite their popularity, these drugs are at best only bacteriostatic, and their real worth has long been suspect and the subject of much controversy. Then, too, mercury causes toxic effects in many people, and in severe cases can be grossly destructive to both soft tissue and bone. Therefore, in patients who are sensitive to mercury, the use of these compounds should be avoided.

Iodine

The USP tincture and other iodine preparations are ordinarily rapid and efficient in disinfecting tissues. However, iodine, especially the alcoholic (and some aqueous) solutions, frequently causes acute pain and irritation when applied to abraded areas. Inflammatory changes at the wound edges interfere with healing and may produce adhesions or other cicatricial changes.

Iodophors

These are aqueous complexes of iodine usually combined with a detergent (povidone, etc.) to produce potent surgical scrubs (Betadine, Septodyne, Prepodyne, etc.) of low irritation to the skin and high activity against both gram-positive and gram-negative bacteria.

Alcohol (Isopropyl and Ethyl)

Seventy per cent is the most effective strength but is quickly vaporized and is drying to human tissues. It is an acceptable temporary antiseptic agent only for its activity against gram-positive and gram-negative bacteria.

Chlorhexidine

Hibiclens is a new preparation which promises to be the most effective yet. It covers the same range as the iodines but is quicker and longer lasting in action. In a recent study, it was significantly more effective than other preparations and there was no irritation.

Chlorhexidine resembles the iodophors in activity against gram-negative and gram-positive bacteria but has the added advantage of cumulative or persistent action in the skin, while the iodophors dry the integument!

Boric Acid

This old standby drug, despite its prevalent use, is vigorously condemned as worthless from a therapeutic standpoint by many of our leading pharmacologists. Boric acid may be absorbed from mucous membranes and denuded areas, and, because it is neither irritating nor painful to the tissues, many people consider it to be innocuous and apply the powder or solution in gross quantities. Nothing could be further from the truth, because boric acid is one of the most toxic of all the drugs in use today. In reviewing the literature, the Goldblooms (1953) found 55 per cent mortality in 109 cases of boric acid poisoning. The usual toxic symptoms are vomiting, diarrhea, rash and desquamation of the skin, hypothermia, hematuria, and signs of meningeal irritation. Regression may end at any of these stages, but unless the trend is reversed, circulatory collapse ensues, leading to a fatal termination.

Hydrogen Peroxide

This familiar nostrum in the pure form, and as the active agent in Sodium Perborate and other proprietary compounds, is found in most dental offices. It oxidizes organic matter and loosens debris and pus by effervescence during the release of nascent oxygen. It is claimed to be highly germicidal, but the action is fleeting or transient.

Toxicity is not a real problem, but extended use of this drug often results in a rebound effect which aggravates rather than relieves the tissue symptoms.

Benzalkonium Chloride (Zephiran)

This was once the best and at the same time the least toxic of all the cold sterilizing agents. It has detergent, keratolytic, and emulsifying actions; therefore, soap is unnecessary prior to its application to instruments or tissues. In fact, soap film will negate or reduce Zephiran's disinfectant power.

Toxicity is negligible when this drug is properly used. Its major drawback is its ineffectiveness against some gram-negative bacilli, especially *Pseudomonas aeruginosa* (common in hospitals and offices) and tubercle bacilli.

Hexachlorophene (pHisoHex)

This drug is used primarily in detergent soaps or creams for preparation of a surgical area and as a preoperative scrub agent for the surgeon's hands. It is active mainly against gram-positive organisms. Some toothpastes now contain this agent. Dermatoses have been noted subsequent to its use, but these are thought to be largely the fault of the detergent.

Silver Salts

Silver nitrate and Argyrol are venerable bacteriostatic agents which have largely been replaced by newer, better, and less toxic drugs.

TOOTHPASTES AND MOUTHWASHES

Before this chapter is ended, a brief comment on toothpastes and mouthwashes is in order.

Since practically all of these compounds contain a detergent and a flavoring agent, they are capable of generating sensitivity reactions in some patients. Detergents such as sodium lauryl sulfate, whether in toothpaste or soap, frequently are guilty of producing persistent and occasionally disabling skin eruptions and other allergic manifestations. Cinnamic aldehyde and methyl salicylate are two common flavoring agents which frequently cause gingivitis, glossopyrosis, and similar symptoms throughout the oral cavity.

While we may expect such reactions from products which contain antibiotics or strong astringents, these two lesser known factors frequently are ignored but will be etiologic for the above complaints in many patients.

Finally, in what is probably one of the most fraudulent and certainly one of the most objectionable areas of television and magazine advertising, a light is shining. In an order dated September 1970, the FDA finally zeroed in on mouthwash commercials. Ten leading brands were ordered to furnish real proof of germicidal power and banishment of halitosis or to cease their outlandish claims. The alternative was a government suit and banishment from the shelves. Hopefully most clinicians are aware that the average mouthwash is clinically worthless and that its promoters deal in the realm of fantasy![54]

SUMMARY

It is assumed that any practitioner who prescribes or administers a certain drug or compound to a patient knows the normal dosage of that agent; therefore the purpose of this chapter is not to list dosages, but to increase the doctor's awareness of the gross and the subtle toxic manifestations which may erupt with catastrophic suddenness or emerge slyly after long-term therapy.

The maze of new compounds and their questionable worth in some cases has been emphasized, along with the fact that an understanding of the pharmacology of all prescribed drugs is mandatory for the successful prophylaxis of drug intoxication. Mention has been made of the site and duration of action, relative strength, potentiation, metabolism and excretion, antagonism, and chemical structure as factors which determine the toxic potential or effects of a great number of drugs individually and in compatible compounds. Disease states which alter the effects of drugs and physiologic conditions which require dosage variant from the normal have been cited and discussed along with the advisability of a cautious approach in the administration of any drug to patients who are on delicate to strict regimens of chemotherapy.

A significant clue to the formidable nature of the problem of drug toxicology and its complexities is that while great progress has been made in recognizing and treating toxic responses to known chemical agents, there is emerging a brand new class of iatrogenic or "physician-made" drug diseases complete with appropriate and different signs, symptoms, and responses. Also, because of this, increasing scientific attention is being focused on the subject of teratology. Studies of teratogenicity are demonstrating that a fairly impressive number of drugs, when administered to laboratory animals (generally at doses substantially exceeding the comparable human dose), produce malformations among the offspring.

These phenomena no doubt lend substance and some respectability to that old adage, "The cure is sometimes worse than the disease."

The following material has been reproduced (with permission) from Medical Letter, Vol. 17, No. 5 (Issue 421), February 28, 1975.

ADVERSE INTERACTIONS OF DRUGS°

This article brings up to date material last reviewed in The Medical Letter in Volume 15, p. 77, 1973.

Two or more drugs administered at the same time or in close sequence may act independently, interact to increase or diminish the intended effect of one or both of the drugs, or may cause a new unexpected reaction.

°Extensive reviews of confirmed or suspected interactions between drugs are provided in P. D. Hansten, *Drug Interactions*, Philadelphia: Lea & Febiger, 2nd ed., 1973; American Pharmaceutical Association, *Evaluations of Drug Interactions*, 1973, Suppl. 1974.

DETECTION OF INTERACTIONS — The following table represents many reports and a consensus of views of many consultants; it lists only major interactions that have been observed clinically and is offered as a guide that may help to prevent unwanted interactions. Because of the risks of interactions, physicians should prescribe as few drugs as possible for concurrent use. Patients should also be asked routinely what prescriptions or over-the-counter medications they have been taking.

MECHANISMS OF INTERACTIONS — Many interactions result from changes in the metabolism of drugs caused by inhibition or induction of hepatic microsomal enzyme activity, changes in the binding of drugs with plasma protein or tissue receptor sites, changes in the distribution of drugs to the active receptor site, or changes in excretion. Genetic differences can also affect drug metabolism and interactions, and an interaction may occur with high doses of some drugs but not with smaller doses.

INTERACTIONS OF ALCOHOL — Interactions of alcohol with other drugs vary from one individual to another, with the amount of alcohol consumed, and with the duration of use of large amounts of alcohol. Concurrent use of excessive and sometimes ordinary doses of central-nervous-system depressants and intoxicating or large amounts of alcohol can lead to coma and death. When a person drinks an intoxicating amount of alcohol, hepatic metabolism of many drugs may be inhibited, leading to increased therapeutic or toxic effects of the drugs (E. Rubin and C. S. Lieber, Science, 162:690, 1968). On the other hand, in some individuals who drink more than eight ounces of 80-proof whiskey or the equivalent daily for a prolonged period, hepatic metabolism of drugs may be enhanced, which will diminish the therapeutic effects of many drugs, including some of those enhanced by acute intoxication with alcohol (Medical Letter, Vol. 16, p. 91, 1974).

Adverse Interactions of Drugs

Interacting Drugs	Adverse Effect	Probable Mechanism
ALCOHOL, with:		
Antabuse (disulfiram)	Abdominal cramps, flushing, vomiting, psychotic episodes, confusion	Inhibits intermediary metabolism of alcohol
Anticoagulants, oral	Diminished anticoagulant effect with chronic alcohol abuse	Enhanced metabolism
	Enhanced anticoagulant effect with acute intoxication	Reduced metabolism
Anticonvulsants		
Phenytoin (Dilantin; and others)	Diminished anticonvulsant effect with chronic alcohol abuse	Enhanced metabolism
	Enhanced anticonvulsant effect with acute intoxication	Reduced metabolism
Antimicrobials		
Chloramphenicol (Chloromycetin; and others)	Minor Antabuse-like symptoms	Inhibits intermediary metabolism of alcohol
Isoniazid	Increased incidence of hepatitis	Not established
	Diminished isoniazid effect in some patients with chronic alcohol abuse	Enhanced metabolism
Quinacrine (Atabrine)	Minor Antabuse-like symptoms	Inhibits intermediary metabolism of alcohol
Hypoglycemics[1]		
Chlorpropamide (Diabinese)	Minor Antabuse-like symptoms	Inhibits intermediary metabolism of alcohol
Phenformin (DBI; Meltrol)	Lactic acidosis	Synergy
Tolbutamide (Orinase)	Diminished hypoglycemic effect with chronic alcohol abuse	Enhanced metabolism
	Enhanced hypoglycemic effect with ingestion of alcohol, particularly in fasting patients	Suppression of gluconeogenesis
	Minor Antabuse-like symptoms	Inhibits intermediary metabolism of alcohol

Adverse Interactions of Drugs (Continued)

Interacting Drugs	Adverse Effect	Probable Mechanism
MAO inhibitors[2] (With Chianti wine and some other alcoholic beverages)	Hypertensive crisis	Inhibit metabolism of tyramine, resulting in increased release of norepinephrine
Salicylates	Gastrointestinal bleeding	Additive
Sedatives and Hypnotics		
Barbiturates	Diminished sedative effect with chronic alcohol abuse	Enhanced metabolism
	Enhanced central-nervous-system depression with acute intoxication	Additive; reduced metabolism
Chloral hydrate (Noctec; and others)	Prolonged hypnotic effect	Mutual potentiation
Diazepam (Valium)	Enhanced central-nervous-system depression	Additive
Meprobamate (Miltown; and others)	Diminished sedative effect with chronic alcohol abuse	Enhanced metabolism
	Enhanced central-nervous-system depression with acute intoxication	Additive; reduced metabolism

ANTIBIOTIC, CHEMOTHERAPEUTIC, & ANTIPARASITIC AGENTS

Interacting Drugs	Adverse Effect	Probable Mechanism
Aminoglycoside antibiotics,[3] with:		
Cephaloridine (Loridine)	Nephrotoxicity	Not established
Cephalothin (Keflin)	Nephrotoxicity	Not established
Curariform drugs[4]	Neuromuscular blockade	Additive
Ethacrynic acid (Edecrin)	Ototoxicity	Additive
Polymyxins (Aerosporin; Coly-Mycin)	Nephrotoxicity	Additive
Aminosalicyl acid (PAS), with:		
Probenecid (Benemid)	Aminosalicylic acid toxicity	Inhibition of renal excretion
Amphotericin B (Fungizone), with:		
Curariform drugs[4]	Increased curariform effects	Hypokalemia
Digitalis drugs	Increased digitalis toxicity	Hypokalemia
Cephaloridine (Loridine), with:		
Aminoglycoside antibiotics[3]	Nephrotoxicity	Not established
Ethacrynic acid (Edecrin)	Nephrotoxicity	Additive
Furosemide (Lasix)	Nephrotoxicity	Additive
Probenecid (Benemid)	Increased cephaloridine toxicity	Inhibition of renal excretion
Cephalothin (Keflin), with:		
Aminoglycoside antibiotics[3]	Nephrotoxicity	Not established
Chloramphenicol (Chloromycetin; and others), with:		
Alcohol	Minor Antabuse-like symptoms	Inhibits intermediary metabolism of alcohol
Anticoagulants, oral	Increased anticoagulant effect with dicumarol	Inhibition of microsomal enzymes
Hypoglycemics[1]	Increased sulfonylurea hypoglycemia	Inhibition of microsomal enzymes
Phenytoin (Dilantin; and others)	Increased phenytoin toxicity	Inhibition of microsomal enzymes
Griseofulvin (Fulvicin-U/F; and others), with:		
Anticoagulants, oral	Decreased anticoagulant effect with warfarin	Induction of microsomal enzymes
Isoniazid, with:		
Alcohol	Increased incidence of hepatitis	Not established
	Diminished isoniazid effect in some patients with chronic alcohol abuse	Enhanced metabolism

DRUGS: USE AND ABUSE   213

Adverse Interactions of Drugs *(Continued)*

Interacting Drugs	Adverse Effect	Probable Mechanism
Aluminum antacids	Decreased isoniazid effect	Inhibition of isoniazid absorption
Antabuse (disulfiram)	Psychotic episodes, ataxia	Alteration of catecholamine metabolism
Phenytoin (Dilantin; and others)	Increased phenytoin toxicity	Inhibition of microsomal enzymes
Lincomycin (Lincocin), with:		
Kaolin-pectin (Kaopectate)	Decreased lincomycin effect	Inhibition of lincomycin absorption
Nalidixic acid (NegGram), with:		
Anticoagulants, oral	Increased anticoagulant effect	Displacement from binding sites
Polymyxins (Aerosporin; Coly-Mycin), with:		
Aminoglycoside antibiotics[3]	Nephrotoxicity	Additive
Curariform drugs[4]	Neuromuscular blockade	Additive
Quinacrine (Atabrine), with:		
Alcohol	Minor Antabuse-like symptoms	Inhibits intermediary metabolism of alcohol

ANTIBIOTIC, CHEMOTHERAPEUTIC, & ANTIPARASITIC AGENTS

Rifampin (Rifadin, Rimactane), with:		
Anticoagulants, oral	Decreased anticoagulant effect	Induction of microsomal enzymes
Contraceptives, oral	Diminished contraceptive effect	Increased estrogen metabolism
Probenecid (Benemid)	Increased rifampin toxicity	Decreased hepatic uptake of rifampin
Sulfonamides, long-acting, with:		
Anticoagulants, oral	Increased anticoagulant effect	Displacement from binding sites
Hypoglycemics[1]	Increased sulfonylurea hypoglycemia	Not established
Tetracyclines, with:		
Antacids, oral	Decreased effect of tetracyclines	Inhibition of tetracycline absorption
Barbiturates	Decreased doxycycline (Vibramycin) effect	Induction of microsomal enzymes
Carbamazepine (Tegretol)	Decreased doxycycline (Vibramycin) effect	Induction of microsomal enzymes
Iron, oral	Decreased effect of tetracyclines	Inhibition of tetracycline absorption
Methoxyflurane (Penthrane)	Nephrotoxicity	Not established

ANTICOAGULANTS, ORAL, with:

Alcohol	Diminished anticoagulant effect with chronic alcohol abuse	Enhanced metabolism
	Enhanced anticoagulant effect with acute intoxication	Reduced metabolism
Allopurinol (Zyloprim)	Increased anticoagulant effect	Inhibition of microsomal enzymes
Anabolic and androgenic steroids	Increased anticoagulant effect	Not established
Barbiturates	Decreased anticoagulant effect	Induction of microsomal enzymes
Chloral hydrate (Noctec; and others)	Increased anticoagulant effect	Displacement from binding sites
Chloramphenicol (Chloromycetin; and others)	Increased anticoagulant effect with dicumarol	Inhibition of microsomal enzymes
Cholestyramine (Questran)	Decreased anticoagulant effect	Decreased absorption
Clofibrate (Atromid-S)	Increased anticoagulant effect	Displacement from binding sites
Contraceptives, oral	Decreased anticoagulant effect	Increase in activity of some clotting factors
Dextrothyroxine (Choloxin)	Increased anticoagulant effect	Not established
Disulfiram (Antabuse)	Increased anticoagulant effect	Inhibition of microsomal enzymes
Glutethimide (Doriden)	Decreased anticoagulant effect	Induction of microsomal enzymes
Griseofulvin (Fulvicin-U/F; and others)	Decreased anticoagulant effect with warfarin	Induction of microsomal enzymes
Hypoglycemics[1]	Increased sulfonylurea hypoglycemia with dicumarol	Inhibition of microsomal enzymes

Adverse Interactions of Drugs *(Continued)*

Interacting Drugs	Adverse Effect	Probable Mechanism
Nalidixic acid (NegGram)	Increased anticoagulant effect	Displacement from binding sites
Phenylbutazone (Butazolidin; Azolid) and oxyphenbutazone (Tandearil; Oxalid)	Increased anticoagulant effect	Displacement from binding sites
Phenytoin (Dilantin; and others)	Increased phenytoin toxicity with dicumarol	Inhibition of microsomal enzymes
Rifampin (Rifadin; Rimactane)	Decreased anticoagulant effect	Induction of microsomal enzymes
Salicylates	Increased anticoagulant effect	Reduction of plasma prothrombin
Sulfonamides, long-acting	Increased anticoagulant effect	Displacement from binding sites
Thyroid hormones	Increased anticoagulant effect	Increased clotting factor catabolism
ANTIDEPRESSANTS, TRICYCLIC,[5] with:		
Barbiturates	Decreased antidepressant effect	Induction of microsomal enzymes
Guanethidine (Ismelin)	Decreased antihypertensive effect	Blockade of uptake at target site
MAO inhibitors[2]	Hyperpyrexia, convulsions	Not established
Sympathomimetic amines[6]	Hypertensive crisis	Inhibition of norepinephrine uptake by neuron
ANTIHYPERTENSIVE DRUGS, with:		
Anesthetics, general	Hypotension	Usually additive
Antidepressants, tricyclic[5]	Decreased antihypertensive effect of guanethidine	Blockade of uptake at target site
Hypoglycemics[1]	Increased hypoglycemia with guanethidine	Not established
Phenothiazines	Hypotension	Blockade of dopamine; additive
Sympathomimetic amines[6]	Decreased hypotensive effect	Inhibition of norepinephrine uptake by neuron
BARBITURATES, with:		
Alcohol	Diminished sedative effect with chronic alcohol abuse	Enhanced metabolism
	Enhanced central-nervous-system depression with acute intoxication	Additive; reduced metabolism
Anticoagulants, oral	Decreased anticoagulant effect	Induction of microsomal enzymes
Antidepressants, tricyclic[5]	Decreased antidepressant activity	Induction of microsomal enzymes
Corticosteroids	Decreased steroid effect	Induction of microsomal enzymes
Tetracyclines	Decreased doxycycline (Vibramycin) effect	Induction of microsomal enzymes
CONTRACEPTIVES, ORAL, with:		
Anticoagulants, oral	Decreased anticoagulant effect	Increase in activity of some clotting factors
Rifampin (Rifadin; Rimactane)	Diminished contraceptive effect	Increased estrogen metabolism
CURARIFORM DRUGS,[4] with:		
Aminoglycoside antibiotics[3] and polymyxins (administered parenterally)	Neuromuscular blockade	Additive
Amphotericin B (Fungizone)	Increased curariform effects	Hypokalemia
Diuretics (causing potassium loss)	Increased curariform effects	Hypokalemia
Narcotic analgesics	Increased respiratory depression	Additive
Quinidine	Increased curariform effects	Additive
DIGITALIS DRUGS, with:		
Amphotericin B (Fungizone)	Increased digitalis toxicity	Hypokalemia
Cholestyramine (Questran)	Decreased digitoxin effect	Binding in intestine
Diuretics (causing potassium loss)	Increased digitalis toxicity	Hypokalemia
Sympathomimetic amines[6]	Enhanced tendency to cardiac arrhythmias	Additive effect on pacemaker

Adverse Interactions of Drugs *(Continued)*

Interacting Drugs	Adverse Effect	Probable Mechanism
DIURETICS		
Ethacrynic acid (Edecrin), with:		
Cephaloridine (Loridine)	Nephrotoxicity	Additive
Furosemide (Lasix), with:		
Cephaloridine (Loridine)	Nephrotoxicity	Additive
Potassium-losing diuretics, with:		
Corticosteroids	Enhanced potassium loss	Additive
Curariform drugs[4]	Increased curariform effects	Hypokalemia
Digitalis drugs	Increased digitalis toxicity	Hypokalemia
Spironolactone (Aldactone), with:		
Potassium salts	Hyperkalemia	Additive
Salicylates	Decreased natriuresis	Not established
Triamterene (Dyrenium), with:		
Potassium salts	Hyperkalemia	Additive
HYPOGLYCEMICS,[1] with:		
Alcohol, see ALCOHOL		
Anabolic steroids	Increased hypoglycemia	Not established
Chloramphenicol (Chloromycetin; and others)	Increased sulfonylurea hypoglycemia	Inhibition of microsomal enzymes
Dicumarol	Increased sulfonylurea hypoglycemia	Inhibition of microsomal enzymes
Guanethidine (Ismelin)	Increased hypoglycemia	Not established
MAO inhibitors[2]	Increased hypoglycemia	Not established
Phenylbutazone (Butazolidin; Azolid) and oxyphenbutazone (Tandearil; Oxalid)	Increased sulfonylurea hypoglycemia	Inhibition of microsomal enzymes
Propranolol (Inderal)	Increased hypoglycemia	Not established
Salicylates	Increased hypoglycemia	Displacement from binding; additive
Sulfaphenazole and possibly other long-acting sulfonamides	Increased sulfonylurea hypoglycemia	Not established
LEVODOPA (Dopar; and others), with:		
MAO inhibitors[2]	Hypertensive crisis	Increase in storage and release of dopamine, norepinephrine, or both
Phenothiazines	Decreased antiparkinson effect	Inhibition of dopamine uptake
Pyridoxine	Decreased antiparkinson effect	Enhancement of decarboxylation of levadopa at periphery
MAO INHIBITORS,[2] with:		
Alcohol (Chianti wine and some other alcoholic beverages)	Hypertensive crisis	Inhibit metabolism of tyramine, resulting in increased release of norepinephrine
Antidepressants, tricyclic[5]	Hyperpyrexia, convulsions	Not established
Hypoglycemics[1]	Increased hypoglycemia	Not established
Levodopa (Dopar; and others)	Hypertensive crisis	Increase in storage and release of dopamine, norepinephrine, or both
Meperidine (Demerol; and others)	Hypertension; or hypotension and coma	Not established
Sympathomimetic amines[6]	Hypertensive crisis	Increase in storage and release of norepinephrine
Tyramine in foods[7]	Hypertensive crisis	Inhibit metabolism of tyramine, resulting in increased release of norepinephrine

Adverse Interactions of Drugs *(Continued)*

Interacting Drugs	Adverse Effect	Probable Mechanism
SALICYLATES, with:		
Anticoagulants, oral	Increased anticoagulant effect	Reduction of plasma prothrombin
Hypoglycemics[1]	Increased hypoglycemia	Displacement from binding; additive
Methotrexate	Increased effect and toxicity of methotrexate	Displacement from binding sites
Probenecid (Benemid)	Decreased uricosuric effect	Not established
Spironolactone (Aldactone)	Decreased natriuresis	Not established
SYMPATHOMIMETIC AMINES,[6] with:		
Antidepressants, tricyclic[5]	Hypertensive crisis	Inhibition of norepinephrine uptake by neuron
Antihypertensive drugs	Decreased hypotensive effect	Inhibition of norepinephrine uptake by neuron
Cyclopropane and halogenated hydrocarbon anesthetics	Cardiac arrhythmias	Not established
Digitalis drugs	Enhanced tendency to cardiac arrhythmias	Additive effect on pacemaker
MAO inhibitors[2, 8]	Hypertensive crisis	Increase in storage and release of norepinephrine
THYROID HORMONES, with:		
Anticoagulants, oral	Increased anticoagulant effect	Increased clotting factor catabolism
Cholestyramine (Questran)	Decreased absorption of thyroid	Binding of hormone in intestine
MISCELLANEOUS DRUGS		
Allopurinol, with:		
Anticoagulants, oral	Increased anticoagulant effect	Inhibition of microsomal enzymes
Azathioprine (Imuran)	Azathioprine toxicity	Inhibition of azathioprine metabolism
Cyclophosphamide (Cytoxan)	Cyclophosphamide toxicity	Inhibition of cyclophosphamide metabolism
Mercaptopurine (6-MP)	Mercaptopurine toxicity	Inhibition of mercaptopurine metabolism
Cholestyramine (Questran), with:		
Anticoagulants, oral	Decreased anticoagulant effect	Decreased absorption
Digitalis drugs	Decreased digitoxin effect	Binding in intestine
Thyroid hormones	Decreased absorption of thyroid	Binding of hormone in intestine
Methotrexate, with:		
Salicylates	Increased effect and toxicity of methotrexate	Displacement from binding sites
Neostigmine, parenteral (Prostigmin), with:		
Quinidine	Decreased neostigmine effect	Anticholinergic effect of quinidine
Phenytoin (Dilantin; and others), with:		
Alcohol	Diminished anticonvulsant effect with chronic alcohol abuse	Enhanced metabolism
	Enhanced anticonvulsant effect with acute intoxication	Reduced metabolism
Chloramphenicol (Chloromycetin; and others)	Phenytoin toxicity	Inhibition of microsomal enzymes
Dicumarol	Phenytoin toxicity	Inhibition of microsomal enzymes
Isoniazid	Phenytoin toxicity	Inhibition of microsomal enzymes
Probenecid (Benemid), with:		
Aminosalicylic acid (PAS)	Aminosalicylic acid toxicity	Inhibition of renal excretion
Cephaloridine (Loridine)	Increased cephaloridine toxicity	Inhibition of renal excretion
Rifampin (Rifadin; Rimactane)	Increased rifampin toxicity	Decreased hepatic uptake
Salicylates	Decreased uricosuric effect	Not established

Footnotes—Adverse Interactions of Drugs

1. Hypoglycemics include insulin, phenformin (DBI; Meltrol), and the sulfonylureas (acetohexamide [Dymelor]; chlorpropamide [Diabinese]; tolazamide [Tolinase]; tolbutamide [Orinase]). Any drug with marked stimulant effect on the sympathetic nervous system can potentiate insulin release and consequently the action of sulfonylureas.
2. MAO inhibitors include furazolidone (Furoxone), isocarboxazid (Marplan), pargyline (Eutonyl), phenelzine (Nardil), and tranylcypromine (Parnate).
3. Aminoglycoside antibiotics include gentamicin (Garamycin), kanamycin (Kantrex), neomycin and streptomycin.
4. Curariform drugs include d-tubocurarine, gallamine, and succinylcholine.
5. Tricyclic antidepressants include amitriptyline (Elavil), desipramine (Norpramin; Pertofrane), doxepin (Sinequan), imipramine (Tofranil; Presamine), nortriptyline (Aventyl), and protriptyline (Vivactil).
6. Sympathomimetic amines include amphetamines, ephedrine, epinephrine (Adrenalin), isoproterenol (Isuprel), methylphenidate (Ritalin), norepinephrine (Levophed), phenylephrine (Sudafed; and others), and many appetite-depressing drugs; also amines in many over-the-counter cough, cold, and sinus remedies, including nasal decongestants.
7. Foods containing tyramine include aged cheeses, Chianti wines, beer, sherry, pickled herring, yeast extracts, chicken liver, chocolate, broad beans, sour cream, canned figs, raisins, and soy sauce.
8. Of the sympathomimetic amines (footnote 6), the most dangerous in patients on MAO inhibitors would be amphetamines, ephedrine, phenylephrine, and phenylpropanolamine.

Partial List of Trade Names

Acenocoumarol—(see Anticoagulants)
Aerosporin—Polymyxin
Aldactone—Spironolactone
Anisindione—(see Anticoagulants)
Antabuse—Disulfiram
Aspirin—(see Salicylates)
Atabrine—Quinacrine
Atromid-S—Clofibrate
Azolid—Phenylbutazone
Benemid—Probenecid
Bishydroxycoumarin—(see Anticoagulants)
Butazolidin—Phenylbutazone
Chloromycetin—Chloramphenicol
Choloxin—Dextrothyroxine
Colistin—(see Polymyxins)
Coly-Mycin—(see Polymyxins)
Coumadin—(see Anticoagulants)
Cytoxan—Cyclophosphamide
Danilone—(see Anticoagulants)
DBI—Phenformin
Demerol—Meperidine
Diabinese—Chlorpropamide
Dicumarol—(see Anticoagulants)
Dilantin—Phenytoin
Diphenylhydantoin—(see Phenytoin)
Dopar—Levodopa
Doriden—Glutethimide
Dyrenium—Triamterene
Edecrin—Ethacrynic acid
Fulvicin-U/F—Griseofulvin
Fungizone—Amphotericin B
Grifulvin—Griseofulvin

Hedulin—(see Anticoagulants)
Imuran—Azathioprine
Inderal—Propranolol
Ismelin—Guanethidine
Keflin—Cephalothin
Lasix—Furosemide
Lincocin—Lincomycin
Loridine—Cephaloridine
Meltrol—Phenformin
Miltown—Meprobamate
Miradon—(see Anticoagulants)
NegGram—Nalidixic acid
Noctec — Chloral hydrate
Orinase—Tolbutamide
Oxalid—(see Phenylbutazone)
Oxyphenbutazone—(see Phenylbutazone)
Panwarfin—(see Anticoagulants)
PAS — Aminosalicylic acid
Penthrane—Methoxyflurane
Phenindione—(see Anticoagulants)
Prostigmin—Neostigmine
Questran—Cholestyramine
Rifadin—Rifampin
Rimactane—Rifampin
Sintrom—(see Anticoagulants)
6-MP—Mercaptopurine
Tandearil—(see Phenylbutazone)
Tegretol—Carbamazepine
Valium—Diazepam
Vibramycin—Doxycycline
Warfarin—(see Anticoagulants)
Zyloprim—Allopurinol

REFERENCES

1. Adriani, J.: The Chemistry and Physics of Anesthesia. 2nd ed., Springfield Ill., Charles C Thomas, 1970.
2. Adriani, J.: The Pharmacology of Anesthetic Drugs: A Syllabus for Students and Clinicians. 5th ed., Springfield, Ill., Charles C Thomas, 1970.

3. Adriani, J.: Techniques and Procedures of Anesthesia. 3rd ed., Springfield, Ill., Charles C Thomas, 1969.
4. Adriani, J.: Fundamentals of General Anesthesia for Students and Practitioners of Dentistry. Springfield, Ill., Charles C Thomas, 1958.
5. Adriani, J.: Selection of Anesthesia: The Physiologic and Pharmacologic Basis. Springfield, Ill., Charles C Thomas, 1955.
6. Artusio, J. F., and Mazzia, V. P. B.: Practical Anesthesiology. St Louis, C. V. Mosby, 1962.
7. Beckman H.: Pharmacology — The Nature, Action, and Use of Drugs. 2nd ed., Philadelphia, W. B. Saunders Co., 1961.
8. Brady, E. S.: A Calculated Risk. Alumni Review, University of Southern California, November, 1964.
9. Birch, A. A., and Tolmie, J. D.: Anesthesia for the Uninterested. Baltimore, University Park Press, 1976.
10. Brechner, Verne L.: Pathological and Pharmacological Consideration in Anesthesiology. The Proceedings of the Twelfth Biennial Western Conference on Anesthesiology. U. of Utah Press, 1972.
11. Burton, A. C.: Physiology and Biophysics of the Circulation. 2nd ed., Chicago, Year Book Medical Publishers, 1972.
12. Catron, D. C.: The Anesthesiologist's Handbook. 2nd ed., Baltimore, University Park Press, 1976.
13. Chas. Pfizer & Co., Inc.: Package inserts, May 1966.
14. Cohen, D. D., and Dillon, J. B.: Anesthesia for Outpatient Surgery. Springfield, Ill., Charles C Thomas, 1970.
15. Cutting, W. C.: Handbook of Pharmacology. 2nd ed. New York, Appleton-Century-Crofts, 1964.
16. DeJong, R. H.: Physiology and Pharmacology of Local Anesthesia. Springfield, Ill., Charles C Thomas, 1970.
17. Dornette, W. H. L.: Anatomy for the Anesthesiologist: A Stereoscopic Atlas '63.
18. Drug Bulletin — L.A.C.–U.S.C. Medical Center, L. A., California, 8/10/77.
19. Drugs in Breast Milk. The Medical Letter. Vol. 16, No. 6, March, 1974.
20. Eastman, J. W., and Cohen, S. N.: Hypertensive crisis and death associated with phencyclidine poisoning. J.A.M.A., 231:1270–1271, 1975.
21. Farr, R. S.: Denver National Jewish Hospital, Denver, Colorado, 1970.
22. Fragen, R. J., and Caldwell, N.: Lorazepam premedication: Lack of recall and relief of anxiety. Anesth. Analg. (Cleve.) 55(6):792, 1976.
23. Garb, S., and Crim, B. J.: Pharmacology and Patient Care. New York, Springer Publishing Co., 1962.
24. Gold, M. I.: Tranquilizers and anesthesia. J.A.D.S.A., April, 1967.
25. Goth, A.: Medical Pharmacology, 5th ed., St. Louis, C. V. Mosby Co., 1970.
26. Greenfield, W.: Anesthesia progress. J.A.D.S.A., 23 (4): July-Aug, 1976.
27. Handbook of Non-Prescription Drugs, 1969 edition.
28. Hunter, A. R., and Bush, G. H.: General Anesthesia for Dental Surgery. Springfield, Ill., Charles C Thomas, 1971.
29. LaDu, B. H.: New York University School of Medicine.
30. Laskin, J. L., Wallace, W. R., and DeLeo, B.: Use of bupivacaine hydrochloride in oral surgery —a clinical study. J. Ortho. Surg., 35:25, 1977.
31. Lee, J. A.: A Symposium of Anesthesia. Chicago, Year Book Medical Publishers, 1973.
32. Libman, R. H.: Anesth. Prog., Sept-Oct, 1976.
33. Lorhan, P. H.: Anesthesia for the Aged. Springfield, Ill., Charles C Thomas, 1971.
34. McCarthy, F.: Emergencies in Dental Practice. 3rd ed., Philadelphia, W. B. Saunders Co., 1979.
35. Medical Letter: Vol. 15 (23), Issue 387, November 9, 1973.
36. Medical Letter: Vol 17 (5), Issue 421, February 28, 1975.
37. Monheim, L. M.: General Anesthesia in Dental Practice. St. Louis, C. V. Mosby Co., 1960.
38. Monheim, L. M.: Local Anesthesia and Plain Control in Dental Practice. 2nd ed. St. Louis, C. V. Mosby Co., 1961.
39. Mulay, D. N., and Urbach, F.: Local therapy of oral leukoplakia with vitamin A. A.M.A. Arch. Dermat., 78:637, 1958.
40. National Prescription Audit, 12th ed. Philadelphia. Lea and Febiger, 1972.
41. Ngai, S. H., and Papper, E. M.: Metabolic Effects of Anesthesia. Springfield, Ill., Charles C Thomas, 1962.
42. Olson, R. E., Morello, J. A., and Kreff, E. D.: Antibiotic treatment of oral anaerobic infections. J. Ortho. Surg., 33;. Aug. 1975.
43. Parke-Davis & Co.: Package inserts.
44. Powell, W. F.: Comprehensive Background for Anesthesiology. Springfield, Ill., Charles C Thomas, 1966.
45. Pricco, D. E.: J. Ortho. Surg., 35:129, 1977.

46. Pryor, W. J., and Bush, D.C.T.: A Manual of Anesthetic Techniques. 4th ed., Chicago, Year Book Medical Publishers, 1973.
47. Saidman, J., and Moya, F.: Complications of Anesthesia. Springfield, Ill., Charles C Thomas, 1970.
48. Salter, F. J.: University of Michigan Hospital Pharmacy Letter for Physicians, Vol. 5, No. 1. Jan., 1970.
49. Schwartz, H., Ngai, S. H., and Papper, E. M.: Manual of Anesthesiology for Residents and Medical Students. 2nd ed., Springfield, Charles C Thomas, 1962.
50. Shore, M. F.: Drugs can be dangerous during pregnancy and lactation. Can. Pharm. J., Dec., 1970. Reprinted by Upjohn Co.
51. Smith, J. W.: Manual of Medical Therapeutics, 19th ed. Boston, Little, Brown and Co., 1969.
52. Smith, R. H.: Pathological Physiology for the Anesthesiologist. Springfield, Ill., Charles C Thomas, 1966.
53. Sohn, D. M.: Valium. Anesth. Prog., May-June, 1975.
54. Steiner, R. B., and Thompson, R. D.: Oral Surgery and Anesthesia. Philadelphia, W. B. Saunders Co., 1977.
55. Stephen, C. R., Ahlgren, E. W., and Bennett, E.: Elements of Pediatric Anesthesia. 2nd ed., Springfield, Ill., Charles C Thomas, 1970.
56. The Medical Letter on Drugs and Therapeutics. New York, Drug and Therapeutic Information, Inc., 1970.
57. Thienes, C. H., and Haley, T. J.: Clinical Toxicology. 4th ed., Philadelphia, Lea & Febiger, 1969.
58. Vereby, K., Volavka, J., Mulé, S. J., et al.: Naltrexone: disposition, metabolism, and effects after acute and chronic dosing. Clin. Pharmacol. Ther. 20:315–328, 1976.
59. Walton, J. G., and Thompson, J. W.: Pharmacology for the Dental Practitioner. British D. J., Vol. 127, 1969.
60. Wynn, R. L., and Kohn, M. W.: The Pharmacology of Intravenous Sedation. Am. Soc. Ortho. Surg. 1976
61. Young, J. A.: The Medical Messiahs. Princeton, Princeton University Press, 1967.

Part 2

TREATMENT OF
SERIOUS MEDICAL
EMERGENCIES

6

BASIC LIFE SUPPORT AND PARENTERAL DRUG ADMINISTRATION

the late
JOHN HAGEN
and
STANLEY F. MALAMED

INTRODUCTION

This chapter is the first in the section on the treatment of serious medical emergencies. While subsequent chapters will discuss specific causes of medical emergencies and their treatment, we will review procedures which are essential to the management of most of these potentially life-threatening situations.

These procedures include the maintenance of a patent airway in the unconscious patient, techniques for delivering oxygen to conscious or unconscious patients, and monitoring of two very important vital signs, the blood pressure and the heart rate (pulse), which give us information concerning the functional status of the cardiovascular system. Taken together, these three procedures constitute the ABC's of basic life support; A for airway, B for breathing, and C for circulation. When all three procedures (ABC) are employed together the technique is termed cardiopulmonary resuscitation (CPR). It is only on rare occasions, fortunately, that the dental practitioner will be called upon to perform cardiopulmonary resuscitation within the dental office. (CPR is discussed in depth in Chapter 9.) However, the dental doctor will more than likely be presented with several occasions during his or her practice lifetime which will require implementation of the steps of basic life support.

With proper management most of these emergency situations will be readily correctable. Proper management is the vital key to success in most of these situations, and a thorough working knowledge of the procedures of basic life support is obligatory for proper management to occur.

This chapter will conclude with a description of techniques for parenteral drug administration. Two techniques for drug administration will be reviewed: the intramuscular and the intravenous routes. Specific drugs to be employed in the management of medical emergency situations will be discussed in later chapters. It must be stated clearly and be well understood that *the administration of drugs, in most medical emergency situations, should be secondary to the performance of the procedures of basic life support.* Once the ABC's have been satisfactorily accomplished the doctor can then give attention to the specific cause(s) of the emergency and give consideration to drug therapy to assist the patient's recovery.

MANAGEMENT OF THE UNCONSCIOUS PATIENT

Loss of consciousness is a common occurrence in the dental office. Whatever the precipitating factor, loss of consciousness always presents the practitioner with a potentially life-threatening emergency, demanding immediate and effective treatment if the victim is to be expected to recover. Loss of consciousness is assumed to represent cardiac arrest until proven otherwise.

Because of possible medicolegal implications, case reports of deaths during dental therapy are rarely observed in dental journals in the United States. However, much valuable information may be readily obtained from both dental and medical journals published in Great Britain. When these articles and reports are examined, an item which is seen to recur quite frequently is anoxia secondary to an obstructed airway, which goes unnoticed until permanent damage has occurred.[11, 12, 14, 19]

In response to these reports, the British Dental Journal published a letter which stated in part: ". . . at a lecture/demonstration a few years ago, not one dental surgeon participating knew how to give the 'kiss of life' correctly and, therefore, could not have resuscitated the patient. In reading accounts of death occurring under general anesthesia and that the 'kiss of life' was administered with no result in some of these cases, I hesitate, but wonder whether the method of resuscitation chosen was correctly applied."[17]

Loss of consciousness need not occur only in the patient receiving general anesthetic agents; indeed the most common cause of unconsciousness in dentistry is vasodepressor syncope (common faint) due to fear and apprehension, in unmedicated patients. The initial treatment in most circumstances of unconsciousness is essentially the same. One possible exception is the acute anaphylactic reaction, in which case the administration of epinephrine as soon as possible may well prove to be the single most important life-saving measure.

Unconsciousness is accompanied by muscular relaxation, and it is this muscular relaxation which is responsible for the associated problems of hypoxia and/or anoxia. In the unconscious patient, hypopharyngeal obstruction by the base of the relaxed tongue occurs always when the head is in the midposition (Fig. 6–1). As stated by Safar: complete airway obstruction leads to asphyxia and cardiac arrest within five to 10 minutes; while partial airway obstruction, through other more complex pathways, may lead to the same result.[18]

In all cases of unconsciousness, immediate treatment consists of the recognition of airway obstruction and the effective management of this problem. Once a patent airway has been secured, only then can the dental practitioner proceed to more definitive life-support measures (cardiac massage; drug administration). It is well to keep in mind the objectives of ventilation, as stated by Coryllos: life is continued as long as exchanges of oxygen and carbon dioxide in the tissues are carried on in a normal way.[9]

The establishment of a patent airway therefore becomes the primary objective of treatment in all cases of unconsciousness.

TECHNIQUES OF AIRWAY MAINTENANCE

Immediately upon the recognition of unconsciousness it is recommended that the following sequence be carried out until one is satisfied that a patent airway exists:

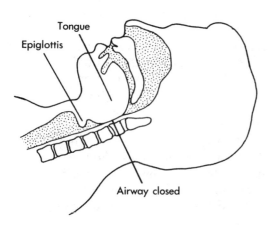

Figure 6–1 Airway obstruction. In flexed position, the tongue acts to produce obstruction, either partial or complete, in the unconscious patient. (From Malamed, S. F., Handbook of Medical Emergencies in the Dental Office. Saint Louis, C. V. Mosby, Co., 1978.)

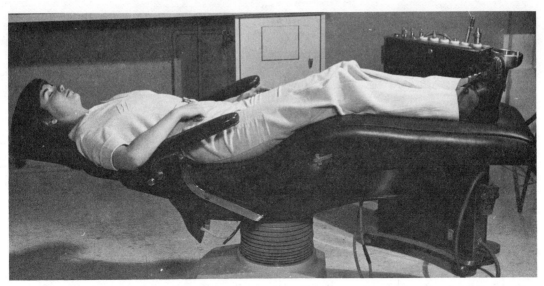

Figure 6-2 Positioning of the unconscious patient. The unconscious patient is placed in a supine position with the chest and abdomen parallel to the floor, the head and legs elevated slightly. (From Malamed, S. F.: Handbook of Medical Emergencies in the Dental Office. Saint Louis, C. V. Mosby Co., 1978.)

1. Positioning of patient
2. Backward tilt of head
3. Check for airway, breathing
4. Forward displacement of mandible, if necessary
5. Check for airway, breathing, if necessary
6. Artificial ventilation, if necessary

    1. Positioning of Patient (Fig. 6-2). An unconscious patient should be placed in the *supine* position. The chest and head should be horizontal to aid in delivery of blood to the brain, and the feet should be elevated slightly, aiding in return of blood to the heart.

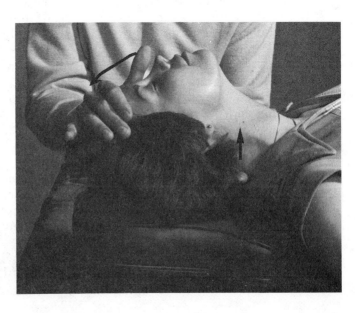

Figure 6-3 Head tilt. The rescuer places one hand beneath the victim's neck, lifting the neck; the second hand, placed on the victim's forehead, pushes the forehead back.

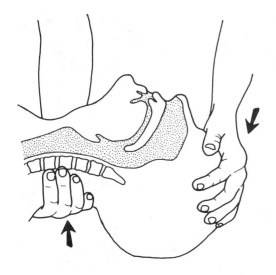

Figure 6–4 Head tilt. Lifting the neck and pushing the forehead back serves to stretch the tissues in the pharynx, lifting the tongue off of the posterior pharyngeal wall. (From Malamed, S. F.: Handbook of Medical Emergencies in the Dental Office. Saint Louis, C. V. Mosby Co., 1978.)

2. Backward Tilt of Head (Head-Tilt, Fig. 6–3). This is perhaps the single most effective step to take in the creation of a patent airway in an unconscious patient. One hand is placed under the patient's neck, lifting it, while the other at the patient's forehead pushes the head back. This simple maneuver stretches the tissues between the larynx and mandible (Fig. 6–4), lifting the base of the tongue from the posterior pharyngeal wall. Elevation of the patient's shoulders (achieved by placing a towel or pillow under the shoulders) may be a further aid in tilting of the patient's head.

When properly carried out, this step alone provides an open airway in about 80 per cent of unconscious patients.

3. Check for Airway Breathing. An evaluation of airway patency may rapidly be made by *looking* and *listening*.

Look: look for movements of the chest and abdomen.

Listen: listen and *feel* for air flow at the mouth and nose. This may be quickly accomplished by placing your ear one inch from the patient's nose and mouth and the palm of one hand on the upper part of the patient's abdomen. If no air exchange is immediately detectable, a gentle push will establish patency of the airway (Fig. 6–5).[8] This airway patency maneuver was first utilized by dental practitioners administering intravenous anesthesia in the early 1940's.

Two types of airway obstruction may be evidenced: complete obstruction and partial obstruction. As mentioned above it takes only a period of between five and 10 minutes for complete airway obstruction to cause biological (non-reversible) death.

Complete airway obstruction will be recognized by the inability to *hear* and *feel* air flow at the mouth or nose, and by *seeing* inspiratory retraction in the intercostal and supraclavicular areas. In the absence of spontaneous breathing movements (apnea), complete airway obstruction will be recognized by the inability to inflate the lungs during attempts at artificial respiration.

Partial airway obstruction will usually be recognized by *noisy* air flow during spontaneous or artificial respiration. Depending upon the degree of obstruction present, retraction may or may not be present. Prolonged partial

Figure 6–5 Evaluation of airway maintenance. Maintaining head tilt, the rescuer evaluates the patency of the airway and spontaneous respiration by placing his or her ear approximately one inch from the victim's mouth and nose, hearing and feeling for respiration, and looking at the victim's chest, looking for spontaneous respiratory movement.

obstruction causes the respiratory center to become less sensitive to the usual stimulus from a buildup of carbon dioxide, leading ultimately to respiratory failure and cardiac arrest. In cases of partial obstruction, various degrees of noisy air flow may be elicited, depending upon the degree of obstruction and the cause of the obstruction. Table 6–1 lists several common causes of noisy respiration.

4. Forward Displacement of Mandible. In approximately one out of five patients, the previously described steps will not result in an open airway. In this instance, the mandible should be displaced forward. This may be accomplished by placing the thumbs on the posterior border of the ascending ramus and lifting the mandible anteriorly until a prognathic state is achieved (Fig. 6–6). This procedure may be made less fatiguing if the forearms are allowed to rest on the patient's shoulder.[2] Forward displacement may also be achieved by placing your thumb in the patient's mouth and pulling the mandible forward (Fig. 6–7).

TABLE 6–1 PARTIAL AIRWAY OBSTRUCTION – CAUSES

Sound Heard	Probable Cause
Snoring	Hypopharyngeal obstruction by tongue
Wheezing	Bronchial obstruction (as seen in asthma)
Crowing	Laryngospasm (partial)
Gurgling	Foreign matter (blood, water, vomitus) in the airway

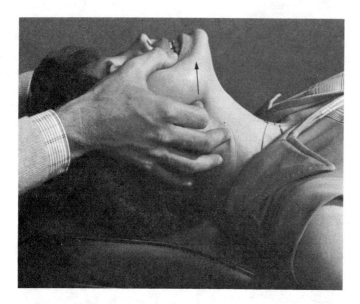

Figure 6–6 Forward displacement of mandible. The rescuer, positioned at the head of the victim, places his or her fingers on the posterior border of the ramus, pushing the ramus in a superior direction (arrow). Fingers placed in the corners of the mouth aid in maintaining a patent airway.

5. Check for Airway Patency and Breathing. Repeat procedure described in step 3. If the airway is now patent and the victim breathing spontaneously, the rescuer need only maintain the patency of the airway and proceed to the further diagnosis and treatment of the cause(s) of the unconscious state. In the absence of spontaneous respiratory movements the doctor must apply artificial ventilation.

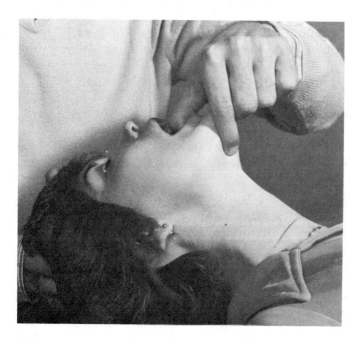

Figure 6–7 Forward displacement of mandible. The rescuer may grasp the anterior portion of the mandible. The mandible is pulled forward, lifting the tongue from the posterior wall of the pharynx. *Caution:* this procedure is employed primarily in edentulous patients; the rescuer risks self-injury when using it in patients with natural teeth.)

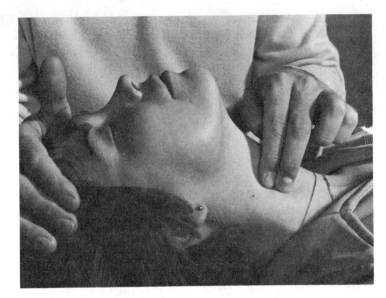

Figure 6–8 Monitoring of carotid pulse. The rescuer places his or her fingers in the groove on the lateral side of the neck. A minimum of 10 seconds is necessary to determine the presence, absence, and quality of the pulse.

ARTIFICIAL VENTILATION

In the absence of spontaneous respiratory movements (apnea) the rescuer immediately begins artificial ventilation of the victim. The goal of artificial ventilation is to supply oxygen to the blood in sufficient quantity to prevent cellular (biologic) death from occurring. Several techniques of artificial ventilation are available. These include exhaled air ventilation, atmospheric air ventilation, enriched oxygen ventilation, and positive pressure oxygen ventilation. Each of these will be discussed. The technique of exhaled air ventilation will serve as an example of airway maintenance and artificial ventilation.

Exhaled Air Ventilation

Following a determination of apnea, the rescuer maintains head tilt, pinches off the victim's nares, opens his mouth widely, sealing it securely over the victim's, and blows exhaled air into the victim's lungs. This first ventilatory attempt with exhaled air (which contains approximately 16 per cent oxygen) consists of four quick ventilations of the victim. Effective artificial ventilation is noted by observing the victim's chest rise with each ventilatory effort. Expiration is a passive procedure, the rescuer removing his mouth from the victim's, allowing the lungs to deflate.

Immediately following this initial ventilatory procedure the adequacy of the cardiovascular system must be assessed (C of the ABC's). The carotid artery, located in a groove on the side of the neck, is palpated for approximately 5 to 10 seconds (Fig. 6–8). If a palpable pulse is not found, external cardiac compression is commenced (see Chapter 9). In the more likely event that a palpable pulse is present, the rescuer continues to maintain a patent airway and administer artificial ventilation as indicated.

In the adult victim, artificial ventilation is applied at a rate of one ventilation every five seconds (12 per minute), while in younger victims the respiratory rate is more rapid (20 per minute, or one every three seconds). In all patients, regardless of age, adequacy of ventilation is indicated by elevation of the chest with each breath.

Following institution of the ABC's of basic life support the rescuer can seek to determine the cause of the emergency situation. If the victim does not recover spontaneously, then definitive therapy may be indicated. If the cause of the medical problem is known (e.g., hypoglycemia), then drugs may be administered (i.e., IV 50% dextrose or IM glucagon). The ABC's must still be carefully adhered to during this period of time. Should a diagnosis or drugs be unavailable, basic life support is maintained and medical assistance sought.

A variation of mouth to mouth ventilation is the mouth to nose technique. It is equally effective and is of use in instances in which mouth to mouth ventilation is difficult to perform, such as when the victim's mouth cannot be opened; when it is impossible to ventilate through the victim's mouth, and when it is difficult to achieve a tight seal around the victim's mouth. In this technique head tilt is maintained; however, the hand under the neck is moved so that it now lifts the victim's mandible upward, sealing the lips. The rescuer takes a deep breath, seals his lips around the victim's nose, and blows in until the victim's lungs expand. The rescuer removes his mouth and passive exhalation occurs.

Atmospheric Air Ventilation

Artificial ventilation with atmospheric air enables the rescuer to deliver approximately 21 per cent oxygen to the victim's lungs, an improvement over the 16 per cent delivered in exhaled air ventilation. To deliver atmospheric air to the victim, however, requires the utilization of adjunctive devices. These devices are not difficult to use, but they do require advanced training in order to be employed effectively. The device most often used to deliver atmospheric oxygen is the self-inflating bag-valve-mask unit (Fig. 6–9). Carden and Hughes[8] and Carden and Friedman[7] have tested those

Figure 6–9 Bag-valve-mask device. The self-inflating bag enables the rescuer to deliver atmospheric air to the victim. Enriched oxygen may be administered by attaching the oxygen tube to the opening at the back of the bag device (arrow).

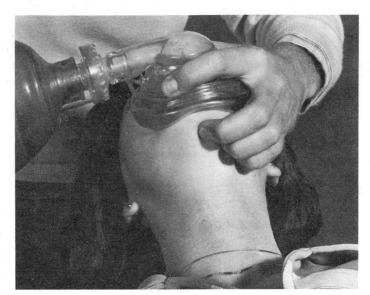

Figure 6-10 Proper use of the bag-valve-mask device requires the rescuer to maintain head tilt and an air tight seal of the mask with but one hand.

devices which are currently being marketed and have concluded that the AMBU, PMR, Laerdal Resusci 2 Resuscitator and Hope 2 Resuscitator are acceptable devices.

In order for these devices to be effectively employed, the operator must be able to maintain a patent airway and maintain an airtight seal between the mask and the patient's face using but one hand. Two fingers, usually thumb and index finger, are used to hold the mask in position while the other fingers are hooked around the lower border of the mandible. The mask is held tightly against the victim's face, and the mandible is pulled backward, producing head tilt (Fig. 6-10). The opposite hand is used to squeeze the self-inflating bag at a rate of once every 5 seconds (adult) or once every 3 seconds (child). Adequate ventilation is ensured by observing the chest inflate with each ventilatory effort.

If the mask is not held securely, leakage will result which diminishes the volume of air reaching the victim's lungs.

Advanced training in the proper use of this and other adjunctive devices is strongly recommended. The face mask which is part of this device is available in a variety of sizes (Fig. 6-11). Several sizes should be avail-

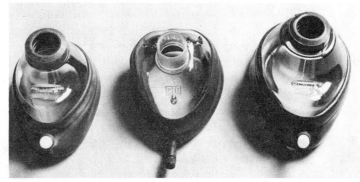

Figure 6-11 Full face masks. Full face masks are available in a variety of sizes. They should be constructed of clear plastic so that the rescuer can observe the victim's mouth at all times.

able in the dental office for use in emergency situations. An additional factor concerning the face mask is the material from which it is manufactured. Until recently, face masks were solid, usually black rubber. While effective for ventilation, the use of solid masks made it impossible for the rescuer to see the victim's mouth for evidence of foreign materials, vomitus, blood, etc. Face masks are available today which are fabricated from clear plastics and rubber, which make it possible to view the victim's mouth during resuscitation efforts. These masks are highly recommended.

Enriched Oxygen Ventilation

Connecting a compressed gas cylinder of oxygen to a self-inflating bag-valve-mask device enables us to deliver oxygen concentrations in excess of atmospheric air to the victim. This is termed enriched oxygen ventilation, with concentrations ranging up to 100 per cent oxygen.

Oxygen is available as a compressed gas in cylinders. A wide range of cylinder sizes are available and are listed by letter according to their volume. An A cylinder contains 76 liters of oxygen, D cylinders 396 liters, E cylinders 659 liters, and an H cylinder 6931 liters. When used for resuscitation in enriched oxygen ventilation, a flow rate of approximately 10 to 20 liters per minute will be employed. However, when used as 100 per cent oxygen for positive pressure ventilation (see below) the flow rate will be increased to approximately 78 liters of oxygen per minute. For this reason the E size cylinder represents the minimal size of cylinder recommended for use in emergency situations. Empty oxygen cylinders are worthless. The larger cylinder (H) is too heavy to be portable. Canisters of oxygen produced by chemical reaction produce minimal flows and volumes of oxygen, are without merit, and ought not to be considered for use in emergency situations.

Specific devices such as pressure reducing valves, flow-rate controls, and connecting tubing must be added to the oxygen cylinder to adapt it for use with the self-inflating bag-valve-mask device. All of the recommended b-v-m devices have outlets for oxygen connectors (Fig. 6–9).

Positive Pressure Oxygen

For purposes of resuscitation, the delivery of 100 per cent oxygen is ideal. The Robertshaw Resuscitator (Fig. 6–12) and the Elder Demand Valve are devices operated by compressed oxygen which deliver oxygen on demand and also provide for intermittent positive pressure breathing. For positive pressure breathing, the face mask is held in the same manner as the self-inflating bag-valve-mask device. Positive pressure oxygen is then delivered by pressing a button on the mask. Oxygen is delivered at a flow rate of approximately 78 liters per minute. Overinflation of the lungs is prevented through an automatic cut-off when airway pressure of 54 cm of water is reached. Respiratory rates are 12 per minute for an adult, and 20 per minute for the child.

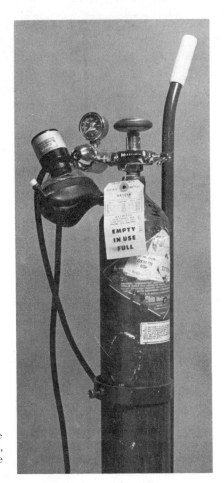

Figure 6-12 Positive pressure oxygen device. Full face mask attached to E-cylinder of oxygen. When properly employed, this device is capable of delivering 100 per cent oxygen to the patient.

If the patient is capable of maintaining his or her own respiratory cycle, positive pressure oxygen is not necessary, but supplemental oxygen can be used to assist the patient during any emergency situation in which he is physiologically depressed. With the mask placed over the patient's face, a minimal inspiratory effort of (−) 1 cm of water will trigger the device to deliver an oxygen flow adequate to ventilate the patient at rest. At (−) 3 cm H_2O the demand valve provides approximately 150 liters of oxygen per minute.

It must always be kept in mind that while higher percentages of oxygen are beneficial to our patients, the devices which operate from compressed gas cylinders will be effective only as long as oxygen remains in the cylinder. With the E cylinder this equates to approximately 30 minutes of positive pressure breathing. Once oxygen is depleted from the cylinder other methods of ventilation must be employed (atmospheric or exhaled air). Artificial ventilation must never be delayed while one seeks an oxygen cylinder. Commence mouth to mouth ventilation, switching to other techniques only when they become available and only if the rescuer is well versed in their use.

ADJUNCTIVE EQUIPMENT

Many devices are available to aid in the maintenance of a patent airway. All of these devices are used to supplement basic life support (ABC), therefore the ABC steps must not be delayed while seeking adjunctive equipment. The simplicity of basic life support, in that it requires no adjunctive equipment, is one of its most positive attributes. The more commonly used adjunctive devices will be reviewed. The use of these devices does entail a degree of risk and will require additional training of the doctor and staff members in order to become proficient in their use.

Artificial Airways

Artificial oral airways (Fig. 6–13) may become necessary to hold the base of the tongue forward and to maintain the teeth and lips in an open position. Oropharyngeal airways may be valuable adjuncts when prolonged airway maintenance is necessary. When it is difficult to open a patient's mouth, a nasopharyngeal airway may be inserted. The nasopharyngeal tube is less likely to stimulate vomiting in an unconscious patient than the oropharyngeal airway. In addition, an oral airway may, on rare occasion, extend beyond the pharynx and obstruct the air passage by forcing the epiglottis onto the trachea.

Artificial airways should be utilized *only* if maintenance of a patent airway without one is difficult, because unnecessary insertion may cause gagging, laryngospasm, and a delay in ventilation of the patient. Several sizes of oropharyngeal airway should be available to accommodate individual patient variation.

Esophageal Obturator Airway

The esophageal obturator is a plastic tube which is sealed at one end and which contains multiple small holes through its length (Fig. 6–14).

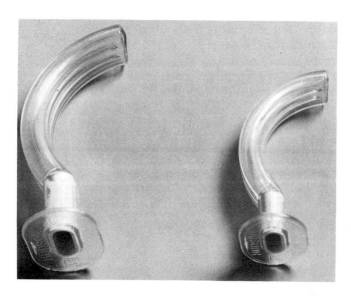

Figure 6–13 Oropharyngeal airways. Available in several sizes, oropharyngeal airways lie between the base of the tongue and the posterior pharyngeal wall, maintaining a patent airway. (*Caution:* proper use of this device requires specialized training.)

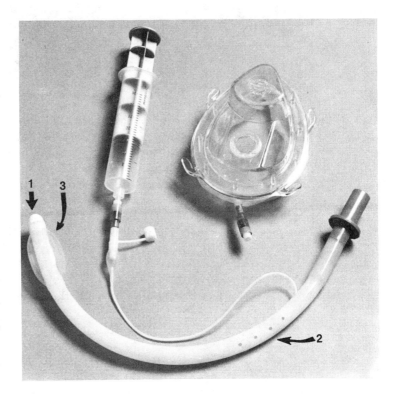

Figure 6-14 Esophageal obturator airway. The esophageal airway is a plastic tube sealed at one end (1), with multiple holes throughout its length (2). When the tube is properly placed in the esophagus, air delivered into the tube will enter the victim's trachea. A balloon (3) prevents the forcing of air into the esophagus. (Courtesy of Littel's Oxygen Inc. 13006 Saticoy, North Hollywood California.

In clinical practice the closed end of the obturator airway is inserted blindly into the patient's mouth and posteriorly into the esophagus. A cuff on the closed end of the tube is inflated, sealing off the esophagus and lower GI tract from the laryngeal area. Artificial ventilation is applied through the open end of the tube, air being forced through the openings along the tube into the oropharynx, trachea, and lungs.

Difficulties encountered in the use of this device include its inadvertent insertion into the trachea. This situation, which has been reported to occur in approximately 8 per cent of insertions, leads to total airway obstruction as air is forced into the esophagus and stomach. A second and more commonly observed adverse reaction is the disturbing propensity for regurgitation or vomiting to occur when the obturator airway is removed. Acidic stomach contents may produce airway obstruction, or might be aspirated into the trachea and bronchi, producing aspiration pneumonitis, which may be fatal. The esophageal obturator airway should not be used by untrained persons.

Endotracheal Intubation

Placement of a cuffed tube from the mouth into the trachea allows for an unobstructed airway. Endotracheal intubation isolates the airway, keeps it patent, prevents aspiration, and ensures delivery of a high concentration of oxygen to the lungs. However, because of the difficulties, delays, and complications in properly placing an endotracheal tube, the American Heart Association recommends that its use be restricted to medical personnel who are highly trained or who use endotracheal intubation frequently (anesthesiologists).[3]

MONITORING OF VITAL SIGNS

An integral part of the management of all medical emergency situations is monitoring the vital signs of the victim. One vital sign, respiration, has been evaluated previously during airway maintenance, with artificial ventilation being started, if needed. Following these ventilations the status of the cardiovascular system must be evaluated. Two vital signs aid in this evaluation: the pulse or heart rate and the blood pressure. The pulse allows for a rapid determination of cardiovascular function. Absence of pulse for a period of from 5 to 10 seconds is an indication for initiation of closed chest cardiac compression in the unconscious, apneic victim. Blood pressure may also be monitored in emergencies. Recordings on a patient should be compared to those observed prior to the emergency. These are termed baseline values and provide an indication of the severity of the problem faced.

PULSE (HEART RATE)

The arterial pulse may be recorded at any site in which an artery lies superficially under the skin. Several areas are readily available on the clothed

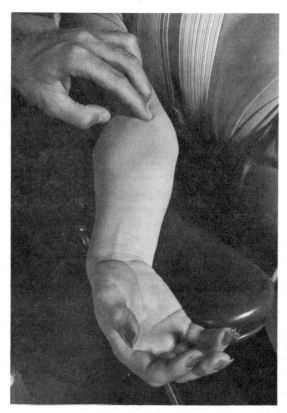

Figure 6-15 Brachial artery. The brachial artery is located on the medial aspect of the antecubital fossa.

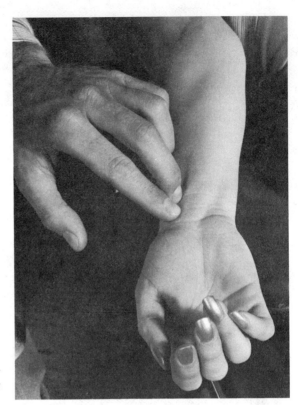

Figure 6-16   Radial artery. The radial artery
is located on the lateral aspect (thumb side) of the
ventral surface of the wrist.

dental patient: the carotid artery, the brachial artery, and the radial artery. For
routine (non-emergency) monitoring of the heart rate the brachial or radial
arteries are suggested. In emergencies the carotid artery becomes of greater
significance because a weak pulse is more likely to be detected at this site.

The brachial artery (Fig. 6–15) may be palpated in the antecubital fossa
at the elbow. It is located on the mesial aspect of the fossa. This artery is not as
superficial as the radial, so that more pressure must be applied to locate it.

The radial artery (Fig. 6–16) lies superficially on the lateral aspect
(thumb side) of the ventral surface of the wrist. It may be located by placing
the fingers on the radius (bone on the thumb side of wrist) and moving the
fingers just slightly onto the wrist. The radial artery is located in a depression
just medial to the radius.

The carotid artery is located in the neck in a groove located anterior to the
sternocleidomastoid muscle. It is located by the doctor's placing two fingers
on the thyroid cartilage (Adam's apple) and then sliding the fingers along the
side of the neck until they reach the groove formed by the sternocleidomastoid muscle posteriorly. Gentle pressure is then applied (Fig. 6–17A and B).

Several important facts follow concerning pulse monitoring. The thumb
should never be employed. The thumb contains a fair-sized artery which may
easily be palpated and mistaken for the victim's pulse. It is suggested that the
fleshy portions of the first two fingers be used for pulse monitoring. Pulse is
recorded in beats per minute. Whenever possible (non-emergency situations),

a full 60 seconds should be used to record the pulse. In emergency situations in which the primary objective is to determine if a functionally adequate pulse exists, not less than 10 seconds should be employed. In the absence of an adequate pulse, external cardiac compression must be started immediately. Evaluation of the pulse consists of determining not only the rate but also the quality of the pulse (thready, bounding, or weak) and the rhythm (skips, prematurities, flutters). Any deviation from a normal, full, regular pulse should be considered pathologic until a more explicit diagnosis is made.

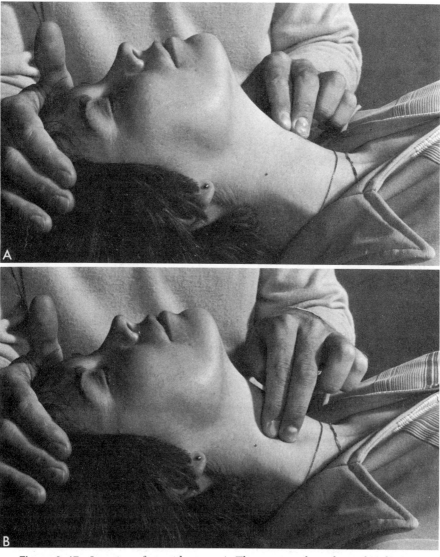

Figure 6–17   Location of carotid artery. *A*, The rescuer places his or her fingers over the thyroid cartilage (Adam's apple) of the victim. *B*, The carotid artery is located in the groove on the side of the neck between the thyroid cartilage and the sternocleidomastoid muscle. (*Note:* head tilt must be maintained throughout this procedure.)

Evaluation of the Pulse

To better understand the more common cardiac irregularities, a description of the normal cardiac mechanism is presented for review.

The heart beat is initiated by stimulation of the sinoatrial node. The impulse spreads as a wave through the atrial musculature and is followed by contraction. When the impulse reaches the atrioventricular node it passes down the bundle of His, the bundle branches, and the Purkinje system into the ventricular musculature, resulting in a contraction. Disruption or impairment of this sequence will manifest as an irregularity in the heart beat which can at times be noted in the arterial pulse. See the conduction system diagram in the chapter on *monitoring*; also, further information on arrhythmias.

The following is a classification and description of the more common cardiac disturbances:

1. *Sinus arrhythmia.* This is noted in most healthy young patients and consists of an increase in the heart rate during inspiration and slowing during expiration.

2. *Premature beats.* These may arise in the atrium, the junctional tissues, or, more frequently, the ventricles. When occurring in the absence of organic heart disease, premature beats may be due to emotional stress, hypoglycemia, or excessive use of stimulants. The premature beat is usually recognized readily because it consists of a contraction before the next beat would normally occur, and is followed by a pause longer than the usual interval.

One special type of premature beat warrants mention. This is bigeminal rhythm, a state in which every alternate beat is premature. It should not be confused with pulsus alternans, a rhythmic disorder in which every alternate beat is feeble and which denotes a grave prognosis.

3. *Atrial fibrillation.* The paroxysmal form of this arrhythmia is most frequently seen in thyrotoxicosis, in rheumatic heart disease with mitral stenosis, or in senile heart disease. The attacks have the characteristics of all types of paroxysmal heart action, with the onset and end being sudden.

When the rate is rapid (120 or more) the diagnosis is made readily, because atrial fibrillation is the only common condition in which one has the combination of a well marked tachycardia with a gross irregularity.

Because of the complexity of the cardiac mechanism, many variables can arise, and the diagnosis and subsequent treatment must become the responsibility of the cardiologist. The pulse coupled with the blood pressure is essential for screening patients for possible cardiovascular disease.

BLOOD PRESSURE

The value of the measurement and recording of blood pressure as a means of preventing medical emergencies and as a valuable guide to the management of those that do occur within the practice of dentistry has been demonstrated by many authors[1, 5] and recognized by the American Dental Association.[15]

Physiology

The arterial blood pressure is the result of the discharge of a volume of blood by the heart into the arterial system which cannot all escape through the arterioles and capillaries into the venous system before the next heart beat occurs. Thus the arterial system is always overfilled and this causes the elastic peripheral vessels to be in a constant state of distention, creating a measurable pressure. This pressure will vary with beating of the heart, rising to a maximum during ventricular contraction (systole) and falling when the ventricles relax (diastole).

Maintenance of normal blood pressure is dependent on two main factors: cardiac output and the caliber of the peripheral vessels. An increased volume of blood discharged into the arterial system can only be accommodated by further stretching of the arterial walls, causing an increase in both the systolic and diastolic pressures. Likewise, constriction of the peripheral vessels will cause an increased arterial pressure by reducing the outflow of blood into the venous system. The pressure will rise until the quantity of blood entering the venous system equals the amount pumped into the arterial system by the heart. The opposite effect occurs when these vessels dilate. The pressure will fall until the arterial outflow is equalized by a proportionate inflow from the heart.

Aside from these factors, variances in the total blood volume, blood viscosity, and the elasticity of the arterial walls as a result of hemorrhage or disease will have varying degrees of influence on the blood pressure.

Under normal conditions these factors all interact in a reflexive compensatory manner to offset extreme changes in the blood pressure. For example, when there is a moderate reduction of cardiac output or blood volume, a reflex constriction of the small vessel walls occurs, and the peripheral resistance is increased. Conversely, when there is an increase in the blood volume or viscosity, the increased blood pressure is counteracted by vasodilatation.

Since arterial pressures cannot be measured precisely with a sphygmomanometer, it is important that this basic inefficiency not be increased by added error due to equipment or technique. Because normal blood pressure readings vary so widely between individuals, a base line or pretreatment determination should be established. This can be used as a comparison should an emergency arise with its attendant blood pressure changes.

Equipment

The sphygmomanometer consists of a compression bag surrounded by a cuff for application to the arm, a manometer by which the applied pressure is read, and an inflating bulb with a controllable exhaust.

In the selection of an instrument, certain points should be considered that will enhance the accuracy desired. The inflatable bag should be about 20 per cent wider than the diameter of the arm, and for an adult 12 cm is adequate. The aneroid type of manometer is preferred for dental office use because of the ease in storage and in reading the blood pressure.

To complete the apparatus requirements, a stethoscope with a diaphragm device is needed to determine blood pressure by auscultation.

For a more comprehensive discussion of the equipment used in recording blood pressure the reader is referred to Burch and DePasquale,[6] and to The American Heart Association's Recommendations for Human Blood Pressure Determinations by Sphygmomanometry.[4]

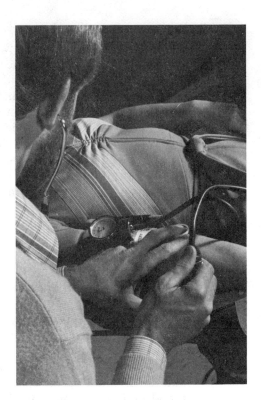

Figure 6–18 The stethoscope ear pieces are placed securely in the ears, facing anteriorly; the diaphragm is placed firmly against the skin over the medial portion of the antecubital fossa.

Technique

The patient may be either in a recumbent position or comfortably seated. The arm should be bared, slightly flexed, and abducted. In the sitting position the forearm should be supported at heart level.

The compression bag must be placed directly over the brachial artery, one inch above the antecubital fossa. After placing the cuff snugly, the radial pulse is palpated while the cuff is rapidly inflated until the pulse is no longer felt. Pressure in the cuff is now released. The point at which the radial pulse disappears is termed the palpatory systolic blood pressure.

After waiting 15 seconds to permit vascular congestion in the arm to diminish, the recorder places the ear pieces of the stethoscope in his ears. They should be placed facing anteriorly, creating a firm seal to block out extraneous sounds. The diaphragm of the stethoscope is now placed firmly against the skin on the medial portion of the antecubital fossa over the brachial artery (Fig. 6–18). If the diaphragm is not held securely against the skin sounds will not be magnified, and extraneous sounds will cause interference.

The pressure in the cuff is inflated to a level 30 mm Hg above that of the palpatory systolic blood pressure. The blood pressure recorder listens carefully for sounds. With the cuff inflated above the systolic blood pressure no blood will pass the cuff, therefore sounds will not be heard.

Release the pressure in the cuff so that the manometer is reduced approximately 2 mm per second. If the pressure is reduced too rapidly errors will appear in the measured blood pressure. When the pressure within the blood pressure cuff equals that of the systolic blood pressure, blood begins to squirt past the cuff into the artery, creating sounds which may be heard through the stethoscope. These sounds, which were first studied by Korotkoff, are called the Korotkoff sounds. Systolic blood pressure is recorded as the point at which these first sounds, a rhythmic tapping or thudding coincident with the heart beat, are heard. As pressure in the cuff is deflated further the sounds change in intensity until they disappear entirely. The point of disappearance is considered to be the diastolic blood pressure.

Following disappearance of the sounds, permit the cuff to deflate totally, and remove the cuff from the patient's arm.

Blood pressure is recorded as a fraction, systolic pressure over diastolic pressure, which is written as 130/80, for example. All blood pressures are measured in millimeters of mercury, mm Hg, but this need not be written. In addition there are no odd numbers on a manometer, so blood pressure readings are always recorded in even numbers.

Evaluation of Blood Pressure

For screening purposes, McCarthy and Malamed[13] have established four levels of blood pressure elevation. Category I is the patient with consistent measurements below 140 and 90 mm Hg. This represents the upper limit of normal blood pressure for adults. Pressures below these limits do not require additional monitoring, consultation, or precautions. Category II includes blood pressures between 140 and 160 mm Hg systolic and/or 90–95 mm Hg diastolic. It is recommended that blood pressures in this category be re-evaluated prior to each dental appointment. If three consecutive recordings occur above 140/90, medical consultation is indicated. Routine dental therapy may proceed with possible modification and special considerations.

Blood pressures between 160 and 200 mm Hg systolic and/or 95–115 mm Hg diastolic are Class III. The blood pressure should be retaken in approximately 5 minutes, and if still elevated medical consultation is indicated. In addition, modifications such as stress-reduction procedures (i.e., psychosedation, length of appointment) are warranted. See Chapter 2 regarding the USC physical evaluation system.

Class IV blood pressures include any systolic pressure in excess of 200 mm Hg and/or diastolic greater than 115 mm Hg. Recommended management includes medical consultation; no elective dental therapy until elevated blood pressure is corrected or found to be uncorrectable; emergency therapy (pain and/or infection) to be treated with medication and/or minimal operative intervention; and referral to hospital if immediate stressful dental therapy is indicated.

PARENTERAL DRUG ADMINISTRATION

Following the successful initiation of the ABC's of basic life support, the rescuer may now begin to consider the underlying cause(s) of the emergency situation being faced. If a cause is readily evident, if the problem is correctable through drug administration, and if the rescuer is knowledgeable in drug administration and pharmacology of the drug(s) to be administered, and is able to manage any adverse actions of the drugs, then parenteral drug administration is advisable. Should these criteria not be met, basic life support should be continued until medical assistance becomes available.

Two parenteral routes of drug administration are available: intravenous and intramuscular.

THE INTRAVENOUS ROUTE

The intravenous administration of drugs affords the dental practitioner an effective means of supportive treatment in many acute emergencies. Drugs administered intravenously act more rapidly than when given by other routes of administration, and their actions are far more predictable. However, venipuncture is an acquired skill which requires training to develop proficiency. Practice on normal, healthy patients is essential if success is to be expected in emergency situations. The dental doctor who is not experienced with the intravenous route should feel no moral or legal compulsion to attempt its use during an emergency.

Equipment

This suggested list of items is readily available and easily stored in the dental operatory:

1. emergency drugs for injection
2. sterile, disposable syringes (5 ml with 1 1/2", 20 gauge needle attached)
3. alcohol and gauze wipes
4. tourniquet
5. adhesive tape
6. optional — intravenous infusion (5% dextrose and water)
7. optional — intravenous tubing

Technique

The most convenient sites for venipuncture are usually located in the antecubital fossa and on the dorsum of the hand.

As a general rule it is best to select the largest vein available. The tourniquet is placed around the arm to obstruct venous flow and thereby distend the veins. Care should be taken not to stop arterial flow to the area. The patient should then open and close the hand several times and finally keep it closed until the venipuncture is complete (Fig. 6–19).

When veins are small, inadequate distention may occur. Gentle slapping of the vein or application of heat will induce a reflex dilatation of the vessel walls. Nitrous oxide/oxygen sedation will also assist dilatation.

After the injection site has been prepared with a skin disinfectant, the vein is ready for entry. This is achieved by placing the needle, with the bevel up, beside the vein with the needle parallel to the long axis of the vein. The thumb of the other hand is positioned so that with slight tension on the skin, the vein is stabilized (Fig. 6–20).

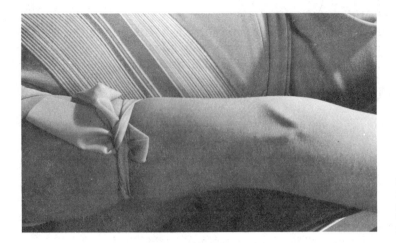

Figure 6–19 A tourniquet, impeding venous return to heart, is placed above the antecubital fossa. If arterial blood flow into the arm is unimpeded, the veins in the arm will distend.

The needle is placed at a 45 degree angle to the skin, and, with a gliding motion, is introduced into the vein. A backflow of blood into the syringe indicates venous entry. Now the needle is cautiously advanced well within the lumen of the vein (Fig. 6–21).

The tourniquet is released, the fist is unclenched, and the selected drug or drugs injected slowly. It is always well to titrate drugs into the blood stream while noting the patient's reactions. If an unfavorable reaction occurs before the entire dose is injected, stopping the procedure will minimize the untoward effects of the drug.

After the needle is withdrawn, firm pressure must be placed over the area to prevent the extravasation of the venous blood through the mechanically created rent in the vessel wall.

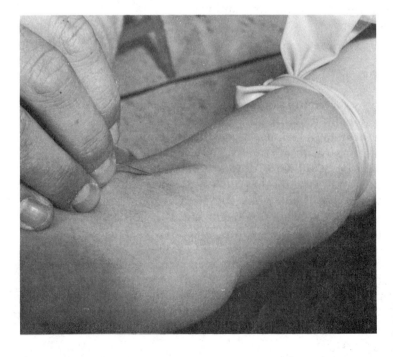

Figure 6–20 The needle is placed at a 45 degree angle directly over the vein. The bevel of the needle is facing up.

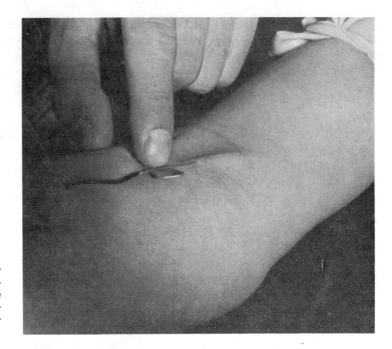

Figure 6-21 Blood flow into the tubing indicates successful venipuncture. The needle is carefully advanced into the vein while tourniquet remains in place.

If a continuous infusion is used the needle must be secured by tape (Fig. 6-22).

Complications

If the needle penetrates the vessel wall after entry into the vein and a portion of the drug is injected into the extravascular tissue, a wheal will form. The needle should be withdrawn and moist heat applied.

On rare occasions a superficial artery may be entered, and the operator

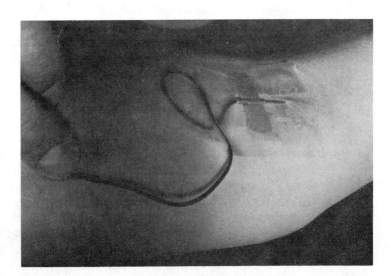

Figure 6-22 If the needle is to remain in the vein it must be secured. Tape is placed over each wing of the needle and across a loop of tubing.

will note a forceful backflow of bright-red blood into the syringe. Certain drugs, if injected, can cause a reflex arterial constriction with possible localized ischemia. If this occurs, the area distal to the injection site may become blanched and quite painful. An injection of 1 per cent procaine solution into the same needle will help to overcome the reflex mechanism.

Phlebitis may be a consequence of irritation by the needle (from prolonged position in the vein) or occur as a reaction to caustic drugs. The patient will complain of pain in the area for several days after injection, and, if the condition is allowed to continue, a thrombus may develop. The inflammation is best controlled by applications of moist heat three or four times daily. This is continued until the area is asymptomatic.

INTRAMUSCULAR ROUTE

When it is not feasible to utilize the intravenous route of administration because of vascular collapse, veins of poor quality, or lack of training, the intramuscular route offers an alternate choice for drug administration. Also, when prolonged action is preferred, a drug injected in a muscle will be more gradually absorbed into the blood stream.

Many sites are available, but the deltoid, gluteus maximus, and vastus lateralis muscles are the most commonly used.

Equipment

5 cc sterile disposable syringe; 20 to 23 gauge, 1 1/2 inch needle; cotton; alcohol; 2 × 2 gauze.

Technique

Deltoid Muscle.   If the deltoid muscle is the site of choice, the skin is first cleansed with an antiseptic and allowed to dry. The muscle is then bunched with the thumb and fingers of the left hand, which will raise the muscle away from the underlying nerves, vessels, and bone. The syringe is held in the right hand by the thumb and first two fingers (Fig. 6–23). Entry into the muscle is made by a quick thrust with the needle perpendicular to the skin. The needle should be advanced only three fourths of its length, because, should the needle break, the cannula can be readily grasped with a hemostat. With the needle in the muscle, the syringe is held by the left hand, and negative pressure is applied to the plunger with the thumb and index finger of the right hand. If no blood appears in the syringe, the left hand is returned to its former position of raising the muscle, and the injection is made slowly. After the needle is withdrawn, the area is vigorously massaged to enhance absorption by greater distribution of the drug in the muscle.

Gluteal Area.   The upper outer quadrant of the gluteal area is most commonly used for intramuscular administration, and the gluteus maximus is the muscle usually injected.

It is imperative that the upper outer quadrant be properly located, be-

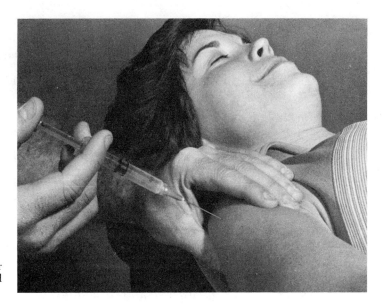

Figure 6-23 Intramuscular injection into the mid-deltoid region.

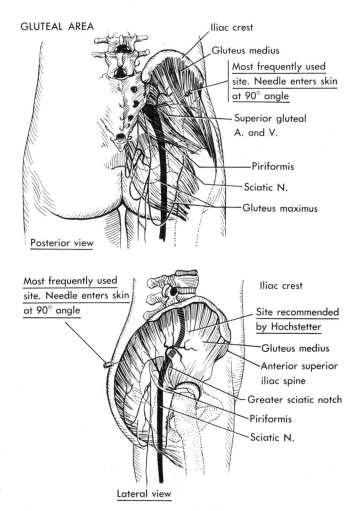

GLUTEAL AREA

Iliac crest

Gluteus medius

Most frequently used site. Needle enters skin at 90° angle

Superior gluteal A. and V.

Piriformis

Sciatic N.

Gluteus maximus

Posterior view

Most frequently used site. Needle enters skin at 90° angle

Iliac crest

Site recommended by Hochstetter

Gluteus medius

Anterior superior iliac spine

Greater sciatic notch

Piriformis

Sciatic N.

Lateral view

Figure 6-24 The anatomical location of the "safe zone" for gluteal injections. (Redrawn from *Spectrum*, Winter 1964-65, Pfizer Laboratories.)

cause vessels and nerves (particularly the sciatic nerve) are abundant in the upper and lower inner quadrants, and nerve damage here could have grave effects on the extremity. It is recommended that the patient be lying face down with toes in. This position helps to obtain maximum relaxation, and the patient is less likely to see the approach of the needle.

D. J. Hanson[10] recommends that the point of insertion of the needle be lateral and superior to a line drawn from the posterior superior iliac spine to the greater trochanter (Fig. 6–24). Such a line would be lateral to and parallel with the course of the sciatic nerve and any injection lateral and superior to this line will be well away from the nerve.

Before injection, the skin is thoroughly cleansed with alcohol and a needle of adequate gauge and length must be chosen. It should be long enough to penetrate the belly of the muscle, thus avoiding injection into deep subcutaneous tissue which could result in persistent, painful nodules.

Hold the syringe by the index finger and thumb and with the other hand draw the skin of the buttock taut. With the needle perpendicular to the skin, drive the needle into the skin and muscle in a single movement, as though it were a dart. Aspiration should be continued for a few seconds, particularly if the needle has a narrow gauge.

Medications should be expelled slowly to allow time for distention of an accommodating space within the muscle and thereby to avoid pain from pressure-sensitive nerves within muscle tissue.

Vastus Lateralis. The area for injection is a narrow band extending from a handbreadth below the great trochanter to the same distance above the knee

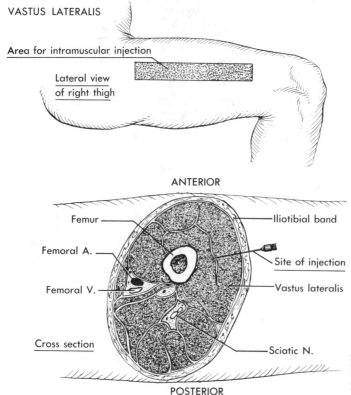

Figure 6–25 The injection site for drug administration in the vastus lateralis muscle. (Redrawn from *Spectrum*, Winter 1964–65, Pfizer Laboratories.)

(Fig. 6–25). It is readily available when the patient is either prone or supine. The needle is inserted to a depth of one inch parallel to the floor.

Serious complications are unlikely in this location, as there are no important nerves or vessels in the area. One other advantage in using this site is that it can readily accept larger quantities of fluid in a single dose than the gluteal muscles.

Wherever the injection is given and whoever gives it, careful training, a knowledge of anatomy, and awareness of the dangers are all prime essentials.

COMMENT

Loss of consciousness is assumed to represent cardiac arrest until proven otherwise. Every dental health professional is obliged to understand and be able to apply at a moment's notice the principles of basic life support. Included in basic life support are airway management, artificial ventilation, administration of positive pressure oxygen, cardiac compression, and monitoring of vital signs. Every dental practitioner must be capable of parenteral drug administration, at least by the intramuscular route. Drug administration is secondary to basic life support. Do not neglect to maintain life by the ABC's while shaking hands fumble with an ampule or a syringe.

REFERENCES

1. Abbey, L. M.: Screening for hypertension in the dental office. J.A.D.A., 88:563, 1974.
2. Allen, G.: Dental Anesthesia and Analgesia. Baltimore, Williams & Wilkins Co., 1972.
3. American Heart Association: Standards for Cardiopulmonary Resuscitation (CPR) and Emergency Cardiac Care (ECC). J.A.M.A., 227 (suppl):833, 1974.
4. American Heart Association: Recommendations for human blood pressure determinations by sphygmomanometry. 1967.
5. Berman, C. L., Guarino, M. A., and Giovannoli, S. M.: High blood pressure detection by dentists. J.A.D.A., 87:359, 1973.
6. Burch, D. E., and DePasquale, N. P.: Primer of Clinical Measurement of Blood Pressure. St. Louis, C. V. Mosby, 1962.
7. Carden, E., and Friedman, D.: Further studies of manually operated self-inflating resuscitation bags. Anesth. Analg., 56:202, 1977.
8. Carden, E., and Hughes, T.: An evaluation of manually operated self-inflating resuscitation bags. Anesth. Analg., 54:133, 1975.
9. Coryollos, P. N.: Mechanical resuscitation in advanced forms of asphyxia: A clinical and experimental study in different methods of resuscitation. Surg. Gynecol. Obstet., 66:698–722, 1938.
10. Hanson, D. J.: Intramuscular injection injuries and complications. Gen Pract., 27:109, 1963.
11. Legal Correspondent. Another death during dentistry. Br. Med. J., 2:352–354, November, 1974.
12. Legal Correspondent. Death during dentistry. Br. Med. J., 2:419–420, August, 1974.
13. McCarthy, F. M., and Malamed, S. F.: Physical Evaluation Manual. University of Southern California School of Dentistry, 1975.
14. Milner, L., Letter: Deaths During Dentistry. Br. Med. J., 2:225–26, October, 1974.
15. Minutes of the House of Delegates, ADA Trans. 1974:643.
16. Mulkey, T. F., and Hayden, C. L.: Monitoring. In McCarthy, F. M. (ed.): Emergencies in Dental Practice. 2nd ed., Philadelphia, W. B. Saunders Co., 1972, Chap. 3.
17. Nicholas, K. E., Letter: An unnecessary hazard in dentistry. Br. Dent. J., 1:83, February, 1975.
18. Safar, P.: Recognition and management of airway obstruction. J.A.M.A., 208:1008–1011, May, 1969.
19. Tomlin, P. J.: Death in outpatient dental anaesthetic practice. Anaesthesia, 29:551–570, 1974.

7

EMERGENCY DRUGS AND ALLERGY

W. HOWARD DAVIS

This chapter is intended to present a practical and safe approach to the potentially serious reactions, primarily allergic, that may occur with drugs used in the dental office. It is felt that a dental practitioner should be prepared to cope with these reactions immediately, because occasions do arise when moments may mean the difference between life and death.

ALLERGIC REACTIONS

Introduction

Allergic reactions are usually caused by defects in the immune system. Knowledge in the field of immunology has greatly expanded, but significant gaps in the total picture are still present. The following seem to be important recent contributions: the identification and complex interaction of T and B lymphocytes in the production, utilization, and inhibition of antibodies; the molecular configuration of antibodies; biochemical pathways in the cell which influence mediating and inhibiting substances in allergic reactions;[37, 39] the identification of the elements and role of complement; the identification of more than one histamine type receptor;[3] etc.

Because allergic reactions are incompletely understood, it is not surprising that they are imprecisely defined. The term *allergy* (Greek *allos*, other, and *ergos*, action) seems appropriate to describe the response to a substance when that response is completely different from its usual effect

248

(as penicillin allergy). The terms *sensitivity* and *hypersensitivity* are best used to describe a reaction wherein one responds or is "sensitive" to a substance to which the majority of the species is not responsive (as ragweed sensitivity). However, through custom, the terms *allergy* and *hypersensitivity* are often used interchangeably.

Semantics continues to be a plague when allergic reactions are subdivided, because the terms do not fit all situations. One classification is used that is based on the mechanisms of tissue damage, as suggested by Gell and Coombs[15] (see Table 7–1). Another commonly used classification has two categories based on the speed of onset of the reaction or the presence or absence of antibodies in the serum. One category is *delayed* or *cellular* or *bacterial* and the other is *immediate* or *humoral* or *atopic*.

The cellular (or delayed or bacterial) type reaction appears to be mediated by specifically sensitized lymphocytes reacting with the exciting substance and does not seem to require the presence of *circulating* antibody[4] (the antibodies appear to be attached to the surface of the lymphocyte).[30] The clinical lesions of cellular allergy may proceed from erythematous papules to serum-filled vesicles to oozing areas with crusting. Microscopically, these lesions show a highly cellular perivascular infiltrate of mononuclear cells. Histamine does not play a significant role in this process, and thus antihistamine drugs are not of specific value in cellular (or delayed or bacterial) type reactions. Many contact allergies fall into this category (as poison ivy) as well as bacterial skin tests (as tuberculin tests), graft versus host reactions, and viral exanthema. Because the cellular (or delayed or bacterial) type allergy is slowly progressive, it does not fall into the category of an emergency and will not be further discussed in this chapter.

The other gross category of allergic reactions is the humoral, immedi-

TABLE 7–1 CLASSIFICATION OF ALLERGIC REACTIONS BASED ON MECHANISMS OF TISSUE DAMAGE (AFTER GELL AND COOMBS)[29a]

Type	General Term	Immune Reactant	Suggested Mechanism of Tissue Damage
I	Anaphylactic	Reaginic antibody; primarily Ig E	Mediators from Ig E-sensitized mast cells cause increased vascular permeability, edema, and smooth muscle contraction
II	Cytotoxic	Ig G or Ig M antibody against cell-surface antigens	Antibody (generally with complement) reacting with cell-surface or cell-attached antigens results in cell destruction
III	Toxic antigen-antibody complex	Immune complexes	Immune complexes fix complement, which attracts leukocytes; mediators released from these cells produce inflammation
IV	Cell-mediated	Lymphocyte	Lymphocytes reacting with antigens release lymphokines, which produce cellular inflammation

ate or atopic. All the reactions in this category appear to be involved with appropriate antibodies, usually circulating in the serum.

Some diseases such as Arthus reactions, serum sickness, and possibly polyarteritis and glomerulonephritis, feature the deposition of antigen-antibody complexes in or near vessel walls and perivascular collections of polymorphs. These conditions are sometimes classified as humoral or immediate because of the relation of this category to antigen-antibody involvement, but they fall poorly within the classification of immediate reactions.

More appropriate to the classification of humoral or immediate are those reactions related to anaphylaxis. Anaphylaxis is not a well-defined term and is applied by some only to allergic (anaphylactic) shock, whereas by others it is broadly used to include local reactions. Among the conditions broadly included in anaphylaxis are anaphylactic shock, allergic rhinitis, gastrointestinal allergy, urticaria and angioedema (angioneurotic edema), and some aspects of serum sickness and bronchial asthma. Anaphylaxis in this chapter will be used broadly and anaphylactic shock as a specific. These lesions are characterized by perivascular serum accumulation with very few cells.

There are several mediating substances involved in anaphylactic reactions, such as skin-sensitizing antibody, histamine, slow-reacting substance of anaphylaxis (SRS-A), serotonin, bradykinin, and others.

Skin-sensitizing antibodies (reagin, atopic antibody) are immune globulins of the IgE class[20] which react with antigens and release histamine from mast cells[22] (and probably from basophils as well). Skin-sensitizing antibody (SSA) is so called because it can be detected in a patient's serum by passive skin tests (Prausnitz-Küstner test). It is probable that SSA interacts with other substances in an anaphylactic reaction.

The actions of histamine are probably responsible in part for many (but not all) of the manifestations of anaphylaxis, such as urticaria, angioedema, blood pressure fall, headache, and bronchial constriction.

Slow-reacting substance of anaphylaxis (SRS-A) is similar in action to histamine. Its action is slower and causes more bronchiolar constriction.[6] SRS-A is not antagonized by antihistamine drugs. Bradykinin and serotonin have questionable roles in human anaphylaxis. The precipitation of cardiac arrhythmias may be a part of anaphylactic shock.[5]

Some light has been shed on the mechanism of antigen formation. High molecular weight substances such as proteins and polysaccharides[1] can act as an antigen without modification. However, low molecular weight substances must fix themselves to a high molecular weight substance such as a protein to act as an antigen (haptenic reaction). Furthermore, more than one of these low molecular weight substances must combine with a protein (polyvalent) to act as an antigen.[7] As a matter of fact, if this low molecular weight substance is present without combining with a protein on a multiple basis, it will *block*[13] this specific antigen-antibody precipitation. Penicillin is a low molecular weight substance which seems unable to attach itself irreversibly to a protein, and thus it cannot act as a haptenic antigen.[12] But degradation products of penicillin can fix themselves to a protein and thus act as an antigen.[10] On this basis, reagents are being formulated to test for penicillin allergy using degradation products of penicillin. The most promising agents are penicilloyl-polylysine[27] and minor determinate mixture. Penicilloyl is a metabolite of penicillin, and when it is combined with polymerized lysine, penicilloyl-polylysine is formed. This substance seems to induce little or no allergenicity[27] and thus is acceptable as a testing agent.

TESTS FOR ALLERGY

Because testing for allergy is not completely reliable, a patient's history of allergic reactions becomes quite important. If a patient reports no allergic reaction to the medications that may be used, no further testing is required. If an allergic reaction is reported to a medication for which a substitute can be prescribed, no further testing is required. Fortunately, most medications used in dentistry have adequate substitutes. For example, erythromycin can usually be substituted for penicillin, and procaine can be substituted for lidocaine. Rarely a patient will report allergies to almost all medications or all local analgesic agents, etc. A careful history and investigation will often reveal that the patient is exaggerating or the patient has been told he or she is allergic to medications when the reactions were not true allergies. This is a common finding when a patient has had fainting episodes associated with local analgesia, or nausea with analgesic medications. However, when the history indicates that medications must be used to which the patient may be allergic, testing should be carried out.

A practical approach would be to begin the testing process using the radioallergosorbent test (RAST). This test is an in vitro assay of the patient's reagenic antibodies (IgE) to a specific antigen.[41] The RAST test is probably the most practical present day in vitro method to test for humoral (immediate, atopic) type allergies. A RAST panel would be appropriate, including several agents for the class of medications desired. For example, a local analgesic panel might include methylparaben (a common preservative), lidocaine, prilocaine, mepivacaine, procaine, etc., or an antibiotic panel might include penicillin G, ampicillin, phenoxymethyl penicillin (penicillin V), nafcillin, cephalexin, erythromycin, tetracycline, and clindamycin. Although the RAST test usually correlates well with the clinical response to a drug, it is not completely predictive. Thus, skin testing is a logical succeeding test after the RAST tests have suggested the least likely allergenic medications.

A scratch or prick test is done first. The scratch test involves making a shallow scratch through the epidermis (not drawing blood) of the volar surface of the forearm. A dilute solution of the agent to be tested is then applied to the scratch. The dilution of the solution should be related to the potential severity of a possible reaction. In the case of penicillin, for example, the dilution could be 5 to 1000 units/ml, related to the history and the RAST results.[19] The prick test is favored by some over the scratch test. The prick test is performed by placing a drop of the test solution on the forearm and puncturing the skin through the liquid. If the scratch or prick test is positive, a wheal and flare should occur within 20 minutes. If a systemic reaction occurs, a tourniquet may be applied proximal to the test site (although this has questionable value) and epinephrine and other drugs administered as described later in the chapter. If a very dilute solution was used initially, such as 5 units of penicillin per ml, and the test was negative, the test should be repeated with a more concentrated solution (10,000 units per ml of penicillin,[36] for example).

If the scratch or prick test proves negative, it would be appropriate to follow with an intracutaneous test. A minute amount of the test solution (about 0.02 ml) is injected in the epidermis of the forearm and the site observed for 20 minutes for the possible wheal and flare reaction.

A detailed description of a serial dilution method of subdermal testing is described by Incaudo, et al.[19a]

If the cutaneous tests are negative, it is reasonable to proceed with judicious administration of the drug, keeping in mind that skin tests are not completely reliable.

Skin testing may elicit misleading results in several ways. For example, if the *test* material is old and contains breakdown products of penicillin which readily fix with proteins (as discussed above), it may be easy to elicit a positive allergic response, whereas the actual *therapeutic* product may be fresh and not contain such breakdown products. Likewise the *test* material may contain an allergenic substance in the diluent[35] which is not present in the *therapeutic* material, or vice versa. A pure fresh product used as a test material may give a negative scratch test because no degradation products are present, but when placed in the body tissue it may break down and form antigenic material, giving a serious reaction. This is why it would be desirable to use substances such as penicilloyl-polylysine and minor determinate mixture intradermally[38] after a scratch test. From the above considerations, it is easy to see why a scratch test is not completely reliable.

Testing of drugs on mucous membranes is similar to scratch testing, but generally more dangerous, because most drugs are more readily absorbed from mucous membranes than from skin, and a tourniquet cannot be placed to limit circulation in mucous membrane areas.

The *indirect basophil degranulation* test is less commonly used since the advent of the RAST test, but its mechanism is as follows. In the presence of an antigen-antibody reaction, rabbit or human basophils will release granules which contain histamine.[32, 33] This change of the basophils can be roughly calibrated by someone with cytologic training. Unfortunately the reading of the basophilic degranulation is not simple, and the results are less than perfect. It does have a place in analyzing a patient who has had an allergic reaction while taking several drugs.[33]

A *passive transfer* (Prausnitz-Küstner) test is also useful for identifying an offending substance when there are several possibilities.[18] A nonallergic human or monkey is injected intradermally with the patient's serum. This area is later challenged with the substances to be tested, and usually will give a wheal and flare reaction to the offending agent. This test has obvious drawbacks for mass use.

Hemagglutination tests[40] require much time and are useful primarily for research.

MANIFESTATIONS OF IMMEDIATE (HUMORAL) ALLERGIES

Urticaria (hives) — a pruritic (itching) wheal.

Angioedema (angioneurotic edema) — an edematous swelling of localized area such as one eyelid. The eyelids, lips, tongue, and glottis are common sites, although most parts of the body can be affected.

Macular or *papular rash* or *flushing* accompanied by pruritis is suggestive of allergy.

Anaphylactic shock — a loss in vascular tone indicated by a fall in blood pressure usually caused by an injected allergen. Prodromal skin signs such as urticaria, flushing, or respiratory signs are often present.

Rhinitis — a pale, boggy swelling of the nasal mucosa with sneezing and watery discharge.

Nausea and/or *diarrhea* — when related to an immediate type allergy, the onset may be close enough to the ingestion of the allergen to help in the diagnosis. The diagnosis is otherwise often difficult to make.

Fever — fever related to an immediate type allergy is not common.

Blood dyscrasias — thrombocytopenic purpura or hemolytic anemia are uncommon with immediate allergies.

Cardiac dysrhythmias — may be a manifestation of allergy that is difficult to define owing to lack of initial diagnosis or spontaneous remission.

Certain allergenic drugs will be discussed in this chapter in varying degrees of detail according to the author's impressions in the light of today's usages and problems.

Aspirin and Angioedema

Aspirin, because of its ubiquitous use and its low incidence of allergic reaction, is commonly overlooked as a cause of allergy.[32] Allergy to aspirin may take several forms, but it is usually of the angioedema or asthmatic[29] type. Although edema of the glottis can be a primary lesion, it frequently follows edema of other areas, such as the lip or tongue. Because of the possible obstruction of the airway by a swelling of the glottis, angioedema must be recognized and promptly treated no matter where the primary lesion occurs.

Another interesting facet of angioedema is the ease with which the lip lesion can be confused with a periapical abscess of an adjacent tooth. When there is swelling of the lip because of a periapical abscess, one can palpate a continuous swelling from the lip to the apical area of the offending tooth; with angioedema, there will be no such swelling over the apex of the tooth.

A familial (autosomal dominant) variety of angioedema deserves attention because of the high incidence (about 30 per cent[24]) of death from laryngeal edema which may be precipitated by dental trauma. This form of angioedema appears to be related to an actual or functional deficiency of C1 esterase inhibitor which results in edema by complex mechanisms. Prophylactic treatment by epsilon-aminocaproic acid (EACA), tranexamic acid,[31] Danazol,[26] and fresh frozen plasma is usually effective, whereas treatment after the edema has occurred is often ineffective.[9a]

Penicillin and Anaphylactic Shock

Penicillin is a notoriously allergenic drug. At the present time, all the chemical variations of penicillin can still be lumped together as far as allergic potential is concerned, although ampicillin more commonly causes skin rashes than other penicillins.

The symptoms of penicillin allergy are extremely variable, but the most common sign is the skin lesion urticaria (hives). The skin lesions can rarely proceed to a dangerous exfoliative dermatitis. The respiratory tract may be affected with angioedema, as described above, or allergic bronchial asthma. The most serious problem is alteration of the circulatory system. Although any of the allergic manifestations can be serious, some warning is usually apparent before a patient is in extremis. This, however, may not be true with the circulatory system. A fatal drop in blood pressure may occur in seconds with no warning. This is anaphylactic shock, and must be dealt with immediately. It is a true medical emergency, in which proper treatment in the first few minutes may mean life or death.

With a condition as serious as anaphylaxis one must consider prevention. In the case of penicillin, an area of prevention worthy of consideration involves the mode of administration. Thousands of cases of anaphylactic shock have been reported after intramuscular injection of penicillin, whereas after oral administration only a relatively few cases have been reported.[23, 25] Using the oral route does not seem to decrease the total incidence of general allergy to penicillin — only the occurrence of anaphylactic shock. Because penicillin can be administered effectively by the oral route in most patients, intramuscular injection of penicillin should be discouraged unless an indication for this route is present.

Allergic nausea or diarrhea is very uncommon with penicillin, but may occur after oral administration and may herald anaphylactic shock, particularly if severe nausea or diarrhea occurs very shortly after orally administered penicillin.

Local Analgesic Agents

Procaine and related esters are capable of inducing the range of allergic reactions just discussed with penicillin. Local procaine reactions are discussed elsewhere in this book. Although systemic reactions to procaine are rare, they sometimes are manifest by such unusual signs and symptoms as prostration, nervousness, disorientation, etc. These unusual reactions to some local analgesics make the diagnosis of allergy to these drugs very difficult. Downs[11] reported a case of procaine reaction which seemed to be due to a lack of cholinesterase function. Kalow[21] and others reported the incidence of 1 in every 2820 persons in whom there is a poorly functional atypical cholinesterase. This results in an inability of these patients to normally hydrolyze the ester types of such local analgesics as procaine. Thus a relatively small dose may produce a toxic reaction.

The diagnosis of allergic versus toxic reactions to local analgesics is further complicated by the fact that the mouth is a very psychically charged area and therefore evokes many emotional episodes of syncope. Because syncope involves a derangement of the peripheral vascular system, it is not possible at first to differentiate syncope from other peripheral vascular disturbances arising from allergic or toxic causes. After having carefully questioned many patients who reported being allergic to various local analgesics, the author found that many times the symptoms and signs were indistinguishable from a marked episode of syncope. One should be very judicious before labeling a patient "allergic" on the basis of such inconclusive signs and symptoms. The probability of a patient's needing local analgesics is so high that a patient with a suspected allergy to a local analgesic agent should be carefully evaluated before a judgment is made.[19a]

Lidocaine and related amides cause rare allergic manifestations, such as angioedema or anaphylactic shock.

Vasoconstrictors

Allergy to the vasoconstrictors is unlikely. Since epinephrine is a normal hormone, allergic reactions should not occur but patients vary markedly in their susceptibility to this group of drugs.

Antibiotics Other Than Penicillin

Even though the reported incidence of allergic reactions to the sulfonamides is somewhat less than with penicillin, such reactions as blood dyscrasias, drug fever, and the common manifestations of allergy have occurred.

The tetracyclines have a low allergenicity, and reactions, when they do occur, usually are limited to mild skin eruptions. Erythromycin estolate (Ilosone) has rarely caused a disturbance of liver function, but only after prolonged use and returned to normal after discontinuance of the drug. This is similarly true of troleandomycin (TAO) except that after previous exposure, prolonged use is not necessary to cause liver dysfunction in those rare patients who are susceptible to this problem. Because it apparently occurs after previous exposure, it is postulated that the reaction may be on an allergic basis.

A cross allergy between penicillin and the cephalosporins (Keflex and Keflin) may occur.

Barbiturates

Relative to allergy, an interesting phenomenon occurs with the barbiturates: the shorter acting the drug, the less likely it is to cause allergy. Allergy to the ultra-short-acting barbiturates, such as thiopental sodium (Pentothal) and methohexital sodium (Brevital), is almost unheard of; allergy to such short-acting barbiturates as pentobarbital sodium (Nembutal) or secobarbital (Seconal) is rare; but allergy following prolonged use of phenobarbital is more common. The allergy to phenobarbital usually takes the form of a measles type rash.

Other Drugs

Some of the more common dental drugs that have demonstrated allergic problems are codeine and related compounds; meperidine (Demerol); morphine; antihistamines; corticosteroids; iodine; mercurials (Merthiolate, Metaphen, etc.); proteolytic drugs (Orenzyme, Chymoral, Ananase, Chymolase); ataraxics (Atarax, Compazine, Equanil, Librium, Miltown, Phenergan, Valium, Vistaril, etc.) Mentioning these drugs may seem superfluous, but it is easy to develop a contempt for their allergic potential when they are used day in and day out with no problems.

TREATMENT

Many signs arising from other causes resemble allergic signs, and rapid differential diagnosis between allergy and other causes may be impossible.[28] Therefore immediate treatment may be essentially symptomatic. Fortunately this is usually safe and effective.

When we discuss allergic phenomena we are frequently speaking of life-threatening reactions. Because some reactions are, may become, or may end as very serious problems, it is important to adopt procedures which will bear scrutiny. With this in mind, our approach will be to suggest therapy that will maximize safety. It goes without saying that many of the succeeding situations will require medical management after initial emergency treatment.

Anaphylactic Shock

Since circulatory failure takes precedence over other situations, it will be dealt with first. It may not be possible at first to distinguish syncope from the first stages of anaphylactic shock, and we will start our outline for treatment as if we were dealing with mild circulatory embarrassment, and then proceed as if the patient were not responding to therapy. The outlined steps should be followed expeditiously, utilizing a team, if possible, until the patient responds.

PALLOR

A common sign that suggests a failing of the circulatory system is pallor although a flush may be prodromal. This will be used as a starting point for treatment.

Place the patient in a supine position. Do not use the head between the knees technique as this could cause serious damage if, for example, cerebrovascular bleeding has occurred.

Next, test the patient's pulse. The carotid artery (just medial to the sternocleidomastoid muscle) is a better location than the radial pulse. If no pulse is present, cardiopulmonary resuscitation should be started immediately (as covered elsewhere in this book). If a pulse is present, proceed to the next step.

Elevate the legs above the torso. Considerable blood can be pooled in the great muscle tissue of the legs, and elevating the legs will return much of this blood to active circulation.

Administer oxygen. These first few steps can be accomplished within seconds by use of assistants.

If the patient is not responding well, the blood pressure should be taken. When the systolic pressure is above 80 mm of mercury and there is no suspicion of allergy, continuation of the above procedures is in order (except for the patient with pre-existing marked hypertension, as discussed below). However, if allergy is suspected as the cause of the fall in blood pressure because other signs of allergy are present, such as urticaria or wheezing respiration, *or* a notoriously allergenic drug was administered, then the immediate therapy for allergy must be instituted (as described below).

INADEQUATE CIRCULATION

If the systolic pressure is below 80 mm/Hg *or* allergic signs are present, consideration should be given to additional therapy. The figure 80 is rather arbitrary and debatable. An article by Cohn and Luria[9] suggests that cuff blood pressure readings which show little or no systolic pressure can be erroneous. They demonstrated this by comparing cuff readings with direct intra-arterial pressure using the femoral artery. One patient, for example, showed no peripheral pressure with a cuff reading, whereas a pressure of 110/70 was demonstrated in the femoral artery. Because it is not practical to measure intra-arterial pressure immediately, we must still rely on cuff readings, but we should probably be more cautious and less energetic in the use of vasopressors.

Notable exceptions to this caution are patients with marked arteriosclerosis or marked hypertension. These patients may require a blood pressure near their average to maintain vital functions.

For the patient with a systolic pressure of less than 80 or when allergic signs are present, the following therapy is suggested. Oxygen should be continued. Now is one of the few times we should depart from symptomatic treatment and make a differential diagnosis; that is, before the selection of a vasopressor.

If you feel that this drop in blood pressure is due to allergy (anaphylactic shock), because of the administration of an allergenic drug or the presence of allergic signs, epinephrine should be administered immediately. Epinephrine has three actions that are desirable in these circumstances: it is a vasopressor; it has an antihistaminic action; it is a bronchodilator. In addition, its action is quite rapid in onset. The dosage range for epinephrine in an adult will vary depending on the severity of the anaphylactic reaction. The drug may be administered intramuscularly or intravenously. When the intravenous route is used, it is probably best to inject fractionally. That is, inject slowly 0.05 mg for minimal blood pressure fall to 0.2 mg for severe blood pressure fall of a 1:10,000 dilution and wait two minutes to evaluate the effect. Repeat this procedure *if necessary* until the patient is improving or the cardiac status suggests the cessation of therapy by exceeding a rate of 150 beats per minute or becomes irregular. The effect of the

IV administration may last only a few minutes, so the IV epinephrine may be followed with 0.3 mg (1/3 ml of 1:1000) IM. The dosage range may be exemplified as follows. If a patient has a pressure of 70/40, an intramuscular dose of 0.3 mg or a slow titration of 0.05 mg per increment would be prudent. The other extreme of the dosage range would be exemplified by a patient who has little or no pulse or demonstrable blood pressure (CPR will be used concurrently if the patient is unconscious and there is *no* pulse). This patient should receive epinephrine intravenously, if possible, in increments of 0.2 mg or more; for various reasons, it might not be possible to use the intravenous route, so the next best thing is to give a 0.5 to 1.0 mg dose intramuscularly. Any accessible muscle mass is acceptable as a depot, including the tongue. If it is possible to enter a vein, it would be well to maintain this route by attaching a drip of 500 ml of 5 per cent dextrose in water, dripping at least 30 drops per minute or more in frank shock. Establishing such a drip while the patient still has adequate intravascular pressure will facilitate subsequent treatment, particularly if the patient's condition deteriorates to the point that intravascular pressure is very low and finding a vein will be difficult. The physician who follows your treatment will be especially appreciative of a patent intravenous infusion.

In treating circulatory dysfunction, it is important to be aware of the difference in treatment that is desirable if the cause of the fall in blood pressure is something other than allergy. As described, epinephrine has beneficial actions related to allergic problems, but its capacity to produce tachycardia and arrhythmia and to raise the blood pressure above normal is especially undesirable for many hypotensive conditions. For example, it is considered undesirable to elevate blood pressure above normal in myocardial infarction or cerebrovascular bleeding. Therefore, unless one is competent to manage the potent vasopressive drugs, it is probably wisest to use a mild vasopressor, such as mephentermine (Wyamine). It is less potent, but relatively safer because it will usually not raise blood pressure above normal. It may be given in doses of 15 to 30 mg intramuscularly or intravenously, depending on the degree of the circulatory problem. When blood pressure is severely depressed, it is usually desirable to use a rapid intravenous infusion of dextrose 5 per cent (and/or lactated Ringer's) in water until improvement is noted, then slow to approximately 60 drops per minute.

After the administration of epinephrine or mephentermine (Wyamine), a corticosteroid may be considered, for it is often beneficial in peripheral vascular problems. It is used secondarily because it may take as long as one hour to act[8, 17] and may not be efficacious. Cortisone is relatively safe for one-dose administration. A product should be used that can be given slowly intravenously or intramuscularly, such as methylprednisolone (Solu-Medrol), 125 mg, or dexamethasone (Decadron),[16] 4 to 20 mg.

An antihistamine may be beneficial in anaphylactic shock in combating histamine release. Chlorpheniramine maleate (Chlor-Trimeton), 10 to 20 mg., brompheniramine maleate (Dimetane) in 10 to 20 mg, or diphenhydramine (Benadryl), 25 to 50 mg may be given intramuscularly or slowly intravenously.

If at any time there is a complete loss of pulse or blood pressure, cardiopulmonary resuscitation should be instituted.

Respiratory Insufficiency Without Circulatory Failure

This usually involves bronchial or bronchiolar constriction owing to edema and/or spasm, and breathing is usually accompanied by an asthmatic, wheezing sound. Another cause of respiratory impairment is edema of the laryngeal area with resultant obstruction.

The strenuousness of treatment should be predicated on the degree of obstruction. If a mild respiratory wheeze is present, inhalation therapy is appropriate. Epinephrine, isoproterenol, and metaproterenol (Alupent) are commonly used. Metaproterenol[14] may be administered as follows: one inhalation is used; if a second inhalation is necessary, two minutes should be allowed before the second inhalation. No more than three inhalations should be used. This therapy is particularly effective for respiratory symptoms secondary to aspirin intolerance. If obstruction is marked, epinephrine is the drug of choice, with the dose of 0.3 ml (0.3 mg of 1:1000 solution) intramuscularly or subcutaneously and repeated every 10 to 15 minutes. If there appears to be complete obstruction of the glottic area by edema, an immediate coniotomy should be done. Because a coniotomy is done through the cricothyroid membrane, it is much more easily accomplished than an emergency tracheotomy. See the chapter on *emergency airway*.

Antihistamines are sometimes effective for glottic edema but may not be effective for bronchial constriction. If appropriate, diphenhydramine (Benadryl) may be used in a dose of 25 to 50 mg intravenously or intramuscularly, depending on severity.

A corticosteroid may be useful. Methylprednisolone (Solu-Medrol) 125 mg or a comparable product used slowly intravenously or intramuscularly is suggested.

Allergic rhinitis can be categorized with skin reactions relative to treatment.

Allergic Skin Reaction

The skin reactions that fall into the potential *emergency* category are those of the anaphylactic type, such as urticaria or flushing with pruritus or angioedema. These skin reactions should be treated promptly because if untreated they may progress to a serious problem such as exfoliative dermatitis, or more important, these lesions may be prodromal to anaphylactic shock, bronchial constriction, or obstructive glottic edema. Recognition and adequate treatment of skin reactions will usually abort these serious problems.

The most important element in evaluating the potential seriousness of an allergic reaction is the interval of time between the administration of the exciting substance and the appearance of the lesion. The shorter this time period, the greater the probability that the reaction will be heralding anaphylactic shock.

Treatment will be related to this criterion. A reaction which occurs over one hour after the administration of the allergen will usually, but not invariably,[2] be of a *nonemergency* nature. Always have the patient available for treatment for at least 24 hours and, if serious signs begin, treat as described under *rapid onset*. The usual treatment for slow onset allergy can be begun with an intramuscularly or orally administered antihistamine such as diphenhydramine (Benadryl) 25 mg intramuscularly or 50 mg orally every six hours. If additional therapy is needed, the patient's physician or allergist should probably be called upon for care.

A potentially serious reaction may be anticipated if the anaphylactic type lesions are produced within one hour (rarely longer[2]) of the administration of an allergenic substance. This situation demands immediate attention as it is a true medical emergency. Three tenths mg epinephrine (0.3 ml of a 1:1000 dilution) should be given intramuscularly or subcutaneously and repeated if necessary. No additional epinephrine should be used if the heart rate exceeds 150 beats per minute or is irregular. Intravenous titration of epinephrine may be used prior to IM administration by giving 0.05 mg (0.5 ml of 1:10,000) slowly with repetition every two minutes until signs are controlled. The intravenous infusion is maintained with dextrose 5 per cent in water.

Then an antihistamine, such as chlorpheniramine (Chlor-Trimeton) or brompheniramine (Dimetane), 10 to 20 mg or diphenhydramine (Benadryl), 25 to 50 mg is given intramuscularly or intravenously.

After the epinephrine and the antihistamine have been administered, a corticosteroid may be used. Eight mg of dexamethasone (Decadron), or 125 mg of methylprednisolone (Solu-Medrol), or a comparable dose of any similar adrenocorticosteroid prepared for intravenous use is acceptable.

Stimulation or Recurrent Convulsions

If during the course of an allergic reaction marked stimulation or convulsions occur, primary attention should be directed to the cardiorespiratory system wherein the cause of the convulsions probably lies. If convulsions persist, a short-acting or ultra-short-acting barbiturate or diazepam (Valium) may be used to control the convulsions.

It is important to use the sedative in a fashion that allows controlled dosage. Because a depressed, exhausted state may follow a series of convulsions, it is important to administer only enough sedative to control the convulsion and not incur the summation effect of drug sedation and the patient's depression. The most controllable form of administration of the sedative is by small incremental intravenous doses. If the intravenous approach is not possible, as will usually be the case during a convulsion, the intramuscular route should be used. To elucidate the intravenous route: diazepam (Valium) 5 mg is administered and a waiting period of 2 minutes is allowed. During this time the full degree of sedation is manifest. This procedure is repeated (5 mg being injected and a 2 minute waiting period) until the desired degree of sedation is achieved. If the intramuscular route is used 10 mg or more may be used.

Reassuring the patient who is excited is also highly important.

Emesis

If a patient vomits while unconscious, as in a convulsion, or in syncope just as he is lapsing into unconsciousness, the elimination of vomitus from the mouth and pharynx is an absolute must. Earlier it was stated that circulatory failure takes precedence over other situations; however, expelling the vomitus of an unconscious patient momentarily preempts even circulatory failure. See the chapter on *general anesthetic emergencies* for detailed treatment.

OUTLINE OF IMMEDIATE ALLERGIC TREATMENT

Keep a copy of this outline (or its equivalent) with your emergency drugs. Have a consultant follow your initial treatment when appropriate.

I. Circulatory problems: Because the etiology of circulatory depression may not at first be apparent, this outline allows a symptomatic approach to therapy
    A. Pallor — quickly do the following (utilize a team if possible)
        1. Supine position
        2. Elevate legs.
        3. Pulse (at common carotid — medial to sternocleidomastoid muscle): if none, begin cardiopulmonary resuscitation
        4. Oxygen
        5. Blood pressure — if systolic pressure is above 80, continue this treatment except as follows: if blood pressure stays low for more than a few minutes *or* if allergy is suspected, *or* if there is a history of marked hypertension or arteriosclerosis, then use "inadequate circulation" treatment and seek consultation
    B. Inadequate circulation (have team member contact consultant)
        1. Continue oxygen
        2. Vasopressor
           a. Allergic cause probable (signaled by allergic signs or allergenic drug given moments before reaction)
           Use epinephrine first:
             If systolic pressure is above 60 mm Hg.
             If IV is possible, titrate dosage by giving slowly 0.05 mg (0.5 ml of 1:10,000) epinephrine. Follow with 0.3 mg (0.3 ml of 1:1000 epinephrine subcutaneously or IM for sustained effect. Stop administration if heart rate exceeds 150 or becomes irregular
             If IV is not possible, give 0.3 mg (0.3 ml) of 1:1000 solution IM.
            Systolic pressure below 60:
             If IV is possible, administer 0.2 ml (2 ml of 1:10,000) epinephrine and repeat every two minutes until patient is improving or heart rate exceeds 150 or becomes irregular. Concurrently use rapid IV infusion of dextrose 5 per cent in water until patient is improving, then slow to 60 drops per minute. Follow with 0.3 mg (1/3 ml of 1:1000) epinephrine IM or subcutaneously.
           Use antihistamine after epinephrine
             Depending upon severity, use 25 to 50 mg IV or IM of diphenhydramine (Benadryl) or equivalent
           b. Nonallergic cause probable
           If etiology of circulatory problem is known, be as specific as possible with treatment
           If etiology is unknown, use mephentermine (Wyamine). If the systolic pressure is 60 to 80, or *relatively* low in the hypertensive or arteriosclerotic patient, use 15 mg IM
           If the systolic pressure is below 60, use 30 mg IV or IM; also use rapid IV infusion of dextrose 5 per cent in water

3. Establish and maintain infusion of dextrose 5 per cent in water at 30 drops per minute (except as noted above)

4. Use corticosteroid —methylprednisolone (Solu-Medrol) 125 mg or dexamethasone, 8 to 12 mg slowly IV, if possible, or IM (or any equivalent product for intravenous use)

C. Cardiac arrest — no pulse (use carotid artery to test). Immediately begin cardiopulmonary resuscitation. Use epinephrine early if allergic cause

II. Respiratory insufficiency: Use oxygen and be sure of patient airway

A. Mild

Use metaproterenol (Alupent) or equivalent, one inhalation, and wait two minutes. May repeat two more inhalations if necessary

B. Severe

1. Use epinephrine, 0.3 mg (0.3 ml of 1:1000) IM, and repeat as necessary

2. Follow with antihistamine if impairment of airway is due to glottic edema — diphenhydramine (Benadryl) 25 to 50 mg IV or IM, depending on severity

3. Follow with corticosteroid — methylprednisolone (Solu-Medrol) 125 mg, or dexamethasone (Decadron), 8 mg slowly IV or IM

III. Skin reactions (urticaria or angioedema): Observe for many hours

A. Slow onset — beginning one hour or longer after offending drug is administered

Use antihistamine — may begin with oral preparation, such as diphenhydramine (Benadryl) 50 mg every six hours, or begin with an intramuscular dose of diphenhydramine (Benadryl) 25 mg or equivalent, and follow with oral preparation

B. Rapid onset — beginning within one hour (usually within 15 minutes) after administration of offending drug or whenever serious signs develop

1. Use epinephrine, 0.3 mg (0.3 ml of 1:1000) IM or subcutaneously and repeat as necessary

2. Follow with antihistamine — diphenhydramine (Benadryl) 25 to 50 mg IV or IM, depending on severity

3. Follow with corticosteroid — methylprednisolone (Solu-Medrol) 125 mg or dexamethasone (Decadron), 8 mg slowly IV or IM

IV. Marked excitement or recurrent convulsions

Allergic convulsions are usually due to circulatory and/or respiratory inadequacy. Treat these problems appropriately

When using a full face mask, continually check for emesis and patency of airway.

If these measures fail to control convulsions or marked stimulation must be controlled, use:

Diazepam (Valium)

If IV is possible, give 5 to 10 mg over one minute and wait two minutes before administering an additional 5 to 10 mg

If IV not possible, give 10 mg IM

Reassure patient who is excited

V. Emesis while unconscious

Immediately lower patient's head and shoulders below waist, in a prone (not supine) position

Keep mouth open by elevating patient's forehead

A few pertinent notes:

Call a consultant whenever appropriate.

Doses listed are for adults. Proportionately smaller doses should be used for children.

It is helpful to read literature accompanying the drug and underline the part appropriate to your use. This then becomes a quick reminder of pertinent facts that can be reviewed at a glance.

EMERGENCY DRUG TRAYS

As one would suspect, there is no standardized drug regimen to manage emergencies. It, therefore, behooves each practitioner to select the drugs felt to be appropriate for emergency management. Thus, it follows that a commercial drug "kit" will not be applicable for everyone, or perhaps anyone.

It is anticipated that a patient may require emergency care in the office for up to one half hour until the patient can be transported to the hospital if necessary. With this in mind, two sample drug lists have been prepared: one for those practitioners who do not feel comfortable with intravenous medication and another for those who do.

A common indication is listed with each drug along with an average initial dose, but it is imperative that one should review in much greater detail the indications, dosage, and hazards of each drug.

It is helpful to read the literature accompanying a drug and underline the part that would be applicable in an emergency.

Drug doses are listed for adults, and proportionately smaller doses should be used for children.

Substitutions can be made for most of the medications with equivalent products.

Ideally, each practitioner should make an outline of the medications he or she would consider using for possible emergencies and keep this outline with the medications.

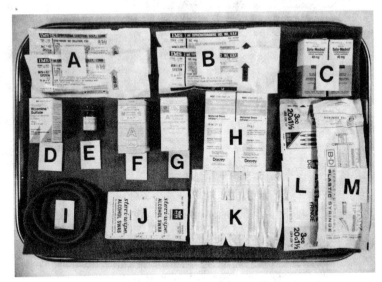

Figure 7–1 Illustrated is a set of emergency drugs which may be appropriate for a practitioner who does not feel comfortable with the use of the intravenous route. The drugs shown illustrate both the prefilled syringe type and the multiple dose vials. When the preloaded syringes are used, it is probably wise to keep a duplicate of the dose needed in case of accidental damage to one dose. This could easily happen considering the nervousness that might accompany a severe emergency. (Illustrated are: A, epinephrine; B, diphenhydramine; C, methylprednisolone; D, mephentermine; E, nitroglycerin; F, morphine; G, atropine; H, metaproterenol; I, tourniquet; J, alcohol sponges; K, needles, L, 3 cc syringe; M, 5 cc syringe.)

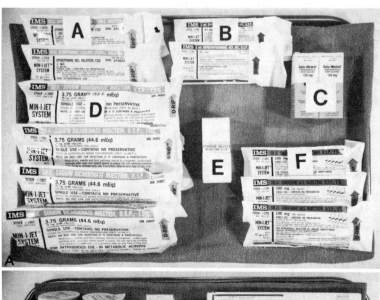

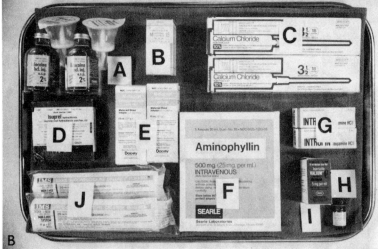

Figure 7–2 The above trays illustrate emergency drugs which may be appropriate for a practitioner who is proficient with the intravenous route. The drugs related to cardiac arrest are those recommended for Advanced Life Support by the American Heart Association in 1977.

A, A, epinephrine; B, diphenhydramine; C, methylprednisolone, D, sodium bicarbonate; E, atropine; F, lidocaine.

B, A, lidocaine; B, morphine; C, calcium chloride; D, isoproterenol; E, metaproterenol; F, theophylline; G, dopamine; H, nitroglycerin; I, diazepam; J, succinylcholine.

Illustration continued on the following page.

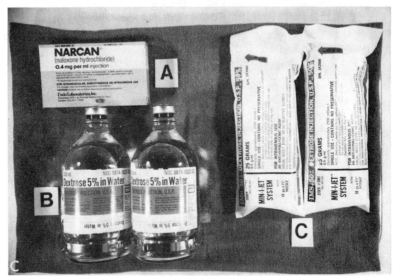

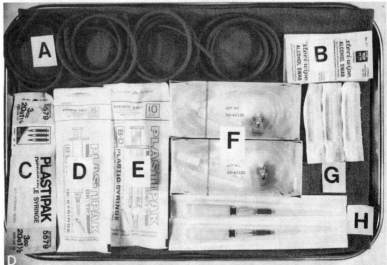

Figure 7-2 *Continued.*

C, A, naloxone; B, dextrose 5% in water; C, dextrose 50%.

D, A, tourniquets; B, alcohol sponges; C, 3 cc syringe; D, 5 cc syringe; E, 10 cc syringe; F, IV infusion sets; G, needles; H, IV catheter needles.

It is suggested that a standard be established within the office to routinely check the medications to be sure they are always present and not outdated. Many manufacturers of drugs will replace outdated medications at no charge.

Figure 7–1 illustrates possible drugs and equipment for the *non-intravenous* routes, while Figure 7–2 illustrates intravenous capability.

Sample Drug List for Office Emergencies When the Intravenous Route Will Not Be Available

1. Oxygen, 100 per cent
   With and without positive pressure
2. Epinephrine
   For anaphylaxis
   Dosage, 0.3 to 1.0 mg intramuscularly
   Have two doses available of l mg/ml (1:1000 solution)
3. Diphenhydramine (Benadryl)
   For anaphylaxis
   Dosage, 25 to 50 mg intramuscularly
   Have two doses available of 50 mg/ml
4. Methylprednisolone (Solu-Medrol)
   For anaphylaxis, aspiration, or shock generally
   Dosage, 125 mg or more intramuscularly
   Have two doses available of 125 mg/vial
5. Mephentermine (Wyamine)
   For hypotension that requires treatment
   Dosage, 15 to 30 mg intramuscularly
   Have two doses available of 15 mg/ml
6. Nitroglycerin (Nitrostat)
   For angina pectoris
   Dosage, 0.3 mg (1/200 grain) to 0.6 mg (1/100 grain) sublingually
   Have at least six fresh tablets available of 0.3 mg
7. Morphine
   For myocardial infarction
   Dosage, 10 mg intramuscularly
   Have at least three doses available of 10 mg/ml
8. Atropine
   For marked bradycardia, accompanied by hypotension, which is symptomatic
   Dosage, 0.5 mg intramuscularly
   Have at least three doses available of 0.5 mg/ml
9. Metaproterenol (Metaprel)
   For mild bronchial asthma
   Dosage, one inhalation 0.65 mg repeated every 3 minutes up to three inhalations
   Have available two inhalers
10. Syringes, needles, tourniquets, and alcohol sponges
11. Sugar packets
    For insulin reaction

Sample Drug List for Office Emergencies when the Intravenous Route Will Be Available

1. Oxygen, 100 per cent
   With and without positive pressure
2. Epinephrine
   For severe bronchospasm
   Dosage, 0.2 to 0.5 mg subcutaneously

For anaphylaxis
Dosage, 0.3 to 1.0 mg intramuscularly or titrate intravenously 0.05 mg every 2 minutes until signs controlled
For cardiac arrest
Dosage, 0.5 mg intravenously and repeated every 5 minutes as needed
Have two doses available of 1.0 mg/ml and two doses of 1.0 mg/10 ml
3. Diphenhydramine (Benadryl)
For anaphylaxis (not for asthma)
Dosage, 20 to 50 mg intramuscularly or slowly intravenously
Have two doses available for 50 mg/ml
4. Methylprednisolone (Solu/Medrol)
For anaphylaxis including asthma, aspiration, or shock generally
Dosage, 125 mg or more intramuscularly or intravenously
Have three doses available of 125 mg/vial
5. Sodium bicarbonate
For acidosis secondary to cardiac arrest
Dosage 1 mEq/kg as an intravenous bolus and repeated as appropriate
Have four doses available of 50 mEq/50 ml
6. Atropine
For marked bradycardia accompanied by hypotension which is symptomatic
Dosage, 0.5 mg as an intravenous bolus repeated as necessary
Have four doses available of 0.4 or 0.5 mg/ml
7. Lidocaine
For ominous ventricular dysrhythmias or ventricular fibrillation
Dosage, 100 mg as an intravenous bolus followed by IV drip of 1 to 4 mg/min
IV drip prepared by adding 2 gm of lidocaine to 500 ml of 5% dextrose in water giving 4 mg/ml
Have available:
2 doses of 100 mg/5ml
2 units of 2 gm/50ml
8. Morphine
For myocardial infarction or acute pulmonary edema
Dosage, 10 to 15 mg intramuscularly or 5 to 10 mg intravenously
Have available three doses of 10 mg/ml
9. Calcium chloride
For cardiac arrest when myocardial action is weak and patient is not digitalized
Dosage, 5 ml of 10 per cent solution
Have available two units of 10 ml of a 10 per cent solution
10. Isoproterenol (Isuprel)
For symptomatic third degree block or sinus bradycardia not responsive to atropine
Dosage, titrate at 2 to 20 µg/min until patient is asymptomatic
IV drip prepared by adding 1 mg of isoproterenol to 500 ml of 5% dextrose in water, giving 2 µg/ml
Have available two units of 1.0 mg vials
11. Metaproterenol (Metaprel)
For mild bronchial asthma
Dosage, one inhalation 0.65 mg repeated every 3 minutes up to three inhalations
Have available two inhalers
12. Theophylline (Aminophylline)
For severe bronchial asthma
Dosage, titrate at 12.5 mg/min intravenously until symptoms abate
Have available two units of 250 mg/20 ml (12.5 mg/ml)
13. Dopamine (Intropin)
For cardiogenic shock
Dosage, start infusion at about 400 µg/min, prepared by adding 200 mg dopamine to 500 ml of 5% dextrose in water. Titrate very carefully to restore peripheral blood pressure to about 90 mm Hg
Have available two ampules of 200 mg

14. Nitroglycerin (Nitrostat)
    For angina pectoris
    Dosage, 0.3 mg sublingually
    Have available at least six tablets
15. Diazepam (Valium)
    For status epilepticus or severe recurrent convulsions
    Dosage, 5 mg/min intravenously (if possible) until seizures controlled
    Have available 10 doses of 5 mg/ml
16. Succinylcholine (Anectine)
    For laryngeal spasm
    Dosage, 10 to 20 mg intravenously and repeated as needed
    Have available five doses of 20 mg/ml
17. Naloxone (Narcan)
    For reversing narcotic excess
    Dosage, titrate 0.1 mg intravenously every 2 minutes until desired effect
    Have available at least two doses of 0.4 mg/ml
18. Dextrose 50%
    For hypoglycemic coma
    For initial use in any seizure disorder
    Dosage, 50 mg intravenously
    Have available three doses of 25 mg/50 ml
19. Dextrose 5% in water
    For diluting drugs for slow intravenous dosage, for correction of hypovolemia,
    for maintaining a patent intravenous route
    Have available two units of 500 ml
20. Alcohol sponges, IV infusion sets, syringes, IV needles including IV catheter-
    needles
21. Tourniquets
    Have available four tourniquets long enough to use around limbs in acute
    pulmonary edema
22. Sugar packets
    For insulin reaction

ACKNOWLEDGMENT

I should like to acknowledge the assistance of Dr. Joseph Tulumello, Dr. Elaine Cooper, Frances Ishii, Janice Frembling, and Kathleen Incardona.

COMMENT

It is emphasized that each preceding sample list of emergency drugs and equipment is exactly that, a *sample* of what the clinician might choose. Neither list should be considered as a suggested standard of care, nor is it intended to be so considered. The intricacies and unknowns of emergency medicine, and the varying training and experience of practitioners, make standardization of drug kits both impossible and undesirable. The real consistencies of emergency medicine are constant change and the inability of experts to agree on standards.

The general practitioner is not expected to perform as a medical specialist in the event of a life-threatening emergency but *is* expected to act promptly in supplying non-drug life support (ABC's of resuscitation), followed by drug support as circumstances and individual training and experience allow.

The general practitioner, rather than choosing the drugs on the "non-intravenous sample" list, might feel more comfortable with a modification, such as: aromatic spirits of ammonia, sugar packets, nitroglycerin, oxygen (with and without positive pressure), epinephrine, and diphenhydramine.

REFERENCES

1. Austen, K. F.: Systemic anaphylaxis in man. J.A.M.A., *192*:116, 1965.
2. Barnard, J. H.: Nonfatal results in third-degree anaphylaxis from Hymenoptera stings. J. Allerg., *45*:94, 1970.
3. Black, J. W., et al.: Definition and antagonism of histamine H_2-receptors. Nature, *236*:385, 1972.
4. Bloom, B. R., and Chase, M. W.: Transfer of delayed-type hypersensitivity. A critical review and experimental study in the guinea pig. Progr. Allerg., *10*:151, 1967.
5. Booth, B. H., Patterson, R.: Electrocardiographic changes during human anaphylaxis. J.A.M.A., *211*:627, 1970.
6. Brocklehurst, W. E.: Slow reacting substance in anaphylaxis (SRS-A). *In* Wolstenholme, G. E. W., and O'Connor, C. M. (eds.): Ciba Foundation Symposium on Histamine. Boston, Little, Brown & Co., 1956, p. 175.
7. Campbell, D. J., and McCasland, G. E.: In vitro anaphylactic response to polyhaptenic and monohaptenic simple antigens. J. Immunol. *49*:315, 1944.
8. Cochrane, G. C., et al.: Evaluation of adrenal steroids administered intravenously, intramuscularly, and orally. J. Clin. Endocrinol., *13*:933, 1953.
9. Cohn, J. N., and Luria, M. H.: Studies in clinical shock and hypotension. J.A.M.A., *190*:113, 1964.
9a. Delfino, J., et al.: Management of a patient with hereditary angioneurotic edema. J. Oral Surg., *36*:890, 1978.
10. de Weck, A. L., and Eisen, H. N.: Some immunochemical properties of penicillenic acid. An antigenic determinate derived from penicillin. J. Exper. Med., *112*:1227, 1960.
11. Downs, J. R.: Atypical cholinesterase activity. J. Oral Surg., *24*:256, 1966.
12. Eisen, H. N., et al.: Elicitation of delayed allergic reactions with haptens: the dependence of elicitation on hapten combination with protein. J. Exper. Med., *95*:473, 1952.
13. Farah, F. S., et al.: Specific inhibition of wheal-and-erythema responses with univalent haptens and univalent antibody fragments. J. Exper. Med., *112*:1211, 1960.
14. Garra, B., et al.: A double-blind evaluation of the use of nebulized metaproterenol and isoproterenol in hospitalized asthmatic children and adolescents. J. Allergy Clin. Immunol., *60*:1, July 1977.
15. Gell, P. G. H., and Coombs, R. R. A.: Clinical Aspects of Immunology. 2nd ed., Philadelphia, F. A. Davis, 1968, p. 580.
16. Grater, W. C.: Cortical steroid choice analogy. Ann. Allergy, *21*:454, 1963.
17. Grater, W. C.: Intravenous hydrocortisone in allergy. Ann. Allergy, *13*:191, 1955.
18. Harris, M. C., and Shure, N.: Sudden death due to allergy tests. J. Allergy, *21*:208, 1950.
19. Imber, W. E.: Allergic skin testing: A clinical investigation. J. Allergy Clin. Immunol., *60*:47, July 1977.
19a. Incaudo, G., et al.: Administration of local anesthetics to patients with a history of prior adverse reaction. J. Allergy Clin. Immunol., *61*:339, May 1978.
20. Ishizaka, K., Ishizaka, T., and Hornbrook, M.: Allergen-binding activity of IgE, IgG and IgA antibodies in sera from atopic patients. In vitro measurements of reaginic antibody. J. Immunol., *98*:490, 1967.
21. Kalow, W.: Hydrolysis of local anesthetics by human serum cholinesterase. J. Pharmacol. Exper. Therap., *104*:122, 1952.
22. Keller, R.: Mast cells and anaphylaxis. Experientia, *18*:286, 1962.
23. Kern, R. A., and Wimberly, N. A., Jr.: Penicillin reactions: Their nature, growing importance, recognition, management and prevention. Am. J. Med. Sci., *226*:357, 1953.
24. Landerman, N. S.: Heredity angioneurotic edema. I. Case reports and review of literature. J. Allergy, *33*:316, 1962.
25. Maganzini, H. C.: Anaphylactoid reactions to penicillin administered orally. N. Engl. J. Med., *256*:52, 1957.
26. NIH: Male hormone prevents hereditary angioedema, corrects inherited abnormality which may be cause. J.A.M.A., *238 (19)*:2010, 1977.
27. Parker, C. W., et al.: Hypersensitivity to penicillinic acid derivatives in human beings with penicillin allergy. J. Exper. Med., *115*:821, 1962.
28. Prickman, L. E.: Anaphylactic reactions. Minnesota Med., *45*:905, 1962.
29. Salvaggio, J. E., et al.: Aspirin induced bronchial asthma. J.A.M.A., *188*:323, 1964.
29a. Schatz, M., et al.: Immunopathogenesis of hypersensitivity pneumonitis. J. Allergy Clin. Immunol., *60*:27, 1977.
30. Sell, S., and Asofsky, R.: Lymphocytes and immunoglobulins. *In* Kallos, P., and Waksman, B. A. (eds.): Progress in Allergy, White Plains, N.Y., Phiebig, 1968, Vol. 12, P. 135.
31. Sheffer, A. L., et al.: Tranexamic acid: preoperative prophylactic therapy for patients with hereditary angioneurotic edema. J. Allergy Clin. Immunol., *60*:38, July 1977.
32. Shelley, W. B.: Birch pollen and aspirin psoriasis. J.A.M.A., *189*:986, 1964.
33. Shelley, W. B.: Indirect basophil degranulation test for allergy to penicillin and other drugs. J.A.M.A., *184*:171, 1963.

34. Shelley, W. B.: New serologic test for allergy in man. Nature, *195*:1181, 1962.

35. Siegel, B. B.: Studies in penicillin hypersensitivity. V. J. Allergy, *33*:349, 1962.

36. Testing for penicillin allergy with aqueous penicillin, G. Medical Newsletter, *17*:84, Sept. 26, 1975.

37. Vane, J. R.: Inhibition of prostaglandin synthesis as a mechanism of action for aspirin-like drugs. Nature New Biology, *231*:232, 1971.

38. Voss, H. E., et al.: Clinical detection of the potential allergic reactor to penicillin by immunologic tests. J.A.M.A., *196*:679, 1966.

39. Walker, J. L.: The regulatory role of prostaglandins in the release of histamine and SRS-A from passively sensitized human lung tissue. Advances Biosci., *9*:235, 1973.

40. Watson, K. C.: Effect of various penicillin compounds on haemagglutination of penicillin-coated erythrocytes. Immunology, *5*:610, 1962.

41. Wide, L.: Clinical significance of measurement of reaginic (IgE) antibody by RAST. *In* Clinical Immunology — Allergy — in Paediatric Medicine. London, Blackwell Scientific Publications, 1973.

8

CARDIOVASCULAR AND OTHER MEDICAL EMERGENCIES

JOHN J. LYTLE

INTRODUCTION

A proper pretreatment physical evaluation will avoid most encounters with a medical emergency in the dental office. Nonetheless you must be prepared to cope with any emergency that may arise. The two most important requirements in the treatment of an office emergency are good judgment and an adequate supply of oxygen.

Certain broad groups of diseases will be discussed from the standpoint of pathologic physiology, symptomatology, and office treatment during acute episodes. A knowledge of various risk diseases seen in dental practice will allow you to provide a better service to your patient, and could prove to be lifesaving.

"Doctor, I'm feeling pain in my chest." Every dental practitioner should be prepared to respond intellectually, emotionally, and actively in an appropriate manner to that complaint.

Chest pain is not a clinical finding but a subjective symptom which may indicate that a life-threatening emergency is about to take place in your office. A rush of thoughts should flash through your mind, computing again the patient's age, previous history of cardiovascular disease, the apparent severity, onset, duration, and possible radiation of this pain. You will simultaneously be aware of the patient's skin and mucosal color, noting any developing pallor or diaphoresis (profuse sweating). Quite possibly you will be recalling the patient's preoperative blood pressure, or, more likely, be wishing that one had been obtained.

At this point you may remember that experienced older hands always said, "keep calm." Your composure and attitude toward the patient can markedly affect the progression of events. Keeping calm is usually a function of understanding the cause of the problem and the course of treatment to be undertaken. This requires preparation before the emergency arises, which is why you are reading this chapter.

BRONCHOPULMONARY DISEASES

PULMONARY EMPHYSEMA

The pulmonary emphysema patient who is ASA Class II or III (review the ASA classification in Chapter 2) will be treated in the office without special concern, except possibly for pharmacosedation. When using inhalation sedation, do not deliver less than 30 per cent oxygen; when supplying oxygen enrichment only, deliver 3 liters per minute via nasal cannula. *No* oxygen supplementation should be supplied to the ASA Class IV emphysema patient (rest dyspnea) if emergency dental care is given in the office.

An emphysema crisis is uncommon, but may occur. Should severe rest dyspnea with cyanosis and tachycardia occur, withhold oxygen if possible and call for assistance. The emphysema patient tolerates a very high arterial carbon dioxide tension. Lowering the carbon dioxide tension by administration of 100 per cent oxygen may cause cessation of breathing. If circumstances force the use of 100 per cent oxygen, be prepared to artificially ventilate the patient until transfer to competent paramedical or medical personnel.

BRONCHIAL ASTHMA

Bronchial asthma is a chronic reversible lung disease characterized by episodes of dyspnea produced by bronchospasm, mucosal edema, and the accumulation of secretions in the tracheobronchial tree. The patient's medical history will almost certainly reveal previous episodes of asthmatic attacks.

If a patient develops an acute asthmatic attack *without* a previous history of asthma the clinician should be thinking of a possible acute allergic reaction to medication and the possibility that the reaction will progress to anaphylaxis with circulatory collapse.

Clinical Findings

The patient will become aware of difficulty in breathing. Inspiration occurs without difficulty, but expiration will become prolonged and associated with characteristic "wheezing." The patient may become cyanotic and will want to sit up and perhaps lean forward to assist ventilation. The patient may become very restless and agitated if no remedial action is taken.

Treatment of a Severe Asthmatic Attack

1. Position the patient in a sitting position — leaning forward if that increases comfort.
2. Administer oxygen 100 per cent by an appropriate full face mask at a comfortable rate.
3. Begin monitoring blood pressure and pulse rate at frequent intervals.
4. Administer epinephrine, 0.3 ml of a 1/1000 aqueous solution subcutaneously.
5. If the patient fails to improve dramatically within 10 minutes of the epinephrine injection, transfer to an acute care hospital facility by ambulance.
6. Be prepared to support collapse of the cardiovascular system in the event the asthmatic attack represents the prodrome of an anaphylactic reaction.

CARDIOVASCULAR DISEASES

CONGESTIVE HEART FAILURE

Congestive heart failure (CHF) is that clinical syndrome occurring when the heart is unable to pump enough blood to meet the metabolic demands of the body. Usually the condition develops slowly and can result from a great variety of disease entities affecting the cardiovascular system. It may develop rapidly in the patient who suffers a myocardial infarction in your office. The prudent dental practitioner should not find himself treating the final decompensating stages of slowly developing CHF. Patients presenting with dyspnea, extreme fatigue, neck vein distention, pitting edema of the lower extremities, and rales in the lung bases on auscultation should be referred for medical management. Dental care should be deferred until the patient has been returned to a state of reasonable cardiac compensation.

During 20 years of dental practice, I have had two patients in serious stages of cardiac decompensation present for dental treatment. Both of these patients felt bad teeth was the cause of their extreme fatigue, dyspnea, and ankle swelling. One 38 year old woman with longstanding mitral valve incompetence tried, unconvincingly, to have me remove several grossly carious teeth. Her uncompensated congestive failure was so severe I urged immediate hospitalization for management of the cardiac problem. She expired the following day at home.

The other patient I vividly recall was a 67 year old man who had recently moved across the country to live with his family on the West Coast. He had a long history of coronary artery disease and had congestive heart failure requiring digitalis and diuretics. His selection of a physician in this new environment unfortunately resulted in one who attempted to manage the cardiovascular problem with diet and herbal preparations. During a six month period without his former medications he slowly decompensated and presented in my office short of breath, extremely fatigued, and concerned that an abscessed tooth was at the bottom of all his trouble. Pitting edema of the lower extremities, prominent neck veins, a positive hepato-jugular reflex, and basilar rales were present, and this patient was advised that the tooth was not the "root" of his problem. I referred him to an internist who reversed his decompensating cardiovascular status and one month later the oral problem was treated without incident.

Patients with a history of congestive failure who appear well compensated and adequately medicated, usually with a diuretic, a low sodium diet, and a digitalis preparation, can be managed very safely in the office environment. The well compensated patient does not suddenly and precipitously decompensate due to the stress associated with a dental procedure unless another problem such as an acute myocardial infarction supervenes. However, the borderline patient (ASA Class III) may decompensate in the office as a result of the emotional and physical stresses of dental treatment. See Chapter 2 for review of ASA classification.

Symptoms and Findings in Congestive Heart Failure

The well compensated patient with a history of previous congestive failure episodes usually can be managed uneventfully and will not present with the findings that follow. These findings may develop slowly as a result of chronic progressive cardiovascular disease or rapidly if this is an acute problem, such as a myocardial infarction affecting the heart's ability to pump blood.

The extreme fatigue that may be noted cannot be attributed to just one side of the heart but must be attributed to both. Decreased peripheral blood flow to the brain can produce mental confusion and stupor. Decreased circulation to the lower limbs can result in deep vein thrombosis. Decreased renal blood flow will result in blood chemistry alterations such as creatinine and blood urea nitrogen elevations. The chronically congested liver produces cardiac cirrhosis characterized by impaired liver function. Fibrosis of the liver occurs with the passage of time.

It is suggested that you review the pathologic physiology of congestive heart failure in Chapter 2 before proceeding.

Treatment of Congestive Heart Failure

Slowly developing congestive heart failure will respond favorably to the following:

1. *Bed rest:* This alone may correct any acute bout of CHF by reducing the demands on the heart.
2. *Low salt diet:* Since CHF initiates powerful sodium retaining mechanisms and these to some extent are responsible for the edema in the lungs and lower extremities, limitation of sodium intake greatly aids in the resolution of CHF.

3. *Diuretics:* Thiazide diuretics, mercurial diuretics, and Lasix (furosemide) mobilize edema fluid and aid in the excretion of sodium. Electrolyte imbalance is a potential complication of diuretic use which may be avoided by regular blood chemistry determinations.
4. *Digitalis:* This agent causes increased strength of myocardial contraction and improves cardiac output in low output failure. There are many different digitalis preparations available. They may be given intravenously, intramuscularly, or orally.

Treatment of Rapidly Developing Congestive Heart Failure

Rapidly developing heart failure occurring in the dental office should be managed as follows:

1. Administer oxygen 100 per cent by full face or nasal mask.
2. Apply rotating tourniquets to the four extremities. This bloodless phlebotomy can effectively reduce circulating blood volume by trapping as much as 700 ml in the extremities. Release one tourniquet for 5 minutes at a time, and continue this rotation.
3. Morphine sulfate 10 mg to 15 mg will specifically improve circulatory dynamics and reduce apprehension.

The decision on how far to carry treatment of rapidly developing CHF will be up to the individual clinician. It is appropriate to transport the patient with rapidly developing congestive heart failure to an acute hospital as quickly as possible. There, the underlying cause of pump failure can be determined and specific therapy directed toward the etiology as well as symptomatic treatment of the failing pump.

CORONARY HEART DISEASE

Angina Pectoris

In Chapter 2 angina pectoris and myocardial infarction were described and recommendations were made for managing the patient with a history of either disorder. Elderly individuals, known diabetics, and patients who describe previous anginal episodes, previous myocardial infarctions, and relief of chest pain with nitroglycerin are more likely to develop a cardiovascular emergency than are young people or those with no history of cardiovascular problems or diabetes. This does not mean that the latter do not develop cardiovascular emergencies, it is just less likely that they will. You will be much more concerned about the sudden onset of severe substernal pain in an elderly diabetic with a history of angina pectoris and a previous myocardial infarction than you might be if a 21 year old, healthy football player describes substernal (precordial) chest pain. We have all read accounts of sudden cardiovascular collapse in a previously healthy young individual, but it is far less likely than in the elderly, medically compromised patient.

The proper management of patients with a known history of cardiovascular disease must be individualized. These patients will benefit from careful preoperative assessment of cardiac reserve and control of preoperative anxiety with appropriate oral or parenteral sedation. Profound local analgesia, short, relatively atraumatic procedures, the availability of oxygen, and careful postoperative management of anxiety and pain are all important considerations. Even after carefully following these principles, a patient may develop chest pain and require immediate management.

MANAGEMENT OF CHEST PAIN OF SUSPECTED CARDIOVASCULAR ORIGIN

Any time chest pain develops before, during, or after dental treatment, one's attention should be focused upon obtaining pain relief for the patient. One of the most significant anxiety-producing factors for the distressed patient is an anxious attitude on the part of the clinician and his or her auxiliaries. It is imperative that you remain calm and stay with the patient until the immediate problem is resolved. An apparently calm doctor transmits confidence to staff and patient. This does not mean that the doctor should act unconcerned. One can demonstrate concern and still minimize anxiety-producing factors in the patient. The dental therapy should be interrupted until the anginal episode is past, and it might be unwise to proceed with elective treatment after the pain has subsided.

Loosen tight collars, coat buttons, scarves, corsets, or brassieres if present, and remove plastic aprons which may cause discomfort by retaining

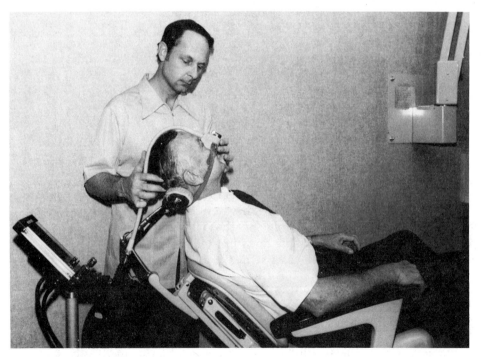

Figure 8–1 Patient seated in reclining position, head above chest, receiving oxygen by mask and being carefully observed.

body heat. Administer oxygen at a comfortable rate through an appropriate, comfortably fitting nasal hood, nasal cannula, or carefully held full face mask. This is comforting and reduces anxiety, and may in itself stop the pain. Be certain the patient is in a comfortable position. Generally, this is not lying flat, but is usually obtained by raising the head somewhat above the chest to a semi-reclining position (Fig. 8–1).

TREATMENT OF ANGINA PECTORIS

Give nitroglycerin from the patient's own fresh supply or from your emergency supply if the patient has none. In Chapter 2, it was suggested that the 0.30 mg strength be given from your fresh supply (not over six months old) if you are premedicating a patient to prevent angina. Once a full-blown anginal attack has occurred, 0.45 mg or 0.6 mg can be given. Two tablets from your office supply (0.30 mg), normally used for prophy- laxis, can be safely given. If the patient is experiencing increasingly severe pain and your initial nitroglycerin dose is not effective within two to three minutes, amyl nitrite may be administered by inhalation. This is a potent vasodilator which can produce the side effects of headache, flushing, and occasionally syncope. I recommend reserving amyl nitrite for the most se- vere pain of unquestioned origin. If no relief is obtained within 10 to 15 minutes of your active intervention, including the administration of oxygen, you may assume that a myocardial infarction has occurred. Immediate transportation to the hospital is imperative. Further material on angina pec- toris is included under Myocardial Infarction.

Myocardial Infarction

The patient with myocardial infarction usually describes severe, unre- mitting, crushing, substernal (precordial) pain. It is vise-like and may radi- ate down the left arm, up toward the jaw or to the neck. Less frequently, the pain radiates to the back or to the right side. The patient may become nauseated and weak and may express fear of imminent death. He or she should be placed in. a position of comfort. All tight garments should be loosened and oxygen should be administered immediately.

The clinical signs become apparent quickly. The patient may develop an ashen pallor. The blood pressure may drop precipitously and an arrhyth- mia may develop. One should immediately call for outside assistance. If a well trained paramedic group is available in your community, this service is the best source to contact. An emergency telephone number should be available for instant use. Minutes are important in the early management of myocardial infarction. If an arrhythmia is present, the paramedics can begin immediate electrocardiographic monitoring, start an intravenous infusion, and continue the blood pressure monitoring and the oxygen administration which you initiated.

If paramedics are not available, it may be possible to develop a work- ing agreement with a nearby physician who will respond to an emergency should it arise. However, it seems that these agreements are subject to many shortcomings. The most obvious is that the physician may not be available when you need him. According to a corollary of Murphy's Law, a severe cardiovascular emergency would be most likely to occur when the physician is unavailable.

An ambulance service without paramedic capabilities would be the second most effective agency to call for assistance in managing the problem of acute myocardial infarction occurring in the office. It is imperative that you stay with the patient to supervise supportive care and to continue monitoring until that responsibility can be transferred to an emergency room physician.

Each practitioner must decide how far he or she will go in the management of an acutely ill patient with suspected myocardial infarction. To monitor the pulse, blood pressure, and state of consciousness, to administer oxygen, and to be prepared to provide basic life support, ventilation, and closed chest cardiac massage are the *inescapable* basic responsibilities of all dental practitioners.

More advanced care, including the administration of pain relieving narcotic drugs, the support of blood pressure, and the management of arrhythmias may be beyond the scope of the general practitioner's expertise. However, the clinician who utilizes intravenous sedation and ultralight general anesthesia should be prepared to provide advanced life support. This will include the support of blood pressure, electrocardiographic monitoring, the treatment of arrhythmias with appropriate pharmacologic agents, and the management of cardiac arrest, including defibrillation of an electrically and functionally incompetent myocardium.

SUMMARY OF STEPS IN MANAGING ANGINA PECTORIS

1. Stop the dental treatment and direct your attention toward abolishing the pain.
2. Immediately administer nitroglycerin from the patient's own supply or from your fresh emergency supply. Give 0.6 mg (two 0.3 mg tablets).
3. Simultaneously administer 100 per cent oxygen by nasal cannula, through an appropriate nasal hood, or via a comfortable full face mask (Fig. 8–2).
4. Make certain the patient is comfortable, loosen restricting garments, remove plastic patient throws, rubber dam, etc.

This should resolve the anginal episode and you and the patient should decide whether or not to continue dental therapy. This is a judgment decision, and will depend upon the severity of the attack. If any doubt exists, do not perform further elective treatment at that appointment.

5. If the pain does not subside following the nitroglycerin administration within 3 to 4 minutes or, if the pain is very intense initially, an amyl nitrite ampule should be broken and the contents inhaled. This should produce pain relief within 30 seconds.
6. If relief is not obtained following these steps, you must assume that you are facing a more serious problem; perhaps a myocardial infarction has occurred and the patient should be removed as quickly as possible to a hospital emergency room facility.

Nitrous oxide in a concentration of 35 per cent has been shown to ame-

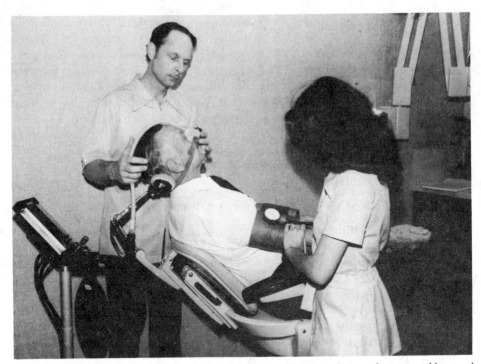

Figure 8-2   Patient seated in reclining position with oxygen being administered by nasal mask. Nurse checking blood pressure. Nitroglycerin may be easily administered with this arrangement.

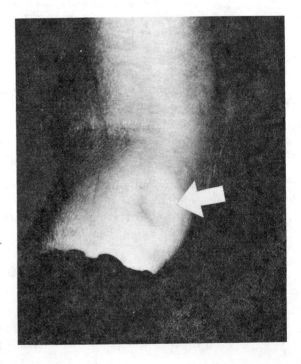

Figure 8-3   Pitting edema of the lower extremities. Note that thumb pressure on the dorsum of the foot leaves a noticeable depression on the edematous foot which remains for several minutes.

liorate the pain of acute myocardial infarction. This use of nitrous oxide has not been accompanied by hemodynamic changes or significant adverse reactions. While this treatment is not a standard of care, it would be perfectly proper to utilize the agent in the dental office for relief of angina pectoris or acute myocardial infarction pain, the balance of the gas mixture being 65 per cent oxygen. It is my opinion that the favorable action of nitrous oxide in this instance results primarily from sedative rather than analgesic action.

SUMMARY OF FINDINGS AND MANAGEMENT OF MYOCARDIAL INFARCTION

Usually several, but not necessarily all, of the following are present:

1. crushing substernal (precordial) pain with or without radiation to arms, jaw or back
2. pain is not relieved by coronary artery vasodilators, oxygen, and rest
3. fear of impending death
4. nausea
5. ashen pallor
6. thready pulse
7. arrhythmia
8. drop in blood pressure
9. unconsciousness

EMERGENCY TREATMENT

1. Position patient comfortably, usually not supine, but with the head slightly elevated.
2. Monitor the pulse and blood pressure.
3. Give 100 per cent oxygen by mask.
4. Give nitroglycerin or amyl nitrite (nitroglycerin: two tablets, 0.3 mg size) (amyl nitrite, via ampule).
5. Transfer the patient to an acute emergency facility as soon as possible.

Optional treatment which may be indicated:

6. Begin an intravenous infusion of 5 per cent dextrose in water. Run very slowly just to maintain the intravenous route.
7. A narcotic can be given if pain is overwhelming and more than 10 to 15 minutes will elapse between onset and transfer to an emergency room. Demerol, 25 to 75 mg, or morphine sulfate, 6 to 10 mg, may be given IM.
8. Cardiopulmonary resuscitation may be necessary if arrest occurs, and one must be prepared to provide that treatment if required.
9. Stay with the patient until transfer to a physician's care in an appropriate emergency facility has been accomplished.

CEREBROVASCULAR DISEASES

CEREBROVASCULAR ACCIDENT

Patients may sustain a cerebrovascular accident or "stroke" in the dental office. Intracranial hemorrhage produces 25 per cent of cerebrovascular accidents. This emergency is most likely to occur while an individual is active during the day — perhaps visiting your office. The remaining 75 per cent of cerebrovascular accidents result for the most part from cerebral ischemia, have significantly different symptoms and findings, usually develop more slowly, and are not likely to present as a medical emergency in the dental office.

Intracranial Hemorrhage

The primary cause of this problem is hypertensive cerebrovascular disease. Other causes are atherosclerotic vascular disease, cerebral aneurysm, arteriovenous malformations, head trauma, and miscellaneous unusual causes such as ingestion of methamphetamine, or "speed," and blood dyscrasias. The untreated hypertensive patient beyond age 55 should be considered a potential candidate. Intracerebral hemorrhage classically presents with the onset of a sudden extremely severe headache. Nausea, vertigo, and severe neurologic deficit such as hemiplegia and/or coma may develop. The rapidity and severity of the developing neurologic symptoms is related to the amount and rate of intracranial bleeding.

The patient should be positioned as comfortably as possible, with slight elevation of the head and upper body. Tight garments should be loosened and oxygen via a full face mask should be given at a comfortable rate to an awake patient. If the patient loses consciousness, an oral airway should be placed and careful observation of respiration should be maintained and assisted ventilation instituted if respiration slows or stops.

These patients should be transferred to an acute care hospital facility as rapidly as possible by ambulance. As soon as you suspect the possible development of the sequence of events described above, a call should be made to obtain an ambulance. The practitioner should avoid giving medications to sedate the patient or to ease the pain if an intracranial hemorrhage is suspected because this may mask rapidly changing neurologic symptoms resulting from the hemorrhage.

This series of events is most likely to occur in older hypertensive patients; however, it may occur in young adults, suggesting rupture of a berry aneurysm, or in a child, suggesting bleeding from an arteriovenous malformation. Your primary responsibility as a dental practitioner is to recognize the potential seriousness of sudden onset of severe headache, nausea, and rapidly developing neurologic deficit, to protect the patient's airway if unconsciousness occurs, to support respiration, and to transport the patient by ambulance to a hospital as rapidly as possible.

Cerebral Ischemia

Ischemia of cerebral vessels makes up the vast majority (75 per cent) of cerebrovascular accidents. Neurologic deficit is usually slower in developing. Headache, nausea, and vomiting are not prominent. Frequently the patient awakens in the morning to discover the neurologic deficit which has resulted from ischemia occurring during the night.

Patients presenting for dental treatment with a history of weakness, change in gait, loss of speech, or any other serious neurologic deficit of very recent origin should be carefully evaluated prior to any dental treatment. Elective treatment should be deferred until there has been stabilization of deteriorating neurologic status.

Cerebral Embolism

This type of cerebrovascular accident makes up a very small per cent of problems. Sudden onset of deteriorating neurologic function usually occurs, without severe headache and with a systemic medical problem such as endocarditis; recent myocardial infarction, or congenital heart disease capable of producing a thrombus would lead one to suspect this possible cause of cerebrovascular accident.

Emergency treatment of both ischemic cerebrovascular disease and embolic cerebrovascular disease is the same. Should sudden deterioration of neurologic status occur in the dental office, support the vital functions of respiration and transfer the patient by ambulance as rapidly as possible to a hospital facility.

VASODEPRESSOR SYNCOPE

Vasodepressor syncope is defined as a transient loss of consciousness resulting from decreased cerebral blood flow following a drop in blood pressure evoked by anxiety or pain. This entity is the common faint and has also been called vasodepressor shock, hysterical reaction, and psychic reaction.

Syncope is a minor cardiovascular emergency that every dental practitioner will see on numerous occasions during his or her professional career. Diagnosis and treatment are straightforward and relatively simple. If fainting occurs during or after the administration of medications, the doctor should be concerned that what appears to be a syncopal episode may be a reaction to the medication. It is important to differentiate between syncope and toxic or allergic reactions. If an elderly patient with known cardiovascular or cerebrovascular problems experiences a syncopal episode, differentiation from cerebrovascular insufficiency of more serious etiology, such as cerebrovascular accident, must be considered.

In the minds of many persons anxiety and fear of pain are associated with dental treatment despite our efforts to minimize the discomforts associated with dental procedures. In offices where every effort is made to conceal all dental instruments, where patients never see blood and never are subjected to sounds or odors which may evoke syncope, a few patients still faint.

I have made every effort to minimize anxiety-producing factors in my practice, and I have the impression that a pleasant environment without the sights, sounds, and smells associated with pain does reduce the number of patients fainting, but it does not eliminate the problem entirely. Patients may be extremely fatigued or debilitated, or they may have fasted for an excessive period prior to their visit and sensitized their vasopressor mechanism to react to the slightest anxiety-producing factor such as entering a dental office.

Preoperative sedation, short or no preoperative waiting in the reception area, pleasant, concerned personnel, and complete pain control in a pleasant nonthreatening environment enable concerned clinicians to manage the syncope-prone individual once he or she has been identified.

Clinical Findings in Syncope

Pallor of the skin or oral mucosa is often the first indication of impending syncope. The patient may then volunteer that he feels weak, and perspiration may appear and is sometimes profuse. The patient may experience nausea, and some may regurgitate gastric contents.

If no corrective measures are taken the patient will become unconscious. Convulsions may accompany the lapse of consciousness. A marked drop in blood pressure will be noted. The pulse which initially may have been rapid and thready slows markedly (bradycardia). The pupils may be dilated. Cardiac arrest must be assumed until proven otherwise.

Treatment of Syncope

The patient should immediately be placed in a reclining position with his head at or slightly below the level of the heart. One hundred per cent oxygen should be administered via an appropriate full face mask. The blood pressure and pulse rate should be monitored, and aromatic spirits of ammonia may be inhaled intermittently. The patient should immediately begin to regain consciousness and may be momentarily confused (Fig. 8–4).

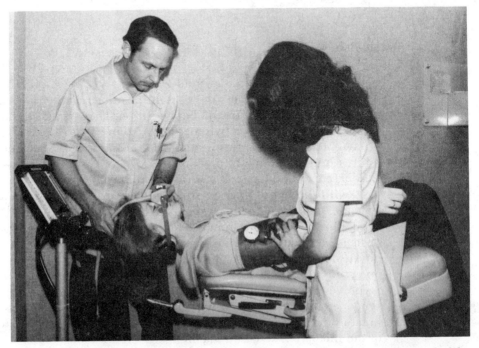

Figure 8–4 Patient in dental chair fully reclined with head at or below the level of the heart. Oxygen is being administered by mask, and blood pressure is being monitored.

The practitioner and auxiliaries should remain calm and reassure the patient that the situation is under control. The patient should be made comfortable by loosening tight or warm garments. A cool, moist towel applied to the forehead or to the back of the neck may be helpful.

The patient should not be allowed to stand quickly or walk unattended. If the faint has occurred in a location such as the reception room or in the doorway, he or she should be assisted to a more appropriate recovery area. The decision to proceed or to initiate planned dental treatment that day depends on the individual. In some instances, it will be possible to continue dental therapy but in others it may well be indicated to appoint the patient for another time and perhaps to utilize a different anesthetic approach or to suggest preoperative sedation. If syncope occurs before or during a sedative procedure, elective treatment should be discontinued. The cardiovascular system requires some hours to fully recover from complete syncope.

SUMMARY OF FINDINGS

1. The patient feels weak.
2. The patient may feel nauseated.
3. Perspiration appears on the brow.
4. Skin and mucosa are noticeably blanched.
   This is followed by:

5. Dilatation of the pupils.
6. Initial tachycardia which proceeds to bradycardia.
7. Marked hypotension.
8. Unconsciousness.
9. Occasionally convulsions precede or accompany the lapse of consciousness.

Differential Diagnosis

1. Orthostatic hypotension is an autonomic disorder in which syncope occurs when the patient assumes the upright position, as after a lengthy dental appointment in the semirecumbent position. There is a sharp fall in arterial blood pressure, followed by syncope, but there is no drop in pulse rate and no symptoms of pallor, sweating, and nausea. Consciousness quickly returns in the recumbent position.
2. Cardiac conduction defects such as the Adams-Stokes syndrome (pulse rate of 40 with short periods of asystole), reflex cardiac standstill, carotid sinus syncope, ventricular tachycardia, paroxysmal tachycardia, and ventricular fibrillation show no prodromal symptoms of vasodepressor syncope. Diagnosis is based upon sudden syncope, history, pulse evaluation, and other physical signs. Air hunger should be treated with oxygen. See the chapter on *cardiopulmonary arrest*.
3. Hyperventilation syndrome usually produces faintness, but not actual syncope, and is associated with acute anxiety. It is readily controlled by breath-holding or rebreathing into a paper bag or a reservoir (pressure) bag of the inhalation sedation machine.
4. Cough syncope follows a paroxysm of explosive coughing usually associated with bronchitis. Syncope is brief and there are no residua. It is caused by

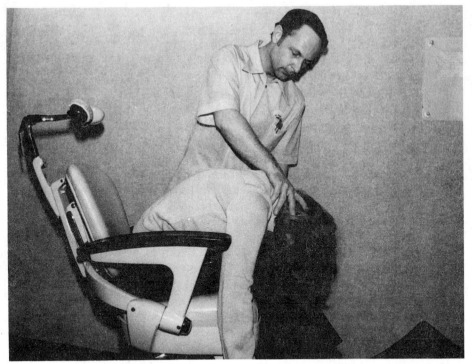

Figure 8–5 Do not press the patient's head forward between the knees. This illustrates the incorrect way to treat syncope in the dental chair. The patient cannot be monitored, observed, or have respiration assistance with oxygen in this position.

a marked increase in intrathoracic and intra-abdominal pressures, causing a sharp elevation of cerebrospinal fluid pressure with resultant fleeting cerebral hypoxia.

5. Hysterical fainting is usually seen in young women with emotional illness. The attack commonly occurs in the presence of others, the patient gracefully crumpling to the floor without injury. There are no irregularities of pulse, blood pressure, or skin color.
6. Hypoglycemia. See insulin shock under diabetes mellitus.

MANAGEMENT OF PATIENT IN SYNCOPE

1. Position the patient in the supine position with the head at or slightly below the level of the heart. *Do not* press the patient's head forward between the knees in the sitting position (Fig. 8–5).
2. Administer 100 per cent oxygen by full face mask.
3. Monitor the blood pressure, pulse, and respirations. This is especially important if medications have been given immediately prior to syncope.
4. Intermittent administration of spirits of ammonia by inhalation during recovery may be useful.
5. Loosen tight clothing.
6. A cool, moist towel may be applied for patient comfort.

ENDOCRINE DISEASES

DIABETES MELLITUS

It is estimated that 5 per cent of the population are predisposed to diabetes mellitus. Two per cent are overt diabetics, 2 per cent are undiagnosed, and 1 per cent are undiagnosed and probably unrecognizable by available testing methods.

Diabetes is a heritable metabolic disease which most dramatically affects carbohydrate metabolism. Most commonly, insulin production by the beta cells in the islets of Langerhans of the pancreas decreases or stops entirely, and the classic clinical signs and symptoms of the disease are seen. In younger persons with rapid clinical expression of the disease process, weight loss, fatigability, excessive thirst (polydipsia), and excessive urination (polyuria), associated with a ravenous appetite (polyphagia) occur when alternate metabolic pathways, primarily for utilization of fats, are called upon to produce energy normally supplied by carbohydrate metabolism.

In older persons, diabetes is frequently associated with obesity, and the decreased insulin production is not as dramatic as in young individuals. In older diabetics the changes that take place in the cardiovascular system, the kidneys, the nervous system, and the eyes may be more distressing to the patient and of more concern to the dental practitioner. See Chapter 2 for diabetes classification.

The medical history obtained by the clinician and his or her auxiliary staff should uncover the known diabetic who presents for care. With current emphasis on education of the diabetic patient to enable him to understand and live with his disease, management of dental procedures in these patients should pose minimal problems for the knowledgeable practitioner.

Emergencies Associated with Diabetes Mellitus

The most frequent emergency the clinician is likely to encounter in treating diabetics is related to insulin overdose (hypoglycemic coma). A knowledgeable diabetic may take a normal dose of insulin and, owing to the fear or anxiety associated with impending dental treatment, fail to eat a sufficient amount of food. This individual may feel nervous, begin to perspire, become agitated, and become unconscious and convulse if not given carbohydrate in the form of sugar, orange juice, or candy, which can be quickly utilized.

Physicians treating patients who present unconscious in a hospital emergency room are impressed and gratified to see a patient respond dramatically to an intravenous dextrose bolus. You should have available a source of readily absorbable carbohydrate to prevent insulin reactions in anxious diabetic patients.

The second way a diabetic patient may become unconscious in your office is by developing diabetic (hyperglycemic) coma. This is extremely unlikely, but possible. A known diabetic, perhaps a teenager rebelling against an unwanted disease, may not take sufficient insulin to prevent ketoacidosis. This patient would probably be stuporous upon presentation in the dental office but may be seeking help for an acute infectious process which increases metabolic demands and leads the patient to think that dental treatment alone would improve his fatigue, lassitude, thirst, excessive urination, and acetone breath. It will not.

Treatment should consist first of recognizing that a potential medical emergency is developing in your office. The patient should be placed in a supine position, vital signs should be carefully monitored, oxygen should be administered, and a determination made as to the quickest way to transfer this patient by ambulance to an acute care hospital facility. If circulatory collapse seems imminent, based on low blood pressure, an intravenous route should be established if possible.

A frequent area of concern in managing the unconscious diabetic relates to the administration of glucose to a patient in diabetic coma, *not* one experiencing an insulin reaction. If you suspect that the problem may be related to hypoglycemia, give intravenous dextrose. This will not significantly adversely affect a patient in diabetic coma, but it will be immensely helpful in reversing an insulin overdose.

A final area of concern to the practitioner managing diabetics relates to the effects of the disease process on the cardiovascular system. Diabetic patients may develop occlusive vascular problems which predispose to premature myocardial infarction and to cerebrovascular accidents as well as to peripheral vascular problems. These patients should be managed more conservatively than the average patient. Follow the stress reduction protocol outlined in Chapter 2.

ADRENOCORTICAL INSUFFICIENCY

Hydrocortisone and aldosterone are two of the hormones produced by the adrenal cortex which are required for cardiovascular homeostasis (normal state). Patients presenting for dental care may have, either slowly or rapidly, lost the ability to produce these hormones for many reasons such as adrenal tuberculosis or idiopathic adrenal failure, or following adrenalectomy. These patients tolerate stress poorly and may decompensate under stress of dental treatment.

Recognizing the Patient with Adrenocortical Insufficiency

The medical history obtained by the clinician is the primary tool for establishing the presence of this problem. Patients with a well documented history of loss of adrenal function will under almost all circumstances be taking steroids on a regular basis. Generally these patients are managed without altering their regular steroid dose.

The most potentially serious problems are related to patients who have been given steroids for suppression of inflammatory responses associated with a multitude of metabolic, autoimmune, arthritic, or asthmatic conditions. The steroids are tapered off and discontinued as soon as practical, often leaving the patient with a suppressed endogenous steroid production mechanism. This patient may feel weak, tired, chronically nauseated and may relate all symptoms to bad teeth. Here again, the carefully taken medical history will alert the practitioner to the potential problem. After consultation with a physician, steroid supplements should be administered prior to dental procedures.

Treatment of an Acute Hypotensive Episode Related to Adrenocortical Insufficiency

1. Place the patient in a supine position with the head comfortably elevated.
2. The legs should be elevated at least to the level of the heart.
3. Monitor the vital signs and record the blood pressure and pulse rate at frequent intervals.
4. Administer 100 per cent oxygen via a suitable full face mask.
5. If possible, start an intravenous drip of isotonic saline and run in as rapidly as possible. Monitor the blood pressure response to intravenous fluids. Four to five liters of isotonic saline may be required to obtain a therapeutic response.
6. Administer hydrocortisone (Solu-Cortef) as an IV push or alternately dexamethasone (Decadron) immediately.
7. Transfer the patient by ambulance to an acute care hospital facility.

CONVULSIVE DISORDERS

GRAND MAL EPILEPSY

Epilepsy is characterized by spontaneously occurring clinical seizures resulting from abnormal neuronal discharge which spreads throughout the brain. It may develop without apparent cause, sometimes has a genetic link, and may follow brain injury, infections, or tumor.

Patients occasionally experience isolated convulsions as a result of a toxic amount of a drug such as lidocaine, occasionally during a syncopal episode, and occasionally with an intracerebral hemorrhage (rare). Children may experience a convulsion with a sudden temperature elevation associated with a systemic infection. These types of convulsions are not related to epilepsy.

The patient's medical history is the most important tool the dental practitioner has at his or her disposal to identify the patient with epilepsy. When a patient indicates that epilepsy is present, the clinician should be certain that the individual is taking an anticonvulsant agent on a regular basis. The most common agent in use is Dilantin, frequently used in combination with phenobarbital, but many other agents are also commonly in use.

Dental treatment should be planned so the patient is fully rested and perhaps sedated at the office visit.

Recognition of a Grand Mal Seizure

A grand mal seizure is characterized by a series of events which are certain to impress any first time observer. The patient may experience an aura, described as a visual, auditory, gustatory, or olfactory sensation which precedes the loss of consciousness. The patient falls to the ground if standing and becomes rigid in extension, the "tonic" phase. Classically, the patient undergoes a "clonic" phase in which rhythmic contraction and extension of the extremities occurs and the patient thrashes about uncontrollably and can sustain injury. The patient then enters a postictal, somnolent phase and may sleep for variable periods of time, sometimes hours. During the tonic and clonic phase the patient may bite his tongue, and a protective bite block, a gauze roll, or even a towel or washcloth placed between the teeth may be useful. The patient may appear cyanotic, and occasionally excess saliva appears as a frothing of the mouth.

Treatment of Grand Mal Seizure

1. Protect the patient from injury. This may include gently restraining the patient in the dental chair or on the floor. It will include protecting the tongue from injury during the active tonic and clonic phases with an appropriate bite block or other device (Fig. 8–6).
2. Oxygen administration may decrease central nervous system ischemia and reduce the partial neuronal death which accompanies every grand mal seizure to some extent (Fig. 8–7).
3. Intravenous diazepam (Valium) 5 to 10 mg may be given if the clinician is equipped to administer medications by this route and is able to treat any respiratory depression that could result.

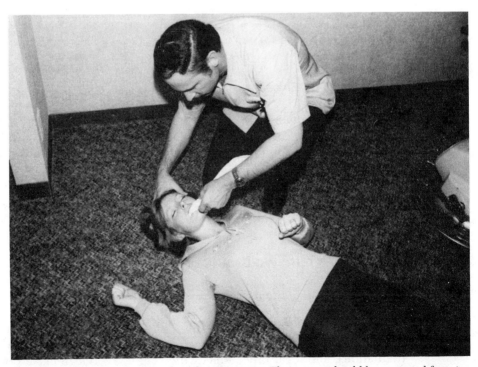

Figure 8–6 Patient on the floor during seizure. The tongue should be protected from injury by teeth with the use of a mouth prop. In this illustration, a tightly rolled cloth towel is employed.

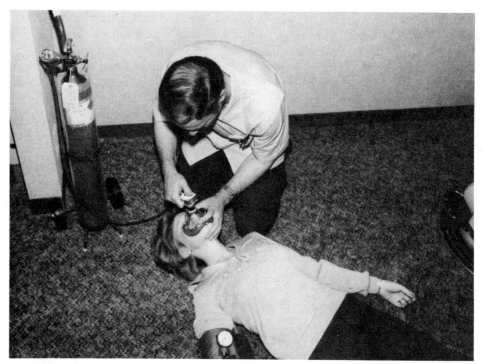

Figure 8–7   Patient on the floor with the airway supported and oxygen being administered through a full face mask.

4.   Hospitalization may be indicated. It is suggested that you seek medical advice following the seizure.

OTHER TYPES OF EPILEPSY

There are numerous other types of seizure disorders which may occur. Petit mal disorders, or small seizures involving transient loss of consciousness or awareness of surroundings, are common and may actually go unrecognized. Focal, or jacksonian, seizures involving a single limb may occur during dental treatment. Patients with these disorders do not require emergency medical management, although it is important that the practitioner recognize these problems and refer the patient for proper management when required.

MANAGEMENT IN PREGNANCY

Treating the pregnant woman with dental disease can be extremely difficult. The dental problem itself is usually straightforward, complicated by temporarily altered physiology. Superimposed on this modestly more complicated circumstance is a group of factors, popular superstitions, governmental regulations, and legal precedents which collectively can make dental care of the pregnant female a harrowing experience.

Pregnancy is not a disease state. The condition normally persists for 10 lunar or nine calendar months. Nine of 10 pregnancies conclude successfully with the birth of a healthy offspring. For many reasons, approximately one of 10 pregnancies does not conclude successfully. Medications, maternal pathology, and other environmental factors can affect the developing fetus unfavorably.

The treating clinician must first assess the dental complaint. Is the problem one which requires definitive treatment immediately to protect or restore the patient's well being? What will the result of not treating the patient be? Can temporary treatment be undertaken and definitive therapy completed after delivery of the child?

Secondly, the practitioner must assess maternal health. Is the mother basically healthy? Is this a normal pregnancy uncomplicated by threatened abortion or other pathological processes which could result in fetal damage whether or not dental treatment is undertaken? Is this an unusually valuable pregnancy? I define an unusually valuable pregnancy as one occurring for the first time in a woman who has been attempting to achieve pregnancy for more than three years and who has finally developed this desired condition.

Having obtained favorable answers to the basic questions relating to the magnitude of the dental disease and the actual state of the pregnancy, I then want to assess the intangible factors which may cause the biggest problem in patient management.

Does the patient understand the facts of her pregnancy? Is she unusually fearful of the effects of anesthetic agents on the fetus? Has she been misinformed as to the effects of her dental disease on fetal development? Is she unusually apprehensive about the effects of dental treatment on the fetus?

If the patient has a significant dental complaint, such as a painful, abscessed tooth which requires extraction, and has an uncomplicated pregnancy and no unusual superstitions or anxieties which militate against treatment, I manage the patient exactly as I manage any other, non-pregnant woman.

Generally, a pregnant woman beyond the first trimester of pregnancy who has no history of previous abortions and who currently has no complications of pregnancy (spotting or cramping), can undergo needed dental treatment without the dental practitioner being open to criticism. Problems in management arise when the clinician finds himself or herself in a position to be criticized by the patient, her family, her physician, or her attorney if the pregnancy is unsuccessful and the dental treatment can be implicated, which it invariably can, since such a complaint is rarely based upon either facts or reason.

The medications commonly used in dentistry such as local analgesics, narcotics, barbiturates, and antibiotics do not produce problems in the developing fetus if used in reasonable therapeutic amounts for the short periods usually necessary to accomplish the goals of dental therapy.

Package inserts must indicate that safe use of a particular medication has not been established unless carefully controlled studies have proved that a particular drug has no effect on the developing fetus. Since these experiments have frequently not been done, an appropriate warning to that effect is included in the package insert. Food and Drug Administration regulations, coupled with a tremendous glut of eager professional liability attorneys, place the practitioner in a precarious position. Much anguish and harm has been visited upon patients and health practitioners by extrapolating animal experimentation to the human experience. One example of such fuzzy thinking is yogurt-induced cataracts in rats. Rats on a 100 per cent yogurt diet develop cataracts because they cannot tolerate galactose, which makes up 1.5 to 2 per cent of commercial yogurt. An occasional human cannot metabolize galactose. It has been suggested that a warning label be placed on yogurt containers.

The patient must be apprised of all potential problems and risks before treatment is instituted. It seems prudent to obtain a signed consent for treatment from pregnant patients which spells out the fact that potential risks have been explained prior to any planned dental procedure.

The practitioner should inquire into the patient's attitude about radiographs, medications, antibiotics, and regional or general anesthetics before embarking on a course of treatment. The patient who requests extraction of a difficult tooth, but who refuses radiographic study or antibiotic administration, places the clinician in a compromised position should these agents be required.

Generally, from a professional liability defense posture, elective dental procedures should be deferred until the patient delivers. If the practitioner and patient mutually decide to undertake an elective procedure, the treatment should be performed during the second trimester of pregnancy.

In summary, I would say that this area of dental practice can be successfully managed if the dental practitioner carefully evaluates the patient and her family's attitudes toward dental care. The patient should make the decision as to whether a procedure should be undertaken. If the doctor perceives that the patient may not be willing to accept all of the necessary aspects of the procedure, such as radiographic studies and/or antibiotic therapy, these facts should be carefully discussed and documented on the record, and it might be wise to refuse treatment. The patient cannot give up her rights to legal redress by agreeing to care which the practitioner feels is substandard.

Further views on the perplexing problem of management in pregnancy are given in Chapter 5.

COMMENT

Laryngeal, bronchial, and esophageal foreign bodies are reviewed in Chapter 2; the Heimlich maneuver is presented in Chapter 12, while cricothyrotomy is covered also in Chapter 12. Allergic manifestations are reviewed in Chapter 7, with emphasis upon anaphylactic shock and surgical shock. Chapter 6 is devoted primarily to basic life support, while Chapter 9 covers cardiopulmonary resuscitation in depth.

Certain other diseases are not covered in this chapter because the possibility of an attendant life-threatening emergency in the dental office is so remote. For example, a sickle cell crisis or polycythemia vera CVA will be treated symptomatically until the patient is transported to the hospital. Good judgment, a calm attitude, and judicious utilization of oxygen will help the practitioner to hold the fort until the patient can be moved. The reader is reminded to refrain from administering 100 per cent oxygen to the emphysema patient with rest dyspnea.

SUGGESTED READING

1. Cahill, G. F.: Diabetes mellitus. *In* Beeson, P. B., and McDermott, W. (eds.): Textbook of Medicine. 14th ed., Philadelphia, W. B. Saunders Co., 1975, Chap. 806, pp. 1599–1618.
2. Crevasse, L.: Congestive heart failure. *In* Conn, H. F. (ed.): Current Therapy 1977. Philadelphia, W. B. Saunders Co., pp. 197–201.
3. Dack, S., Acute myocardial infarction. *In* Conn, H. F. (ed.): Current Therapy 1977. Philadelphia, W. B. Saunders Co., 1977, pp. 221–226.
4. Earp, H. S., and Ney, R. L.: Adrenal insufficiency. *In* Conn, H. F. (ed.): Current Therapy. Philadelphia, W. B. Saunders Co., 1977, pp. 487–488.
5. Forcheimer, L. L.: Yogurt induced cataracts in rats, J.A.M.A., *217*:1113, 1971.
6. Glasser, G. H.: The epilepsies. *In* Beeson, P. B., and McDermott, W. (eds.): Textbook of Medicine. 14th ed., Philadelphia, W. B. Saunders, 1975, Section 16, pp. 723–743.
7. Heyman, A.: Syncope. *In* Beeson, P. B., and McDermott, W. (eds.): Textbook of Medicine. 14th ed., Philadelphia, W. B. Saunders, 1975, Chap. 353, pp. 626–629.
8. Innes, I. R., and Nickerson, M.: Norepinephrine, epinephrine and the sympathomimetic amines. *In* Goodman, L. S., and Gilman, A. (eds.): The Pharmacological Basis of Therapeutics. 5th ed., New York, Macmillan, 1975, Chapter 24, pp. 477–511.
9. Lyon, L. Z., and Wishan, M. S.: Management in pregnancy. *In* McCarthy, F. M. (ed.): Emergencies in Dental Practice. 2nd ed., Philadelphia, W. B. Saunders Co., 1972, pp. 487–488.
11. Skelton, C. L.: Angina pectoris. *In* Conn, H. F. (ed.): Current Therapy 1977. Philadelphia, W. B. Saunders Co., 1977, pp. 168–172.
10. Ojemann, R. G.: Intracerebral and intracerebellar hemorrhage. *In* Youmanns, J. R. (ed.): Neurological Surgery. Philadelphia, W. B. Saunders Co., 1973, Vol. 2, Chap. 38, pp. 844–851.
11. Skelton, C. L.: Angina pectoris. *In* Conn, H. F. (ed.): Current Therapy 1977. Philadelphia, W. B. Saunders Co., 1977, pp. 168–172.
12. Thompson, P. L., and Lown, B.: Nitrous oxide as an analgesic in acute myocardial infarction. J.A.M.A., *235*:924–927, 1976.

9

CARDIOPULMONARY ARREST

THOMAS W. QUINN

INTRODUCTION

Cardiac arrest can occur in the dental office. It is imperative that *all* dental practitioners and their assistants be familiar with the emergency measures associated with cardiopulmonary resuscitation. This chapter will review the proper management of cardiac arrest in the office.

For the clinician who does not utilize the intravenous route, basic life support is in order. For those practitioners who administer intravenous agents for sedation or general anesthesia, a program of advanced life support will be outlined.

DIAGNOSIS OF CARDIAC ARREST

When a patient collapses in the dental office, emergency resuscitative efforts must be instituted immediately. It is mandatory to differentiate between cardiac arrest and other forms of the unconscious state, such as vasodepressor syncope (common faint) or profound hypotension.

The patient who is in a state of cardiac arrest has an ashen-gray appearance. The skin is cold and clammy, and there is an absence of pulsation in the large arteries. There is also an absence of heart sounds and respiration. Observation of the eyes later in the arrest indicates that the eyes are fixed with pupils dilated. The signs of cardiac arrest can appear when the heart is in complete standstill (asystole), when the heart is in ventricular fibrillation, or when the heart rate is so slow and ineffective that there is inadequate perfusion of vital organs.

BASIC LIFE SUPPORT

Basic life support is an emergency first aid procedure that consists of recognizing respiratory and cardiac arrest and starting the proper application of cardiopulmonary resuscitation. The basic life support procedure maintains life until the victim recovers sufficiently to be transported or until advanced life support is available. The ABC steps of cardiopulmonary resuscitation refer to the following: A= airway, B = breathing, C = circulation.

Because of the extreme importance of the ABC's of basic life support, there will be some duplication of material on airway management, artificial ventilation, and oxygen therapy which has been presented in Chapter 6. The reader is invited to review that section at this time.

AIRWAY AND BREATHING

When respiratory arrest occurs, gas exchange between the blood stream and lungs ceases. This produces an immediate accumulation of carbon dioxide, resulting in respiratory acidosis. The lack of oxygen and tissue hypoxia leads to anaerobic metabolism and lactic acidosis (i.e., metabolic acidosis). At the same time the body responds with increased sympathetic nervous system activity which results in an increase in the pulse rate, peripheral vasoconstriction, and restlessness. Hypoxia and acidosis depress the heart, reducing cardiac output, and eventually produce cardiac dysrhythmias which can lead to cardiac arrest.

The dental chair should be positioned so that the patient is supine with the feet slightly elevated. It is recommended that an emergency oxygen source that has been regularly checked be available in all offices. Also there should be an oral airway and a full face mask available to administer oxygen under positive pressure. A mask attached to a self-inflating reservoir bag, intermittently compressed by hand, is also acceptable. No time should be lost in assisting respiration. The clinician or assistant should immediately initiate ventilation of the lungs by the mouth-to-mouth technique. It is imperative to elevate the mandible, thereby drawing the tongue away from the posterior pharyngeal wall to provide a patent airway. A solid obstruction of the airway may be dislodged by a forceful thrust upward into the epigastrium, as in the Heimlich maneuver, which is described in Chapter 12.

If vomiting has occurred, it is necessary to remove the vomitus by placing the patient's head to one side and by using fingers, gauze and suction, drawing out all foreign material in the oropharynx. Following removal of the vomitus, adequate ventilation can be carried out.

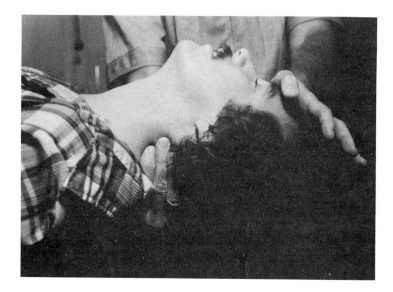

Figure 9–1 The head in a position of maximum backward tilt.

Mouth-to-Mouth Ventilation

The practitioner or assistant responsible for respiratory assistance places one hand behind the patient's neck to maintain the head in a position of maximum backward tilt (Fig. 9–1). The patient's nostrils are pinched together with the thumb and index finger while pressure is exerted on the forehead to maintain the backward tilt (Fig. 9–2). The patient's mouth is opened as widely as possible, the resuscitator takes a deep breath, makes a tight seal with the lips around the patient's mouth, and then blows

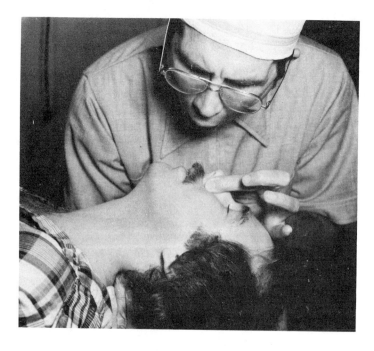

Figure 9–2 The nostrils are pinched together while pressure is exerted on the forehead to maintain maximum backward tilt.

into the patient's mouth. The patient is allowed to exhale passively. Observation of the chest to determine adequate respiratory movement is essential.

In some cases mouth-to-nose ventilation is more effective than mouth-to-mouth ventilation. Mouth-to-nose ventilation is recommended for the small child or in those cases where it is impossible to ventilate the patient through the mouth.

Resuscitation with Positive Pressure Oxygen

Oropharyngeal Airway. When an oxygen source is available, an oral airway should be inserted and a tight-fitting, full face mask applied. The oropharyngeal airway is a semicircular-shaped apparatus made of plastic or rubber. It is curved to fit over the back of the tongue, and in this position it will hold the tongue away from the pharynx. It is more easily inserted into the mouth upside down. As the airway approaches the posterior wall of the pharynx near the back of the tongue, it should be rotated into its proper position. If the oropharyngeal airway is not inserted properly, it is possible to push the tongue posteriorly, thus obstructing the airway. Proper head position must be maintained even with the use of a properly positioned airway.

One hundred per cent oxygen is administered to the patient, whose head is in the same backward tilt position with the mandible forward. Observation of the thoracic cage to determine effective ventilation is mandatory. A clear, full face mask to observe the presence of vomitus is recommended. As mentioned previously, a resuscitator bag with atmospheric air as the inflating gas, or attached to an oxygen source, can also be utilized.

Esophageal Airway. Another method of ventilating the patient is with an esophageal airway. The esophageal airway is a tube approximately 15 inches long which is open at the top and has a blind end at the bottom. The lower end is inserted into the esophagus. An inflatable cuff is located just above the blind end. There are several side holes located near the upper end which allow air from the interior of the tube to enter the pharynx. Pressurized air enters the upper end of the esophageal airway and exits through the side holes in the pharynx. The inflated cuff prevents air from entering the esophagus and allows the air to pass into the trachea, inflating the lungs. See Chapter 6 for further information on the esophageal obturator.

CIRCULATION

As mentioned previously, the mechanisms leading to cardiac arrest are ventricular standstill, ventricular fibrillation, and cardiovascular collapse.

Examples of ventricular standstill in patients undergoing dental treatment are: vagal stimulation with increased parasympathetic activity, drug overdose, or absence of electrical activity in patients with diseases of the conduction system of the heart.

Ventricular fibrillation may be seen in patients with acute myocardial infarction, hypoxia, or digitalis toxicity.

Cardiovascular collapse could occur when there is inadequate mechanical strength of the heart (cardiogenic shock) or inadequate filling of the heart (vasomotor collapse).

In all cases, external cardiac compression is initiated in an attempt to restore cardiac output. Although the cardiac output may be only one fourth or one third that of normal, it can be lifesaving.

Precordial Thump

A sharp blow to the mid-sternum has traditionally been recommended to establish a normal heart beat in cases of ventricular tachycardia, ventricular fibrillation, or heart block of recent onset. It is now questionable as to the value of the precordial thump as one of the initial steps in basic life support.

The precordial thump has been successfully employed to terminate ventricular tachycardia in the monitored patient. However, in studies on experimental animals, no beneficial effects resulted from the precordial thump to correct ventricular fibrillation or asystole. Precordial thumping of an hypoxic myocardium, whether active or in asystole, may produce ventricular fibrillation, a situation that is apparently irreversible in the absence of a defibrillator and is not recommended as a routine procedure on the unmonitored patient.

External Cardiac Compression

The patient is in a supine position in the dental chair. If the chair does not have a firm backrest, it is recommended that a 12″ × 24″ board be placed under the patient's back (Fig. 9–3). *Do not move the patient to the floor!* It is extremely awkward to attempt resuscitation when the patient is on the floor. Most dental operating rooms are small, and the dental chair occupies most of the room. It is much easier to carry out adequate CPR with the patient in the dental chair, provided there is adequate back support.

To effectively carry out external cardiac compression, it is essential that the lower sternum be depressed from 1½ to 2 inches. The individual responsible for cardiac compression is positioned on the side of the patient and places the heel of one hand over the lower half of the sternum. To determine the exact position, it is essential to palpate the xiphoid process and then advance the heel of the hand superiorly about 1½ inches. The other hand is now placed on top of the first one; the shoulders are directed over the patient's sternum. The arms remain straight, and a downward vertical pressure is exerted to compress the sternum 1½ to 2 inches. The compressions are continuous, regular, and at a rate of approximately 60 to 80 per minute. The heel of the first hand should remain in contact with the chest wall during relaxation when the sternum returns to a normal resting position between compressions.

After each 5 compressions of the sternum, one breath of air by mouth-to-mouth or oxygen under positive pressure is administered. If the practitioner or assistant is alone when cardiac arrest occurs, the following outline is suggested:

One-Person Resuscitation

Artificial ventilation and compression must be accomplished utilizing a 15 to 2 ratio. This consists of two quick lung inflations followed by 15 chest compressions. The two full lung inflations must be delivered in rapid succession within a period of five or six seconds, without allowing full exhalation between the breaths. If the time for full exhalation were allowed, the additional time required would reduce the number of compressions and ventilations that could be achieved in a one-minute period.

Infants and Children

The cardiac compression technique is similar for children (ages two to 10 years) except that only the pressure of the heel of one hand is required. The ventricles of small children lie higher in the chest, and external pressure should be exerted over the mid-sternum. Young children require 3/4 to 1½ inch compression of the sternum. The compression rate should be 80 to 100 per minute with breaths delivered as quickly as possible after each five compressions.

EMERGENCY SERVICES

It is important that at the time of any cardiovascular collapse, the following be adhered to:

1. The time of collapse must be recorded and an emergency flow chart activated. This flow chart is a modified form of a CPR chart that can be used in the dental office (Fig. 9–10).

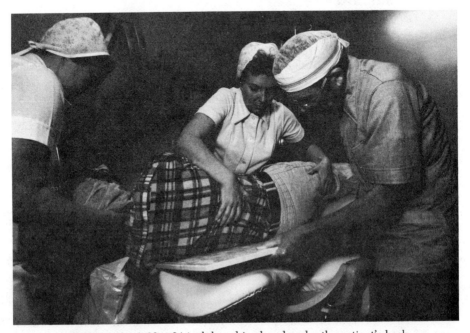

Figure 9–3 A 12 × 24 inch board is placed under the patient's back.

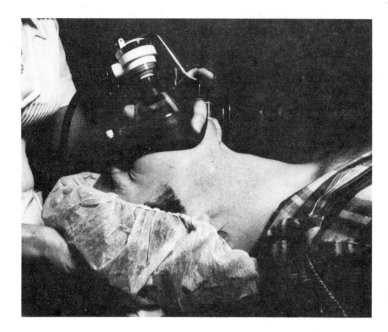

Figure 9–4 A clear, full face mask with oral airway is applied to administer positive pressure oxygen.

2. An emergency ambulance service with appropriate CPR equipment and qualified personnel should be called immediately. The emergency room of a local hospital should be instructed that a patient who has collapsed is being transported to the emergency room for immediate care.

ADVANCED LIFE SUPPORT IN THE OFFICE SETTING

The following is an outline for advanced life support prior to transportation to a hospital.

In the offices of those practitioners who utilize IV sedation or general anesthesia, an intravenous line is standard procedure. If a catastrophe should occur under local analgesia, or in cases where an IV is not in place, it is important that an intravenous line be established if possible; this should not interfere with cardiac compression and ventilation. A continuous drip of 5 per cent dextrose in water or lactated Ringer's should be administered. If the patient can be adequately ventilated by means of a full face mask with oral airway, there is no need for endotracheal intubation (Fig. 9–4). If this method does not provide adequate respiratory exchange, then endotracheal intubation is recommended. The endotracheal tube should be attached to a non-rebreathing valve with a source of oxygen supplied for resuscitation.

EMERGENCY DRUGS

Oxygen. Oxygen is considered an essential in resuscitation. An increase in arterial oxygen tension is required; and, therefore, oxygen must

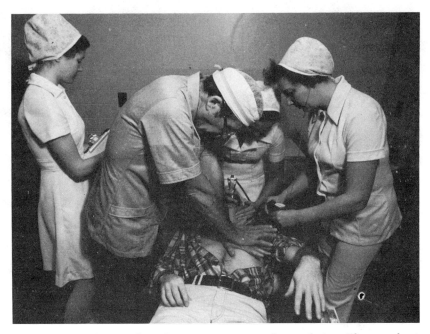

Figure 9–5 External cardiac compression with ventilation. The anesthesia assistant is checking the carotid pulse while the surgical assistant attempts to obtain the blood pressure.

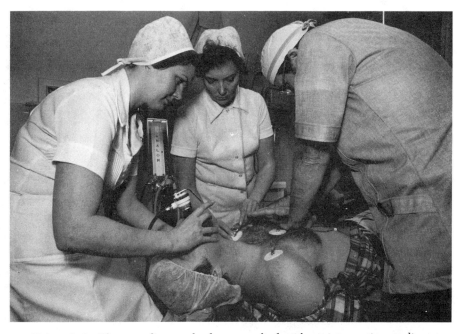

Figure 9–6 Electrocardiogram leads are applied without interrupting cardiac compression and ventilation.

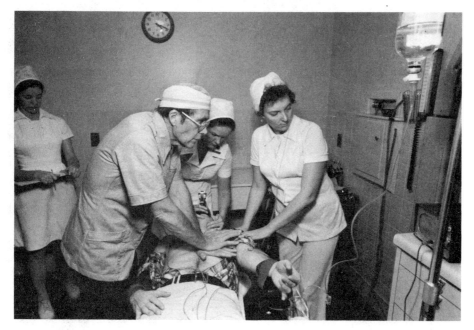

Figure 9–7   The CPR team observing the ECG monitor while the circulating nurse records all necessary information on the emergency flow chart.

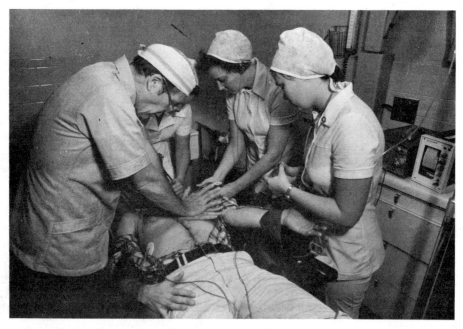

Figure 9–8   Administration of emergency drugs by an assistant under the direction of the leader of the CPR team.

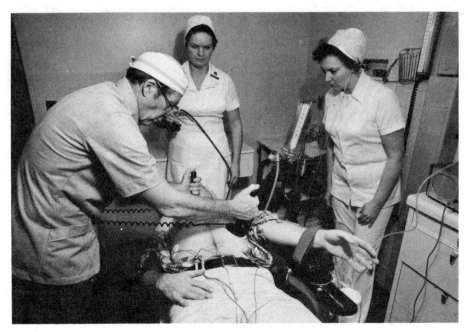

Figure 9–9   Application of defibrillator paddles; 4 × 4 inch gauze pads are dampened with saline and placed under the paddles.

be administered in the presence of suspected hypoxemia of any cause and especially in cardiopulmonary arrest.

Na Bicarbonate.   Profound metabolic acidosis occurs within a few minutes in circulatory collapse. To overcome this acidosis, 44.5 mEq of sodium bicarbonate or 1 ampule (50 ml) of the disposable syringe type should be administered intravenously if the heart has not resumed rhythm approximately 30 seconds after arrest. This dose should be repeated every 5 minutes prior to transportation to the hospital. The maintenance of a normal pH renders the myocardium more responsive to circulating and administered catecholamines.

Epinephrine.   Epinephrine is the most effective drug used in cardiopulmonary resuscitation. The immediate intracardiac injection of epinephrine in the dental office is not recommended. This drug should be administered intravenously in dilutions of 1:10,000, approximately 5 ml every 5 minutes.

MONITORING

In offices where general anesthesia is used, an ECG or cardioscope should now be applied in such a way as to not interfere with cardiac compressions or ventilation (Fig. 9–6). The only evidence for effective circulation is a readily palpable carotid or femoral pulse, a satisfactory blood pressure, and reactive pupils. Rhythmic electrical activity alone does not indicate effective circulation. The ECG, however, will allow differentiation between asystole, ventricular fibrillation, or dysrhythmia resulting from ineffectual

Name:_____   Time CPR started:_____
                                       Time ambulance called: _____
Date: _____   Time ambulance arrived: _____
                                       Time hospital called:_____
                                       Time patient left office: _____

TIME

	0	5	10	15	20	25	30	35	40	45	50	55	60			
BP																
Pulse																
Respiration																
EKG																
Pupils																
Epinephrine																
NA Bicarb.																
Lidocaine																
CA Chloride																
Solu-cortef																
Defibrillation																

Comments: _____   Personnel: _____
_____   _____
_____   _____
_____   _____
_____
_____
_____
_____
_____
_____

Figure 9–10   Emergency flow chart.

heart action. If fibrillation is diagnosed, defibrillation should be carried out as soon as possible. In all offices utilizing general anesthesia, a defibrillator should be avaialble.

DEFIBRILLATION

The defibrillator paddles are applied using electrode jelly or preferably 4″ × 4″ gauze pads dampened with saline. One electrode is placed just below the right clavicle at the right sternal border and a second is placed just beyond the cardiac apex below the left breast (Fig. 9–9). The optimum amount of electrical energy for defibrillation of the adult patient is usually in the area of 400 joules, or watt seconds, for cases of ventricular fibrillation. Lower settings are frequently effective in converting ventricular fibrillation and ventricular tachycardia and produce less myocardial damage. The damage resulting from the defibrillator shocks is usually proportional to the energy used; and maximal settings, where not required, may further impair an already damaged myocardium. All monitoring devices attached to an electrical wall outlet should be disconnected prior to defibrillation. All personnel should avoid contact with the patient or chair during defibrillation.

A single defibrillatory shock does not produce serious functional damage to the myocardium, so there is no reason to withhold it in the unconscious, apneic, pulseless adult when a direct-current defibrillator is available, *even though the patient is unmonitored.* In these circumstances, unmonitored defibrillation with a single shock may be performed by the practitioner or assistant; but it is emphasized that this single shock must not delay the prompt application of basic life support measures in any way. Unmonitored defibrillation is not recommended for children.

In cases where there is an apparent cardiac arrest secondary to prolonged anoxia or drug overdose, CPR for a period of two minutes or more is recommended with re-evaluation prior to the delivery of an unmonitored defibrillator shock.

ADJUNCTIVE DRUGS

Atropine. Atropine sulfate is a parasympatholytic drug which reduces vagal tone and thereby accelerates the rate of discharge of the SA node. It may also improve atrioventricular conduction by this vagolytic action. It is useful in treating severe bradycardia with hypotension. Dosage is 0.5 mg intravenously every 5 minutes until the desired rate of around 60 beats per min is achieved. The total dose should not exceed 2.0 mg.

Lidocaine. Lidocaine is used to reduce the irritability of the myocardium. Fifty to 100 mg of lidocaine is administered intravenously and may be repeated every 5 minutes. This is useful to control multifocal, premature beats and episodes of ventricular tachycardia.

Calcium Chloride (Adults Only). Calcium chloride is a cardiotonic stimulant that is given slowly by the intravenous route, and this drug is used to increase the amplitude of organized electrical complexes on the ECG. The usual recommended dose of calcium chloride is 2.5 ml to 5 ml of a 10 per cent solution. This is injected intravenously as a bolus at intervals of 10 minutes. Calcium gluconate provides less ionizable calcium per unit value. Large doses of calcium may elevate calcium blood levels with detrimental effects. Calcium must not be administered together with sodium bicarbonate, since this mixture results in the formation of a precipitate.

TRANSPORTATION TO HOSPITAL

Other vasoactive compounds plus diuretics and steroids can be administered when the patient has been transferred to a local hospital. Monitoring of urine output, central venous pressure, blood gases, and electrolytes is more effectively carried on in this type of advanced care facility.

The practitioner should always accompany the patient to the hospital, and the new life support team should be informed as to the type and amount of emergency drugs that have been administered.

TERMINATION OF BASIC OR ADVANCED LIFE SUPPORT

The decision to terminate resuscitative efforts depends upon the assessment of the cerebral and cardiovascular status of the patient. It is important to continue CPR procedures until the patient is transported to a hospital setting where a final decision is made to continue with the CPR treatment or to terminate resuscitative efforts.

SUMMARY

It is important to recognize that a cardiac emergency in the dental office presents a serious problem that requires immediate resuscitative efforts in an attempt to restore adequate, spontaneous circulation. This includes basic life support with utilization of the fundamental ABC's of resuscitation, alerting a nearby hosptial or advanced life support unit, and arranging transportation of the patient to this facility as rapidly as possible. When advanced life support is carried out in the dental office, there should be a greater chance for success because of the introduction of essential drugs as well as adequate cardiopulmonary resuscitative efforts. Monitoring of cardiac rhythms is also an advantage to enable the practitioner to determine which emergency drugs are essential. The utilization of defibrillators to reverse ventricular fibrillation should increase the chance of survival. Even though advanced life support procedures are carried out in the dental office, it is also imperative that a local hospital be advised that a patient has collapsed in the office and cardiopulmonary resuscitative efforts are being carried out; and the patient should be transferred to the intensive care unit immediately.

SUGGESTED READING

1. Dripps, R. D., Eckenhoff, J. E., and Vandam, L. D.: Introduction to Anesthesia. Philadelphia, W. B. Saunders Co., 1977.
2. Heimlich, H. J.: A life-saving maneuver to prevent food choking. J.A.M.A., 234:398, 1975.
3. Pennington, J. E., Taylor, J. and Lown, B.: Chest thump for reverting ventricular tachycardia. N. Engl. J. Med., 283:1192–1195, 1970.
4. Sprone, C. W., and Mullanney, P. J. (eds.): Emergency Care: Assessment and Intervention. St. Louis, C. V. Mosby Co., 1974.
5. Standards for cardiopulmonary resuscitation (CPR) and emergency cardiac care (ECC). J.A.M.A., 227:833–868, 1974.
6. Yakaitis, R. W., and Redding, J. S.: Precordial thumping during cardiac resuscitation. Crit. Care Med., 1:22–26, 1973.

10

COMPLICATIONS FROM LOCAL ANALGESIA

JESS HAYDEN, JR.

and the late

NIELS BJORN JORGENSEN

INTRODUCTION
LOCAL COMPLICATIONS
SYSTEMIC COMPLICATIONS

DISCUSSION
PROPHYLAXIS AND TREATMENT
SUMMARY AND CONCLUSIONS

INTRODUCTION

The purpose of this chapter is to set forth in a classified form and to discuss the complications which may accompany or follow the injection of local analgesic solutions.* The classification is that of the writers, and the discussion relates to our observations made in the course of the clinical practice of dentistry.

The basic format and information in this chapter were prepared in co-operation with the late Niels Bjorn Jorgensen. Over the years of his associa-tion with Loma Linda University's Schools of Medicine and Dentistry, Dr. Jorgensen established a model program for the teaching of local analgesia, and inhalation and intravenous sedation to the candidates for a degree in dentistry. A man of great humility, his teaching nevertheless brought inter-national recognition both to him and to the University he devotedly served. It is a great tribute to his foresight that a majority of the concepts which he pioneered were incorporated in the American Dental Association's "Guide-lines for Teaching the Comprehensive Control of Pain and Anxiety in Den-tistry."[19] The title of one of his films, "The Comfort of the Patient," sig-nified the thrust of his academic and professional achievement. The story of his struggle to realize the goals he envisioned are revealed elsewhere.[21, 24]

In the United States, local analgesia undoubtedly is the most used mo-dality for the control of pain during dental treatment. In fact the use of local analgesia in dentistry has become such a routine procedure that one is

---

*In the United States, the term local anesthesia is generally employed rather than the precise term, local analgesia.

apt to ignore possible hazards in its employment. Although it does appear to be without dangers, local or systemic complications occasionally do happen. These complications have been classified below as: I. Local, and II. Systemic.

A more extensive bibliography is readily available in *Accepted Dental Therapeutics*,[1] which is conveniently divided into sections concerning: (1) the general principles of medication, including emergency treatment and sterilization; (2) therapeutic agents, which includes suggestions for certain clinical problems; (3) preventive agents; and (4) indexes.

LOCAL COMPLICATIONS

A. *Bacterial contamination* occurs when a needle tip inadvertently touches any tissue or object without the oral cavity, usually the clinician's or assistant's finger or the patient's lip. If the needle is used for deep injections, a serious infection may result. Bacterial contamination always occurs when the needle touches the mucous membrane in a relatively dirty mouth.

Since all mouths contain myriad bacteria, and it is not feasible to assess the patient's (host's) resistance to these, a routine preparation of the tissues should precede each injection. Such a preparation is described in connection with the inferior alveolar injection. Aerosols from the area of treatment are spread some distance from the oral cavity, depending on the techniques of dentistry employed and the immediate physical environment. Therefore, a routine must be established to insure the continued sterility of needles, syringes and cartridges, and ampules or vials of local analgesics. For instance, in the Pediatric Dental Clinic, Dental Science Building of the University of Iowa, random samples, which were then cultured, revealed that on the average, one out of 10 diaphragms of local analgesic cartridges were contaminated. For test purposes, the cartridges were left in their original container, with the lid removed, sitting on the operatory bench. Thereafter, immediately before insertion into a cartridge syringe, the diaphragm of each cartridge was swabbed with merthiolate and rubbed dry with a sterile gauge 2 × 2 sponge. The usual sequela of contamination is a low-grade infection, whether confined to the area of the attached periodontal tissues, or deeply situated in the pterygomandibular space. Improper techniques of sterilizing and storing needles or methods of handling by the assistant or doctor lead to varying degrees of contamination.[2] *Chemical deposits* on the needle are due to sterilizing solutions, or perhaps to chemical vapor sterilization. Inflammation and pain are frequent after-effects.

B. *Local reactions to topical or injected solutions* are usually seen as *epithelial desquamation* following the application of topical analgesics. Such desquamation usually results from too long an application of the topical analgesic, but may be due to a heightened sensitivity of the tissue. All local analgesics are toxic. The after-effects usually are transitory. *Sterile abscesses* or gangrene may result owing to ischemia resulting from injecting an excess of analgesic solution, with its contained vasoconstrictor, into the firm, hard tissue of the palate. *Local allergic reactions,* such as blisters on the oral mucosa or lips, are to be considered as a sign of warning, and further use of the causative agents should be accompanied with suitable precautions and a change to a local analgesic of different chemical structure.[2] Emphatically, clinicians are not immune to contact dermatitis. *Trismus and pain* follow the injection of solutions into muscles and tendons, and they are among the variety of local tissue changes produced by local analgesics. Much of the soreness frequently attributed to post-surgical operative causes is simply the result of improper administration of solutions.

The anatomical structures basic to local analgesia were incorporated into clinical textbooks shortly after the discovery of the benefits of local analgesia. As Allen[25] in his foreword wrote, "There is no substitute for the correctly placed needle tip for achieving local anesthesia". Improper placement in one instance led to a patient's inability to open the mouth following a mandibular (inferior alveolar?) block and resulted in a $75,000 award to the patient.[29] A further complication, similarly related in some instances to failure to adhere to principles of injection based on morphology, is post-injection anesthesia, *paresthesia* and/or *neuritis* caused by the needle's penetrating the nerve.[18, 39] Steiner and Thompson[37] (p. 511–512), as additional sequelae of "repeated and inaccurate plunging of the needle into a helpless patient," list: exhausted buffering capacity, myositis, hemorrhage with hematoma or ecchymosis, fibrosis, and edema.

C. *Breakage of needles* is seldom a problem. Needles available today possess physical qualities which should prevent such a mishap. When breakage does occur, it usually is the result of the needle's impaling muscular tissue or passing beneath the periosteum and being snapped off during sudden closure of the mouth. Kennett, Curran, and Jenkins[27] describe such needle breakage in a five year old. The needle was a "short 27 gauge." Although many advocate short 27 gauge needles as being less painful, and have not experienced needle breakage, reason would appear to dictate the use of long hubs and long needles for deep injections.

D. *Lip-chewing* is a complication caused by the use of long-acting local analgesics for children. The after-effects can be most unpleasant for the child, his parents, and the practitioner. Many clinicians routinely employ long-acting analgesics in order to obtain profundity of effect. The child should always be premedicated prior to the injection if dismissal from the dental office long precedes the dissipation of the analgesic action. For brief appointments, the use of short-acting solutions for block analgesia should be routine. Even so, a cotton roll should be placed between the lips, or tied in the vestibule by means of dental floss or sutures passed through the dental embrasures if analgesia exists at the time of dismissal. Verbal warnings should be given to the child or accompanying adult, but may be futile if not reinforced by the cotton roll. A small, oval, self-adhesive, red luminescent sticker warning "WATCH ME PLEASE, MY LIPS AND CHEEK ARE NUMB" may be affixed to the child's forehead. *

E. *Emphysema uncommonly occurs after an injection.*[44] An example is that of a 10-year-old boy who received an inferior alveolar injection. Within two hours of his dismissal, he returned to the office exhibiting homolateral swelling and crepitation in the anterior triangle of the neck and the face.

---

*Professional Education Products, 8519 North 48th St., Omaha, Nebraska 68152.

His consulting pediatrician shared the amazement at this dental treatment sequela, and prescribed antihistaminics on the basis of a possible allergic response. Questioning revealed that the boy had been blowing up balloons immediately after his dental treatment. The manner in which the symptoms subsided suggested that air in the fascial planes, rather than allergy, was the cause.

F. *The trauma of injection* comprises the vast majority of local complications. Reactions from the supraperiosteal technique generally are minor, consisting of edema, after-pain, and sometimes slight ulceration of the puncture point. The former are due to infection, too rapid injection, or injecting too large a volume; the latter is due to an infection. The unpleasantness generally passes in a few days. Hematomas may result from nicking an artery. Usually the effects are seen in connection with the posterior superior alveolar artery, and less commonly the facial. Obviously, any of these local complications can result in swelling and pain. Two common techniques of administration often cause pain, the first because of lack of skill of administration; the second is irrevocably tied to morphology and physiology: the complications from palatine injections are mostly immediate pain from the needle insertion; subperiosteal injections may result in lifting the periosteum from the bone, causing after-pain and even infection. From a physiologic standpoint, this injection probably is contraindicated.

The use of long beveled, thin, pointed disposable needles predisposes to hematomas and trismus, for arteries, nerve trunks, and muscles or tendons are easily penetrated with these much too flexible instruments.

G. *Bleeding due to hemophilia* or anticoagulant therapy is always a hazard. The first is readily recognized by both the patient and clinician. The latter is much more prevalent, but is not as well recognized. It is a particular danger when deep block injections are required for the relief of pain in an active ambulatory patient. See the chapter on *physical evaluation* for further information on handling of the anticoagulant-treated patient.

SYSTEMIC COMPLICATIONS

A. *Allergic reactions* are extremely uncommon. *Anaphylaxis* presents the gravest challenge, for the opportunity to render support to the patient is so fleeting that death usually results. Fortunately, anaphylactic shock is known by the rarity of its response to analgesic solutions. *Skin eruptions* occasionally may be a manifestation of allergy. Methylparaben, a preservative in many local analgesics, may cause an allergic or hypersensitivity reaction.[14, 28] See the chapter on *emergency drugs and allergy* for more information on anaphylactoid and toxic reactions.

B. *Toxic reactions* are expressed systemically if too large an amount of an analgesic drug is absorbed too rapidly into the system. Shane, et al.[34] reported that 12 cartidges of 2 per cent lidocaine with epinephrine 1:100,000 were injected into a four year old child. The child became lethargic and required artificial ventilation with oxygen for 55 minutes before recovering. We know of other instances in which the death of a child ensued and local analgesia toxicity was evident. (The recommended dose of an amide local analgesic with vasoconstrictor is approximately 7 mg per kg, or 3 mg per lb. It is incumbent in the administration of a local analgesic to be familiar with the doses recommended by the manufacturer.) Absorption is increased when too much solution is injected too rapidly into the highly vascular circumoral tissues. Further, "If a doctor accidentally injects a cartridge of procaine intravenously over a period of five seconds, the rate is fifteen times that which is considered safe, or over two hundred times more toxic."[2] It is noteworthy that all the amide local analgesics, used in the same concentration as procaine, are more toxic than procaine. Further, two reactions may simultaneously occur, those caused by (1) the local analgesic and (2) the vasoconstrictor. Adriani and Campbell[3] reported that spray or paste topical analgesics may simulate the effect of intravenous injection. Spray products apparently are no more effective in producing analgesia than those applied with a swab; but sprays do have several disadvantages which may introduce unnecessary hazard in their use.[2] In any case, the toxic reaction sequence may take the form of stimulation, convulsions, and depression.

In addition, the report of Allen and co-workers[4] indicates that the amount of epinephrine 1:100,000 in a 1.8 ml cartridge is sufficient to affect the heart's stroke volume. Epinephrine effects are directly dose related and care should be taken to inject minimal quantities.

C. *Psychic reactions* are exhibited by most patients, but clinicians usually notice only those signs which immediately precede *syncope*. Certainly catecholamine levels are elevated in the very anxious or phobic patient.[15] Fortunately, first-aid procedures for syncope are so ingrained into most people, and the recuperative powers of the body are such that shock seldom ensues.

Acute asthmatic attacks may follow the administration of a local analgesic. Such attacks are considered to be due to allergy or emotional stress.

D. *Viral Hepatitis.* From our reading of the literature and consultation with dental and medical doctors, it presently appears that viral hepatitis is caused by at least two immunologically distinct infectious agents: virus A, the etiologic agent of infectious, epidemic, or short incubation hepatitis (HA), and virus B, which is responsible for serum hepatitis, or long-term incubation hepatitis (HB). In the case of acute viral hepatitis it may be impossible to make a specific diagnosis, and it is therefore designated type unspecified. Several other viral agents are now being classified as "non-A, non-B" if the distinction can be made.

The prevalence of hepatitis A (HAV) is decreasing, while that of hepatitis B (HBV) is increasing. Virus B (HBV) is of the greatest concern to the staff of a dental office. The "carrier" rate in the United States among the general population is about 0.5 per cent. Among health care workers it is 1 to 2 per cent. It is estimated that general dental practitioners have two to four times the risk of acquiring type B hepatitis than do persons not in the health care professions. The risk is higher among oral surgeons. In the United Kingdom, the "carrier" rate of the hepatitis B surface antigen (HB_sAg) ranges from 1 in 500 to 1000 among Europeans to as high as 1 in 5 for Afro-Asians. The "carrier" state occurs after some 5 to 10 per cent of acute infections. The groups that pose the highest risk of transmitting HBV when they present to the dental practitioner for treatment are: those undergoing chronic renal hemodialysis; the mentally retarded and institutionalized, particularly those with Down's syndrome; leukemics (and some other dyscrasias); individuals treated with radiation and immunosuppressives; hemophiliacs or others who receive large volumes of blood or its derivatives, or those transfused with blood from paid donors; drug addicts, particularly those who share syringes for parenteral inoculation of illicit drugs; male homosexuals and prostitutes; the tattooed; and individuals who have been transfused in or recently returned from countries with a high background prevalence of hepatitis B. The list is not exhaustive. Perhaps the greatest cause of exposure to HBV for the clinician and staff is puncture of the skin with contaminated instruments. The risk of developing hepatitis B after an accidental puncture by a hepatitis B contaminated needle is 6 to 7 per cent.

It now appears that "carriers" of type B hepatitis do not present as great a risk to casual contacts as was believed in the late 1960's. Nevertheless, for the practitioner or staff member who acquires hepatitis B, the result is 100 per cent. Therefore, care should be taken to minimize exposure. There is a voluminous literature concerning hepatitis A and B. For an informative survey related to dental practice see the recommendations in the reports and publications of the American Dental Association's Council on Dental Therapeutics, the Dental Health Committee of the British Dental Association, and the report of surveys by Mosley and White.[5, 10, 31]

DISCUSSION

To better illustrate what may happen during the deep injection of local analgesic solution, the path of the needle during deep injections is described:

A. When administering the *inferior alveolar* injection the mucous membrane at the area of the needle insertion should be wiped clean with sterile gauze, and an antiseptic, such as tincture of merthiolate, applied. If saliva flows copiously at the time of needle insertion, bacteria may be introduced into the deeper structures, and though these may be relatively harmless to the host, low-grade infection and after-pain may result. To prevent this invasion, a roll of sterile gauze should be placed in the upper vestibule blocking the parotid duct, and a second pad of gauze placed underneath the tongue over the salivary caruncula. Bacteria of a more harmful nature also may be introduced by the inadvertent touch of the needle point to any foreign object, such as a finger, the lips, etc. As mentioned before, a serious infection within the pterygomandibular space may result.

1. The path of the needle is through loose areolar tissue. If the needle is inserted or directed too far medially, it will enter the medial pterygoid muscle, resulting in trismus, after-pain, and probably incomplete or no analgesia.

2. If the needle is directed too far laterally, it will penetrate the deep tendon of the temporalis muscle. Trismus and after-pain may be expected. Furthermore, if the needle is continued in this too-lateral path, it will be rammed against the periosteum, and the result will be pain and a reflex action by the patient which may result in needle breakage.

3. If the needle is directed in a path diverging inferiorly from a plane through the coronoid notch, the deepest point of the concavity of the an-

terior border of the ramus, it will have to penetrate the sphenomandibular ligament, which covers the mandibular sulcus. If the entire bevel of the needle is not lateral to the sphenomandibular ligament, solution is deposited along its medial aspect, and incomplete anesthesia is the result.

The inferior alveolar nerve or the lingual nerve may be traumatized by the needle. These nerves, if accidentally rammed by the needle, do not slide away, as is generally supposed, since they are both attached firmly to the interpterygoid fascia, a structure which continues forward from the anterior border of the sphenomandibular ligament to the lateral pterygoid lamina. As the inferior alveolar nerve runs downward toward the foramen it is attached to the lateral surface of this fascia. The lingual nerve is attached to the medial surface, but farther anteriorly. When the mouth is kept wide open, the interpterygoid fascia is stretched and holds the two nerves quite firmly, as if on a trellis.[25]

To avoid injury to the lingual nerve the needle must be inserted at the proper level, relative to the coronoid notch, kept close to the medial aspect of the deep tendon of the temporalis muscle and lateral to the pterygomandibular raphe. It must be clearly understood that injury of a nerve does not necessarily indicate a fauly approach but may be related to the long, beveled, pointed thin needles which are now in vogue and demand, and which make it impossible to detect and follow necessary anatomical landmarks.

As the needle advances toward the mandibular sulcus, it may easily injure or penetrate the inferior alveolar nerve. To avoid this, the needle should enter the sulcus over the lingular notch; it should touch the periosteum just before reaching the notch, and then slide gently over this saddle-like bony surface into the anterior part of the sulcus. A heavy, rigid needle with a short bevel is required if this is to be easily accomplished. If the lingual and inferior alveolar nerves are injured, paresthesia or post-analgesic neuritis may result. If the needle is advanced posteriorly into the mandibular sulcus, the inferior alveolar artery or vein may be punctured and injected into. The result may be a local hematoma or a systemic toxic reaction from the injected drug. This can be avoided by confining the needle tip to the anterior part of the sulcus. Injection into the vessel must be avoided by aspirating before injecting.[23, 25, 35]

B. *The posterior superior alveolar nerve block* is a simple and effective injection that recently has been abondoned by many practitioners because of the frequent occurrence of hematomas. These are due to the characteristics of thin, usually disposable needles (see above). From just distal of the zygomatic process the needle point must be advanced medially, superiorly, and posteriorly along the periosteum toward the foramina located halfway between the upper and lower borders of the maxilla. Here the tuberosity makes a sharp turn medially, and if the needle advances farther the pterygoid venous plexus or the maxillary artery may be punctured. If the syringe and needle are kept in a plane parallel with the sagittal plane, the maxillary artery and/or the lateral pterygoid muscle may be invaded. Obviously, trismus and hematoma are possible complications of this injection if the needle deviates from the proper path, and it will with a thin flexible needle. Only with a heavy rigid needle with a short bevel can the correct anatomical pathway routinely be followed, as with a probe.

C. When the *maxillary nerve* block is administered through the pterygopalatine canal, care must be exercised that the needle does not penetrate the thin medial wall of the canal and enter the nasal cavity. Not only will there be no anesthesia, but infection also may result. When directed laterally, the needle and solution may through the pterygomaxillary fissure enter the infratemporal space and the pterygoid muscle. Trismus will result. If the needle is in the correct path but advanced too far, the orbital cavity may be entered. Solution injected here may temporarily paralyze the muscles of the eyeball; even the optic nerve may be anesthetized, resulting in temporary blindness. In checking the path through the pterygopalatine canal in approximately 200 skulls, bony obstructions were found in 15 per cent of the cases. If obstructions are encountered when giving this injection, the needle should not be forced, or needle fracture may result. The alternative path is along the tuberosity. The commonest complication will be severe hematoma if the maxillary artery is punctured. Also, the orbit might be entered if the needle is advanced too far. These complications can be avoided by following Smith's[36] and Jorgensen's[22, 25] technique for a determination of the depth of needle insertion.

A most serious complication is post-injection infection; asepsis must be maintained when using this technique.

D. The treatment of patients with *hypertensive, cardiovascular,* or *cerebrovascular* disease is increasingly common. Specific considerations regarding evaluation, routine management, and precautions are covered in detail in Chapter 2.

Hypertensives are a special problem because they exhibit a great lability of blood pressure. The anticipation of dental treatment causes an initial elevation of their blood pressure, which may be heightened by the stimulus of an injection or dental treatment.

Patients with a history of cardiovascular or cerebrovascular disease suffer an elevation in blood pressure after any noxious stimulus. Obviously, any rise in blood pressure may be dangerous for these patients. The reports of Cheraskin and Prasertsuntarasai,[12] McCarthy,[30] and observations of dental clinic patients at Loma Linda University since 1955 confirm that the blood pressure is not elevated by the small amount of epinephrine (1:100,000 to 1:50,000) contained in the most commonly employed dental analgesic solutions unless they are injected intravenously. In addition, a special report of the New York Heart Association in 1954 concluded that there is no hazard for the cardiac patient if no more than 0.2 mg of epinephrine is utilized at a single dental appointment.[41] The total maximum dose of 0.2 mg of epinephrine is equal to 20 ml of local analgesic solution containing epinephrine in the amount of 1:100,000 (0.01 mg per ml). It is stated that 0.5 mg of epinephrine is the effective dose for positive or pressor effects in man when injected subcutaneously.[43] This is two and one-half times the maximum amount of epinephrine advised by the New York Heart Association, and it represents 50 ml of epinephrine 1:100,000.

Warnings against the use of vasoconstrictors such as epinephrine are still heard. Many of these are repetitions based on early teaching, such as those expressed by Berlove.[7] However, it is recognized that some hypertensive patients are extremely sensitive to epinephrine, and recommendations are seen in the literature against the use of epinephrine in such cases.[11] One reported death that occurred in the dental office was due to a burst

cerebral aneurysm following sedation and the injection of four 2.2 ml ampules of lidocaine with 1:80,000 noradrenaline.[42] Still it is our belief that the
hypertensive patient who is so sensitive that as little as 0.02 mg of epinephrine (2 ml of 1:100,000 solution) could not be administered is rare
indeed, if he exists at all. We continue to recommend the routine use of
epinephrine for sedated hypertensive patients in order to achieve the deepest level of analgesia. Inadequate analgesia resulting from a local analgesic solution without epinephrine results in the pain-produced release of
significant amounts of endogenous epinephrine, thus subjecting the patient
to the risk of a hypertensive episode. Again it must be remembered that
very anxious patients will exhibit similar outpourings of catecholamines.[15]
It is our belief that considerable research is needed on the effect of epinephrine in the dental patient.

Adequate *sedation* is the single most important prophylactic measure
in preventing adverse systemic responses in the hypertensive patient during dental treatment. Proper administration of the local analgesic solution is
mandatory: 25 gauge or larger needle, aspirating syringe or cartridge, and
slow administration.

With regard to aspiration, Harris'[20] classic paper is still significant.
Harris remarked that aspiration was not universally practiced because (1)
"It is evidently thought by some that, when a needle point is in a blood
vessel, blood will enter, or can be 'teased,' into a nonaspirating cartridge,"
(2) "So little has been said about it in the literature that many dentists
believe the incidence of puncturing blood vessels is insignificant in dental
injections." (3) "The hazards of intravascular injection are not sufficiently
appreciated by the profession." A final quotation is warranted: "One of the
most insidious dangers in therapeutics is the complacency which develops when undesirable reactions are infrequent. . . . If any of these deaths
might have been prevented by ordinary or even extraordinary precautions,
that they occurred at all seems inexcusable." It is not easy to ascertain the
prevalence of deaths due to local analgesia, but they have not ceased,[9, 38, 42]
and Harris' statement is still valid.

Slow administration of minimal amounts of local analgesic 0.5 to 1 ml
over 1 to 2 minutes permits the tissues to adequately buffer the local analgesic solution; greater profundity and duration of effect is obtained and the
risk of toxic or allergic reaction to the local analgesic, vasoconstrictor, or
preservative is minimized. A review of fundamental biochemical phenomena such as the Henderson-Hasselbalch equation will substantiate the efficacy of the injection of minimal amounts of local analgesia over a maximal
time.[14]

Another facet of the epinephrine controversy has arisen with the introduction of the monoamine oxidase inhibitors. It has been suggested that
patients taking these agents should not be given epinephrine-containing
compounds because of the possibility of increased sensitivity to epinephrine.[11] Monoamine oxidase inhibitors are true antidepressants and are utilized in the treatment of melancholia and depressive states. The monoamine oxidase inhibitors include Nardil, Niamid, Parnate, and Marplan.
They inhibit monoamine oxidase, the enzyme which destroys neurohor-
monal substances such as serotonin and norepinephrine. The mode of antidepressant action is not understood.

Diverse side effects from monoamine oxidase inhibitors have been reported, among which are postural hypotension, potentiation of CNS depressants, and hypertensive episodes.[6, 32] While hypertensive episodes are uncommon, it is recognized by us that great care should be taken when administering epinephrine in local analgesic solutions to the hypertensive or cardiac patient who is taking a monoamine oxidase inhibitor. Since reports of these side effects are sparse and conflicting at this time[14] we do not feel that the use of epinephrine should be flatly discontinued in such patients for the same reasons already enumerated regarding alleged epinephrine hypersensitivity. We suggest the continued use of epinephrine, the usual precautions of administration, and that extreme caution be used in the administration of sedative drugs due to potentiation by the MAO inhibitors.

PROPHYLAXIS AND TREATMENT

The treatment and prophylaxis of many of the local complications have been altered by the introduction of disposable needles. For instance, if the precautions outlined under *Bacterial contamination* (p. 308) and *Inferior alveolar* injection (p. 312) are followed, then bacterial infections will be noted for their uncommon rarity. The best practical prophylaxis is the establishment of a precise routine for the handling of cartridges, needles and syringes, and the preparation of the tissues of the patient for a meticulously administered injection. Trauma from tearing of the tissue would seem a thing of the past. At the same time, however, the extraordinary sharpness of the needles does increase the hazard of inadvertently entering tissues that should be avoided. The passage for the needle in deep injections such as the inferior alveolar, the tuberosity, or the infraorbital, is through loose, fatty, areolar tissue. In our opinion, thin needles with long, pointed bevels cannot be used as probes, and may easily invade a muscle, artery, or nerve. Trismus and after-pain, hematoma, paresthesia, or post-anesthetic neuritis may follow.

A brief discussion of needle bevels, gauges and lengths is appropriate to the foregoing and following remarks regarding prophylaxis. Smith[36] (p. 306, Fig. 178) depicted for block injections the "correct" needle, with a short bevel, and the "incorrect" needle, with a long, pointed bevel. Today, manufacturers distribute similar long, pointed bevels. A "Status report on dental anesthetic needles and syringes"[13] provides photographs of long, pointed bevels deformed by barbs or burrs following inferior alveolar and long buccal nerve blocks. A deformed or burred needle may cause damage as it is withdrawn from the area of deepest penetration. The type and angle of the needle bevel must be considered in relation to the needle tip strength, and what the needle tip is expected to perform. Reportedly,[33] a short, 45 degree bevel offers strength, is sharp, and will offer a full diameter cutting surface with drag-free insertion and withdrawal of the cannula. The long, tapered, multibeveled point, such as is designed for venipuncture, not only has reduced wall thickness and is prone to hook and burr when striking bone but also fails to incise the full diameter of the cannula; therefore, dragging and tearing of the tissues may result when it is used for dental block injections.

Lumen size, of course, is related to the caliber of the needle and there-fore affects both the strength of the needle and the probability of aspira-tion. The Hagen-Poisuelle law of laminar flow in tubes states that the flow rate is proportional to the fourth power of the diameter. A small increase in the diameter of the lumen of the cannula will markedly increase the flow and the possibility of aspiration.

The reported prevalence of aspiration of blood following intravascular injection varies from 2.4 to 5 per cent, and may be greater.[8] However, it is not infrequently observed that a 21 gauge or larger needle in a hand or arm vein may not permit aspiration, although fluid administered via the needle indicates that the needle is in the vein. For this reason, it seems logical to propose that the smaller the gauge of the dental needle tip, the greater the possibility of similar occlusion.

The length of the needle is related to its strength; longer needles are stronger. At present, needle lengths are not standardized; for example, the length of a needle designated as ¾, 1, or 1¼ inch may vary widely (Council report, p. 1173).[13] A longer needle provides a desirable margin of safety; that is, it prevents penetration up to the hub. If there is breakage, the por-tion remaining outside of the oral tissue may be grasped and the broken remains extracted.

The rigidity of a needle is a combination of caliber size and length. A heavier gauge or conical needle will not deflect, whereas a thin needle may deviate up to 3 millimeters.[13] Thus, if the needle tip is not placed precisely at the lingula for an inferior alveolar injection, a deviation of from 6 to 10 mm from the lingula to the needle tip may result, enough to place the needle in the medial or lateral pterygoid muscle. Although the intimate relation of the pterygoid muscles to the mandibular foramen is not general-ly recognized by the clinician, it has long been depicted in adults in ana-tomical atlases, such as those by Kampmeier, Cooper and Jones[26] and Truex and Kellner.[40]

There is at present no complete set of standards for the needles, car-tridges, and syringes used in dentistry. However, the American Dental As-sociation, in cooperation with the American National Standards Institute, has established a subcommittee to propose such standards.

The *prophylaxis for trismus* is to adhere strictly to the correct anatomic route for the needle, which we find is impossible without the use of a heavy rigid needle with a short bevel.

In regard to needle size, it will be noted from Table 10–1 that a dispos-able 25 gauge needle has an outside diameter only 0.10 mm greater than the 27 gauge, which is too flexible for deep injections. Thus, by using the 25 gauge needle, the dental practitioner gains the advantages of far greater rigidity and an increase of approximately 0.05 mm (one fourth larger) in in-side diameter, which may enhance the opportunity for positive aspiration.

However, in our opinion, for deep injections of the mouth, the needle of choice is either the Mizzy, Inc., conical needle or the 23 gauge needle, even though these needles require sterilization by autoclaving. If a well trained staff is available, a large gauge needle may be cleaned, sterilized, and reused;[16] if not, the needles may be sterilized preoperatively, used once and discarded; this is probably the most practical approach when cir-

TABLE 10–1 APPROXIMATE DIMENSIONS OF SEVERAL CARTRIDGE TYPE NEEDLES°

Size Gauge	Length mm	Outside Diameter Limits mm	Inside Diameter Minimum at point	Length ≅ Inches
30	25	0.30–0.31	0.13	1
27	25	0.39–0.41	0.19	1
27	35	0.39–0.41	0.19	1¼
25	25	0.49–0.52	0.24	1
25	35	0.49–0.52	0.24	1¼
23	41	0.62–0.64	0.32	1⅝
Conical	41	0.62–0.64	0.24	1⅝
		0.41–0.44°°		

Dimensions of Cannula

°Dimensions from drafts proposed by the Subcommittee on Needles, Cartridges, and Syringes Used in Dentistry of the American National Standards Committee MD-156, and by courtesy of Ernst Fanta, Mizzy, Inc. Clifton Forge, VA. (For this table the lengths are given to the nearest millimeter.)
°° at point

cumstances permit. The outside diameter at the tip of the very rigid 23 gauge needle is only 0.23 mm greater than the outside diameter of the tip of the disposable 27 gauge needle, but the inside diameter is 0.13 greater. At the tip the outside of the conical needle is about the same size as that of a 27 gauge needle, while the inside diameter is about the same as that of a 25 gauge needle.

The *proper treatment for trismus and neuritis,* in our experience, is infrared irradiation. The paresthesia which may follow the injury to the nerve will pass in 2 to 8 weeks, though we are now observing paresthesia lasting for several years associated with the use of long, pointed bevels. We are convinced that hematomas can largely be avoided by the use of a heavy, rigid needle with a short bevel which will transmit a sensation if it touches the resistant wall of an artery. The needle can then be slightly withdrawn and a new path taken. A vein may also be entered, but this does not result in hematoma. However, aspiration must be done to avoid systemic reactions.[1, 2, 23, 25, 35] If the technique is careless, infection may result. This can be serious and at times very difficult to control. Mizzy conical needles were used by dental students in the Oral Surgery Department of Loma Linda University for approximately ten years, during which time only one hematoma was observed. When disposable needles became mandatory for student use, seven hematomas occurred during the first trial period of 500 injections. The disposable needles were 23 gauge, with a *long, pointed bevel.* The treatment of a *hematoma* in the region of the maxillary tuberosity starts with control of the bleeding by placing gauze, packed under pressure, in the buccal vestibule, and extraoral pressure over the swollen area. Later treatment includes the use of infrared rays.

As mentioned, *allergic* reactions to local analgesics may happen, though rarely.

Careful questioning of the patient who is to receive the injection of a drug may either reveal a history of allergy or raise the suspicion that one may exist. In the first instance, the patient may be aware of the drug causing the reaction; in the second instance skin testing may be indicated. There is often expressed uncertainty as to the value of such procedures. In such an instance it is of value to consider the opinion of DeJong:[14] "While skin testing may give a high yield of false positives (due to the irritancy of anesthetics such as tetracaine) it has been convincingly demonstrated that subjects not reacting to intracutaneous testing may be given the local anesthetic with reasonable impunity."

The first treatment for a fall in blood pressure is the administration of oxygen, followed, if necessary, by pressor drugs and a suitable corticosteroid intravenously. Antihistamines are also to be administered. Subsequent analgesics should be of a different chemical structure[14] (see the chapter on *emergency drugs and allergy*).

The treatment for *syncope, convulsions* or *shock* is to place the patient in a horizontal position and to administer oxygen, with positive pressure if necessary. If the convulsions do not cease when this method is employed, intravenous injection of diazepam should be made slowly, using just barely enough to stop the convulsion. Because of the usual depression which follows the convulsion, it is advisable to continue the administration of oxygen for some time. If the blood pressure has dropped and does not come back by this method, then a pressor drug such as mephentermine or phenylephrine should be administered intravenously. It has also been suggested that the administration of a corticosteroid is useful.

Worth noting is the possibility that syncope, or all of these untoward events, may often be prevented by positioning the patient in a semi-supine position in the dental contour chair during the time of injection and treatment. The report of Forsyth, Allen, and Everett,[17] in regard to the effects of posture on the cardiorespiratory system warrants careful study and further evaluation. Some patients may become syncopic as a result of hypoglycemia induced by fasting, drugs, ethanol, or other cause. The prophylaxis is simply a preoperative high carbohydrate meal. Two to four ounces of honey may also be administered preoperatively. The point is that prevention is simple, and treatment of hypoglycemic syncope is time consuming. Shane and co-workers[34] reported a classic example of this presumed complication, based on elicited history. .

Acute asthmatic attacks should be treated with epinephrine. The drug should be slowly and cautiously administered, either intramuscularly or intravenously.

The prophylaxis for dental patients with *hypertension, cardiovascular,* or *cerebrovascular disease* is to control, by careful sedation, the rise in blood pressure caused by endogenous epinephrine.[12, 15, 30, 42] Only light sedation is induced, but the elevated blood pressure reverts to the patient's usual level and does not subsequently rise after the use of local analgesic solutions with vasoconstrictors and the surgical or restorative treatment. At Loma Linda University, dental patients with these diseases are *always* sedated.

The transmission of hepatitis B (HBV) is most likely to occur during those procedures in which blood may be transferred from patient to clinician or assistant, patient to patient, and clinician to patient. With regard to parenteral injections of local anesthetics for sedation the most likely carrier of HBV will be the needle, and/or needle-tracked drug abuser.

Hepatitis B can be prevented by thoroughly cleansing and then sterilizing instruments which penetrate the soft tissues. Needles should be autoclaved at 121° C, for 15 to 30 minutes, or by exposure to dry heat at 160° C for 2 hours or 170° C for 1 hour. The Council on Dental Therapeutics of the American Dental Association has further recommended that if blood may inadvertently, or as a result of positive aspiration, be drawn into a non-disposable syringe, the syringe should be exposed to boiling water (100° C.) for 30 minutes. Individual dose cartridges or ampules of local analgesic solutions are recommended, which in the words of the *Accepted Dental Remedies* of 1966, "... of course, should never be used for more than one patient" (p. 38)! Neither needles, syringes nor carpules or ampules should be stored in disinfectant solution which might become contaminated with pathogenic microorganisms through careless handling. Rather the articles should be kept in the containers in which they were sterilized.[1]

Care should be taken to avoid accidental puncture of the skin with used needles when cleaning the instrument tray. The discarded needles should be in a container which does not permit their inadvertent sticking of individuals disposing of the container.

SUMMARY AND CONCLUSIONS

Much patient distress could be avoided by the use of 25 gauge or heavier short-bevel needles, aspirating syringes, or cartridges, and the slow administration of minimum volumes of local analgesic solution. In the treatment of toxic or psychic reactions, the administration of oxygen usually is best. No dental office is adequately equipped unless the dentist can immediately administer oxygen under pressure. If the patient does not recover rapidly, medical assistance should be summoned. The spread of serum hepatitis can be prevented in the dental office by the use of sterilized needles and syringes and by never using a portion of any one analgesic cartridge on more than one patient.

Finally, the best way to prevent local complications, such as trismus, neuritis, or cellulitis, is to adhere strictly to the principles of asepsis and anatomy. An understanding of human physiology, coupled with a careful history and observation of the patient's vital signs, can minimize or prevent complications ranging from mild allergy to total collapse.

REFERENCES

1. Accepted Dental Therapeutics. 37th ed. Chicago, American Dental Association, 1977.
2. Accepted Dental Therapeutics, 36th ed. Chicago, American Dental Association, 1975.
3. Adriani, J., and Campbell, D.: Fatalities following topical application of local anesthetics to mucous membrane. J.A.M.A., 162:1527, 1956.
4. Allen, G. D., et al.: The cardiorespiratory effects of epinephrine and local anesthetics for dentistry. Anesth. Prog. 20:152, 1973.
5. American Dental Association Council on Dental Therapeutics: Type B serum hepatitis and dental practice. J.A.D.A., 92:153, 1976.
6. Ayd, F. J., Jr.: The treatment of everyday depressive patients with nialamide. Clin. Med., 6:1569, 1959.
7. Berlove, I. J.: Dental-Medical Emergencies and Complications. Chicago, Year Book Publishers, Inc., 1959, p. 128.
8. Bos, A. L., Coppes, E. J., et al.: Aspiration control in the administration of local anesthesia in dentistry. Netherlands D. J. (Supp. 6), 78:24, 1971.
9. Bourne, J. G.: Deaths with dental anesthetics. Anesthesia, 25:473, 1970.

10. British Dental Association, Dental Health Committee: The prevention of transmission of serum hepatitis in dentistry. Br. Dent J., *137*:28, 1974.
11. Burch, G. E., and DePasquale, N. P.: Arterial hypertension and the dental patient. J.A.D.A., *73*:102, 1966.
12. Cheraskin, E., and Prasertsuntarasai, T.: Use of epinephrine with local anesthesia in hypertensive patients. IV. Effect of tooth extraction on blood pressure and pulse rate. J.A.D.A., *58*:61, 1959.
13. Council of Dental Materials and Devices and Council on Dental Therapeutics of the American Dental Association, Joint Report. J.A.D.A. 89:1171, 1974.
14. DeJong, R. H.: Local Anesthetics, 2nd ed., Springfield, Ill., Charles C Thomas, 1977.
15. Edmondson, H. D., et al.: Biochemical evidence of anxiety in dental patients. Br. Med. J. 4:7, 1972.
16. Feinberg, Larry. Personal communication, 15 July 1978.
17. Forsyth, W. D., Allen, G. D., and Everett, G. B.: An evaluation of cardiorespiratory effects of posture in the dental outpatient. Oral Surg. Oral Med. Oral Path, *34*:562, 1972.
18. Gibilisco, J. A., et al.: The differential diagnosis of atypical facial pain. Lancet, *85*:450, 1965.
19. Guidelines for teaching the comprehensive control of pain and anxiety in dentistry. Chicago, Council on Dental Education. American Dental Association, 1971.
20. Harris, S. C.: Aspiration before injection of dental local anesthetics. J. Oral Surg., *15*:299, 1957.
21. Hayden, J., Jr.: The limits of excellence: What one man can do. 1st Annual N. B. Jorgensen Memorial Lecture, 29 February, 1976, Loma Linda University, Loma Linda, Calif. Anesth. Prog. 25:75, 1978.
22. Jorgensen, N. B.: Measurements for intra-oral block of the maxillary nerve. J. Oral Surg., 6:1, 1948.
23. Jorgensen, N. B.: Accidental intravenous injection of procaine in dentistry. J. South. California Dent. Assoc., *20*:17, 1952.
24. Jorgensen, N. B.: Pain Control. *In* Royer, R. Q. (ed.): Current Therapy in Dentistry. St. Louis, C. V. Mosby Co., 1970, Vol. IV, p. 371.
25. Jorgensen, N. B., and Hayden, J., Jr.: Sedation, Local and General Anesthesia in Dentistry. 2nd ed. Philadelphia, Lea and Febiger, 1972.
26. Kampmeier, O. F., Cooper, A. R., and Jones, T. S.: A frontal section anatomy of the head and neck. Urbana, University of Illinois Press, 1957, Frontal Section 9.
27. Kennett, S., Curran, J. B., and Jenkins, G. R.: Management of a broken hypodermic needle: Report of a case. Anesth. Prog., *20*:48, 1973, and J. Can. Dent. Assoc., 38:414, 1972.
28. Larson, C. E.: Methylparaben — an overlooked cause of local anesthetic hypersensitivity. Anesth. Prog., *24*:72, 1977.
29. Litigation California jury awards $75,000 to patient with locked jaw. J.A.D.A., 89:983, 1974.
30. McCarthy, F. M.: Clinical study of blood pressure responses to epinephrine-containing local anesthetic solutions. J. Dent. Res., 36:132, 1957.
31. Mosley, J. W., and White, E.: Viral hepatitis as an occupational hazard of dentists. J.A.D.A., *90*:992, 1975.
32. Parker, S.: Effect of nialamide when used alone and with other therapies in the treatment of depression. Dis. Nerv. System, (Sec. 2), *20*:591, 1959.
33. Personal Communication. Mizzy Corporation, Clifton Forge, VA.
34. Shane, S. M., et al.: Intravenous Amnesia — an appraisal after seven years and 10,500 administrations. Anesth. Prog., *21*:36, 1974.
35. Sicher, H., and DuBrul, E. L.: Oral Anatomy. 5th ed. St. Louis, C. V. Mosby Co., 1970, p. 420.
36. Smith, A. E.: Block Anesthesia and Allied Subjects. St. Louis, C. V. Mosby Co., 1920.
37. Steiner, R. B., and Thompson, R. D. (eds.): Oral Surgery and Anesthesia. Philadelphia, W. B. Saunders Co., 1977.
38. Tomlin, P. J.: Death in outpatient dental anesthetic practice. Anesthesia, 29:551, 1974.
39. Trieger, N.: Pain Control. Chicago, "Die Quintessenz," 1974.
40. Truex, R. C., and Kellner, C. E.: Detailed Atlas of Head and Neck. New York, Oxford University Press, 1948, Fig. 111a, p. 103.
41. Use of epinephrine in connection with procaine in dental procedures. J.A.D.A., *50*:108, 1955.
42. What may happen...? SAAD Digest, 2:75, 1973 (London).
43. White, J. C., Smithwick, R. H., and Simeone, F. A.: The Autonomic Nervous System. New York, The Macmillan Co., 1952, p. 98.
44. Worth, H. M.: Principles and Practice of Oral Radiologic Interpretation. Chicago, Year Book Publishers, Inc., 1963, p. 212.

11

GENERAL ANESTHETIC EMERGENCIES AND COMPLICATIONS

JOHN B. McVEIGH

INTRODUCTION

This chapter is concerned with the safe administration of general anesthetics to ambulatory patients. It is widely recognized that the administration of general anesthesia entails certain risks, some of which are life threatening. The reader should notice that emphasis is placed first on the prevention of emergencies and complications associated with general anesthesia, and second on the prompt recognition and proper treatment of such undesirable occurrences.

Outpatient anesthesia for dental patients enjoys an enviable safety record (See mortality records in Chapter 2).[18, 41] The low incidence of mortality and morbidity demonstrates the safety and acceptance of this procedure. Unexpected, serious events sometimes occur, however, and will continue to do so. Those who are concerned with general anesthesia are aware of this fact and dedicate themselves to the prevention of such occurrences.

Emergencies in anesthetized patients are directly related to the survival of vital body organs. Irreversible brain damage occurs after four to five minutes of cerebral anoxia. Prompt recognition of adverse changes and immediate corrective therapy are essential to prevent brain damage or death. While anesthetized the patient's normal physiology is altered, and protective reflexes are reduced or abolished, leaving him or her relatively defenseless. It is incumbent, therefore, upon those involved with the safety of the patient to exercise the greatest care until he or she has completely recovered from the anesthetic.

Successful anesthesia and surgery or operative dentistry demand coordinated teamwork. Each member of the anesthesia team has definite responsibilities and must be alert to recognize any abnormal signs. It must be stressed that prevention of emergencies and complications is much to be preferred to their treatment. Impending emergencies or complications may be avoided or at least diminished in severity by early recognition and immediate application of corrective measures.

RESPIRATORY EMERGENCIES AND COMPLICATIONS

RESPIRATORY OBSTRUCTION

Most general anesthetic emergencies are related to respiratory tract obstruction. The respiratory tract, including the anatomic dead space, extends from the lips and nares to the pulmonary alveolar membrane. Obstruction of the flow of air or gases can occur at any level within these limits. The usual sites of obstruction are the lips, oropharynx, nasopharynx, glottis, vocal cords, trachea and large bronchi, bronchioles, and alveoli. *The prevention of respiratory obstruction by the maintenance of a patent airway is the greatest single factor in the administration of a safe and satisfactory general anesthetic.*

Respiratory obstruction is characterized by any or a combination of the following signs:

1. Reduced or inadequate gaseous exchange, as evidenced by weak expansion of the anesthetic reservoir bag or weakness in respiratory sounds.
2. Noisy respiration, unless obstruction is complete.
3. Cyanosis. (See under Respiratory Emergencies, *Apnea.*)
4. Strong diaphragmatic activity and excessive abdominal movement.
5. Exaggerated activity of the secondary muscles of respiration.

Respiratory obstruction prevents adequate gaseous exchange, resulting in hypoxia and, if not corrected, will ultimately lead to cardiac arrest. *It has been estimated that 90 per cent of deaths associated with general anesthesia are related to improper management of the airway.*[14]

Anatomic and Mechanical Considerations

The Lips. During general surgery hindrance of air flow past the lips may occur in patients whose dentures have been removed or in patients with thick, full lips. The use of an oral or nasal airway or endotracheal tube in more difficult instances will correct this obstruction. In operations within the oral cavity the lips are not a significant factor in airway obstruction, as the mouth is held open by a mouth prop and the lips are retracted.

The Oropharynx. The oropharynx is the most frequent site of upper airway obstruction. When the tongue and jaw relax under anesthesia they tend to fall backward and may occlude the space between the base of the tongue and the posterior pharyngeal wall. This is corrected by supporting the angle of the mandible and properly positioning the oropharyngeal pack to elevate the tongue. These procedures will bring the tongue forward and away from the posterior pharyngeal wall. This type of obstruction is extremely dangerous if unrecognized, as the airway is almost completely occluded. If obstruction persists, a pharyngeal airway or endotracheal tube should be placed.

The Nasopharynx. Obstruction at this level is usually due to one of the following: edema of the nasal mucous membrane, deviated nasal septum, enlarged turbinates, or hypertrophied adenoid tissue. With nasopharyngeal obstruction an oropharyngeal or oroendotracheal tube should be placed; as in dental procedures the mouth is open and the oropharynx is packed.

The Glottis. Restriction of air flow at the glottis is most often due to obstruction by foreign bodies too large to enter the larynx. These may be gauze sponges, fragments of broken dentures, dental bridgework, and so forth. All removable appliances should be removed prior to induction of anesthesia. A properly positioned oropharyngeal pack will help prevent this form of obstruction.

The Larynx. Interruption of air flow in the larynx may be due to the presence of teeth, parts of teeth, dental materials, or other small foreign bodies in the area, or to partial or complete adduction of the vocal cords (laryngospasm). Reflex adduction of the vocal cords in response to an irritant is a protective mechanism to prevent contamination of the lower respiratory tract. (See under Respiratory Emergencies, *Laryngospasm.*)

The Trachea and Large Bronchi. Obstruction at this level is usually the result of aspiration of foreign matter such as vomitus, whole teeth or tooth fragments, dental materials or devices, etc.

The Bronchioles. The smooth muscle of the bronchioles may contract, resulting in bronchospasm. This may occur in some patients while under light anesthesia, particularly those with a history of asthma, or contraction may be precipitated by the use of certain sensitizing drugs. (See under Respiratory Emergencies, *Bronchospasm.*)

The Alveoli. Emphysematous changes or atelectasis (lung collapse) will result in obstruction of the alveoli. With alveolar obstruction there will be an increase in the pulse rate, lag of the chest wall on the affected side, and progressive cyanosis. Assisting respiration with 100 per cent oxygen under positive pressure will aid in oxygenating the blood.

Laryngospasm

Laryngospasm is a reflex protective mechanism to prevent contamination of the lower respiratory tract. In laryngospasm there is partial or complete adduction of the vocal cords. With partial adduction, a crowing sound will be heard and a moderate hypoxia will result from the impaired airway. If this partial adduction is not promptly and properly treated, it will often develop into complete adduction of the vocal cords and result in complete obstruction of the airway, severe anoxia, and cyanosis. Complete obstruction must be relieved promptly to prevent cardiac arrest. Laryngospasm is an infrequent complication in the properly prepared patient receiving a well-administered ultralight general anesthetic.

CAUSES

1. Irritation of the vocal cords by blood, mucus, or debris.
2. Improper administration of parasympathomimetic drugs, such as a barbiturate, particularly in the unpremedicated patient.
3. Sudden high concentrations of inhalation anesthetic agents.

PREVENTION

1. Many premedicate with atropine or scopolamine, unless contraindicated; others do not feel it is necessary.
2. Properly position the oropharyngeal pack to prevent irritation of the vocal cords by blood, mucus, or debris passing beyond the pack.
3. Maintain adequate depth of anesthesia to obtund reflex mechanisms that may be stimulated during surgery.
4. Maintain a patent airway and provide adequate oxygenation.

TREATMENT

Frequently this respiratory emergency is improperly managed. It is not uncommon to see the inexperienced anesthetist who is confronted with a patient experiencing laryngospasm to reach hurriedly for succinylcholine, administer 20 to 40 mg intravenously, and follow this with 100 per cent oxygen via a full face mask without attempting to determine the cause of the spasm. While doing this, any blood, mucus, or debris in the pharynx will either be aspirated when the vocal cords relax or will remain to act again as an irritant and set up a second spasm.

Laryngospasm can be properly managed in the following manner:

1. Grasp the tongue with gauze and draw forward.
2. Using a tonsil tip, suction the pharynx and oral cavity free of all debris.
3. Replace the soiled pack with a fresh oropharyngeal pack.
4. Administer 100 per cent oxygen via nasal mask.
5. If surgery is completed, lighten the level of anesthesia; if more surgery

is contemplated, some anesthetists prefer to slightly deepen the anesthetic level; others do not.

These measures will suffice to alleviate the laryngospasm in nearly all instances. If the spasm persists, however, administer 10 to 20 mg of succinylcholine slowly intravenously (succinylcholine chloride should be injected slowly to minimize muscular fasciculations and resultant postoperative muscle pain). After the laryngospasm is broken, respiration should be assisted if necessary by manual compression of the thorax or by intermittent positive pressure applied by hand to a bag of oxygen connected to a tight-fitting nasal mask. Intubation should not be attempted while the patient is in laryngospasm as the cords will be tightly adducted and the intubation procedure would be extremely difficult and unduly traumatic. The time wasted in attempting intubation with the cords adducted would increase the hypoxia and no doubt result in unfortunate sequelae. Artificial respiration is ineffective in severe laryngospasm and should be avoided until the airway is established, as it would tend to evacuate the remaining oxygen from the lungs. Air will not enter the lungs on the release of pressure on the chest wall until the airway is clear. Succinylcholine should not be used indiscriminately and without adequate resuscitative drugs and equipment on hand. Its administration is certainly justified in relieving severe laryngospasm that does not respond to the treatment measures outlined above. Even here, however, the minimal effective dose should be employed. If a general anesthetic is properly administered to a properly prepared patient, and the causes of laryngospasm are clearly understood and appreciated, respiratory obstruction in this area will rarely occur.

Bronchospasm

Bronchospasm is a condition of partial or complete contraction of the bronchiolar musculature. Partial bronchospasm is not uncommon in patients under general anesthesia, and it is not difficult to control. Total bronchospasm, which fortunately is rare, is a very serious emergency. Its treatment will be described below. It is most frequently encountered in patients with a history of bronchial asthma or chronic bronchitis. When there is contraction of the bronchiolar musculature, and a resulting hypoxia, the patient is said to have a bronchospasm. The chest is fixed in a position of inspiration.[26] In partial bronchospasm an expiratory wheeze, such as is heard in bronchial asthma, will be heard. In total bronchospasm, usually no sounds are heard from the lungs.

CAUSES

Bronchospasm may be due to several factors:

1. Vagal stimulation by mucus, blood, aspirated gastric contents, or surgery.
2. Histamine release.
3. Mechanical stimulation by an endotracheal tube.
4. Irritating vapors.

PREVENTION

1. A careful medical history is important. Those individuals with chronic bronchitis or bronchial asthma are more susceptible to bronchospasm.
2. The parasympathetic nerves cause constriction of the bronchiolar musculature. Premedication with atropine, a parasympatholytic agent, may help to prevent bronchospasm in susceptible patients.
3. Provide a smooth induction of anesthesia.
4. Avoid irritating inhalation agents.

TREATMENT

Epinephrine is an excellent bronchodilator in normal individuals. The moribund asthmatic, however, is invariably resistant to epinephrine and isoprenaline. In the event of severe bronchospasm Gold[26] and others[15, 53] recommend the slow IV injection of 250 to 500 mg of aminophylline (i.e., given over a 5 minute period). Aminophylline must be injected slowly, as a marked hypotension will result with rapid administration. Hydrocortisone, 100 mg, IV, remains the most effective treatment of a severe and protracted bronchospasm. In total bronchospasm, cyanosis appears very rapidly, and one's natural inclination is to force oxygen into the lungs at any cost. Dickson[15] feels that this is wasted effort, and, more important, wasted time. Every second is important, and even if some oxygen is forced into the lungs it will at best relieve the hypoxia and cyanosis only momentarily. It will still be impossible to remove carbon dioxide from the lungs, and cardiac arrest may follow rapidly. If hydrocortisone and aminophylline are administered in the dosage given above immediately after the diagnosis is made, the chances for recovery are good.[53]

Aspiration of Vomitus

Vomiting under anesthesia, particularly with the use of inhalation agents, is not an uncommon occurrence. Fortunately the material is rarely aspirated and the only problem is one of debridement. However, if vomitus is aspirated, one is confronted with a most serious emergency. In addition to the obvious hazard of airway obstruction, which results in anoxia and possible death if treatment is mismanaged, there is the often unrecognized sequence of events leading to aspiration pneumonitis. Aspiration of gastric contents constitutes a grave emergency, the frequency of which can be minimized by appropriate preventive measures. The most obvious preventive measure is to avoid general anesthesia in a patient who is suspected to have food in the stomach. Nearly all dental or oral surgical procedures can be delayed for some time if necessary. If emergency surgery is needed, a local analgesic technique should be employed if the patient has recently eaten. It usually requires about 4 hours for most food to pass through the stomach, but if the patient is quite apprehensive or in considerable pain, 10 to 12 hours or longer may be required. Other preventive measures include insuring adequate oxygen levels being supplied to the patient to prevent nausea and maintaining meticulous observation from the point of induction to the time of complete recovery from the anesthetic. The patient should not be moved from the surgery room to the recovery room until protective reflexes are present.

INCIDENCE

Deaths from aspiration were reported soon after the introduction of ether and chloroform for surgical anesthesia. The first death reported to be related to aspiration was in 1848. Historically, aspiration into the tracheo-bronchial tree was recognized early as a cause of morbidity and mortality. Aspiration of vomitus has been reported[34] as the primary cause of death in 0.03 to 26.3 per cent of anesthetized patients. The incidence is higher in obstetric patients, apparently because of relatively poorer preparation and greater likelihood of a full stomach as compared with general surgical patients. Edwards et al.,[20] in a report on 1000 anesthetic deaths, considered 110 to be due to aspiration of vomitus. In a recent paper by Cameron et al.,[10] the clinical records of 47 patients with documented aspiration were reviewed. The overall mortality was 62 per cent. If only one lobe was involved on x-ray, mortality was 41 per cent. If two or more lobes on one or both sides were involved, mortality increased to 90 per cent.

DIAGNOSIS

The diagnosis of aspiration of vomitus requires a high index of suspicion, as the original episode may have gone unnoticed, or its immediate effects may have been masked by the anesthetic state. If vomitus appears in the mouth or pharynx, the possibility of aspiration should be considered and investigated. Aspiration may cause immediate circulatory collapse and respiratory apnea or spasm of reflex origin, but the onset of severe illness may be more subtle and occur after a latent period; sometimes even 6 to 8 hours after the initial features have subsided or passed unobserved. Aspiration of solids is diagnosed by the presence of obstruction of the airway or by signs of lung collapse. Liquid aspirate is not always easily diagnosed. Cyanosis, tachycardia, and tachypnea, possibly associated with bronchospasm or respiratory distress, may occur immediately or at a variable interval. If, during anesthesia, there is difficulty in maintaining the patient's color and there is an increase in the inflationary pressure, aspiration must be suspected. Endotracheal aspiration may be diagnostic. Acute pulmonary edema in a severe case of aspiration is revealed by a profuse serosanguinous froth pouring from the airway. X-ray examination may show widespread infiltration of the lung, more often affecting the right side and the lower lobes, but changes are usually more marked 24 hours later. Progressive hypotension with low venous pressure, a rising hematocrit, hypoxemia, and acidosis may lead to a state of shock and death.[44] Stetson[60] emphasizes the importance of pre-anesthetic evaluation and preparation along with scrupulous observation of the patient to prevent this disaster.

Aspiration Pneumonitis. Except for the situations of obvious asphyxiation which lead to sudden death, there was little significance attached to the aspiration of small quantities of vomitus that did not cause sudden death, but that later resulted in aspiration pneumonitis. In these cases death was usually attributed to secondary pulmonary infection. In the

1860's it was finally realized that something besides infection was going on in the lungs. Winternitz[67] injected HCl into the bronchi of anesthetized rabbits and unknowingly described what is now accepted as the typical picture of acute aspiration pneumonitis. Other studies, for example, those of Mendelson[45] in 1946 and Teabeaut[62] in 1952, clarified the pathologic sequence of events occurring in the lungs after aspiration. The pulmonary reaction to the aspiration of gastric contents is directly related to the nature and volume of the aspirated material. Experimental studies evaluating the significance of what is aspirated, such as enzymes, pH, bacteria, blood, fecally contaminated gastric juice, alcohol, and various combinations thereof, including the addition of solid food, have been conducted using experimental animals. From these studies the pH of the material aspirated was considered the most important factor in determining the degree of pneumonitis. Normal gastric juice is acidic and ranges from pH 1.5 to 2.4. When the pH was less than 1.2, patchy atelectasis and hemorrhagic areas with occasional frank necrosis occurred in the lungs as well as air leaks from the lung surface and pulmonary edema. In experimental studies using isolated perfused ventilated lungs, gastric juice containing methylene blue, after being introduced into the trachea, appeared on the lung surface within 12 to 18 seconds. When we realize the rapidity of distribution of material within the lungs, it follows that the treatment of aspiration must be rapid and correct. Aspiration can occur from two distinct sources caused by two different mechanisms. These are vomiting and regurgitation. A distinction between these two actions should be made before describing prevention and treatment. One is an active phenomenon; the other is passive. Regurgitation is a passive act with a high and often unrecognized incidence during anesthesia. It occurs when the intra-abdominal pressure exceeds the intrathoracic pressure and there is an associated incompetence of the gastroesophageal closing mechanism. If the patient is in the supine position and someone inadvertently exerts pressure on the abdomen, there is the possibility that regurgitation, which is silent, may occur. There is no retching or other muscular movement which would warn the surgeon or anesthesiologist of the regurgitation episode. Vomiting, however, is an active phenomenon caused by a different mechanism and is equally as hazardous as regurgitation. Nausea, which precedes the act of vomiting, may be masked by the anesthetic state. The alert anesthetist, however, can recognize such objective signs of an impending vomiting episode as increased salivation, sweating, repetitive swallowing, increased pulse rate, and variations in the character of respiration. Recognizing these signs may allow as much as a minute's advance warning of vomiting. Bannister and Sattilaro[4] described the microscopic findings following the aspiration of matter with a low pH. After 24 hours there is usually a peribronchial infiltration of polymorphonuclear leukocytes, followed later by mononucleated cells predominating. If the aspirated material is contaminated, lung abscesses will also be evident.

TREATMENT

Successful treatment of this emergency depends on prompt recognition. Once the diagnosis is made, treatment is begun immediately. The patient should be placed in the Trendelenburg position with the head down at least 15 degrees. The patient is then rolled onto his right side to aid in the drainage of vomitus from the mouth and to help confine any aspirated material to the dependent right lung. The right lung is more often affected because of the configuration of the main bronchi. This position will, therefore, tend to localize the aspiration to the right side while the airway is being cleared and the patient is being oxygenated. The oropharynx should be cleared digitally with gauze placed over the fingers and by the use of suction. When the pharynx is clear, roll the patient onto his back and intubate. A rapidly acting muscle relaxant, such as succinylcholine, 20 mg IV, may be helpful if needed. Intubation will facilitate the administration of high oxygen concentrations and tracheobronchial irrigation and suction, and will prevent additional aspiration of any material inadvertently left in the mouth. Following intubation, the patient is placed in a slight Fowler position, that is, with the head above the horizontal plane. Normal saline in 5 to 10 cc increments is introduced through the endotracheal tube to facilitate the removal of particulate matter. This is followed by suction and ventilation with oxygen. *This procedure should be reserved for selected cases as the instillation of saline could conceivably force aspirated material deeper into the pulmonary tree.* The main advantage of introducing saline is that it tends to dilute and thereby elevate the pH of highly acidic vomitus. Lavage using large volumes of fluid has been shown to increase the spread of acid and, therefore, is contraindicated. Maintenance of a patent airway for adequate ventilation with oxygen is of primary importance. Within the last decade numerous authors have advocated the use of corticosteroids to combat pneumonitis.[4, 31, 42] A satisfactory dosage schedule would be 100 mg of hydrocortisone (Solu-Cortef) given intravenously as soon as practicable, then 100 mg every eight hours for three days, followed by 25 mg every six hours for an additional two days.[16] It should be pointed out that since hydrocortisone may reduce the patient's defense mechanisms against bacterial infection, adequate doses of antibiotics should be considered. In addition, there should be symptomatic treatment for other complications such as vasopressors to support circulation, bronchodilators such as aminophylline (250 mg given IV in 500 ml of dextrose and water every eight hours), and digitalis for heart failure and pulmonary edema.[4] Tracheostomy should be considered in severe cases in which continued support of respiration is deemed advisable. Nicholl et al.[50] encourage tracheostomy also in that it reduces the anatomic dead space.

The paper of Mucklow and Larard[48] lends additional support to the treatment described above. They based their technique on experience gained from working in a busy casualty department where many patients were admitted in coma caused by drug overdosage, trauma, or diabetes, together with seven cases in which aspiration of vomitus was associated with anesthesia. They used lavage in 40 cases, six of which were patients under anesthesia, with apparent clinical success. They further advocated the intravenous administration of aminophylline, 250 mg slowly, to reduce or prevent the element of bronchospasm which is frequently present. Hydrocortisone was also employed in the same dosage schedule mentioned above. After the patient has sufficiently recovered from this initial treatment, he or she should be hospitalized for further indicated treatment and observation.

RESPIRATORY ABNORMALITIES

Alterations of the normal respiratory pattern are most often encountered during the induction phase of anesthesia. Respiratory abnormalities include the following:

Tachypnea. Usually associated with light anesthesia, particularly with the inhalation agents, and with surgical stimulation before adequate anesthesia is achieved. The tidal volume is reduced and ventilation becomes inadequate. This results in respiratory acidosis, hypoxemia, and hypercapnia.

Shallow Breathing. Sometimes seen with deep anesthesia, halothane use, muscle relaxants, etc. Respirations should be assisted until the normal respiratory pattern returns.

Slow Breathing. Slow, deep breathing is characteristic of overdosage of opiates.

Apnea. Apnea is a state of "no breathing" characterized by an increase in the pulse rate, progressive hypoxia, and cyanosis. If breathing is not promptly restored, hypoxia will become severe and result in irreversible brain damage or death.

Apnea may be caused by any of the following:

1. High concentration of inhalation agents.
2. Irritating vapors.
3. Overdosage of anesthetic agents.
4. Depletion of carbon dioxide.
5. Muscle relaxants.

Simple breath-holding is frequently seen during induction by "pushing" a high concentration of inhalation agents, or by stimulation from irritating vapors. Smooth induction will most often prevent breath-holding. When apnea occurs, the mask should be removed from the patient's face and the gas machine flushed promptly with oxygen to remove the irritating agent. The mask should then be reapplied snugly and respirations assisted by rhythmic contraction of the bag. If you are unable to ventilate the patient by this procedure, remove the mask and examine the patient for a possible obstruction in the airway. Laryngospasm or bronchospasm should also be considered as possible causes of inability to inflate the lungs. These conditions have been discussed earlier in this chapter.

If the lungs can be inflated but the patient's condition does not improve, there may be a mechanical failure in the anesthetic machine or an incorrect hookup of the oxygen and gas tanks. Fatalities have occurred in some instances when nitrous oxide was administered instead of the intended oxygen. In this situation the anesthetic machine should be discarded and mouth-to-mouth resuscitation performed until the error can be detected. The pulse should be monitored to determine if the circulation is still intact, as artificial respiration is useless unless the circulation is maintained.

Apnea resulting from an overdosage of anesthetic agent can occur for several reasons. Premedication with meperidine, morphine, or barbiturates will result in a certain degree of expected respiratory depression. Intravenous anesthetic agents also have a depressant effect on respiration. The combination of premedication and intravenous anesthesia has an additive effect, and may lead to respiratory depression and apnea. This problem is infrequently encountered in anesthesia for the ambulatory patient, as minimal premedication and light planes of anesthesia are usually employed. The goal in outpatient anesthesia is a safe anesthetic with a level no deeper than the surgical stimulus requires. Overdosage sometimes occurs in elderly patients as their metabolic rate is lower and their circulation time is somewhat longer than in younger individuals, and additional increments of intravenous agents may be mistakenly administered when the effect of the initial injection is not readily realized. Overdosage may occur also in patients with impaired liver function.

Apnea resulting from a depletion of carbon dioxide is seen rarely, but may be encountered in the induction phase of inhalation anesthesia in a child. No treatment is indicated, as carbon dioxide accumulates during the apneic state, and respirations will resume quickly.

Apnea may occur as the result of painful stimulus in light planes of anesthesia. The anesthetic level should be deepened and respiration assisted, using 100 per cent oxygen.

Apnea is commonly seen when muscle relaxants are employed. This can be minimized by using the minimal effective dose for the purpose desired. Treatment here is to manually assist respirations with 100 per cent oxygen until normal breathing returns.

As apnea, if allowed to persist, will lead to hypoxia and cyanosis, it is felt that the problem of cyanosis should be discussed. The appearance of cyanosis of the skin or mucous membranes will, in the absence of certain heart diseases or blood dyscrasias, indicate either peripheral vascular stasis or inadequate oxygenation of arterial blood in the lungs. Cyanosis may result from airway obstruction, incorrect gas-oxygen mixture, deficient pulmonary ventilation, or interruption of oxygen transfer from the alveoli to the pulmonary capillaries. Since the appearance of cyanosis depends on the presence of a minimum of reduced hemoglobin (approximately 5 gm), it may be late in onset or absent in states associated with anemia. Furthermore, there is an appreciable element of observer's error involved in its recognition. Its *absence* is therefore of little value for judging the state of the circulation. When it suddenly develops, however, it is a sign of the greatest importance. Whether its primary cause is circulatory or respiratory, its continuance is an indication that insufficient oxygen is reaching the vital body organs. The sudden appearance of cyanosis warns of the existence of an emergency situation requiring immediate action to restore a normal circulation and assure a patent airway and normal pulmonary gaseous exchange. It should be noted that the disappearance of cyanosis following ventilation with 100 per cent oxygen does not necessarily imply an adequate oxygen supply to the body, as the blood may be fully oxygenated but not have sufficient flow to provide an adequate amount of oxygen to the vital organs.

Coughing. Coughing may be initiated by irritating vapors during induction with inhalation agents. Coughing may also be encountered during intravenous anesthesia in heavy smokers or those with inflammation of the air passages. Adequate premedication and a smooth induction will reduce excessive mucus flow, a factor in reflex coughing. If marked coughing develops during anesthesia and persists afterward, the patient may have aspirated and should be referred for thoracic consultation without delay.

Hiccup. Hiccup is a state of intermittent spasm of the diaphragm accompanied by sudden closure of the glottis. Respiratory exchange is diminished to some extent and may lead to hypoxia. Jerking movements accompanying hiccup often make surgery difficult or impossible. Hiccup usually will respond to the administration of 10 to 20 mg of succinylcholine followed by ventilation with oxygen under positive pressure.

DECREASED OXYGEN CONCENTRATION

Oxygen is essential to life, but, unfortunately, there is no store of oxygen in the body to be drawn upon in an emergency. The brain is particularly sensitive to oxygen lack, and irreversible brain damage occurs after 4 to 5 minutes of oxygen deprivation. An excellent practice is to administer 30 to 100 per cent oxygen to the patient immediately after starting intravenous anesthesia and to continue to do so during the procedure to increase the oxygen saturation of the blood. If a respiratory emergency should later arise, precious time is added for treating the problem.

Decreased oxygen concentration usually results from one or more of the following:

1. Any cause of respiratory obstruction, as noted above.
2. Incorrect oxygen-to-gas ratio resulting from an improper mixture setting of the gas machine, accidental crossing of anesthetic lines or tanks, or depletion of oxygen at the tank.
3. Inadequate flow of oxygen from the gas machine to the patient.

CARDIOVASCULAR EMERGENCIES AND COMPLICATIONS

ALTERATIONS OF PULSE RATE

Tachycardia. Tachycardia signifies a pulse rate greater than 100 beats per minute. Sinus tachycardia is more common than ventricular tachycardia. The rate is usually 100 to 180 beats per minute, with normal P-R intervals and QRS complexes. It is important to distinguish between supraventricular (atrial) tachycardia and ventricular paroxysmal tachycardia, as the treatment and prognosis of each are different. Electronic monitoring of cardiac rate and rhythm is a matter of routine in many offices. An atrial tachycardia will often respond to vagal stimulation (carotid sinus or eyeball pressure) and to methoxamine, phenylephrine, or neostigmine. Tachycardia is generally well tolerated in the absence of myocardial disease. Treatment is indicated when hypotension develops or there is cardiac failure. Ventricular tachycardia, particularly when accompanied by multiple premature ventricular contractions (PVCs), may lead to ventricular fibrillation.

Bradycardia. Bradycardia is characterized by a pulse rate less than 60 beats per minute with normal P-R intervals and QRS complexes. It is most often due to an increase in vagal tone. Vagal tone may be increased reflexly by pain, or by pressure on the carotid sinus, the eyeballs, or the posterior pharyngeal wall. Uncomplicated bradycardia produces no symptoms unless it is extreme, when it may lead to syncope or convulsions. Bradycardia may be treated by atropine, 0.4 to 0.8 mg intravenously.

CARDIAC ARRHYTHMIAS

An arrhythmia is any deviation from the normal cardiac rhythm. Minor arrhythmias, usually arising in the S-A node, such as sinus tachycardia, sinus bradycardia, or sinus arrhythmia, in the absence of other symptoms, do not preclude general anesthesia. Other arrhythmias, arising in the atria, the conduction system, or the ventricles should be pursued and corrected prior to the administration of a general anesthetic. Cardiac arrhythmias seen in patients under general anesthetic are the result of multiple factors acting on the pacemaker, the conduction system, and the myocardium. Arrhythmias may produce an emergency situation if cardiac filling is so impaired that there is a sharp decrease in cardiac output. In such a case hypotension would follow and the resultant myocardial hypoxia would further reduce the force of cardiac contraction.

Predisposing Factors

Factors contributing to arrhythmias during general anesthesia and surgery include the preoperative condition of the heart, length of surgery, type of surgery, type and duration of anesthesia, age of patient, metabolic considerations, and, most important, duration and degree of hypoxia.

Ventricular arrhythmias may be insignificant, such as an isolated PVC, or they may be of sufficient magnitude to cause death. Patients with serious ventricular arrhythmias obviously are not candidates for general anesthesia. Fatal arrhythmias may be prevented by recognition and prompt treatment of prefatal disturbances.

Four ventricular arrhythmias are considered prefatal: Ventricular bigeminy or trigeminy, multiple (more than six per minute) PVCs, R on T phenomena, and multifocal PVCs.

Bigeminy.   This is a rhythm in which every other beat is premature, so that each two beats appear coupled. In *trigeminy*, two premature beats follow each normal beat, or two normal beats are followed by a premature beat. These beats can lead to other ventricular dysrhythmic problems. When bigeminy is suspected, surgery should be discontinued and a diagnosis established. If the coupled beats do not disappear and the patient's condition continues to worsen, lidocaine, 1 mg per kg, should be administered intravenously along with oxygen under positive pressure.

Multiple PVCs.   This arrhythmia can lead to ventricular tachycardia, a potentially fatal arrhythmia. More than five PVCs per minute is a matter of concern. Ventricular tachycardia is frequently followed by ventricular fibrillation. Ventricular tachycardia may also result in a sudden loss of blood pressure and shock. Restoration of blood pressure with vasopressors and fluids along with 400 watt-seconds of countershock to the precordium may be suitable treatment for this problem.

R on T Phenomena.   The R on T phenomenon relates to ventricular contraction while the heart is repolarizing and is in its most vulnerable period. A cardiac contraction during the vulnerable period can initiate ventricular fibrillation.

Multifocal PVCs.   These are initiated from different areas of the ventricles. These may also lead to ventricular fibrillation.

Prevention and Treatment

When alterations of cardiac rhythm are accompanied by cardiovascular changes such as hypotension, they require prompt diagnosis and corrective therapy. The usual treatment consists of discontinuing anesthetic administration, hyperventilating the lungs with oxygen under positive pressure, followed by measures to correct hypotension, and, in the small number of patients who fail to respond to these primary measures, administration of an antiarrhythmic drug. There are several useful drugs available for the prevention and treatment of arrhythmias. Tolas and Allen[63] in a controlled study involving 124 patients demonstrated rather conclusively that the beta-adrenergic drug propranolol (Inderal) was effective in the prevention of cardiac arrhythmias associated with anesthetic induction. They warned, however, because of the potency of the beta blockade, that it be used with caution. Fukushima et al.[25] studied the effects of propranolol on blood pressure, heart rate, and cardiac rhythm during ventricular arrhythmias initiated by hypercarbia on 13 patients. Propranolol was considered effective in all subjects. The successful use of propranolol suggests the mechanism of ventricular arrhythmias produced by hypercarbia to be related to beta-adrenergic receptors. Blockade of these receptors by propranolol decreased the sensitization of the myocardium to sympathetic stimulation. Morrow[47] suggests the intravenous administration of lidocaine, 1 to 2 mg per kg. Harrison et al.,[30] in discussing the antiarrhythmic properties of lidocaine, stated that lidocaine is effective and also has little effect on systemic arterial pressure and little or no effect on the contractile force of the heart. Underhill and Tredway[64] feel it futile to attempt to control arrhythmias in the presence of hypotension. They stated further that ventricular and atrial arrhythmias which failed to respond to cardiac depressants often reverted when the blood pressure was raised to normal levels with norepinephrine. Presumably the increased coronary flow results in improved myocardial stability. The value of pressor amines in the control of ventricular tachycardia appears to lie in their ability to accelerate the basic idioventricular pacemaker, thereby suppressing ectopic activity. Payne[51] stated that Pronethalol blocks the cardiac effects of both catecholamines and sympathetic activity. When given in moderate doses of 2.5 to 10 mg intravenously, it is capable of completely abolishing extrasystoles associated with respiratory acidosis and catecholamine release. One per cent procaine administered intravenously frequently has been used to control arrhythmias. Quinidine lactate injected intravenously in doses of 100 to 300 mg often will correct some ventricular arrhythmias refractory to procaine. The external electrical defibrillator is sometimes effective in reversing ventricular fibrillation if the myocardium is well oxygenated. Premedication with appropriate dosages of atropine is useful in inhibiting reflex vagal activity. Drugs which act as general depressants of cardiac irritability may aid materially in protecting the heart from arrhythmias. They are useful also in restoring an irregular rhythm to normal.

See the chapter on *monitoring* for discussion of the cardiac conduction system and of the cardioscope.

HYPOTENSION

Hypotension occurring during anesthesia, regardless of cause, may develop into an acute emergency. When hypotension exists to a mild degree preoperatively there is little concern if the patient is asymptomatic. If the patient presents with a more marked preoperative hypotension, a medical consultation is deemed advisable. With the patient under anesthesia, the anesthetic team must be constantly aware of his condition, as it has been demonstrated often the morbidity and mortality resulting from severe hypotension are directly related to the length of time the patient is in shock. Therefore, prompt recognition of a hypotensive state and immediate corrective therapy are required to prevent cardiovascular collapse. Hypotension has been reported in anesthetized patients who previously had been receiving antihypertensive therapy,[11, 49] and adrenal insufficiency with marked hypotension is sometimes seen in anesthetized patients who have previously been receiving corticosteroids.[58] Miscellaneous causes of hypotension would include excessive blood loss, air embolism, severe hypoxia, and overdosage of an anesthetic agent.

Shock may be regarded as a state of cardiovascular collapse often associated with insufficient venous return to the heart and complicated by a persisting deficiency of blood flow to the peripheral tissues. Various forms of shock are well known. In this chapter, however, we are concerned only with shock as a complication associated with the use of a general anesthetic. Certain anesthetic agents such as halothane may cause peripheral vasodilation and a resultant fall in systemic blood pressure. In general, the miscellaneous causes of hypotension listed above may result in shock in the anesthetized patient.

Rauwolfia Alkaloid Therapy

Reserpine and similar drugs are commonly used in the treatment of hypertension and psychiatric disorders. Reduction of blood pressure produced by intramuscular reserpine is gradual in onset and usually moderate, but significant. In addition, the drug possesses a behavioral effect, causing sedation which allows the patient to rest and yet be easily aroused for nursing care.[2] The action of reserpine depends on its ability to lower the level of catecholamine and serotonin content in all organs where these mediators are normally stored. The major storage areas, central and peripheral, include the lower centers of the brain, the adrenal medulla, sympathetic ganglia and nerves, cardiac muscle, and vascular and intestinal walls.[68]

The onset of hypotensive effect is one to two hours after intramuscular administration, after which the blood pressure falls gradually over a period of an hour and then slowly returns to pretreatment levels over a widely variable period of several hours to as much as several days.[24] At times the reduction of blood pressure achieved with reserpine alone is not sufficient to control the blood pressure at the desired level. In such instances hydralazine may be added. Parenteral hydralazine should be given only when the drug cannot be given orally.[52] The initial dose recommended is 10 mg, t.i.d., and is gradually increased to 100 mg t.i.d., over a period of four weeks. It is well known that the surgical and anesthetic risk is higher in the hypertensive patient.

There have been differences of opinion over the years regarding the delay of surgery in patients who are or have been recently receiving antihypertensive drugs. Freis[24] feels that surgery should be delayed until the blood pressure has been controlled for at least several days and symptoms of heart failure have cleared entirely. Others[68] are of the opinion that reserpine is potentiated by anesthetic agents and that extreme hypotension may result if the catecholamine level has previously been lowered. They feel that elective surgery should be delayed for two weeks after the drug is discontinued, this being the time required to return the catecholamine level to near normal in most patients. Present thought is that patients on reserpine therapy present few problems that are fundamentally new and would not be encountered in nontreated hypertensives. As an example of this concept, Morrow and Morrow[47] carried out corrective cardiac operations in five normotensive males, aged 16 to 35, each of whom had received oral reserpine for 38 to 68 days preoperatively up to the day preceding operation. None of the patients had significant changes in blood pressure or heart rate when anesthesia was induced, at the time of endotracheal intubation, or during maintenance of anesthesia. No patient required a vagolytic or vasopressor compound during operation. All had uncomplicated postoperative courses. The results of this study provide at least indirect evidence that the difficulties encountered in the anesthetic management of hypertensive patients receiving reserpine are attributable to their underlying hypertensive cardiovascular disease rather than to the pharmacologic effects of reserpine. In addition, Munson and Jamicek[49] stated that hypertensive individuals not receiving reserpine may have unstable blood pressures. They felt that this was commonly due to the loss of cardiovascular homeostatic mechanisms secondary to arteriosclerotic changes. Hamelberg[29] points out that no essential difference exists in the incidence of hypotension during anesthesia between the treated and nontreated patients. Opinion now tends to favor maintaining patients on their antihypertensive medication. No matter by which view one chooses to abide, he should be aware of the fact that catecholamine-depleted tissues are sensitive to exogenous catecholamine.[9] Bosomworth[6] states that his personal experience indicates that phenlyephrine and norepinephrine are the most reliable vasopressors when hypotension occurs in the reserpine-treated patient. The general feeling currently held regarding patients receiving antihypertensive drugs is that careful attention to anesthetic technique and an understanding of the pharmacologic action of these drugs make the postponement of surgery unnecessary.

Steroid Therapy

Patients receiving steroids or who have previously been on steroid therapy are being seen more frequently in practice today. In the patient with organic adrenal insufficiency any stressful procedure, such as surgery or anesthesia, was frequently fatal prior to the introduction of desoxycortisone acetate and adrenal cortical extract.[29] Steroids combined with careful attention to electrolyte balance increased the patient's chance to survive surgical procedures and anesthesia. Although a blessing for patients with adrenal cortical insufficiency, corticosteroids became a hazard when used for other diseases. Several men[33, 58] reported unresponsive hypotension and fatalities in this group of patients. There is evidence that this state of shock is the outcome of adrenal cortex depression induced by corticosteroid therapy.[40, 55] In one study[58] shock was successfully treated in 80 per cent of patients by further administration of cortisone.

It has been suggested that cortisone be administered to any patient about to undergo surgery who has had parenteral corticosteroid therapy within six months to a year.[8] Brown states that the usual course of therapy employed for the patient who is on maintenance or who has a history of having been on cortisone is to change the patient's daily dose to 200 mg of cortisone orally, beginning on the day prior to operation.[8] Cortisone or hydrocortisone, 150 mg diluted in 1000 ml. of 5 per cent glucose, is slowly infused. This infusion is discontinued in the recovery period if no signs of adrenal crisis appear. Maintenance on 200 mg of steroid per day is continued for two to three days postoperatively, and the dose is gradually reduced to the previous maintenance level. Close cooperation between the dental practitioner and physician must be maintained when confronted with these patients.

Although the prophylactic preparation of patients on steroids at the time of surgery is still recommended, one author questions this concept in those patients who have discontinued their steroids.[54] He based his remarks on recent studies measuring the plasma levels of 17-hydroxycorticosterone. In his study steroid therapy was discontinued, and within 48 hours normal values of 17-hydroxycorticosterone were present. Further, these patients responded to stressful situations without difficulty. It should be mentioned that caution must be exercised in this concept, because in the early reports of mortalities from iatrogenic adrenal insufficiency the cardiovascular instability did not occur until some six to twelve hours after the operative procedure.[40] It has been suggested that in patients whose steroid therapy has been discontinued steroids should be administered because of an unexplained cardiovascular instability. In these patients, 200 mg of hydrocortisone is given in one injection, followed by 100 mg by intravenous drip every eight hours. This dose is large enough to fully saturate the binding properties of transcortin and should correct the cardiovascular instability of adrenal insufficiency.[56] No one appears to have exact data which would indicate how long a patient must be receiving steroids before significant adrenal depression results. Also, Bosomworth[6] feels that it cannot be stated with certainty how long after discontinuance of cortisone therapy adrenal function can be considered normal. The consensus today appears to be that steroid therapy be adjusted and continued in those patients receiving steroids at the time of surgery, but reinstitution of therapy in patients who have discontinued therapy for some time is not routinely required.

Miscellaneous Causes of Hypotension

As with most emergency situations, prevention is the best cure. This is particularly true in the prevention of hypotension from miscellaneous causes. If heavy bleeding is expected, the patient should be hospitalized and replacement blood ordered. A dramatic hypotension may follow air embolism; therefore extreme care should be exercised during intravenous administration of drugs. If sufficient air is inadvertently injected, the patient becomes cyanotic, gasps for breath, and usually develops hypotension. Once this condition is recognized, the patient should be immediately placed on his left side to confine the air to the right side of the heart where it may gradually be absorbed. Anesthetic errors that may precipitate marked hypotension are severe hypoxia and overdosage of anesthetic agents.

HYPERTENSION

Hypertension carries with it the danger of increased bleeding, rupture of cerebral vessels, and pulmonary edema. It therefore follows that the surgical and anesthetic risk is high in patients with severe hypertension. Hypertension is usually a chronic disease for which patients can be treated with oral medication. Occasionally, however, crises arise during anesthesia whereby the patient's blood pressure rises acutely to dangerously high levels, and prompt treatment with parenteral medication is necessary to prevent serious complications. Physiologically, acute regulation of arterial pressure is effected primarily in the nervous system, the shift of fluid between interstitial space and blood, and the stress-relaxation mechanism of the vascular system. However, these factors, even including the nervous system, seem to be unimportant for the long-term regulation of arterial pressure. Long-term regulation has been found to depend almost entirely on the kidneys.[28] In the case of a hypertensive crisis Baldini[3] suggests intermittent intravenous injections of 2.5 mg of chlorpromazine at intervals of two to four minutes with frequent repeated determinations of blood pressure until the desired reduction of blood pressure is achieved. Other men[2, 24, 68] feel that reserpine is the drug of choice for most hypertensive emergencies. Scherbakova[57] states that patients with marked hypertension must receive a preliminary course of antihypertensive drugs (reserpine, dibazole, or euphylline). Whenever potent antihypertensive drugs are being administered, a solution of levarterenol or a similar drug should be available for immediate use should excessive blood pressure drop occur. Elective surgery should be delayed until the blood pressure level has been controlled for at least several days.

CARDIAC ARREST

Cardiac arrest is the most urgent general anesthetic emergency. Circulatory arrest occurs with both ventricular fibrillation and asystole, and the clinical picture is essentially the same.

Clinical Picture [17]

1. Absence of carotid or peripheral pulse.
2. Sudden pallor and cyanosis.

3. Absence of heart sounds.
4. Wide dilatation of the pupils *later* in the arrest.
5. Absence of bleeding.
6. Dark blood in operative site.
7. Loss of consciousness.
8. Convulsion.
9. Electrocardiographic evidence of asystole or ventricular fibrillation.

Cause

Circulatory arrest is usually due to one or a combination of the following:[13]

1. Progressive hypoxia leading to anoxia of the myocardium.
2. An accumulation of certain chemicals in the heart, such as carbon dioxide, potassium, epinephrine, or agents which depress the myocardium.
3. Cardiac reflexes.

Prevention

A thorough preoperative evaluation of the patient is essential as the first step in the prevention of cardiac arrest. Serious arrhythmias that may lead to ventricular fibrillation or asystole might be expected to develop in the following individuals: (a) those in the older age group; (b) those with a past history of ectopic rhythms; (c) patients with advanced heart disease; (d) those with coronary artery disease; and (e) patients with W-P-W syndrome, A-V heart block, or bundle branch block.

Anesthetics that predispose to the development of ventricular fibrillation should be avoided. Lidocaine increases the ventricular fibrillation threshold and is considered the drug of choice in treating premonitory arrhythmias. There are many offices where electronic monitoring is performed. By early detection and correction of less serious arrhythmias, fatal ventricular arrhythmias may be prevented. Adequate oxygenation of the patient from induction to complete recovery from the anesthetic must be insured.

Treatment[5]

1. Start cardiopulmonary resuscitation immediately.
2. Oxygen under positive pressure.
3. If ventricular fibrillation is identified by ECG, immediate defibrillation should be tried using 400 joules (watt-seconds).
4. Sodium bicarbonate, one ampule (44 mEq), intravenously every 5 minutes or so during CPR.
5. Calcium gluconate or calcium chloride, one ampule intravenously, if indicated.
6. Epinephrine 5 to 10 ml of 1:10,000, intravenously, prior to repeated cardioversion.

The patient should be transferred to the hospital as soon as possible for observation and additional care.

For more information see chapter on *Cardiopulmonary Arrest.*

ACCIDENTAL INTRA-ARTERIAL INJECTION

The accidental injection of intravenous anesthetic agents into an artery may lead to gangrene and ultimate amputation of tissue supplied by the injured artery. Many theories[1, 12, 35, 36, 61] have been proposed in regard to the pathologic response to intra-arterial barbiturate injections. These theories include arterial spasm, intimal damage and thrombosis, blockage of the lumen of arterioles by acid crystals, and release of norepinephrine. The necrosis was first thought to be a result of severe arterial spasm, possibly from the high alkalinity of the barbiturate, but there is little laboratory evidence to support this theory. Kinmonth and Shepherd[35] found that the period of vasoconstriction following injection is too short to produce the resulting necrosis. Waters[66] discounted thrombosis as a cause because thrombosis is a slow process and could not effect the changes that occurred shortly after injection. He reported that crystals of thiopental separated out in arterial blood and could block arterioles mechanically on reaching them, and could be responsible for the initial symptoms seen. The stagnation could lead to subsequent thrombosis. The mechanism of thrombosis is controversial, but biopsy has shown that, regardless of cause, thrombosis develops in all cases where tissue necrosis occurs.

Incidence

The true incidence is unknown, having been reported from a high of 1:3500[19] to a low of 1:200,000.[18] Many cases cause only minor injury and go unreported.

Clinical Picture

After intra-arterial injection of barbiturate there is a sudden onset of severe burning pain extending peripherally from the injection site. This severe pain may continue or gradually subside after a few minutes and usually will persist as a burning sensation for several hours. The involved extremity may become edematous and cyanotic. The prognosis is poor if these changes develop rapidly.[27]

Prevention

Most often accidental intra-arterial injection occurs in the antecubital fossa. Engler[23] suggested that the lateral aspect of the antecubital fossa be selected over the medial aspect, where the branches of the ulnar and brachial arteries are more superficial and close to the vein and are easily entered. One must be particularly careful when reinserting a needle in an anesthetized patient, as intra-arterial injection would not elicit pain and the emergency might go unrecognized. An excessively tight tourniquet and hypotension might mask arterial pulsations. Dependence cannot be placed on the color of the blood; arterial blood may sometimes be darker than expected. Release of the tourniquet may allow arterial pressure to push back the plunger. If there is still doubt, a very small amount of medication may be injected at first, waiting for any untoward reaction or pain before completing the injection.

Treatment

Intra-arterial injection constitutes a serious emergency. Any but emergency surgery should be cancelled. Treatment aimed at preventing thrombosis should begin immediately. Efforts to re-establish circulation are rarely successful after thrombosis has occurred.[12] No single treatment has been consistently successful. It is almost universally agreed, however, that injection of 1 to 2 per cent procaine, several milliliters through the same needle in place, may be of value. Immediate heparinization is advocated by many writers.[27, 35, 39] In experiments using rabbits Kinmonth and Shepherd[35] showed that heparinization reduced the area of gangrene. They reported the most critical factor regarding tissue loss was the concentration of the barbiturate injected. A concentration of 10 per cent caused an area of gangrene averaging 14.8 cm², one of 5 per cent resulted in an area of 10.4 cm², and a concentration of 2.5 per cent produced an area of only 0.15 cm². Stellate ganglion block or general anesthesia with halothane may be tried to promote vasodilation. Other measures include arteriography, to determine the extent of injury, and thrombectomy, to re-establish pulses. Amputation of areas of tissues necrosis may be necessary. The patient should be hospitalized as soon as possible for the above treatment by a vascular surgeon. In spite of therapy, some patients have developed gangrene and suffered amputation, particularly with higher concentrations of agent. Awareness of the possibility of this complication and a careful intravenous technique should do much to prevent this tragic accident.

NEUROLOGICAL EMERGENCIES AND COMPLICATIONS

CONVULSIONS

Convulsions contributed significantly to the anesthesia associated death rate in the past, but with better understanding of their causes and with the introduction of intravenous anesthetic agents this emergency is infrequently encountered today.

Clinical Picture

Convulsions are characterized by sudden involuntary tonic and clonic contractions of the arms and legs. In addition, the patient exhibits forced expiration and a rigid rib cage, and sometimes experiences laryngospasm.

Causes

Cerebral hypoxia is the most frequent cause of convulsions in the anesthetized patient. Other common causes are carbon dioxide retention, overdosage of local analgesic agents, epilepsy, or air embolism.

Prevention

Proper premedication to allay fear and apprehension in the overly anxious patient, along with a smooth induction and a well-administered anesthetic, will keep the incidence of this emergency at a minimum.

Treatment

Artificial respiration while the patient is convulsing is ineffective in inflating the lungs. Treatment consists of stopping the convulsion, relieving laryngospasm if present, maintaining respiration, and supporting the circulation, which soon fails in the untreated patient. Any drug used to control convulsions may lead to respiratory depression; therefore, it is advisable to use only the smallest effective dose. Intravenous barbiturates have been used to control convulsion, but they augment the depression seen following convulsions and may produce a difficult problem in managing the depressed state. Small doses of succinylcholine (10 to 20 mg), intravenously, are usually sufficient to control the convulsing patient. Respiration must be supported with 100 per cent oxygen.

TREMORS

Occasionally a pronator spasm may occur in the arm receiving an injection of barbiturate. This is usually eliminated by deepening the anesthetic and adding nitrous oxide and oxygen. Minor jactitations are often associated with hypoxia and are easily controlled by supporting respirations with 100 per cent oxygen.

MISCELLANEOUS EMERGENCIES AND COMPLICATIONS

Malignant Hyperthermia

Malignant hyperthermia is a rare emergency associated with general anesthesia, having an incidence of about 1:75,000. It was seen by Lee in the mid 1930s in some patients under ether anesthesia.[38] Most of today's cases involve children who have received halothane and succinylcholine. It is a condition in which the body temperature rises progressively and will terminate in death in the absence of adequate treatment. In susceptible individuals, any potent inhalation anesthetic agent such as methoxyflurane, halothane, diethyl-ether and cyclopropane, or any skeletal muscle relaxant such as succinylcholine, decamethonium, gallamine, and d-tubocurarine can precipitate an acute crisis characterized by fever, often malignant. Temperatures of 111.2° F (44° C) have been reported.[32]

Cause

The exact cause of malignant hyperthermia is unknown, but recent studies strongly suggest it is most likely to occur in a patient with an inherited sarcoplasmic defect.[59, 65] The inheritance is as an autosomal dominant. Members of susceptible families have minor muscle abnormalities such as ptosis, squint, or kyphoscoliosis and may have moderate elevation of creatine phosphokinase and serum aldolase levels, possible evidence of a subclinical myopathy.[22] This relationship between malignant hyperthermia and inherited muscular defects was demonstrated in a report by Ellis.[21] It was shown that musculoskeletal abnormalities and surgery to correct them are common in patients with myopathy. Many patients who developed malignant hyperthermia have had surgery for squints, ptosis, hernias, or orthopedic abnormalities. Triggering agents appear to release stored calcium to the cytoplasm. This, in turn, causes sustained myofibrillar contraction, mobilization of glycogen from the liver, and acceleration of lactic acid and carbon dioxide production. Once this rapid process resulting in malignant hyperthermia has started it is almost impossible to halt. The overall mortality rate is about 64 per cent and is unchanged in recent years in spite of aggressive therapy.[56]

Clinical Signs

Often the first indications of developing trouble are violent fasciculations followed by skeletal muscle rigidity after the administration of succinylcholine. The most consistent early sign is a ventricular arrhythmia-tachycardia. Other early findings are rapid, deep respirations, hot skin, profuse sweating, rigidity, and a mottling cyanosis.[7]

Late events of ominous prognostic significance are hemolysis, consumption coagulopathy, acute left heart failure, and decerebration. The latter is characterized by fixed and dilated pupils, loss of deep tendon reflexes, convulsions, coma, and loss of central temperature regulation. Returning consciousness and hyperactivity of deep tendon reflexes are favorable signs.

Prevention

Unexplained deaths associated with anesthesia should be investigated with the malignant hyperthermia syndrome in mind. Relatives should have their creatine phosphokinase levels determined. Normal levels are less than 100 units per liter in males and less than 60 in females.[38] If the history and investigations indicate a patient is likely to develop malignant hyperthermia, careful thought must be given to the planning of anesthesia or sedation. Local analgesia should be used wherever possible, but lignocaine should not be used; the local analgesia of choice is procaine HCl. If general anesthesia is unavoidable, inhalation agents, particularly halothane, are contraindicated in conjunction with succinylcholine and atropine. Sodium pentothal, Brevital, promethazine and diazepam are probably safe, as are nitrous oxide and a non-depolarizing relaxant technique.[22] The patient should be hospitalized for general anesthesia when the probability of this condition exists.

Treatment

Treatment must be aggressive if the patient is to survive. Should this emergency occur in the office, anesthesia and surgery must be terminated immediately. Give 100 per cent oxygen by positive pressure while arrangements are being made to transfer the patient to a hospital. The patient should be transferred to the hospital as soon as possible. The present position with regard to treatment is as follows:

1. Hyperventilate with 100 per cent oxygen (8 to 10 L O_2 flow), if necessary by IPPV.
2. Actively cool the patient by aggressive methods.
    a. IV iced saline (not Ringer's lactate) 1000 ml/10 minutes for 30 minutes.
    b. Lavage of stomach, bladder, rectum, peritoneal and thoracic cavities with iced saline.
    c. Extracorporeal circulation and heat exchange (femoral to femoral).
    d. Surface cooling with ice and hypothermia blanket.
3. Administer sodium bicarbonate, 100 mEq stat, and up to 600 mEq over time, guided by arterial pH and pCO_2. Since increasing the blood pH drives potassium into cells, sodium bicarbonate is highly effective in reversing the severe hyperkalemia.
4. Maintain urine output. Mannitol should be given IV to dislodge myoglobin from the renal tubules.
5. Procine amide 15 mg/kg over 5 to 10 minutes with ECG control.
6. Administer insulin to shift potassium back into cells and to improve glucose uptake.
7. Support circulation with isoprenaline, using blood pressure and ECG monitoring.
8. Discontinue cooling when the temperature reaches 101° F.

AIR EMBOLISM

Accidental entrance of air as a complication of general anesthesia could occur during intravenous infusion or during intravenous injection.

Clinical Picture

When air enters a vein in sufficient quantity, it travels to the right heart and lung and may set up an obstruction within the pulmonary artery. This may be followed by a loud precordial murmur. A precordial stethoscope will elicit the characteristic bubbling or so-called "mill wheel murmur" sounds. A sudden cyanosis will develop, followed rapidly by hypotension, tachycardia, engorged neck veins, and irregular, gasping respiration, progressing through tachypnea and hypopnea, and if not treated promptly will lead to cardiac arrest.

Treatment

1. Prevent further entrace of air into the vein.
2. Tilt the chair back steeply and lower the head to keep air out of the cerebral vessels.
3. Turn the patient onto the left side so that bubbles of air are carried away from the pulmonary artery.
4. Give 100 per cent oxygen and stop nitrous oxide. N_2O is more soluble than nitrogen in blood and would thus increase the size of the emboli.
5. Infuse large volumes of intravenous fluid to wash out froth.
6. Papaverine, 30 to 60 mg to dilate pulmonary vessels.
7. Vasopressors.[38]

Prevention here, as elsewhere, is stressed. Strict observance of proper technique will prevent this complication.

INJURIES TO SOFT TISSUES AND TEETH

Ocular Injury

Corneal abrasion is a painful injury usually resulting from careless application of the face or nasal mask. In the hospital, with the patient supine and covered with drapes, the eyelids are usually taped shut. This precaution is not necessary in outpatient procedures where the head is not covered with drapes. Care should be taken, however, to insure that there is no drying of the cornea, which may contribute to ulceration, and that masks are properly applied.

The eyes should be checked after surgery for any inadvertent injury. If any injury is found, the patient should be referred for ophthalmic consultation. If corneal abrasions are treated promptly, they usually re-epithelialize within 24 hours.

Extravascular Injection

Extravasation of injected medication is a common complication of intravenous anesthesia. It is due either to a faulty intravenous technique or to displacement of the needle during anesthesia. Extravasation is followed by pain and swelling at the site of injection. The pain is intense if the solution is alkaline, acid, or hypertonic. In the anesthetized patient extravasation can only be detected by careful observation, and could go unnoticed.

TREATMENT

1. Remove the needle immediately.
2. Inject 5 to 10 ml of 1 per cent procaine into the involved area to dilute the barbiturate. Sloughing has occurred with such medications as Levophed or Pentothal. Brevital rarely produces a slough.
3. Massage the area to disperse the irritant.
4. Heat application may be dangerous if skin circulation is poor.

Chipped or Loosened Teeth

The upper anterior teeth are particularly prone to injury by the laryngoscope blade during intubation. The teeth should never be used as a fulcrum for the laryngoscope blade. It is wise to protect the anterior teeth with a thin lead strip such as can be fashioned easily from the lead backing in an occlusal film packet. Another source of injury to anterior teeth is the damaged mouth prop. Whenever the internal metal portion of the mouth prop shows through the rubber it should be discarded immediately. Here, as with most other injuries, prevention is the key.

Injuries to the Tongue and Lips

Injuries to the tongue are most often due to impingement of the tongue between the mouth prop and teeth. Injuries to the lips are frequently the result of impingement of the lips between the teeth and a dental forceps or the laryngoscope blade. Both the operator and the surgical assistant must be aware of the problem and prevent pressure on the soft tissues by instruments and teeth.

POSTOPERATIVE EMERGENCIES AND COMPLICATIONS

RESPIRATORY

Airway Obstruction

Airway obstruction in the postoperative period is most often the result of the tongue falling back against the posterior pharyngeal wall when the patient is in the supine position and the jaw is relaxed (Fig. 11–1). Examination of the patient reveals hyperactivity of the secondary muscles of respiration, flaring of the nares, and little or no elevation of the thoracic wall. Auscultation will demonstrate inspiratory stridor or, in some cases, no sounds at all. While the patient is in the supine position, simple elevation of the mandible is usually sufficient to draw the tongue away from the posterior pharyngeal wall and thus clear the airway (Fig. 11–2). A gauze pack in the mouth to aid in clot formation is also a potential source of airway obstruction. It is suggested that the gauze pack be large enough to protrude from the mouth for easier observation. Although the procedure described will relieve obstruction in the supine

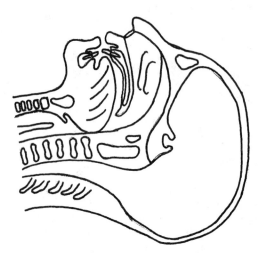

Figure 11–1 Head not extended, mandible retruded. This position causes the tongue to fall backward against the posterior pharyngeal wall, occluding the airway.

patient, obstruction will recur unless the patient is constantly being helped. It is far better to turn the patient onto his side, flex the knees, and place a pillow behind the back to maintain the side position. In this position the jaw does not tend to fall back and, in fact, tends to fall forward, opening the airway. In any case, close observation of the patient is essential in the postoperative period.

Laryngospasm. Laryngospasm may develop in the postoperative period and is usually caused by irritation of the vocal cords by mucus or blood. Oxygen under positive pressure should be administered after suctioning the mouth and pharynx and changing the oropharyngeal pack. This will usually relieve the spasm. If the spasm persists, small doses of succinylcholine, 10 to 20 mg, should be given intravenously. The mouth should then be resuctioned and the patient ventilated with 100 per cent oxygen under positive pressure.

Bronchospasm. Bronchospasm in the postoperative period is most likely to be the result of irritation of the airway or misplacement of the endotracheal

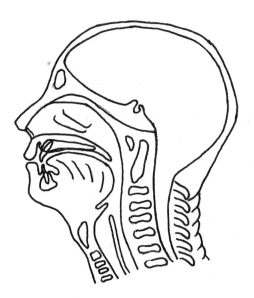

Figure 11–2 Head extended, mandible drawn upward. This maneuver elevates the tongue away from the posterior pharyngeal wall and opens the airway.

tube. Heavy smokers and those with chronic bronchitis are more prone to postoperative bronchospasm. Aminophylline will relieve the problem but entails a certain risk in the hypoxic or hypercarbic patient. Isoethrane may be effective as an aerosol. In severe instances of bronchospasm, intravenous isoproterenol or epinephrine should be effective, whereas an aerosol would not.

Aspiration of Vomitus.   This subject is discussed elsewhere in this chapter; however, a few remarks are in order here. The patient should not be removed from the surgery room to the recovery room until protective reflexes are present. If the patient in recovery is placed onto his side, as described above under postoperative airway obstruction, the danger of aspirating after vomiting is greatly reduced. A reliable source of suction and oxygen should be immediately available in the recovery room for both emergency use and for the prevention of emergencies. Many offices have seat belts attached to the recovery bunks to prevent undue movement and falling.

Hypercarbia

Postoperative hypercarbia can result from an inadequate respiratory drive or increases of CO_2. Inadequate respiratory drive may result from the residual effects of the anesthetic agent or depression of respiration from premedication with narcotics. Increased CO_2 production is seen with shivering or emergence delirium. Respiratory depression due to the residual effects of anesthetic agents is best combatted by controlled ventilation with oxygen until the anesthetic agents are detoxified and the patient is able to control his own respirations. If the depression is due to narcotic medication, intravenous injection of a narcotic antagonist such as naloxone 0.2 to 0.4 mg will result in immediate elimination of respiratory depression followed by arousal and awakening. The patient must be carefully observed, as the narcotic's duration of action may be considerably longer than that of naloxone. Naloxone may have to be repeated once or twice to maintain wakefulness.

CARDIOVASCULAR

Hypotension

Postoperative hypotension constitutes one of the most common complications encountered in the recovery room and may result from various causes.[43] A mild hypotension in the early postoperative period is frequently due to a change in position or to physical movement during transport to the recovery area. This postural hypotension is a result of a lack of efficiency of the patient's compensatory mechanisms caused by the effects of anesthetic, analgesic, tranquilizing, or antihypertensive drugs. The underlying mechanism appears to be pooling of blood in the lower extremities or other peripheral regions with subsequent reduction in arterial pressure.

CLINICAL SIGNS

Clinical signs of hypotension are as follows:

1.   The skin is pale or gray.

2. The skin is cold, clammy and diaphoretic (profuse sweating).
3. The pulse is rapid and thready.
4. Respirations are rapid and shallow.
5. There are signs of cerebral ischemia which include disorientation, restlessness and anxiety.

These clinical signs are often difficult to recognize as they may be masked by residual anesthetic drugs.

TREATMENT

When hypotension is recognized, corrective therapy is started immediately. Therapy includes parenteral administration of fluids, oxygen under positive pressure, and a vasopressor agent. If the patient is sitting, he should be layed down and placed onto his side. The blood pressure should be checked at frequent intervals until stable.

Arrhythmias

Serious arrhythmias may occur after surgery and anesthesia. Often these disappear without treatment. If a serious arrhythmia persists, it may lead to a reduction of cardiac output and severe hypotension. For treatment of the various more common arrhythmias see *Cardiac Arrhythmias*, in this chapter.

MISCELLANEOUS COMPLICATIONS

Emergence Delirium

Emergence delirium is a condition of muscular activity and excitement during the immediate postoperative period. It is most often seen in healthy teenagers recovering from an intravenous barbiturate anesthetic. There may be uncontrolled thrashing about accompanied by loud vocalization. Although the problem is not dangerous, it is most troublesome. It is well known that barbiturates possess no analgesic properties and are therefore unable to dull the pain of recent surgery. This and the lingering effects of the anesthetic on cortical function result in a patient who is restless, confused, and unable to cope with any pain following surgery. Local analgesia given to prevent postoperative pain will often avert this problem. Narcotics in conservative doses may be helpful in stubborn cases. It is important to prevent injury to the patient, but mechanical restraints often do more harm than good. A reassuring voice along with minimal control of movement is frequently helpful.

Shivering

Shivering after operation may occur with most anesthetic agents but is most common with halothane and is frequently seen after anesthesia with barbiturates. Pyramidal tract signs mimicking convulsions may sometimes be seen. This condition usually responds to the administration of methylphenidate (Ritalin), 20 mg.

Pain

Some pain is inevitable after operation. Its effects are exaggerated in the unstable patient. Opiates must be given with caution in the immediate post-operative period, as there is danger of hypotension and hypoventilation. Morphine, 5 mg, or meperidine, 50 mg, given intramuscularly, is generally satisfactory for the average adult.

Prolonged Recovery

Prolonged recovery from dental or oral surgical procedures is an infrequent complication. When it does occur it is usually related to overdosage of anesthetic agents or premedication agents, or it occurs after relatively lengthy procedures. Clinical observation leads me to believe that Orientals are more prone to prolonged recovery than others. Some experts feel that prolonged recovery may be minimized by supplementing general anesthesia with local analgesia; others do not.

DISCHARGING THE PATIENT

Before discharging the patient, oral and written post-operative instructions should be given to the patient and the individual accompanying the patient home. Under no circumstances should the patient be allowed to drive himself. He should be driven home by a competent adult. The patient is never discharged until vital signs are stable, until all bleeding is controlled, and until he can walk without difficulty.

EMERGENCY EQUIPMENT

The life-endangering nature of general anesthetic emergencies requires that the necessary drugs and equipment be readily available. The emergency tray should be checked at least monthly to be certain that batteries and lights for the laryngoscope are functioning properly and that all drugs are within their date limit.

Electronic monitoring equipment is now found in many offices, and no doubt electronic monitoring will become standard practice. It should be recognized that the cardioscope only registers electrical activity of the heart and does not indicate adequacy of circulation. The pulsemeter, however, requires the presence of a pulse to function and thus gives evidence of circulatory perfusion.

Emergency situations may arise suddenly and require immediate action. For this reason it is strongly urged that periodic "emergency drills" be practiced to familiarize each member of the anesthesia team with emergency treatment and equipment.

* * * * * *

Perhaps the most valuable result of all education is the ability to make yourself do the thing you have to do, when it ought to be done, as it ought to be done, whether you like to do it or not.

THOMAS HUXLEY

REFERENCES

1. Albo, D., Jr., et al.: Effect of intra-arterial injection of barbiturates. Am. J. Surg., 120:676, 1970.
2. Alper, M. H., Flacke, W., and Krayer, O.: Pharmacology of reserpine and its implications for anesthesia. Anesthesiology, 24:524, 1963.
3. Baldini, E., and Lincoln, J. R.: Treatment of acute hypertensive crises in surgical patients. J.A.M.A., 190:157, 1964.
4. Bannister, W. K., and Sattilaro, A. J.: Vomiting and aspiration during anesthesia. Anesthesiology, 23:251, 1962.
5. Benson, D. W., Jude, J. R., and Kouwenhoven, W. B.: External cardiac massage. Anesth. Analg., 42:132, 1963.
6. Bosomworth, P. P.: Discussion of reference 29. Anesth. Analg., 43:107, 1964.
7. Britt, B. A.: Recent advances in malignant hyperthermia. Anesth. Analg., 51:841, 1972.
8. Brown, E. S.: Steroids and the anesthesiologists. Connecticut Med., 26:227, 1962.
9. Burn, J. H., and Rand, M. J.: The action of sympathomimetic amines on animals treated with reserpine. J. Physiol. (Lond.), 144:314, 1958.
10. Cameron, J. L., Mitchell, W. H., and Zuidema, G. D.: Aspiration pneumonia. Clinical outcome following documented aspiration. Arch. Surg., 106:49, 1973.
11. Coakley, C. S., Alpert, S., and Boling, J. S.: Circulatory responses during anesthesia of patients on rauwolfia therapy. J.A.M.A., 161:1143, 1956.
12. Cohen, S. M.: Accidental intra-arterial injection of drugs. Lancet, 2:409, 1948.
13. Collawn, T. H.: Causes and prevention of cardiac arrest. North Carolina Med. J., 23:336, 1962.
14. Cullen, S. C.: Anesthesia. 6th ed. Chicago, Year Book Medical Publishers, 1961, p. 48.
15. Dickson, D. N.: Total bronchospasm. So. Afr. Med. J., 38:108, 1964.
16. Dines, D. E., Baker, W. G., and Scantland, W. A.: Aspiration pneumonitis — Mendelson's syndrome. J.A.M.A., 176:229, 1961.
17. Dripps, R. D.: Introduction to Anesthesia. 5th ed., Philadelphia, W. B. Saunders Co., 1977, p. 452.
18. Driscoll, E. J., and American Society of Oral Surgeons Committee on Anesthesia. ASOS anesthesia morbidity and mortality survey. J. Oral Surg., 32:733, 1974.
19. Dundee, J. W.: Thiopentone and Other Barbiturates. London, Livingston Ltd., 1956.
20. Edwards, G., Morton, H. J., Pask, E. A., and Wylie, W. D.: Deaths associated with anaesthesia. Anaesthesia, 11:194, 1956.
21. Ellis, F. R.: Malignant hyperpyrexia. Anaesthesia, 28:245, 1973.
22. Ellis, F. R., Keaney, N. P., and Harriman, D. G.: Histopathological and neuropharmacological aspects of malignant hyperpyrexia. Proc. Roy. Soc. Med., 66:66, 1973.
23. Engler, H. S., et al.: Gangrenous extremities resulting from intra-arterial injections. Arch. Surg., 94:644, 1967.
24. Freis, E. D.: Hypertensive emergencies. Med. Clin. North Amer., 46:353, 1962.
25. Fukushima, K., et al.: Effect of propranolol on the ventricular arrhythmias induced by hypercarbia during halothane anesthesia in man. Brit. J. Anaesth., 40:53, 1968.
26. Gold, M. I.: Treatment of bronchospasm during anesthesia. Anesth. Analg., 54:783, 1975.
27. Goldsmith, D., and Trieger, N.: Accidental intra-arterial injection: A medical emergency. Anesth. Prog. 22:180, 1975.
28. Guyton, A. C., et al.: Physiologic control of arterial pressure. Bull. New York Acad. Med., 45:811, 1969.
29. Hamelberg, W.: Current concepts on antihypertensive drugs and steroids. Anesth. Analg., 43:104, 1964.
30. Harrison, D. C., Sprouse, J. H., and Morrow, A. G.: The antiarrhythmic properties of lidocaine and procaine amide. Clinical and physiologic studies of their cardiovascular effects in man. Circulation, 28:486, 1963.
31. Hausmann, W., and Lunt, R. L.: Problem of treatment of peptic aspiration pneumonia following obstetric anesthesia. Obstet. Gynaec., Brit. Emp. 62:509, 1955.
32. Hawthorne, A. T., Richardson, M. E., and Whitfield, G. T.: Fulminating hyperthermia and general anesthesia. Brit. Med. J., 4:750, 1968.
33. Hays, M. A.: Surgical treatment as complicated by prior adrenal cortical steroid therapy. Surgery, 36:945, 1956.
34. Heironimus, T. W.: Regurgitation and aspiration during anesthesia. Virginia Med. Monthly, 90:162, 1963.
35. Kinmonth, J. B., and Shepherd, R. C.: Accidental injection of thiopentone into arteries; studies of pathology and treatment. Brit. Med. J., 2:914, 1959.
36. Klatt, E. C., Brooks, A. L., and Rhamy, R. K.: Toxicity of intra-arterial barbiturates and tranquilizing drugs. Radiology, 92:700, 1969.

37. Lee, J. A.: A Synopsis of Anaesthesia. 7th ed., Chicago, Year Book, 1976, p. 801.
38. Lee, J. A.: A Synopsis of Anaesthesia. 7th ed., Chicago, Year Book, 1976, p. 825.
39. Lindell, T. D., Porter, J. M., and Langston, C.: Intra-arterial injection of drugs. N. Engl. J. Med., 287:1132, 1972.
40. Lundy, J. S.: Cortisone problems involving anesthesia. Anesthesiology, 14:376, 1953.
41. Lytle, J. J.: Anesthesia morbidity and mortality survey of the Southern California Society of Oral Surgeons. J. Oral Surg., 32:739, 1974.
42. Marshall, B. M., and Gordon, R. A.: Vomiting and aspiration in anesthesia. II. Canad. Anaes. Soc. J., 5:438, 1958.
43. Marx, G. F., et al.: Postoperative hypotension. New York J. Med., 67:1893, 1967.
44. McCormick, P. W.: Immediate care after aspiration of vomit. Anaesthesia, 30:658, 1975.
45. Mendelson, C. L.: The aspiration of stomach contents into the lungs during obstetric anesthesia. Am. J. Obstet. Gynecol., 52:191, 1946.
46. Morrow, D. H., and Logic, J. R.: Management of cardiac arrhythmias during anesthesia. Anesth. Analg., 48:748, 1969.
47. Morrow, D. H., and Morrow, A. G.: The responses to anesthesia of nonhypertensive patients pretreated with reserpine. Brit. J. Anaesth., 35:313, 1963.
48. Mucklow, R. G., and Larard, D. G.: The effects of the inhalation of vomitus on the lungs: Clinical considerations. Brit. J. Anaesth. 35:153, 1963.
49. Munson, W. M., and Janicek, J. A.: Effect of anesthetic agents on patients receiving reserpine therapy. Anesthesiology, 23:741, 1962.
50. Nicholl, R. M., Holland, E. L., and Brown, S. S.: Mendelson's syndrome: Its treatment by tracheostomy and hydrocortisone. Brit. Med. J., 2:745, 1967.
51. Payne, J. P.: Pronethalol in treatment of ventricular arrhythmias during anesthesia. Brit. Med. J., 1:603, 1964.
52. Physician's Desk Reference.
53. Rees, L. T.: Bronchospasm during anaesthesia. Anaesthesia, 18:103, 1963.
54. Robinson, B. H., Mattingly, D., and Cope, C. L.: Adrenal function after prolonged corticosteroid therapy. Brit. Med. J., 1:1579, 1962.
55. Salassa, R. M., Bennett, W. A., and Keating, F. R.: Postoperative adrenal cortical insufficiency: Occurrence in patients previously treated with cortisone. J.A.M.A., 512:1509, 1953.
56. Sandberg, A. A., and Slaunwhite, W. R.: Transcortin, a corticosteroid binding protein. J. Clin. Invest., 38:384, 1959.
57. Scherbakova, L. S.: Anesthesia for hypertensive patients. Eksp. Kchir. Anest. (Russian), 3:67, 1964.
58. Slavey, G., and Brooke, B. N.: Post-operative collapse due to adrenal insufficiency following cortisone therapy. Lancet 1:1167, 1957.
59. Steers, A. J. W., Tallach, J. A., and Thompson, D. E.: Fulminating hyperpyrexia during anaesthesia in a member of a myopathic family. Brit. Med. J. 2:341, 1970.
60. Stetson, J. B.: Patient safety: Prevention and prompt recognition of regurgitation and aspiration. Anesth. Analg., 53:142, 1974.
61. Stone, H. H., and Donnelly, C.: The accidental intraarterial injection of thiopental. Anesthesia. 22:995, 1961.
62. Teabeaut, J. R.: Aspiration of gastric contents. Experimental study. Am. J. Path., 28:51, 1952.
63. Tolas, A. G., and Allen, G. D.: Comparison of effects of methods of induction of anesthesia on cardiac rhythm. J. Oral Surg., 25:54, 1967.
64. Underhill, W. L., and Tredway, J. B.: Treatment of paroxysmal tachycardia with isoproterenol. Ann. Int. Med., 60:680, 1964.
65. Wang. J. K.: Acute hyperthermia with anesthesia. Minn. Med. 55:618, 1972.
66. Waters, D. J.: Intra-arterial thiopentone: A physiochemical phenomenon. Anaesthesia. 21:343, 1966.
67. Winternitz, M. C., Smith, G. H., and McNamara, F. P.: Effect of intrabronchial insufflation of acid. J. Exper. Med., 32:199, 1920.
68. Ziegler, C. H., and Lovette, J. B.: Operative complications after therapy with reserpine and reserpine compounds. J.A.M.A., 176:916, 1961.

12

ESTABLISHING AN EMERGENCY AIRWAY

LEO KORCHIN

RECOGNITION OF OBSTRUCTION
NONSURGICAL MANEUVERS TO RE-
LIEVE OBSTRUCTION
  Abdominal and Chest Thrust
  Mouth-to-Mouth Breathing

ESTABLISHMENT OF AN EMERGENCY
  AIRWAY
  Cricothyroid Membrane Puncture
    Anatomic Considerations
    Surgical Considerations
    Technique

There is no provision for the storage of oxygen in the body, and oxygen deprivation is tantamount to strangulation. Permanent brain damage or death will be produced by total airway obstruction lasting three to five mintues. Partial airway obstruction is not so critical, yet it too will produce permanent brain damage and even death unless early and rational treatment is instituted. Preparation for this unhappy situation could place one in the position of saving a life which, in the absence of a preconceived plan, might be lost.

Many substances placed in a patient's mouth during a dental procedure can be aspirated. Since pharyngeal reflexes are abolished during general anesthesia, the ease of aspiration is greater than when local analgesia or no anesthesia is used. It might be well to state at this time that the type of emergency situation with which this chapter is concerned is that which might occur to a patient who receives treatment under local analgesia or no anesthesia. While the treatment of acute foreign body obstruction is the same for a patient under general anesthesia, there are other considerations involved that are beyond the scope of this presentation. The subject material is applicable, however, to patients who are recovering from general anesthesia. Following are some of the materials that might be aspirated and produce obstruction: vomitus, fragments of teeth or whole teeth, amalgam fillings or particles of amalgam, gold inlays, crowns, prosthetic appliances, impression material, sponges, packs, drains, cotton rolls, broken instruments, etc. A convulsive seizure may occur in the waiting room or operatory, and one of the hazards of this circumstance is the aspiration of vomitus.

Aspiration most frequently does not produce acute respiratory obstruction. After initial symptoms of choking, coughing, gagging, and wheezing, the material is expelled or passed through the larynx to lodge in the trachea or a bronchus. Unless present in massive amount, the complications produced by a foreign body in the deeper air passages do not become manifest at once. If the fragment is not soon removed, however, tracheobronchial or pulmonary disease subsequently becomes evident. When a foreign body disappears from the oral cavity and is accompanied by signs of laryngeal and bronchial irritation, it must be presumed to have passed into the respiratory passage until proved otherwise. These patients should be referred at once to a physician. However, if total airway obstruction occurs, immediate definitive treatment should be rendered with equipment at hand. An airway must be reestablished within three to five minutes from onset in order to avoid permanent brain damage. See chapter 2 for further information on laryngeal, bronchial, and esophageal foreign bodies.

There are three basic steps for the restoration of ventilation in critical airway emergencies: (1) prompt recognition of obstruction; (2) nonsurgical maneuvers to relieve obstruction; and (3) establishment of an emergency surgical airway. This plan of action is rational and provides an orderly series of steps for the emergency treatment of airway obstruction in the dental office.

RECOGNITION OF OBSTRUCTION

A patient gasping for breath with great effort, possibly clutching his throat or chest, demonstrating suprasternal retraction, and unable to obtain air exchange is presumed to have an upper respiratory tract obstruction, and nonsurgical maneuvers to relieve the obstruction should be initiated.

The clinician faced with an apneic patient must determine whether this is a late effect of obstruction or whether there is some other cause. Ordinarily this is not difficult, because if there is obstruction the foreign body might have been seen to disappear into the pharynx, the patient will be unable to speak and/or the patient will have demonstrated signs of respiratory distress. However, the apnea of anxiety-induced hyperventilation, particularly if accompanied by cyanosis,[3] might be puzzling until its true nature was determined. This and other respiratory disturbances, such as those which might follow the intravascular injection of a local anesthetic agent, or the depressant effect of barbiturates and other depressant drugs on the respiratory center, can be distinguished from obstructive phenomena because resistance to air or oxygen during resuscitative efforts is not encountered.

NONSURGICAL MANEUVERS TO RELIEVE OBSTRUCTION

When respiratory obstruction occurs in the conscious patient, protective mechanisms are activated which attempt to eject the obstructing object. The patient will cough, wheeze, gag, choke, and make great efforts to expel the respiratory block. Attempts at removal by the doctor might be actively resisted. Nevertheless such an attempt should be made, although force must not be used. If the obstruction is large, the attempt at removal may be successful. A general anesthetic should not be administered, because removal of the voluntary respiratory effort may result in immediate asphyxia.

ABDOMINAL AND CHEST THRUST

If the attempt to manually remove the obstruction is not successful, a rapid series of thrusts to the upper abdomen (Heimlich maneuver[6]) is done. This maneuver can be accomplished with the patient seated while turned in the chair, standing, or lying supine. In the seated and standing positions, the doctor places himself behind the patient. He grasps one fist with his other hand, the thumb side of the fist against the patient's abdomen, between the xiphoid and the umbilicus, and the other hand placed on top of the first (Fig. 12–1). If the patient is in the supine position with the doctor kneeling beside or astride him, the heel of the doctor's one hand is placed between the xiphoid and the umbilicus and the other hand is placed on top of the first (Fig. 12–2). Now pressure is exerted upward into the epigastrium by means of a quick upward thrust. The sudden elevation of the diaphragm compresses the lungs and increases the air pressure within the tracheobronchial tree. This pressure is forced out through the trachea and acts to eject a foreign body occluding the airway. If the patient is grossly obese or in a state of advanced pregnancy, the same maneuver can be perfomed by means of a backward thrust with the arms around the lower chest. In this position, the thumb side of the fist should be on the lower sternum, not on the xiphoid process.[2]

The possibility of a rib fracture and damage to the internal organs, such as rupture or laceration of the abdominal viscera, is a significant consideration in performing these maneuvers, but the possible iatrogenic effects

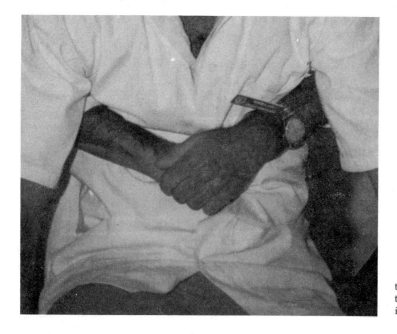

Figure 12–1 Abdominal thrust. Position of hands when the patient is seated or standing.

should not be a deterrent when a life can be saved. However, it is important to stress that pressure must never be placed on the xiphoid process of
the sternum or on the lower margins of the rib cage.

   If this maneuver is unsuccessful, the unconscious patient should be
placed in a head-down position, fluid aspirated, and the mouth and pharynx
explored with the fingers, removing any foreign bodies encountered. (If not
attempted on the conscious patient, the Heimlich maneuver can now be
performed.) The mandible should be held forward to prevent occlusion of
the pharynx by the tongue. This also can be accomplished by grasping the
tongue with a gauze sponge and pulling it forward. Many obstructions will
be relieved at this time, and respiration may begin spontaneously. The airway should remain supported until the patient is conscious. If respiration
cannot be started, mouth-to-mouth resuscitation should be initiated at once.

MOUTH-TO-MOUTH BREATHING

   If obstruction is not complete, it is possible for enough air to reach the
lungs by means of mouth-to-mouth breathing so that life can be maintained.
Mouth-to-mouth breathing should be continued until the patient is in the
hands of a professional person capable of accepting responsibility for the
further conduct of the case, or until the patient recovers. During this procedure it is important to support the mandible in a forward position so that
the airway is not further obstructed by the base of the tongue. If resuscitative efforts are successful, the chest will be observed to rise and fall rhyth-

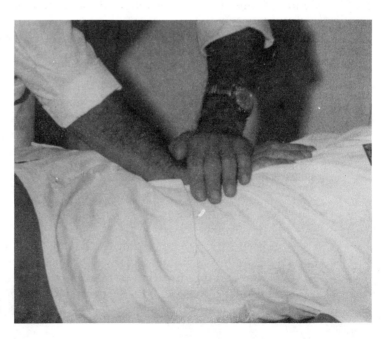

Figure 12–2 Abdominal
thrust. Position of hands when
patient is supine.

mically as the rescuer breathes into the patient's mouth and allows for passive exhalation, about 12 to 18 times a minute.

It is important to check the carotid arterial pulse and the pupils of the eyes. If a pulse is absent and the pupils are dilated, closed chest cardiac massage must be instituted concurrently with mouth-to-mouth breathing. See the chapter on *cardiopulmonary arrest*.

Inability to inflate the lungs because of complete obstruction or absence of expiration owing to a check-valve type of obstruction will become evident after a few breaths. Without delay an emergency surgical airway must be established.

ESTABLISHMENT OF AN EMERGENCY SURGICAL AIRWAY

CRICOTHYROID MEMBRANE PUNCTURE

Anatomic Considerations

The cricoid cartilage lies directly below the thyroid cartilage, forming a complete ring around the larynx below the vocal cords. It is the only complete cartilaginous ring in the respiratory passage and can be palpated in the midline of the neck as the smaller protuberance below the thyroid cartilage. Posteriorly the cricoid becomes wider and thicker, a safety factor impeding accidental posterior perforation into the esophagus during cricothyroid membrane puncture. The thyroid and cricoid cartilages are connected anteriorly by the cricothyroid membrane. This membrane is superficial, covered only by skin and thin layers of adipose tissue and fascia. It is elliptical in shape, and its average useful dimensions are 0.5 to 1.2 cm vertically at the midline, and 3 cm transversely.[4] An instrument passed through the skin and cricothyroid membrane immediately enters the space of the larynx below the vocal cords. Since no important blood vessels overlie the membrane, it can be pierced with little or no bleeding. Some practice is required to locate the cricothyroid membrane quickly. This can best be done with the neck in the normal or slightly flexed position. In men, where the thyroid cartilage is prominent, the palpating finger is placed on this structure and carried down the midline to the soft depression between the thyroid and cricoid cartilages. In women and children, where the thyroid cartilage is not so prominent, the palpating finger is carried superiorly along the midline from the suprasternal notch to the prominent cricoid cartilage.

Surgical Considerations

Technically, the approach to the tracheal space through the cricothyroid membrane is influenced by the character of the skin, the mobility of the larynx, and the direction of the fibers in the elastic membrane.

The skin is loose, tough, and resistant. Forceful attempts at penetration by a sharp, pointed object and sudden release might transfix the posterior shield of the cricoid cartilage, overcoming this protective barrier and producing a perforation into the esophagus. Extreme upward or downward position might also produce esophageal perforation. If a trocar and cannula are used, the cannula edge is apt to catch on the skin. Since the skin is loose, the manipulation used to free the cannula might change its direction and result in a sudden, forceful penetration of the tissues lateral to the trachea. These complications can be avoided by incising the skin over the cricothyroid membrane with a scalpel or by pinching the skin and snipping through with scissors.

The cricothyroid membrane is also resistant to penetration, although considerably less so than the skin. Since the larynx is not firmly fixed, it must be stabilized while the cricothyroid membrane is punctured.

The objective of cricothyroid membrane puncture is to provide an opening, a stoma large enough to restore normal ventilation. This is accomplished by spreading the fibers of the membrane at right angles to their course with the blades of the instrument used for the initial penetration. The dilation of the stoma in the transverse plane is the maneuver that opens the trachea to the outside. If the instrument is held in position to prevent collapse of the stoma, the objective of providing an opening to restore normal ventilation will have been attained. Refinement of the procedure provides for the passage of a firm rubber, plastic, or metal tube between the blades of the dilating instrument into the tracheal lumen. The dilator is then withdrawn.

Technique

Because they are time consuming, and since each second is of lifesaving importance, normal surgical requirements of aseptic technique, local analgesia, and hemostasis are disregarded.

The patient is placed in a head-down position and the neck is moderately hyperextended. This can be accomplished easily in the dental chair by lowering the headrest. In those dental chairs without a movable headrest the neck is hyperextended by placing a roll behind the shoulders. To produce extension of the neck when the patient is on the floor, he is placed on his back and his shoulders are supported and elevated by means of a roll. The chin and sternal notch are held in the median plane. A 2-cm. incision through skin only is made over the cricothyroid membrane. A scissors can be used to make this incision by pinching the skin and snipping through (Fig. 12–3). The larynx is stabilized by grasping it between the left thumb and middle finger. The left index finger is pressed into the cricothyroid membrane through the incision. A fine-pointed hemostat or scissors is passed along the fingernail and forced through the membrane into the tracheal space. An episode of coughing usually accompanies entrance into the trachea. After the membrane is perforated, the beaks of the instrument are spread and the airway dilated transversely (Fig. 12–4). A tube is inserted between the beaks of the dilating instrument (Fig. 12–5), and the instrument is removed (Fig. 12–6).

Figure 12–3

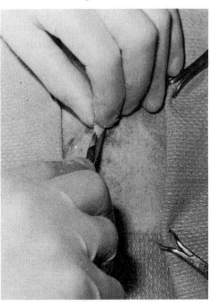

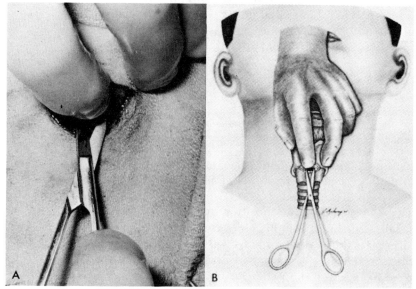

Figure 12–4

Figure 12–3 Skin pinched and snipped through with scissors.
Figure 12–4 Blades of instrument spread to dilate membrane.

To prevent dislodgement of the tube by coughing or movement, and also to prevent its aspiration into the trachea, it must be held firmly in place. A firm rubber or plastic tube can be sutured to the skin or secured with adhesive tape. A metal tube can be made with a flange which serves the double purpose of preventing its aspiration and providing anchorage for tapes which are tied around the neck (Fig. 12–7). This approach is essentially the same as that recommended by Ruhe, Williams, and Proud,[7] who have designed special instruments to facilitate the procedure (Fig. 12–8).

Figure 12-5

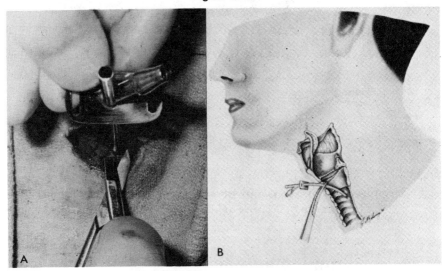

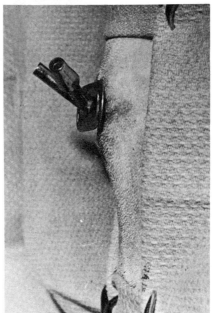

Figure 12-6

Figure 12-5 Tube inserted between blades of scissors into trachea.
Figure 12-6 Tube extending into trachea through the cricothyroid membrane.

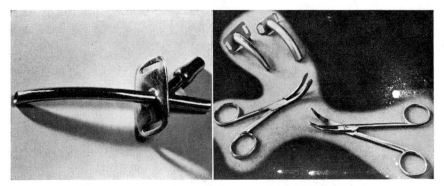

Figure 12-7   **Figure 12-8**

Figure 12-7 Tube with oxygen adaptor designed for use in cricothyroid membrane puncture.
Figure 12-8 Commercial instruments designed for cricothyroid membrane puncture. (Storz Instrument Co., St. Louis, Mo.)

The complications that may result from cricothyroid membrane puncture are infection and pressure necrosis of the cricoid cartilage. Some degree of laryngeal stenosis may occur if the tube is not removed within 48 to 72 hours.

COMMENT

For many years needle puncture through the cricothyroid membrane with a 13-gauge needle has been advocated as an emergency procedure, and would appear to be a simple and direct method of providing an airway.

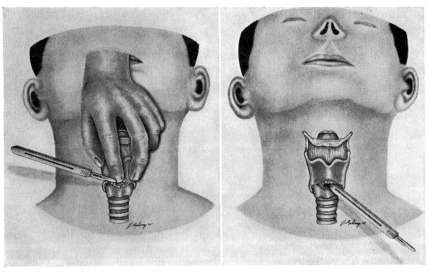

Figure 12-9   **Figure 12-10**

Figure 12-9 Opening into trachea obtained rapidly by incising the cricothyroid membrane.
Figure 12-10 Stoma maintained by placing handle of scalpel between the cricoid and thyroid cartilages.

A large bore needle of this type, however, is not ordinarily available in a dental office. If required for more than a very short time, one 13 gauge needle will not permit adequate air exchange,[1] and the rapid accumulation of secretions probably would limit the effectiveness of two or even three such needles.

In an extreme emergency, an airway can be produced within a few seconds by making an incision through the cricothyroid membrane and then placing the handle of the scalpel or some other flat object between the thyroid and cricoid cartilages to keep the wound open (Figs. 12–9 and 12–10). This method, while rapid, is apt to produce damage to the cricoid cartilage, and may cause subsequent laryngeal stenosis. The possibility of this complication is minimized if a low tracheostomy is performed as soon as the patient's condition permits.

SUMMARY

The approach to a patient with acute airway obstruction should consist of an orderly series of steps: (1) Prompt recognition of obstruction. (2) Non-surgical maneuvers to relieve obstruction. 3) Establishment of an emergency surgical airway.

Under emergency conditions an airway can be established rapidly, safely, and easily through the cricothyroid membrane. If it is necessary for an artificial airway to remain in place, a low tracheotomy should follow within 48 to 72 hours so that laryngeal stenosis will be avoided.

REFERENCES

1. Allison, M. L.: Personal communication.
2. American Heart Association: Statement on first aid for foreign body obstruction of the airway (Interim Recommendations), April 9, 1976.
3. Best, C. H., and Taylor, N. B.: The Physiological Basis of Medical Practice. 6th ed. Baltimore, Williams & Wilkins Co., 1955, p. 413.
4. Caparosa, R. J., and Zavatsky, A. R.: Practical aspects of the cricothyroid space. Laryngoscope, 67:577, 1957.
5. Chipps, J. E.: The dentist's role in the management of foreign bodies. Dent. Clin. North Amer., July 1957, p. 393.
6. Heimlich, H. J.: A life-saving maneuver to prevent food-choking. J.A.M.A. 234:398, 1975.
7. Ruhe, D. S., Williams, G. V., and Proud, G. O.: Emergency airway by cricothyroid puncture or tracheotomy: Comparative study of methods and instruments. Trans. Am. Acad. Ophthalmol., 64:182, 1960.

13

LEGAL ASPECTS OF EMERGENCIES

G. A. SHEPPARD

DEFINITION AND EFFECT

When the dental practitioner is confronted with an unforeseen combination of circumstances that calls for immediate action, this is an emergency. This may be bizarre or common, does not arrive gift wrapped, and the degree of severity is widely fluctuating. A word of caution: The law does not allow the operator to falsely proclaim an emergency just so "extra work" can be justified or to "explain away" a mistake.[1] An attempt will be made here to illustrate only the common and frequent happenings and the probable legal consequences that flow therefrom. By airing the various problems, it is intended to encourage the prevention of disastrous dental eventualities.

Many practitioners like to play "ostrich" and place their heads in the sand about being responsible for office emergencies. The time is long past when just a hope and a prayer will shield those clinicians from malpractice litigation. Thinking and acting preventively lets practitioners deliver better quality care to their patients.

364

This chapter is a *very* brief compilation of what the writer understands to be legally accepted standards, gathered from all states. In no way is it meant to be interpreted as a rule of law. Also, each state has its own "standards of care" pronounced through judicial interpretation of specific cases. These change *constantly*.

Let there be no mistake, the writer in no way means that what is cited as a "rule — standard — doctrine" will *always* be true, even when similar facts are litigated. The adequacy of counsel, preparation of the case, selection of dental and medical experts, choice of trial attorney, etc., govern any given result. The "situations" cited are for educational purposes only, in that, from actual experience, we know, with proper records, preparation, etc., that most like situations are defensible and won for the practitioner when tried before a jury.

This chapter presupposes that the reader has already been exposed to and understands the use of such terms as liability, negligence, fault, duty, proof, res ipsa loquitur, malpractice, and standard of care.

This writer also believes that the following commonly known factors have a major influence on the continuing rise in claims and lawsuits against health practitioners for alleged malpractice and lack of informed consent:

A. The pervasive idea that one can get something for nothing.
B. The consumerism vogue, with its obvious attendant philosophy of cheaper prices rather than quality of care.
C. Expanded duties by dental auxiliaries.
D. Third party factors that dilute the true doctor–patient relationship.
E. Contingent fee arrangements between patients and attorneys.
F. Changing public moral and ethical standards.
G. Tax free (not even "reportable" to the IRS) recovery by plaintiff when he or she prevails in trial and receives a monetary judgment or verdict against the clinician.

Dental practice often requires that decisions and actions be taken under circumstances of stress and immediacy, and courts tend to evaluate these decisions and actions less critically than decisions and actions accomplished under "normal conditions."[2]

The above presupposes, of course, that there is a *true* emergency such as a broken needle,[3] or a tooth or foreign object that has been aspirated.[4]

The courts also look most favorably when *immediate* consultation is accomplished.[5]

A "decision," made in an emergency, *not* to attempt the removal of a broken needle so that more damage might be prevented, or because more anesthesia might jeopardize the patient, is praiseworthy and might avoid liability.[6]

The foregoing is most pregnant because of the following legal doctrines:

1. The original "incident" may submit the practitioner to liability for additional harm (even death) resulting from later negligent care and treatment addressed to the original injury.[7]
2. The original "incident" may submit the practitioner to liability for additional harm (even death) resulting from later care and treatment (not negligent).[8]

3. The original "incident" may submit the practitioner to liability for additional harm (even death) resulting from later care and treatment, when an inherent risk, like *infection*, is the aftermath.[9]

Courts recently have become prone to *not* call an emergency an emergency. One leading case stated that even cardiac arrest during the treatment might not be classified as an emergency, owing to the fact that it might be considered a complication that could be and should be foreseen.[10]

EVERYDAY EMERGENCIES

Quite frequently every clinician will be confronted with so-called emergencies that exist, at least in the minds of his patients, in regard to hypersensitive teeth, minor abrasions to the mouth, side effects from drugs, and the like. These, of course, call for specific knowledge as to what product the patient should buy, usually without prescription, and which would be applicable to his particular problem.

If prescriptions are utilized, the amounts must be carefully controlled and the cumulative effects of the drugs known, as a recent case awarding over $1,500,000 in damages was upheld on appeal, where these facts were involved.[11]

More important would be the instant knowledge and use of the correct size and gauge of needles, asepsis, the standard of care in regard to disposable needles, disposable needle with suture, and so forth. Remember that the law is well settled: emergencies can be of any nature, and if there is peril to life and health, then lightning action is required. The clinician must have at his fingertips the exact knowledge of how to treat and with what equipment and products.

Modern "advertising" includes, many times, the information by manufacturers of drugs concerning printed material explaining the product. These data are held to be known by the prescribing doctor and the pamphlet allowed in evidence if distributed with the product.[12] This is why it is so important that the dental practitioner have immediate knowledge of the need for a particular product, know its limitations and any contraindications, antidotes, etc.

Courts usually hold that it is a matter of the doctor's judgment whether a tooth he is attempting to save can be saved or filled. Just because, at a later date, the tooth becomes diseased and has to be extracted is no reason to hold the doctor liable.[13]

The above is based on the presumption that the doctor acted in good faith and had reasonable justification in his attempt to save the tooth in the first instance. To help bolster and prove his judgment, a phone call to another clinician who agrees with the diagnosis and prognosis is most helpful. To the same effect is having another clinician view any x-rays and verify the reading. These precautions should be commonplace, and the results entered on the patient's chart.

What knowledge is known is to be promptly imparted to the patient. Assume there is a finding of a possibility of cancer; the patient must be notified *immediately* if liability is to be avoided.[14] To the same effect is the requirement that if the patient's address is faulty, the doctor is under a high duty to *find* the patient.

One of the most frequent "emergency" areas centers around infection. The doctor must, of course, have an adequate health history to determine how many months pregnant the patient is and to guide her actions accordingly, or else liability ensues.[15] Postoperative care and treatment and "developing" infection always require proof of the methods of sterilization, procedures, etc., and when these are adequately explained there usually is no liability in a later suit even when death ensues following placement of immediate dentures.[16]

Many doctors ignore the seriousness of the legal consequences *subsequent* to an emergency, i.e., that if found liable in court for allowing a broken tooth to become lodged in the lung, the patient's loss of profits, wages, etc., while off work, are part of damages to be awarded.[17]

Because the law looks favorably upon the doctor's efforts during an emergency is no excuse not to proceed with due caution *during* the emergency. Proceeding "blindly" by clamping an artery is contraindicated because of the possible damage to other structures and if done "blindly" liability may lie.[18] Thus the operator cannot panic, but must proceed with the commensurate care due the emergency. Just because, for instance, a fistula later occurs, this can often be explained as an inherent risk of the procedure for which no liability should attach.[19] But if an infection following an operation *cannot* be explained, the jury should have a right to decide the issue of malpractice.[20]

Just because the doctor has an emergency, and there is a fracture, does not excuse him from not having sterile instruments immediately at hand.[21]

The price and availability of disposable needles makes an "old" method of sterilization a problem at the very least. When infection arises after injection and the old "flaming" method of sterilizing the needle was followed, the court can find that the cause of the ultimate infection was an unsterile instrument.[22] It is interesting to note that disposable needles are responsible for an increasing number of post-injection paresthesias (lingual and inferior alveolar nerves), with attendant malpractice allegations.

The basic problem in this area of the law is that the plaintiff-patient need not exclude every possibility that the infection-injury might have been caused by some means other than the doctor's actions,[23] whether the result is cellulitis or osteomyelitis.

As time goes on and more knowledge is gained, it *sometimes* is best in an emergency *not* to operate further. This is especially true when needles break or roots are broken off. Facts now tend to show that more damage is done by attempting to remove broken roots (paresthesia, etc.) than by leaving them alone.[24] Generally it is very difficult not to have malpractice "found" by the jury when foreign bodies are found in the stomach after an operation.[25]

It is imperative that the doctor know the capabilities of the local analgesic utilized, what type of inherent risk is involved, and what percentage of people have reactions. A recent case in which Ravocaine (by aspirating technique) was given as a mandibular block points this up. The patient immediately felt uncomfortable; a headache developed, with rapid pulse and a feeling of faintness. The doctor took her to the recovery room, and thereafter had her husband take her to her physician. The condition did not improve and she was hospitalized. The doctor involved could justify his use of the local analgesic and its capability, and he provided an adequate medical history. The court held that under the circumstances there should be no liability.[26] To the same effect is the doctrine that even when death ensues after a local analgesic (Xylocaine), if the nature and purpose of the analgesic were proper, the injection itself was within the standard of care, and a proper health history and informed consent were gained, no liability is involved.[27] But when paralysis results from a local analgesic and there is *conflicting* evidence as to the standard of care in the case, there is possible liability.[28]

Cases are constantly seen wherein the teeth and gums are so involved that the patient complains of inability to eat. This should warn the doctor to be certain that a correct dietary supplement is utilized. How often we hear from the patient's attorney about the "cruelness" of the doctor's action resulting in severe loss of weight.

A more serious instance would be the action necessary to remedy a cut lip. With high-speed equipment more lacerations of major consequence are seen. (And, you guessed it, the plaintiff's attorney is always there in time to get a color photograph of the swelling and discoloration.) Instant know-how would seem to be mandatory in this type of situation, with immediate referral to a sympathetic plastic surgeon. If the patient is left to his or her "own devices," invariably the plastic surgeon seen by the plaintiff will have a lack of understanding, or keloids will form, etc.

Sometimes even the method of injection (in one particular case, mandibular rather than local infiltration) can be a suspected cause of the infection/osteomyelitis that follows.[29]

To the same effect is the emergency occurrence in which the warning on the label of the local analgesic has not been heeded by the doctor, who did not inquire as to the state of the patient's blood pressure prior to the injection.[30]

Often emergencies arise when too much time elapses while the doctor attempts to perform an unsuccessful extraction, as exemplified by trismus, hospitalization, undue pain, etc.[31] The same emergencies are often present when nerves are severed, when adjacent teeth are broken, or when needles are broken.[32]

The importance of the injection as opposed to the agent injected becomes most important when there is evidence to prove correct skill in making the injection but the product itself may be shown to be the cause of the anaphylactic reaction.[33]

Probably the knowledge of what to do and how to do it would be mandatory if the crown of the tooth broke off and protection were needed for the pulp. The same could be true if a wrong tooth were extracted, making an implant necessary. The examples could be endless in the necessity of proper knowledge of technique and products to be used in such emergencies. The same would be true of procedures that the doctor is required to know and prescribe with regard to home care after any of a variety of accidents imparted to the patient to control bleeding. The courts have held that failure to give a patient proper instructions as to his home care will create liability.[34]

Wrongful *diagnosis* of an emergency type condition "caused" from dental care and treatment can make a practitioner liable.[35] In this situation, after an extraction the doctor failed to diagnose (after local analgesic—

Novocain — and extraction) the swelling and pain. The doctor stated the patient had the mumps. The real cause, though, was acute osteomyelitis and cellulitis. The court was very plain in stating that not only was the diagnosis in error but the doctor also endangered the plaintiff in refusing to acknowledge his error.

Even if the patient is referred to a doctor after an emergency, the receiving doctor must be cognizant of what to do and how to do it, or be held liable.[36] In one instance, after extraction, the patient developed undue trismus. By "missing" the diagnosis (a broken jaw was diagnosed), the "wrong" treatment was prescribed and the patient's condition deteriorated from an *infection,* the true condition. Suppose a root is broken during an extraction. The doctor is held accountable for deciding whether or not it should be removed or left. Suppose further that the cavity shows disease. When death subsequently ensues, the court can hold the doctor liable either for failing to curette or for not referring the patient on.

What can be more common to the doctor than an injection for local analgesia? But the possible consequences are seldom realized.

A patient might appear with complaint of great pain, and the matter may seem an emergency. If in the process, though, the injection is into an infected area, liability might be predicated[38] upon the theory that the invasion of the infected area might have caused the infection to spread.

Suppose under the same circumstances a *wrong* substance is injected, instead of the intended local analgesic. Then of course there would be liability.[39] This latter matter involved a dental practitioner utilizing a local pharmacy to make up the local analgesic, and instead Lysol was prepared and injected.

Doctors often ask about their liability via law to control an infection that occurs after extraction. All that can be stated in a general way is that if an injection is done properly and if the substance is proper, there should not be any problem. But the exception always points up the dilemma. When the injection is intravenous in the arm and the vein is missed, causing pain and swelling, liability might ensue[40] when the condition worsens and a physician's care is required.

The law states that if one does not have the training or equipment to give definitive treatment, he is then inadequate to treat emergencies, and liability will ensue.[41] The matter might not be a major emergency, but even in the care of immediate denture work there may be a limitation of diet. Malnutrtion can be a very serious allegation, and one should be able to suggest the correct supplement.

If the person treating lacks the necessary skill or equipment, he or she is obligated to perform no treatment at all, but rather to immediately refer the patient to the proper person.[42]

X-RAYS AND BIOPSIES

Seemingly, each day, science and the healing arts become more sophisticated in their ability to think of tests, procedures, and so forth, that are to benefit the patient. Dental practitioners must be aware of all these advances and methods, often including x-rays, cultures, biopsies, blood gas tests, warnings via updated PDR, etc.

Failure to diagnose figuratively is "thrown at" the defendant doctor as a cause of the plaintiff's alleged injuries and damage. Realizing that there are recoveries by plaintiff on this ground, the doctor should remind himself that whenever there is the least doubt about any diagnosis, further tests should be considered, and a colleague should review with him all factors and mark this review on the patient's chart.

Jurors have found, on the basis of "failure to diagnose," liability running the gamut from aspirin poisoning[43] to x-ray burn[44] to suspected fractures[45] to nausea[46] to cancer[47] to neuromas[48] to embolism[49] to foreign objects[50] to broken bur[51] to tumor.[52]

Delay in taking x-rays in many cases results in the fixing of liability on the doctor. Each factual situation is unique, but a week's or month's delay often is enough to cause liability.[53] One case in which the doctor was held liable turned on the fact that while treating the patient via an emergency extraction a small root portion was broken off at the time of the surgery; the doctor was unaware of this. Postoperatively the patient complained of pain and remained infected. No postoperative x-ray was taken and several days later the subsequent treating doctor x-rayed the area and easily spotted the small root tip; upon its removal the plaintiff became "well."[54]

In the same vein, failure to initiate tests and failure to take biopsies are "easy grounds" for injuries to find a doctor liable.[55]

Suppose the slides and report from a biopsy are to be forwarded to someone else. Liability has been found when there is a delay in sending them on (death case — 6 week delay).[56]

Jurors have no trouble fixing responsibility on the doctor when infrequent x-rays are taken and the patient has a suspected periodontal problem — that even when x-rays are taken but misread liability follows.[57]

Some very disturbing legal results have involved liability being placed upon the doctor for not following the label instructions on products or the admonitions in the PDR, in cases of:

1. Prescribing a drug without warning of side effects.
2. Improper dilutions of solutions.[59]
3. Use of a product in an abnormal way (doctor used extraoral impression material to obtain fingertip impressions, with resultant loss of fingers).[60]
4. Use of drug that caused tooth discoloration.[61]

Needless to say, any "experimental" use of a product, technique, or equipment should be avoided. Each jurisdiction has its own rules and possibly regulations regarding procedures such as acupuncture and hypnotism. Wherever a doctor practices, he or she should make certain that procedures used are *not* experimental and *are* within the standard of care. This writer, in representing doctors, has had experience in cases involving both acupuncture and hypnotism, including the doctor's failure to gain complete anesthesia, and including not "awakening" the patient following hypnosis. To date, very little record of litigation on these subjects exists, but what there is fixes liability on the doctor.[62]

Most states have recently adopted, or are in the process of adopting, dental radiation laws covering such subjects as exposure, adequate instruction and licensing of operators, shielding, leakage. combs, space frames, timer control, protective barriers, etc. Remember that violation of a law or ordinance is negligence per se, which means, in effect, strict liability.

Adequate x-rays are necessary to show enough of the area to allow one to proceed if there is an emergency. It must be remembered that in the absence of any agreement to the contrary, x-rays form a part of the doctor's records and are his, even though they might be paid for by the patient.[63] X-rays should never be billed separately, as this frequently misleads the patient as to ownership.

In this latter regard, the doctor must never let the patient tell him what to do or how to do it. If the patient refuses to be x-rayed and films are needed for proper diagnosis, then by all means they must be taken or the patient not treated. Remember — doctors by law must practice the proper standard of care, and a patient cannot require a practitioner to do otherwise. The doctor might be consenting to a violation of the law if he or she condescends.

The doctor's assistants, of course, must be adequately trained and be given proper procedures to follow. They cannot act as primary health providers. If the doctor himself wants to use hypnosis, he must certainly be qualified and properly trained, and he must be absolutely certain that it is an accepted technique and the acceptable standard of care.

Often after an emergency some settlement is attempted directly with the doctor by or in behalf of a minor. Be reminded that only the court can approve any release or settlement.[64]

If an emergency occurs, such as a fractured root, root in the antrum, cracked tooth, etc., good judgment and the standard of care seemingly evidence the necessity of postoperative x-rays. The same is true if the patient returns after an operative procedure and has complaints in the area wherein the treatment was rendered. Besides other testing, these x-rays should help to ascertain any possible disease. As mentioned before, the x-rays are the doctor's records and should be kept with his other records at all times and the originals *never* be given to the patient under any circumstances. Not that it isn't advisable to let some other practitioner borrow them under proper circumstances; but the patient should never be the bearer. We have seen lost x-rays, defaced x-rays, stolen x-rays, substituted x-rays, etc., always to the doctor's detriment.

The use of x-rays points up a very pregnant possibility of failing: i.e., failure to use x-rays for diagnostic purposes and, even more important, alleged failure to keep abreast of progress.[65] Courts have also found that it is negligence when the doctor fails to use an x-ray in locating a piece of steel left imbedded, or when he fails to use the x-ray in locating the source of pain, e.g., a broken fragment of tooth.[66] The importance of the use of x-rays and proper equipment cannot be stressed too heavily.

Besides declaring liability in the failure to make use of x-rays for tests,[67] courts state that if the proper x-ray procedures are not followed, liability may be imposed.[68] Many doctors would like to laugh at the problem of overexposure and dental laws, but let me remind you of a decision in which a plaintiff sued for personal injuries allegedly as a result of an overdose of dental x-ray. The court felt that the patient's resulting complaints of nervousness could certainly have been caused by the x-ray exposure.[69] Of course in proved areas wherein there is no dispute as to the requirement that an x-ray be taken, the mere failure to take the x-ray might be malpractice in itself.[70]

The proper attitude of the doctor would thus seem to be dictated by the factual questions involved and by the particular patient's problem. It is probably malpractice to fail to remove a root or a piece of tooth from a jaw, if it may *"easily"* be recovered.[71]

Most doctors like to advise conservative treatment, and generally this is fine. But assume that the patient continues to complain after an extraction. This should raise a red flag in the doctor's mind if the situation persists. X-rays would normally be deemed necessary, and if not taken postoperatively under these circumstances, liability might ensue.[72]

Because an "emergency" occurs is no excuse not to *correctly* diagnose via proper reading of x-rays.[73]

X-rays often give a dental practitioner a basis for his diagnosis-prognosis, and without the film he would be in a most difficult position explaining the reasons for his care and treatment. Thus x-rays are like *gold*. Normally, testimony based on x-rays is *not* admissible when the x-rays are not produced.[74]

Often there is a conflict between a radiologist and the practitioner as to the reading of an x-ray or even as to whether or not the patient was advised of the results learned from the film (fracture).[75] This graphically points to the reason for keeping good records and entering on the chart all findings and advice given to the patient.

Akin to this is the failure to use modern methods for gaining pathologic examinations such as biopsies to determine malignancies. Courts have held that failure to utilize proper procedures and tests may give rise to liability.[76]

A common problem of liability is due to postponement in treatment caused by a delay in recognizing or biopsying the suspicious area. Some cases go so far as to hold that the failure of prompt diagnosis and biopsy might result in the failure of possible cure of a malignancy and thus create liability.[77]

If the laboratory report on the biopsy is in any way ambiguous, the doctor must take further steps for diagnosis, for if not, liability for later death of the patient may be affixed.[78]

EMPLOYEE EMERGENCY

New laws are rapidly being enacted in some jurisdictions granting auxiliary employees varying degrees of activity that traditionally were classified as only being done by the doctor. Each clinician must be cognizant of what these rights and limitations are in his own jurisdiction.

The majority of jurisdictions still do not permit dental assistants or other employees to treat pyorrhea, to fill teeth, to take impressions, to adjust bridges, etc., and declare this to be an unlawful practice of dentistry.[79] An emergency should not change this rule. Prior laws went even so far as to make certain the doctor couldn't have a "manager" who would advise patients as to type of dentures or assist in any "facial correction" or even quote fees.[80]

A dental assistant or dental hygienist also has an independent duty to the patient, and that is to use reasonable skill and care, just as medical nurses need observe their own standard of care.[81]

The dental assistant or nurse should be acting under the direct supervision of the employer.[82] The doctor cannot allow an unlicensed practitioner to perform operations. Doctors' employees cannot examine an appliance in the mouth of the patient with a view to replacement or correction.[83]

Recently, a clinician had his wife in the office helping him. The patient made them *both* defendants, when, during endodontic therapy, a broach slipped and was swallowed by the patient.[84]

What should be done under these circumstances is legal and lengthy, and will not be presented here. The preventive techniques and admonitions are uniform for all jurisdictions and if not taught in all dental schools should be made mandatory. Swallowed objects are a most common emergency, and this writer has personally assisted in legal cases concerning swallowed or aspirated crown, ear ring, denture, x-rays, watch crystal, button, broken glass from lamp, plaster from ceiling, contact lens, clamp, bur, file, tooth; you name it and it has been swallowed or aspirated.

For liability purposes, "volunteers" in the office are classified as employees.[85]

Following are only a few examples in which the employee becomes involved, followed, naturally, by the employer doctor:

1. When the employee dispenses drugs.[86]
2. When the employee fails to relay to the doctor the patient's current health history.[87]
3. When the hygienist employee fails to inform the doctor of the depth of the periodontal pockets.[88]
4. When the employee doctor who assisted without the knowledge of the plaintiff, was unlicensed.[89]
5. When the employee positions the patient "improperly" and injury results therefrom.[90]

EMERGENCY RESTRAINT OVER FEE — NO VISITORS

A doctor had a dispute with the patient over his fee. This of course was to him an *emergency*, and he grabbed the patient, locked her up in a room, and wouldn't let her go until he called the Marshal. The doctor had told the patient, "Leave the teeth or pay the price," and kept the patient from leaving. As fate would have it, the patient-plaintiff later had a miscarriage, and the court was most lenient in granting general damages plus punitive damages.[91] The court was most positive in its approach that there is no excuse for this type of procedure; although even today many doctors' actions parallel this, there is no justification for it.

It has been clear for many years that when a mother suffers mental upset and illness from seeing intentional injury to her child liability on the part of the injurer has been created.[92] This points up a rule most doctors follow: the parents or friends of the patient will not be allowed in the operating room. It is easily seen from newspaper reports of alleged manhandling of children and alleged assault and battery that if "Mama" were allowed to view the treatment, and an untoward incident occurred, there might be an additional cause of action for her supposed mental grievances, besides those that the minor-patient urges for himself.[93] It must be remembered that monetary damages in personal injuries are tax free.

Assault and battery charges will lie against a doctor who takes back the dentures to insure payment of a "debt." What is significant is that the law allows *punitive* damages under these circumstances.[94]

For the uninitiated, punitive damages are those that are assessed against the defendant when he is being "punished" for his actions. They are in addition to the usual "pain or suffering" damages, which are classified as general or compensatory damages. They are "important" in that they are *not* covered by the usual professional liability insurance.

Recovery by the patient's spouse, mother, or father for "their" emotional distress has now been extended to cases in which they are not even present when the alleged "negligent act" by the doctor takes place, but are only in some theoretical "zone of danger," and even when the "act" is negligent, not intentional (injection case).[95]

A word of caution regarding the collection of fees. Judgment should be used as to whether or not it is advisable to collect a fee from a patient who suffered from an untoward incident during dental care and treatment. Also, when attempting to collect fees, courts (usually of monetary jurisdictional limits up to $1000) where we attorneys are not allowed to practice should be the method of choice. Suing through collection agencies usually forces your ex-patient to hire an attorney. So frequently we then see the counterclaim for malpractice as "retaliation" to the collection attempt.[96]

Recently new laws, both federal and state, have been enacted, limiting doctors' rights in collection, and also limiting collection agencies' methods. When there is a violation of the law, we often see countersuits for interference with contract, invasion of privacy, intentional causing of emotional distress, and so on ad nauseam. Be forewarned!

As a corollary, most states have laws making it illegal to record telephone conversations when one party lacks knowledge of the recording. Also, most states allow a cause of action when a person is threatened with criminal actions while attempting to gain advantage in any civil action.[97]

Most jurisdictions have laws regarding who has legal responsibility for dental bills. The writer will not attempt to set forth these rules here, but suffice to say that they involve age, contract, divorce, custody, bankruptcy, etc. To try to collect from a person who doesn't legally owe the debt often leads to a countersuit against the doctor.[98]

PRESCRIPTIONS IN EMERGENCIES

There is a great tendency among doctors to prescribe medicines for patients in emergencies, rather than referring them to a specialist. The danger in not gaining someone else's opinion is that if something goes wrong there is no one to back the doctor up.

Probably in most jurisdictions it is illegal not to write prescriptions for certain drugs. Practice has it that the phone is so easy and some pharmacists are so trustworthy that the law is overlooked. Let me assure you that liability in these regards happens with some frequency; as often as not the doctor will prescribe XYZ over the phone, the pharmacist will write ABC, and the lawsuit follows. The doctor is placed in the position of having no written record, whereas the pharmacist has his written prescription as taken over the phone. The answer to this is, always, whether an emergency or not, write down the prescription, the date and how prescribed on the prescription pad, and place it with the patient's chart. It cannot be stressed enough that if some habit-forming drug is prescribed, extreme caution should be used to avoid being blamed for any addiction that might be formed.

As this chapter is being prepared the FDA has ordered a reassessment of the prescribing practices for Librium and Valium. The "improper" use of a product most certainly may cause liability. The agents, their instructions and contraindications, and the PDR inserts all must be understood and be kept up to date. Recently, the medical doctors who treated Freddie Prinze during his life (he shot himself to death) were sued on the theory that they negligently "prescribed for" him during his life.

More than once a year this writer defends a dental practitioner against the allegation that a prescribed drug caused death, suicide, or addiction.

Science has yet to satisfactorily inform the doctor of all the synergistic and potentiating actions of the various drugs and agents. Therefore, a constant reminder — whatever drug or agent is used, its effect and contraindication should be well known. Lack of tests on the patient, when called for as determined by the health history and/or agent utilized, and when the patient suffers from these tests not being performed, may constitute liability.[99]

It should go without saying that in most jurisdictions it is illegal (a crime) to prescribe certain drugs over the telephone and without seeing the patient. A doctor will usually be held liable for any adverse effects of this practice.

Wrong drugs are often prescribed. Questions also arise as to the site and depth of the injection, allergy, failure to heed the warning of a health history, overdosage, disregard of premedication elements, lack of sterile procedure, no aspiration, unsuitable vasoconstrictor, nonfresh product etc.

The law makes it mandatory that the doctor know the applicable health history of the patient. If the patient is extremely nervous, the doctor is held to know that certain commonly used drugs in dentistry may cause hallucinations, etc. The list of possibilities is endless.

Doctors have been warned about the use of antidepressant drugs and the contraindications of some food such as chicken livers, sherry, etc. The result of not knowing the health history of a patient under these circumstances could well be disastrous — high blood pressure crises. Other common-knowledge drug contraindications are endless, such as aspirin with an anticoagulant, oral contraceptives with an anticoagulant, digitalis drugs with laxatives, etc.

Even a labeled cosmetic may be a "drug" and temporarily affect the skin.[100]

Some dental schools now teach their students to take blood and urine tests to aid in recognizing diseases that influence a person's health. This is important owing to the disease and drug counterparts, such as diabetes, because those afflicted are more susceptible to infections and are slow healers.

When the harmful effects of the drug are not told the patient, and a later injury occurs, the statute of limitations does not run against the patient until the patient discovers the cause of the injury.[101]

Stanford University linked a widely used anesthetic (trade name in the United States, Penthrane) to kidney disturbances. This, of course, again reflects the absolute necessity of knowing the drug's side effects and presupposes the doctor's taking an adequate health history from the patient.

The doctor must be on *constant* alert to be certain that a drug he might be utilizing is not "new" or experimental so as to avoid liability from injury by a patient's use.[102]

A doctor's license may be challenged by the appropriate authorities when he is alleged to have been prescribing without proper prescriptions.[103]

Also, a dental practitioner might be charged with illegally selling narcotics when he dispenses dangerous drugs.[104]

FOREIGN BODIES

Some jurisdictions have held against the doctor for negligence in allowing some particle, tooth, bur, x-ray film, etc., to drop into the patient's throat and be swallowed.[105]

In order to alleviate any possible future aggravation, it would seem best to have the patient referred to an M.D. to be certain of the placement of the foreign body and have the M.D. continue x-raying until the foreign body has been evacuated. If a tooth lodges in an area where it won't pass, consideration must be given to the probabilities and potential danger to the patient. This at all times must be discussed with the patient so that he or she may have an intelligent voice in the proceedings.

The cases of foreign bodies, whether a needle, a broken tooth, or a root, are quite frequent. More often than not the doctor is held accountable for such an experience.[106]

The vital point to realize in such an emergency is that if a standard of care requires proceeding immediately to remedy the situation, then one must either be competent to do so or immediately refer the patient to a specialist. Experiences have shown that with modern disposable needles of proper gauge, length, etc., there are fewer broken needles every year. Difficulty arises when doctors attempt to remove the broken piece when they are not qualified and do not have the equipment to proceed properly. In this latter situation it must be recalled that any prolongation of time in holding the patient's mouth open gives serious rise to possible joint problems, trismus, etc. Often there is more damage done to the joint than could ever possibly be anticipated in the tracing of a needle by too long an operation for the recovery. It appears now that the standard of care would call for a competent operator who has been trained in such procedures as obtaining proper x-rays, using tracer needles, etc., so as to block any later attack on the operator's adequacy.

It must also be stressed that records must evidence what instructions are given the patient following an untoward incident. If the patient was properly instructed to use an antibiotic and has failed to follow the instructions, the court probably will state that there is nothing to show any liability on the part of the defendant.[107]

The law places the burden on the professional person to have his instructions understood. The import is that instructions are no good if not understood, or if there is a language barrier, mental block, minority, etc. If the patient once had difficulty with a procedure, the doctor is accountable to act accordingly later. Recently there was a matter in which all proper instructions and preparations were made for multiple extractions. The patient had not eaten for the prescribed length of time, but yet under the general anesthetic there was great regurgitation, and x-rays evidenced vomitus injected into the lungs. The next time the patient was to return for treatment the doctor would be held to the knowledge that at the prior visit the usual time allowed for eating did not suffice, and this patient must have extra time allowed. In a more precautionary vein, probably prior to any further work there should be an O.K. from an M.D. and if at all possible, a local analgesic should be given.

PRE-EMERGENCY PRECAUTIONS

It used to be thought that in an emergency the standard of care would be that of the community in which one practiced. It recently has become apparent that the courts will not allow anyone to practice below a certain minimum standard of care, no matter what type of practice might be prevalent in any one community. The theory is that the day of the horse and buggy is gone and that everyone has access to written material, seminar courses, etc.[108]

As far as can be determined, the courts seemingly hold that it is a factual question whether there is any malpractice in allowing a patient, when under a sedative or awakening from anesthesia, to climb over restraining bars when there was no safety strap in place.[109]

Malpractice jurisprudence advises that instructions put down in the pamphlet of any drug or antibiotic had better be understood and followed (unless there could be contrary conclusive evidence that the drug usage was a departure from what was the standard of care in the community when utilized), because the instruction pamphlet will be admissible in evidence as setting the standard of care.[110]

It would appear advisable, owing to the seeming liberalization of rules within which doctors are found liable, if a doctor is performing operative work of any kind, and if there might be some emergency later, whether it be reaction to a drug, excessive pain, bleeding, infection, etc., that a telephone exchange be available for patients on a 24-hour basis, seven days a week.

With the ease of answering service communication, it now appears apparent that the doctor should be available (or have another doctor on call) at all times, and when not in the office, be able to be reached by phone. If not, liability may ensue if this causes injury to the patient.[111]

Needless to say, a duty is placed on the general practitioner to refer the patient to a specialist if it is the standard of care to so do.[112] Most states have jury instructions that succinctly state this rule. It is not true that all jurisdictions require the general practitioner, if he is doing the work of a specialist, to practice the standard of care of that specialist when he undertakes that specialty type of work for the patient. It is true, unequivocally, though, that if the doctor holds himself out to be a specialist, he is held to that higher standard of care.[113] In one case, the defendant doctor claimed to be a specialist in endodontia. The reamer was swallowed. Usual conflicting versions followed. The patient stated that the doctor said, at the time of the incident, "I dropped it, I dropped it." The doctor said the patient "moved," causing the problem. "Untoward" statements are so very crucial, as will be pointed out later in more detail.

Once control is assumed over the patient, a duty is owed not only to the patient but to third parties. Recently we have seen premedication at home prior to coming to the office. Owing to the circumstances of an improper health history, the premedication was contraindicated, and such patients had auto accidents which involved injuries to other persons.

A patient should not be allowed to leave the office while still under some sedation or not fully conscious and alert after an anesthetic. A patient might not know what he was doing and cause tragic circumstances to others and himself.

It is appalling to note that in some dental offices oxygen is not readily available. It is common knowledge that there are approximately as many cardiac arrests from apprehension *and emotional upset* when local analgesics are used as when a general anesthetic is given. Oxygen, of course, is standard equipment, and it is felt by many that the failure to have it available or not know how to use it would create liability. The entire office staff should be trained for all emergencies, including cardiac arrest, etc.

Existing or prior health problems will govern as to the choice of local analgesic utilized, its strength, and whether a vasoconstrictor is to be used. The manufacturer's instructions show how to control any unusual sensitivity or convulsions. This alerts the doctor that he must have the knowledge, competence, equipment, and supplies with which to operate. It would seem certain that the standard of care should be such that before any local analgesic is administered, the blood pressure be taken — at least that is the indication of the case of Quanital v. Laurel Grove Hospital.[114]

As will be discussed later in detail, consent (informed) must be gained from the *patient,* not his or her spouse, and medication cannot be forcibly administered without liability.[115]

In some jurisdictions, when you injure one spouse the other may also sue for loss of consortium, i.e., loss of society, companionship, conjugal affections and physical assistance. Damages may run high.[116]

OPERATIVE EMERGENCY

In effect, as discussed before, the "emergency doctrine" allows a different and probably lesser standard of care. In reality, this means that treatment under those circumstances need be accomplished within the "emergency doctrine" standard of care. What is this standard? It is most difficult to describe, because each set of facts is different. In general, though, the doctor in the emergency situation must act as others would under the circumstances and proceed onward if he is competent to so do.[117] Certainly the doctor is not required to stop to gain express consent to proceed,[118] and if the emergency situation clearly calls for referral to a specialist, this must be accomplished. Any unneeded delay might be interpreted as aggravating the original incident and be adverse to the doctor's case.[119]

Cases that go to juries seemingly make it very clear what is expected of practitioners in emergencies. The practitioner should be trained in emergency care itself, with accompanying knowledge as to drug usage and administration, CPR, etc. If a doctor does not have the proper equipment, such as differing size oxygen face masks, laryngoscope, etc., he will certainly be open to criticism by the plaintiff's attorney.

If the doctor knows he does not have the capability to handle the situation, it is quite clear there is a duty for immediate referral.[120]

If a doctor decides to tackle the emergency situation himself, he must be properly equipped, and have trained personnel to give him adequate assistance. Without these precautions he lays himself open to grave criticism.[121] Never give assurances like "everything will be all right," and do not "abandon" the patient.[122]

If this sounds like the dental office in which all employees should act like a team and "drill" on various possible emergencies, that is absolutely correct. These could run the gamut from cuts to respiratory collapse to aspirated foreign bodies.

Most dental practitioners do some oral surgery, i.e., extractions of teeth, etc., and must at all times be cautious with regard to hemorrhage. It is now probably standard procedure that the proper health history is utilized by anyone doing operative procedures when a regional or general anesthetic is used.

If the patient is a bleeder, he must of course be asked if he is taking or has recently taken any drugs. If there is any doubt at all, laboratory tests are in order. Usually, though, the patient knows if he suffers from hemophilia. If major dental surgery is involved, the doctor should be prepared for any emergency and be competent to handle it.

Operative procedure probably demands that the doctor be prepared for the possibility of a cut cheek, floor of the mouth wound, or lip laceration. These highly vascular soft tissues bleed easily, and the operator must be competent to control any hemorrhage. The doctor, for example, is held accountable for knowing that the roots of the mandibular third molars are especially close to the inferior alveolar vessels. When these vessels are ruptured, severe hemorrhage often occurs.

There should be a set routine in the office for periodic inspection of all equipment, running from necessary flashlight batteries to the sterilization of equipment. If not done, the ever-alert plaintiff's attorney will certainly crucify the defendant on his office procedure and training of employees.

The doctor should know, in general, how to diagnose shock and what type of shock is involved. Certain types of shock point to specific action.

When the operative result entails infections, and when there is more than one method to treat this and the wrong selection of method is made and followed, this does not mean there is malpractice.[123] This signifies the importance of never criticizing a prior doctor's care and treatment or result, as perhaps there were different alternatives available that are not known at the present time. Also, seldom is the doctor afforded all the facts from the patient, and even if given "most" of the facts, they are often hazy and/or colored or mistaken.

One doctor should not "cause" the termination of a treatment by another doctor whose treatment would prolong life (cancer case). It might result in murder charges.[124]

DECLARED EMERGENCIES

Jurisdictions that have not provided for the protection of their health practitioners should immediately proceed to give them such immunity during times they render services when there is a state of emergency or disaster or when they have been requested by a state official or agency or local disaster counsel to give treatment.[125]

A like situation is the "Good Samaritan" rule. Most states have such rules; in effect, they state that if a doctor helps a person who is in distress and as an emergency, and if the work is in good faith, there will be no liability.[126] To the same effect, where there is a declared emergency in a hospital, then the dental practitioner is given a waiver of liability for his work.[127]

Of course, if a jury finds that there is *no* emergency, then there is *no* waiver of liability.[128] Thus, the afforded protection is not absolute and is subject to after-the-fact interpretation. Very comforting, eh what!

STATEMENTS IN EMERGENCIES

Doctors are human, like anyone else. When faced with an untoward incident and shaken by a result that might be most disastrous, the doctor often lets certain words slip that he will remember the rest of his life, and would probably give a million dollars to retract and erase. Recall the case of the doctor who, after giving a hypodermic injection and extracting teeth (with alleged unsterilized instruments, for the patient-plaintiff ended up with a severe infection on her arm), told his nurse: "I wonder if Mrs. Dimock will ever forgive me for wrecking her arm."[129]

In the same vein, can you picture the doctor, after extracting a tooth and breaking the patient's jaw, stating to the patient: "I did break your jaw; I guess I hit you a little too hard."[130]

Office personnel should be trained so that when an untoward event occurs, the dental assistant won't be saying, "Oh, what a terrible cut," or, "Gee, you goofed that time, didn't you, Doctor?" The doctor can certainly be sympathetic, and teach his employees to be the same, but statements regarding cause, severity, etc., are to be avoided at all times.

If, after the operation is over, the nurse or dental assistant has to admit that the doctor had charged her with the failure to properly sterilize the instruments (and an infection did develop), the liability will, naturally, be against the doctor.[131]

In the cases in which we talk of admissions or exclamations by the doctor and his employees, and how deadly they may be, courts have permitted these items to be relied upon by the plaintiff in establishing liability.[132]

Often the most devastating evidence of malpractice comes from the lips of the doctor, such as, "Boy, I sure made a mess of things."[133]

To the same effect is an improper expression of regret, such as: "He did not blame her husband for being angry about the occurrence."[134]

Can you imagine the effect on a patient who has suffered postoperative complications to hear a doctor say, after reopening the area, "Well, I'll be darned, it is a piece of cotton." And how much consolation is given a patient who, after seeing the doctor be fidgety and grouchy, is cut and then hears the doctor say, "I'm sorry — but these kids have upset me. They have been in here all afternoon."

If the reader were a patient who had just had a mandible fractured, he or she would not be very happy to hear the doctor say, "It gave me the most difficulty I've had in forty years."

There is always a reverse twist to these situations, and invariably, as Murphy's law so decrees, one is likely to hear a judge say, as in one orthodontic matter being tried, that he "felt the dentist's failure to take certain steps . . . constituted negligence!"

POST-EMERGENCY RAPPORT

After some event has occurred which might tend to upset the rapport of the doctor-patient relationship, if the patient still decides to continue with the dental services, ordinarily the doctor's refusal would constitute malpractice.[139] The general rule of mutual cooperation on the part of the patient and the doctor is that the patient must return for treatment often enough to give the practitioner a reasonable opportunity to give postoperative care.[140] Of course, if the doctor is employed for one item of treatment or for some specific matter, there would be no duty to continue thereafter, if he has satisfactorily treated the patient for the contracted service.[141]

It is also true that if the work is badly done, the patient is not required to allow the doctor a second chance.[142] In this particular case the doctor undertook to fit jackets on the teeth and inferentially promised that the color would match the natural teeth; but they didn't. The patient contended that they were a darker color, and that she was the subject of ridicule by her friends. The doctor stated, yes, they were a different color, but that he expected the patient to return. When the jury saw the jackets and the teeth, they decided that the plaintiff was under no duty to allow the doctor to attempt to continue.

Of course it should be noted that if at any time there is an agreement between the doctor and patient that the treatment would be mutually discontinued, it should be put in writing and entered on the chart.

Assuming that there isn't a minor, or incompetent, etc., involved, the doctor is not always blessed with a patient forever. Probably he can discuss the matter with the patient and suggest that dental services can be provided by another doctor, that the rapport has been ruptured, and give the patient a reasonable opportunity to secure the services of another doctor. This does not mean that when a doctor has the emergency of an infection after an extraction, and when it is proved that there was some failure in the sterilization technique, he could shun the problem and send the patient on. To the contrary, those postoperative services are a necessary part of the originally contracted dental care.[143]

Assume that the emergency is "over" and the "result" lingers on, as for example an oroantral fistula. If healing and closure do not progress right on schedule, the failure to refer might be held against the doctor.[144] The logical "next step" is that the doctor will be liable if, after the emergency is treated, a precautionary referral is not accomplished.[145] Cases representative of this dilemma range from orthodontic "failure" to as little as time lost by failure to telephone.

ADVICE RE MISHAP

It has been held that a cause of action will lie against the doctor for allegedly leaving roots of six teeth in the jaw after extractions when he knew it and didn't tell the plaintiff.[146] Later x-rays showed the condition, and the patient suffered pain and generally rundown health. The court's theory is that the patient has the ability to understand the knowledge imparted by the doctor and that this must be passed to him. This particular case also stands for the proposition that the statute of limitations for any alleged negligent act will not begin to run until the time the patient learns of the condition.

A most intriguing case is Furniss v. Fitchett.[147] In the New Zealand case, a doctor disclosed to the patient's husband the patient's mental condition; thereafter, when the patient learned of this, she suffered a severe reaction. The doctor was held liable. A like case in the United States is the well-known "cancer phobia" case,[148] wherein a patient claimed damages following the disclosure that x-ray burns negligently caused by the defendant might result in cancer. In another case, the patient suffered from a malignant disease which required surgery. The court held the doctor liable for emotional distress because the doctor had advised the patient that the surgery would not be advisable now because of the damage done to her heart through his prior negligence.

In the emergency in which some foreign object is left in a patient's person, whether it be a broken needle, root tip, etc., some courts will permit a jury to infer negligence just by the presence of that foreign object.[149]

A doctor and his assistants' manner after the emergency has occurred will be much more important than the requisite dental skill. Human nature being what it is, the patient expects added attention and personal contact. There is nothing wrong in stating that one is sorry for an incident, but that of course does not mean admitting liability for the act. Public relations and kindness go a long way to alleviate problems which might otherwise arise in the mind of the patient. What with the tendency toward more frequent and larger dental malpractice judgments, the practitioner must do more than just practice dentistry.

EMERGENCY REFERRAL

As stated before, the duty of the doctor in referring a patient to a specialist only arises if, under the same circumstances, a reasonable, careful, and skillful general dental practitioner would so act. Elements that can be given attention in considering the need for a specialist include the patient's mental and emotional condition.[150] If at any time there is an emergency and the doctor realizes his own lack of competence in the particular area, he has the duty to advise the patient to employ someone more skilled and to refer the patient on.[151]

In one case it has been held that the doctor who is making dentures and is so intent that he fails to treat an opening into the antrum will be liable.[152]

LOCAL ANALGESIA

A chapter could be written on the legal aspects of local analgesia. Why? Because thousands of injections are given each working day, and various problems naturally arise from them.

It goes without saying that any "incorrect" method of needle insertion may be a cause for liability.[153]

The doctor is held to know the correct type of local analgesic and its contraindications, the percentage that should be used, whether a vasoconstrictor should be included, the injection amount, the size and gauge of the needle, and so on into infinity. The patient's health, age, weight, etc., are the factors that decide the "correctness," and there certainly can be no "general" or "standard" dosage. For your own edification, read the insert that comes with the product to check the contraindications, the *time* that should be taken to inject the solution, and how aspiration is necessary.

Every year there are many deaths from local analgesia; and there are also many other problems involved in its use, so do not be lulled into a false sense of security by the success and apparent ease of administration you normally enjoy.

Let us assume that a patient is seen as an emergency, swollen and in pain. If the local analgesic is injected into an infected area, liability may be predicated upon the theory that invasion of the infected area might have caused the infection to spread.[154]

In a recent case in which the patient broke his arm during a local analgesic injection, the patient claimed that he probably "held on too tight" and that the doctor was to blame because he improperly positioned the patient's arms.[155]

Although an entire chapter could also be written about nitrous oxide, suffice it to say that, from the author's personal experience, every calamity from death to hallucinations can and does occur with its use. Again, just read the literature to remind yourself of the admonitions concerning health history, extreme nervousness, and so on. *Records* about this subject will be covered later in this chapter.

What is worrisome to those of us who defend in dental malpractice matters is the declaration by some courts that when nitrous oxide is used the patient is considered to be "under the influence" and hence not responsible for his or her acts, thus depriving us of affirmative defenses such as contributory negligence, assumption of risk, comparative negligence, etc.[156]

POST-EMERGENCY TREATMENT

If there has been a prior operation on a patient and a complication of the same or a like condition is now in question, the law requires that, before proceeding, the professional person who last treated the patient must be contacted.[157]

A doctor may not induce the nonhiring of a troublesome patient.[158]

Perhaps every day each doctor sees a patient who has suffered some incident at the hands of a fellow practitioner's. It would appear that a few cardinal rules should govern:

1. Don't attempt to judge the other doctor's efforts — even judges and juries have difficulties in this endeavor.
2. Don't make conclusionary statements about the prior doctor's work; just do the best possible. Tell the truth in a factual and dental way.
3. Don't assume to know the condition of the patient when originally treated, nor the handicaps or instructions given.
4. Always call the other doctor before proceeding.
5. Avoid giving conclusions as to what might have been done or what should have been done. Always explain, and this is true, that there are many different methods and techniques that are proper in regard to the same problem, all of which are acceptable and constitute good practice. The law allows no guarantee to the patient.

If in treating the emergency or treating someone else's emergency, there is some question in mind, by all means call in a consultant or verify, whether it be by phone or otherwise, the plan or procedure.

DEATH

The recent decisions regarding alleged malpractice causing cardiac arrest while under an anesthetic state startling principles.[159] The child who suffered the cardiac arrest was six years old and was normal except that he had a runny nose, he was very apprehensive, his eyes turned inward a bit, and he had a slight temperature. When all vital signs ceased, the doctor knew something had to be done but didn't feel qualified to give resuscitation. Because of this a lengthy interval passed until someone else was found to give open heart massage. The court stressed that there is always a calculated risk of cardiac arrest when a patient is given a general anesthetic. The court stated that there should be qualified personnel immediately available in order to handle emergency resuscitation attempts. It also stated that great attention should be given to the health history, paying special regard to any slight rise in temperature and any slight apprehension. It is known that apprehension is an emotional state which causes epinephrine to be pumped into the circulatory system, which increases the sensitivity of the heart, which in turn can cause a reaction to the vagus nerve. The court stated that both apprehension and temperature increase are danger signals. The time element in regard to being prepared and competent to handle the rescue effort was all important. The court concluded that the doctrine of res ipsa loquitur might well be given to the jury, and if it applied there would be an inference of negligence.

The humane issues at death far outweigh any of the legal issues, but some legal conclusions will be set forth:

1. Do not volunteer to take care of everything, and state that the body will be preserved, etc. If someone else takes care of the remains and directions are not followed, and the next of kin notices this and suffers shock, the doctor will be liable for damages.[160]

2. The next of kin has the right to bury and/or preserve the remains; one cannot allow this to be done by someone else without the next of kin's consent.[161]

3. The surviving spouse is the person who has the right to control the disposition, not other relatives.[162]

4. Probably the fact that the doctor authorized an autopsy without gaining the proper consent would create liability.[163]

5. No arrangement should be made with anyone but the next of kin as to the retention of body organs, brain, etc. Although retention of body parts might enhance the advancement of science, this does not negate the next of kin's rights, and when this right is violated, damages for mental suffering are proper.[164]

The foregoing does not vitiate the instructions in a decedent's will, of course. California has now set out an Anatomical Gift Act, allowing the deceased to dispose of the whole or any part of his body.[165]

A wrongful death action may be brought by a deceased man's illigitimate children.[166]

Failure to promptly attempt to find and tell the next of kin of the death can cause liability.[167]

A false notice of death can create liability.[168]

Allowing undue display of the deceased *body* creates liability.[169]

The "secret" burial of the deceased creates liability.[170]

As a corollary to the foregoing, just because there is an inability to determine the cause of death is no excuse for failing to gain permission for the autopsy.[171]

This section of the chapter is *meant* to be cursory. The reason is that the causes, agents utilized, lack of health histories, types of damages, *who* recovers damages, lack of equipment, inadequacy of training for CPR, and so on, are so extensive that they should not be treated except in *great* depth. Please believe the writer, death or "vegetable cases" do occur, under any and all circumstances and to any and all age groups and under any and all health conditions. Prevention and recognition of the problem, and the legal difficulties and solutions should be taught in every dental school.

At the time this chapter was being prepared a jury awarded the heir 2.8 million dollars in a death case allegedly arising from "contaminated equipment." The latest and largest malpractice verdict noted was 7.6 million dollars in an x-ray radiation case.

RECORDS

The proper preparation and maintenance of records can be a doctor's salvation in a lawsuit. These can include the patient's chart, medical history, x-rays, consent, data, etc. Records—meaning adequate records—are expected of the doctor, and if he does not keep them he may possibly be guilty of malpractice. The reason for this stems from the fact that although the patient does not have property rights to the records themselves, he does have a right to expect that proper records will be kept of his case.

Experience repeats itself many times over as to how a witness' memory will fade with time. Adequate records will refresh a doctor's recollection.

From the writer's own practical experience, a recent lawsuit was won because of detailed records the doctor had kept. The case in question involved a broken needle in the jaw, but more specifically, whether or not the patient was told of the incident. The doctor said yes; the patient said no. The patient claimed he had been discharged and was not told of any problem. The doctor alleged the plaintiff gave a phone number where he could be reached, so as to make the appointment for the plaintiff to go to the hospital for the removal of the needle fragment. The plaintiff denied this, but the records of the defendant showed a phone number written on the x-ray envelope, which, under investigation and proper presentation into the evidence, was proved to be that of the manager of the apartment house wherein the plaintiff resided. This little penciled notation undoubtedly played a major part in gaining a verdict for the defendant.

Records that are offered and accepted into evidence are physical in nature; they are tangible, not illusory. They may be viewed by the jury. The jury frequently will forget or discount what has been said two or three days before, but if they can take the physical evidence into the jury room during deliberation, they cannot ignore those items.

Records, if kept in the usual business of the doctor, need not be personally entered by the doctor, but may be put down by whoever usually does those chores. The importance of this is shown when the patient suffers a cut cheek. If the patient's chart evidences that the patient moved after being warned, this could go a long way toward providing a complete defense. Assume, in the same case, that the patient's chart evidences only that the doctor and the assistant were present. It forecloses the frequent allegation that there was some other witness present. These allegations usually state that a friend of the patient was present who will testify, "Oh, the doctor acted carelessly or fumbled about."

In another instance in the writer's practice, the patient died in the dental chair after having been administered a local analgesic. As luck would have it, the inevitable plaintiff's attorney showed up stating that he represented the widow and that he believed that filing a dental malpractice suit would be a fine idea. He was shown the records of the doctor, and on the plaintiff's chart was a signed health history, including a question asking about prior cardiac conditions. The deceased had lied and stated that he had none, when as a matter of fact, he had been under the constant care of a physician for the past few years. The deceased had signed the health chart, and with that, of course, the claim and threatened litigation ended.

The proper time to prepare records is at or near the time of the emergency itself. At no other time will the doctor have so fresh in his mind the facts to be recorded. At a later date an entry should not be recorded, as there are adequate methods to determine that the entry was not made at or about the time of the treatment. This writer well remembers the doctor whose records were adequate. The defendant-doctor's deposition had been taken and the records properly marked and photostated. Later at the time of trial the doctor appeared with his records for final review. He had "doctored" and changed the records, stating that he thought this would be a truer reflection of the facts and would help his case. A winning case thus became questionable.

The public policy of keeping records even outweighs provisions in a doctor's will to destroy or bury all his patients' records.[172]

When it comes to proof in court about the patient's complaints (opening into sinus), records, when kept properly, can be a good defense.[173]

If a patient refuses help from an employee in sitting down, leaving the office, etc., this should be marked on the chart and would be proof of assumption of risk on the patient's part if an injury later occurs.[174]

The *records* must show the *age* of a minor (assuming a valid informed consent is gained from the proper person), for if the patient is a minor and prescriptions for drugs are provided, the doctor may be guilty of contributing to the delinquency of a minor.[175]

The problems of records and minors are always troublesome to the doctor. California has adopted *modern* laws addressed to the subject. California allows a pregnant minor to seek dental care as if an adult.[176] California also allows a minor over 15, under certain conditions, to give valid consent to the doctor.[177]

An adequate history is of course a most vital and important "record" regarding the patient. It should be signed by the patient and taken before any care and treatment are rendered.[178] A good history will "catch" the use of drugs or the mixing of medications.[179]

An adequate history should allow the doctor a *correct* choice of local analgesic, or *correct* sedation, etc., covering such important considerations as use of vasoconstrictor, aspirin, etc.

False records can be absolutely disastrous and subject the doctor to punitive damages.[180]

When the examination by the doctor might have called for a different type of operative procedure and this was not entered on the record, liability might follow.[181]

Courts have become very strict when any dental surgery is performed without a signed adequate health history. An allegation by plaintiff that the failure to take the history caused an aggravation of a pre-existing cardiac valvular lesion and subacute bacterial endocarditis will allow the jury to determine whether or not this constitutes malpractice.[182]

Some dental practitioners utilize a voluminous medical history such as shown in Figure 13–1. Individual questioning of the patient seems to be an absolute must. The reader is referred to chapter 2 for a discussion of the merits of brief vs. long medical histories.

Adequate records must be kept in order to defend against allegations of fraud in Medicare actions.[183] Records are necessary to show the plaintiff's present health condition and his or her condition before care and treatment was undertaken. In a recent case handled by this author, a postoperative complaint following an injection was involuntary muscle tremors. The patient's health history was utilized to prove that the patient had a long-standing history of alcoholism, and that this condition predated any treatment supplied by the defendant.

Properly and adequately prepared records can show the true cause of a residual foreign body and help prove affirmative defense of the statute of limitations. Records can prove the doctor's acts and reasons in cases of mandatory reporting to the authorities regarding the "battered child" or "contagious disease" patient.

Dental records often reflect and uncover the fact that severe pain in the oral cavity is referred pain from the cardiac area as a result of heart attack.

Text continued on page 393

MEDICAL/DENTAL HEALTH HISTORY

PATIENT NAME_____AGE_____

DATE OF BIRTH_____PLACE OF BIRTH_____

HEIGHT_____WEIGHT_____

DIRECTIONS: ALL QUESTIONS WILL REQUIRE A "NO" ANSWER OR A POSITIVE
             RESPONSE IN ONE OR MORE WORDS. PLEASE FILL IN COMPLETELY
             AND ANSWER ALL QUESTIONS.

EXAMPLES: A. DO YOU HAVE A TOOTHACHE?___YES, FOR 3 DAYS_____
            B. HAVE YOU BEEN HOSPITALIZED?__1970, APPENDECTOMY_____
            C. DO YOU HAVE PAIN AT THIS TIME?___No_____

MEDICAL

1. Have you been examined by a physician within the past year?_____

    For what reason?_____

2. Has there been any change in your general health in the past year?_____

    _____

3. Are you currently being treated by a physician for a medical problem?_____

    _____

4. Please list any prescribed medications taken within the past year:_____

    _____

5. Have you ever been seriously ill?_____

6. Please list dates and reasons for all hospital admissions:_____

    _____

7. Have you had radiation treatment for any tumor or growth?_____

8. Do you often feel exhausted or fatigued?_____

Figure 13–1

9. Have you ever had any of the following diseases or conditions? **Please list** dates:

Hepatitis_____Colitis_____

Tuberculosis_____Thrombophlebitis_____

Stomach Ulcers_____Diabetes_____

Epilepsy_____Arthritis_____

Porphyria_____Other_____

CARDIOVASCULAR

1. Have you ever had a heart attack or stroke?_____

_____

2. Do you have high blood pressure?_____

3. Have you ever had rheumatic fever?_____

4. Do you have a heart murmur or any heart defect?_____

_____

5. Do you have chest pain (angina) with physical exertion?_____

_____

6. Do you have any blood disorder such as anemia (thin blood)?_____

_____

7. Have you ever had an excessive bleeding problem?_____

_____

8. Do your ankles ever swell?_____

RESPIRATORY

1. Do you have a persistant cough?_____

2. Are you ever short of breath with mild exertion?_____

3. Do you have asthma?_____

4. Do you have emphysema?_____

5. Do you have bronchitis?_____

Figure 13–1 *Continued*

Illustration continued on following page

ALLERGIES

1. Have you ever experienced an unfavorable reaction to any of the following
    medications? If yes, please indicate type of reaction:

    Valium_____Percodan_____

    Penicillin_____Aspirin_____

    Atropine_____Codeine_____

    Demerol_____Talwin_____

    Erythromycin_____Sodium Pentothal_____

    Sodium Brevital_____Other_____

NEUROLOGICAL

1. Do you have numbness or tingling in any part of your body?_____

    _____

2. Has any part of your body ever been paralyzed?_____

3. Do you ever have convulsions?_____

4. Do you have frequent severe headaches?_____

5. Have you ever had psychiatric treatment?_____

6. Do you have a tendency to faint?_____

7. Do you consider yourself to be a nervous person?_____

8. Have you ever suffered from severe nervous exhaustion (breakdown)?_____

    _____

9. Do you often feel unhappy and depressed?_____

10. Do you often cry?_____

11. Do you have a profound fear of dental treatment?_____

DISABILITY

1. Do you wear contact lenses?_____

2. Do you use a hearing aid?_____

3. Are you disabled in any way?_____

    _____

Figure 13–1 *Continued*

DENTAL

1. Have you ever experienced an unfavorable reaction to a local anesthetic (Xylocaine or Novocain)?_____

2. Have you ever had Sodium Pentothal or Sodium Brevital in an Oral Surgery office?_____

3. Have you ever had an unfavorable reaction to any dental treatment?_____

_____

4. Do you have difficulty in opening your mouth wide?_____

_____

5. Have you ever had an injury to the face, jaws or neck?_____

_____

6. Does your jaw ever "click", "pop", or give you a sharp pain or discomfort?

_____

7. Do you have regular dental care?_____

8. Have you had orthodontic care?_____

9. Would you like a referral to a general dentist for further care?_____

PERSONAL

1. Do you smoke or use tobacco frequently?_____

2. Do you drink alcohol frequently?_____

3. Have you ever been addicted to any drug?_____

FOR THE LADIES ONLY

1. Are you pregnant?_____

2. Have you passed through menopause?_____

3. Have you had a hysterectomy or ovariectomy?_____

GENERAL

1. How do you consider your health to be?

    Excellent_____Good_____Average_____Fair_____Poor_____

Figure 13-1 *Continued*

Illustration continued on following page

2. Please list all medications that you are now taking:_____

_____

_____

_____

_____

3. Are you currently experiencing dental pain or swelling?_____

_____

4. Do you prefer general anesthesia (Sodium Brevital) or local anesthesia

(Xylocaine or Novocain)?_____

5. Please indicate any important medical or dental information not already

covered by this questionnaire:_____

_____

_____

_____

_____

_____

_____

PLEASE SIGN AND DATE BELOW:

_____
SIGNATURE (Patient, or parent if minor)   Date

_____
Reviewed by: Nurse   Doctor

Figure 13–1 *Continued*

Within six months of this writing the author has handled eight trial matters for dentists involving local analgesic reaction (epilepsy), mandible fracture, local analgesic fear (cancer), lingual and inferior alveolar paresthesia, root canal-apico, crown and bridge, periodontal operation, and full-mouth reconstruction. In each instance, on each doctor's chart, there were notations regarding advice given and not followed, alternate choices, referral to specialists, offers to redo the work, etc. In *each* trial, after the jury rendered their verdict for the defendant, they related the *huge* influence on their decision by the doctor's records. In *each* instance these records and x-rays were placed in evidence, marked as exhibits, and taken by the jury into their private deliberation chamber.

Some interesting asides:

1. Some jurisdictions hold that an unseated bridge belongs to the patient.[184]
2. Since records are available to the patient, their content is held to be in the knowledge of the patient when the statute of limitations is involved.[185]

Number 2, above, is a most common help in defense of the doctor's claim that the plaintiff knew of the condition at a specific time, in which case the chart may help to convince the plaintiff's attorney not to file suit, or, if suit is filed, the records are concrete evidence for jurors to refer to. Records can also be utilized to show that an emergency was involved, thus calling into effect that particular doctrine.

INFORMED CONSENT

The cocoon of confidence is not embodied in this legal doctrine. This area of law is the fastest growing within malpractice litigation. The reader would do well to confer with the attorney in his own state who specializes in defense of dental malpractice matters, as each jurisdiction is developing its own law on the subject.

In general, *at least*, the patient must be advised concerning projected dental care and treatment as to the following:

1. Reasons for care and treatment
2. Diagnosis
3. Prognosis
4. Alternatives
5. Nature of care and treatment
6. The risks involved (inherent included)
7. Expectancies of success
8. Possible results if care and treatment are not undertaken

The problem confronting the doctor is normally most perplexing in that his guidelines as to gaining informed consent from the patient come from legal language in court decisions — a veritable "professional gap." One of the "early" leading cases[186] used language as follows: ". . . (professional person) violates his duty to his patient and subjects himself to liability if he withholds any facts which are necessary to form the basis of an intelligent consent by the patient to the proposed treatment . . . may not minimize the known dangers of a procedure or operation in order to induce his patient's consent... is to explain to the patient any risks attendant... no matter how remote...."

Contrast the foregoing with the language of another state court as to all that is needed in informed consent, wherein merely stating "It's a serious operation, not done without risks" was found to be sufficient.[187]

A continuing problem of "decision" lies with the situation of a patient whose psychological and emotional conditions (depressed, nervous, unstable, etc.) are in question. How far should the doctor go? To alarm the patient might generate reactions that increase the hazards to the patient. The law has become most *exacting* in these circumstances and unrelenting in demanding that informed consent be gained even when the patient was "upset, agitated, anxious, depressed, crying, and had been drinking and having marital difficulties."[188] To the same effect the law seems clear that if the risk is "high" of an untoward result, informed consent is mandatory.[189]

Some jurisdictions appear to hold that informed consent need address itself only to "probable" risks and not "possible" risks.[190] Very often there is an "overlap" between informed consent and the question of the balance of surgery as against other treatment, but invariably the issue is still treated as malpractice and liability will be imposed.[191]

The farthest reaching court language on imposing a duty of informed consent to "possible risks" is as follows: "... explain every risk to the patient... full disclosure of facts...."[192] By the very nature of some treatment (cobalt irradiation), even expert evidence is not necessary to establish liability when there is *silence* as to any risks.[193] To the same effect is the statement by the doctor that "no danger can result."[194]

When a drug (antibiotic) is prescribed that has dangerous side effects, the patient must be "warned" and informed consent gained or the doctor will be liable.[195] Likewise, any "deliberate" misleading of the patient or "playing down" the risk may bring liability.[196]

The courts have become most stringent in stating that the patient must "understand" the informed consent, the meaning of words, etc., and it is incumbent on the doctor to make certain that his warnings are fully comprehended or else liability ensues.[197]

There is one case that gives solace to dental practitioners in Montana. It specifically held under the facts of that case that the doctor was *not* liable for failure to warn the patient that the mandible might fracture on the extraction of a tooth.[198] A word of caution: every case stands or falls on its own peculiar facts, testimony, experts, and judge or jury.

The law is well settled that the patient in order to make an intelligent choice must be informed of the various types of treatment possible and must give *valid* consent to his choice. The courts hold that the patient must be informed when there is offered a more hazardous type of operation so that he might select a less dangerous type of treatment.[199]

It is generally recognized that when the practitioner is confronted by an emergency of an unanticipated condition (and it would be impracticable and impossible to obtain consent) he will be allowed to proceed with what the occasion demands without gaining express consent.[200] The theory is that there is implied consent to go forward.[201]

In a case in which the mandible fractured during an attempted extraction of an infected wisdom tooth, it was alleged that the repair of the fracture was without consent because the patient-plaintiff was still under the anesthetic. In this case[202] the court stated that because of the emergency it would be impractical to bring the patient to consciousness; thus consent was implied. An interesting aside was that the court held as a matter of law that alleged rough method and discourteous manner would not prove malice. Also, the court stated that just because an operation in dentistry is painful does not mean that it is intentionally cruel so that punitive damages will be assessed against the doctor.

In the same vein, many professional people have attempted to formulate a consent that is all inclusive, like a panacea; but in reality it turns out to be a Pandora's box of troubles. The courts have held, when there are utilized the words "consent to any and all surgery," etc., that this is not valid, that it is too broad, and that it will have no more effect than to allow only the operation that was discussed with the plaintiff.[203]

It seems fairly apparent nowadays that informed consent should be gained from a patient before any operative treatment is performed. The courts say that the doctor must disclose to the patient all the facts which mutually affect his rights and interests. If this is not done, there is no intelligent consent, and any consent given is without foundation and *invalid*.[204]

The deadly effect of the informed consent doctrine is most graphically illustrated by the following: (1) If the patient is not given an informed consent and understands same, the performance of the care and treatment constitutes a technical battery.[205] (2) The defendant doctor will be liable for all damages proximately resulting, whether or not they could be anticipated.[206]

Figure 13–2 is an example of the form used for informed consent for surgery, and Figure 13–3 is an example of the informed consent form for orthodontia, formulated by the doctor and this writer. For each specialty or type of treatment we have attempted to do likewise. A word of caution: these forms are only part of the office records and should not be utilized alone. Office procedure and other records are necessary in order to make informed consents effective and practical. They, and the other planning that makes them work, have proved to be very effective in fending off litigation, and, as a bonus, are a great public relations plus for the doctor.

It is impossible in the space allotted to render a complete account of the many facets of informed consent. I *would* like to point out that there are exceptions to the mandatory requirements of informed consent, but they are minor.

Many practitioners still scoff at the legal requirements of the Informed Consent Doctrine. Let me remind you that it has been imposed by law that the patient be fully apprised, in advance of treatment, of information that will allow him or her to make an intelligent decision.

The language of the instruction by a judge to the jury in a dental malpractice case on the subject might give credence to "think preventively," and, as the old Boy Scout motto proclaims, "Be Prepared." In California the law reads as follows:

It is the duty of a dentist to disclose to his patient all relevant information to enable the patient to make an informed decision regarding the proposed operation of treatment.

There is no duty to discuss minor risks inherent in common procedures, when such procedures very seldom result in serious ill effects.

Text continued on page 399

CONSENT FOR SURGERY/ANESTHESIA

This is my consent for Dr. _____ or any dentist or physician who may be employed by Dr. _____, to perform the oral surgery indicated on my examination chart, as previously explained to me, and any other procedure deemed necessary or advisable as a corollary to the planned operation. I also agree to the use of a local and/or ultralight general anesthetic, sedation, and analgesic, depending upon the judgment of the dentists involved with my care.

I have been informed, and understand, that occasionally there are complications of the surgery, drugs and anesthesia, including pain, infection, swelling, bleeding, discoloration, numbness and tingling of the lip, tongue, chin, gums, cheeks and teeth, pain and numbness and tingling, and thrombophlebitis (inflammation of a vein) from intravenous and intramuscular injection, injury to and stiffening of neck and facial muscles, change in occlusion or temporomandibular joint difficulty, injury to the adjacent teeth or restorations in other teeth, or injury to other tissues, referred pain to ear, neck and head, nausea, vomiting, allergic reaction, bone fractures, bruises, delayed healing, sinus complications, and nasal antral fistulas and openings.

Medications, drugs, anesthetics and prescriptions may cause drowsiness and lack of awareness and coordination which can be increased by the use of alcohol or other drugs; thus, I have been advised not to operate any vehicle or hazardous devices, or work, while taking such medications and/or drugs, or until fully recovered from the effects of same. I understand and agree not to operate any vehicle or hazardous device for at least twenty-four (24) hours, or until further recovered from the effects of the anesthetic, medication and drugs that may have been given to me in the office for my care.

I acknowledge the receipt of pre-operative instructions, and understand that I should have nothing to eat or drink for at least six hours prior to receiving a general anesthetic. In addition, I acknowledge the receipt of, and understand, post-operative instructions and have been given a specific appointment date to return to the office. It has been explained to me, and I understand, that there is no warranty or guarantee as to any result and/or cure. *I understand that I can ask for a full recital of possible risks attendant to all phases of my care merely by asking.*

The following were used as an aid in the explanation of the surgery and anesthesia:
Radiographs (x-ray)_____
Drawings_____
Audiovisual media_____

_____
SIGNATURE (Patient, or parent if minor)   Date

When the patient is a minor or incompetent to give consent, signature should be of a person authorized to consent for the patient.

_____
Witness

Figure 13–2

ADDENDUM TO CONSENT FOR SURGERY/ANESTHESIA

I acknowledge that my health history has revealed the following conditions:

1. _____

2. _____

3. _____

4. _____

Because of these medical conditions, it has been thoroughly explained to me, and I completely realize, that any surgical procedure may, therefore, be classified as a risk procedure. The risk involved is defined as a greater *possibility* of experiencing morbidity (the relative incidence of disease) and mortality (the proportion of deaths to population) during the surgical procedure than a person in good health. These complications which can occur during surgery may involve more than the average amount of post-operative discomfort, increased pain and swelling, and delayed healing.

I fully acknowledge that these possible complications have been *EXPLAINED IN DETAIL TO ME*. With clear knowledge of all of these possible complications, I have requested that the surgical procedure be performed in the office environment, rather than a hospital. However, it is my understanding that additional precautions will be made during my surgical procedure that will include the use of oxygen for several minutes prior to the commencement of the procedure, and electronic monitoring of the cardiovascular system by an ECG machine.

I may request further explanations of the *risks involved and possible outcome of the procedure, merely by asking.*

_____

SIGNATURE (Patient, or parent if minor)   Date

When the patient is a minor or incompetent to give consent, signature should be of a person authorized to consent for the patient.

_____

Witness

Figure 13–2 *Continued*

Illustration continued on following page

INFORMED CONSENT

I hereby authorize that all necessary orthodontic treatment be given for_____
_____. This shall include the taking of necessary diagnostic records and the administration of necessary medications. I understand that all records may be used for reproduction in scientific publications and books, for exhibit under the auspices of a scientific group, and for teaching purposes at established dental schools.

I understand that orthodontic treatment cannot succeed through the efforts of the orthodontist alone, but rather through the joint cooperation of all parties involved and together we may achieve the best possible result. In many instances, lack of co-operation in the requested use of headgear, elastics, retainers and positioners will make a successful completion of treatment or maintenance of treatment result impossible.

I understand that treatment time varies with the difficulty of the problem, cooperation of the patient, and individual physiological response to treatment. Treatment time can be prolonged by broken appointments, broken appliances, poor oral hygiene, poor diet. I further understand that for the best orthodontic result progress records may be taken to evaluate treatment and make a progress diagnosis which may involve a change in the treatment plan. Occasionally, due to lack of cooperation and/or the severity of the problem a rediagnosis may require maxillofacial surgery and/or selected teeth to be removed to obtain the best possible treatment result.

I understand that during orthodontic treatment there is a possibility the following may occur: cold sores; canker sores; irritation or injury to the oral mucosa or skin; periodontal involvement; root involvement; decalcification; decay or staining under or around the orthodontic appliances; chipped or broken teeth; tooth sensitivity and mobility; loss of teeth; undesired facial changes; temporomandibular joint problems; allergic reactions to dental materials or medications; possible need for crown and/or bridgework; possible need for endodontic and/or periodontal treatment; aspiration or swallowing of dental materials, appliances or portions of appliances; eye damage; heart involvement; hepatitis.

I understand my responsibility in maintaining a well-balanced soft textured diet which is free of hard, sticky, and high sugar foods as well as maintaining a hygiene program of three brushings a day. I understand that regular dental check-ups are necessary so that the general dentist may check for decay and clean the teeth, if necessary. It is also my responsibility to immediately report any faulty appliances and insure the wearing of any supplemental appliances or retainers as instructed. If it becomes evident that further orthodontic treatment will endanger oral health or if lack of cooperation will prevent completion of a satisfactory result treatment may be discontinued.

I understand that Dr._____ will use his knowledge, skill and training to do his very best but that there is no guarantee of success of treatment and that relapse of treatment results is possible.

I understand what the problem is and the reason for treatment; the alternatives have also been explained to me, one of which is no treatment and the possible results if nothing is done. The treatment plan and the type of appliances to be used have been explained to me.

It has been explained to me, and I understand there is no specific warranty or guarantee as to any result and/or cure, and I understand I can ask for a full recital of all possible risks attendant to phases of _____
orthodontic care and treatment by just asking.

I understand the variables associated with the degree of success to be achieved and have read and understood the above.

_____   _____
(date)   (signature)

Figure 13–3

However, when a procedure inherently involves a known risk of death or serious bodily harm, it is the dentist's duty to disclose to his patient the possibility of such outcome and to explain in lay terms the complications that might possibly occur. The dentist must also disclose such additional information as a skilled practitioner of good standing would provide under the same or similar circumstances.

There is no duty to make disclosure of risks when the patient requests that he not be so informed or where the procedure is simple and the danger remote and commonly understood to be remote.

Also, a dentist has no duty of disclosure beyond that required of dentists of good standing in the same or similar locality when he relied upon facts which would demonstrate to a reasonable man that the disclosure would so seriously upset the patient that the patient would not have been able to rationally weigh the risks of refusing to undergo the recommended treatment.

Notwithstanding the patient's consent to a proposed treatment or operation, failure of the dentist to inform the patient as stated in this instruction before obtaining such consent is negligence and renders the dentist subject to liability for any injury (proximately) (legally) resulting from the (treatment) (operation) if a reasonably prudent person in the patient's position would not have consented to the (treatment) (operation) if he had been adequately informed of all the significant perils.

Recent court decisions have interpreted this requirement to definitely include alternative treatment options.

To translate informed consent into actual practice, let us assume the following has been properly accomplished:

A. Adequate x-rays
B. Complete health history, up to date and signed.
C. The patient is capable of understanding what is to be explained to him.

Let us further assume the doctor's skill and judgment tell him that what is dentally desirable is a deep filling on a lower molar tooth, a crown on an upper first molar, and an extraction of an upper bicuspid. For all three procedures, numbers 1 and 2 of the Informed Consent are almost self-explanatory.

Listed are some possible explanations, as examples, and are not complete, for the *deep filling* with the corresponding numbers from the Informed Consent form numbered items listed on page 393:

No. 3. Crown? Root Canal? Onlay? Inlay? Extraction? etc.
No. 4. A reasonable explanation of the future.
No. 5. A reasonable percentage of usefulness and longevity.
No. 6. A full explanation of what is being attempted.
No. 7. Pain, sensitivity, swelling, possible later root canal and/or apico and/or extraction, etc.
No. 8. The explanation of pain, infection, medical harm possibilities, etc.

Listed are some possible explanations, as examples, and are not complete, for the *crown* with corresponding numbers from the Informed Consent form numbered items listed on page 393:

No. 3. Onlay? Inlay? Extraction? etc.
No. 4. A reasonable explanation of the future.
No. 5. A reasonable percentage of usefulness and longevity.
No. 6. A full explanation of what is being attempted.
No. 7. Pain, swelling, sensitivity, infection, later root canal, later apico, later extraction, later partial or bridge, etc.
No. 8. The explanation of pain, infection, medical harm possibilities, etc.

Listed are some possible explanations, as examples, and are not complete, for the extraction of the *upper first molar,* with corresponding numbers from the Informed Consent form numbered items listed on page 393:

No. 3.   Attempted root canal, apico, etc.
No. 4.   A reasonable explanation of the future.
No. 5.   A reasonable percentage regarding a "good" result.
No. 6.   A full explanation of what is being attempted.
No. 7.   Pain, swelling, bleeding, infection, discoloration, opening into antrum, etc.
No. 8.   The explanation of pain, infection, medical harm possibilities, etc.

Needless to say, the Informed Consent doctrine knows no age limits, whether pediatric or geriatric. Some 15 year olds can comprehend, while some 50 year olds cannot. Proceed with caution.

A signed and dated Informed Consent is needed for *each* different procedure and, like the health history, it must be "up to date."

NO DELAY IN EMERGENCY

The law states generally that when a person is unconscious the operator must take great precaution to see that no injury occurs.[207] Emergency as a defense will do the operator no good if there is any delay or indecision in his actions. By this is meant that if a matter is one that should be referred to a specialist, this must be done immediately, and any delay may be taken into consideration as an aggravation of the original incident and play heavily against the professional person's interest.[208] In the case just referred to, the doctor had left a root in the mandible, and there later developed infection and a joint problem. There was a delay in referring the matter to the proper specialist, which made the doctor liable.

The emergency treatment must be within the standard of care for like emergencies,[209] and if this is not met, then of course liability should lie.

If there is hemorrhage from an extraction, this emergency calls for keeping the patient under constant observation as long as necessary in order to control the problem.[210]

THE FUTURE?

Legal concepts change with great rapidity. It used to be that a patient could be refused treatment, for any reason.[211] Now statutes are being promulgated that under certain circumstances (including an emergency) it becomes obligatory to accept a patient.[212]

Recovery of monetary damages is now becoming "possible" when a parent, seeing her child injured, suffers shock, fright, and emotional trauma.[213] The courts have even gone farther, and it is now "possible" for a child, seeing her sister injured, to recover for "shock, fright, and emotional trauma."[214]

Patient-plaintiffs continually attempt to hold the doctor liable on the theory of *strict liability,* said doctrine, in effect, making the doctor liable even when there is no malpractice, the basis being that the doctor "caused" the injury.[215]

Further attempts are being pressed to hold that supplying items such as blood, drugs, etc., is a sale of a product (and not a service) and if the item is defective, there will be strict liability with no need to show negligence or malpractice.[216]

Can a doctor foresee how long any projected treatment will take with any accuracy? The courts now seemingly hold that the operator is held to know how long he will need the anesthetic, and if he misjudges and it begins to wear off, liability can be predicated on this fact.[217]

The dangers of treating a "mentally disturbed" patient are exemplified by cases that, in effect, state if the patient is not "controlled" and suicide follows, a wrongful death suit may be proper.[218]

An area of concern to most doctors is whether the doctor can sue the plaintiff's attorney and plaintiff for malicious prosecution. Each jurisdiction has its own "rules," but usually, in order to do this, the defendant must first *win* his own malpractice suit. Some doctors now believe they can avoid awaiting this outcome and sue for Abuse of Process and Libel and Slander. Again, each state has its own laws, and attorneys specializing in these matters should be consulted.

Some states now allow a practitioner to be sued when he writes a report about a patient and the patient later complains that it isn't "accurate." This can be true even if the letter by the doctor is to the plaintiff's attorney.

Arbitration is thought of by some health practitioners as relief from the malpractice onslaught. It may well be, but it is *very* technical and is fraught with the danger of we attorneys arbitrating your dental matter, and that may be bad! Jurors seemingly do fine with dental malpractice matters, when the case is prepared properly and thoroughly. Not always so with judges (who are attorneys).

Comparative Negligence is a new doctrine that states, in effect, that there may be some percentage of fault by the patient and some percentage of fault by the doctor. This means, for instance, that in cases where the patient is admonished to sit still, and does not and moves, and is cut, the defense of Contributory Negligence no longer bars the plaintiff from recovery against the doctor. This new doctrine is another way of allowing the plaintiff to prevail, at least in some percentage of his claim for damages, whereas before he would have lost the suit because he was at fault for moving after being warned, as his own actions caused the injury. Woe is me!

Ever encroaching on the doctor-patient relationship are third party influences, whether in dollar allowances, or in what treatment can be done. Please heed the warning: no matter what third party, government or not, allows by way of payment on work to be accomplished, that is *not* the standard of care. It is the doctor's judgment that sets the standard of care and just because it cannot be "paid for" or the work not done more than once a year, or every five years, or whatever, that doesn't excuse the doctor from practicing the proper standard of care and apprising the patient of what is needed. The law does not allow the clinician to practice below the standard of care, *even* if the patient agrees to this in advance, or *even* if the patient gives a "release" to this maneuver. Be forewarned, suits on these facts are being handled now by the writer.

Last, and perhaps most important, is the State Board of Dental Examiners' action in each jurisdiction. This is an increasing hazard to the dental practitioner. It is separate and apart from malpractice. It is disciplinary in nature, is initiated by the governing body or by the patient, and is closely akin to being criminal in nature. Professional liability insurance does not cover this challenge and proceeding, which may end up in a separate time and trial. It is distasteful and embarrassing, and may end up with a loss of the doctor's license. At the first hint of involvement in this type of proceeding, every practitioner should contact an attorney specializing in dental malpractice defense, in that the basis for the State Board involvement, at least ostensibly, is concerned with the standard of care practiced on the patient or patients.

Most jurisdictions are faced with an avalanche of dental malpractice litigation. In order to provide a winning defense, planning is all important. One of the most significant tools to utilize is the protection afforded by law. Different states give varying degrees of protection to the client (dental practitioner) when he makes confidential communications to his attorney. This is highly important in that recent law in most state jurisdictions is to the effect that the plaintiff will have wide latitude in discovering reports, communications, records, etc., while (1) figuring out if he has a case, or (2) planning strategy to prove malpractice against the doctor.

One way to avoid this problem is by the use of all legal and moral defenses and by the discriminating use of the attorney-client privilege. If on the happening of an "incident" or notice of potential problem the doctor contacts an attorney who specializes in dental malpractice defense, the dealings between the two will be clothed with the attorney-client privilege. The proper attorney-client privilege states that all confidential communications from the client to the attorney will be clothed with an absolute privilege so that no one may delve into the private matters at hand.[219]

Malpractice insurance should be arranged so that there is no intermediary between the doctor and the attorney, thus providing the best possible opportunity to prepare a timely defense. The attorney can then notify the insurance company and/or broker.

EDITOR'S COMMENT

To the dental practitioner as yet uninitiated to the courtroom, and to the predoctoral or auxiliary student, the doctrine of informed consent and the various records and suggested policies must appear to be utterly incredible. Yet enormous efforts by the plaintiff's attorney to achieve big-dollar awards must be met by equal effort on the part of potential defendants. The doctor who innocently places his or her faith in total devotion to the highest quality of patient care, and who does not practice defensively, is headed for a very rude awakening. It is unfortunate that the additional time spent by the doctor in defense before the fact must be borne in the final analysis by additional patient costs, but such is the system.

To those health professionals who feel that the full details of informed consent would be shattering to patients, including the risk of death during treatment, may I state that the goriest of warnings rarely faze the patient.

Malpractice *does* occur, and the patient should be compensated in full and proper measure. Until a system of fair compensation is adopted on a "no-fault" or workmen's compensation type basis, we shall have to live with a monster which is vastly increasing costs to the patient, and which is causing a significant number of health professionals in high-risk specialties to seek other employment.

It is the rare reader who will finish this chapter without a sinking feeling regarding his or her choice of the health professions as a life endeavor. However, take heart, most dental malpractice suits are won by the defendant, particularly the doctor-defendant who has had the foresight to follow the three R's: records, rapport, and reason, and who has the courage to prevail.

Further, 691 malpractice claims were filed in California in 1977 against medical and dental practitioners as compared to a high of 874 in 1975. Preventive measures *are* effective.

REFERENCES

So that there be a sense of propriety, the names and citations of the cases will not be included. Only the state from which the decision arose will be listed.

1. Louisiana
2. Delaware–Mississippi
3. Washington, D.C.
4. Louisiana
5. Maine
6. Kentucky
7. California
8. Louisiana–Massachusetts
9. California
10. Massachusetts
11. Florida
12. California
13. California
14. Minnesota
15. Kentucky
16. New Jersey–Michigan–Nebraska
17. Tennessee
18. California
19. California
20. New Mexico
21. Illinois
22. Massachusetts
23. Virginia
24. Washington, D.C.
25. Oregon–Louisiana
26. California
27. California
28. California
29. New Jersey
30. New Jersey
31. Kansas–Minnesota
32. Vermont–Washington, D.C.–California
33. California
34. Wyoming
35. Nebraska
36. New Jersey
37. Georgia
38. California–New Jersey
39. Michigan
40. California
41. California
42. Massachusetts
43. Georgia
44. California
45. California–Illinois
46. Alabama
47. New York–Iowa
48. California
49. California
50. Pennsylvania
51. Michigan
52. California
53. California
54. Florida
55. California–New York–Kentucky
56. Kansas
57. New York
58. Pennsylvania
59. Maryland
60. Minnesota
61. Washington
62. Delaware
63. Michigan
64. California
65. California
66. California–Kentucky
67. Michigan
68. Idaho
69. California
70. Virginia
71. California
72. Louisiana–Oregon
73. Arizona
74. Illinois
75. Michigan
76. November
77. California–Arizona
78. Arizona
79. California
80. California
81. California
82. California
83. Georgia–New York
84. Washington
85. Missouri
86. Arkansas
87. Maryland
88. California
89. Michigan
90. Oregon
91. Utah
92. California
93. California
94. Wisconsin
95. California–New York
96. Louisiana

97. California
98. New York
99. New York–California
100. Washington
101. California
102. Washington, D.C.
103. California
104. Arizona
105. California
106. California
107. California
108. Florida–North Carolina–Washington
109. California
110. Idaho
111. California
112. Washington, D.C.
113. Michigan
114. California
115. Michigan
116. Ohio–Kentucky
117. Ohio
118. California–Louisiana–Washington–Kansas
119. California
120. Maine
121. Arkansas
122. Washington–Florida
123. California
124. California
125. California
126. California
127. California
128. New Mexico
129. California
130. New York
131. California
132. California
133. California
134. California
135. Louisiana
136. New Jersey
137. Washington, D.C.
138. California
139. California
140. Connecticut
141. North Carolina
142. Rhode Island
143. California
144. Washington, D.C.
145. Illinois–California–Montana
146. California
147. New Zealand
148. New York
149. California
150. California
151. Maine
152. Oregon
153. California–Louisiana
154. California–New Jersey–Michigan
155. Louisiana
156. Kansas
157. California
158. California

159. California
160. California
161. California
162. California
163. Oklahoma–Kentucky
164. New York
165. California
166. New Jersey
167. California
168. New York
169. Tennessee
170. Pennsylvania
171. Florida
172. New York
173. Washington
174. Connecticut
175. Utah
176. California
177. California
178. Nebraska
179. Illinois
180. New Jersey
181. Tennessee
182. Ohio
183. Washington, D.C.
184. Louisiana
185. California
186. California
187. North Carolina
188. Missouri
189. North Carolina–Florida
190. Louisiana–Texas–Colorado
191. Georgia
192. California
193. Kansas
194. New Mexico
195. West Virginia
196. Rhode Island–Michigan–California
197. Tennessee–Pennsylvania
198. Montana
199. Massachusetts
200. California
201. Louisiana–Washington, D.C.–Kansas
202. California
203. California
204. California
205. California
206. California
207. Missouri
208. California
209. Ohio
210. Montana
211. Louisiana
212. California
213. California
214. California
215. New Jersey
216. Florida–California
217. California
218. California
219. California

INDEX

Note: in this index, page numbers in *italic* type refer to illustrations; page numbers followed by (t) refer to tables.

Anticoagulant therapy, following acute myocardial infarction, 39–40

Antidepressants, adverse interactions of, 214

Antihistamines, characteristics and effects of, 171–173
classification of, 172
in allergic bronchial constriction, 259
in pregnant women, 138

Antihypertensives, 142–144
adverse interactions of, 214

Antimicrobials, adverse interactions of, 211

Antiparasitic agents, adverse interactions of, 212–213

Antiprotozoan drugs, effects of, 191–192

Antiseptics, effects of, 207–209

Antiviral drugs, effects of, 190–191

Aortic aneurysm, ASA classification of, 42
dissecting, as cause of sudden death, 4(t)
treatment modification for, 25(t)

Aortic stenosis, as cause of sudden death, 4(t)

Apnea, in general anesthesia, 331–332

Apoplexy, cerebral. See Cerebrovascular accident.

Appendicitis, 82

Arrhythmias, in general anesthesia, 350
pathological, 121–125
physiological sinus rhythm and, 120–121
pulse rate in, 99

Arterial blood gas saturation, monitoring of, 109

Arterial hypertension, 41–42
treatment modification for, 25(t)

Arterial hypotension, 41

Arteriosclerosis, 78–79

Artificial airways, 232, 232

Artificial ventilation, of unconscious patient, atmospheric air, 228–230
exhaled air, 227–228

ASA classification, acute myocardial infarction, 38–39
adrenocortical insufficiency, 50
anemia, 50
angina pectoris, 36–37
blood pressure, 54
body temperature, 56
bronchial asthma, 32
bronchiectasis, 30
cerebrovascular accident, 44
chronic renal insufficiency, 45
convulsive disorders, 52
diabetes mellitus, 48
emphysema, 31
epilepsy, 52
hepatitis, 46
Hodgkin's disease, 51–52
hyperthyroidism, 49
hypothyroidism, 48
leukemia, 51
patients having coronary artery bypass surgery, 40
peptic ulcer, 45
polycythemia vera, 51
pulse rate and rhythm, 55

ASA classification (Continued)
regional enteritis, 46
respiratory rate, 57
sickle cell anemia, 51
ulcerative colitis, 46

ASA physical status classification, guidelines for, 25–26, 26(t)

ASA physical status classification system, 25, 25(t)

Ascites, 53
in hepatitis, 46

Asphyxia, as cause of sudden death, 4(t)

Aspiration of foreign bodies, 29
malpractice liability, 376–377

Aspiration pneumonitis, 328–329

Aspirin, and angioedema, 253

Asthma, bronchial, 32

Asthmatic attacks, during local analgesia, treatment of, 319
local analgesia and, 311
treatment of, 273

Atarax, 167–168

Atelectasis, 71

Atherosclerosis, coronary artery, in sudden death profile, 7
stress and, 225

Atrial fibrillation, 76, 122–123, 123, 237

Atrial flutter, 122, 122

Atrial tachycardia, 76, 122, 122

Atrioventricular node, 75

Atrium, definition of, 32

Atropine, effects of, 197
in treatment of cardiac arrest, 305
taken with digitalis, 142

Auscultation, in physical examination, 65
of anesthetized patient, 95

Bacitracin, effects of, 193

Bacterial contamination, in local analgesia, 308

Bacterial diseases, 28

Bacterial endocarditis, subacute, 79–80

Bag-valve-mask device for atmospheric air ventilation, 228

Barbiturates, adverse interactions of, 214
allergies to, 255
characteristics and effects of, 159
classification, structure, and dosages of, 160(t)

Basal cell carcinoma, 68

Bemegride, effects of, 199

Benzalkonium chloride, effects of, 209

Benzodiazepines, contraindications to, 167

Bigeminy, 334

Biliary cirrhosis, 83

Biopsy, malpractice liability in, 369–372

Blood, diseases of, 50–52
monitoring color of, during anesthesia, 100

Blood dyscrasias, as allergic response, 253

Blood pressure, and heart disease, 78
ASA classification of, 54
before anesthesia, 99
evaluation of, 240